Lecture Notes in Computer Science   **9478**

Commenced Publication in 1973
Founding and Former Series Editors:
Gerhard Goos, Juris Hartmanis, and Jan van Leeuwen

Editorial Board

David Hutchison
Lancaster University, Lancaster, UK
Takeo Kanade
Carnegie Mellon University, Pittsburgh, PA, USA
Josef Kittler
University of Surrey, Guildford, UK
Jon M. Kleinberg
Cornell University, Ithaca, NY, USA
Friedemann Mattern
ETH Zurich, Zürich, Switzerland
John C. Mitchell
Stanford University, Stanford, CA, USA
Moni Naor
Weizmann Institute of Science, Rehovot, Israel
C. Pandu Rangan
Indian Institute of Technology, Madras, India
Bernhard Steffen
TU Dortmund University, Dortmund, Germany
Demetri Terzopoulos
University of California, Los Angeles, CA, USA
Doug Tygar
University of California, Berkeley, CA, USA
Gerhard Weikum
Max Planck Institute for Informatics, Saarbrücken, Germany

More information about this series at http://www.springer.com/series/7410

Sushil Jajodia · Chandan Mazumdar (Eds.)

Information Systems Security

11th International Conference, ICISS 2015
Kolkata, India, December 16–20, 2015
Proceedings

 Springer

Editors
Sushil Jajodia
Center for Secure Information Systems
Fairfax, VA
USA

Chandan Mazumdar
Jadavpur University
Kolkata
India

ISSN 0302-9743   ISSN 1611-3349   (electronic)
Lecture Notes in Computer Science
ISBN 978-3-319-26960-3   ISBN 978-3-319-26961-0   (eBook)
DOI 10.1007/978-3-319-26961-0

Library of Congress Control Number: 2015955354

LNCS Sublibrary: SL4 – Security and Cryptology

Springer Cham Heidelberg New York Dordrecht London

Printed on acid-free paper

Springer International Publishing AG Switzerland is part of Springer Science+Business Media
(www.springer.com)

General Chairs' Message

We are indeed delighted and honored to be associated with the 11th International Conference on Information Systems Security (ICISS 2015), held during December 16–20, 2015, at Jadavpur University, Kolkata. Since its inception in 2005, the decade-long perseverance and dedication of information security researchers in India and the consistent support of friends and well-wishers, like Prof. Sushil Jajodia and other experts from different countries, have contributed to the acceptance of this conference as a major venue to exchange ideas in the frontier areas of information systems security.

After the successful completion of the 10th edition of the conference in 2014 at Hyderabad, when it was decided that a team of young researchers from Jadavpur University would take the lead to bring the conference back to its birthplace, we were sure that the event would take place again without any glitch. The Program Committee under the stewardship of Prof. Sushil Jajodia and Prof. Chandan Mazumdar was quickly formed and the committee took steps to attract contributions from across the globe and to get the papers reviewed by experts within the stipulated period. We extend our sincere thanks to the program chairs, the members of the Program Committee, and the reviewers, without whose help the excellent technical program for this conference would not have been completed.

We are indebted to Profs. Pierangela Samarati, Stefano Paraboschi, Vincenzo Piuri, and Vinod Ganapathy, who kindly accepted our invitation to share their experience and to deliver the keynote lectures. It is heartening to note that the invited speakers also contributed to the volume with their research papers. The conference included tutorial sessions on different aspects of information security with participation from academia and industry. We are grateful to the tutorial speakers. The participants definitely benefitted from their lectures. We are thankful to Prof. Sarmistha Neogy for organizing such lively tutorial sessions.

The Publicity Chairs Sara Foresti and Manoj S. Gaur contributed significantly in promoting the conference to the information security community across the globe. The Organizing Committee led by Mridul Sankar Barik and Sanjoy K. Saha along with Finance Chairs Anirban Bhaduri and Anirban Sengupta ensured that different events of the conference were adequately handled. We take this opportunity to record our appreciation for their effort. We would also like to thank the sponsors for their contributions.

December 2015

Arun Kumar Majumdar
Aditya Bagchi

Preface

This volume contains the papers presented at the 11th International Conference on Information Systems Security (ICISS 2015), held December 16–20, 2015, in Kolkata. The conference initiated in 2005 to cater to cyber security research in India successfully entered its 11th edition and has been providing an attractive international forum on information system security for academics, industry, business, and government.

This year, the conference attracted 133 submissions from 17 countries. Given the high quality of the submissions, the Program Committee (PC) accepted 24 full papers and eight short papers after a rigorous review process with multiple reviews for each paper. We thank all the expert reviewers for their invaluable support. We are grateful to the PC members who put in enormous efforts in reviewing and selecting the papers. Without the untiring efforts of the PC members/reviewers and the contributions of the authors of 133 papers, the conference would not have been possible.

The entire process of submission, refereeing, e-meetings of the PC for selecting the papers, and compiling the proceedings was done through the EasyChair system. Thanks go to the architects of EasyChair for providing a highly configurable conference management system.

One of the hallmarks of the ICISS conference series is the high quality of plenary/invited presentations. This year we were fortunate to have four eminent speakers give invited presentations: Pierangela Samarati (University of Milan), Stefano Paraboschi (University of Bergamo), Vincenzo Piuri (University of Milan), and Vinod Ganpathy (Rutgers University). It is indeed a great pleasure for us to thank the invited speakers who agreed to present at the conference coming from far-off places in mid-December. All of the invited speakers have also contributed to the volume by providing their papers. We are grateful to them for their time and efforts.

Owing to the keen interest in information system security, the conference also included several tutorials on various topics in cyber security and also short talks to facilitate discussion on emerging topics.

We thank all the members of the Organizing Committee for making all the arrangements for the conference. We are grateful to Jadavpur University for all the support provided for running the conference. In particular, Dr. Anirban Sengupta helped us at key points including the maintenance of the conference website.

Last but not least, thanks go to Alfred Hofmann from Springer for readily agreeing to publish the proceedings in the LNCS series. Thanks go to his team and in particular Anna Kramer for preparing the proceedings meticulously and in time for the conference.

December 2015

Sushil Jajodia
Chandan Mazumdar

Organization

Steering Committee

Sushil Jajodia	George Mason University, USA
Chandan Mazumdar	Jadavpur University, India
Aditya Bagchi	ISI, Kolkata, India
Somesh Jha	University of Wisconsin, USA
Arun Kumar Majumdar	IIT Kharagpur, India
Venu Govindaraju	SUNY Buffalo, USA
Atul Prakash	University of Michigan, USA
A.S. Ramasastri	IDRBT, Hyderabad, India
Pierangela Samarati	University of Milan, Italy
R.K. Shyamasundar	IIT Bombay, India

Advisory Committee

Suranjan Das	Vice Chancellor, Jadavpur University, India
Bimal Kumar Roy	ISI, Kolkata, India
B.J. Srinath	DeitY, India
G. Athithan	DRDO, India
Phalguni Gupta	NITTTR, Kolkata, India
Sivaji Bandyopadhyay	Dean-FET, Jadavpur University, India

General Chairs

Aditya Bagchi	ISI, Kolkata, India
A.K. Majumdar	IIT, Kharagpur, India

Program Chairs

Sushil Jajodia	George Mason University, USA
Chandan Mazumdar	Jadavpur University, India

Organizing Chairs

Mridul Sankar Barik	Jadavpur University, India
Sanjoy K. Saha	Jadavpur University, India

Publicity Chairs

Sara Foresti   Universitá degli Studi di Milano, Italy
Manoj S. Gaur   MNIT, India

Tutorial Chair

Sarmistha Neogy   Jadavpur University, India

Finance Chairs

Anirban Bhaduri   Jadavpur University, India
Anirban Sengupta   Jadavpur University, India

Program Committee

Vijay Atluri   Rutgers University, USA
Mridul Sankar Barik   Jadavpur University, India
Prithvi Bisht   UIC, USA
Lorenzo Cavallaro   Royal Holloway, University of London, UK
Rajat Subhra   IIT Kharagpur, India
  Chakraborty
Samiran Chattopadhyay   Jadavpur University, India
Subhasis Dasgupta   Indian Statistical Institute, India
Anupam Datta   Carnegie Mellon University, USA
William Enck   North Carolina State University, USA
Earlence Fernandes   University of Michigan, USA
Sara Foresti   Universitá degli Studi di Milano, Italy
Vinod Ganapathy   Rutgers University, USA
Manoj Gaur   Malaviya National Instotute of Technology, Jaipur, India
Soumya Ghosh   Indian Institute of Technology, Kharagpur, India
K. Gopinath   Indian Institute of Science (IISc), Bangalore, India
Vikram Goyal   IIIT-Delhi, India
Gaurav Gupta   Ministry of Communications and Information Technology
                               (Government of India), India
Phalguni Gupta   Indian Institute of Technology Kanpur, India
Ravishankar Iyer   Coordinated Science Laboratory, USA
Sushil Jajodia   George Mason University, USA
Ram Krishnan   University of Texas at San Antonio, USA
Yingjiu Li   Singapore Management University, Singapore
Subhamoy Maitra   Indian Statistical Institute, India
Anish Mathuria   DA-IICT, India
Chandan Mazumdar   Jadavpur University, India
Samrat Mondal   Indian Institute of Technology Patna, India

Debdeep Mukhopadhyay	IIT Kharagpur, India
Ruchira Naskar	National Institute of Technology, Rourkela, India
Goutam Paul	Indian Statistical Institute, India
Phu H. Phung	University of Illinois at Chicago, USA
Indrajit Ray	Colorado State University, USA
Indrakshi Ray	Colorado State University, USA
Chester Rebeiro	IIT Madras, India
Dipanwita Roy Chowdhury	IIT Kharagpur, India
Anirban Sengupta	CDC-JU, India
Sandeep Shukla	IIT, Kanpur, India
Anoop Singhal	NIST, USA
Witawas Srisa-An	University of Nebraska-Lincoln, USA
Scott Stoller	Stony Brook University, USA
Shamik Sural	IIT, Kharagpur, India
S.P. Suresh	Chennai Mathematical Institute, India
Vinod Yegneswaran	SRI International, USA
Stefano Zanero	Politecnico di Milano, Italy

Additional Reviewers

Adhikari, Avishek
Albrecht, Martin
Banik, Subhadeep
Barnwal, Rajesh
Battula, Ramesh Babu
Chakraborty, Suvradip
Chang, Bing
Chatterjee, Ayantika
Cheng, Yao
Chung, Keywhan
Dash, Santanu Kumar
De Capitani di Vimercati, Sabrina
Faruki, Parvez
Fazzini, Mattia

Ghosh, Nirnay
Gupta, Phalguni
Kumar, Suresh
Li, Yan
Maggi, Federico
Paupore, Justin
Polino, Mario
Quarta, Davide
Singh, Bhupendra
Somani, Gaurav
Wang, Lingyu
Wijesekera, Duminda
Yu, Xingjie

Contents

Information Flow Control

Sensor Networks and Cognitive Radio

Watermarking and Steganography

Short Papers

Invited Talks

Data Security Issues in Cloud Scenarios

Sabrina De Capitani di Vimercati, Sara Foresti, and Pierangela Samarati$^{(\boxtimes)}$

Computer Science Department, Università degli Studi di Milano, 26013 Crema, Italy
{sabrina.decapitanidivimercati,sara.foresti,pierangela.samarati}@unimi.it

Abstract. The amount of data created, stored, and processed has enormously increased in the last years. Today, millions of devices are connected to the Internet and generate a huge amount of (personal) data that need to be stored and processed using scalable, efficient, and reliable computing infrastructures. Cloud computing technology can be used to respond to these needs. Although cloud computing brings many benefits to users and companies, security concerns about the cloud still represent the major impediment for its wide adoption.

We briefly survey the main challenges related to the storage and processing of data in the cloud. In particular, we focus on the problem of protecting data in storage, supporting fine-grained access, selectively sharing data, protecting query privacy, and verifying the integrity of computations.

1 Introduction

The wide use and advancements of Information and Communication Technologies (ICTs) have profoundly changed our lives. The proliferation of any kind of smart devices that can easily connect to the Internet together with the availability of (almost free) wireless connections anywhere have led to a more distributed computing environment, which is expected to grow in the near future. In this context, modern applications and services provide increase user functionality with support of advanced user's authentication and identity protection [4,27,37]. At the same time, however a huge amount of data is generated, collected, and processed, which introduces the need of developing scalable, efficient, and reliable computing infrastructures. Cloud computing is a collection of technologies and services that provides an answer to these needs, making virtually unlimited storage space and computing power available at affordable prices. Users and companies can therefore store their data at external cloud providers, access reliable and efficient services provided by third parties, and use computing power available in multiple locations across the network. Although the use of cloud computing has clear economic advantages, the collection, storage, processing, and sharing of (often personal) data in the cloud pose several security concerns (e.g., [3,25,32–35,43,44]). In particular, when data are moved to the cloud, the data owner loses control over them and often even knows neither the location where the data are stored nor the organizations responsible for their management.

S. Jajodia and C. Mazumdar (Eds.): ICISS 2015, LNCS 9478, pp. 3–10, 2015.
DOI: 10.1007/978-3-319-26961-0_1

It is important to observe that the protection of data is a key aspect not only for the success of today's cloud infrastructures but also for the proper development of applications in emerging areas such as Internet of Things and Big Data analytics, which are characterized by huge amounts of data that need to be shared and processed by different parties. In addition to data privacy, another important concern is the security and privacy of the data processing that may involve different parties with the need of sharing information and performing distributed computations. Ensuring that the data processing is carried out securely is a significant challenge. The goal of this paper is to provide an overview of the data protection challenges that need to be addressed when using the cloud to store and process data, and to illustrate existing proposals addressing them. In particular, we focus on the problem of protecting data in storage while supporting fine-grained access, selectively sharing data among different users/data owners, supporting query privacy, and verifying the integrity of data computations.

2   Protection of Data in Storage and Fine-Grained Access

A well-known problem that characterizes the use of a cloud infrastructure is the *loss of control* over data. A data owner storing her data in the cloud often knows neither where her data are stored nor the organizations involved in their management. Encryption services are therefore at the basis of current solutions for protecting the confidentiality and integrity of the data from malicious users and from the providers themselves (e.g., [7,25,43]). Encryption can be applied both at the server side or at the owner side. In the first case, data owners have full trust in the cloud provider managing their data (e.g., Google Cloud Storage, iCloud), which has full access to their data, and can enjoy full functionality. In the second case, the data are encrypted before outsourcing them to a cloud provider (e.g., Boxcryptor, SpiderOak), and data owners can enjoy protection but limited functionality. In fact, the cloud provider cannot access the data it stores in plaintext, and hence cannot directly evaluate queries or execute computations, because they would require operating on encrypted data. Current approaches enabling the execution of queries on encrypted data are based on: the use of specific cryptographic techniques supporting keyword-based searches (e.g., [8]); homomorphic encryption supporting any operation but with high performance overhead (e.g., [29]); different layers of encryption each supporting specific operations [40]; or indexes, that is, metadata attached to the data and used for fine-grained information retrieval and execution of specific queries, depending on the kind of index (e.g., [9,31,46]).

Although all these approaches provide the capability of evaluating queries on encrypted data, they make query evaluation more expensive or not always possible. To avoid this problem, alternative solutions to encryption use *data fragmentation* to protect data confidentiality. Data fragmentation is based on the observation that often data are not sensitive per se but the association among data is sensitive and needs to be protected. For instance, while a list of names and a list of illnesses are not sensitive, the association of each name in the first list with a illness in the second list needs to be kept confidential. In this case, encrypting both names and illnesses may not be necessary. Data fragmentation comes at this point: the use of encryption is limited or avoided by splitting data in different *fragments* (e.g., [1,10–12,15]). Fragments are computed in such a way that sensitive associations, called *confidentiality constraints*, are broken. To guarantee that sensitive associations cannot be reconstructed, fragments are designed in such a way to guarantee their unlinkability or are stored at different cloud providers.

Besides protecting data confidentiality and integrity, attention has been also dedicated to solutions aimed at proving to remote parties that the management of data by a cloud provider complies with the service level agreement, guaranteeing their availability (e.g., [6,36]).

3   Selective Information Sharing

The proposals aimed at protecting the confidentiality of the data in the cloud are typically based on the implicit assumption that any authorized user can access the whole data content. This assumption, however, is in contrast with the nature of today's open and dynamic scenarios, where different users might need to have different views on the outsourced data (e.g., [2,18]). Since neither the cloud provider storing the data nor the data owner can enforce the access control policy for confidentiality and efficiency reasons, respectively, existing solutions are based on the use of *attribute-based encryption* (ABE) and *selective encryption* techniques. ABE is a public-key encryption schema that regulates access to resources on the basis of policies defined on *descriptive attributes* associated with users [30,48]. ABE-based approaches have been recently widely investigated, and several solutions have been proposed for improving the support of policy updates (e.g., [28,42]). Selective encryption is based on the idea that different resources are encrypted with different keys and that a key derivation strategy (e.g., [5]), which relies on the definition of a *key derivation hierarchy*, is adopted to translate read access privileges into the ability of users to derive the encryption keys used to protect the data they are authorized to access [19,20]. To easily support changes to the access control policy on a resource (i.e., grant/revoke operations) without downloading the resource, decrypting it, changing the key derivation hierarchy, and re-encrypting the resource with the new key, two layers of encryption (each characterized by its own encryption policy) are used. One layer is managed by the data owner, while the other is managed directly by the cloud provider and access to data is granted to users who know the encryption keys of both the layers. Therefore, the management of grant and revoke operations can be partially delegated to the cloud provider storing the data.

Few works have also extended the selective encryption techniques to enforce write privileges (e.g., [14,41,42]), to support the presence of multiple data owners selectively sharing their data among each other (e.g., [17]), and to support the release of data according to a subscription-based policy [13].

4   Query Privacy

Several efforts have been dedicated to the development of efficient techniques for protecting *access confidentiality* and *pattern confidentiality*. Access confidentiality means that an observer (including the cloud provider storing the data) should not be able to infer the target of an access singularly taken. Pattern confidentiality means that an observer should not be able to infer whether the target of two different accesses is the same. Private Information Retrieval (PIR) techniques have been traditionally used to provide both these protection guarantees but they are computationally expensive and operate on plaintext data, therefore not protecting data confidentiality. Recent alternative solutions enhance existing index structures (e.g., B+-trees and Oblivious RAM [9,26,49]) to protect confidentiality of data, accesses, and patterns thereof. However, these solutions, while more efficient than PIR approaches, cause an overhead in access times (either for each access or when triggering expensive reordering of the underlying data structure), which make them not always applicable in real-life scenarios. Dynamically allocated data structures (e.g., [22–24,45,51]) represent a different approach to provide data, access, and pattern confidentiality, while guaranteeing a limited overhead in query evaluation and supporting concurrent accesses to the data. The basic idea of these solutions consists in moving the physical location where data are stored after each access (without leaving traces of such reallocations) so that an observer cannot make any inference on the data accessed.

5   Integrity of Computations

When data are elaborated by cloud providers that are not fully trustworthy, there is the problem of verifying the integrity of such a computation, that is, verifying whether the result is *correct*, *complete*, and *fresh*. A result is: correct if the computation involves only genuine data; complete if the computation has been performed on the whole data collection and includes all resources satisfying the computation; fresh if the computation has been performed on the most recent version of the data. At a high level, existing solutions addressing this problem can be divided into two main classes: *deterministic* and *probabilistic*. Deterministic approaches are based on the definition of *authenticated data structures*, which are structures built over specific attributes (e.g., Merkle hash trees or signature chaining schemas [38,39]). A user submits a query to a cloud provider that executes it and returns the query result along with the information necessary for the user to verify the correctness and completeness of the query result. Such an information, called *verification object*, is computed with the help of an authenticated data structure. These techniques provide deterministic integrity guarantees but only for queries with conditions on the attribute(s) on which the data structure has been built. Probabilistic approaches complement the data with fictitious information or checks whose absence in a query result signals an integrity violation (e.g., [21,47,50]). Probabilistic approaches can detect an integrity violation for any query but with only probabilistic guarantees. This means that while the absence of the expected fictitious information implies an integrity violation, their presence does not provide full guarantees of the integrity of the query result (the cloud provider might have just not missed the fictitious information inserted by the data owner). The possible presence of multiple providers in the computation complicates the scenario and requires the use of additional controls (e.g., [16]).

6   Conclusions

The adoption of cloud technologies to store and process huge amount of data, while bringing many benefits, also introduces novel security risks on the data. In this paper, we described challenges related to the management of data in the cloud, and described current solutions.

Acknowledgements. This work was supported in part by: the EC within the 7FP under grant agreement 312797 (ABC4EU) and within the H2020 under grant agreement 644579 (ESCUDO-CLOUD); the Italian Ministry of Research within PRIN project "GenData 2020" (2010RTFWBH).

References

1. Aggarwal, G., Bawa, M., Ganesan, P., Garcia-Molina, H., Kenthapadi, K., Motwani, R., Srivastava, U., Thomas, D., Xu, Y.: Two can keep a secret: a distributed architecture for secure database services. In: Proceedings of the 2nd Biennial Conference on Innovative Data Systems Research (CIDR 2005), Asilomar, CA, USA, January 2005
2. Ardagna, C., De Capitani di Vimercati, S., Paraboschi, S., Pedrini, E., Samarati, P., Verdicchio, M.: Expressive and deployable access control in open web service applications. IEEE Trans. Serv. Comput. (TSC) **4**(2), 96–109 (2011)
3. Ardagna, C.A., Jhawar, R., Piuri, V.: Dependability certification of services: a model-based approach. Computing **97**(1), 51–78 (2013)
4. Ardagna, C., Jajodia, S., Samarati, P., Stavrou, A.: Providing users' anonymity in mobile hybrid networks. ACM Trans. Internet Technol. (TOIT) **12**(3), Article 7, 1–33, May 2013
5. Atallah, M., Frikken, K., Blanton, M.: Dynamic and efficient key management for access hierarchies. In: Proceedings of the 12th ACM Conference on Computer and Communications Security (CCS 2005), Alexandria, VA, USA, November 2005
6. Ateniese, G., Burns, R., Curtmola, R., Herring, J., Khan, O., Kissner, L., Peterson, Z., Song, D.: Remote data checking using provable data possession. ACM Trans. Inf. Syst. Secur. (TISSEC) **14**(1), 12:1–12:34 (2011)
7. Bowers, K., Juels, A., Oprea, A.: Hail: a high-availability and integrity layer for cloud storage. In: Proceedings of the 16th ACM Conference on Computer and Communications Security (CCS 2009), Chicago, IL, USA, November 2009
8. Cao, N., Wang, C., Li, M., Ren, K., Lou, W.: Privacy-preserving multikeyword ranked search over encrypted cloud data. In: Proceedings of the 30th IEEE International Conference on Computer Communications (INFOCOM 2011), Shanghai, China, April 2011

9. Ceselli, A., Damiani, E., De Capitani di Vimercati, S., Jajodia, S., Paraboschi, S., Samarati, P.: Modeling and assessing inference exposure in encrypted databases. ACM Trans. Inf. Syst. Secur. (TISSEC) **8**(1), 119–152 (2005)

10. Ciriani, V., De Capitani di Vimercati, S., Foresti, S., Jajodia, S., Paraboschi, S., Samarati, P.: Fragmentation and encryption to enforce privacy in data storage. In: Biskup, J., López, J. (eds.) ESORICS 2007. LNCS, vol. 4734, pp. 171–186. Springer, Heidelberg (2007)

11. Ciriani, V., De Capitani di Vimercati, S., Foresti, S., Jajodia, S., Paraboschi, S., Samarati, P.: Keep a few: outsourcing data while maintaining confidentiality. In: Backes, M., Ning, P. (eds.) ESORICS 2009. LNCS, vol. 5789, pp. 440–455. Springer, Heidelberg (2009)

12. Ciriani, V., De Capitani di Vimercati, S., Foresti, S., Jajodia, S., Paraboschi, S., Samarati, P.: Combining fragmentation and encryption to protect privacy in data storage. ACM Trans. Inf. Syst. Secur. (TISSEC) **13**(3), 22:1–22:33 (2010)

13. De Capitani di Vimercati, S., Foresti, S., Jajodia, S., Livraga, G.: Enforcing subscription-based authorization policies in cloud scenarios. In: Cuppens-Boulahia, N., Cuppens, F., Garcia-Alfaro, J. (eds.) DBSec 2012. LNCS, vol. 7371, pp. 314–329. Springer, Heidelberg (2012)

14. De Capitani di Vimercati, S., Foresti, S., Jajodiac, S., Livraga, G., Paraboschi, S., Samarati, P.: Enforcing dynamic write privileges in data outsourcing. Comput. Secur. **39**, 47–63 (2013)

15. De Capitani di Vimercati, S., Foresti, S., Jajodia, S., Livraga, G., Paraboschi, S., Samarati, P.: Fragmentation in presence of data dependencies. IEEE Trans. Dependable Secure Comput. (TDSC) **11**(6), 510–523 (2014)

16. De Capitani di Vimercati, S., Foresti, S., Jajodia, S., Livraga, G., Paraboschi, S., Samarati, P.: Integrity for distributed queries. In: Proceedings of the 2nd IEEE Conference on Communications and Network Security (CNS 2014), San Francisco, CA, USA, October 2014

17. De Capitani di Vimercati, S., Foresti, S., Jajodia, S., Paraboschi, S., Pelosi, G., Samarati, P.: Encryption-based policy enforcement for cloud storage. In: Proceedings of the 1st ICDCS Workshop on Security and Privacy in Cloud Computing (SPCC 2010), Genova, Italy, June 2010

18. De Capitani di Vimercati, S., Foresti, S., Jajodia, S., Paraboschi, S., Psaila, G., Samarati, P.: Integrating trust management and access control in data-intensive web applications. ACM Trans. Web (TWEB) **6**(2), 6:1–6:43 (2012)

19. De Capitani di Vimercati, S., Foresti, S., Jajodia, S., Paraboschi, S., Samarati, P.: Over-encryption: management of access control evolution on outsourced data. In: Proceedings of the 33rd International Conference on Very Large Data Bases (VLDB 2007), Vienna, Austria, September 2007

20. De Capitani di Vimercati, S., Foresti, S., Jajodia, S., Paraboschi, S., Samarati, P.: Encryption policies for regulating access to outsourced data. ACM Trans. Database Syst. (TODS) **35**(2), 12:1–12:46 (2010)

21. De Capitani di Vimercati, S., Foresti, S., Jajodia, S., Paraboschi, S., Samarati, P.: Integrity for join queries in the cloud. IEEE Trans. Cloud Comput. (TCC) **1**(2), 187–200 (2013)

22. De Capitani di Vimercati, S., Foresti, S., Paraboschi, S., Pelosi, G., Samarati, P.: Efficient and private access to outsourced data. In: Proceedings of the 31st International Conference on Distributed Computing Systems (ICDCS 2011), Minneapolis, MN, USA, June 2011

23. De Capitani di Vimercati, S., Foresti, S., Paraboschi, S., Pelosi, G., Samarati, P.: Supporting concurrency in private data outsourcing. In: Atluri, V., Diaz, C. (eds.) ESORICS 2011. LNCS, vol. 6879, pp. 648–664. Springer, Heidelberg (2011)

24. De Capitani di Vimercati, S., Foresti, S., Paraboschi, S., Pelosi, G., Samarati, P.: Distributed shuffling for preserving access confidentiality. In: Crampton, J., Jajodia, S., Mayes, K. (eds.) ESORICS 2013. LNCS, vol. 8134, pp. 628–645. Springer, Heidelberg (2013)

25. De Capitani di Vimercati, S., Foresti, S., Samarati, P.: Selective and fine-grained access to data in the cloud. In: Jajodia, S., et al. (eds.) Secure Cloud Computing. Springer, New York (2014)

26. Ding, X., Yang, Y., Deng, R.: Database access pattern protection without full-shuffles. IEEE Trans. Inf. Forensics Secur. (TIFS) **6**(1), 189–201 (2011)

27. Donida Labati, R., Genovese, A., Piuri, V., Scotti, F.: Touchless fingerprint biometrics: a survey on 2D and 3D technologies. J. Internet Technol. **15**(3), 325–332 (2014)

28. Zhao, F., Nishide, T., Sakurai, K.: Realizing fine-grained and flexible access control to outsourced data with attribute-based cryptosystems. In: Bao, F., Weng, J. (eds.) ISPEC 2011. LNCS, vol. 6672, pp. 83–97. Springer, Heidelberg (2011)

29. Gentry, C.: Fully homomorphic encryption using ideal lattices. In: Proceedings of the 41st ACM Symposium on Theory of Computing (STOC 2009), Bethesda, MD, USA, May–June 2009

30. Goyal, V., Pandey, O., Sahai, A., Waters, B.: Attribute-based encryption for fine-grained access control of encrypted data. In: Proceedings of the 13th ACM Conference on Computer and Communications Security (CCS 2006), Alexandria, VA, USA, October–November 2006

31. Hacigümüş, H., Iyer, B., Li, C., Mehrotra, S.: Executing SQL over encrypted data in the database-service-provider model. In: Proceedigs of the 21th ACM SIGMOD International Conference on Management of Data (SIGMOD 2002), Madison, WI, USA, June 2002

32. Jhawar, R., Piuri, V.: Fault tolerance management in IaaS clouds. In: Proceedings of the IEEE Conference in Europe about Space and Satellite Telecommunications (ESTEL 2012), Rome, Italy, October 2012

33. Jhawar, R., Piuri, V., Samarati, P.: Supporting security requirements for resource management in cloud computing. In: Proceedings of the 15th IEEE International Conference on Computational Science and Engineering (CSE 2012), Paphos, December 2012

34. Jhawar, R., Piuri, V., Santambrogio, M.: A comprehensive conceptual system-level approach to fault tolerance in cloud computing. In: Proceedings of the 2012 IEEE International Systems Conference (SysCon 2012), Vancouver, Canada, March 2012

35. Jhawar, R., Piuri, V., Santambrogio, M.: Fault tolerance management in cloud computing: a system-level perspective. IEEE Syst. J. **7**(2), 288–297 (2013)

36. Juels, A., Kaliski, B.: PORs: Proofs of retrievability for large files. In: Proceedings of the 14th ACM Conference on Computer and Communications Security (CCS 2007), Alexandria, VA, USA, October–November 2007

37. Labati, R.D., Piuri, V., Scotti, F.: Touchless Fingerprint Biometrics. Series in Security. CRC Press, Hoboken (2015)

38. Li, F., Hadjieleftheriou, M., Kollios, G., Reyzin, L.: Authenticated index structures for aggregation queries. ACM Trans. Inf. Syst. Secur. (TISSEC) **13**(4), 32:1–32:35 (2010)

39. Pang, H., Jain, A., Ramamritham, K., Tan, K.: Verifying completeness of relational query results in data publishing. In: Proceedings of the 24th ACM SIGMOD International Conference on Management of Data (SIGMOD 2005), Baltimore, MD, USA, June 2005
40. Popa, R., Redfield, C., Zeldovich, N., Balakrishnan, H.: CryptDB: protecting confidentiality with encrypted query processin. In: Proceedings of the 23rd ACM Symposium on Operating Systems Principles (SOSP 2011), Cascais, Portugal, October 2011
41. Raykova, M., Zhao, H., Bellovin, S.: Privacy enhanced access control for outsourced data sharing. In: Proceedings of the 16th International Conference on Financial Cryptography and Data Security (FC 2012), Kralendijk, Bonaire, February–March 2012
42. Ruj, S., Stojmenovic, M., Nayak, A.: Privacy preserving access control with authentication for securing data in clouds. In: Proceedings of the 12th IEEE/ACM International Symposium on Cluster, Cloud and Grid Computing (CCGrid 2012), Ottawa, Canada, May 2012
43. Samarati, P.: Data security and privacy in the cloud. In: Huang, X., Zhou, J. (eds.) ISPEC 2014. LNCS, vol. 8434, pp. 28–41. Springer, Heidelberg (2014)
44. Samarati, P., De Capitani di Vimercati, S.: Cloud security: issues and concerns. In: Murugesan, S., Bojanova, I. (eds.) Encyclopedia on Cloud Computing. Wiley, New York (2016)
45. Stefanov, E., van Dijk, M., Shi, E., Fletcher, C., Ren, L., Yu, X., Devadas, S.: Path ORAM: an extremely simple oblivious RAM protocol. In: Proceedings of the 20th ACM Conference on Computer and Communications Security (CCS 2013), Berlin, Germany, November 2013
46. Wang, H., Lakshmanan, L.: Efficient secure query evaluation over encrypted XML databases. In: Proceedings of the 32nd International Conference on Very Large Data Bases (VLDB 2006), Seoul, Korea, September 2006
47. Wang, H., Yin, J., Perng, C., Yu, P.: Dual encryption for query integrity assurance. In: Proceedings of the 17th Conference on Information and Knowledge Management (CIKM 2008), Napa Valley, CA, USA, October 2008
48. Waters, B.: Ciphertext-policy attribute-based encryption: an expressive, efficient, and provably secure realization. In: Proceedings of the 14th IACR International Conference on Practice and Theory of Public Key Cryptography (PKI 2011), Taormina, Italy, March 2011
49. Williams, P., Sion, R.: Single round access privacy on outsourced storage. In: Proceedings of the 19th ACM Conference on Computer and Communications Security (CCS 2012), Raleigh, NC, USA, October 2012
50. Xie, M., Wang, H., Yin, J., Meng, X.: Integrity auditing of outsourced data. In: Proceedings of the 33rd International Conference on Very Large Data Bases (VLDB 2007), Vienna, Austria, September 2007
51. Yang, K., Zhang, J., Zhang, W., Qiao, D.: A light-weight solution to preservation of access pattern privacy in un-trusted clouds. In: Atluri, V., Diaz, C. (eds.) ESORICS 2011. LNCS, vol. 6879, pp. 528–547. Springer, Heidelberg (2011)

Automated Border Control Systems: Biometric Challenges and Research Trends

Ruggero Donida Labati, Angelo Genovese, Enrique Muñoz, Vincenzo Piuri[✉],
Fabio Scotti, and Gianluca Sforza

Department of Computer Science, Università degli Studi di Milano,
Via Bramante 65, 26013 Crema, Italy
{ruggerodonida.labati,angelo.genovese,enrique.munoz,vincenzo.piuri,
fabio.scotti,gianluca.sforza}@unimi.it

Abstract. Automated Border Control (ABC) systems automatically
verify the travelers' identity using their biometric information, without
the need of a manual check, by comparing the data stored in the electronic document (e.g., the e-Passport) with a live sample captured during the crossing of the border. In this paper, the hardware and software
components of the biometric systems used in ABC systems are described,
along with the latest challenges and research trends.

1 Introduction

The number of travelers in the world is constantly increasing [12] and International Border Crossing Points (BCP) are required to increase the passenger
throughput, without sacrificing security or comfort. In this context, Automated
Border Control (ABC) and surveillance systems can be deployed for an automatic, secure, fast, and user-friendly crossing procedure [5,50,51,60].

ABC systems, or e-Gates, typically include three steps: (i) the document
(e.g., the e-Passport) is checked for authenticity; (ii) the identity of the traveler
is verified based on his biometric traits; (iii) the validity of the traveler authorization (e.g., the visa) is checked. Face and fingerprint recognition techniques
are used in most of the e-Gates, with some systems using also the iris. If the
biometric recognition is not successful, a manual check of the traveler identity is
performed [23].

Three types of automated border crossing procedures are possible: (i) one-
step process; (ii) integrated two-step process; (iii) segregated two-step process
[50]. In a one-step process, the document, the identity, and the authorization are
verified at the same time, inside the e-Gate. In an integrated two-step process,
the validity of the document is checked before letting the traveler go inside the
e-Gate for the identity verification and for checking his travel authorization. In a
segregated two-step process, the validity of the document and the travel authorization can be checked also at a different time and place of the border crossing.

In order to perform the required steps, four subsystems are used: (i) the Document Authentication System (DAS), which checks the validity of the

© Springer International Publishing Switzerland 2015
S. Jajodia and C. Mazumdar (Eds.): ICISS 2015, LNCS 9478, pp. 11–20, 2015.
DOI: 10.1007/978-3-319-26961-0_2

document; (ii) the Biometric Verification System (BVS), which captures live biometric samples and compares them with the ones contained in the document; (iii) the Central Systems Interface (CSI), which handles communication with external systems; (iv) the Border Guard Maintenance System (BGMS), which is used by the officers to monitor the ABC system.

In order to check if the traveler is authorized for passage across the border, the ABC system checks with three external systems: (i) the Visa Management Systems (VMS), which contains the visa information [46]; (ii) the Registered Traveler Program (RTP), which contains the personal and biometric data of frequent travelers who voluntarily enrolled in the program; (iii) the Entry-Exit Management Systems (EEMS), which contains the information about which borders the travelers cross, in order to detect overstayers, illegal immigration, and collect statistical information. In particular, the EU is proposing to officially adopt the RTP and EES in the ABC systems [2,3,44,45].

2   Biometric Verification in ABC Systems

This section describes the biometric verification procedures using the face, the fingerprint, and the iris, which are the biometric traits used in ABC systems, as recommended by the ICAO [61]:

- *Face recognition* is the primary biometric trait adopted in e-Gates [61], since it is socially accepted, non-intrusive, and does not require special training. The biometric face verification consists of six steps: (i) the system chooses the camera position based on the traveler's height; (ii) information is displayed to instruct the traveler about how to position its head; (iii) illumination is automatically adjusted based on environmental lights; (iv) the face image is captured; (v) a quality assessment module is used to determine if the image complies with the ISO recommendations [61,64]; (vi) the matching between the live image and the sample in the document is performed.
- *Fingerprint recognition* is an optional biometric technology in e-Passports and e-Gates [61], features high recognition performances and good social acceptance, and is widely adopted. The biometric fingerprint verification consists of four steps: (i) information is displayed to instruct the traveler about how to position the finger on the sensor; (ii) the fingerprint image is captured; (iii) a quality assessment module is used to determine if the image meets the required ISO recommendations [63]; (iv) the matching between the live image and the sample contained in the document/database is performed. Minutiae-based matching algorithms are the most widespread [55,58,67,72]. Moreover, second generation European e-Passports store both face and fingerprint traits, which can be combined to increase the recognition accuracy [4,22,74].
- *Iris recognition* is optional in e-Gates [61] and, while featuring very high recognition performances, is intrusive and has limited social acceptance, and for these reasons is not widely adopted. The biometric iris verification consists of four steps: (i) information is displayed to instruct the traveler about where to place his head near the camera; (ii) a near-infrared light pulse is used to

illuminate the eye, as well as control the gaze direction and the dilation of the pupil; (iii) the iris image is captured; (iv) the live image and the sample contained in the document/database are matched.

3   Challenges

The most important challenges in the design of ABC systems regard the development of better anti-spoofing techniques, compatibility between systems, scalability of biometric systems, and methods for allowing the use of the e-Gates also to people with reduced mobility and visual impairments. Moreover, other challenges regard the capture of higher quality face and fingerprint images, and the design of less-intrusive iris biometric recognition technologies:

- *Better anti-spoofing techniques*, in particular liveness-based methods, are important to avoid cheating attempts that use, for example, printed face images [69], fake fingers made with silicone [68], or synthetic irises [14]. Recent projects studied enhanced anti-spoofing techniques for biometric systems [1], however the data about impostors trying to gain authorized access in e-Gates are not publicly available.
- *Compatibility between systems* should be realized by adopting a common biometric data format [63–65], in order to facilitate the adoption of ABC systems. The type of data exchanged (sample or template) must be chosen according to bandwidth and privacy requirements [7,8,11,16,17,20,21,40,79]. Moreover, a common standard for cryptographic interoperability could help the widespread adoption of security and privacy protection techniques [40].
- *Scalable biometric systems* must be designed, so that ABC systems are able to work efficiently on a large scale [56,57].
- *The design for people with reduced mobility and visual impairments* could help people in a wheelchair, with muscular dystrophy, or with walking aids in accessing the e-Gate and interacting with the biometric sensors. Similarly, it could help visually impaired people when they can not see the information displayed to instruct them about the correct procedures.
- *Higher quality face images* greatly increase the recognition performances, but require the users to stand looking directly in front of the camera, which must be placed at the correct height. Moreover, the illumination must be uniform and able to compensate for environmental variations [78].
- *Higher quality fingerprint images* also increase the performance of fingerprint recognition technologies, and can be obtained by enhancing both the usability of the system and the algorithms for the quality estimation [24,28,38], without increasing the acquisition time.
- *Less-intrusive iris recognition techniques* could help in extending the field of use iris-based systems, since they are currently the most accurate, but have high costs and intrusiveness. At the moment, iris recognition systems are not considered in e-Passports [71] and require additional systems for their use.

4   Research Trends

The most promising research trends in the design of innovative ABC systems regard the use of multibiometrics and less-constrained recognition:

– *Multibiometrics* can increase biometric recognition accuracy, usability, and robustness to spoofing attacks, by combining multiple biometric sources [74, 80]. Several studies demonstrate the increase of accuracy fusing face and fingerprint biometrics [77], also in the case of ABC systems [22,62]. Moreover, the non-universality or low discriminative power of some biometric traits (e.g., soft biometrics) can be compensated by fusing multiple traits [6,15,52–54,66], which can then be used in automated border control and surveillance [73]. However, multibiometric systems are bigger, more complex, and handle more sensitive data, thus requiring more robust data protection schemes [18,19].
– *Less-constrained recognition* could increase the usability and social acceptance of biometric systems [70]. In fact, since they allow a touchless recognition, it would be possible to perform the biometric verification at higher distances, with natural light conditions, and while the traveler is moving, by using the fingerprint [25,26,29,30,32–35,39,41], the palm [59], or the iris [27,37,42,70, 75,76]. A study showed that touchless fingerprint technologies would be preferred over touch-based systems [35], thus allowing for an increased confidence and adoption of biometric recognition [43]. Moreover, less-constrained biometric recognition techniques using innovative traits are being researched [13,31,36], and the advances in three-dimensional reconstruction techniques [9,10,47–49] could allow the use of three-dimensional modeling methods for accurate, less-constrained biometric systems [34,35,59,81].

5   Conclusions

The paper presented the biometric technologies adopted in ABC systems for the traveler's recognition, with a particular focus on the systems based on the face, the fingerprint, and the iris.

Moreover, the challenges of biometric systems in the context of ABC systems were discussed, with specific attention to their usability and to anti-spoofing techniques. The current issues of face, fingerprint, and iris recognition systems were also presented.

Lastly, the paper introduced the most promising research trends for a more accurate, usable, and socially accepted biometric recognition for travelers in ABC systems, with a specific focus on multibiometrics and less-constrained systems.

Acknowledgements. This work was supported in part by: the EC within the 7FP under grant agreement 312797 (ABC4EU); the EC within the H2020 program under grant agreement 644597 (ESCUDO-CLOUD); and the Italian Ministry of Research within PRIN 2010-2011 project "GenData 2020" (2010RTFWBH).

References

1. TABULA RASA - trusted biometrics under spoofing attacks - EU FP7 project (2010). https://www.tabularasa-euproject.org/
2. FastPass - a harmonized, modular reference system for all European automated border crossing points - EU FP7 project (2013). https://www.fastpass-project.eu
3. ABC4EU - automated border controls for europe - EU FP7 project (2014). http://abc4eu.com
4. Fiumicino is the first airport in Italy to automate border controls (2014). http://www.futuretravelexperience.com/2014/11/romes-fiumicino-airport-trialling-automated-border-control-e-gates
5. Amato, A., Di Lecce, V., Piuri, V.: Semantic Analysis and Understanding of Human Behavior in Video Streaming. Springer, Bücher (2012)
6. Azzini, A., Marrara, S., Sassi, R., Scotti, F.: A fuzzy approach to multimodal biometric continuous authentication. Fuzzy Optim. Decis. Making **7**(3), 215–302 (2008). 1568–4539
7. Barni, M., Bianchi, T., Catalano, D., Di Raimondo, M., Donida Labati, R., Failla, P., Fiore, D., Lazzeretti, R., Piuri, V., Scotti, F., Piva, A.: Privacy-preserving fingercode authentication. In: Proceedings of the 2010 ACM Workshop on Multimedia and Security, pp. 231–240, New York, NY, USA, September 2010
8. Barni, M., Bianchi, T., Catalano, D., Raimondo, M.D., Donida Labati, R., Failla, P., Fiore, D., Lazzeretti, R., Piuri, V., Scotti, F., Piva, A.: A privacy-compliant fingerprint recognition system based on homomorphic encryption and FingerCode templates. In: Proceedings of the 2010 IEEE International Conference on Biometrics: Theory Applications and Systems (BTAS), pp. 1–7, Washington, DC, USA, September 2010
9. Bellocchio, F., Borghese, N.A., Ferrari, S., Piuri, V.: 3D Surface Reconstruction: Multi-scale Hierarchical Approaches. Springer, New York (2013)
10. Bellocchio, F., Ferrari, S., Piuri, V., Borghese, N.A.: Hierarchical approach for multiscale support vector regression. IEEE Trans. Neural Netw. Learn. Syst. **23**(9), 1448–1460 (2012)
11. Bianchi, T., Donida Labati, R., Piuri, V., Piva, A., Scotti, F., Turchi, S.: Implementing FingerCode-based identity matching in the encrypted domain. In: Proceedings of the 2010 IEEE Workshop on Biometric Measurements and Systems for Security and Medical Applications (BioMS), pp. 15–21, Taranto, Italy, September 2010
12. Boeing: current market outlook: 2014–2033 (2014). http://www.boeing.com
13. Bonissi, A., Donida Labati, R., Perico, L., Sassi, R., Scotti, F., Sparagino, L.: A preliminary study on continuous authentication methods for photoplethysmographic biometrics. In: Proceedings of the 2013 IEEE Workshop on Biometric Measurements and Systems for Security and Medical Applications (BioMS), pp. 28–33, Napoli, Italy, September 2013
14. Burge, M.J., Bowyer, K.: Handbook of Iris Recognition. Springer Science and Business Media, Heidelberg (2013)
15. Cimato, S., Gamassi, M., Piuri, V., Sana, D., Sassi, R., Scotti, F.: Personal identification and verification using multimodal biometric data. In: Proceedings of the 2006 IEEE International Conference on Computational Intelligence for Homeland Security and Personal Safety (CIHSPS), pp. 41–45, Alexandria, VA, USA, October 2006

16. Cimato, S., Gamassi, M., Piuri, V., Sassi, R., Scotti, F.: Privacy issues in biometric identification. In: Touch Briefings, pp. 40–42 (2006)
17. Cimato, S., Gamassi, M., Piuri, V., Sassi, R., Scotti, F.: A biometric verification system addressing privacy concerns. In: Proceedings of the 2007 International Conference on Computational Intelligence and Security (CIS), pp. 594–598, Harbin, China, December 2007
18. Cimato, S., Gamassi, M., Piuri, V., Sassi, R., Scotti, F.: Privacy-aware biometrics: design and implementation of a multimodal verification system. In: Proceedings of the 2008 Annual Computer Security Applications Confernece (ACSAC), pp. 130–139, Anaheim, CA, USA, December 2008
19. Cimato, S., Gamassi, M., Piuri, V., Sassi, R., Scotti, F.: A multi-biometric verification system for the privacy protection of iris templates. In: Corchado, E., Zunino, R., Gastaldo, P., Herrero, A. (eds.) Proceedings of the International Workshop on Computational Intelligence in Security for Information Systems (CISIS). Advances in Soft Computing, vol. 53, pp. 227–234. Springer, Heidelberg (2009)
20. Cimato, S., Gamassi, M., Piuri, V., Sassi, R., Scotti, F.: Privacy in biometrics. In: Boulgouris, N.V., Plataniotis, K.N., Micheli-Tzanakou, E. (eds.) Biometrics: Theory, Methods, and Applications. Computational Intelligence, pp. 633–654. Wiley-IEEE Press, New York (2009)
21. Cimato, S., Sassi, R., Scotti, F.: Biometrics and privacy. Recent Pat. Comput. Sci. 1, 98–109 (2008). 1874-4796
22. Cuesta Cantarero, D., Perez Herrero, D.A., Martin Mendez, F.: A multi-modal biometric fusion implementation for ABC systems. In: Proceedings of the 2013 European Intelligence and Security Informatics Conference (EISIC), pp. 277–280, Uppsala, Sweden, August 2013
23. Donida Labati, R., Genovese, A., Muñoz, E., Piuri, V., Scotti, F., Sforza, G.: Advanced design of automated border control gates: biometric system techniques and research trends. In: Proceedings of the 2015 IEEE International Symposium on Systems Engineering (ISSE), Rome, Italy, September 2015
24. Donida Labati, R., Genovese, A., Muñoz, E., Piuri, V., Scotti, F., Sforza, G.: Automatic classification of acquisition problems affecting fingerprint images in automated border controls. In: Proceedings of the 2015 IEEE Symposium on Computational Intelligence in Biometrics and Identity Management (CIBIM 2015), Cape Town, South Africa, December 2015
25. Donida Labati, R., Genovese, A., Piuri, V., Scotti, F.: Measurement of the principal singular point in contact and contactless fingerprint images by using computational intelligence techniques. In: Proceedings of the 2010 IEEE International Conference on Computational Intelligence for Measurement Systems and Applications (CIMSA), pp. 18–23, Taranto, Italy, September 2010
26. Donida Labati, R., Genovese, A., Piuri, V., Scotti, F.: Fast 3-D fingertip reconstruction using a single two-view structured light acquisition. In: Proceedings of the 2011 IEEE Workshop on Biometric Measurements and Systems for Security and Medical Applications (BioMS), pp. 1–8, Milan, Italy, September 2011. ISBN: 978-1-4577-0765-0
27. Labati, R.D., Genovese, A., Piuri, V., Scotti, F.: Iris segmentation: state of the art and innovative methods. In: Liu, C., Mago, V.K. (eds.) Cross Disciplinary Biometric Systems. ISRL, vol. 37, pp. 151–182. Springer, Heidelberg (2012)
28. Donida Labati, R., Genovese, A., Piuri, V., Scotti, F.: Quality measurement of unwrapped three-dimensional fingerprints: a neural networks approach. In: Proceedings of the 2012 IEEE-INNS International Joint Conference on Neural Networks (IJCNN), pp. 1123–1130, Brisbane, Australia, June 2012

29. Donida Labati, R., Genovese, A., Piuri, V., Scotti, F.: Two-view contactless fingerprint acquisition systems: a case study for clay artworks. In: Proceedings of the 2012 IEEE Workshop on Biometric Measurements and Systems for Security and Medical Applications (BioMS), pp. 1–8, Salerno, Italy, September 2012

30. Donida Labati, R., Genovese, A., Piuri, V., Scotti, F.: Virtual environment for 3-D synthetic fingerprints. In: Proceedings of the 2012 IEEE International Conference on Virtual Environments, Human-Computer Interfaces and Measurement Systems (VECIMS), pp. 48–53, Tianjin, China, July 2012

31. Donida Labati, R., Genovese, A., Piuri, V., Scotti, F.: Weight estimation from frame sequences using computational intelligence techniques. In: Proceedings of the 2012 IEEE International Conference on Computational Intelligence for Measurement Systems and Applications (CIMSA), pp. 29–34, Tianjin, China, July 2012

32. Donida Labati, R., Genovese, A., Piuri, V., Scotti, F.: Accurate 3D fingerprint virtual environment for biometric technology evaluations and experiment design. In: Proceedings of the 2013 IEEE International Conference on Computational Intelligence and Virtual Environments for Measurement Systems and Applications (CIVEMSA), pp. 43–48, Milan, Italy, July 2013

33. Donida Labati, R., Genovese, A., Piuri, V., Scotti, F.: Contactless fingerprint recognition: a neural approach for perspective and rotation effects reduction. In: Proceedings of the IEEE Workshop on Computational Intelligence in Biometrics and Identity Management (CIBIM), pp. 22–30, Singapore, April 2013

34. Donida Labati, R., Genovese, A., Piuri, V., Scotti, F.: Touchless fingerprint biometrics: a survey on 2D and 3D technologies. J. Internet Technol. **15**(3), 325–332 (2014)

35. Donida Labati, R., Genovese, A., Piuri, V., Scotti, F.: Toward unconstrained fingerprint recognition: a fully-touchless 3-D system based on two views on the move. IEEE Transactions on Systems, Man, and Cybernetics: Systems (2015)

36. Donida Labati, R., Piuri, V., Sassi, R., Sforza, G., Scotti, F.: Adaptive ECG biometric recognition: a study on re-enrollment methods for QRS signals. In: Proceedings of the IEEE Workshop on Computational Intelligence in Biometrics and Identity Management (CIBIM), pp. 30–37, Orlando, FL, USA, December 2014

37. Donida Labati, R., Piuri, V., Scotti, F.: Neural-based iterative approach for iris detection in iris recognition systems. In: Proceedings of the IEEE Symposium on Computational Intelligence for Security and Defence Applications (CISDA), pp. 1–6, Ottawa, Canada, July 2009

38. Donida Labati, R., Piuri, V., Scotti, F.: Neural-based quality measurement of fingerprint images in contactless biometric systems. In: Proceedings of the 2010 IEEE-INNS International Joint Conference on Neural Networks (IJCNN), pp. 1–8, Barcelona, Spain, July 2010

39. Donida Labati, R., Piuri, V., Scotti, F.: A neural-based minutiae pair identification method for touchless fingeprint images. In: Proceedings of the 2011 IEEE Workshop on Computational Intelligence in Biometrics and Identity Management (CIBIM), pp. 96–102, Paris, France, April 2011

40. Labati, R.D., Piuri, V., Scotti, F.: Biometric privacy protection: guidelines and technologies. In: Obaidat, M.S., Sevillano, J.L., Filipe, J. (eds.) ICETE 2011. CCIS, vol. 314, pp. 3–19. Springer, Heidelberg (2012)

41. Donida Labati, R., Piuri, V., Scotti, F.: Touchless Fingerprint Biometrics. Security, Privacy and Trust. CRC Press, Hoboken (2015)

42. Donida Labati, R., Scotti, F.: Noisy iris segmentation with boundary regularization and reflections removal. Image Vis. Comput. Spec. Iss. Iris Images Segmentation **28**(2), 270–277 (2010)

43. El-Abed, M., Giot, R., Hemery, B., Rosenberger, C.: A study of users' acceptance and satisfaction of biometric systems. In: Proceedings of the 2010 IEEE International Carnahan Conference on Security Technology (ICCST), pp. 170–178, San Jose, CA, USA, October 2010

44. European commission: proposal for a regulation of the european parliament and of the council establishing a registered traveller programme (2013). http://ec.europa.eu

45. European commission: proposal for a regulation of the european parliament and of the council establishing an entry/exit system (EES) to register entry and exit data of third country nationals crossing the external borders of the member states of the European union (2013)

46. European parliament: regulation (EC) no. 767/2008 of the European parliament and of the council of 9 July 2008 concerning the visa information system (VIS) and the exchange of data between member states on short-stay visas (2008)

47. Ferrari, S., Bellocchio, F., Piuri, V., Alberto Borghese, A.: A hierarchical RBF online learning algorithm for real-time 3-D scanner. IEEE Trans. Neural Netw. **21**(2), 275–285 (2010)

48. Ferrari, S., Ferrigno, G., Piuri, V., Alberto Borghese, N.: Reducing and filtering point clouds with enhanced vector quantization. IEEE Trans. Neural Netw. **18**(1), 161–177 (2007)

49. Ferrari, S., Frosio, I., Piuri, V., Alberto Borghese, N.: Automatic multiscale meshing through HRBF networks. IEEE Trans. Instrum. Measur. **54**(4), 1463–1470 (2005)

50. Frontex agency: best practice operational guidelines for automated border control (ABC) systems. Technical report, European Agency for the Management of Operational Cooperation at the External Borders of the Member States of the European Union (2012). http://frontex.europa.eu

51. Frontex agency: best practice technical guidelines for automated border control (ABC) systems. Technical report, European Agency for the Management of Operational Cooperation at the External Borders of the Member States of the European Union (2012). http://frontex.europa.eu

52. Gamassi, M., Lazzaroni, M., Misino, M., Piuri, V., Sana, D., Scotti, F.: Accuracy and performance of biometric systems. In: Proceedings of the 2004 IEEE Instrumentation and Measurement Technology Conference (IMTC), pp. 510–515, Como, Italy, May 2004

53. Gamassi, M., Lazzaroni, M., Misino, M., Piuri, V., Sana, D., Scotti, F.: Quality assessment of biometric systems: a comprehensive perspective based on accuracy and performance measurement. IEEE Trans. Instrum. Measur. **54**(4), 1489–1496 (2005)

54. Gamassi, M., Piuri, V., Sana, D., Scotti, F.: A high-level optimum design methodology for multimodal biometric systems. In: Proceedings of the 2004 IEEE International Conference on Computational Intelligence for Homeland Security and Personal Safety (CHISPS), pp. 117–124, Venice, Italy, July 2004

55. Gamassi, M., Piuri, V., Sana, D., Scotti, F.: Robust fingerprint detection for access control. In: Proceedings of the Workshop RoboCare, CNR, Rome, Italy, May 2005

56. Gamassi, M., Piuri, V., Sana, D., Scotti, F., Scotti, O.: Scalable distributed biometric systems - advanced techniques for security and safety. IEEE Instrum. Measur. Mag. **9**(2), 21–28 (2006)

57. Gamassi, M., Piuri, V., Sana, D., Scotti, O., Scotti, F.: A multi-modal multi-paradigm agent-based approach to design scalable distributed biometric systems. In: Proceedings of the 2005 IEEE International Conference on Computational Intelligence for Homeland Security and Personal Safety (CIHSPS), pp. 65–70, Orlando, FL, USA, April 2005

58. Gamassi, M., Piuri, V., Scotti, F.: Fingerprint local analysis for high-performance minutiae extraction. In: Proceedings of the 2005 IEEE International Conference on Image Processing (ICIP), vol. 3, pp. 265–268, Genoa, Italy, September 2005

59. Genovese, A., Piuri, V., Scotti, F.: Touchless Palmprint Recognition Systems. Advances in Information Security, vol. 60. Springer, Switzerland (2014)

60. Gorodnichy, D., Yanushkevich, S., Shmerko, V.: Automated border control: problem formalization. In: Proceedings of the 2014 IEEE Symposium on Computational Intelligence in Biometrics and Identity Management (CIBIM), pp. 118–125, Orlando, FL, USA, December 2014

61. International civil aviation organization: Doc 9303, machine readable travel documents. Part 1, vol. 2 (2006). http://www.icao.int/publications/pages/publication.aspx?docnum=9303

62. International organization for standardization (ISO: ISO/IEC 24722:2007, Information technology - Biometrics - Multimodal and other multibiometric fusion (2007)

63. International Organization for Standardization (ISO): ISO/IEC 19794-4:2011, Information technology - Biometric data interchange formats - Part 4: finger image data (2011)

64. International organization for standardization (ISO): ISO/IEC 19794-5:2011, Information technology - Biometric data interchange formats - Part 5: face image data (2011)

65. International organization for standardization (ISO): ISO/IEC 19794-6:2011, Information technology - Biometric data interchange formats - Part 6: Iris image data (2011)

66. Jain, A.K., Ross, A.: Multibiometric systems. Commun. ACM **47**(1), 34–40 (2004)

67. Maltoni, D., Maio, D., Jain, A.K., Prabhakar, S.: Handbook of Fingerprint Recognition, 2nd edn. Springer, London (2009)

68. Marasco, E., Ross, A.: A survey on antispoofing schemes for fingerprint recognition systems. ACM Comput. Surv. **47**(2), 1–36 (2014)

69. Marcel, S., Nixon, M.S., Li, S.Z.: Handbook of Biometric Anti-spoofing: Trusted Biometrics Under Spoofing Attacks. Advances in Computer Vision and Pattern Recognition. Springer, London (2014)

70. Matey, J.R., Naroditsky, O., Hanna, K., Kolczynski, R., LoIacono, D.J., Mangru, S., Tinker, M., Zappia, T.M., Zhao, W.Y.: Iris on the move: acquisition of images for iris recognition in less constrained environments. Proc. IEEE **94**(11), 1936–1947 (2006)

71. Palmer, A.J., Hurrey, C.: Ten reasons why IRIS needed 20:20 foresight: some lessons for introducing biometric border control systems. In: Proceedings of the 2012 European Intelligence and Security Informatics Conference (EISIC), pp. 311–316, Odense, Denmark (2012)

72. Piuri, V., Scotti, F.: Fingerprint biometrics via low-cost sensors and webcams. In: Proceedings of the 2008 IEEE International Conference on Biometrics: Theory, Applications and Systems (BTAS), pp. 1–6, Washington, DC, USA, September 2008

73. Reid, D., Samangooei, S., Chen, C., Nixon, M.S., Ross, A.: Soft biometrics for surveillance: an overview. In: Machine Learning: Theory and Applications, vol. 31, pp. 327–352. Elsevier (2013)
74. Ross, A., Nandakumar, K., Jain, A.: Handbook of Multibiometrics. International Series on Biometrics, vol. 6. Springer, USA (2006)
75. Scotti, F.: Computational intelligence techniques for reflections identification in iris biometric images. In: Proceedings of the 2007 IEEE International Conference on Computational Intelligence for Measurement Systems and Applications (CIMSA), pp. 84–88, Ostuni, Italy, June 2007
76. Scotti, F., Piuri, V.: Adaptive reflection detection and location in iris biometric images by using computational intelligence techniques. IEEE Trans. Instrum. Measur. **59**(7), 1825–1833 (2010)
77. Snelick, R., Indovina, M., Yen, J., Mink, A.: Multimodal biometrics: issues in design and testing. In: Proceedings of the ACM International Conference on Multimodal Interfaces (ICMI), pp. 68–72, Vancouver BC, Canada, November 2003
78. Spreeuwers, L.J., Hendrikse, A.J., Gerritsen, K.J.: Evaluation of automatic face recognition for automatic border control on actual data recorded of travellers at Schiphol airport. In: Proceedings of the International Conference of the Biometrics Special Interest Group (BIOSIG), pp. 1–6, Darmstadt, Germany, September 2012
79. Unisys: entry-exit feasibility study - final report. Technical report, European Commission (2008). http://www.europarl.europa.eu
80. Wei, H., Chen, L., Ferryman, J.: Biometrics in ABC: counter-spoofing research. In: Proceedings of the Frontex Global Conference on Future Developments of Automated Border Control (ABC), Warsaw, Poland (2013)
81. Zhang, D., Lu, G.: 3D Biometrics: Systems and Applications. Springer Publishing Company, Incorporated, New York (2013)

Extending Mandatory Access Control Policies in Android

Stefano Paraboschi[✉], Enrico Bacis, and Simone Mutti

Department of Management, Information and Production Engineering,
Università degli Studi di Bergamo, Bergamo, Italy
{parabosc,enrico.bacis,simone.mutti}@unibg.it

Abstract. Solutions like SELinux have recently regenerated interest toward Mandatory Access Control (MAC) models. The role of MAC models can be expected to increase in modern systems, which are exposed to significant threats and manage high-value resources, due to the stronger protection they are able to offer. Android is a significant representative of these novel systems and the integration of MAC models is an important recent development in its security architecture. Opportunities indeed exist to further enrich the support offered by MAC models, increasing their flexibility and integrating them with other components of the system. We discuss a number of proposals that have recently been made in this domain.

First, we illustrate the integration of SELinux and SQLite, named *SeSQLite*, which permits to apply MAC permissions at a fine granularity into relational databases, offering both a schema-level and row-level support. Then, *AppPolicyModules* are presented, which let app developers specify extensions to the system-level policy that protect the resources of each specific app. Finally, an integration between SELinux and the interprocess communication services is proposed, to further regulate the cooperation among separate apps and services. All these enhancements lead to a stronger and more detailed support of the complex security requirements that characterize modern environments.

1 Introduction

A clear long-term trend in computer security is the increasing complexity of the systems that have to be controlled, with a significant increase in terms of the attack surface, resource value, and complexity of user needs. In terms of the attack surface, larger software stacks and the presence of pervasive network connections increase the exposure of a system and the number of components whose failure may lead to a compromise of a system. The growth in resource value derives from the adoption of computer systems to support most activities. The wider impact of IT solutions also leads to the need to offer access to a larger number of users, each with the need to operate over a specific fraction of the system resources. In many domains the use of computers would indeed be even stronger in the absence of security worries. It can be argued that security management is a bottleneck to the development of modern information systems.

S. Jajodia and C. Mazumdar (Eds.): ICISS 2015, LNCS 9478, pp. 21–35, 2015.
DOI: 10.1007/978-3-319-26961-0_3

The construction of systems able to offer adequate protection has to consider a large variety of aspects [1, 5, 11]. At a high-level, it is necessary that components of IT systems are built using a security-by-design approach, giving to security the role of critical requirement considered in the first phases of the project. Each of the elements, at every level of the architecture, has then to provide robust behavior. An element that is perceived to increase in importance is the use of modern access control models and policy languages. These classical security tools require to be extended in order to meet the stringent requirements of novel applications.

The Android operating system is a representative example of modern computer systems, with novel challenges and the need to extend current security techniques and models. Android has become the most widely deployed operating system, with an impact on a variety of application domains (smartphones, embedded devices, domotics, automotive, etc.). In this paper we mostly refer to the use of Android in the smartphone domain, but the other domains can also benefit from the enhancements that we propose.

Android has to face an extensive collection of security challenges. One of the most visible threats in Android is represented by the installation of potentially malicious apps. Much of the utility of a smartphone derives form its ability to execute apps that suit specific user needs. Apps can be retrieved from monitored markets, like Google's Play Store, or from user-chosen repositories, which may host malicious apps. The risk associated with user-chosen repositories is far greater, but the design of Android has to assume that users will be able and will install potentially malicious apps. The goal is then to reduce the damage that a malicious app can do to the system. The problem can be considered a variant of classical multi-user operating systems, where users are assumed to potentially misbehave and access control aims at restricting the damage potential. Indeed, in Android each app is associated in the Linux kernel with a specific *uid* and *gid*, adapting to apps the Discretionary Access Control (DAC) services of Linux that were originally designed to support multiple users. At the file system level, each app is then able to label its files with *acl*s that will be consistent with the protection needs of each app.

The DAC model alone is insufficient to deal with the security challenges Android has to face. An important recent evolution in Android is the development of SEAndroid, which integrates SELinux into the design of the operating system [15]. SELinux implements a type-based Mandatory Access Control (MAC) model in Linux. The advantages of MAC models are particularly beneficial to Android. The presence of SELinux offers a strictly enforced central policy, able to limit the power (and abuses) of privileges. The availability of SELinux permits Android to better support the security principle of "isolation", containing the installed apps within a restricted space and limiting their ability to compromise system resources.

SEAndroid already provides significant benefits, but we see additional opportunities to extend its use in Android. The paper summarizes a few recent advances in this domain that could lead to an increase in the security of the system. A first aspect is the inability of the SQLite database to support fine granularity in the access to resources. An effort has been directed to the integration in SQLite of the support for MAC labels, allowing a table-level and row-level enforcement of access restrictions on the content of the database. Another research line considers the introduction of the ability of apps to be protected by SELinux. The current architecture mainly uses SELinux to protect system resources from the vulnerabilities and misbehaviors of system components and apps. Apps that are not considered part of the core system are all contained together in a single *untrusted_app* domain. An app interested in getting protection cannot receive support from the MAC system. Developers of apps that process sensitive data may instead be interested in getting this protection. To allow app developers to specify ad-hoc policies for their apps requires to satisfy several critical requirements, with a need for the correct management of policy modules that goes beyond what current systems provide. The proposal of AppPolicyModules wants to provide a mechanism that lets apps to be enriched with an ad-hoc MAC policy for their resources, with guarantees about the fact that this addition to the policy is not going to weaken the system MAC policy. The availability of this technology also opens the door to the realization of a more robust support of Android permissions.

2 Overall Android Architecture

The Android architecture is composed by three layers (see Fig. 1): (a) a Linux kernel (b) a middleware framework and (c) an application layer. The first layer (i.e., the Linux kernel) provides low-level services and device drivers to other layers and differs from a traditional Linux kernel. The Android team has taken the Linux kernel code and modified it to run in an embedded environment, thus it does not have all the features of a traditional Linux distribution. The second layer is composed by native Android libraries, runtime modules (e.g., Dalvik Virtual Machine) and an application framework.

The third layer is composed by applications. They can be divided into two categories (i) core applications (e.g., browser, dialer phone) installed by default and (ii) common applications, written in Java, installed by the user. Each application is composed by different *app components*. There are four different types of app components: (a) *Activities*, typically each screen shown to a user is represented by a single *Activity component* (b) *Services*, provide the background functionalities (c) *Content Providers* used to share data among applications and (d) *Broadcast Receivers* used to receive event notifications both from the system and from other applications.

2.1 Android Security Architecture

Android provides a *permission mechanism* that enforces restrictions on the specific operations that a particular process can perform. Basically, by default, an application has no permissions to perform any operation (e.g., reading or writing the user's private data, keep the device awake, performing network access).

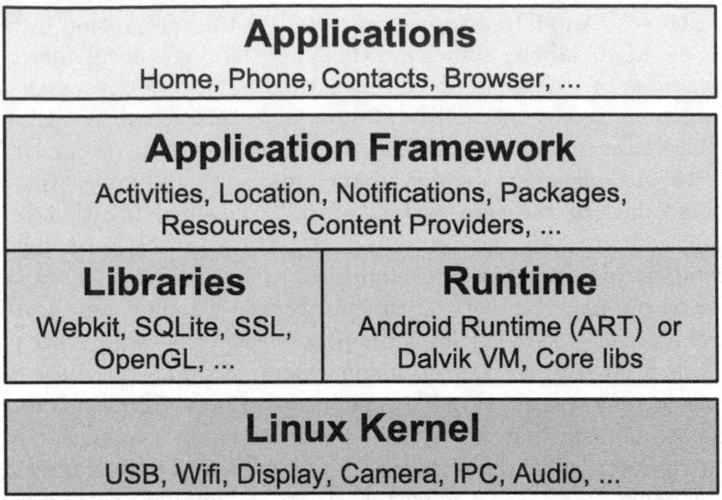

Fig. 1. Android Architecture overview.

Furthermore, Android isolates applications from each other, with a sandbox. The sandbox mechanism relies on the use of *certificates*. All Android applications must be signed with a certificate whose private key is held by their developer and is a prerequisite for inclusion into the official Android Market. The purpose of certificates in Android is twofold: (a) to distinguish application authors; and (b) to grant or deny access to signature-level permissions.

Android assigns a unique user id (UID) and a group id (GID) to each app. Each installed application has a set of data structures and files that are associated with its UID and GID. Only the application itself and the superuser (i.e., root) have the permissions to access these structures and files.

2.2   SELinux

SELinux originally started as the Flux Advanced Security Kernel (FLASK) [7] developed by the Utah University Flux team and the US Department of Defense. The development was enhanced by the NSA and released as open source software. SELinux policies are expressed at the level of *security context* (also known as *security label* or just *label*). SELinux requires a security context to be associated with every process (or subject) and resource (or object), which is used to decide whether access is allowed or not as defined by the policy. Every request that a process generates to access a resource will be accepted only if it is authorized by both the classical DAC access control service and by the SELinux policy. The advantages of SELinux compared to the DAC model are its flexibility (the design of Linux assumes a *root* user that has full access to DAC-protected resources) and the fact that process and resource labels can be assigned and updated in a way that is specified at system level by the SELinux policy (in the DAC model, owners are able to fully control the resources). SELinux uses a closed world assumption, so the policy has to explicitly define rules to allow a *source* (the process) to perform a set of *actions* on a *target* (the resource). The rule also specifies the class of target on which the rule has to be applied (e.g., file, directory). An SELinux rule has the following syntax:

```
allow  source_t  target_t : class  {actions};
```

3   SeSQLite

Android provides several ways to store apps data. For example, apps can store text files both in their own files directory and in the phone SD card. Sometimes, however, an app needs to be able to carry out complex operations on persistent data, or the volume of data requires a more efficient method of management than a flat text file. To this end Android provides a built-in *SQLite* database[1].

SQLite is the most widely deployed in-process library that implements a SQL database engine. It offers high storage efficiency and small memory footprint. A SQLite database is represented by a single disk file and anyone who has direct access to the file can read the whole database content. Usually, due to the fact that SQLite has no separate server, the entire database engine library is integrated into the application that needs to access a database. Furthermore, SQLite does not provide any kind of access control mechanism, it only provides a few proprietary extensions (e.g., database encryption).

Modern DBMSs provide their own authorization mechanisms [4,6], with a corresponding set of SQL constructs, which permit access control at the level of tables, columns or views. DBMSs use a permission model that is similar to, but separate from, the underlying operating system permissions. Current information systems often make a limited use of these database access control facilities and tend to embed access control directly in the application program used to access the database. This choice derives from the perceived difficulty in keeping the database users aligned with the user population in the application, and from the flexibility obtained in the construction of the application thanks to the absence of access control restrictions to the database. (Our expectation is that this is going to change, but it will take a long time.)

The integration of the MAC model, defined at the level of the operating system, and the access control services, internal to the DBMS, promises to reduce the above obstacles and lead to an increase in the security of the system. Such integration would also provide *system-wide consistency*, because all the access control decisions would be guaranteed to be compliant with the system-level MAC policy. To realize such integration in Android it is necessary to extend SQLite with the support for SELinux controls.

---

[1] https://www.sqlite.org/.

3.1 SQLite and Content Provider

In the Android platform, SQLite is used to store several types of information, like contacts, SMS messages, and web browser bookmarks. In order to let an app consume these types of information, Android provides specific components, called *Content Providers*. The Content Providers are daemons that provide an interface to the SQLite library, for sharing information with other applications.

Due to the fact that SQLite does not provide any security mechanism, access control is embedded directly into the Content Provider used to access the database. The Content Provider code that handles a query can explicitly call the system's permission validation mechanism, using the *Android Permission Framework*, to require certain permissions.

Besides the Content Provider, at the Linux kernel level Android provides both *DAC* and *MAC* access control [15]. Both DAC and MAC are designed to provide protection against an attempt to directly access the database by a process that is not the Content Provider.

3.2 SeSQLite Architecture

The file-level granularity provided by DAC is not sufficient if we want to provide a fine grained access control over SQLite databases. To this end, we introduced *Security-Enhanced SQLite* [10] (SeSQLite), which extends SQLite and integrates it with SELinux in order to provide fine-grained mandatory access control. In this way we can ensure that access control policies are consistently applied to every user and every application.

The requirements leading the implementation of SeSQLite are the following:

R.1 - Backward Compatibility SeSQLite is designed to maintain backward-compatibility with common SQLite databases (i.e., no modification to the SQL syntax);

R.2 - Flexibility SeSQLite is designed to provide everything needed to successfully implement a Mandatory Access Control module, while imposing the fewest possible changes to SQLite. Moreover, it is designed to be easily adapted to different implementation of MAC (e.g., *SELinux* or *SMACK* [14]);

R.3 - Performance SeSQLite must keep negligible the overhead on computational time and database size.

3.3 Access Control Granularity

In a SQLite database there are different types of SQL object, which can be grouped in two granularity levels: the *Schema Level* and the *Tuple Level*. To supply per-SQL object protection, SELinux requires that SQLite provides support for security labeling. However, a distinction among the approaches used to manage schema and tuple object is needed, since schema and tuple objects address different needs and belong to different logical models, as it will be presented in the following.

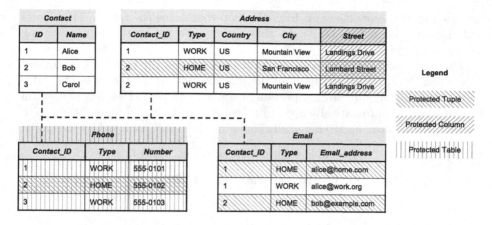

Fig. 2. Example of an access policy defined on a database of contacts leveraging both SeSQlite schema checks and tuple checks. An application that wants to issue a SELECT query over the shadowed parts needs an additional privilege.

Schema Level. All SQL statements must be compiled before their execution. In SQLite, the compilation process follows the sequence of steps below:

1. Syntax check;
2. Semantic check;
3. Expansion;
4. Code generation.

The output of the compilation process is a piece of program containing the information about all the tables and attributes that have to be accessed.

Example 1. Consider the *Address* table in Fig. 2 and the following query:

```
SELECT Country, City, Street FROM Address WHERE Contact_ID=1;
```

The statement accesses four columns within the *Address* table. The *Country*, *City* and *Street* attributes appear in the target list directly as a part of the query. The *Contact_ID* is used in the *WHERE* clause.

Using this information, SeSQLite introduces a *schema check* to control if the query complies with the SELinux policy, i.e., the user can access all the tables and columns specified in the query. An error is immediately raised if the user does not have all the privileges needed to perform the query.

According to the example policy in Fig. 2, the check will raise an error if the issuer is not granted the access privilege, since the user does not have the privileges to select the attribute *Street*. The same approach can be applied to INSERT, DELETE and UPDATE statements.

Row Level. At tuple level, the query is made to be always compliant with the policy. In fact, tuple level access control operates as a *filter* that automatically excludes any unaccessible tuple from the loop that scans the tables. This allows SeSQLite to process only the tuples that can be accessed by the user, according to the action requested.

Query rewriting is the most common mechanism used to provide fine-grained access control at tuple level because the modifications are internal to the database and do not require any adaptation at application level. Essentially this can be compared to automatically appending conditions to a SQL query's *WHERE* clause as it executes, and dynamically changing the result returned by the query.

Example 2. Consider the table *Email_address* in Fig. 2 and the query:

```
SELECT Type, Email_address FROM Email WHERE Contact_ID=1;
```

Table 1. Result of the query in Example 2 without *check_tuple()*.

Type	Email_address
HOME	alice@example.com
WORK	alice@example.org

The output of the query is shown in Table 1. However, if we consider the same query and we want to enforce that a user can select only non protected tuples, with query rewriting the query becomes:

```
SELECT Type, Email_address FROM Email
WHERE Contact_ID=1 AND check_tuple();
```

The *check tuple()* function appends to the *WHERE* clause the predicate responsible to perform the access control filter. The query output is presented in Table 2.

Table 2. Result of the query in Example 2 with *check_tuple()*.

Type	Email_address
WORK	alice@example.org

SeSQLite uses a modified version of traditional query-rewriting, with the following traits:

1. Due to the fact that SQLite does not provide a multi-user database, the decision to allow or deny the access to a SQL object depends on the policy provided by the *SELinux Security Server*. This design provides a characteristic feature called system-wide consistency in access control, which means that SELinux provides all the access control decisions based on a single declarative policy.

2. In order to maintain a negligible overhead, SeSQLite uses two different *query rewriting* approaches, based on the number of SELinux contexts used in the database (the experimental results can be found in Table 3):
   - The first approach is based on a custom SQL function, which checks for each row if its security context can be seen by the issuer of the query. This approach is selected when a substantial number of different SELinux contexts is used in the database.
   - The second approach is used when a limited number of SELinux contexts is present in the database (the most common case). Before starting the table scan, the visibility of all the contexts present in the database is computed based on the issuer of the query. The ones that can be accessed are enclosed in a SQL *IN* operator, so that only those tuples are accessed.

Table 3. Total CPU time and overhead for a suite of common operation in SeSQLite.

	Time	Overhead
SQLite	5.846 s	–
SeSQLite (2 contexts)	6.132 s	+4.8 %
SeSQLite (100 contexts)	6.741 s	+15.3 %
SeSQLite (1000 contexts)	6.749 s	+15.4 %

4   AppPolicyModules

SeSQLite assumes that different Android application use different SELinux contexts, so that it is possible to use this information in the access control checks.

Unfortunately, at the moment all the apps share a single SELinux context[2]: *untrusted_app*. We recently proposed the concept of *AppPolicyModules* (*APMs*) [2], which aim at providing the full benefits given by the use of Mandatory Access Control to third-party apps.

4.1   Providing Mandatory Access Control to Apps

APMs follow the principles of the Android security model, which aims at strengthening the boundaries among apps, introducing an additional mechanism to guarantee that apps are isolated and cannot manipulate the behavior of other apps. The additional mechanism is obtained with an adaptation of the services of the MAC model introduced by SELinux.

The introduction of APMs improves the definition and enforcement of the security requirements associated with each app. However, apps become known

---

[2] There is also the context *google_app* used only for the apps signed by Google.

to the system only when the user asks for their installation. For this reason, the MAC policy has to be dynamic, with the ability to adapt to the installation and deletion of apps. This requires modularity and the capability to incrementally update the security policy, letting an app be able to specify the policy module it is associated with. In this way app developers, who know the service provided by the app and its source code, can benefit from the presence of a MAC model, letting them define security policies that increase the protection the app can get against attacks coming from other apps, which may try to manipulate the app and exploit its vulnerabilities.

It is to note that many app developers will either be unfamiliar with the SELinux syntax and semantics, or will not want to introduce strict security boundaries to the app beyond those associated with *untrusted_app*. However, we observe that the app developers that can be expected to be most interested in using the services of the MAC model are expert developers responsible for the construction of critical apps (e.g., apps for secure encrypted communication, or for key management, or for access to financial and banking services).

We consider here how it is possible to use APMs to enforce a stricter model on the management of Android permissions, relying on the automatic generation of APMs. If we consider the structure of the *AndroidManifest.xml* file provided by each app, it already contains the definition of security requirements through the use of the tag `<use-permission>`. For example, if an app developer wants to write on the SD card, she has to explicitly request the associated Android permissions (e.g., *android.permission.WRITE_EXTERNAL_STORAGE*), which corresponds both to a set of concrete actions at the OS level and to a set of SELinux rules.

The system already offers both a high-level and a low-level representation of permissions, but they are not integrated. Furthermore, in the absence of policy modularity, the apps are associated only with the *untrusted_app* domain, which is allowed to use the actions that correspond to the access to all the resources that are invokable by apps, essentially using for protection only the functions of Android permissions. The integration of security policies at different levels offers a more robust enforcement of the app policy. This can be realized introducing a mechanism that bridges the gap between different levels, through the analysis of the high-level policy (i.e., the permissions asked by the app within the Android Permission Framework) and the automatic generation of an APM that maps those Android permissions to a corresponding collection of SELinux rules.

In general, with the availability of *appPolicyModules*, the system could evolve from a scenario where each app is given at installation time access to the whole *untrusted_app* domain at the SELinux layer, to a scenario where each app is associated with the portion of *untrusted_app* domain that is really needed for its execution, with a better support of the classical "least-privilege" security principle. It is to note that Android M provides the feature to drop Android permissions at runtime. This confirms that APMs and more generally domain specialization identify a concrete need and that Android is evolving in this direction.

Example 3. Most mobile browsers (e.g., Chrome, Firefox) store confidential information such as *usernames* and *passwords* in a SQLite database. Following Google's
best practices for developing secure apps, the password database is saved in the
app data folder, which should be accessible only to the app itself. However, this is
not enough to protect the password database by other apps with root privileges.

The use of MAC support offers protection even against threats coming from
the system itself, like a malicious app that abuses root privileges. The app can
protect its resources from other apps, specifying its own types and defining in
a flexible way which system components may or may not access the domains
introduced by the APM.

Figure 3 shows an example where the *untrusted_app* domain does not hold
any permission on the file labeled as *password_file*, which is accessible only by
the *browser1* domain.

It is to note that both *browser1* and *password_file* are typebounded (see [9]),
thus *browser1* is not violating any restriction defined on the parent domain (i.e.,
untrusted_app). Greater flexibility derives from the possibility to freely manage
privileges for internal types over internal resources, building a MAC model that
remains completely under the control of the app.

The management of policy modules provided by apps and integrated within
the system-level SELinux policy has to satisfy four crucial requirements.

Req1, No impact on the system policy: the app must not change the system
policy and only have an impact on processes and resources associated
with the app itself;

Req2, No escalation: the app cannot specify a policy that gives more privileges
than those given to *untrusted_app*;

Req3, Flexible internal structure: the app can define and activate separate
domains, to limit potential vulnerabilities deriving from internal flaws,
adopting the principle of "least privilege" and fragmenting its structure
in a way that each component is only given the minimum amount of
privileges it needs to execute properly;

Req4, Protection from external threats: the app can protect its resources
from other apps, specifying its own types and then defining SELinux
restrictions on them.

We refer to [2] for an extensive discussion of these principles and their impact
on the realization of APMs.

5   SEIntentFirewall

In order to cross the process boundaries (i.e., inter-process communication) an
app can use a messaging object to request an action from another app or system
component. The messaging object is called *Intent*.

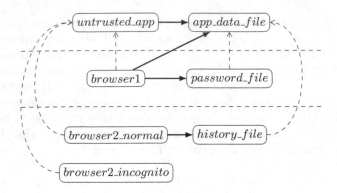

Fig. 3. Isolation of two applications using typebounds.

5.1   Android Intents

Formally, Intents are asynchronous messages that allow application components to request functionality from other Android components. This mechanism has been denoted as *Inter-Component Communication* (ICC). Intents represent the high-level *Inter-process Communication* (IPC) technique of Android, while the underlying transport mechanism is called *Binder*.

Binder is a customized implementation of *OpenBinder* for Android. It has the facility to provide bindings to functions and data from one execution environment to another. The *OpenBinder* implementation runs under Linux and extends the existing IPC mechanisms. Android provides two types of intent:

Implicit intent: specifies the action that should be performed and optionally the data for the action. If an implicit intent is used, Android searches for all components that are registered for the specific action and the provided data type;

Explicit intent: explicitly defines the component that should be called by the Android system (i.e., using the Java class as identifier).

Intents can be used to: start *Activities*; start, stop, and bind *Services*; and, broadcast information to *Broadcast Receivers*. All of these forms of communication can be used with either explicit or implicit Intents.

5.2   SEIntentFirewall Architecture

Unfortunately, Intent messages can be intercepted by a malicious app, as shown in previous research [3,12,13], due to the fact that there is no guarantee that the Intent will be received by the intended recipient, and launch a malicious Activity in place of the intended Activity. To address this problem, Google has introduced the *Intent Firewall* component since Android 4.3. As it is explicit in the name, the *Intent Firewall* is a security mechanism that regulates the exchange of *Intents* among apps.

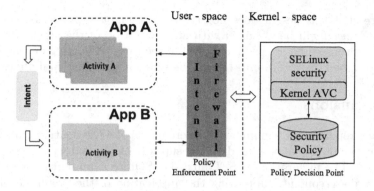

Fig. 4. Overview of the architecture used by SEIntentFirewall.

Although this approach provides several advantages in the protection against Intent-based attacks, it introduces two major drawbacks. Firstly, the *Intent Firewall* policy can be modified only by the root user (i.e., uid 0). Secondly, due to the fact that the system has to manage a new policy language, it introduces *policy fragmentation*.

SEIntentFirewall [8] is a built-in enhancement of *IntentFirewall*, providing fine-grained Mandatory Access Control (MAC) for Intent objects (see Fig. 4). This approach leads to a more powerful control on the communication among apps. This aims at strengthening the barriers among apps, introducing an additional mechanism to guarantee that apps are isolated and cannot manipulate the behavior of other apps.

The SELinux decision engine will then operate as the Policy Decision Point. This choice offers a well-defined policy language and engine, leads to a simpler and better structured code base, and minimizes the implementation effort. It

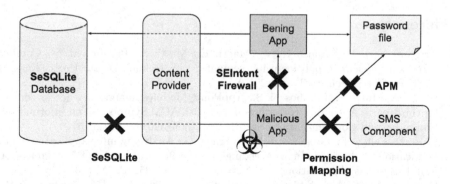

Fig. 5. A malign app is blocked in manifold ways thanks to the wide adoption of SELinux. The SeSQLite database blocks the retrieval of sensitive data; SEIntentFirewall intercepts malicious Intents; the APM specifies which app has access to the password file, while the permission mapping strengthens the permission control.

is to note that this design does not require to adapt apps source code. The *SEIntentFirewall* will be obtained with an adaptation of the services provided by APMs, discussed before [2]. This way, the security-demanding developers will be able to embed their SEIntentFirewall rules jointly with the AppPolicyModule.

6   Conclusions

The paper reported on a number of interconnected investigations, all characterized by the objective of extending the support of Mandatory Access Control in Android. The integration of SELinux and SQLite extends the use of labels to the database content, supporting the application of the system-level policy to the structured data contained in the many existing databases. The support for AppPolicyModules offers to app developers the opportunity to protect with stronger guarantees their apps and data from vulnerabilities in other apps or system components. The introduction of the SEIntentFirewall finally lets the MAC model cover also the invocation of services.

As it is shown in Fig. 5, all these elements support each other and permit the construction of a more robust operating environment, with the possibility to control the behavior of the system in different phases, all following the specifications of a modular policy applied at every access request.

Acknowledgments. The authors would like to thank Ivo Carminati, Paolo Carrara, Stefano Cattaneo, Valentina Centurelli, Andrea Durelli, Kevin Gotti, Niccoló Mangiagalli, Giada Mariani, Francesco Marrazzo, Simone Opreni, Jacopo Ratti, Marco Rosa, Gabriele Scotti, Paolo Vavassori, and Davide Vimercati for support in the implementation of the systems and in the experimental evaluation. This work was partially supported by a Google Research Award (winter 2014), by the Italian Ministry of Research within the PRIN project "GenData 2020" and by the EC within the 7FP and H2020 program, respectively, under projects PoSecCo (257129) and EscudoCloud (644579).

References

1. Arrigoni Neri, M., Guarnieri, M., Magri, E., Mutti, S., Paraboschi, S.: Conflict detection in security policies using semantic web technology. In: Proceedings of IEEE ESTEL - Security Track (2012)
2. Bacis, E., Mutti, S., Paraboschi, S.: AppPolicyModules: mandatory access control for third-party Apps. In: Proceedings of the 10th ACM Symposium on Information, Computer and Communications Security, pp. 309–320. ACM (2015)
3. Chin, E., Felt, A.P., Greenwood, K., Wagner, D.: Analyzing inter-application communication in Android. In: Proceedings of the 9th International Conference on Mobile Systems, Applications, and Services, pp. 239–252. ACM (2011)
4. Denning, D.E., Akl, S.G., Morgenstern, M., Neumann, P.G., Schell, R.R., Heckman, M.: Views for multilevel database security. In: 1986 IEEE Symposium on Security and Privacy, p. 156. IEEE (1986)
5. Guarnieri, M., Arrigoni Neri, M., Magri, E., Mutti, S.: On the notion of redundancy in access control policies. In: Proceedings of the 18th ACM Symposium on Access Control Models and Technologies, pp. 161–172. ACM (2013)

6. Knox, D.: Effective Oracle Database 10g Security by Design. McGraw-Hill Inc., New York (2004)

7. Lepreau, J., Spencer, R., Smalley, S., Loscocco, P., Hibler, M., Andersen, D.: The flask security architecture: system support for diverse security policies. In: Secure Computing Corp, Saint Paul, MN (2006)

8. Mutti, S., Bacis, E., Paraboschi, S.: An SELinux-based Intent manager for Android. In: IEEE Conference on Communications and Network Security, Florence, Italy, September 2015

9. Mutti, S., Bacis, E., Paraboschi, S.: Policy specialization to support domain isolation. In: SafeConfig 2015: Automated Decision Making for Active Cyber Defense, Denver, Colorado, USA, October 2015

10. Mutti, S., Bacis, E., Paraboschi, S.: SeSQLite: security enhanced SQLite. In: Annual Computer Security Applications Conference 2015 (ACSAC 2015), Los Angeles, California, USA, December 2015

11. Mutti, S., Neri, M.A., Paraboschi, S.: An eclipse plug-in for specifying security policies in modern information systems. In: Proceedings of the Eclipse-IT (2011)

12. Ongtang, M., McLaughlin, S., Enck, W., McDaniel, P.: Semantically rich application-centric security in Android. Secur. Commun. Netw. 5(6), 658–673 (2012)

13. Sbîrlea, D., Burke, M.G., Guarnieri, S., Pistoia, M., Sarkar, V.: Automatic detection of inter-application permission leaks in Android applications. IBM J. Res. Dev. 57(6), 10:1–10:12 (2013)

14. Schaufler, C.: Smack in embedded computing. In: Proceedings of the Ottawa Linux Symposium (2008)

15. Smalley, S., Craig, R.: Security Enhanced (SE) Android: bringing flexible MAC to Android. In: Network and Distributed System Security Symposium (NDSS 13) (2013)

Reflections on the Self-service Cloud Computing Project

Vinod Ganapathy$^{(\boxtimes)}$

Department of Computer Science, Rutgers University, Piscataway, NJ, USA
vinodg@cs.rutgers.edu

Abstract. Modern cloud computing infrastructures use virtual machine monitors (VMMs) that often include a large and complex administrative domain with privileges to inspect client VM state. Attacks against or misuse of the administrative domain can compromise client security and privacy. Moreover, these VMMs provide clients inflexible control over their own VMs, as a result of which clients have to rely on the cloud provider to deploy useful services, such as VM introspection-based security tools.

This paper discusses the self-service cloud computing (SSC) project that addresses these two shortcomings. SSC splits administrative privileges between a system-wide domain and per-client administrative domains. Each client can manage and perform privileged system tasks on its own VMs, thereby providing flexibility. The system-wide administrative domain cannot inspect the code, data or computation of client VMs, thereby ensuring security and privacy. SSC also allows providers and clients to establish mutually trusted services that can check regulatory compliance while respecting client privacy. We have used a prototype implementation of SSC atop the Xen hypervisor to build user domains to perform privileged tasks such as memory introspection, storage intrusion detection, and anomaly detection.

1 Introduction

Over the last four years, the author has his collaborators have been working on a project called *Self-service Cloud Computing* (SSC) [1–3]. SSC aims to improve the state of client security on public cloud platforms. This paper discusses the key ideas of SSC and reflects on some of the design decisions and implications of SSC.

The SSC project begins with the observation that Modern cloud infrastructures rely on virtual machine monitors (VMMs) to flexibly administer and execute client virtual machines (VMs). VMMs implement a trusted computing base (TCB) that virtualizes the underlying hardware (CPU, memory and I/O devices) and manages VMs. In commodity VMMs, such as Xen and Hyper-V, the TCB has two parts—the hypervisor and an administrative domain. The hypervisor directly controls physical hardware and runs at the highest processor privilege level. The administrative domain, henceforth called dom0, is a privileged VM

© Springer International Publishing Switzerland 2015
S. Jajodia and C. Mazumdar (Eds.): ICISS 2015, LNCS 9478, pp. 36–57, 2015.
DOI: 10.1007/978-3-319-26961-0_4

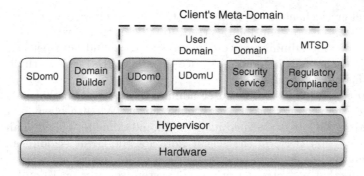

Fig. 1. The design of a Self-service Cloud (SSC) computing platform. SSC splits the TCB of the system (indicated using the shaded components) into a system-level TCB, with the hardware, the SSC hypervisor, and the domain builder, and a client-level TCB, with the Udom0 and service domains.

that is used to control and monitor client VMs. Dom0 has privileges to start/stop client VMs, change client VM configuration, monitor their physical resource utilization, and perform I/O for virtualized devices.

Endowing dom0 with such privileges leads to two problems:

- *Security and privacy of client VMs.* Dom0 has the privilege to inspect the state of client VMs, *e.g.,* the contents of their vCPU registers and memory. This privilege can be misused by attacks against the dom0 software stack (*e.g.,* because of vulnerabilities or misconfigurations) and malicious system administrators. This is a realistic threat [4–10], since dom0 typically executes a full-fledged operating system with supporting user-level utilities that can be configured in complex ways.

- *Inflexible control over client VMs.* Virtualization has the potential to enable novel services, such as security via VM introspection [11,12], migration [13] and checkpointing. However, the adoption of such services in modern cloud infrastructures relies heavily on the willingness of cloud service providers to deploy them. Clients have little say in the deployment or configuration of these services. It is also not clear that a "one size fits all" configuration of these services will be acceptable to client VMs. For example, a simple cloud-based security service that checks network packets for malicious content using signatures will not be useful to a client VM that receives encrypted packets. The client VM may require deeper introspection techniques (*e.g.,* to detect rootkits), which it cannot deploy on its own. Even if the cloud provider offers such an introspection service, the client may be reluctant to use it because dom0's ability to inspect its VMs may compromise its privacy.

SSC aims to simultaneously address the problems of security/privacy and inflexbile control by observing that both of the above problems are a direct consequence of the way in which commodity hypervisors assign privilege to VMs. SSC introduces a novel privilege model that reduces the power of the administrative domain and gives clients more flexible control over their own VMs. SSC's privilege model splits the responsibilities traditionally entrusted with dom0 between a new system-wide administrative domain, called Sdom0, and per-user administrative domains, called Udom0s, service domains (SDs) and mutually-trusted service domains (MTSDs).

Udom0 (User dom0) is a per-user administrative domain that can monitor and control the set of VMs of a particular client. When a client attempts to start a VM in SSC, it is assigned its own Udom0 domain. This domain creates the user VMs that perform the actual work for the client (UdomUs). Udom0 can delegate its privileges to service domains (SDs), which are special-purpose user domains that can perform privileged system services on UdomUs. Clients can leverage SDs to implement services such as memory introspection to verify VM integrity, intrusion detection, and storage encryption. In a traditional cloud, these services would be implemented in dom0, and would have to be deployed by the cloud provider. Thus, SSC allows clients to flexibly deploy new services and control their own VMs using SDs.

Sdom0 (System dom0) is the system-wide administrative domain in SSC. Sdom0 retains the privileges to start/stop Udom0 domains upon request by clients, and to run drivers for virtualized devices. Sdom0 manages resources, including scheduling time-slices and I/O quotas. SSC's privilege model disallows Sdom0 from inspecting the state of the client's domains (Udom0s, SDs, and UdomUs), thereby ensuring the security and privacy of client VMs.

Although this privilege model allows SSC to achieve our stated goals, in practice, cloud providers typically require some ability to control client VMs for regulatory compliance. For example, providers may wish to ensure that clients are not misusing their cloud infrastructure to host malicious software [14]. To do so, the cloud provider must have the ability to inspect client VMs, but this may conflict with the client's privacy goals. There is often such a tension between the client's privacy policies and the cloud provider's need to retain control over client VMs executing on its platform.

SSC resolves this tension by introducing mutually-trusted service domains (MTSDs). The cloud provider and the client mutually agree upon policies and mechanisms that the provider will use to control the client's VMs. The cloud provider implements its code in a MTSD, which runs similar to a SD, and can therefore inspect a client's VMs. Clients can leverage trusted computing technology [15–17] to verify that a MTSD only runs code that was mutually agreed-upon with the cloud provider. Clients that have verified the trustworthiness of the platform and the MTSD can rest assured their privacy will not be compromised. Likewise, the cloud provider can ensure liveness of MTSDs for regulatory compliance.

Figure 1 depicts the design of SSC. We use the term *meta-domain* to refer to the collection of a client's domains (Udom0, UdomUs, SDs, and MTSDs). Only Udom0 holds privileges over UdomUs in its meta-domain, but can delegate specific privileges to SDs to carryout specialized services. To bootstrap meta-domains, SSC employs a specialized domain builder (domB). DomB is entrusted with the task of creating VMs, a privilege that no longer resides with the system-wide administrative domain (Sdom0). Section 3 presents a detailed overview of the design of SSC.

We have implemented an SSC-compliant VMM by modifying Xen (v3.4.0) and have demonstrated its utility by showing that SDs can be used to implement a variety of services [1,2]. This paper mainly focuses on the main ideas underlying the design of SSC, and we refer the reader to the original papers on SSC for detailed experimental evaluations.

2   Threat Model

SSC's threat model is similar to those used in recent work on protecting client VMs in the cloud [18–20], and differentiates between cloud service providers and cloud system administrators. Cloud providers are entities such as Amazon EC2 and Microsoft Azure, who have a vested interest in protecting their reputations. On the other hand, cloud system administrators are individuals entrusted with system tasks and maintaining the cloud infrastructure. To do so, they have access to dom0 and the privileges that it entails.

We assume that cloud system administrators are adversarial (or could make mistakes), and by extension, that the administrative domain is untrusted. Administrators have both the technical means and the monetary motivation to misuse dom0's privileges to snoop client data at will. Even if system administrators are benign, attacks on client data can be launched via exploits directed against dom0. Such attacks are increasing in number [4–9] because on commodity VMMs, dom0 often runs a full-fledged operating system, with a complex software stack. Likewise, misconfigured services in dom0 can also pose a threat to the security and privacy of client data.

SSC protects clients from threats posed by exploits against Sdom0 and cloud administrators who misuse Sdom0's privileges. SSC prevents Sdom0 from accessing the memory contents of client VMs and the state of their virtual processors (vCPUs). This protects all of the client's in-memory data, including any encryption keys stored therein. SSC's core mechanisms by themselves do not prevent administrators from snooping on network traffic or persistent storage. Security-concious clients can employ end-to-end encryption to protect data on the network and storage. Packet headers need not be encrypted; after all, network middleboxes inspect and mangle packet headers.

SSC assumes that the cloud service provider is trusted. The provider must supply a TCB running an SSC-compliant VMM. We assume that the physical hardware is equipped with an IOMMU and a Trusted Platform Module (TPM) chip, using which clients can obtain cryptographic guarantees about the software stack executing on the machine. The cloud provider must also implement procedural controls (security guards, cameras, auditing procedures) to ensure the physical security of the cloud infrastructure in the data center. This is essential to prevent hardware-based attacks, such as cold-boot attacks, against which SSC cannot defend. SSC does not attempt to defend against denial-of-service attacks. Such attacks are trivial to launch in a cloud environment, *e.g.*, a malicious administrator can simply configure Sdom0 so that a client's VMs is never scheduled for execution, or power off the server running the VMs. Clients can ameliorate the impact of such attacks via off-site replication. Finally, SSC does not aim to defend against subpoenas and other judicial instruments served to the cloud provider to monitor specific clients.

3   Design and Implementation of the SSC Platform

We now describe the design and implementation of the SSC platform, focusing on the new abstractions in SSC, their operation, and SSC's privilege model. As Fig. 1 shows, an SSC platform has a single system-wide administrative domain (Sdom0) and a domain-building domain (domB). Each client has its own administrative domain (Udom0), which is the focal point of privilege and authority for a client's VMs. Udom0 orchestrates the creation of UdomUs to perform client computations, and SDs, to which it delegates specific privileges over UdomUs. SSC prevents Sdom0 from inspecting the contents of client meta-domains.

- CREATE_UDOM0 (BACKEND_ID, NONCE, ENC_PARAMS, SIGCLIENT)
  Description: This hypercall is issued by Sdom0 to initiate a client meta-domain by creating a Udom0. The BACKEND_ID argument is a handle to a block device provided by Sdom0 to the client to pass Udom0 kernel image, ramdisk and configuration to domB. The NONCE supplied by the client is combined with the vTPM's measurement list, which is returned to the client for verification following domain creation. ENC_PARAMS denotes a set of parameters that are encrypted under the vTPM's AIK public key. SIGCLIENT is the client's digital signature of key parameters to the CREATE_UDOM0 call. These parameters are used by the protocol in Figure 3(a) to bootstrap a secure communication channel with the client after Udom0 creation.

- CREATE_USERDOMAIN (BACKEND_ID, NONCE)
  Description: Issued by Udom0 to provide VM images of SDs or UdomUs to domB. The parameters BACKEND_ID and NONCE are as described above.

- CREATE_MTSD (CLIENT_ID, BACKEND_ID, NONCE_PROVIDER, NONCE_CLIENT, PRIVILEGE_LIST)
  Description: Sdom0 uses this hypercall to start an MTSD within a client's meta-domain. The configuration parameters, which are included in the block device specified by BACKEND_ID, contain the command-line arguments used to initiate the service provided by the MTSD. MTSDs are also assigned specific privileges over UdomUs in the client meta-domain. This hypercall returns an identifier for the newly-created MTSD. It also returns two signed vTPM measurements, each appended with the nonces of the provider and the client.

- GRANT_PRIVILEGE (SD_ID, UDOMU_ID, PRIVILEGE_LIST)
  Description: This hypercall is used by Udom0s to delegate specific privileges to a SD over an UdomU. Udom0s can issue this hypercall only on SDs and UdomUs within their own meta-domain.

Fig. 2. Summary of new hypercalls introduced to enable SSC. Figure 3 shows their usage.

One of the main contributions of the SSC model is that it splits the TCB of the cloud infrastructure in two parts, a ***system-level TCB***, which consists of the hypervisor, domB, BIOS and the bootloader, and is controlled by the cloud provider, and a ***client-level TCB***, which consists of the client's Udom0, SDs, and MTSDs. Clients can verify the integrity of the system-level TCB using trusted hardware. They are responsible for the integrity of their client-level TCBs. Any compromise of a client-level TCB only affects that client.

Sdom0 runs all device drivers that perform actual I/O and wields authority over scheduling and allocation decisions. Although these privileges allow Sdom0

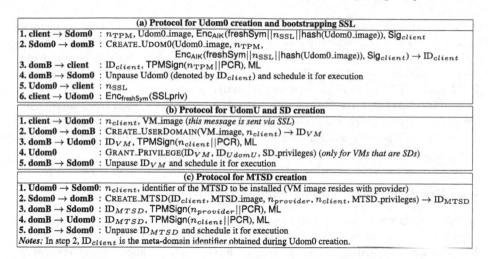

(a) Protocol for Udom0 creation and bootstrapping SSL
1. client → Sdom0 : n_{TPM}, Udom0_image, Enc$_{AIK}$(freshSym$\|n_{SSL}\|$hash(Udom0_image)), Sig$_{client}$
2. Sdom0 → domB : CREATE_UDOM0(Udom0_image, n_{TPM},   Enc$_{AIK}$(freshSym$\|n_{SSL}\|$hash(Udom0_image)), Sig$_{client}$) → ID$_{client}$
3. domB → client : ID$_{client}$, TPMSign($n_{TPM}\|$PCR), ML
4. domB → Sdom0 : Unpause Udom0 (denoted by ID$_{client}$) and schedule it for execution
5. Udom0 → client : n_{SSL}
6. client → Udom0 : Enc$_{freshSym}$(SSLpriv)

(b) Protocol for UdomU and SD creation
1. client → Udom0 : n_{client}, VM_image (*this message is sent via SSL*)
2. Udom0 → domB : CREATE_USERDOMAIN(VM_image, n_{client}) → ID$_{VM}$
3. domB → Udom0 : ID$_{VM}$, TPMSign($n_{client}\|$PCR), ML
4. Udom0   : GRANT_PRIVILEGE(ID$_{VM}$, ID$_{UdomU}$, SD_privileges) (*only for VMs that are SDs*)
5. domB → Sdom0 : Unpause ID$_{VM}$ and schedule it for execution

(c) Protocol for MTSD creation
1. Udom0 → Sdom0: n_{client}, identifier of the MTSD to be installed (VM image resides with provider)
2. Sdom0 → domB : CREATE_MTSD(ID$_{client}$, MTSD_image, $n_{provider}$, n_{client}, MTSD_privileges) → ID$_{MTSD}$
3. domB → Sdom0 : ID$_{MTSD}$, TPMSign($n_{provider}\|$PCR), ML
4. domB → Udom0 : ID$_{MTSD}$, TPMSign($n_{client}\|$PCR), ML
5. domB → Sdom0 : Unpause ID$_{MTSD}$ and schedule it for execution
Notes: In step 2, ID$_{client}$ is the meta-domain identifier obtained during Udom0 creation.

Fig. 3. Protocols used in SSC for the creation of Udom0, UdomUs, SDs and MTSDs.

to perform denial-of-service attacks, such attacks are not in our threat model; consequently, Sdom0 is not part of the TCB.

The components of SSC must be able to communicate with each other for tasks such as domain creation and delegating privileges. In our prototype, VMs communicate using traditional TCP/IP sockets. However, domB receives directives for domain creation through hypervisor-forwarded hypercalls (see Figs. 2 and 3). Images of domains to be created are passed by attaching storage volumes containing this information.

3.1 Bootstrapping

Hosts in the cloud infrastructure are assumed to be equipped with TPM and IOMMU hardware, which is available on most modern chipsets. We assume that the TPM is virtualized, as described in prior work [15]. The supporting user-level daemons for the virtualized TPM (vTPM) run within domB, which is in the TCB, and interact with the hardware TPM on the physical host. The protocols described in this section assume client interaction with a vTPM instance. We use the vTPM protocols as described in the original paper [15], although it may also be possible to use recently-proposed variants [21]. The vTPM can cryptographically attest the list of software packages loaded on a system in response to client requests; such attestations are called *measurements* [22].

During system boot, the BIOS passes control to a bootloader, and initializes the hardware TPM's measurement. In turn, the bootloader loads our modified version of the Xen hypervisor, Sdom0's kernel and ramdisk, and domB's kernel and ramdisk. It also adds entries for the hypervisor and domB to the measurement stored in the TPM's PCR registers. The hypervisor then builds Sdom0 and domB. Finally, it programs the IOMMU to allow Sdom0 access to only the pages that it owns. Following bootstrap and initialization, the hypervisor unpauses Sdom0 and schedules it for execution. Sdom0 then unpauses domB, which awaits client requests to initialize meta-domains. SSC forbids Sdom0 from directly interacting with the TPM; all TPM operations (both with the hardware TPM and vTPM instances) happen via domB.

Sdom0 starts the XenStore service, which is a database used traditionally by Xen to maintain information about virtual device configuration. Each user VM on the system is assigned its own subtree in XenStore with its virtual device configurations.

3.2 Building Client Meta-Domains

In SSC, domB receives and processes all requests to create new domains, including Udom0s, UdomUs, SDs, and MTSDs. Client requests to start new meta-domains are forwarded to domB from Sdom0. In response, domB creates a Udom0, which handles creation of the rest of the meta-domain by itself sending more requests to domB (*e.g.,* to create SDs and UdomUs). To allow clients to verify that their domains were built properly, domB integrates domain building with standard vTPM-based attestation protocols developed in prior work [15,22].

Udom0. Upon receiving a client request to create a new meta-domain, Sdom0 issues the CREATE_UDOM0 hypercall containing a handle to the new domain's bootstrap modules (kernel image, ramdisk, *etc.*). DomB builds the domain and returns to the client an identifier of the newly-created meta-domain. In more detail, the construction of a new meta-domain follows the protocol shown in Fig. 3(a). This protocol achieves two security goals:

(1) *Verified boot of Udom0.* At the end of the protocol, the client can verify that the Udom0 booted by the SSC platform corresponds to the image supplied in step 1 of Fig. 3(a). To achieve this goal, in step 1, the client supplies a challenge (n_{TPM}) and also provides hash(Udom0_image), encrypted under the vTPM's public key (AIK). These arguments are passed to domB, as part of the CREATE_UDOM0 hypercall in step 2. In turn, DomB requests the vTPM to decrypt the content enciphered under its public key, thereby obtaining hash(Udom0_image). DomB then creates the domain after verifying the integrity of the VM image (using hash(Udom0_image) and Sig_{client}), thereby ensuring that Sdom0 has not maliciously altered the VM image supplied by the client. It then returns to the client an identifier of the newly-created meta-domain, a digitally-signed measurement from the vTPM (containing the contents of the vTPM's PCR registers and the client's challenge) and the measurement list. The client can use this to verify that the domain booted with the expected configuration parameters.

(2) *Bootstrapping SSL channel with client.* In SSC, the network driver is controlled by Sdom0, which is untrusted, and can eavesdrop on any cleartext messages transmitted over the network. Therefore, the protocol in Fig. 3(a)

also interacts with the client to install an SSL private key within the newly-created Udom0. This SSL private key is used to authenticate Udom0 during the SSL handshake with the client, and helps bootstrap an encrypted channel that will then be used for all further communication with the client.

Installation of the SSL private key proceeds as follows. In step 1, the client supplies a fresh symmetric key (freshSym), and a nonce (n_{SSL}), both encrypted under the vTPM's public key. In step 2, domB creates Udom0 after checking the integrity of the Udom0 image (using Sig_{client}). When domB creates Udom0, it requests the vTPM to decrypt this content, and places freshSym and n_{SSL} in Udom0's memory, where SSC's privilege model prevents them from being accessed by Sdom0. Recall from Sect. 3.1 that Sdom0 cannot directly access the TPM or vTPM (only domB can do so), and therefore cannot obtain the value of freshSym. In step 5, Udom0 sends n_{SSL} to the client, which responds in step 6 with the SSL private key encrypted under freshSym. Udom0 can now decrypt this message to obtain the SSL private key. Assuming that both freshSym and n_{SSL} are random and generated afresh, the protocol allows the client to detect replay attempts.

This protocol has been carefully designed to restricts the power of certain kinds of attacks launched by malicious SDom0s. We refer the reader to [1] for a discussion of these attacks and a security analysis of the protocol.

UdomUs and SDs. Udom0 accepts and processes client requests to start UdomUs and SDs. Clients establish an SSL connection with Udom0, and transmit the kernel and ramdisk images of the new domain to Udom0. Udom0 forwards this request to domB, which then builds the domain.

We aim for Udom0s and SDs to be stateless. They perform specialized tasks, and do not need persistent state for these tasks. The lack of persistent state eases the clients' task of verifying the integrity of these domains (*e.g.,* via inspection of their code), thereby minimizing risk even if they are compromised via attacks directed against them. The lack of state also allows easy recovery upon compromise; they can simply be restarted [23]. In our design, we do not assign persistent storage to SDs. They are neither extensible nor are they allowed to load kernel modules or extensions outside of the initial configuration. All relevant configuration values are passed via command line parameters. This design does require greater management effort on the part of clients, but is to be expected in SSC, because it shifts control from the provider to clients.

We have implemented SDs and Udom0s in our prototype using a carefully-configured paravirtualized Linux kernel; they only use ramdisks. The file system contains binaries, static configuration and temporary storage. SSC elides any unnecessary functionality in SDs and Udom0s to minimize their attack surface. Udom0s in our prototype integrates a replica of the xend Python-based toolstack for end-user interaction and to provide an administrative interface to the meta-domain.

MTSDs. Like SDs, each MTSD belongs to a client meta-domain. MTSDs can be given specific privileges (via the CREATE_MTSD hypercall) to map the state of client VMs, checkpoint, fingerprint, or introspect them. This allows the cloud provider to inspect client domains for regulatory compliance. Both the cloud provider and client cooperate to start the MTSD, as shown in the protocol in Fig. 3(c). The client initiates the protocol after it has agreed to start the MTSD in its meta-domain. DomB creates the MTSD, and both the provider and the client can each ensure that the MTSD was initialized properly using signed measurements from the vTPM. The provider or the client can terminate the protocol at this point if they find that the MTSD has been tampered with.

3.3 SSC Privilege Model

At the heart of SSC is a new privilege model enforced by the hypervisor. This model enables clients to administer their own VMs securely, without allowing cloud administrators to eavesdrop on their data. For purposes of exposition, we broadly categorize the privileged operations performed by a VMM into six groups.

(1) *VM control operations* include pausing/unpausing, scheduling, and destroying VMs.
(2) *Privacy-sensitive operations* allow the mapping of memory and virtual CPU registers of a VM.
(3) *Read-only operations* expose non-private information of a VM to a requester, including the number of vCPUs and RAM allocation of a VM, and the physical parameters of the host.
(4) *Build-only operations* include privacy-sensitive operations and certain operations that are only used during VM initialization.
(5) *Virtual I/O operations* set up event channels and grant tables to share memory and notifications in a controlled way for I/O.
(6) *Platform configurations* manage the physical host. Examples of these operations include programming the interrupt controller or clock sources.

In addition to these operations, VMMs also perform hardware device administration that assigns PCI devices and interrupts to different VMs. We expect that

Table 1. Actors and operations in the privilege model. Each ✓ in the table denotes that the actor can perform the corresponding operation.

	Sdom0	domB	Udom0	SD/MTSD
VM control (**C**)	✓		✓	✓
Privacy-sensitive (**P**)			✓	✓
Read-only (**R**)	✓		✓	✓
Build-only (**B**)		✓		
Virtual I/O (**I**)	✓		✓	✓
Platform config. (**L**)	✓			

hardware device administration may rarely be used in a dynamic cloud environment, where VM checkpointing and migration are commonplace, and leave for future work the inclusion of such operations in the SSC privilege model.

In SSC, Sdom0 has the privileges to perform VM control, read-only, virtual I/O and platform operations. VM control operations allow VMs to be provisioned for execution on physical hardware, and it is unreasonable to prevent Sdom0 from performing these tasks. A malicious system administrator can misuse VM control operations to launch denial-of-service attacks, but we exclude such attacks from our threat model. Sdom0 retains the privileges to access read-only data of client VMs for elementary management operations, *e.g.,* listing the set of VMs executing in a client meta-domain. Sdom0 executes backend drivers for virtual devices and must therefore retain the privileges to perform virtual I/O operations for all domains on the system. As discussed earlier, SSC also admits the notion of driver domains, where device drivers execute within separate VMs [24]. In such cases, only the driver domains need to retain privileges to perform virtual I/O. Finally, Sdom0 must be able to control and configure physical hardware, and therefore retains privileges to perform platform operations.

The domain builder (domB) performs build-only operations. Building domains necessarily involves some operations that are categorized as privacy-sensitive, and therefore includes them. However, when domB issues a hypercall on a target domain, the hypervisor first checks that the domain has not yet accrued a single cycle (*i.e.,* it is still being built), and allows the hypercall to succeed only if that is the case. This prevents domB from performing privacy-sensitive operations on client VMs after they have been built.

Udom0 can perform privacy-sensitive and read-only operations on VMs in its meta-domain. It can also perform limited VM control and virtual I/O operations. Udom0 can pause/unpause and destroy VMs in its meta-domain, but *cannot* control scheduling (this privilege rests with Sdom0). Udom0 can perform virtual I/O operations for UdomUs in its meta-domain. Udom0 can delegate specific privileges to SDs and MTSDs as per their requirements. A key aspect of our privilege model is that it groups VMs by meta-domain. Operations performed by Udom0, SDs and MTSDs are restricted to their meta-domain. While Udom0 has privileges to perform the above operations on VMs in its meta-domain, it cannot perform VM control, privacy-sensitive, and virtual I/O operations on MTSDs executing in its meta-domain. This is because such operations will allow Udom0 to breach its contract with the cloud provider (*e.g.,* by pausing, modifying or terminating an MTSD that the Udom0 has agreed to execute). Tables 1 and 2 summarize the privilege model of SSC.

In our SSC prototype, device drivers execute within Sdom0, thereby requiring clients to depend on Sdom0 to perform I/O on their behalf. Naïvely entrusting Sdom0 with I/O compromises client privacy. In SSC, we modified XenStore to allow domB to create subtrees for newly-created VMs, and give each Udom0 access to the subtrees of all VMs in its meta-domain. Udom0 uses this privilege to customize the virtual devices for its UdomUs. For instance, it can configure

Table 2. Actors, objects, and operations in the privilege model. Each column denotes an actor that performs an operation, while each row denotes the object upon which the operation is performed. Operations are abbreviated as shown in Table 1.

	Sdom0	domB	Udom0	SD	MTSD
Hardware	L				
Sdom0					
domB	C,R,I		I		
Udom0	C,R,I	B			
SD	C,R,I	B	C,P,R,I	C,P,R,I	C,P,R,I
MTSD	C,R,I	B	R,I	R,I	R,I
UdomU	C,R,I	B	C,P,R,I	C,P,R,I	C,P,R,I

a UdomU to use Sdom0 as the backend for virtual I/O. Alternatively, it can configure the UdomU to use an SD as a backend; the SD could modify the I/O stream. An SD can have Sdom0 as the backend, thereby ultimately directing I/O to physical hardware, or can itself have an SD as a backend, thereby allowing multiple SDs to be chained on the path from a UdomU to the I/O device. We also modified XenStore to allow Sdom0 and Udom0 to insert block devices into domB. This is used to transfer kernel and ramdisk images during domain building.

We implemented this privilege model in our prototype using the Xen Security Modules (XSM) framework [25]. XSM places a set of hooks in the Xen hypervisor, and is a generic framework that can be used to implement a wide variety of security policies. Security policies can be specified as modules that are invoked when a hook is encountered at runtime. For example, XSM served as basis for IBM's sHype project, which extended Xen to enforce mandatory access control policies [25]. We implemented the privilege described in this section as an XSM policy module.

4   Examples of SDs and MTSDs

We now illustrate the utility of SSC's privilege model using a number of example SDs and MTSDs that we implemented atop our prototype.

Storage SDs. Cloud providers supply clients with persistent storage. Because the actual storage hardware is no longer under the physical control of clients, they must treat it as untrusted. They must therefore have mechanisms to protect the confidentiality and integrity of data that resides on cloud storage. Such mechanisms can possibly be implemented within the client's VMs itself (*e.g.,* within a custom file system). However, virtual machine technology allows such services to be conveniently located outside the VM, where they can also be combined flexibly. It also isolates these services from potential attacks against client

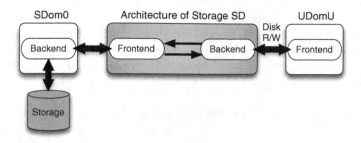

Fig. 4. Storage SD architecture.

VMs. Because all I/O from client VMs is virtualized, storage encryption and integrity checking can easily be implemented as cloud-based services offered by the provider.

Cloud providers would normally implement such services as daemons within dom0. However, this approach entails clients to trust dom0, and hence cloud administrators. SSC provides clients the ability to implement a variety of storage services as SDs without trusting cloud administrators. We describe two such SDs below, one for integrity checking and another for encryption. Our implementation of both SDs is set up as illustrated in Fig. 4. Each SD executes as a VM. When Udom0 starts a UdomU that wants to avail the service offered by an SD, it configures the UdomU to advertise the SD as the backend driver for disk operations. The SD itself executes a frontend driver that interfaces within a backend driver running within Sdom0. When UdomU attempts to perform a disk operation, the data first goes to the SD, which is the advertised backend for the UdomU. The SD performs the advertised service, and passes it to the frontend executing within the SD. In turn, the frontend forwards the (possibly modified) data block to Sdom0's backend, which interacts with the disk to store data persistently.

This setup can also be used to chain SDs, each offering its own service. For example, an encryption SD (see below) can serve as the I/O backend for UdomU. In turn, a checkpointing SD can serve as the I/O backend for the encryption SD. This would allow clients to easily produce disk checkpoints that store encrypted data.

Encryption SD. Storage encryption protects the confidentiality of client data by enciphering it before storing it on disk. Using SSC, clients can deploy their own storage encryption SD that enciphers their data before it is transmitted to Sdom0, which stores it on disk (or further processes the encrypted data, *e.g.,* to implement replication). Conversely, Sdom0 reads encrypted data from disk, and passes it to the SD, which decrypts it and passes it to the client. SSC ensures that Sdom0 cannot access the encryption keys, which are stored in client VM memory, thereby protecting client data.

Udom0 initiates the storage encryption SD using a key passed as a kernel parameter, and an initialization script that starts the SD with a crypto loopback device. The SD encrypts client data before it reaches Sdom0, and decrypts enciphered disk blocks fetched by Sdom0. Data is never presented in the clear to the cloud provider, and the encryption key is never exposed to Sdom0. In our implementation, the crypto loopback device in the SD uses AES 128-bit encryption.

Integrity Checking SD. Our integrity checking SD offers a service similar to the one proposed by Payne *et al.* [26]. The SD implements a loopback device, which runs as a kernel module. This device receives disk access requests from UdomUs at the block level, enforces the specified integrity policy, and forwards the requests to/from disk.

In our prototype SD, users specify important system files and directories to protect. The SD intercepts all disk operations to these targets, and checks that the SHA256 hashes of these disk blocks appear in a database of whitelisted hashes. Since all operations are intercepted at the block level, the SD needs to understand the high-level semantics of the file system. We use an offline process to extract known-good hashes at the block level from the client VM's file system, and populate the hash database, which the SD consults at runtime to check integrity.

Memory Introspection SD. Memory introspection tools (*e.g.*, [27–30]) rely on the ability to fetch and inspect raw memory pages from target VMs. In commodity cloud infrastructures, memory introspection must be offered by the provider, and cannot be deployed independently by clients, who face the unsavory option of using the service but placing their privacy at risk.

Using SSC, clients can deploy memory introspection tools as SDs. We illustrate such an SD by implementing an approach developed in the Patagonix project [30]. Patagonix aims to detect the presence of covertly-executing malicious binaries in a target VM by monitoring that VM's page tables. As originally described, the Patagonix daemon runs in dom0, maps all the memory pages of the target VM, and marks all pages as non-executable when the VM starts. When the target VM attempts to execute a page for the first time, Patagonix receives a fault. Patagonix handles this fault by hashing the contents of the page (*i.e.*, an md5sum) requested for execution, and comparing it against a database of hashes of code authorized to execute on the system (*e.g.*, the database may store hashes of code pages of an entire Linux distribution). If the hash does not exist in the database, Patagonix raises an alarm and suspends the VM.

We implemented Patagonix as an SD. Each Patagonix SD monitors a target UdomU, a reference to which is passed to the SD when the UdomU boots up. Udom0 delegates to Patagonix SD the privileges to map the UdomU's pages, and mark them as non-executable. The SD receives and handles faults as the UdomU executes new code pages. Our Patagonix SD can detect maliciously-executing binaries with the same effectiveness as described in the original paper [30].

System Call Monitoring SD. There is a large body of work on system call-based anomaly detection tools. While we will not attempt to summarize that work here (see Giffin's thesis [31] for a good overview), these techniques typically work by intercepting process system calls and their arguments, and ensuring that the sequence of calls conforms to a security policy. The anomaly detector executes in a separate VM (dom0), and capture system call traps and arguments from a user VM for analysis. Using SSC, clients can implement their own system call anomaly detectors as SDs. The SD simply intercepts all system calls and arguments from a target UdomU and checks them against a target policy.

Checkpointing SD. It is commonplace for cloud service providers to checkpoint client VMs for various purposes, such as live migration, load balancing and debugging. On commodity cloud architectures, checkpointing is implemented as a user daemon within dom0, which copies client VM memory pages and stores them unencrypted within dom0. If dom0 is untrusted, as is usually the case, it is challenging to create trustworthy checkpoints [32]. SSC simplifies checkpointing by allowing it to be implemented as an SD. The SD maps the client's memory pages, and checkpoints them akin to the dom0 checkpointing daemon (in fact, we reused the same code-base to implement the SD). As previously discussed, clients can chain the storage encryption SD with the checkpointing SD to ensure that the checkpoint stores encrypted data.

Memory Deduplication SD. When multiple VMs have memory pages with identical content, one way to conserve physical memory using a mechanism where VMs share memory pages [33]. Such a mechanism benefits cloud providers, who are always on the lookout for new techniques to improve the elasticity of their services. It can also benefit cloud clients who may have multiple VMs on the cloud and may be billed for the memory consumed by these VMs. Identifying and exploiting memory sharing opportunities among VMs allows clients to judiciously purchase resources, thereby reducing their overall cost of using the cloud. In commodity cloud computing environments, providers implement memory deduplication to consolidate physical resources, but such services are not exposed to clients, thereby limiting their applicability.

SSC allows clients to deploy memory deduplication on their own VMs without involving the cloud provider. To illustrate this, we implemented a memory deduplication SD. This SD accepts as input a list of domains (UdomUs) in the same meta-domain, and identifies pages with identical content (using their md5 hashes). For each such page, the SD instructs the hypervisor to keep just one copy of the page, and free the remaining copies by modifying the page tables of the domains. The hypervisor marks the shared pages as belonging to special "shared memory" domain. When a domain attempts to write to the shared page, the hypervisor uses copy-on-write to create a copy of that page local to the domain that attempted the write, and makes it unshared in that domain.

Regulatory-Compliance using MTSDs. The SDs discussed so far are deployed within the client's meta-domain, and their output is not visible to cloud administrators. However, cloud administrators may wish to monitor client VMs, *e.g.*, to enforce regulatory compliance. In today's cloud infrastructure, this is achieved via VM introspection tools that execute in dom0. Such tools can inspect and modify client state, and therefore require dom0 to be trusted.

MTSDs offer cloud providers unprecedented power and flexibility in verifying client regulatory compliance while respecting client privacy. As an example, cloud providers can implement the Patagonix SD above as an MTSD to ensure that a client VM is free of malware. In this case, the cloud provider would supply the database of code hashes, which is the regulatory compliance policy. The MTSD itself would execute in the client meta-domain; the manifest of this MTSD simply requests privileges to read client memory pages and registers. The MTSD continuously monitors client UdomUs and reports a violation of regulatory compliance to the cloud provider (*i.e.*, Sdom0) only if the client becomes infected with malware. The cloud provider only learns whether the client has violated regulatory compliance, and cannot otherwise read or modify the content of the client's memory pages.

Clients may wish to ensure that the MTSD's functionality does not compromise their privacy. For example, the client may want to check that an MTSD that reads its VM memory pages does not inadvertantly leak the contents of these pages. One way to achieve this goal is to inspect the code of the MTSD to ensure the absence of such undesirable functionality. However, we cannot reasonably expect most cloud clients to have the economic resources to conduct thorough and high-quality security evaluations of MTSDs.

We therefore limit the amount of information that an MTSD can transmit outside the meta-domain. MTSDs are not given any persitent storage, and can only communicate with the provider (*i.e.*, Sdom0) via the SSC hypervisor. Further, this communication channel is restricted to be a stream of bits whose semantics is well-understood. That is, each 0 bit in the stream denotes a violation of regulatory compliance, while a 1 bit denotes otherwise.[1] The client can set up a user daemon (*e.g.*, within Udom0) that is awakened by the SSC hypervisor upon every new bit transmitted by the MTSD over this channel. An honest client that does not violate the provider's regulatory compliance policies should therefore only expect to see a stream of 1s transmitted to Sdom0. Any 0s in the stream either denote an MTSD attempting to steal information, or an inadvertant compliance violation (*e.g.*, due to malware infection). In either case, the client can terminate its meta-domain.

5   A Retrospective Look at SSC

The previous sections have described the main ideas underlying SSC. After having worked on SSC for nearly four years, we now look back and comment on some of the design decisions in light of recent hardware trends, in particular, the Intel SGX [34,35].

---

[1] Note that a client cannot modify this stream without tampering with the code of the MTSD. The provider ensures that the MTSD was booted correctly (Fig. 3(c)), and SSC's privilege model prevents the client from modifying a running MTSD.

SSC's Threat Model. When we started the SSC project, one of the main foci of the research community was to protect client VMs from co-located VMs belonging to adversarial clients [36]. We instead chose to focus on protecting client data from an adversarial public cloud platform. At the time, one of the main approaches to achieve this goal was to store client data encrypted on the cloud platform and develop techniques to compute on encrypted data. While this approach is promising, general-purpose techniques such as homomorphic encryption are still too expensive to be practical. Domain-specific techniques (*e.g.,* [37]) are a promising way to achieve practical overheads, but must be carefully designed for each specific domain. We were seeking a practical yet general-purpose solution that would work in a broad range of settings.

Unfortunately, this goal is challenging to achieve. The cloud provider controls the entire compute infrastructure and can subvert any security mechanisms that are not grounded in cryptography. As a result, we chose to relax our goals somewhat, and work with the slightly unconventional threat model of differentiating the cloud provider from cloud administrators, and choosing to trust the cloud provider but not cloud administrators. The cost of doing so was that we could not protect against attacks initiated by the cloud provider itself, *e.g.,* via government-issued subpoenas, requiring the cloud provider to gather the client's data. This was a price we were willing to pay. It also seemed like an interesting point in the design space, and other research groups were also concurrently working on related problems assuming a similar threat model [18–20].

However, with the announcement of the Intel SGX, our original goal is no longer challenging to achieve. The SGX provides hardware support for *enclaves*, which are regions in a process address space that are protected from the rest of the process and even the underlying operating system. Building atop the SGX, it should therefore be possible to build virtual machines that are able to protect a client's data from the underlying hypervisor and other software components that are controlled by the cloud provider (*e.g.,* as has been demonstrated by the Haven project [38]).

However, this protection comes at a cost. With SGX enclaves, the cloud provider no longer has visibility into the code and data of the client. While this benefits the client by protecting the confidentiality of its code and data, it also allows malicious clients to execute arbitrary code within their enclaves and violate service-level agreements with the cloud provider. For example, the cloud provider may wish to ensure that the client is not misusing the cloud infrastructure to host a malware (*e.g.,* a botnet command and control server). On traditional cloud platforms, this goal is easy to achieve. If a cloud provider suspects that a client is violating the terms of the SLA, it can simply scan the contents of the client's VMs for traces of any SLA-violating code or data. With enclaves, malicious clients can easily hide their activities from cloud providers, who must then use other means to infer malicious activity. Thus, the SGX "flips" the threat model in favor of clients. It is not clear that this extreme is desirable, either. Later in this section, we briefly discuss a possible solution to this problem using SSC's MTSD abstraction.

MTSDs and Mutual Trust. We introduced MTSDs and the concept of mutual trust in SSC to balance the concerns of the client and the cloud provider. We believe that this notion of mutual trust is novel; to our knowledge, it has only been investigated concurrently in the context of one other project on system administration [39].

Of all new abstractions introduced in SSC, we feel that MTSDs have the potential to have the greatest impact. In our own work, we have demonstrated several novel applications that can be enabled using mutual trust, such as privacy-preserving regulatory compliance [1]. It can also be used to implement trustworthy resource accounting and billing software [2]. On traditional cloud platforms, clients trust the cloud provider to correctly charge them based upon the resources that they consume. If a client has reason to believe that a cloud provider is charging it for more than its share of resources consumed, it cannot prove that the cloud provider is cheating. MTSDs allow the creation of trustworthy services that performs resource accounting. The client and cloud provider agree upon the software that will be used to account for the client's network bandwidth utilization. This metering software executes as an MTSD and serves as the network backend for all of the client's network-facing VMs. The client and cloud provider can both verify that the MTSD was started correctly (using TPM attestations), and the SSC hypervisor ensures that neither the cloud provider nor the client can tamper with the MTSD once it has started execution. Thus, both the cloud provider and the client can trust the network bandwidth utilization reported by the MTSD.

Moving foward, we feel that the idea of mutual trust can also find valuable applications in SGX-enabled platforms. For example, the cloud provider and client could leverage a mutually-trusted library to ensure that the contents of the client's enclaves comply with the cloud provider's SLAs. Investigating how such a mutually-trusted library can be constructed and the guarantees that it can provide are topics for interesting future research.

Reliance on the TPM. Finally, as is clear from the discussion in Sect. 3, SSC's security guarantees rely in a critical way on attestations generated by the TPM. However, like other TPM-based protocols, these attestations only provide guarantees about the software stack during the instant that the attestations were created. It well-known that malicious modifications to the software stack that are introduced after or between attestations can bypass detection, and SSC's bootstrap protocols suffer from the same shortcoming. It would be interesting to investigate whether similar attestation protocols as implemented in the SGX (*e.g.,* to attest the integrity of enclave creation) can be leveraged to extend the boot-time guarantees provided by SSC's protocols.

6   Related Work

Popular cloud services, such as Amazon's EC2 and Microsoft's Azure rely on hypervisor-based VMMs (Xen [40] and Hyper-V [41], respectively). In such

VMMs, the TCB consists of the hypervisor and an administrative domain. Prior attempts to secure the TCB have focused on both these entities, as discussed below.

Historically, hypervisors have been considered to be a small layer of software. Prior work has argued that the architecture of hypervisors resembles that of microkernels [42]. The relatively small code size of research hypervisors [43–45], combined with the recent breakthrough in formally verifying the L4 microkernel [46], raises hope for similar verification of hypervisors. However, commodity hypervisors often contain several thousand lines of code (*e.g.,* 150 KLoC in Xen 4.1) and are not yet within the realm of formal verification. Consequently, researchers have proposed architectures that completely eliminate the hypervisor [18].

The main problem with these techniques is that they often do not support the rich functionality that is needed in cloud computing. Production hypervisors today need to support different virtualization modes, guest quirks, hardware features, and software features like memory deduplication and migration. In SSC, we work with a commodity hypervisor-based VMM (Xen), but assume that the hypervisor is part of the TCB. While this exposes an SSC-based VMM to attacks directed against hypervisor vulnerabilities, it also allows the SSC model to largely resemble commodity cloud computing. Recent advances to strengthen hypervisors against certain classes of attacks [47] can also be applied to SSC, thereby improving the overall security of the platform.

In comparison to hypervisors, the administrative domain is large and complex. To address threats against the administrative domain, the research community has focused on adopting the principle of separation of privilege, an approach that we also adopted in SSC. Murray *et al.* [48] disaggregated the administrative domain by isolating in a separate VM the functionality that builds new VMs. This domain builder has highly-specific functionality and a correspondingly small code-base. This feature, augmented with the use of a library OS enhances the robustness of that code. Murray *et al.*'s design directly inspired the use of domB in SSC. Disaggregation is also advocated by Nova [45]. The Xoar project [23] extends this approach by "sharding" different parts of the administrative toolstack into a set of domains. Previous work has also considered separate domains to isolate device drivers [24], which are more defect-prone than the rest of the kernel.

SSC is similar to these lines of research because it also aims to reduce the privilege of Sdom0, which can no longer inspect the code, data and computation of client VMs. However, SSC is unique in delegating administrative privileges to clients (via Udom0). It is this very feature that enables clients to deploy custom services to monitor and control their own VMs.

The CloudVisor project [19] leverages recent advances in nested virtualization technology to protect the security and privacy of client VMs from the administrative domain. In CloudVisor, a commodity hypervisor such as Xen executes atop a small, trusted, bare-metal hypervisor. This trusted hypervisor intercepts privileged operations from Xen, and cryptographically protects the state of client

VMs executing within Xen from its dom0 VM, *e.g.*, dom0 only has an encrypted view of a client VM's memory.

The main advantage of CloudVisor over SSC is that its TCB only includes the small, bare-metal hypervisor, comprising about 5.5 KLOC, whereas SSC's system-wide TCB includes the entire commodity hypervisor and domB. Moreover, the use of cryptography allows CloudVisor to provide strong guarantees on client VM security and privacy. However, SSC offers three concrete advantages over CloudVisor. First, SSC offers clients more flexible control over their own VMs than CloudVisor. For example, because CloudVisor only presents an encrypted view of a client's VM to dom0, many security introspection tools cannot be implemented within dom0. Second, unlike CloudVisor, SSC does not rely on nested virtualization. Nesting fundamentally imposes overheads on client VMs because privileged operations must be handled by both the bare-metal and nested hypervisors, which can slow down I/O intensive client applications, as reported in the CloudVisor paper. Third, SSC's MTSDs allow the cloud provider and clients to execute mutually-trusted services for regulatory compliance. It is unclear whether the CloudVisor model can achieve mutual trust of shared services.

There has been nearly a decade of research on novel services enabled by virtualization, starting with Chen and Noble's seminal paper [11]. On current cloud infrastructures, deploying these techniques requires the cooperation of the cloud provider, which greatly limits their impact. SSC enables clients to deploy their own privileged services without requiring the cloud provider to do so. The primary advantage of such an approach is that clients need no longer expose their code and data to the cloud provider. At the same time, SSC's MTSDs accommodate the need for cloud providers to ensure regulatory compliance and have some control over client VMs.

The xCloud project [49,50] also considers the problem of providing clients flexible control over their VMs. The original position paper [49] advocated several approaches to this problem, including by extending hypervisors, which may weaken hypervisor security. The full paper [50] describes XenBlanket, which realizes the vision of the xCloud project using nested virtualization. XenBlanket implements a "blanket" layer that allows clients to execute paravirtualized VMMs atop commodity cloud infrastructures. The key benefit of XenBlanket over SSC is that it provides clients the same level of control over their VMs as does SSC but without modifying the hypervisor of the cloud infrastructure. However, unlike SSC, XenBlanket does not address the problem of protecting the security and privacy of client VMs from cloud administrators.

7 Summary

SSC is a new cloud computing model that improves client security and privacy, and gives clients the flexibility to deploy privileged services on their own VMs. SSC introduces new abstractions and a supporting privilege model to achieve these goals. We integrated SSC with a commodity hypervisor (Xen), and presented a number of applications showing SSC's benefits.

Acknowledgments. This paper reports work that was done together with my Ph.D. student Shakeel Butt and collaborators Andres Lagar-Cavilla and Abhinav Srivastava. Portions of this work have appeared in ACM CCS 2012, ACM SOCC 2014, and in Shakeel Butt's Ph.D. thesis. We are thankful to the NSF for their support of parts of this work via grants CNS-0831268, CNS-0915394, CNS-0952128 and CNS-1420815. We also thank Microsoft Research India for their research gift and Sriram Rajamani, Kapil Vaswani, Aditya Nori and Manuel Costa for discussions on SSC and the Intel SGX.

References

1. Butt, S., Lagar-Cavilla, H.A., Srivastava, A., Ganapathy, V.: Self-service cloud computing. In: ACM CCS (2012)
2. Butt, S., Ganapathy, V., Srivastava, A.: On the control plane of a self-service cloud platform. In: ACM SOCC (2014)
3. Butt, S.: Self-service Cloud Computing. Ph.D. thesis, Rutgers University, January 2015
4. CVE-2007-4993: Xen guest root escapes to dom0 via pygrub
5. CVE-2007-5497: Integer overflows in libext2fs in e2fsprogs
6. CVE-2008-0923: Directory traversal vulnerability in the shared folders feature for VMWare
7. CVE-2008-1943: Buffer overflow in the backend of XenSource Xen paravirtualized frame buffer
8. CVE-2008-2100: VMWare buffer overflows in VIX API let local users execute arbitrary code in host OS
9. Kortchinsky, K.: Hacking 3D (and breaking out of VMWare). In: BlackHat USA (2009)
10. Gartner: Assesing the Security Risks of Cloud Computing. http://www.gartner.com/DisplayDocument?id=685308
11. Chen, P.M., Noble, B.: When virtual is better than real. In: HotOS (2001)
12. Garfinkel, T., Rosenblum, M.: A virtual machine introspection based architecture for intrusion detection. In: NDSS (2003)
13. Clark, C., Fraser, K., Hand, S., Hansen, J.G., Jul, E., Limpach, C., Pratt, I., Warfield, A.: Live migration of virtual machines. In: USENIX NSDI (2005)
14. Litty, L., Lagar-Cavilla, H.A., Lie, D.: Computer meteorology: monitoring compute clouds. In: HotOS (2009)
15. Berger, S., Caceres, R., Goldman, K., Perez, R., Sailer, R., van Door, L.: vTPM: virtualizing the trusted platform module. In: USENIX Security (2006)
16. Kauer, B.: OSLO: improving the security of trusted computing. In: USENIX Security (2007)
17. Group, T.C.: TPM main spec., 12 v1.2 r116. http://www.trustedcomputinggroup.org/resources/tpm_main_specification
18. Keller, E., Szefer, J., Rexford, J., Lee, R.: Eliminating the hypervisor attack surface for a more secure cloud. In: ACM CCS (2011)
19. Zhang, F., Chen, J., Chen, H., Zang, B.: CloudVisor: retrofitting protection of virtual machines in multi-tenant cloud with nested virtualization. In: ACM SOSP (2011)
20. Santos, N., Rodrigues, R., Gummadi, K., Saroiu, S.: Policy-sealed data: a new abstraction for building trusted cloud services. In: USENIX Security (2012)
21. Danev, B., Masti, R., Karame, G., Capkun, S.: Enabling secure VM-vTPM migration in private clouds. In: ACSAC (2011)

22. Sailer, R., Zhang, X., Jaeger, T., van Doorn, L.: Design and implementation of a TCG-based integrity measurement architecture. In: USENIX Security (2004)
23. Colp, P., Nanavati, M., Zhu, J., Aiello, W., Coker, G., Deegan, T., Loscocco, P., Warfield, A.: Breaking up is hard to do: security and functionality in a commodity hypervisor. In: ACM SOSP (2011)
24. LeVasseur, J., Uhlig, V., Stoess, J., Gotz, S.: Unmodified device driver reuse and improved system dependability via virtual machines. In: ACM/USENIX OSDI (2004)
25. Sailer, R., Jaeger, T., Valdez, E., Caceres, R., Perez, R., Berger, S., Griffin, J., van Doorn, L.: Building a MAC-based security architecture for the xen hypervisor. In: ACSAC (2005)
26. Payne, B., Carbone, M., Lee, W.: Secure and flexible monitoring of virtual machines. In: ACSAC (2007)
27. Srivastava, A., Giffin, J.T.: Tamper-resistant, application-aware blocking of malicious network connections. In: Lippmann, R., Kirda, E., Trachtenberg, A. (eds.) RAID 2008. LNCS, vol. 5230, pp. 39–58. Springer, Heidelberg (2008)
28. Baliga, A., Ganapathy, V., Iftode, L.: Detecting kernel-level rootkits using data structure invariants. IEEE TDSC 8(5), 670–684 (2011)
29. Payne, B., Carbone, M., Sharif, M., Lee, W.: Lares: an architecture for secure active monitoring using virtualization. In: IEEE Symposium on Security & Privacy (2008)
30. Litty, L., Lagar-Cavilla, H.A., Lie, D.: Hypervisor support for identifying covertly executing binaries. In: USENIX Security (2008)
31. Giffin, J.T.: Model Based Intrusion Detection System Design and Evaluation. Ph.D. thesis, University of Wisconsin-Madison (2006)
32. Srivastava, A., Raj, H., Giffin, J., England, P.: Trusted VM snapshots in untrusted cloud infrastructures. In: Balzarotti, D., Stolfo, S.J., Cova, M. (eds.) RAID 2012. LNCS, vol. 7462, pp. 1–21. Springer, Heidelberg (2012)
33. Waldspurger, C.A.: Memory resource management in VMWare ESX server. In: USENIX/ACM OSDI (2002)
34. Intel: (September 2013) Intel document 329298–001US
35. Hoekstra, M., Lal, R., Pappachan, P., Rozas, C., Phegade, V.: Using innovative instructions to create trustworthy software solutions. In: HASP (2013)
36. Ristenpart, T., Tromer, E., Shacham, H., Savage, S.: Hey, you, get off of my cloud: exploring information leakage in third-party compute clouds. In: ACM Conference on Computer and Communications Security (CCS) (2009)
37. Popa, R., Redfield, C., Zeldovich, N., Balakrishnan, H.: Cryptdb: protecting confidentiality with encrypted query processing. In: ACM SOSP (2011)
38. Baumann, A., Peinado, M., Hunt, G.: Shielding applications from an untrusted cloud with Haven. In: OSDI (2014)
39. Santos, N., Rodrigues, R., Ford, B.: Enhancing the OS against security threats in system administration. In: Narasimhan, P., Triantafillou, P. (eds.) Middleware 2012. LNCS, vol. 7662, pp. 415–435. Springer, Heidelberg (2012)
40. Barham, P., Dragovic, B., Fraser, K., Hand, S., Harris, T., Ho, A., Neugebauer, R., Pratt, I., Warfield, A.: Xen and the art of virtualization. In: ACM SOSP (2003)
41. Microsoft: Hyper-V Architecture. http://msdn.microsoft.com/en-us/library/cc768 520(BTS.10).aspx
42. Hand, S., Warfield, A., Fraser, K., Kotsovinos, E., Magenheimer, D.: Are VMMs microkernels done right? In: HotOS (2005)
43. Seshadri, A., Luk, M., Qu, N., Perrig, A.: SecVisor: a tiny hypervisor to provide lifetime kernel code integrity for commodity OSes. In: ACM SOSP (2007)

44. McCune, J.M., Li, Y., Qu, N., Zhou, Z., Datta, A., Gligor, V., Perrig, A.: TrustVisor: efficient TCB reduction and attestation. In: IEEE Symposium on Security & Privacy (2010)
45. Steinberg, U., Kauer, B.: NOVA: a microhypervisor-based secure virtualization architecture. In: ACM Eurosys (2010)
46. Klein, G., Elphinstone, K., Heiser, G., Andronick, J., Cock, D., Derrin, P., Elkaduwe, D., Engelhardt, K., Kolanski, R., Norrish, M., Sewell, T., Tuch, H., Winwood, S.: seL4: Formal verification of an OS kernel. In: ACM SOSP (2009)
47. Wang, Z., Jang, X.: Hypersafe: a lightweight approach to provide lifetime hypervisor control-flow integrity. In: IEEE Symposium on Security & Privacy (2010)
48. Murray, D., Milos, G., Hand, S.: Improving xen security through disaggregation. In: ACM VEE (2008)
49. Williams, D., Elnikety, E., Eldehiry, M., Jamjoom, H., Huang, H., Weatherspoon, H.: Unshackle the cloud! In: HotCloud (2011)
50. Williams, D., Jamjoom, H., Weatherspoon, H.: The xen-blanket: virtualize once, run everywhere. In: ACM EuroSys (2012)

Access Control

Enforcing Separation of Duty in Attribute Based Access Control Systems

Sadhana Jha[1], Shamik Sural[2]([✉]), Vijayalakshmi Atluri[3], and Jaideep Vaidya[3]

[1] Advanced Technology Development Centre, Indian Institute of Technology,
Kharagpur, India
sadhanajha@sit.iitkgp.ernet.in
[2] School of Information Technology, Indian Institute of Technology, Kharagpur, India
shamik@sit.iitkgp.ernet.in
[3] MSIS Department, Rutgers University, Newark, USA
{atluri,jsvaidya}@rutgers.edu

Abstract. Conventional access control models like discretionary access control and role based access control are suitable for regulating access to resources by known users of an organization. However, for systems where the user population is dynamic and the identities of all users are not known in advance, attribute based access control (ABAC) can be more conveniently used. The set of constraints supported by an access control model acts as a deciding factor for the type of restrictions it can put on unauthorized access. Among the various types of constraints, enforcement of Separation of Duty (SoD) is considered to be the most important in any commercial application. In this paper, we introduce the problem of SoD enforcement in the context of ABAC. We analyze the complexity of the problem and provide a methodology for solving it. Experiments on a wide range of data sets show encouraging results.

Keywords: Attribute based access control · Separation of duty · Mutually exclusive policies · Policy enforcement

1 Introduction

Organizations use access control mechanisms to mitigate the risk of unauthorized access to their data, resources and systems. Depending on the information required for authorization and the process of making decisions, different access control models have been developed. For traditional information systems, where a system provider needs to deal only with a predictable set of users, access control models such as Discretionary Access Control (DAC) [18], Mandatory Access Control (MAC) [17] and Role based Access Control (RBAC) [16] have been proposed. Among these, RBAC, which is based on the notion of roles, has emerged as the most effective one. The primary limitation of these traditional models including RBAC, is their significant dependence on user identity and an inherent lack of extendibility, making them unsuitable for dynamic systems where users from different domains may have to be given access.

© Springer International Publishing Switzerland 2015
S. Jajodia and C. Mazumdar (Eds.): ICISS 2015, LNCS 9478, pp. 61–78, 2015.
DOI: 10.1007/978-3-319-26961-0_5

To handle such dynamic environments, in recent years, Attribute based Access Control (ABAC) has been proposed [9]. ABAC mediates access based on the attributes of users and objects and not on their identity. In addition environmental attributes also play a role in the model. An attribute in the context of ABAC defines a particular characteristic of an entity.

Access decision in ABAC considers a set of authorization policies or rules that consist of predicates over attribute values of the requesting user, requested resources and the environment in which the request is being made. A user can execute an operation on a resource, if and only if, attribute values of the requesting user and that of the requested resource as well as the environment satisfy the authorization policy for that operation. The limitation of extendibility of traditional models in multiple domains can be overcome in ABAC by selecting appropriate attributes for those domains.

To comply with organizational business requirements, authorization policies of access control models often need to be constrained. One of the most common form of constraint in any commercial organization is Separation of Duty (SoD) [19]. A typical SoD constraint (interchangeably called an SoD policy) prevents error and fraud by ensuring that at least two individuals are responsible for the separate steps of any critical task. For example, consider the task of payroll processing, which involves two main activities, namely, accounting and signing of checks. A relevant SoD principle would be that, if an employee is able to do the accounting activity, then she is restricted from signing the checks. A system is said to be *safe* with respect to an SoD policy, if the set of authorization policies of the system does not violate that SoD policy.

While SoD enforcement in RBAC has been studied in the literature [11], to the best of our knowledge, there is no work yet on enforcement of SoD in the context of ABAC. In this paper, we formally define SoD in terms of the various ABAC components. We show that, although directly enforcing SoD in ABAC is intractable, enforcement through mutually exclusive authorization policies can be done efficiently. We also show how to determine the set of such mutually exclusive policies for a given SoD constraint.

The rest of the paper is organized as follows. Section 2 discusses the preliminaries about the various ABAC components and the principle of SoD. Section 3 defines the SoD verification problem in ABAC and analyzes its complexity. In Sect. 4, we provide a methodology for SoD enforcement using mutual exclusion. Section 5 gives the results of experimental evaluation of the proposed approach. Related literature is reviewed in Sect. 6 and finally, Sect. 7 concludes the paper along with some suggestions for prospective future work.

2   Preliminaries

In this section, we first introduce the main components of attribute based access control [4]. We also provide the general definition of Separation of Duty and its implications in the context of ABAC.

2.1 Attribute Based Access Control (ABAC)

ABAC is an access control model based on the notion of attributes of the requesting user, requested object, and the environment in which a request is made. The basic components of ABAC are as follows:

- users ($\mathcal{U}$): A set of authorized users. Each member of this set is represented as u_i, for $1 \leq i \leq |\mathcal{U}|$.
- Objects ($\mathcal{O}$): A set of resources to be protected. Each member of this set is represented as o_i, for $1 \leq i \leq |\mathcal{O}|$.
- Environment ($\mathcal{E}$): A set of environment conditions such as access location and access time, independent of users and objects. Each member of this set is represented as e_i, for $1 \leq i \leq |\mathcal{E}|$.
- $\mathcal{U_A}$: A set of user attribute names that could possibly influence access decisions. A member of $\mathcal{U_A}$ is represented as ua_i, for $1 \leq i \leq |\mathcal{U_A}|$. Each ua_i is associated with a set of values it can acquire. For instance, consider a user attribute *qualification* associated with the set of values { *UG, PG* and *Null*[1] }. Then, every $u_i \in \mathcal{U}$ can have either *UG, PG* or *Null* as the value of the attribute *qualification*.
- $\mathcal{O_A}$: A set of object attributes that could possibly influence access decisions. An element of $\mathcal{O_A}$ is represented as oa_i, where $1 \leq i \leq |\mathcal{O_A}|$. Similar to users, each object attribute oa_i is associated with a set of values it can acquire. For instance, if an object attribute *type* is associated with a set of values { *Binary, Text*} associated with it, then the value of the attribute *type* for each object $o_i \in \mathcal{O}$ can be either *Binary* or *Text*.
- $\mathcal{E_A}$: A set of all environment attributes that could possibly influence access decisions. A member of $\mathcal{E_A}$ is denoted as ea_i, where $1 \leq i \leq |\mathcal{E_A}|$. Each $ea_i \in \mathcal{E_A}$ is associated with a set consisting of all the possible values that ea_i can acquire. For instance, if an environment attribute *workingshift* is associated with a set of values { *DayShift, EveningShift, NightShift, Null*}, then for every $e_i \in \mathcal{E}$, value of the attribute *workingshift* can be either *DayShift, EveningShift, NightShift* or *Null*.
- $\mathcal{F_U}$: $\mathcal{U} \times \mathcal{U_A} \rightarrow \{j|j$ is a user attribute value}. For instance, consider a user *Bob*, who is a *UG* student. Then $\mathcal{F_U}(Bob, qualification) = \{UG\}$.
- $\mathcal{F_O}$: $\mathcal{O} \times \mathcal{O_A} \rightarrow \{j|j$ is an object attribute value}. For instance, consider a file *F1* whose type is *Binary*. Then, $\mathcal{F_O}(F1, type) = \{Binary\}$.
- $\mathcal{F_E}$: $\mathcal{E} \times \mathcal{E_A} \rightarrow \{j|j$ is an environment attribute value}. For instance, consider an environment *e* having value *DayShift* for the attribute named *workingshift*. This is represented as $\mathcal{F_E}(e, workingshift) \rightarrow \{DayShift\}$.
- $\triangle$: A set consisting of all possible operations (actions) on objects allowed in a system. For example, if *read* and *write* are the only two possible actions on a file, then $\triangle = \{read, write\}$. Each member of $\triangle$ is represented as a_i.
- $\mathcal{P}$: A set of authorization policies. Each member of this set is represented as p_i, for $1 \leq i \leq |\mathcal{P}|$.

---

[1] *Null* indicates that the value of the attribute is unknown.

A policy p in ABAC is a 4 - tuple of the form $\langle uc, oc, ec, a \rangle$. Here, uc (respectively oc and ec) is a user condition (respectively, object condition and environment condition) comprising of equalities of the form $n = c$, where n is a user attribute name (respectively, object attribute name and environment attribute name) and c is either a constant or *any*. For an attribute name n, if the value of c is *any*, then the attribute n is not relevant for making the access decisions. $a \in \triangle$ is an action.

When a user makes a request to access an object, the authorization policy set $\mathcal{P}$ is searched for the policies through which the user can get access. If any such policy exists, then access is granted, otherwise denied. As an example, consider an organization having the following requirement: A user having clearance level *high* and designation *Director* can *edit* any file having clearance level *confidential*, from his *office* computer. In ABAC, this requirement can be specified in the form of a policy: <{(clearance level = *High*), (designation = *Director*)}, {(type = *File*), (clearance level = *confidential*)}, {(access location = *Director Office*)}, *edit*>.

We now introduce the notion of an ABAC state. An ABAC state φ is a 4-tuple $< \mathcal{F_U}, \mathcal{F_O}, \mathcal{F_E}, \mathcal{P} >$. Modification in any of the components results in a different state. These components collectively determine access permissions of users to objects. A state is said to be *safe* if it restricts every unauthorized access.

2.2   Separation of Duty

Separation of Duty (SoD) is a security principle that prevents a single user from performing all the steps in a critical task. The idea behind this is that the likelihood of a single person involved in a fraud is higher than that of a group of people being involved. A k-n SoD (k-out-of-n Separation of Duty) policy, which is a generalization of the above statement, states that no less than k users together should get all the n permissions required to perform a task. This definition of SoD is valid irrespective of the underlying access control mechanism. Two different approaches could be used to enforce an SoD policy: Static SoD (SSoD) and Dynamic SoD (DSoD). In the present work, we consider only SSoD in which an SoD policy should hold irrespective of the dynamic environment. Thus, in the rest of the paper, we deal only with the attributes of users and objects as mentioned in Subsect. 2.1 and do not consider environmental attributes as is required in DSoD.

Since a permission in any access control model essentially provides authority to a user to perform actions on certain objects, every permission could be expressed as a 2-tuple (a_i, o_j), where a_i is the name of the action to be performed and o_j is the name of the object on which a_i is to be performed. We denote a pair of action and object as an *access tuple* (hereinafter referred to as a *tuple*). Using this notion of tuples, we can define SoD in ABAC as follows:

Definition 1. *A k-n SoD (k-out-of-n Separation of Duty) policy is expressed as* $sod\langle\{t_1, t_2, \ldots\ldots, t_n\}, k\rangle$, *where each* t_i *is a tuple of the form* (a_i, o_i) *such that* $a_i \in \triangle$, $o_i \in \mathcal{O}$, $1 < k \leq n$.

The above definition of SoD conveys that, for a task that requires n actions to be performed respectively on n objects (not necessarily distinct), no less than k users together should satisfy authorization policies that would give them all the t_1, t_2,......, t_n accesses. An SoD policy $\langle\{t_1, t_2,......, t_n\}, k\rangle$, can be further represented in a compact form as a 2-tuple $\langle Per, k\rangle$, where Per is the set of t_is in the SoD. A set ω of m SoD policies is denoted as $\omega = \{s_1, s_2, ..., s_m\}$.

Given a k-n SoD policy s and an ABAC state φ, if no set of k-1 users in φ together is authorized for t_1, t_2,......, t_n, then we say that φ satisfies s, which is denoted as $satisfies_\varphi[s]$. An ABAC state is said to be *safe*, if for each $s \in \omega$, $satisfies_\varphi[s]$ is *true*, otherwise unsafe, if $satisfies_\varphi[s]$ is *false*.

Example 1. Consider a university *XYZ* having *Dramatics* and *Dance* societies for its students. Every society has got some *committee members*, who are not students. At the start of an academic session, each enrolled *student* is required to apply for the membership of any one of the societies. If a student is already a member of a society, then she can either change the society or can apply for renewal of membership for the same society of which she is already a member. A committee member is not allowed to apply for membership. They can only approve the membership of the applicants. Representative sets of users and objects are shown below:

- $\mathcal{U}$: {Tom, Alice, John}
- $\mathcal{O}$: {Form1, Form2, List1, List2}.

Table 1 gives the names of all the user attributes along with their possible values. Table 2 gives the names of each object attribute and their corresponding values. The set of actions allowed is given by $\triangle = \{apply, verify, approve\}$. Tables 3 and 4 show the $\mathcal{F}_\mathcal{U}$ and $\mathcal{F}_\mathcal{O}$, respectively, while Table 5 shows the set of authorization policies $\mathcal{P}$ for XYZ.

Table 1. User Attributes and their Possible Values

$\mathcal{U}_\mathcal{A}$	Range of $\mathcal{U}_\mathcal{A}$
Designation	{student, null}
Course	{ug, pg, null}
Role	{committee member, applicant, null}
Type	{fresher, member, null}

The SoD requirements for University *XYZ* are as follows:

$$s_1 = <\{(\text{apply, Form1}), (\text{approve, Form1})\}, 2>$$
$$s_2 = <\{(\text{verify, Form1}), (\text{approve, Form1})\}, 2>$$
$$\omega = \{s_1, s_2\}$$

Table 2. Object Attributes and their Possible Values

$\mathcal{O}_A$	Range of $\mathcal{O}_A$
Type	{form, document}
Subtype	{application form, renewal form, new applicant list, renewal applicant list}
Category	{dramatics, dance}
Protection Level	{read-only, read-write}

Table 3. User-User Attribute Assignment

$\mathcal{U}$	Designation	Course	Role	Type
Tom	Student	ug	Applicant	Fresher
Alice	Student	pg	Applicant	Member
John	Null	Null	Committee member	Null

It is observed from Tables 1, 2, 3, 4 and 5 that, while $satisfies_\varphi[s_1]$ is *true*, $satisfies_\varphi[s_2]$ is *false*. This is due to the presence of the policies p_5 and p_6 through which the user *John* is getting authorized to both the tuples (*verify*, *Form1*) and (*approve*, *Form1*). Thus, the ABAC state defined above is not *safe*.

3   Problem Formulation and Complexity Analysis

We next formally define the SoD verification problem in ABAC.

3.1   Problem Definition

Definition 2. *ABAC-VF-SoD (SoD Verification in ABAC): Given an ABAC state φ and a set of SoD policies ω, an instance of ABAC-VF-SoD takes the form $< \varphi, s >$, where $s \in \omega$. It asks whether $satisfies_\varphi[s]$ is true.*

If answer to $satisfies_\varphi[s]$ is *true* for each instance of an ABAC-VF-SoD problem, only then the ABAC state φ is considered to be *safe*. Next, we study the complexity class of ABAC-VF-SoD.

Table 4. Object-Object Attribute Assignment

$\mathcal{O}$	Type	Subtype	Category	Protection Level
Form1	Form	Application form	Any	Read-write
Form2	Form	Renewal form	Any	Read-write
List1	Document	New applicant list	Dance	Read-only
List2	Document	Renewal list	Dance	Read-only

Table 5. ABAC Authorization Policies

p_1 = <(Designation = student, Course = ug, Role = applicant, Type = fresher), (Type = form, Subtype = application form, Category = dance, Protection Level = read-write), (apply)>
p_2 = <(Designation = student, Course = ug, Role = applicant, Type = fresher), (Type = form, Subtype = application form, Category = dramatics, Protection Level = read-write), (apply)>
p_3 = <(Designation = student, Course = pg, Role = applicant, Type = new), (Type = form, Subtype = application, Category = dance, Protection Level = read-only), (apply)>
p_4 = <(Designation = student, Course = pg, Role = applicant, Type = Member), (Type = Form, Subtype = application form, Category = dramatics, Protection Level = read-only), (apply)>
p_5 = <(Designation = any, Course = any, Role = committee member, Type = any), (Type = form, Subtype = application form, Category = any, Protection Level = read-only), (verify)>
p_6 = <(Designation = any, Course = any, Role = committee member, Type = any), (Type = form, Subtype = applicant list, Category = any, Protection Level = read-only), (approve)>

Theorem 1. *ABAC-VF-SoD is coNP complete*

Proof. To prove that ABAC-VF-SoD is coNP complete, we prove that the complement of ABAC-VF-SoD, denoted by ABAC-VF-SoD', is NP-complete. Given a set ω of SoD policies and an ABAC state φ, an instance of ABAC-VF-SoD' problem asks whether $satisfies_\varphi[s]$ is *false*.

ABAC-VF-SoD' is in NP: Suppose a k-n SoD policy $s \equiv \langle Per, k \rangle$ and a set of k' users are given, such that $k' \leq k$ and it is claimed that the given k' users together violate the SoD policy s. This claim can be easily verified by finding the union of the set of tuples accessible by the set of k' users, using the authorization policies $\mathcal{P}$ and then comparing it with the *Per* set of the SoD policy. If the set of tuples accessible by k' users together forms a superset of *Per*, then $satisfies_\varphi[s]$ is *false*. This can be done in polynomial time.

ABAC-VF-SoD' is NP-hard: To prove that ABAC-VF-SoD' is NP-hard, we reduce the decision version of a well known NP-hard problem, namely the set covering problem (D_SCP) [1] to the ABAC-VF-SoD' problem. D_SCP is defined as follows: Given a set of elements called the universe U, a set S of m subsets of U and a value K, does there exist a set of K subsets of S whose union equals U. The steps for constructing a k-n SoD policy from a set covering problem $\langle U, S, K \rangle$ such that $|U| = n$ are as follows:

- Map each element of the universe U to a $t \in$ SoD
- Assign $k = K + 1$.

If the size of the solution for the set covering problem is K, then at least $K + 1$ users are required to cover all the t in the k-n SoD policy. The steps for creating an ABAC state φ are as follows: create a user for each set $N \in$ S. If a set of K subsets together covers all the elements of U, then a minimum of K + 1 users together are required to cover all the (*action*, *object*) pairs in the SoD. The above reduction can be done in polynomial time.

Algorithm 1. CHECK_SoD_BF($s = \langle\{t_1, t_2, \ldots, t_n\}, k\rangle, \mathcal{P}, \mathcal{F}_\mathcal{U}$)

1: **for** each subset S $\in 2^\mathcal{U}$ **do**
2:      accessible_tuples $\leftarrow$ set of tuples $\tau \subseteq \{t_1, t_2, \ldots, t_n\}$ accessible by the members of S
3:      **if** (accessible_tuples $\supseteq \{t_1, t_2, \ldots, t_n\}$ &&|S| $< k$) **then**
4:          **return** *false*
5:      **end if**
6: **end for**
7: **return** *true*

3.2   Brute Force Approach for Solving ABAC-VF-SoD

A brute force algorithm for solving ABAC-VF-SoD is given in Algorithm 1. CHECK_SoD_BF generates all the subsets of $\mathcal{U}$ and then, finds the set of tuples accessible by its members and stores it in *accessible_tuples*. If the cardinality of *accessible_tuples* is less than k and also it contains all the tuples in SoD, then the algorithm returns *false*. The algorithm will return *true* only if SoD is not violated at all. As is obvious, such an algorithm needs an exponential number of iterations and hence, is not practical for reasonable number of users, objects or access control policies.

4   Solving ABAC-VF-SoD Using Mutual Exclusion

As mentioned above, a tuple t in an SoD policy is of the form (a, o). For a user u to be able to perform the action a on the object o, there must be a policy $p \in \mathcal{P}$ that allows u the requested action. We denote such policies which allow a user to perform actions on objects as *valid* for that user. The set *valid*[u] consists of all valid policies for a user u. If a policy p allows access to a tuple t of an SoD policy, then p is said to be *relevant* for t. The set *relevant*[t] contains all such relevant policies. The set of all tuples which can be accessed using a policy p is denoted as *valid_tuples*[p]. Using these notations, the set of all tuples of an SoD policy for which a user is authorized can be represented as:

$$auth\_tuples[u] = \{t|\, \exists p \in valid[u] \wedge t \in valid\_tuples[p]\}$$

An SoD puts a constraint on the set *auth_tuples*[u], which in turn can be enforced by putting a constraint on the set *valid*[u]. The cardinality of the set *valid*[u] for a user u can be restricted by declaring policies to be mutually exclusive. If two policies p_1 and p_2 are declared to be mutually exclusive, then no user can have both of these policies in his *valid* set.

Definition 3. *A t-m MEP (t-out-of-m MEP) policy is expressed as $MEP\langle\{p_1, p_2,......, p_t\}, m\rangle$, where each p_i is an authorization policy and $1 < m \leq t$.*

This definition of MEP conveys that no user in the system can have $|valid[u]| \geq m$. If a user violates an MEP policy e, then it is represented as $violates_e[u]$. The set of MEP policies of an ABAC system can be represented as $\xi = \{e_1, e_2, ..., e_n\}$.

Example 2. Consider that the ABAC system given in Example 1 has a mutual exclusion requirement as follows:

- No user can apply for both *dance* and *dramatics*
- No user can both *apply* and *approve* the *application* form for any of the activities.

From Table 5, the set ξ of the system will have the following mutual exclusion constraints:

$$\xi = \{e_1, e_2, e_3, e_4, e_5, e_6\}, \tag{1}$$

where
$$e_1 = \langle\{p_1, p_2\}, 2\rangle$$
$$e_2 = \langle\{p_3, p_4\}, 2\rangle$$
$$e_3 = \langle\{p_1, p_6\}, 2\rangle$$
$$e_4 = \langle\{p_2, p_6\}, 2\rangle$$
$$e_5 = \langle\{p_3, p_6\}, 2\rangle$$
$$e_6 = \langle\{p_4, p_6\}, 2\rangle$$

It can be easily verified that none of the users violates e_2, e_3, e_4, e_5 and e_6 but the MEP constraint e_1 is violated by *Tom*.

Definition 4. *ABAC-VF-MEP (Verification of MEP in ABAC): Given a set of mutually exclusive policies ξ and the user-user attribute assignment relation $\mathcal{F}_{\mathcal{U}}$, an instance of ABAC-VF-MEP takes the form $< e, \mathcal{F}_{\mathcal{U}} >$, where $e \in \xi$. It asks whether there exists a user $u \in \mathcal{U}$ for which $violates_e[u]$ is true.*

An ABAC state φ is considered *safe* with respect to a set of MEP policies ξ, if and only if, all instances of ABAC-VF-MEP return *false*. The ABAC-VF-MEP problem can be solved using Algorithms 2, 3 and 4.

Algorithm 2. CHECK_MEP_SET($\xi = \{e_1, e_1, ... , e_n\}, \mathcal{F}_{\mathcal{U}}$)

1: flag = *true*
2: **for** each $e \in \xi$ **do**
3:     flag = CHECK_MEP($e, \mathcal{F}_{\mathcal{U}}$)
4:     **if** (flag == false) **then**
5:         **return** *false*
6:     **end if**
7: **end for**
8: **return** *true*

Algorithm 3. CHECK_MEP$(e, \mathcal{F}_\mathcal{U})$

1: **for** each user u $\in \mathcal{U}$ **do**
2:    valid[u] = Find_valid_Set($e, \mathcal{F}_u, u$)
3:    **if** ($|$valid[u]$| > m$) **then**
4:       **return** *false*
5:    **end if**
6: **end for**
7: **return** *true*

Algorithm 4. Find_valid_Set$(e, \mathcal{F}_u, u)$

1: valid[u] $\leftarrow$ *null*
2: **for** each p $\in e$ **do**
3:    **if** (Aval[u] $\supseteq$ USER$_{uan=uav}$ of p) **then**
4:       valid[u] $\leftarrow$ valid[u] $\cup \{p\}$
5:    **end if**
6: **end for**
7: **return** valid[u]

Algorithm 2 takes a set ξ of MEP constraints of the form $e = \langle \{p_1, p_2, \ldots\ldots, p_t\}, m \rangle$ and the user-user attribute assignment relation $\mathcal{F}_\mathcal{U}$ of an ABAC system as input. The algorithm returns *false*, if there exists an $e \in \xi$ and a user u for which *violates$_e$*[u] is *true*. To check whether e is violated or not, it uses the function CHECK_MEP given in Algorithm 3. CHECK_MEP takes a single MEP constraint and the user-user attribute assignment relation $\mathcal{F}_\mathcal{U}$ of φ as input and returns *false*, if there exists any user u for which *violates$_e$*[u] is *true*. The function Find_Valid_Set given in Algorithm 4 finds the *valid* set for users. To find a valid policy for a user, it uses Aval[u], which consists of the set of all user attribute-value pairs for the user u.

Theorem 2. *ABAC-VF-MEP is in* **P**

Proof. One of the possible ways for solving ABAC-VF-MEP is given in Algorithm 2. In the algorithm, the *for* loop of Lines 2–7 is executed at most $|\xi|$ times. For each constraint, the function CHECK_MEP is executed once. In the function CHECK_MEP, the *for* loop of Lines 1–6 is executed at most $|\mathcal{U}|$ times. For each $u \in \mathcal{U}$, it invokes the function Find_Valid_Set once. The *for* loop of Lines 2–6 of Find_Valid_Set is executed at most $|\mathcal{P}|$ times ($|e| \leq |\mathcal{P}|$). Hence, the overall complexity of the algorithm is $O(|\xi||\mathcal{U}||\mathcal{P}|)$.

The fact that ABAC-VF-SoD is intractable while ABAC-VF-MEP is in P, makes the use of ABAC-VF-MEP a suitable approach to solve ABAC-VF-SoD and thus enforce SoD in an ABAC system. However, it should be noted that, while an ABAC-VF-SoD instance takes input in the form of SoD tuples, an ABAC-VF-MEP instance takes input in the form of authorization policies. Thus, one needs to *reduce*, a step that is not required to be performed on-line, an instance of ABAC-VF-SoD to an instance of ABAC-VF-MEP (otherwise, ABAC-VF-SoD would not be in coNP, as already proved). To do so, an instance of ABAC-VF-SoD is initially transformed into an intermediate form, which is based on authorization policies and then from that intermediate form, it is transformed into an instance of ABAC-VF-MEP. Thus, reduction of an instance of ABAC-VF-SoD problem into an instance of ABAC-VF-MEP is a two step process:

– Generation of SoAP (Separation of Authorization Policies, the intermediate form) from SoD
– Generation of MEP from SoAP.

Generation of SoAP from SoD. A SoAP policy puts a constraint on the cardinality of the set *valid* of a user. It can be formally defined as follows:

Definition 5. *A k-n SoAP (k-out-of-n Separation of Authorization Policy) is defined as SoAP⟨{p_1, p_2,......, p_n}, k⟩, where each p_i ∈ P, 1 < k ≤ n.*

This definition of SoAP conveys that to cover every p_i ∈ SoAP, at least k users are required. A p is covered by a user u, if p ∈ *valid*[u]. For a given SoD policy, several SoAP policies can be generated. A minimal SoAP policy for an SoD policy is the one which uses minimum number of authorization policies to enforce the SoD policy.

An algorithm to generate an SoAP policy, which implicitly enforces an SoD policy, is given in Algorithm 5. The algorithm CREATE_SoAP takes an SoD policy *SoD*, the set of authorization policies $\mathcal{P}$ and the user-user attribute assignment relation $\mathcal{F}_{\mathcal{U}}$ as input and generates a reduced set of authorization policies $\mathcal{P}'$. $\mathcal{P}'$ is then passed to a function CREATE_MINIMAL_SoAP to generate the minimal SoAP policy.

Algorithm 5. CREATE_SoAP(SoD <{t_1, t_2,......, t_n}, k>, $\mathcal{P}$, $\mathcal{F}_{\mathcal{U}}$)

1: **for** each t ∈ SoD **do**
2:     find relevant[t]
3: **end for**
4: $\mathcal{P}' = \cup_{t \in SoD}$ relevant[t]
5: SoAP ← CREATE_MINIMAL_SoAP(SoD, $\mathcal{P}'$, $\mathcal{F}_{\mathcal{U}}$)
6: **if** (SoAP != null) **then**
7:     **return** SoAP
8: **end if**
9: **return** *"SoD cannot be enforced"*

The CREATE_MINIMAL_SoAP function given in Algorithm 6 generates all possible subsets of $\mathcal{P}'$. Among all these generated subsets, it returns the set which is of minimal cardinality and also covers all the tuples of the input SoD. If the size of the subset thus found is less than the number of users required in the original SoD, then the algorithm returns *"SoD cannot be enforced"* as the output.

Generation of MEP from SoAP. For a given SoAP policy, various sets of MEPs can be generated. Different MEP constraints put different levels of restrictiveness on the *valid* set of users. Every SoD policy can be enforced using $(|\mathcal{P}|\text{-}2)$ MEP constraints. An algorithm for generating a $t\text{-}m$ MEP constraint from a $k\text{-}n$ SoAP is given in Algorithm 7.

The algorithm GenerateMEP takes a SoAP policy as input and returns the set of MEP constraints which together enforce the input SoAP. To understand the behavior of the GenerateMEP algorithm, consider following cases:

Algorithm 6. CREATE_MINIMAL_SoAP(SoD, $\mathcal{P}'$, $\mathcal{F}_u$)

1: **for** q $\rightarrow$ 0 to $(2^{|\mathcal{P}'|}\text{-}1)$ **do**
2:     policy_set[q] $\leftarrow$ *null*
3:     sod_tset[q] $\leftarrow$ *null*
4:     pset_size[q] $\leftarrow$ *null*
5: **end for**
6: q $\leftarrow$ 0
7: **for each** pset $\in 2^{|\mathcal{P}'|}$ **do**
8:     policy_set[q] $\leftarrow$ pset
9:     pset_size[q] $\leftarrow$ |pset|
10:     sod_tset[q] $\leftarrow$ $\cup_{p \in pset}$ auth_policy[p]
11:     q $\leftarrow$ q + 1
12: **end for**
13: min $\leftarrow \infty$
14: **for** i $\rightarrow$ 0 to q **do**
15:     **if** (sod_tset[q] $\{t_1, t_2,......, t_n\}$) &&(pset_size[q] < min) **then**
16:         min $\leftarrow$ pset_size[q]
17:         location $\leftarrow$ q
18:     **end if**
19: **end for**
20: **if** (min >= k) **then**
21:     return <policy_set[location], k>
22: **end if**
23: return **null**

- SoAP $= < \{p_1, p_2, p_3, p_4, p_5\}, 2 >$. This SoAP policy states that at least two users are required to cover all the authorization policies. In other words, no user can have p_1, p_2, p_3, p_4 and p_5 in its *valid* set. So, the algorithm returns the MEP constraint $< \{p_1, p_2, p_3, p_4, p_5\}, 5 >$
- SoAP $= < \{p_1, p_2, p_3, p_4, p_5\}, 5 >$. This SoAP policy states that at least five different users are required to cover p_1, p_2, p_3, p_4 and p_5 in their *valid* sets. This implies that no user can have more than one authorization policy out of p_1, p_2, p_3, p_4 and p_5 in its *valid* set. So, the algorithm returns $\langle\{p_1, p_2, p_3, p_4, p_5\}, 2\rangle$.
- SoAP $= < \{p_1, p_2, p_3, p_4, p_5\}, 4 >$. This SoAP policy states that at least four different users are required to cover all the p_1, p_2, p_3, p_4 and p_5 in their *valid* set. This means that out of p_1, p_2, p_3, p_4 and p_5 none of the users should have

Algorithm 7. GenerateMEP(SoAP $= < \{p_1, p_1, ..., p_n\}, k >$)

1: **if** (k == 2) **then**
2:     **return** $< \{p_1, p_2, ..., p_n\}, n >$
3: **end if**
4: **if** (k == n) **then**
5:     **return** $< \{p_1, p_2, ..., p_n\}, 2 >$
6: **end if**
7: **return** all size-$(n$-$1)$ subsets of $\{p_1, p_2, ..., p_n\}$ with $m = k$-1 and the set $\{p_1, p_2, ..., p_n\}$ with $m = k$

more than two authorization policies in their *valid* set. In order to ensure this, the algorithm generates all the subsets of $\{p_1, p_2, p_3, p_4, p_5\}$ of cardinality *3* as well as the complete set $\{p_1, p_2, p_3, p_4, p_5\}$, each having m equal to *3*.

We now give an example showing the generation of SoAP from an SoD policy and the generation of MEP constraints from the obtained SoAP policy.

Example 3. Consider an ABAC system having the set of authorization policies $\mathcal{P} = \{p_1, p_2, ..., p_{10}\}$ and two SoD policies $s_1 = <\{t_1, t_3\}, 2>$ and $s_2 = <\{t_1, t_2, t_3\}, 3>$. Let the relevant sets for t_1, t_2 and t_3 be as follows:

- relevant$[t_1] = \{p_1, p_3, p_4\}$
- relevant$[t_2] = \{p_3, p_5\}$
- relevant$[t_3] = \{p_6\}$.

SoAP Generation Using CREATE_SoAP. For s_1, the reduced policy set $\mathcal{P}'$ will have $\{p_1, p_3, p_4, p_6\}$ and the minimal SoAP will be of the form $<\{p_1, p_6\}, 2>$[2]. For s_2, the reduced policy set $\mathcal{P}'$ will be $\{p_1, p_3, p_4, p_5, p_6\}$ and the minimal SoAP will be of the form $<\{p_3, p_6\}, 3>$. For s_2, the algorithm CREATE_SoAP will return "SoD cannot be enforced".

MEP Generation Using GenerateMEP. For the SoAP policy $<\{p_1, p_6\}, 2>$ as mentioned above, the generated MEP is $<\{p_1, p_6\}, 2>$ implying that no user can have more than one policy out of the set $\{p_1, p_6\}$ in his *valid* set.

It can be observed that, while the generation of MEP from an SoAP using the algorithm GenerateMEP can be done in polynomial time, generation of SoAP from SoD using the algorithm CREATE_MINIMAL_SoAP (given in Sect. 4 as Algorithm 6) is not polynomial. However, it may be noted that, the algorithm CREATE _MINIMAL_SoAP would normally be run off-line since the policies in an ABAC system are more stable as compared to the user-user attribute mappings. For any change in user-user attribute mappings as required in a dynamic system, the administrator needs to run only the algorithm CHECK_MEP_SET.

---

[2] The other possible minimal set are $\{p_3, p_6\}$ or $\{p_4, p_6\}$.

5   Experimental Evaluation

To study the run time behavior of both ABAC-VF-SoD and ABAC-VF-MEP, we have built a synthetic data generator that takes the number of users, objects, authorization policies and size of SoD policies as input, and generates user-user attribute mappings, object-object attribute mappings, authorization policies as well as SoD policies for an ABAC system. For the experiments, Java (7.0.1–17) on a Windows 7 system with 64-bit i5 processor @ 2.50GHz and 4GB RAM is used.

The effect of increase in the number of users on the execution time of the brute force approach (Algorithm 1) for solving the ABAC-VF-SoD problem is shown in Fig. 1. The data set used for the analysis consists of 100 authorization policies and 10–5 SoD policies. From the figure, it is seen that the run time of the algorithm increases exponentially with increase in the number of users. This is because the algorithm needs to check every subset of the set USER (see Subsect. 3.2). The execution time is largely dependent on the cardinality of the authorized user set. In the worst case, the size of this set would be same as the number of users in the organization, making direct checking of SoD violation impractical whenever there is a change in the user-user attribute value relation, including assigning user attribute values to new users.

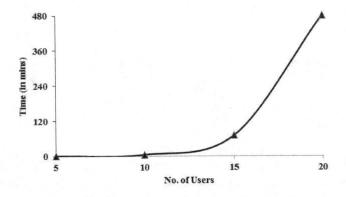

Fig. 1. Variation in execution time of ABAC-VF-SoD with increase in number of users

The effect of increase in the number of users and number of policies on the execution time of the CHECK_MEP algorithm (Algorithm MEPCheck) for solving ABAC-VF-MEP is shown in Figs. 2 and 3, respectively. The figures show that a linear increase in the number of users or the number of policies causes a close to linear increase in the run time of the algorithm.

We also carried out experiments with the sample university data set available from http://www3.cs.stonybrook.edu/~stoller. The smallest size data set consists of 35 users and 10 rules (authorization policies). As the number of authorization policies is fixed to 10 in each data set, we provide only the effect

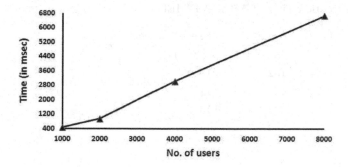

Fig. 2. Execution time of ABAC-VF-MEP with increase in number of users

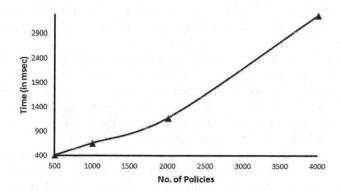

Fig. 3. Execution time of ABAC-VF-MEP with increase in number of policies

of the increase in the number of users on the execution time. Since the smallest data set has 35 users, we were unable to run Algorithm 1 on this data set to completion as even for 20 users, the execution time is in hours (refer to Fig. 1). On this data set, execution time for Algorithm 4 is reported in Table 6. Form the table it can be seen that, even for the largest data set consisting of 330 users, CHECK_MEP takes only a few milliseconds. Thus, this is a practical approach for verifying whether any change in the relation $\mathcal{F}_U$ violates the SoD policies.

6   Related Work

There is a sizable amount of literature on ABAC in general. In [15], a logic based framework for ABAC is proposed in which access policies are specified in the form of free logic programs that admit primitive recursion using the CLP($\mathcal{SET}$) version of set theory. A trust based access control model called TrustBAC is introduced in [12]. It extends the conventional RBAC model with the notion of trust levels. Here, users are assigned to trust levels instead of roles based on their credentials. Trust levels are assigned to roles, which, in turn, are assigned

Table 6. Execution Time of ABAC-VF-MEP with increase in the Number of users

No. of Users	Execution time (in msec)
35	23
132	103
167	117
244	139
330	157

to permissions as in RBAC. In [14], authors introduce ABAC and suggest its use as an access control model for the open environment. The present state and future trends in access control is surveyed, and it is shown that the new trend in access control is part of future communication infrastructure supporting mobile computing.

In [13], the ABAC model has been presented in terms of authorization architecture and policy administration. It is also shown how ABAC can be used to secure web service invocations. Advantages of ABAC over other access control mechanisms for web based services is also demonstrated. Jin et al. [9] show how authorization policies in DAC, MAC and RBAC can be expressed using ABAC. It establishes a formal connection between theses three successful classical models and the ABAC model. In [6], a methodology for integrating modeling and analysis of organizational workflows and ABAC policies is proposed. The proposed methodology helps to identify workflow activities that are not being protected by access control policies and to improve existing access control policies. In [10], an approach to integrate ABAC with RBAC by modeling RBAC in two different levels is introduced. The first level, referred to as the aboveground level, is a standard RBAC model extended with environment, and the second level, referred to as the underground level, is used to represent security knowledge in terms of attribute based policies. Thus, it helps to bring the advantages of RBAC into ABAC. In [4], NIST provides a comprehensive definition for the ABAC model.

Very recently, a few approaches for mining attribute based policies have been proposed. In [8], the authors present a methodology for mining ABAC policies from RBAC policies and attribute data. The proposed methodology splits a role to generate rules. Roles are split in such a fashion that the set of permissions assigned to those roles is the Cartesian product of a set of resources and a set of operations. While splitting, a correspondence between the resulting split roles and the mined rules is preserved. [2] performs policy mining by iterating over tuples of the user-permission relation and uses selected tuples as seeds for constructing candidate rules. The highest-quality candidate rules are selected to be included in the generated policy. In [3], a multi-objective evolutionary approach is used for mining policies. The proposed methodology aims at learning a policy consistent with the input requests and does not use those attributes which uniquely represent user and resource identities and hence, exploits the true potential of the ABAC paradigm.

There is also a significant amount of work towards specifying constraints in an ABAC system. In [9], a policy specification language called ABACα, which can specify policies for authorizing a permission as well as constraints on attribute assignment, is proposed. The set of constraints specified in [9] applies restrictions on the values a subject attribute may take when the subject is created or an object attribute may get when the object is created. A constraint apply only when specific events such as a user modifying a subjects attributes occur. In [7], a policy specification language called ABCL (Attribute based Constraint Specification Language) is proposed. It provides a mechanism to represent different kinds of conflicting relations among attributes in a system in the form of relation sets. While the constraints in ABACα are event specific, the constraints in ABCL are event independent and are to be uniformly enforced no matter what event is causing an attribute value to change. They are specified as restrictions on a single set-valued attribute or restrictions on values of different attributes of the same entity. Nurmamat and Rahman [5] examine the potential relationships between subjects, objects and also the relationships among them. Given an initial ABAC system, a revised system is generated based on subject similarity.

Although a few types of constraints have been studied for ABAC, this paper is the first ever work that comprehensively studies the effect of SoD on ABAC and how one can enforce the same.

7 Conclusion and Future Scope

In this work, we have shown how Separation of Duty can be represented in terms of ABAC components. We introduced two problems, namely, the ABAC-VF-SoD problem and the ABAC-VF-MEP problem. While ABAC-VF-SoD has been shown to be intractable, ABAC-VF-MEP can be efficiently solved in polynomial time. It has been shown that SoD verification can be done efficiently if we can generate a set of mutually exclusive policies corresponding to an SoD policy. As a future work, we plan to formulate a strategy which can effectively determine the set of MEP constraints that are most effective and least restrictive for a given SoD policy.

References

1. Cormen, T.H.: Introduction to Algorithms. MIT press, Cambridge (2009)
2. Xu, Z., Stoller, S.D.: Mining attribute-based access control policies. In: IEEE Transactions on Dependable and Secure Computing (2015)
3. Medvet, E., Bartoli, A., Carminati, B., Ferrari, E.: Evolutionary Inference of Attribute-Based Access Control Policies. In: Gaspar-Cunha, A., Henggeler Antunes, C., Coello, C.C. (eds.) EMO 2015. LNCS, vol. 9018, pp. 351–365. Springer, Heidelberg (2015)
4. Hu, V.C., Ferraiolo, D., Kuhn, R., Schnitzer, A., Sandhu, R., Miller, R., Scarfone, K.: Guide to Attribute Based Access Control (ABAC) Definition and Considerations. NIST Special Publication (2014)

5. Nurmamat, H., Rahman, K.: Attribute based access control constraint based on subject similarity. In: Proceedings of the IEEE Workshop on Advanced Research and Technology in Industry Applications, pp. 226–229 (2014)
6. Lakkaraju, S., Dianxiang, X.: Integrated modeling and analysis of attribute based access control policies and workflows in healthcare. In: Proceedings of the International Conference on Trustworthy Systems and their Applications (TSA), pp. 36–43. IEEE (2014)
7. Zaman, B.K., Krishnan, R., Sandhu, R.: Towards an attribute based constraints specification language. In: Proceedings of the IEEE International Conference on Social Computing, pp. 108–113 (2013)
8. Xu, Z., Stoller, S.D.: Mining attribute-based access control policies from RBAC policies. In: Proceedings of the International Conference and Expo on Emerging Technologies for a Smarter World, pp. 1–6. IEEE (2013)
9. Jin, X., Krishnan, R., Sandhu, R.S.: A unified attribute-based access control model covering DAC, MAC and RBAC. In: Proceedings of the 26th Annual Conference on Data and Applications Security and Privacy, pp. 41–55 (2012)
10. Huang, J., Nicol, D.M., Bobba, R., Huh, J.H.: A framework integrating attribute-based policies into role-based access control. In: Proceedings of the 17th ACM Symposium on Access Control Models and Technologies, pp. 187–196. ACM (2012)
11. Li, N., Tripunitara, M.V., Bizri, Z.: On mutually exclusive roles and separation-of-duty. In: ACM Transactions on Information and System Security (TISSEC) (2007)
12. Chakraborty, S., Ray, I.: TrustBAC: integrating trust relationships into the RBAC model for access control in open systems. In: Proceedings of the Eleventh ACM Symposium on Access Control Models and Technologies, pp. 49–58. ACM (2006)
13. Yuan, E. Tong, J.: Attributed based access control (ABAC) for web services. In: Proceedings of the IEEE International Workshop on Web Services (2005)
14. Ernesto, D., Vimercati, S.D.C.D., Samarati, P.: New paradigms for access control in open environments. In: Proceedings of the Fifth IEEE International Symposium on Signal Processing and Information Technology, pp. 540–545 (2005)
15. Lingyu, W., Wijesekera, D., Jajodia, S.: A logic-based framework for attribute based access control. In: Proceedings of the ACM Workshop on Formal Methods in Security Engineering, pp. 45–55 (2004)
16. Sandhu, R.S., Coyne, E.J., Feinstein, H.L., Youman, C.E.: Role-based access control models. In: IEEE Computer, pp. 38–47 (1999)
17. Osborn, S.: Mandatory access control and role-based access control revisited. In: Proceedings of the 2nd ACM Workshop on Role-Based Access Control, pp. 31–40 (1997)
18. Harrison, M.A., Ruzzo, W.L., Ullman, J.D.: On protection in operating systems. In: Communications of the ACM, pp. 461–471 (1976)
19. Clark, D.D., Wilson, D.R.: A comparision of commercial and military computer security policies. In: Proceedings of the 1987 IEEE Symposium on Security and Privacy, pp. 184–194. IEEE Computer Society (1987)

Modeling of Online Social Network Policies Using an Attribute-Based Access Control Framework

Phillipa Bennett, Indrakshi Ray$^{(\boxtimes)}$, and Robert France

Computer Science Department, Colorado State University,
Fort Collins, CO 80523, USA
{Phillipa.Bennett,Indrakshi.Ray}@colostate.edu

Abstract. People often share sensitive personal information through online social networks (OSNs) to keep in touch with their friends and families. Such sensitive information if leaked inadvertently to malicious third parties may have disastrous consequences on the lives of individuals. Access control policies need to be specified, analyzed, enforced, and managed in a simple manner for the regular OSN users. We demonstrate how this can be done. We first propose a simple model that captures the typical OSN features and show how to represent it using an Entity-Relationship Diagram. The numerous features of an OSN interact with each other in subtle ways – this makes it easy for the naïve user to make misconfiguration errors. Towards this end, we illustrate how our OSN model can be formalized in Alloy and its constraints adequately captured. Alloy has an embedded SAT solver which makes it amenable to analysis. We illustrate how potential misconfigurations caused by the user can be automatically detected by the SAT-solver. Finally, we show how OSN policies can be enforced, managed, and changed through Policy Machine which is an attribute-based access control framework.

1 Introduction

Online Social Networks (OSNs) are used for various purposes and impact society in many different ways. For example, on an individual level, they help families and friends separated by distance keep in touch and thus help mitigate undesirable effects of long distance relationships. Sensitive personal information is often shared through OSNs.

Organizations have used the data generated in OSNs to do targeted advertising campaigns, develop new products, perform market research, trend analysis and reputation monitoring, and vet and hire human resources. Third parties can also misuse this information with disastrous consequences on individuals such as damaged reputation, financial hardships, or compromised physical safety and security. Thus, it is important to protect sensitive information shared in OSNs.

R. France—Involved in the discussion of this work, but now deceased.

© Springer International Publishing Switzerland 2015
S. Jajodia and C. Mazumdar (Eds.): ICISS 2015, LNCS 9478, pp. 79–97, 2015.
DOI: 10.1007/978-3-319-26961-0_6

OSNs have evolved from simple networks of members sharing information to large networks whose differing types of relationships and interactions make them difficult to understand and analyse. Researchers have proposed access control policies [3,4,14] for OSNs. Relationship-based access control (ReBAC) policies for OSNs are based on the structure, and on different models of sharing [2,4,5,9, 15–17]. In a ReBAC system a member will give the right to access, or the right to perform an operation on, private objects they own to other members based on their direct and indirect relationships. In access control for OSNs, a social graph represents the relationships and the links formed among users and artifacts on which access control rules are evaluated. The wide variety of artifacts that are posted by the user together with the various features supported by OSNs makes configuring the access control rules hard.

OSN access control policies on the various artifacts are not necessarily independent, and interact in subtle ways that may give rise to inconsistencies and conflicts. In such cases, the default conflict resolution mechanisms decide which policies have higher priority. Thus, if a user has specified policies in an incorrect manner, his sensitive information may be leaked unintentionally. Researchers have worked on misconfiguration detection, that is, on uncovering situations in which the user's intent is inaccurately mapped to her access control settings [1,11–13].

Correct specification of access control policies is not enough. This is because OSNs are, by their very nature, dynamic. The set of users in an OSN, the resources needing protection, and the policies of users are subject to change. Moreover, OSNs introduce features and capabilities to make them more responsive to the functional needs of the user. However, all of these pose special challenges for specification, enforcement, and management of access control policies of the user. Towards this end, we provide tools and techniques to the naïve user so that he can correctly specify, enforce, and manage his OSN policies.

We start by expressing OSN policies using an Entity Relationship Diagram. Such a diagram is easy to understand and use, but fails to capture all the constraints in the OSN. Moreover, it is also not amenable to automated analysis. Automated analysis is needed to study and understand how the different features of the OSN interact with each other and to detect how such interactions may cause misconfigurations.

We use Alloy [10] for the purpose of automated analysis. Alloy is a formal modeling language capable of expressing complex structural constraints and behaviour. Alloy is supported by an automated constraint solver called the Alloy Analyzer that searches for instances of the model that satisfy modelled system properties. The model is automatically translated into a Boolean expression, which is analysed by SAT solvers embedded within the Alloy Analyzer. A user-specified scope on the model elements bounds the domain, making it possible to create finite Boolean formulas that can be evaluated by the SAT-solver. When a property does not hold, a counter example is produced that demonstrates how it has been violated. Using our Alloy model, we are able to demonstrate how the different features give rise to misconfigurations. The misconfigurations may help the user refine her access control policies.

The access control policies of the user must be enforced and managed in a consistent manner. We demonstrate how this can be done using an attribute-based access control framework. The motivation of using an attribute-based access control framework is three fold. First, attribute-based access control is a more general purpose access control model that can express all the different types of policies associated with a user and is not limited to OSN policies. This obviates the need for the user to learn multiple types of access control models. Second, attribute-based control is gaining maturity and it is most likely going to become the next generation access control standard. Third, it will also provide the ground work needed to compare between expressing OSN policies using relationship-based access control vs. attribute-based access control.

We had a choice of using XACML or using the NIST Policy Machine (PM) [6–8] as our access control framework. XACML provides the language and architecture for supporting attribute-based access control and it is widely used. PM originated for the Enterprise Server Environment and provides a consistent policy enforcement mechanism that supports a wide-range of policies. We decided to use the PM for several reasons. First, the PM provides a more elegant support for administering access control that is needed by the users in OSNs. Specifically, it handles access to data and access to policy governing the data in a uniform manner. Second, it supports policy evolution. Third, it provides a consistent framework that can be used to support the various policies associated with a user.

The rest of the paper is organized as follows. Section 2 provides the OSN policies that are expressed using an Entity Relationship Diagram. Section 3 presents the Alloy model and demonstrates how misconfigurations can be automatically detected using Alloy. Section 4 presents the highlights of the Policy Machine that are relevant to our current work. Section 5 demonstrates how the policies can be expressed using the PM framework. Section 6 concludes the paper with some pointers to future directions.

2   Online Social Network Model

In this section, we describe the various entities and their associations in an OSN. The different entity sets are denoted by *User, Subject, Group, Application, Object,* and *Operation* as shown in Fig. 1. Each of these entity sets and association sets are associated with a set of attributes that describe that set.

2.1   Entity Sets in REBAC

User. This is the set of entities who have an account in the OSN. Each user is associated with a set of attributes. Examples of attributes include *identity* and *profile. identity* gives the identity by which the user is known in the OSN. Although most of the above attributes are defined by the user, some are incorporated by the system. For example, $User = \{Jane, Tim, George, Amy\}$.

Group. This is the set of groups in the OSN, some are user created and others exist in the system by default. *Group = {Photography, Running}*.

Relationship. The set of relationships supported by the OSN. Specifically, these are the categories of relations on which access control are decided. It also includes the category called *customized* where a user can create his own relations. For example, *Relationship = {Friends, Restricts, Blocks, Bans, Follows}*.

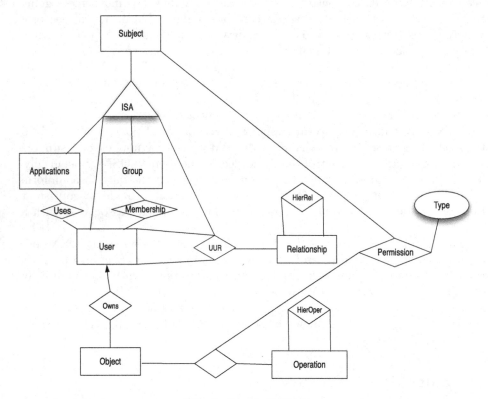

Fig. 1. Simple ReBAC

Application. The set of applications that users can install and use in the OSN. For example, *Application = {Solitaire, GreetingCards}*.

Subject. A user has several attributes and associations (these are discussed in the next section), but only some of these attributes and associations are used in making access control decisions. The set of attributes or associations of a user that determines access control to a resource is termed as *Subject*. For instance, a user may get access to a resource based on his identity, his relationship to the owner of the resource, membership in some groups, or by virtue of executing some applications. In this work, the *id* of the user, *Group*, *Application*, and the relationship that an owner of the object has with the access requester determine the access privilege and we refer to them as *Subject*. For example, the data owner *George* may define the subject as $Subject = \{Running, Amy, Family)\}$.

Object. The set of resources that need protection. Attribute of an object include its *type* which determines the operations on the object. An object can be either a *File* or a *Folder*. Folders are containers that store the individual files. Note that, the objects may be organized in the form of a directory structure through the use of folders.

Operation. This is the set of actions that can be performed on objects. For example, $Operation = \{Tag, View, Share, Search, Comment\}$.

2.2   Relationship Sets

In this case, we have several associations between entity sets some of which we discuss below.

Uses. This association set, *Uses*, connects the entity sets *User* to *Process* and it is a many to many relation. We use tuple notations to denote the individual instances of association sets. Note that, We use a tuple notation (u_i, a_j) to denote instances of this association set. In other words, $(u_i, a_j) \in Uses$. Moreover, $(u_i, a_j) \in Uses \Rightarrow u_i \in Users \wedge a_j \in Applications \wedge a_j \in uses(u_i)$. For example, $Uses = \{(Jane, Solitaire)\}$.

Membership. This association set, *Membership*, connects the entity sets *Users* to *Groups* and it has pairs of the form (u_i, g_m) which indicates that the user u_i is a member of group g_i. $(u_i, g_m) \in Membership \Rightarrow u_i \in Users \wedge g_m \in Groups$. For example, $Membership = \{(George, Running), (Tim, Running)\}$.

UUR. This association gives the user to user relation and contains a set of triples (u_i, u_j, r_m), that specifies that user u_i is related by r_m to user u_j. Note that, two users u_i and u_j can be related by multiple relations. For example, we can have $UUR = \{(Jane, George, Friends), (Jane, Amy, Follows), (Amy, Jane, Bans)\}$.

Mutually Exclusive. This association set *MutuallyExclusive* gives the pairs of relations (r_i, r_j) that are mutually exclusive to each other. It means that two users u_i and u_j cannot be related by two relations that are mutually exclusive to each other. The association is symmetric. In other words, $(r_i, r_j) \in MutuallyExclusive \implies (r_j, r_i) \in MutuallyExclusive$. For example, $MutuallyExclusive = \{(Friends, Blocks), (Blocks, Follows)\}$.

HierRel. Relations may be ordered, where the ordering relation may be referred to as *HierRel* which is transitive and antisymmetric and is defined by the system. For any two relations r_i and r_j, $(r_i, r_j) \in HierRel$ signifies that relation r_i is prerequisite to relation r_j and r_j also gets all the positive permissions given to r_i. $(Friends, Family)$ is an example of hierarchy. Thus, if a user u_k can be in a relationship r_j with u_m only if she is in relationship r_i with u_m. In other words, $(r_i, r_j) \in HierRel \wedge (u_k, u_m, r_j) \in UUR \implies (u_k, u_m, r_i) \in UUR$. We use $HierRel^+$ to denote the transitive closure of $HierRel$.

HierOper. The operations in an OSN forms a partial order where the ordering relation is defined by the system and is referred to as $HierOper$. For any two operations op_i and op_j, $(op_i, op_j) \in HierOper$ signifies that if an entity has the permission to execute op_i on some object r, then it also has the permission to execute op_j on r provided there are no prohibitions defined on it. If the entity is prohibited from executing op_i on object r, then op_j may or may not be prohibited from executing r depending on the type of enforcement. For example, $(View, Tag)$ is an example where the operations are arranged in a hierarchy.

Permissions. This is the set of allowable and prohibitable operations in a system. Each permission is an association between *Subjects*, *Objects* and *Operations* and has an attribute called *kind* which is an enumerated type having values *Allow* and *Deny* corresponding to positive and negative permissions respectively. Permissions may be defined by the user or by the system. Example of a permission is $(u_i, op_i, o_i, Allow)$ which allows user u_i to perform operation op_i on object o_i. Another example is $(r_j, op_j, o_j, Deny)$ which prohibits relation r_j from performing operation op_j on object o_j. Examples of permissions are $(Amy, Share, o_9, Deny)$ and $(Solitaire, Traverse, georgefl, Allow)$.

3   Automated Analysis of OSN Models

We need to formally analyze our Alloy model to detect potential problems with the configuration and to understand how the elements interact. Moreover, automated analysis is desirable as they can reveal problems that the user has missed. Towards this end, we show how to represent such a model in Alloy.

Alloy is a formal modeling language capable of expressing complex structural constraints and behaviour. Alloy is supported by an automated constraint solver called the Alloy Analyzer that searches for instances of the model that satisfy modelled system properties. The model is automatically translated into a Boolean expression, which is analysed by SAT solvers embedded within the Alloy Analyzer. A user-specified scope on the model elements bounds the domain, making it possible to create finite Boolean formulas that can be evaluated by the SAT-solver. When a property does not hold, a counter example is produced that demonstrates how it has been violated.

3.1   Modeling OSN in Alloy

In the following, we show how the OSN can be modeled in Alloy. An Alloy model consists of *signature* declarations, *fields*, *facts* and *predicates*. Each signature consists of a set of *atoms* which are the basic entities in Alloy. Atoms are *indivisible* (they cannot be decomposed), *immutable* (their properties do not change) and *uninterpreted* (they do not have any inherent properties). Each field belongs to a signature and represents a relation between two or more signatures. A relation denotes a set of tuples of atoms. Facts are statements that define constraints on the elements of the model. Predicates are parameterised constraints that can be used within facts or other predicates.

Listing 1.1 shows a partial Alloy model of Facebook's access control policies.

Listing 1.1. OSN Policy

```
sig OSN {
        individuals: set Individual,
        lists: set List,
        objects: set Object,
        folders: set Folder,
        protected_elements: set (Resource),
        owned: set (Resource + Custom),
        owners: individuals -> owned,
        object_location: folders -> objects,
        social_graph: individuals -> individuals -> lists,
        permissions,
                exceptions
        :individuals -> Subject -> protected_elements,
        has_access: Individual -> protected_elements}
{
        protected_elements = objects + folders
        owned = objects + folders + (lists & Custom)
}
```

The model identifies

1. Groups of elements denoting
   (a) the set of **individuals** that have an OSN account; (corresponds to entity *User* in Sect. 2)
   (b) the set of **lists** representing relationship tags including friends, friends of friends; (corresponds to entity *Relationship* in Sect. 2)
   (c) the set of **objects** denoting the different types of objects such as photographs, videos, status updates, etc.; (corresponds to attribute type of entity *Object* in Sect. 2)
   (d) the set of **folders** that contains groups of objects; (corresponds to *Folder* in Sect. 2)
   (e) the set of **protected_elements** representing those elements in the model that are protected under a policy - objects and folders; (corresponds to entity *Object* in Sect. 2) and
   (f) the set of elements in **owned** representing elements that are owned by individuals - objects, folders, and custom lists. (corresponds to association *Owns* in Sect. 2)
2. Relations denoting
   (a) **object_location** shows how objects are arranged in folders;
   (b) **social_graph** shows how individuals denote the kinds of relationships they have with other individuals; for example the tuples *(Jim, Bailey, Blocks)*, and *(Amy, Bailey, Friends)* in the social graph means that *Jim*

blocks *Bailey*, and that *Amy* is friends with *Bailey* respectively. (corresponds to association *UUR* in Sect. 2)

(c) **owners** shows who owns the objects, folders, and custom lists; (corresponds to subset of *User* in Sect. 2)

(d) **permissions** and **exceptions** are the privacy settings for protected elements; in addition to giving access to named individuals, permission and exceptions include giving access to lists (of individuals). For example if the tuple *(Jim, Friends, object1)* exists in *permissions*, and the tuple *(Bill, Acquaintances, object1)* exists in *exceptions*, then all of Bill's friends except acquaintances have access to *object1*; (corresponds to entity *Permission* and its attribute *Type* in Sect. 2) and

(e) The **has_access** relation represents the resolving of the *permissions* and *exceptions* and tells explicitly who has access to particular elements protected under the policy which correspond to positive and negative permissions.

We need additional constraints on the model to faithfully represent OSN policies. For convenience, we use some of the utilities provided by the Alloy Analyzer for 2-tuple relations *(util/relation)*, and 3-tuple relations *(util/ternary)* in our specifications.

Owners. Each owned element has exactly one owner; this makes the owner relation a total injection over the owned elements. We can express this constraint in Alloy through use of the predicate *bijective*. We show this constraint in Listing 1.2.

Listing 1.2. Owners Constraints

```
bijective[osn.owners, osn.owned]
```

Objects and Folders. Each object may be contained in only one folder; this means that the *object_location* relation is *injective* over the objects. In addition, a folder and the objects it contains must belong to the same individual. We show these constraints in Listing 1.3.

Listing 1.3. Constraints for Folders

```
// each object can only be contained in one folder
injective[osn.object_location, osn.objects]
// a folder and the objects it contains has the same owner
all fol: osn.folders, o: osn.objects |
        fol->o in osn.object_location implies
        osn.owners.fol = osn.owners.o
```

Social Graph. The social graph maps the *UUR* relation in Sect. 2 and describes the relationships among individuals, and individuals with interest groups. In the social graph we exclude self relationships - this makes the subgraph of the *social_graph* irreflexive in its first two elements; We show these constraints in Listing 1.4 and use *select12[]* from the *ternary* utilities to select the first and second elements from the social graph.

Listing 1.4. General Constraints for Social Graph

```
// no self relationships in the social graph
irreflexive[select12[osn.social_graph]]
```

We can extract **acquaintances, close friends, family** members, **friends**, those **blocked** or **restricted**, those placed in **custom** lists, **friends of friends**, and those in an **interest group**; we describe them in the paragraphs below.

Friends. A tuple, say *(Amy, Bailey, Friends)* in the social graph means that *Amy* and *Bailey* have established a friendship; such friendships are symmetric, so the tuple *(Bailey, Amy, Friends)* will also exist in the social graph. We can extract those individuals that are friends from the social graph by selecting the firsts two elements where the third element is *Friends*. We show these constraints in Listing 1.5.

Listing 1.5. Constraints for Friends

```
let friends = select12[osn.social_graph & univ->univ->Friends] |
    // symmetry
    symmetric[friends]
```

Individuals denoted as *custom, acquaintance, family*, and *restricted* are first friends with the individuals who marks them as such; for example the tuple *(Bailey, Amy, Acquaintance)* where Bailey marks Amy as an acquaintance is allowed in the social graph because Amy and Bailey are also friends; acquaintances, close friends, family, restricts, and other user defined relationships (custom) may also be extracted from the social graph in the same manner as friends; these relationships are constrained as given in Listing 1.6.

Listing 1.6. Social Graph Relationships that depends on Friends

```
acquaintance in friends
custom in friends
family in friends
restricts in friends
```

Blocks. An individual that is blocked is not a friend. Listing 1.7 has this constraints.

Listing 1.7. Constraints for Blocks

```
no blocks & friends
```

Permissions and Exceptions.

General Constraints for Permissions and Exceptions. A tuple in the permissions relation gives access to protected elements, and the tuples in the exceptions relation prohibit access. In other words, they correspond to positive and negative permissions in the OSN model as shown in Sect. 2. Typically, the owner sets permissions and exceptions. Some rules about permissions and exceptions are given below.

1. When an owner of a resource wants exclusive access or wants everyone else to get access to a resource, she can specify the permission as *Only_me* or *Everyone* respectively. For example, the tuple *(Amy, Only_me, object2)* in *permissions* would indicate that only Amy has access to *object2*. If an owner uses *Only_me* or *Everyone* to specify permissions on objects, the permissions cannot be overridden by exceptions on those objects.
2. Individual can give permissions/exceptions on resources they own to their friends or to their own custom lists.
3. Exceptions can be specified for only those protected elements that have permissions defined on them.

We show a part of the constraints for permissions and exceptions for protected elements, custom lists, and implications of Only_me and Everyone permissions in Listing 1.8.

Listing 1.8. General Constraints for Permissions and Exceptions

```
// each protected element has at least one permission defined
surjective[perms13, osn.resources]

// each protected element has at least one permission defined
surjective[perms13, osn.resources + osn.copies]

// permissions/exceptions for owned custom lists
all
        i: osn.individuals |
let
        c = osn.lists & Custom,
        ic = i->c | {
(ic in (perms12 + excepts12)) implies
(ic in osn.owners) }

// Implications for Only_me and Everyone permissions
all
        r: res |
some (Only_me->r + Everyone->r) & perms23 implies
(#perms23.r = 1 and  #excepts23.r = 0)
```

Resources. We can extract specific permissions and exceptions for resources and show that any folder and the objects they contain must have the same permissions and exceptions, and that individuals specify permissions only for resources they own. We show this in Listing 1.9.

Listing 1.9. Specific Resource Constraints for Permissions and Exceptions

```
// individuals specify permissions/exceptions for resources they own
((resource_permissions13 + resource_exceptions13) - univ->Friends)
        in osn.owners
// a folder and the objects it contains have the same permissions,
// and the same exceptions
        all
                fol: osn.folders, obj: osn.objects|
        fol->obj in osn.object_location implies (
                perms.fol = perms.obj and excepts.fol = excepts.obj)
```

Access to Protected Elements. Resolving permissions and exceptions with those blocked or restricted by an individual gives the set of users who are able to access a protected element. In the following, we describe how this is done.

1. Extract the permissions and exceptions for a protected element and replacing list with the individuals in the list.
2. Remove those blocked or restricted by the owner of the protected element if the permission for the object and copies that are not public (i.e. Everyone).

We do not show the functions for resolving the access, but show how we constrain the *has_access* relation where *Everyone* denotes the universe of individuals (publicly accessible) where *HaveAccessToResource[]* is the function we use to resolve access for objects.

Listing 1.10. Access to Protected Elements

```
// access to resources
        all
                i: everyone, r: osn.protected_resources |
        let
                perm = i->r | {
        perm in osn.has_access iff
                perm in HaveAccessToResource[osn, r] }
```

3.2   Misconfiguration Detection

The work of [11] identifies that a user's mental model of sharing, i.e. what a user intended to share, may not be actually reflected in the policy configurations. It is important to detect potential misconfigurations in policy rules and notify the user so that he can take some corrective actions. We describe the misconfigurations that can be uncovered through analysis of the Alloy model in the following paragraphs.

Friend(s) Exist in Both the Allowed and Denied List. If this happens, then the individuals will not have access to the resource. We show an example of Fig. 2 where *Individual0* both grants and denies access to *Object* for *Individual1*, and give the Alloy specification for detecting this misconfiguration in Listing 1.11.

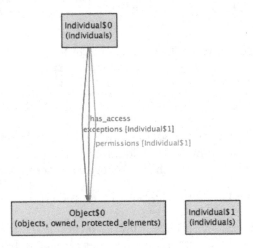

Fig. 2. Misconfiguration: explicit permission and exception for same resource

Listing 1.11. Explicit Allow and Deny

```
pred IndividualHasExplicitPermissionAndExceptionForResource[
      osn: OSN, i: Individual] {
    some o: osn.objects |
          i in ran[osn.permissions.o] and
          i in ran[osn.exceptions.o] }
```

Smartlist Updates. Facebook supports interest groups consisting of a set of members. Members post messages to these groups which are viewable to all other members. We may want existing group members to be notified when new members join the group so that they make informed decisions when submitting their posts. In the following, we show the Alloy code when a member has posted an object to the interest group and an individual who is in the member's restricted/blocked list joins the interest group. Since these scenarios suggest a before and after state in the OSN, we can check when state changes detect that these misconfigurations occur. Alloy specification to check for this misconfiguration is given in Listing 1.12; the state prior to the set of the operations is *osn* and the state after to the set of operations is *osn'*.

Listing 1.12. Interest Group Misconfiguration

```
pred RestrictedNowInInterestGroup [osn, osn': OSN, o: Object,
    restricted: Individual] {
    some
            restrictor: Individual,
            it: Interest_Group |
    let
            restricts = restrictor -> restricted |

    // restrictor is owner of object
    restrictor -> o in osn.owners and
    restrictor -> o in osn'.owners and

    // object is shared with interest group, it
    restrictor -> it -> o in osn.permissions and
    restrictor -> it -> o in osn'.permissions and

    // restriction in both before ans after state of social graphs
    restricts in osn.social_graph.Restricts and
    restricts in osn'.social_graph.Restricts and

    // restrictor's presence in the interest group
    restrictor -> it in univ.(osn.social_graph) and
    restrictor -> it in univ.(osn'.social_graph) and

    // restricted's presence in the interest group
    restricted -> it not in univ.(osn.social_graph) and
    restricted -> it in univ.(osn'.social_graph) and

    // restricted's access
    restricted->o not in osn.has_access and
    restricted->o in osn'.has_access and

    // restrictor's access
    restrictor->o in osn.has_access and
    restrictor->o in osn'.has_access }
```

In this example, we show a textual view of the model found by the Alloy Analyser in Fig. 3; Fig. 3(a) shows that *Individual0* has restricted *Individual1*, *Individualo* has shared *Object2* with *Interest_Group0*, and *Individual1* is not a part of *Interest_Group0*, while Fig. 3(b) shows that *Individual1* is now a part of *Interest_Group0* and now has access to *Object2*.

For lack of space, we do not show other misconfigurations.

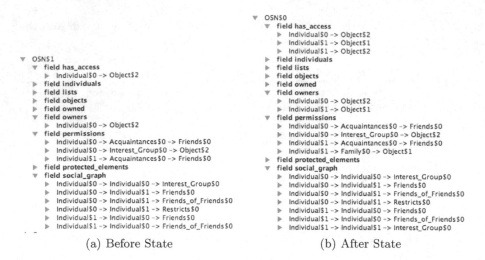

Fig. 3. Misconfiguration: interest group cause restricted individual to have access to object

4   Policy Machine

Enterprise computing applications aim to provide data services (DSs) to its users. Examples of such services are email, workflow management, and calendar management. NIST Policy Machine (PM) [7] was proposed so that a single access control framework can control and manage the individual capabilities of the different DSs. Each DS operates in its own environment which has its unique rules for specifying and analyzing access control. The PM tries to provide an enterprise operating environment in which policies can be specified and enforced in a uniform manner. PM was initially developed for enterprise applications and is targeted at Microsoft Windows Server environment where the Active Directory is responsible for user authentication and authorization. The PM follows the attribute-based access control model and can express a wide range of policies that arise in enterprise applications and also provides the mechanism for enforcing such policies.

We present only the specification constructs in the PM that are needed to model OSN policies. The PM consists of two types of objects: (i) data objects and (ii) policy objects. We have operations defined on these objects. Examples of operations on data objects are read and write. Examples of operations on policy objects are adding users, adding attributes to the users etc. Note that, operations on policy objects alter the access control state and allows for policy evolution.

The policy objects consists of 3 entities: (i) users, (ii) processes, and (iii) objects. *Users* represent the human users in the system who need access to resources. The users access resources through some program. A program invoked by the user is referred to as a *process* and it inherits the privileges of the invoking user. *Objects* are the resources needing protection.

In addition, we have 3 types of containers: (i) user containers, (ii) object containers, and (iii) policy containers. Each container is associated with one or more attributes that characterize the elements contained in them. The containers group and categorize elements contained in them. Each element can be in one or more containers.

In addition, the PM defines links, referred to as associations and prohibitions, between user containers and object containers. Associations describe the access privileges that users belonging to the given user container have over objects belonging to the given object container. Prohibitions describe the rights that are prohibited for users belonging to the user container over the objects belonging to the given container. The links are labeled with the names of operations that are allowed and restricted respectively.

Prohibitions can be specified on a user basis or on a process basis to accommodate prohibition on a session basis. While granting access, all the policies associated with the specific user and process with regards to an object are taken into account. In the case of conflict, prohibition has a higher precedence.

The final component is obligation which describes the sequence of operations that must occur when an access has occurred. Note that, these operations may occur over data objects or policy objects. If such operations occur over policy objects, the access control configuration gets modified.

5   Specifying OSN Model Using PM

In this section, we briefly describe how the OSN model can be represented using the PM. One of the motivation for using PM for OSNs is the ability to provide administrative control to the users with regards to configuring their access control policies. The second motivation for using PM is for automated enforcement of the policies and to avoid misconfigurations by the user.

5.1   Formalization of Containers in Policy Machine

The core of the PM is represented by the notion of containers associated with users and objects. In this work, we formalize the notion of containers and also extend it in order to handle OSN policies.

Definition 1 (Container): *A container is a set of elements. If the elements contained in a container is a set of users, we refer to it as a* user container. *If the elements in a container are objects, the container is an* object container. *If the elements in a container are policies, it is referred to as* policy container *or* policy class.

Each container characterizes its members and has multiple attributes for each of its characteristics. *id* and *owner* are two essential attributes for all containers. *id* uniquely identifies each container in the system. Each container has an attribute called *owner* which identifies the set of users who have administrative control over the container, such as, adding and removing elements contained in them. The owner of a container can be an individual user of the OSN, a group of OSN users having shared rights, or the system user. When the owner of a container is an individual user, we refer to it as a *private container*. When a group of users share administrative privileges over a container, it is referred to as a *shared container*. When the system administrators have ownership, it is referred to as a *system container*.

Two containers can be related by the following relationships, namely, *disjoint*, *contained-in*, and *overlapping* relations. We define these relations below. These relations play a role in access control decisions.

Definition 2 (Disjoint): *If containers A and B are* disjoint, *then elements contained in one of them should not be in the other. Formally, A and B are disjoint, iff* $\forall x \in A, x \notin B \wedge \forall y \in B, y \notin A$. *Disjoint relation is symmetric. Disjoint containers have different sets of elements, so they do not interfere with each other with regards to access control decisions.*

Definition 3 (Overlapping): *If containers A and B are* overlapping, *then elements contained in one of them may also be present in the other. Formally, A and B are overlapping, iff* $\forall x \in A, x \notin B \vee x \in B \wedge \forall y \in B, y \notin A \vee y \in A$. *Overlapping relation is symmetric. For an element existing in two overlapping containers, the privilege is the union of the privileges of the two containers and the prohibition is also the union of the prohibitions of the two containers.*

Definition 4 (Contained-in): *If container A is contained-in container B, then every element in A is also an element in B. Formally, A is contained-in B, iff* $\forall x \in A, x \in B$. *Contained-in relation is transitive. For an element in a container A that is contained in another container B, the privilege and prohibitions of B also apply to the element.*

5.2   Modeling the Entities and Relationships in the OSN Model

We now describe how we map the various entity sets and association sets in the OSN Model to match the PM configuration. The PM defines 3 entity sets, namely, *User*, *Process*, and *Object*. The other entity sets and associations are described using containers, associations, and assignments, as described below.

User in the OSN corresponds exactly with the set *User* as defined by the PM.

Group consists of a set of groups that are defined for the OSN. In the PM framework, we model each group as a container. For the groups *Photography* and *Running*, we create two containers, namely, *PhotographyC* container and a *RunningC* container. This may be a private container or a shared container depending on how the group is managed. Each user can be part of one or more such containers and each container can have multiple users. The relation *Membership* in the OSN model decides which user is in which container. For example, if {*(George, Running), (Tim, Running), (John, Photography)*} ⊆ *Membership*, then {*George, Tim*} ⊆ *RunningC* and {*John*} ⊆ *PhotographyC*.

Application gives the set of application that can be defined for the OSN. Here again each application is modeled as a container and users can be part of one or more such containers. The owner of the application may be the individual or the system depending on what is allowed by the OSN. For the set *Application* = {*Solitaire, GreetingCard*}, we create containers *SolitaireC* and *GreetingCardC*. The association *Uses* in the OSN model is used to propagate the respective containers. For example, *Uses* = {*(Jane, Solitaire)*}, results in user *Jane* being in the container *SolitaireC* which signifies that *Jane* is invoking the application *Solitaire*.

Relationship in the OSN signifies the set of relationships supported by the OSN. Each user has a set of relationships which are modeled as a set of private containers which gives her the authority to add or delete users from these containers. For example, the OSN user *George* may have *FriendsC*, *BlocksC*, *RestrictsC* and *AllowsC* containers. The elements of the association *UUR* in the OSN model are used to populate these containers. Suppose *UUR* = {*(Jane, George, Friends), (Jane, Amy, Follows), (Amy, Jane, Bans)*}. User *Jane* has container *FriendsC* which contains *George* and also has a container *FollowsC* which contains *Amy*. User *Amy* has a container *BansC* which contains *Jane*.

Two relations can be mutually exclusive. Suppose *MutuallyExclusive* = {*(Friends, Blocks), (Blocks, Follows)*}. *(Friends, Blocks)* are mutually exclusive means that user *George* cannot place another user, say *John* on both the *Friends* list and the *Blocks* list. Mutually exclusive relations are modeled as disjoint containers; and can be automatically enforced by the system. Thus, for the above example *FriendsC* and *BlocksC* are disjoint containers. Thus, if *George* places *John* in *FriendsC* container, he will be prohibited from placing John in *BlocksC* container.

Two relations may also be related in a hierarchy as depicted by the *HierRel* in the OSN model. For example, *Friends* and *Family* can form a hierarchy. Hierarchical relations can be modeled as *contained-in* containers. Thus, *Family* is contained-in the *Friends* container. Thus, privileges applicable to members of *Friends* automatically applies to members of *Family*. Note that, *HierRel* is transitive and can easily be modeled by the *contained-in* relation which is also transitive.

Subject is an abstraction that describes the set of attributes that may give a user the access. In the PM, the ownership in the various containers determine the access privilege of a user.

Object in the OSN model is the set of resources needing protection and corresponds to the PM notion of objects. Each object is also contained in one or more containers that determine the operations permitted on it. The containers can be owned by one user, or by multiple users, or by the system.

Operation in the OSN model correspond to the set of actions that can be performed on objects. In addition, the operations may be ordered in a hierarchy through *HierOper*. We have no explicit representation of operations in the PM, but the association *Permissions* can be represented which we discuss later.

We use the *assignment relation* to map users and objects to their respective containers. Note that, the assignment relation is transitive. In addition, we have *labeled associations* that specify the access rights user containers have on the object containers. Some operations are ordered in a hierarchy. For example, *(View, Tag)* is an example of operations arranged in a hierarchy. Thus, if a user has the permission to view an object, she also has the permission to tag it. However, such hierarchies must be flattened and represented as labeled associations. Figure 4 gives a fragment of an OSN policy that is represented using the PM.

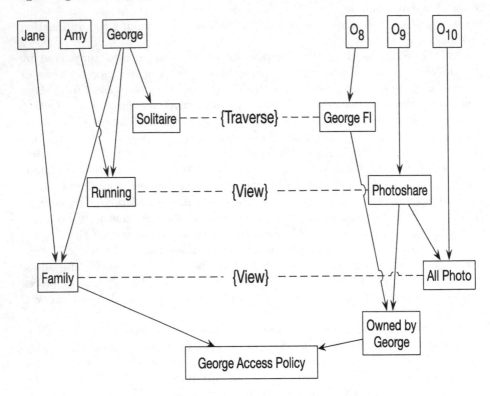

Fig. 4. Using PM to represent OSN policy

6 Conclusion and Future Work

OSNs contain a large amount of sensitive personal information. Inadvertent leakage or disclosure can have disastrous consequences. Adding to the complexity is the fact that OSNs provide numerous features which make it harder for the naïve user to configure his access control settings in the correct manner. Formal models, tools, and enforcement mechanisms are needed for specifying, analyzing, enforcing, and managing the access control settings of the OSN user. We propose a simple model for expressing OSN policies, and demonstrate how such a model can be automatically analyzed using Alloy to detect for potential misconfigurations. We also illustrate how such a model can be enforced and managed using PM which is an attribute-based access control framework developed at NIST. Our future plans involve developing new types of access control models for OSNs that support advanced features like spatio-temporal access control, history-based, and retention policies. We also intend to compare relationship-based access control with attribute-based access control for use in OSNs with respect to expressiveness, ease-of-use, and complexity.

Acknowledgement. This work was is based on research sponsored by NIST under agreement number 70NANB14H059, by an internal grant from Colorado State University, and by NSF under award number CCF-1018711.

References

1. Bennett, P.L., Ray, I., France, R.B.: Analysis of a relationship based access control model. In: C3S2E15 (2015)
2. Bruns, G., Fong, P.W.L., Siahaan, I., Huth, M.: Relationship-based access control: its expression and enforcement through hybrid logic. In: Bertino, E., Sandhu, R.S. (eds.) CODASPY. ACM (2012)
3. Carminati, B., Ferrari, E., Perego, A.: Enforcing access control in web-based social networks. ACM Trans. Inf. Syst. Secur. **13**(1), 6:1–6:38 (2009)
4. Cheng, Y., Park, J., Sandhu, R.S.: Relationship-based access control for online social networks: beyond user-to-user relationships. In: SocialCom/PASSAT, IEEE (2012)
5. Cheng, Y., Park, J., Sandhu, R.: A user-to-user relationship-based access control model for online social networks. In: Cuppens-Boulahia, N., Cuppens, F., Garcia-Alfaro, J. (eds.) DBSec 2012. LNCS, vol. 7371, pp. 8–24. Springer, Heidelberg (2012)
6. Ferraiolo, W.J.D., Gavrila, S.: Policy machine: Features, architecture, and specification. Technical report, NIST, December 2012
7. Ferraiolo, D., Atluri, V., Gavrila, S.: The policy machine: a novel architecture and framework for access control policy specification and enforcement. J. Syst. Archit. **57**(4), 412–424 (2011)
8. Ferraiolo, D.F., Gavrila, S.I., Jansen, W.A.: Enabling an enterprise-wide, data-centric operating environment. IEEE Comput. **46**(4), 94–96 (2013)
9. Fong, P.W.L.: Relationship-based access control: protection model and policy language. In: Sandhu, R.S., Bertino, E. (eds.) CODASPY, pp. 191–202. ACM (2011)
10. Jackson, D.: Software Abstractions: Logic, Language, and Analysis. The MIT Press, Cambridge (2012)
11. Javed, Y., Shehab, M.: Access control policy misconfiguration detection in online social networks. In: SocialCom/PASSAT, pp. 544–549. IEEE, September 2013
12. Johnson, M.L., Egelman, S., Bellovin, S.M.: Facebook and privacy: it's complicated. In: Cranor, L.F. (eds.) SOUPS, p. 9. ACM, July 2012
13. Madejski, M., Johnson, M.L., Bellovin, S.M.: A study of privacy settings errors in an online social network. In: PerCom Workshop, pp. 340–345. IEEE, March 2012
14. Squicciarini, A.C., Xu, A., Zhang, X.(L).: Cope: enabling collaborative privacy management in online social networks. J. Am. Soc. Inf. Sci. Technol. **62**(3), 521–534 (2011)
15. Zhang, R.: Relation Based Access Control. Studies on the Semantic Web, vol. 5. IOS Press, Heidelberg (2010)
16. Zhang, R., Artale, A., Giunchiglia, F., Crispo, B.: Using description logics in relation based access control. In: Grau, B.C., Horrocks, I., Motik, B., Sattler, U. (eds.) Description Logics. CEUR Workshop Proceedings, vol. 477 (2009). CEUR-WS.org
17. Zhang, R., Giunchiglia, F., Crispo, B., Song, L.: Relation-based access control: an access control model for context-aware computing environment. Wirel. Pers. Commun. **55**(1), 5–17 (2010)

Role Mining in the Presence of Separation of Duty Constraints

Prasuna Sarana[1], Arindam Roy[2], Shamik Sural[1]([⊠]), Jaideep Vaidya[3],
and Vijayalakshmi Atluri[3]

[1] School of Information Technology, IIT Kharagpur, Kharagpur, India
saranaprasuna257@gmail.com, shamik@sit.iitkgp.ernet.in
[2] Advanced Technology Development Centre, IIT Kharagpur, Kharagpur, India
arindam.roy@iitkgp.ac.in
[3] MSIS Department, Rutgers University, Newark, USA
{atluri,jsvaidya}@rutgers.edu

Abstract. In recent years, Role Based Access Control (RBAC) has emerged as the most popular access control mechanism, especially for commercial applications. In RBAC, permissions are assigned to roles, which are then assigned to users. The key to the effectiveness of RBAC is the underlying role set that is used. The process of identifying an appropriate set of roles that optimally meets the organizational requirements is called role mining. One of the most useful constraints that can be expressed in RBAC is Separation of Duty (SoD). SoD constraints allow organizations to put a restriction on the minimum number of users required to complete a critical task. However, existing role mining algorithms do not handle SoD constraints and cannot be easily extended to incorporate SoD constraints. In this paper, we consider the problem of role mining when SoD constraints are present. We develop three alternative approaches that can be applied either during or after role mining. We evaluate the performance of all three approaches on several real world data sets and demonstrate their effectiveness.

Keywords: RBAC · Role mining · Separation of duty · SMER constraints

1 Introduction

Resources are protected in organizations by providing appropriate and selective permissions to users. Traditionally, access control policies were directly specified in terms of users and their permissions. However, such an access control method increases the burden on system administrators when the number of users or permissions increases. RBAC (Role Based Access Control) [1,2] reduces this administrative overhead by assigning permissions to users through roles. Roles in RBAC make task re-assignment easier and reduce the complexity as well as chances of error compared to direct assignment of permissions to users.

© Springer International Publishing Switzerland 2015
S. Jajodia and C. Mazumdar (Eds.): ICISS 2015, LNCS 9478, pp. 98–117, 2015.
DOI: 10.1007/978-3-319-26961-0_7

However, RBAC is effective only when the set of roles matches the organization's functional requirements. Therefore, an important step in RBAC deployment is to define the requisite roles. This process, known as role engineering [3], can be carried out using top down, bottom up or hybrid approaches [12]. In the top down approach, roles are formed by identifying independent business processes that are associated with permissions. This approach is often difficult to handle as organizations consist of hundreds of business processes and is also known to be cost intensive. On the other hand, the bottom up approach uses the existing user permission assignments for identifying roles – a procedure referred to as *role mining* [4]. A hybrid approach [3] combines elements of both top-down and bottom-up approaches to include business process knowledge as well as existing user-permission assignment information.

Note that, the user permission assignment (*UPA*) information can be represented as a matrix, in which rows represent users and columns represent permissions. Thus, a value of *1* in the (u_i, p_j) entry of a *UPA* matrix denotes the fact that the permission p_j is assigned to the user u_i. Role mining decomposes the given *UPA* matrix into two boolean matrices: User Assignment matrix (*UA*) and Permission Assignment matrix (*PA*), of which *UA* depicts the assignment of roles to users and *PA* depicts the assignment of permissions to roles. While many different UA and PA combinations exist that can correctly specify the UPA, the main challenge for role mining algorithms is to find the UA and PA that can do so optimally. Here, optimality is in terms of some metric such as the number of roles. Several metrics have been identified in the literature [5,13].

Besides ease of administration, a key benefit of RBAC is that it also allows specification and enforcement of policies with various constraints such as cardinality, prerequisite, and Separation of Duty (SoD), which match real life situations [1]. Cardinality constraints limit the maximum number of roles a user or a permission can belong to, the maximum number of permissions a role can have or the maximum number of users a role can be assigned to. SoD is considered to be an important constraint in computer security for the prevention of fraud. Typically, an SoD constraint (also called an SoD policy) states that at least k users are required to complete a task that requires n number of permissions, for given values of k and n.

While many algorithms have been developed for role mining [4,8], none of these handle the different constraints that can be expressed in RBAC. Harika et al. [14] were the first to comprehensively address cardinality constraints in the process of role mining. However, they also do not address SoD constraints, which are actually the most important constraints that need to be enabled to eliminate fraud. In this paper, we address precisely this problem – how to identify an appropriate set of roles while also taking into consideration the existing SoD constraints.

Note that, while SoD restricts the set of users in terms of permissions, in order to implement it, RBAC uses Statically Mutually Exclusive Roles (SMER) constraints [7]. A t-m SMER constraint ensures that no user is allowed to be a member of t or more roles out of a given set of m roles. It is actually quite challenging to convert a set of SoD constraints into a corresponding set of SMER constraints that can enforce the given SoD constraints. Therefore, it is not straightforward to just use an existing role mining algorithm to identify the UA and PA, and then to generate the SMER constraints over this to precisely enforce the given SoD policies.

Thus, our objective in this paper is to take a *UPA* matrix and a set of SoD constraints as input, and find a *UA* and a *PA* matrix consistent with the *UPA* along with a set of SMER constraints that correctly enforce the given SoD constraints while minimizing the number of roles. We develop three alternative strategies to solve this problem. The developed solutions fall into two broad categories, namely *SoD-aware* and *post-processing*, based on whether constraints are considered during or after the process of role mining.

The rest of the paper is organized as follows: In Sect. 2, we present the preliminaries necessary to understand the rest of the paper. In Sect. 3, we introduce the problem of generating SMER constraints in role mining and describe the proposed algorithms. We present the results of experimental evaluation of our work in Sect. 4. We discuss prior work related to this paper in Sect. 5. Finally, we conclude the paper in Sect. 6 and discuss directions for future research.

2   Preliminaries

We now present some of the basics of the RBAC model, SoD and SMER constraints, and Role Mining.

Definition 1 *RBAC. The Role Based Access Control (RBAC) model comprises the following components [1]:*

- *U, P, R are respectively the sets of users, permissions and roles*
- *UA ⊆ U × R, a many-to-many mapping of users to roles*
- *PA ⊆ R × P, a many-to-many mapping of roles to permissions*
- *Cardinality, Separation of Duty and Prerequisite constraints*

We leave out other components like sessions and role hierarchy as they are not directly related to the work reported in this paper. Also, cardinality constraints have been considered in the context of role mining in recent literature [6,9,14]. We, instead, focus on the Separation of Duty constraints. In this paper, we use the term *UA* (respectively, *PA*) to denote the user-role assignment (respectively, role-permission assignment) relation as well as its representation in the form of a boolean matrix.

Definition 2 *k-n SoD Constraint. A k-n SoD constraint states that at least k users are required together to have a given set of n permissions. It can be expressed as $sod<\{p_1,p_2,...,p_n\},k>$ where each p_i is a permission for $1 \leq i \leq n$, and n, k are integers such that $2 \leq k \leq n$.*

Typically, these n permissions are required to carry out a sensitive task and the constraint specifies that no set of k-1 users should be able to complete it. While this constraint restricts a set of users in terms of their permissions, in RBAC, users get permissions through roles. In order to implement SoD, RBAC uses Statically Mutually Exclusive Roles (SMER) constraints as defined below [7].

Definition 3 *t-m SMER Constraint. A t-m SMER constraint specifies a set of m roles and no user is allowed to be a member of t or more of these m roles. A t-m SMER constraint can be expressed as $smer\langle\{r_1, r_2, ..., r_m\}, t\rangle$, where each r_i is a role for $1 \leq i \leq m$, and t, m are integers such that $2 \leq t \leq m$.*

It has earlier been shown that any t-m SMER constraint can be represented using a set of t-t SMER constraints, which is defined below [7].

Definition 4 *t-t SMER Constraint. A t-t SMER constraint specifies a set of t roles and no user is allowed to be a member of all the t roles. It is expressed as $smer\langle\{r_1, r_2, ..., r_t\}, t\rangle$, where each r_i is a role for $1 \leq i \leq t$, and t is an integer such that $t \geq 2$.*

The problem of determining whether the *UA* and *PA* of an RBAC system together satisfy an SoD constraint has been shown to be coNP-complete [7]. Unlike SoD constraints, which restrict permissions of a set of users, SMER constraints restrict role membership for a single user, and hence, whether an SMER constraint holds in the *UA* of an RBAC system can be checked in polynomial time (*PA* is not required for checking any violation of SMER constraints). However, if SMER constraints are to be used to enforce SoD constraints, one needs to first *generate* a set of SMER constraints (using the PA) that are adequate to enforce a given set of SoD constraints.

We consider the problem of generating SMER constraints from SoD constraints as an added requirement in role mining. In this paper, we present algorithms for generating SMER constraints from SoD constraints concurrently with the process of role mining and also alternatively as a post-processing step after an initial stage of unconstrained role mining. The basic unconstrained Role Mining Problem (RMP) (i.e., role mining without any constraints) is defined as follows [4]:

Definition 5 *Basic Role Mining Problem (RMP). Given a set of users U, a set of permissions P and a user-permission assignment matrix UPA, find a set of roles R, a user-to-role assignment matrix UA and a role-to-permission assignment matrix PA such that the UA and PA are consistent with the UPA and |R| is minimized.*

Basic RMP has been shown to be NP-Complete [4]. Significant work [3–5, 15–17] has already been done to find efficient algorithms for obtaining approximate solutions. However, as mentioned before, none of these handles SoD constraints.

3 Role Mining and SMER Constraint Generation

In this section, we formally introduce the problem of role mining in the presence of SoD constraints (*RMP_SoD*) and present our solution approaches.

3.1 Problem Definition

The *RMP_SoD* problem aims to find an appropriate set of roles that satisfy a given set of SoD constraints. Thus, it can be defined as follows:

Definition 6 *RMP_SoD. Given a set of users U, a set of permissions P, a user-permission assignment matrix UPA and a set E of SoD constraints, find a set of roles R, a user-to-role assignment matrix UA, a role-to-permission assignment matrix PA and a set C of SMER constraints such that the UA and PA are consistent with the UPA, C enforces E, and |R| is minimized.*

The following example illustrates this. Consider a set of users $U = \{u_1, u_2, u_3, u_4, u_5\}$, a set of permissions $P = \{p_1, p_2, p_3, p_4, p_5, p_6\}$, a *UPA* matrix as shown in Table 1 and a set $E = \{e_1, e_2\}$ of SoD constraints as shown below:

$$e_1 = \langle \{p_3, p_5\}, 2 \rangle \tag{1}$$

$$e_2 = \langle \{p_1, p_5, p_6\}, 2 \rangle \tag{2}$$

Table 1. Example UPA matrix

	p_1	p_2	p_3	p_4	p_5	p_6
u_1	0	1	0	0	1	0
u_2	0	1	0	0	1	0
u_3	1	1	0	1	1	0
u_4	1	1	1	0	0	0
u_5	0	0	0	0	0	1

After role mining, a *UA* (depicted in Table 2) and a *PA* (depicted in Table 3) would be generated along with a set $C = \{C_1 \cup C_2\}$ of SMER constraints as shown below:

$$C_1 = \{\langle \{r_1, r_2\}, 2 \rangle\} \tag{3}$$

$$C_2 = \{\langle \{r_1, r_3, r_4\}, 3 \rangle, \langle \{r_2, r_3, r_4\}, 3 \rangle\} \tag{4}$$

A comparison of the *UA* and *PA* matrices as well as the generated set of SMER constraints (Expressions 3 and 4) with the given *UPA* matrix and the set of SoD constraints (Expressions 1 and 2) shows that the decomposition is

Table 2. Generated UA matrix

	p_1	p_2	p_3	p_4	p_5	p_6
r_1	1	1	1	0	0	0
r_2	1	1	0	1	0	0
r_3	0	1	0	0	1	0
r_4	0	0	0	0	0	1

Table 3. Generated PA matrix

	p_1	p_2	p_3	p_4	p_5	p_6
r_1	1	1	1	0	0	0
r_2	1	1	0	1	0	0
r_3	0	1	0	0	1	0
r_4	0	0	0	0	0	1

correct and the SoD policies can be enforced using the SMER constraints. It can be verified that this decomposition is the smallest correct decomposition – i.e., it is not possible to obtain a correct decomposition of the *UPA* into *UA* and *PA* using fewer roles.

3.2   Generating SMER Constraints After Unconstrained Role Mining

We now discuss several alternative *post-processing* approaches that generate SMER constraints after unconstrained role mining. The initial stage of unconstrained role mining can employ any of the existing role mining algorithms that minimize the number of roles [4,8]. In the second stage, SMER constraints are generated, methods for which are discussed in the following sub-sections. Note that for this stage, only the *PA* obtained after unconstrained role mining is used along with the given set of SoD constraints. The output of the second stage is a set *C* of SMER constraints.

Naïve Approach. One possibility is to simply use an existing SMER generation algorithm in conjunction with an existing role mining algorithm. We term this as the naïve approach. As discussed earlier, many role mining algorithms exist. For SMER constraint generation, Li et al. [7]. propose a method that works in two phases. The first phase translates the given SoD constraints into Role-level Static Separation of Duty (RSSoD) requirements, i.e., restrictions on permissions in SoD constraints are mapped to restrictions on role memberships, and the second phase is the generation of SMER constraints from RSSoD requirements using an *SMER-Gen* procedure [7].

Definition 7 *k-n RSSoD Requirement. A k-n RSSoD requirement states that at least k users are required together to have n roles. A k-n RSSoD requirement can be expressed as $rssod\langle\{r_1,r_2,...,r_n\},k\rangle$, where each r_i is a role for $1 \leq i \leq n$, and n, k are integers such that $2 \leq k \leq n$.*

After getting the RSSoD requirements, all singleton sets of *t-m* SMER constraints that are minimal for enforcing the SoD policies are generated. The main drawback of this approach is that, generation of RSSoD requirements involves finding a minimal set of roles having all the permissions in the SoD policy, which is computationally very expensive. The methods proposed in the next two sub-sections avoid this shortcoming.

Generation of 2-2 SMER Constraints. In the first of our proposed post-processing approaches, we generate a set of 2-2 SMER constraints required to enforce the given set of SoD constraints. The input is a PA matrix and a set $E = \{e_1, e_2, ..., e_m\}$ of k-n SoD constraints. The output is a set $C = \{c_1, c_2, ..., c_q\}$ of 2-2 SMER constraints such that C enforces E. Each 2-2 SMER constraint is expressed as: $c = \langle \{r_i, r_j\}, 2 \rangle$, which means that, r_i and r_j are two mutually exclusive roles, i.e., no user is allowed to be a member of both the roles. Although 2-2 SMER constraints are expected to be quite restrictive in nature, we still consider generation of 2-2 SMER constraints as they are sufficient to enforce any enforceable SoD constraint. An SoD constraint e_i is not enforceable, if one of the following conditions hold: (i) all the permissions in e_i are assigned to a single role in the PA matrix and (ii) the given UA matrix already has user assignments violating the generated 2-2 SMER constraints.

To generate 2-2 SMER constraints for an SoD constraint e_i, we first find a set of roles S such that each role in S has at least one permission in e_i. Next, we check whether any role in S has all the permissions in e_i. If so, we declare e_i as not enforceable; otherwise, all valid pairs of mutually exclusive roles in S are generated. If two roles are mutually exclusive, then each role contains at least one mutually exclusive permission which is not present in the other role and permission set of one role is not a subset of the other.

As an example, consider an SoD constraint $\langle \{p_a, p_b, p_c\}, 2 \rangle$ in which p_a, p_b and p_c are three permissions and at least two users are required together to have all these three permissions. If there are two roles of which one role has p_a and p_b, and the other role has p_b and p_c, then we declare the two roles as mutually exclusive as these two roles are not subsets of each other and therefore each role has at least one permission which is not in the other. This can be determined by checking two conditions, namely, (i) $assign\_perms[r_i] \not\subseteq assign\_perms[r_j]$ and (ii) $assign\_perms[r_j] \not\subseteq assign\_perms[r_i]$. $assign\_perms[r]$ contains the permissions of SoD assigned to the role r, which can be found by using the PA matrix.

The algorithm $2\text{-}2\_SMER\_Post\_Processing$ for generating 2-2 SMER constraints from a PA matrix and a set E of k-n SoD constraints is shown in Algorithm 1. Here S denotes the set of roles that are affected by an SoD constraint $e_i \in E$. Lines 5 to 8 of the algorithm determine whether a constraint is enforceable or not. If it is enforceable, then for every pair of roles in S, Line 10 finds whether they should be declared mutually exclusive. Line 11 verifies whether the given UA matrix satisfies the mutual exclusivity constraint. If Line 11 returns false, the SoD constraint is declared as not enforceable. The above steps are repeated for every SoD in E (Lines 3 to 18).

Generating 2-2 SMER constraints for an SoD can be done in polynomial time. If the number of roles in the set S for the SoD is m, then the time complexity of finding whether the SoD constraint is enforceable or not is $O(m)$ and the time

---

Algorithm 1. 2-2_SMER_Post_Processing

1: Required: UA, PA, a set E of $k - n$ SoD constraints
2: C = ϕ
3: **for** each SoD e_i in E **do**
4:     Using PA, find a set S of roles having at least one permission in e_i
5:     **if** any role in S has all the permissions in e_i **then**
6:         Declare e_i as not enforceable
7:         **continue**
8:     **end if**
9:     **for** each pair of roles (r_i, r_j) in S **do**
10:         **if** $assign\_perms[r_i] \not\subseteq assign\_perms[r_j] \land assign\_perms[r_j] \not\subseteq assign\_perms[r_i]$ **then**
11:             **if** UA matrix satisfies $\langle\{r_i, r_j\}, 2\rangle$ **then**
12:                 C = C $\cup \{\langle\{r_i, r_j\}, 2\rangle\}$
13:             **else**
14:                 Declare e_i as not enforceable
15:             **end if**
16:         **end if**
17:     **end for**
18: **end for**

---

complexity for generating mutually exclusive roles is $O(m^2)$. So the total time complexity is $O(m+m^2)$, which is $O(m^2)$.

While 2-2 SMER constraints can be generated quite efficiently as compared to the naïve approach of Sub-sect. 3.2, in some cases too many SoD constraints might become non-enforceable if the UA matrix already has user-role assignments that violate the generated 2-2 SMER constraints. We next present a method which makes an estimate of the highest possible value of t for which a given SoD constraint can be enforced using t-t SMER constraints. This is expected to be less restrictive as compared to using only 2-2 SMER constraints. At the same time, it ought to be more efficient than the naïve approach.

Generation of t-t SMER Constraints. Our second post-processing approach also considers a PA matrix and a set $E = \{e_1, e_2, ..., e_m\}$ of k-n SoD constraints as input and generates a set $C = \{c_1, c_2, ..., c_q\}$ of $t - t$ SMER constraints such that C enforces E. To generate $t - t$ SMER constraints for an SoD e_i, the first step, like the previous algorithm, is to find the set of roles S so that each role in S has at least one permission in e_i. The next step is to determine whether e_i is enforceable or not. Two cases for which an SoD e_i cannot be enforced are: (i) The number of roles in the set S is less than k in e_i and (ii) At least one role in the set S has all the permissions in e_i. If e_i is enforceable, it is checked whether the permission set of any role is a subset of another role (here, by permission set we mean only those permissions of a role that are included in e_i). If so, then only 2-2 SMER constraints can be generated; else, we determine the largest value of t for which the following condition is satisfied.

$$|S| > (k - 1)(t - 1) \tag{5}$$

Algorithm 2. t-t_SMER_Post_Processing

1: Required: UA, PA, a set E of $k - n$ SoD constraints
2: $C = \phi$
3: **for** each SoD e_i in E **do**
4:     Using PA, find a set S of roles having at least one permission in e_i
5:     **if** number of roles in S is less than k of e_i **then**
6:         Declare e_i as not enforceable
7:         **continue**
8:     **end if**
9:     **if** any role in S has all the permissions in e_i **then**
10:         Declare e_i as not enforceable
11:         **continue**
12:     **end if**
13:     **if** permission set of any role is a subset of another (permission set considers only the permissions of e_i that are in the role) **then**
14:         Generate 2-2 SMER constraints similar to Algorithm 1
15:     **else**
16:         Find the largest value of t such that $|S| > (t\text{-}1)(k\text{-}1)$
17:         **for** each subset of roles R of size t from S **do**
18:             **if** UA satisfies $\langle R, t \rangle$ **then**
19:                 $C = C \cup \{\langle R, t \rangle\}$
20:             **else**
21:                 Declare e_i as not enforceable
22:             **end if**
23:         **end for**
24:     **end if**
25: **end for**

Theorem 1 given below establishes the reason for using this condition. Finally, we include every subset of t roles in S as a t-t SMER constraint in the set C. The above steps are repeated for every $e_i \in E$.

The algorithm for generating t-t SMER constraints (t-t_SMER_Post_Processing) is shown in Algorithm 2. Lines 5 to 8 and 9 to 12 determine whether the constraint is enforceable or not. Lines 13–14 generate 2-2 SMER constraints if it is determined that t-t SMER constraints cannot be generated. Line 16 finds the desired value of t. Lines 17–18 verify whether the UA matrix satisfies the t-t SMER constraints. If Line 18 returns false for any of the t-t SMER constraints, the SoD constraint is declared as not enforceable, else, it is included in the set of SMERs.

The time complexity for generating $t - t$ SMER constraints can be computed as follows. If the number of roles in the set S is m, then the time complexity for determining whether a constraint is enforceable or not is $O(m)$. Time complexity to determine whether to generate 2-2 SMER constraints or t-t SMER constraints is $O(m^2)$ and the time complexity for generating all combinations of t out of m roles is $O(m\ ^nC_k)$. So the overall time complexity is $O(m^2 + m\ ^nC_k)$ which is $O(m\ ^nC_k)$.

Theorem 1. *Given a k-n SoD constraint and a set S of roles, the largest value of t for which t-t SMER constraints can be generated to enforce the SoD constraint is given by $|S| > (t\text{-}1)(k\text{-}1)$.*

Proof. Roles in set S are the roles containing permissions required to complete a task needing separation of duty. To enforce a $k\text{-}n$ SoD constraint, the task needs at least k users to get all the n permissions through the roles in S. So, we need to find a value of t such that even if we assign $(t\text{-}1)$ distinct roles to $(k\text{-}1)$ distinct users, these $(t\text{-}1)(k\text{-}1)$ roles should not be equal to the number of roles in S, i.e., $|S| \neq (t\text{-}1)(k\text{-}1)$.

So, after assigning $(t\text{-}1)$ roles to $(k\text{-}1)$ users, at least one role should be left in S which is assigned to the kth user. Hence, $|S| > (t\text{-}1)(k\text{-}1)$.

It may be noted that, the value of t obtained as above is a conservative estimate. However, finding an exact bound for t would require a computationally expensive step of examining all possible subsets of roles actually assigned to users.

3.3   SoD-Aware Role Mining

From the discussions so far, it may be observed that, while the naïve approach of Sub-sect. 3.2 can precisely enforce the given set of SoD constraints, the 2-2 SMERs and the t-t SMERs generated in Sub-sects. 3.2 and 3.2, being more restrictive, might not be enforceable in the UA matrix (which was obtained by an unconstrained role mining algorithm from the given UPA). On the other hand, the naïve approach is computationally expensive and might not be feasible to implement in real-life applications. It may be recalled that the first step in the naïve approach is to find a minimal set of roles in the *PA* that together have n permissions corresponding to a $k\text{-}n$ SoD constraint for generating RSSoD requirements (refer to Definition 7). For this step, initially a set of roles is determined such that, each role in the set has at least one permission in the SoD. However, all the roles are not allowed to be included in the minimal set. The roles that are not included in the minimal set have the same permissions that are covered by the roles in the minimal set. Finding that set takes a substantial amount of time.

As an example, consider that role r_i is included in the minimal set and role r_j is not included in the minimal set. One of the following three cases may arise:

Case 1: r_i and r_j have the same set of permissions. In this case, two RSSoD requirements need to be considered, one including r_i and the other including r_j.

Case 2: Permission set of r_j is a subset of the permission set of r_i.

Case 3: Permission set of r_j is already covered by the remaining roles in the minimal set.

So, if we ensure that the above three cases do not occur while forming the roles, and thus make the role mining step *SoD-aware*, we can avoid the exponential time required for finding the minimal set as mentioned above.

Algorithm 3. SoD_aware_Role_Mining

1: Required: UPA, a set E of $k - n$ SoD constraints
2: Determine $UserUnc[u]$ for all users u and $PermUnc[p]$ for all permissions p from the UPA
3: $\mathcal{U}$ represents the set of selected users and $\mathcal{P}$ represents the set of selected permissions to form a role
4: **while** there exists at least one user u or permission p with uncovered edges **do**
5:    Set $\mathcal{U}=\phi$, $\mathcal{P}=\phi$
6:    Select vertex v with minimum number of uncovered edges
7:    **if** v is a user **then**
8:       Call $UserSelected\_FormRole$ procedure
9:    **else**
10:      Call $PermissionSelected\_FormRole$ procedure
11:   **end if**
12: **end while**

It may be noted that, these conditions could be embedded in any unconstrained role mining algorithm. In this paper, we use the Minimum Biclique Cover (MBC) based approach proposed in [8] as the unconstrained role mining algorithm and show how it can be made SoD-aware. In this approach, the UPA matrix is mapped to an undirected bipartite graph $G = (\{V_1, V_2\}, E)$. The two disjoint sets of vertices V_1 and V_2 in the UPA are U and P (the sets of users and permissions), respectively. The edge set E consists of tuples (u, p) where $u \in U$, $p \in P$ and permission p is assigned to user u in the UPA. The basic Role Mining Problem is mapped to the Minimum Biclique Cover finding problem for this bipartite graph. Each biclique in the minimum biclique cover represents a role. Since MBC is known to be NP-Complete, a number of different heuristics were tried in [8]. It was reported that selecting a vertex with minimum number of uncovered incident edges as the greedy choice in each iteration gives better result. We use the same heuristic in the approach presented below.

To make the MBC approach for solving RMP SoD-aware, whenever a new role $newR$ is formed, for every SoD e_i, we determine which permissions of $newR$ are in e_i. If the common permissions of $newR$ and e_i form a subset of a previously created role r, then we modify $newR$ and r as it leads to one of the three cases described above. The common permissions in $newR$ and r that belong to e_i are removed and a new role is created with these permissions.

After the biclique cover is obtained and the UA and PA get created, we derive RSSoD requirements in linear time by finding the roles having at least one permission in an SoD. Finally, we generate a set of SMER constraints in which every SMER constraint is minimal for enforcing an SoD constraint. It is to be noted that both t-m as well as t-t SMER constraints might get generated using this method.

The overall procedure for SoD-aware role mining is shown in Algorithm 3 ($SoD\_aware\_Role\_Mining$). Initially, determine $UserUnc[]$ and $PermUnc[]$ for all users and permissions. $UserUnc[u]$ contains uncovered permissions for a user

---

Algorithm 4. UserSelected_FormRole

1: **for** each $p \in UserUnc[v]$ **do**
2:     Add p to $\mathcal{P}$
3: **end for**
4: **for** each SoD e_i in E **do**
5:     Determine $perms\_SoD[e_i]$
6:     **for** each role r **do**
7:         **if** $perms\_SoD[e_i] \subseteq assign\_perms[r]$ **then**
8:             Call $Modify\_UA\_PA$ procedure
9:         **end if**
10:     **end for**
11: **end for**
12: **if** $\mathcal{P} \neq \phi$ **then**
13:     Add v to $\mathcal{U}$
14:     **for** each user $u \neq v$ **do**
15:         **if** $\mathcal{P} \subseteq assign\_perms[u]$ and at least one element of $UserUnc[u]$ is an element of $\mathcal{P}$ **then**
16:             Add u to $\mathcal{U}$
17:         **end if**
18:     **end for**
19: **end if**
20: Form a role with $\mathcal{U}$ and $\mathcal{P}$

---

u and $PermUnc[p]$ contains uncovered users for a permission p. $\mathcal{U}$ and $\mathcal{P}$ respectively represent sets of selected users and permissions for the newly formed role. Repeat the process given below until there is no vertex with uncovered edges.

Select a vertex v, which can be either user or permission, with minimum number of uncovered edges. If v is a user, then call $UserSelected\_FormRole$ procedure (Algorithm 4); else, call $PermissionSelected\_FormRole$ procedure (dual of Algorithm 4 - not shown separately). In Algorithm 4, Lines 1 to 3 find uncovered permissions of user v and store them in $\mathcal{P}$. For each SoD e_i in E, determine $perms\_SoD[e_i]$ (Line 5). It contains the permissions that are

---

Algorithm 5. Modify_UA_PA

1: Required: Role r and constraint e_i
2: **for** each permission p common to $perms\_SoD[e_i]$ and $assign\_perms[r]$ **do**
3:     Remove p from $assign\_perms[r]$ and P
4:     Add p to $tempP$
5: **end for**
6: **for** each user $u \neq v$ **do**
7:     **if** $tempP \subseteq assign\_perms[u]$ **then**
8:         Add u to $tempU$
9:     **end if**
10: **end for**
11: Form a role with $tempU$ and $tempP$

---

common to $\mathcal{P}$ and SoD e_i. If there is any role r having the same permissions as in $perms\_SoD[e_i]$ (Lines 6 to 10), then call $Modify\_UA\_PA$ procedure (refer to Algorithm 5). In Algorithm 5, Lines 2 to 5 remove common permissions in $\mathcal{P}$ and role r and store them in $tempP$. Lines 6 to 10 find the users whose permission sets are subsets of $tempP$ and store them in $tempU$. Line 11 forms a role with $tempU$ and $tempP$. It then returns to Algorithm 4. If $\mathcal{P}$ is not null, then find the users whose permission set is a subset of $\mathcal{P}$ and at least one permission must be uncovered (Lines 14 to 18) and store them in $\mathcal{U}$. $assign\_perms[u]$ contains the permissions assigned to the user u. Finally, $\mathcal{U}$ and $\mathcal{P}$ form a role.

4   Experimental Evaluation

All the algorithms presented in Sect. 3 have been implemented in C on a 3.1 GHz Intel i5-2400 CPU having 4 GB RAM. Nine real world data sets [8,14] shown in Table 4 were initially considered for the experiments. However, after studying the data sets, it was found that the Domino, FW1, FW2 and HC data sets cannot be meaningfully used to study the performance of role mining algorithms under SoD constraints (although they can be used for testing unconstrained role mining algorithms) since some sets of users in these data sets have all the permissions assigned to them (thus they will violate any SoD). Hence, valid SoD constraints cannot be generated from them.

Table 4. Data set details

Data sets	# Users	# Permissions	# Roles	Time (s)
Americas-large (AL)	3485	10127	423	78.78
Americas-small (AS)	3477	1587	213	6.31
APJ	2044	1164	456	5.60
Customer (Cus)	10961	284	276	4.66
Domino (Dom)	79	231	20	<0.01
EMEA (EM)	35	3046	34	0.02
Firewall1 (FW1)	365	709	69	0.11
Firewall2 (FW2)	325	590	10	0.15
Healthcare (HC)	46	46	15	<0.01

The rest of the data sets (in the form of UPA matrices) are given as input to the SoD-aware role mining approach. For post-processing approaches, the UA and PA obtained after applying the unconstrained MBC algorithm is given as input. Details of the number of roles generated and execution time needed using the unconstrained MBC algorithm are shown in Table 4. Since the data sets do not inherently contain any SoD constraints, we introduce different k-n SoD constraints using a simulator. In the simulator, for given values of k and n,

Table 5. Average number of SMER constraints generated by SoD-aware role mining, post-processing 2-2 SMER generation and post-processing t-t SMER generation for different number SoD constraints with different values of k and n. (a) 2-2 SoD (b) 2-3 SoD (c) 3-6 SoD (d) 5-10 SoD. Numbers in square brackets represent the percentage of SoD constraints that could be enforced.

(a)

Data set	$2-2\ SoD\ Constraints$					
	20 SoDs			50 SoDs		
	SoD_aware	2-2_post	t-t_post	SoD_aware	2-2_post	t-t_post
AL	20 [100]	984 [95]	984 [95]	50 [100]	2461 [92]	2568 [92]
AS	20 [100]	441 [80]	439 [80]	49 [100]	1279 [84]	1272 [84]
APJ	20 [100]	40 [80]	39 [80]	50 [100]	124 [84]	124 [84]
Cus	19 [100]	19 [95]	15 [80]	48 [100]	48 [96]	36 [78]
EM	19 [100]	57 [80]	54 [80]	48 [100]	142 [84]	138 [84]

(b)

Data set	$2-3\ SoD\ Constraints$					
	20 SoDs			50 SoDs		
	SoD_aware	2-2_post	t-t_post	SoD_aware	2-2_post	t-t_post
AL	20 [100]	3307 [100]	3306 [100]	50 [100]	7697 [98]	7694 [98]
AS	20 [100]	995 [80]	993 [80]	50 [100]	3365 [84]	3360 [84]
APJ	20 [100]	146 [100]	128 [100]	50 [100]	345 [100]	297 [100]
Cus	20 [100]	32 [60]	19 [100]	50 [100]	81 [58]	49 [98]
EM	20 [100]	172 [95]	163 [95]	50 [100]	425 [98]	404 [98]

(c)

Data set	$3-6\ SoD\ Constraints$					
	20 SoDs			50 SoDs		
	SoD_aware	2-2_post	t-t_post	SoD_aware	2-2_post	t-t_post
AL	520 [100]	11334 [90]	11334 [90]	1301 [100]	31155 [88]	31155 [88]
AS	488 [100]	2120 [50]	2120 [50]	1309 [100]	5081 [48]	5081 [48]
APJ	506 [100]	553 [95]	574 [95]	1262 [100]	1498 [94]	1556 [94]
Cus	479 [100]	46 [15]	372 [100]	1196 [100]	97 [14]	929 [100]
EM	430 [100]	696 [100]	697 [100]	1103 [100]	1819 [100]	1831 [100]

(d)

Data set	$5-10\ SoD\ Constraints$					
	20 SoDs			50 SoDs		
	SoD_aware	2-2_post	t-t_post	SoD_aware	2-2_post	t-t_post
AL	5281 [100]	24908 [70]	24908 [70]	13297 [100]	62058 [74]	62058 [74]
AS	4746 [100]	1307 [15]	1307 [15]	11889 [100]	3831 [16]	3831 [16]
APJ	4843 [100]	1459 [85]	1614 [85]	12299 [100]	3924 [90]	4258 [90]
Cus	4531 [100]	7 [5]	2180 [100]	11392 [100]	25 [2]	5461 [98]
EM	3022 [100]	1591 [100]	1594 [100]	7851 [100]	4168 [100]	4178 [100]

Table 6. Average time (in seconds) for the generation of SMER constraints by SoD-aware role mining, post-processing 2-2 SMER generation and post-processing t-t SMER generation for different number SoD constraints with different values of k and n. (a) 2-2 SoD (b) 2–3 SoD (c) 3–6 SoD (d) 5–10 SoD

(a)

Data set	$2-2\ SoD\ constraints$					
	20 SoDs			50 SoDs		
	SoD_aware	2-2_post	t-t_post	SoD_aware	2-2_post	t-t_post
AL	236.43	139.71	144.70	484.39	366.24	379.54
AS	13.68	10.12	10.17	26.04	29.27	30.21
APJ	481.18	0.30	0.44	518.63	0.97	1.28
Cus	279.30	< 0.01	0.24	281.49	< 0.01	0.57
EM	48.32	0.02	0.02	69.77	0.05	0.06

(b)

Data set	$2-3\ SoD\ constraints$					
	20 SoDs			50 SoDs		
	SoD_aware	2-2_post	t-t_post	SoD_aware	2-2_post	t-t_post
AL	246.48	505.56	509.40	531.47	1203.94	1212.81
AS	14.44	30.45	31.84	28.97	89.90	96.28
APJ	486.62	1.58	1.39	527.31	3.61	3.14
Cus	279.27	0.49	0.26	281.48	1.27	0.66
EM	56.16	0.07	0.07	85.03	0.02	0.17

(c)

Data set	$3-6\ SoD\ constraints$					
	20 SoDs			50 SoDs		
	SoD_aware	2-2_post	t-t_post	SoD_aware	2-2_post	t-t_post
AL	274.23	2022.69	2054.26	663.16	5762.90	5861.89
AS	17.34	117.65	143.63	39.96	280.90	337.96
APJ	496.46	6.70	7.10	552.33	17.98	19.65
Cus	279.26	1.18	5.01	281.45	2.69	12.12
EM	72.57	0.29	0.29	131.09	0.76	0.77

(d)

Data set	$5-10\ SoD\ constraints$					
	20 SoDs			50 SoDs		
	SoD_aware	2-2_post	t-t_post	SoD_aware	2-2_post	t-t_post
AL	314.58	6164.60	6267.25	844.92	14667.29	15008.82
AS	22.01	260.65	371.36	51.37	5.89	900.52
APJ	509.36	19.72	23.35	580.08	47.04	59.35
Cus	279.24	0.95	28.19	281.40	2.34	70.54
EM	90.60	0.66	0.67	176.17	1.74	0.67

Table 7. Average number of roles generated for SoD-aware role mining for different number of SoD constraints and different values of k and n (The number of roles for the other approaches is the same as that shown in Table 4. These values are repeated in the first column below for ease of referencing).

Data set	$2 - 2\ SoD$		$2 - 3\ SoD$		$3 - 6\ SoD$		$5 - 10\ SoD$	
	20 SoDs	50 SoDs	20 SoDs	50 SoDs	20 SoDs	50 SoDs	20 SoDs	50 SoDs
AL [423]	443	484	458	519	496	616	550	745
AS [213]	218	254	238	285	257	344	291	411
APJ [456]	461	473	467	481	476	505	489	531
Cus [276]	276	276	276	276	276	276	276	276
EM [34]	48	68	56	83	72	128	90	173

n permissions are chosen randomly from the set of all permissions. We study the approaches for 4 different types of SoD constraints: 2-2 SoD, 2–3 SoD, 3-6 SoD and 5-10 SoD. The number of SoD constraints considered for each of the four types are 20 and 50. Although we use real-world UPA matrices, since the SoDs are synthetically generated, the experiments were repeated 30 times for each combination of parameters. The (rounded off) mean of the results over 30 repetitions are reported in the tables included in this section.

It may be noted that, for comparative study, we had also implemented the naïve approach described in Sub-sect. 3.2 that uses Li et al.'s [7] algorithm. However, generation of RSSoD requirements was found to take an inordinate amount of time. Although, the algorithm would produce an output for small test data sets, for the data sets listed in Table 4, even after running for more than 24 h, the program did not reach completion. Hence, the results could not be meaningfully reported in this paper. On the other hand, all of the proposed approaches worked for large data sets as well.

Table 5 shows the number of SMER constraints generated by the three proposed approaches and Table 6 shows their execution time. The number of SoD constraints that could not be enforced are also reported in Table 5. From the table it is observed that, for both the post-processing approaches, i.e., 2-2 post-processing and t-t post-processing, there are a certain number of SoD constraints that could not be enforced. The SoD-aware approach, however, could enforce all the constraints. The number of SMER constraints generated by the SoD-aware approach is also, in general, less compared to the other two methods. For the cases where some of the SoDs were not enforceable in the post-processing approaches, the number of corresponding SMERs is less. The number of non-enforceable SoDs is usually more for the 2-2 post-processing approach compared to the t-t post-processing approach. A second point to note is that, some of the entries in the two columns *2-2_post* and *t-t_post* are the same, which implies that the value of t was obtained as 2 even in the t-t SMER constraint generation algorithm (Lines 13-14 of Algorithm 2).

A further observation, which is intuitively obvious, is that, the number of SMER constraints (Table 5) and time taken to generate them (Table 6) tend to increase as the number of SoD constraints increases and the length of the SoD increases. The time taken for 2-2 post-processing and t-t post-processing approaches grow rapidly as the length of the SoDs increase. For example, while for 20 2-2 SoDs, it takes 139 s for the AL data set, the time required for 20 5–10 SoDs for the same data set is 6,164 s. The corresponding values for 50 SoDs are 366 and 14,667 s, respectively. On the other hand, the time required for the SoD-aware role mining does not vary so much with the length of the SoD. The time needed for the t-t post-processing approach is comparable with that for 2-2 post-processing. Although it might be felt that the post-processing approaches (2-2 post and t-t post) should take less time than the SoD-aware approach, the main component of execution time in the post-processing approaches goes into checking whether any of the existing users in the UA matrix violates the generated SMER constraint (Line 11 of Algorithm 1 and Line 18 of Algorithm 2).

Table 7 shows the number of roles generated for different lengths of SoD constraints and different number of SoD constraints. We only show the results for the SoD-aware role mining algorithm since for the post-processing approaches, the roles are already generated by the chosen unconstrained role mining algorithm and the number of roles is not changed by either 2-2 post-processing or t-t post-processing algorithms. From the table, it is also observed that, SoD-aware role mining generates more number of roles compared to unconstrained role mining using the MBC approach. This is because, extra roles are created by Algorithm 5 called from Step 8 of Algorithm 4, which in turn, is called from Step 8 of Algorithm 3, to avoid the three cases (Cases 1–3) as explained in Sub-sect. 3.3. Further, there is a significant dependency of the number of roles in the SoD-aware role mining algorithm on the length of the SoD.

By comparing results across the three tables (Tables 5, 6 and 7), one can conclude that the three approaches have their own strengths and shortcomings. While SoD-aware role mining generates more number of roles, it significantly outperforms t-t post-processing in terms of the number of generated SMER constraints, especially when the lengths of the given SoD constraints are short. Execution time for the SoD-aware role mining algorithm is also comparable with t-t post-processing when lengths of SoD constraints are less, and is significantly less when the SoD constraints are longer (except for the APJ and $Customer$ data sets). The number of SMER constraints for 2-2 post-processing approach is much higher compared to SoD-aware role mining. Further, the post-processing approaches often end up in situations where certain constraints are not enforceable, which is their main drawback.

5   Related Work

Role mining is the problem of decomposing a given UPA into UA and PA matrices while optimizing a metric like the number of roles (often called the Basic Role Mining Problem - RMP). Vaidya et al. [4] formally define basic RMP and introduce two different variations of basic RMP, namely $\delta - approx$ RMP and $MinNoise$ RMP. They proved all the problems to be NP-Complete. An approach called Largest Uncovered Tile Mining (LUTM) was proposed in [4] to find roles by mapping RMP to the database tiling problem. Two algorithms named as CompleteMiner and FastMiner were proposed in [10] of which CompleteMiner uses subset enumeration to find interesting roles. As subset enumeration takes exponential time, FastMiner is used to reduce the time complexity by finding the intersection for every pair of users. Lu et al. [5] present a unified framework for modeling the optimal binary matrix decomposition problem using binary integer programming. Zhang et al. [3] use the permission assignment relation *PA* to obtain an optimal role hierarchy graph. It uses the initial *PA* and reduces the number of roles by identifying pairs of roles such that merging and splitting this pair results in a least cost graph. The work in [8] maps the basic role mining problem to the minimum biclique cover finding problem for bipartite graphs.

Some of the cardinality constraints considered during role mining include restricting the number of permissions to a user and the number of permissions to a role. Kumar et al. [9] propose the Constrained Role Miner Algorithm (CRM), which limits the number of permissions that can belong to a role. John et al. [6], propose two alternative approaches for restricting the number of roles for a user. One is the RPA (Role Priority based Approach), which prioritizes roles based on number of permissions and then limits the number of roles assigned to a user, and the other is the CPA (Coverage of Permissions based Approach), which chooses roles by iteratively picking the role having the largest number of permissions that are yet uncovered for that user. Harika et al. [14] impose role-usage cardinality and permission-distribution cardinality constraints in both concurrent and post-processing frameworks. Role-usage cardinality constraint limits the maximum number of roles a user can have and permission-distribution cardinality constraint limits the maximum number of roles a permission can belong to.

Another important constraint is Separation of Duty (SoD), which is used in computer security to prevent fraud. Li et al. [7] introduce how SoD constraints can be implemented in RBAC. It is equivalent to a post-processing approach to role mining under SoD constraints, which generates a set of SMER constraints from a set of SoDs and a given *PA* matrix such that the SMER constraints enforce the SoD constraints. Lu et al. [11] propose Extended Boolean Matrix Decomposition (EBMD), which extends BMD [5] by allowing negative authorizations for implementing SoD constraints to solve the constraint-aware role mining problem. The work presented in the current paper is the first ever attempt to do role mining in the presence of SoD constraints that generates SMER constraints.

6   Conclusion and Future Directions

We have proposed a number of alternative approaches for role mining in the presence of separation of duty constraints. Besides generating the UA and PA matrices from a given UPA matrix as done in any unconstrained role mining algorithm, we also derive a set of SMER constraints that enforce the given set of SoD constraints. After suggesting a naïve way of handling the problem using an existing algorithm, we have introduced three new methods. Two of these generate the SMER constraints from an initial unconstrained decomposition of the UA matrix using any existing role mining algorithm. The third approach considers the SoDs at the time of role mining and the roles are formed in such a way that enforceable SMERs can be easily generated from the set of mined roles. We have evaluated the proposed algorithms on several real world data sets and compared their performance in terms of the number of SMERs, number of roles, as well as their execution time. The experiments show that the naïve approach is not at all scalable and does not work for many data sets. On the other hand, the proposed approaches were able to handle all of the standard real datasets used to evaluate role mining and are quite scalable.

In the future, we plan to consider generation of t-t SMER constraints while doing role mining. Additionally, in this paper we restricted our attention to minimizing the number of roles. In the future, we plan to consider different metrics such as the number of SMER constraints, sum of roles and SMER constraints, Weighted Structural Complexity (WSC) [13], etc.

References

1. Sandhu, R.S., Coyne, E.J., Feinstein, H.L., Youman, C.E.: Role based access control models. IEEE Comput. **29**, 38–47 (1996)
2. Ferraiolo, D.F., Sandhu, R., Gavrila, S., Richard Kuhn, D., Chandramouli, R.: Proposed NIST standard for role-based access control. In: ACM TISSEC, pp. 224–274 (2001)
3. Zhang, D., Kotagiri, R., Tim, E.: Role engineering using graph optimization. In: ACM SACMAT, pp. 139–144 (2007)
4. Vaidya, J., Atluri, V., Guo, Q.: The role mining problem: finding a minimal descriptive set of roles. In: ACM SACMAT, pp. 175–184 (2007)
5. Lu, H., Vaidya, J., Atluri, V.: Optimal boolean matrix decomposition: application to role engineering. In: IEEE ICDE, pp. 297–306 (2008)
6. John, J.C., Sural, S., Atluri, V., Vaidya, J.S.: Role mining under role-usage cardinality constraint. In: Gritzalis, D., Furnell, S., Theoharidou, M. (eds.) SEC 2012. IFIP AICT, vol. 376, pp. 150–161. Springer, Heidelberg (2012)
7. Li, N., Tripunitara, M.V., Bizri, Z.: On mutually exclusive roles and separation of duty. In: ACM TISSEC, pp. 5–39 (2007)
8. Alina, E., William, H., Nikola, M., Prasad, R., Robert, S., Robert, T.E.: Fast exact and heuristic methods for role minimization problems. In: ACM SACMAT, pp. 1–10 (2008)
9. Kumar, R., Sural, S., Gupta, A.: Mining RBAC roles under cardinality constraint. In: Jha, S., Mathuria, A. (eds.) ICISS 2010. LNCS, vol. 6503, pp. 171–185. Springer, Heidelberg (2010)
10. Vaidya, J., Atluri, V., Warner, J.: Role miner: mining roles using subset enumeration. In: ACM CCS, pp. 144–153 (2006)
11. Lu, H., Vaidya, J., Atluri, V., Hong, Y.: Constraint-aware role mining via extended boolean matrix decomposition. In: IEEE TDSC, pp. 655–669 (2012)
12. Coyne, E.J.: Role engineering. In: ACM Workshop on RBAC, pp. 15–16 (1996)
13. Molloy, I., Chen, H., Li, T., Wang, Q., Li, N., Bertino, E., Calo, S.B., Lobo, J.: Mining roles with multiple objectives. In: ACM TISSEC, pp. 1–35 (2010)

14. Harika, P., Nagajyothi, M., John, J.C., Sural, S., Vaidya, J., Atluri, V.: Meeting cardinality constraints in role mining. IEEE TDSC **12**(1), 71–84 (2015)
15. Ye, W., Li, R., Gu, X., Li, Y., Wen, K.: Role mining using answer set programming. In: FGCS (2014)
16. Li, R., Li, H., Gu, X., Li, Y., Ye, W., Ma, X.: Role mining based on cardinality constraints. In: Concurrency and Computation Practice and Experience (2015). doi:10.1002/cpe.3456
17. Ma, X., Li, R., Wang, H., Li, H.: Role mining based on permission cardinality constraint and user cardinality constraint. In: Security and Communication Networks (2014). doi:10.1002/sec.1177

Context-Aware Access Control in Novel Automotive HMI Systems

Simon Gansel[1]([✉]), Stephan Schnitzer[2], Ahmad Gilbeau-Hammoud[2],
Viktor Friesen[1], Frank Dürr[2], Kurt Rothermel[2], Christian Maihöfer[1],
and Ulrich Krämer[3]

[1] System Architecture and Platforms, Mercedes-Benz Cars, Daimler AG,
Stuttgart, Germany
{simon.gansel,viktor.friesen,christian.maihöfer}@daimler.com
[2] Institute of Parallel and Distributed Systems, University of Stuttgart,
Stuttgart, Germany
{schnitzer,hammoud,dürr,rothermel}@ipvs.uni-stuttgart.de
[3] Telemotive AG, Munich, Germany
ulrich.krämer@telemotive.de

Abstract. The growing relevance of vehicular applications like media player, navigation system, or speedometer using graphical presentation has lead to an increasing number of displays in modernf cars. This effectuates the desire for flexible sharing of all the available displays between several applications. However, automotive requirements include many regulations to avoid driver distraction to ensure safety. To allow for safe sharing of the available screen surface between the many safety-critical and non-safety-critical applications, adequate access control systems are required. We use the notion of *contexts* to dynamically determine, which application is allowed to access which display area. A context can be derived from vehicle sensors (e.g., the current speed), or be an application-specific state (e.g., which menu item is selected). We propose an access control model that is inherently aware of the context of the car and the applications. It provides delegation of access rights to display areas by applications. We implemented a proof-of-concept implementation that demonstrates the feasibility of our concept and evaluated the latency introduced by access control. Our results show that the delay reacting on dynamic context changes is small enough for automotive scenarios.

1 Introduction

Within the last 30 years the development of cars in the automotive industry has increasingly depended on electronics and software instead of mechanics [3]. The growing relevance of graphics functions and applications using integrated displays in modern cars is a good indicator for this trend. For instance, the *Head Unit* (HU) uses displays integrated into the backside of the front seats and center console to display multimedia content, navigation system, and web browser. Additionally, the *Instrument Cluster* (IC) uses the instrument and the

© Springer International Publishing Switzerland 2015
S. Jajodia and C. Mazumdar (Eds.): ICISS 2015, LNCS 9478, pp. 118–138, 2015.
DOI: 10.1007/978-3-319-26961-0_8

head-up displays to show car specific information like speed, warnings, and navigation instructions. In order to support these applications, cars are equipped with a growing number of displays of steadily increasing size. The availability of these displays has lead to the desire to use them flexibly, by dynamically mapping applications to display areas. For instance, users desire to customize the *Human-Machine Interface* (HMI), e.g., reduce the size of the speedometer in favor of a larger display area for navigation, or choose between HMI themes. The dynamic mapping of applications to display areas introduces one great challenge: ensuring safety. It is the responsibility of the *Original Equipment Manufacturers (OEMs)* to ensure that graphical outputs from the various applications do not violate safety requirements. Different standards like [15, ISO 26262] and automotive guidelines (e.g., [7]) address the safety aspects of displaying information in vehicles. For example, as regulated by German law (StVZO Sect. 57 [16]), the speedometer must be visible. Additionally, warning messages must be displayed at consistent places on the displays, easily perceivable by the driver (e.g., the brake warning light is statically mapped to a place and guaranteed to be visible).

Most of these requirements apply to specific situations or states of a vehicle, only. For instance, the visibility of the speedometer applies only to moving vehicles, thus the display area of the speedometer could be used for any purpose while the car is parking. Moreover, the display area used by the break warning light could be used for extended radio information. In order to guarantee safe display access, the flexibility must be restricted adequately, using the automotive requirements and guidelines. To this end, we use the notion of *contexts* to dynamically determine at some point in time, which application is allowed to access which display area. A context can be derived from vehicle sensors (e.g., speed, location, or time), or be an application-specific state (e.g., which menu item is selected). Integrating context natively into access control, significantly improves safety, flexibility, and efficiency, since a certified component is in charge.

Moreover, the growing number of applications and the desire to integrate third-party applications (e.g., from Google Play), favors a decentralized developement process. While traditional access control assumes a central authority, e.g., to assign the access control matrix, a decentralized development process requires access control that supports decentralized granting of permissions.

In [10] we proposed an access control model that provides access control to display areas, where access decisions only depend on the applications and reaction on context changes is completely left to the applications in a distributed fashion. However, correctly considering the context of the car or applications often determines whether the automotive requirements are fulfilled or not. Thus, inherent support for contexts is an obvious evolution of the concepts in [10].

In this paper, we extend our approach by concepts for *context-aware* access control, which allow for adapting access permissions based on the context of the car or the applications without compromising on safety. Our model grants permissions to exclusively access certain display areas to applications depending on the current context. In detail, we make the following contributions: (1) A formal definition of the context-aware access control model and the required properties like isolation. (2) A proof-of-concept implementation to show the feasibility of the approach. (3) An evaluation of the performance of our implementation.

The rest of this paper is structured as follows. In Sect. 2 we present our system model. In Sect. 3 we define our context-aware access control model and address correctness in Sect. 4. In Sect. 5 we define the protocol for state transitions and proof the correctness of our protocol. We present our implementation in Sect. 6 and evaluate the latency introduced by access control in Sect. 7. We discuss related work in Sect. 8 and conclude in Sect. 9.

2   System Model

In this section, we introduce our system model (c.f. Fig. 1) for context-based display access control in automotive HMI systems. The *display surface* is a shared resource represented by the set of all available pixels of the connected displays. Applications present their graphical output on *display areas*, which ares defined as subsets of the display surface. The mapping between applications and display areas is dynamic and performed by the *Access Control Layer* depending on the current *context* and the *permissions*. Each application authenticates itself to the Access Control Layer. To this end, each application has a Universally Unique Identifier (UUID). A context represents a distinct situation of the car or of an application and can be set only by the responsible application using the *Context Manager*. A *permission* defines which application is allowed to access which display area in which context. To prevent inconsistencies, each pixel must be mapped to at most one application. In case the visibility of an application is restricted, depending on the context permissions must be revoked if this context is active, e.g., context "car in motion" requires that a video playback must not be visible to the driver. To guarantee conflict-freeness either two permissions do not allow access to the same or part or the same display area or their mapped contexts cannot be active at the same time. If the context changes, the application allowed to access a certain display area might also change.

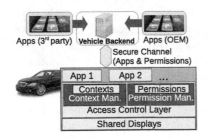

Fig. 1. System model   **Fig. 2.** Context mapping

Figure 2 shows an example where a display area located in the center of the IC display is shared between four applications. Based on the automotive requirements, in such a case the decision which of the four applications gets exclusive access to the display area shall be based on the current set of contexts—namely, "Imminent collision", "Incoming phone call", and "Navigation selected".

To facilitate the software development process, the OEM shall be able to pass context-based usage permissions for display areas to software development companies or even individual developers, which again shall be able to pass usage permissions to others in a hierarchical fashion. This allows the OEM to meet all safety-relevant requirements without being a central certification authority for all applications. Nevertheless, for the sake of security, the deployment of applications is centralized using the *Vehicle Backend* (cf., Fig. 1).

3   Context-Aware Access Control Model

In this section we present our model for access control to display areas based on contexts. First, we present an overview. Then, we define the entities and describe the granting of permissions—constrained by contexts—between applications.

3.1   Overview

Access control mechanisms determine which subjects are allowed to access which objects. In this work, subjects correspond to *applications* and objects to *display areas* whose pixels are accessed by applications. We use *permissions* that allow applications to access *display areas*. Access to display areas is restricted by *contexts* of the car or applications. An application requires a permission restricted to certain contexts—called *constrained-permission*—to access a dedicated display area. Only if the contexts specified in the constrained-permission match the current contexts of the car and applications, access is granted. An application that owns a constrained-permission *cp* can *grant* another application a constrained-permission not exceeding *cp* in both, size and context. Since our model guarantees that at any point in time each pixel is accessed by exactly one application, an application might need to *revoke* a constrained-permission if it wants to access a certain pixel itself. Providing dynamic granting and revoking of constrained-permissions our model suits to a decentralized development process where the OEM delegates the development of certain application components to a contractor, who delegates parts of the application to subcontractors, etc. Next, we define these concepts in a formal model.

3.2   Objects and Subjects

We define a display area (object) as a set of pixels as depicted in Fig. 3. The smallest display area consists of a single pixel called an *atomic object*. The complete display surface is called the *display surface* and consists of all pixels.

Definition 1. $\Lambda = \{\lambda_1, ..., \lambda_n\}$ is a finite set of pixels (atomic objects). A display area is a subset of the set of pixels, formally a display area o is an object $o \in O = \mathcal{P}(\Lambda)\backslash\emptyset$ with O representing the set of all display areas.

An application (subject) requires a permission to access a display area's content.

Definition 2. $S = \{s_1, ..., s_n\}$ is a set of applications (subjects) with $n \geq 1$.

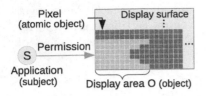

Fig. 3. Subject and objects

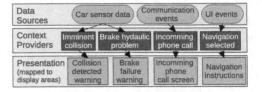

Fig. 4. Contexts

3.3   Contexts

In automotive scenarios setting the graphical content of display areas often depends on context. As depicted in Fig. 4, contexts are identified by three *Data Sources*. The source *car sensor data* provides information about the status of the car (e.g., the RPM of the wheels, or the status of the brakes) or environmental conditions (e.g., the distance to the car in front). The source *communication events* considers events occurring due to incoming information via communication devices, e.g., phone calls, SMS, and mails. Finally, *user interface (UI) events* are triggered by the user input events like selecting the radio in the HU menu. The data from the data sources is interpreted by *Context Providers*, which decide for their contexts whether they are active or inactive. Each context is exclusively mapped to one application which serves as context provider and has an ID, unique within the scope of its application. Next, we define contexts formally.

Definition 3. $C = (S \times \mathbb{N})$ is the set of all contexts, where each context is represented by an application and the context ID. $CTX = \{f : C \to A\}$ is the set of functions that return for each context its status $A = \{active, inactive\}$.

A context (e.g., with id 1) describes a state like "car is in motion" which is determined by the application speedometer s_{sp}, i.e., $(s_{sp}, 1) \in C$. Hence, in case the current speed is above 0 mph, the speedometer sets the status of its context $(s_{sp}, 1)$ to active otherwise to inactive. For instance, if set $ctx \in CTX$ is a set of contexts and the context $(s_{sp}, 1)$ is active then $((s_{sp}, 1), active) \in ctx$. Let $a \in A$. If $a = active$, the function $inv(a) = a'$ returns $a' = inactive$ else $a' = active$.

3.4   Constrained-Permissions

A constrained-permission represents a permission restricted to contexts. An application is only allowed to access a display area if it has a constrained-permission matching the current contexts. We define a constrained-permission as follows.

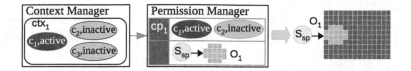

Fig. 5. Example of contexts and constrained-permissions

Definition 4. $CP : CTX \times S \times O$ is the set of constrained-permissions expressing that an application is allowed to access a display area in certain contexts.

We assume the application speedometer s_{sp} shall only be visible in case the car is in motion (i.e., $c_1 = (s_{sp}, 1)$ is active), as depicted in Fig. 5. To this end, s_{sp} has a constrained-permission cp_1 which allows access to display area o_1, iff the current contexts of $ctx_1 \in CTX$ contains $(c_1, active)$ and $(c_2, inactive)$.

Next we define *conflict-freeness* of two constrained-permissions, which guarantees that at no point in time a pixel is accessibly by more than one application. Let $cp = (C_1, (s_1, o_1)) \in CP$ and $cp' = (C_2, (s_2, o_2)) \in CP$. We say two constrained-permissions cp and cp' are *conflict-free*, iff either the intersection of the two objects o_1 and o_2 is empty or a context c is in the set of contexts C_1 and in C_2, and the status of both is different.

Definition 5. cp and cp' are **conflict-free** $\Leftrightarrow cp \sqcap cp' = \emptyset \Leftrightarrow o_1 \cap o_2 = \emptyset \vee \exists cx = (c, a) \in C_1, \exists cx' = (c', a') \in C_2 : c = c' \wedge a \neq a'$. Let $Im(ctx) = \{ctx(c) | c \in C\}$. We say $cp \sqsubseteq cp' \Leftrightarrow Im(ctx_{cp'}) \subseteq Im(ctx_{cp}) \wedge o_{cp} \subseteq o_{cp'}$.

For instance, let $cp_{sp} = (\hat{C}, s_{sp}, o) \in CP$ and $cp_{acc} = (\tilde{C}, s_{acc}, \hat{o}) \in CP$ be constrained-permissions of speedometer and adaptive cruise control, respectively, where o covers $\hat{o}$. In this case, to guarantee conflict-freeness means that $\hat{C}$ and $\tilde{C}$ cannot both match the same set of current contexts.

To increase flexibility of obtaining and releasing constrained-permissions, we next introduce hierarchical granting and revoking of constrained-permissions.

Hierarchical Granting of Constrained-Permissions. An application that received a constrained-permission cp can itself grant a constrained-permission cp' to other applications under the following conditions. First, the display area of cp' is a subarea of the display area of cp. Second, cp' must be at least as constraining (in terms of contexts) as cp. Third, if other constrained-permissions have been granted based on cp, all of them must be conflict-free with cp'. An application is no longer allowed to access any pixels included in one of its granted constrained-permissions which match the current contexts. Formally, we define a set that maps to each application its granted and received constrained-permissions.

Definition 6. $CONS = \{f : S \rightarrow \mathcal{P}(S \times CP) \times \mathcal{P}(S \times CP)\}$ maps to each application two sets $\mathcal{P}(S \times CP)$ that contain mappings of constrained-permissions to applications representing the constrained-permissions an application has *received* and the constrained-permissions it has *granted* to other applications.

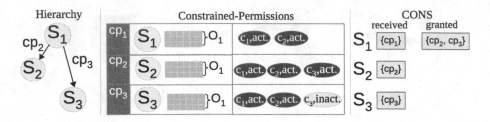

Fig. 6. Example of granting constrained-permissions of S_1 to S_2 and S_3

Let $cons \in CONS, s \in S$. Set $received_{cp}(cons, s) := \{r | (r, g) \in cons(s)\}$ denotes the set of constrained-permissions s has received. Similarly, set $granted_{cp}(cons, s) := \{g | (r, g) \in cons(s)\}$ is the set of constrained-permissions s has granted. Accordingly, $(s', cp') \in received_{cp}(cons, s)$ indicates that application s has received a constrained-permission cp' from application s' and $(s', cp') \in granted_{cp}(cons, s)$ indicates that application s' granted cp' to s'.

In Fig. 6 we depict an example of granting constrained-permissions between the applications s_1, s_2, and s_3. We assume set $cons \subseteq CONS$ contains the current constrained-permissions and s_1 received a constrained-permission cp_1 from application $\hat{s}$ (not depicted in Fig. 6) and granted $\{cp_2\}$ and $\{cp_3\}$ to s_2 and s_3, respectively. Thus, the display areas of cp_1, cp_2, and cp_3 are all the same. The constrained-permissions cp_2 and cp_3 are conflict-free ($cp_2 \sqcap cp_3 = \emptyset$) since the context c_3 must be *active* in cp_2 and *inactive* in cp_3 which cannot happen at the same time. Since each context that matches cp_1 also matches either cp_2 or cp_3, s_1 has no longer access to o_1 in any context (as long as it does not revoke cp_2 or cp_3). Hence, the display area an application can use actually depends on the current contexts and the constrained-permissions it granted to other applications.

We define the comparison operator $<_{cp}$ for applications to indicate the chain of dependencies according to constrained-permissions. An application which received a constrained-permission has a dependency to its granting application.

Definition 7. Let $s, s' \in S; cp \in CP; cons \in CONS$. We say $s <_{cp} s' \Leftrightarrow$

$$\exists s_1, ..., s_n \in S; \exists cp_1, ..., cp_{n-1} \in CP : \tag{7.1}$$

$$s_1 = s' \wedge s_n = s \wedge cp \sqsubseteq cp_{n-1} \wedge \tag{7.2}$$

$$\forall i : 1 \le i < n : (s_i, cp_i) \in received_{cp}(cons, s_{i+1}) \tag{7.3}$$

$$\forall i : 1 \le i < n - 2 : cp_{i+1} \sqsubseteq cp_i \tag{7.4}$$

If an application s has received a constrained-permission cp from application s' or indirect by using a chain of intermediate applications then $s <_{cp} s'$. Hence, s depends on s' according to the constrained-permission cp.

Formally, with $s, s' \in S$, we say $s \neq_{cp} s' \Leftrightarrow \not\exists cp \in CP : s <_{cp} s' \vee s' <_{cp} s$.

4 Safety Property

In this section, we introduce *states* in our model and describe the correctness of our model using a *safety property* defined using states. States are called *safe*, if they fulfill the safety property. A *state* in our model is a set of sets of constrained-permissions and contexts.

Definition 8. $U : CONS \times CTX$ represents the set of contexts, granted and received constrained-permissions. We say $u \in U$ is a *state* in U.

Next, we define a *safety property* which can be satisfied in a state in U or not. States satisfying this property are *safe states* and a sequence of safe states is called *safe state sequence*.

Definition 9. A state satisfies the **Conflict-freeness Property (CFP)**, if each constrained-permission is conflict-free. Let $u - (cons, ctx) \subset U$. u satisfies CFP $\Leftrightarrow$

$$\forall s, s', s_1, s_2 \in S; \forall cp, cp' \in CP : s' \neq_{cp} s \land s' \neq_{cp'} s \land cp \neq cp' \land$$
$$(s_1, cp) \in received_{cp}(cons, s) \land (s_2, cp') \in received_{cp}(cons, s')$$
$$\Rightarrow (cp \sqcap cp' = \emptyset)$$

This means, it exists at most one constrained-permission that allows access to a display area for a given set of contexts at a time. This property implies **exclusive access**, i.e., in each context each display area is accessed by at most one application. Thus, an application that has access to a pixel is guaranteed to be visible if the according context is given.

5 Protocol

In this section, we describe the *requests* that can be issued by applications in order to change contexts or constrained-permissions and are performed by *transitions* using *rules*. Moreover, we discuss the verification of our protocol, i.e., that our defined model fulfills the defined safety property using our transitions.

5.1 Requests and Transitions

A transition is triggered by a request to add or delete a constrained-permission, or to set the status of a context.

Definition 10. A request $r \in \boldsymbol{RP} = RA \times S \times S \times CP$ consists of the operation mode $\boldsymbol{RA} = \{append, discard\}$, grantor, grantee, and the constrained-permission. A request $\boldsymbol{RC} = S \times C \times A$ consists of the application, the context, and the desired status. The set of all possible requests is $\boldsymbol{R} = RP \cup RC$.

We define transitions between states. To maintain consistency, these transitions are restricted by rules. If none of the rules apply then the state does not change.

Definition 11. $trans : U \times R \to U$ is a function which represents the transition from one state to another in U initiated by a request $r \in \boldsymbol{R}$.

The three possible types of request, in particular, grant a constrained-permission, revoke a constrained-permission, and set the status of a context, are described in the following.

To **grant a constrained-permission** cp to another application s', an application s initiates a request $r \in RP$ with $ra = append$. The request is accepted, if s has received a constrained-permission which is an super-set of cp and cp is conflict-free to all granted constrained-permissions of s—expressed by Rule 1.
Rule 1. To satisfy Rule 1, the following condition $cond_1$ has to be fulfilled.

$$cond_1 = (r = (ra, s, s', cp) \in RP \wedge ra = append \wedge cp = (C_1, \hat{s}, \hat{o}) \wedge$$
$$s \neq s' \wedge s' = \hat{s} \wedge [\forall cp' \in \{\hat{cp} \in CP | \exists (\hat{s}, \hat{cp}) \in granted_{cp}(cons, s)\} : cp \sqcap cp' = \emptyset] \wedge$$
$$[\exists \tilde{cp} \in \{\hat{cp} \in CP | \exists (\hat{s}, \hat{cp}) \in received_{cp}(cons, s)\} : cp \sqsubseteq \tilde{cp} = (\tilde{C}, (\tilde{s}, \tilde{o})) \wedge \tilde{s} = s])$$

To perform the grant transition we use the function $add_{cp} : CONS \times S \times S \times CP \to CONS$ that adds a constrained-permission. Let $s, s' \in S; cp = (C_{cp}, s_{cp}, o_{cp}) \in CP$. We say $[cons' = add_{cp}(cons, s, s', cp)] \Leftrightarrow$

$$cons'(s) = (received_{cp}(cons, s), granted_{cp}(cons, s) \cup \{(s', cp)\}) \wedge \quad (5.1.1.1)$$

$$cons'(s') = (received_{cp}(cons, s') \cup \{(s, cp)\}, granted_{cp}(cons, s')) \wedge \quad (5.1.1.2)$$

$$[\forall s'' \in S \backslash \{s', s\} : cons'(s'') = cons(s'')] \quad (5.1.1.3)$$

If the condition $cond_1$ is fulfilled the function add_{cp} adds cp to the set of $received_{cp}$ and $granted_{cp}$ constrained-permissions for s and s' in $cons$ (5.1.1.1), (5.1.1.2). All other applications are not affected by this function (5.1.1.3).

To **revoke a constrained-permission** cp, an application s initiates a request $r \in RP$ with $ra = discard$. If s has granted cp, the request is accepted, and, additionally, constrained-permissions depending on cp will also be revoked—formally expressed by Rule 2.
Rule 2. To satisfy Rule 2, the following condition $cond_2$ has to be fulfilled.

$$cond_2 = (r = (ra, s, s', cp) \in RP \wedge ra = discard \wedge$$
$$(s \neq s' \wedge (s', cp) \in granted_{cp}(cons, s) \wedge (s, cp) \in received_{cp}(cons, s')))$$

To perform the transition we use the function $del_{cp} : CONS \times S \times S \times CP \to CONS$ that deletes a constrained-permission. Let $s, s' \in S; cp = (C_{cp}, s_{cp}, o_{cp}); cp' = (C_{cp'}, s_{cp'}, o_{cp'}) \in CP$. We say $[cons' = del_{cp}(cons, s, s', cp)] \Leftrightarrow$

$$[\forall s_1 \in S : s_1 <_{cp} s \Rightarrow \quad (5.1.2.1)$$

$$received_{cp}(cons', s_1) = received_{cp}(cons, s_1) \backslash \quad (5.1.2.2)$$

$$\{(s_2, cp') \in S \times CP | s_2 <_{cp'} s_1 \wedge cp' \sqsubseteq cp\} \wedge \quad (5.1.2.3)$$

$$granted_{cp}(cons', s_1) = granted_{cp}(cons, s_1)\backslash \qquad (5.1.2.4)$$

$$\{(s_2, cp') \in S \times CS | s_1 <_{cp'} s_2 \wedge cp' \sqsubseteq cp\} \wedge \qquad (5.1.2.5)$$

$$cons'(s) = (received_{cp}(cons, s), granted_{cp}(cons, s)\backslash\{(s', cp)\}) \wedge \qquad (5.1.2.6)$$

$$[\forall s_3 \in S\backslash\{s', s\}; \forall cp' \in CP : cp' \sqsubseteq cp \wedge s \neq_{cp'} s_3 \vee s <_{cp'} s_3 \qquad (5.1.2.7)$$

$$\Rightarrow cons'(s_3) = cons(s_3)] \qquad (5.1.2.8)$$

If the condition $cond_2$ is fulfilled, the function del_{cp} removes cp and all depending constrained-permissions from $received_{cp}$ (5.1.2.2), (5.1.2.3) and $granted_{cp}$ (5.1.2.4), (5.1.2.5). All other constrained-permissions that did not receive or grant a permission depending on cp are not affected by this function (5.1.2.8). To **change the status of a context** c, an application s initiates a request $r \in RC$. The request is accepted, iff s introduced c.

Rule 3. To satisfy Rule 3, the following condition $cond_3$ has to be fulfilled.

$$cond_3 = (r = (s, c, a) \in RC \wedge c = (\tilde{s}, n) \in C \wedge \tilde{s} = s)$$

To perform the transition, we use the function $set_{ctx} : CTX \times C \times A \rightarrow CTX$ which adds a context to the set of current contexts. Formally, $set_{ctx}(ctx, c, a) = ctx' \Leftrightarrow ctx'(c) = a \wedge \forall c' \in C\backslash\{c\} : ctx'(c') = ctx(c')$.

Next, we use the three rules to define the function $trans$. Let $u = (cons, ctx) \in U$, and $r \in R$ with $r = (ra, s, s', cp) \in RP$, or $r = (s, c, a) \in RC$. We define

$$trans(u, r) = \begin{cases} (add_{cp}(cons, s, s', cp), ctx), & \text{if } cond_1 \text{ (Rule 1)} \\ (del_{cp}(cons, s, s', cp), ctx), & \text{if } cond_2 \text{ (Rule 2)} \\ (cons, set_{ctx}(ctx, c, a)), & \text{if } cond_3 \text{ (Rule 3)} \\ u, & \text{otherwise.} \end{cases}$$

5.2 Protocol Correctness Verification

To verify the correctness of our model we use the Conflict-freeness Property (CFP) (cf., Sect. 4) and a *system* that consists of sequences of states and requests. We use this system to define a proposition which we prove by using complete induction over the states. Finally, we prove that the system is safe if the initial state fulfills the CFP. For instance, using an initial state where a single application has a constrained-permission for the whole screen area for a certain context, is a safe state. Our proof implies that using our protocol, only safe states can be reached. Next, we give the formal definitions.

System. In this section, we give the formal definitions for the sequence of states and the system. A *system* consists of all possible *sequences* of requests and the sequence of all states starting from a given initial state. We denote $I^n \subset \mathbb{N}_0$ as a finite set with $I^n = \{0, 1, 2, 3, ..., n\}$.

Definition 12. The set of sequences is a set of n-tuples and defined as $X^{I^n} = \{(x_0, ..., x_i, ..., x_n) | x_i \in X \land i \in I^n \land x_i = f(i) \text{ with } f : I^n \to X\}$.
We say $(x_0, x_1, ..., x_n) \in X^{I^n}$ is a sequence with $x_0 := x_0 \in X$, $x_1 := x_1' \in X$,...,
$x_n := x_n^{(n)} \in X$.
The **operator** $\succ$ indicates whether an element is part of a sequence or not. Let $(x_0, x_1, ..., x_n) \in X^{I^n}$. We define $x \succ (x_0, x_1, ..., x_n) \Leftrightarrow \exists i \in I^n : x = x_i$.

This means, a sequence is an ordered list of elements and the **operator** $\succ$ indicates whether an element is part of that sequence. After the generic definition of sequences we next define sequences of requests and sequences of states.

Definition 13. For a **sequence of requests** $(r_0, ..., r_{n-1}) \in R^{I^{n-1}}$ the **sequence of states** generated by $(r_0, ..., r_{n-1})$ is defined as $(u_0, u_1, ..., u_n) \in U^{I^n}$ with $\forall i \in I^{n-1} : u_{i+1} = trans(u_i, r_i)$.

Using the definition of sequences of requests and states we next define a *system* that consists of an initial state and all possible states that can be reached by using sequences of requests. In addition, we define the **operator** $\gg$ that indicates whether a transition (u, r, u') is part of a *system* or not.

Definition 14. A **system** $\Psi(u_{start}) \subset R^{I^n} \times U^{I^n}$ is generated by initial state u_{start}. Let $x_r = (r_0, ..., r_{n-1}) \in R^{I^{n-1}}$; $x_u = (u_0, ..., u_n) \in U^{I^n}$.
We define $(x_r, x_u) \in \Psi(u_{start}) \Leftrightarrow$

$$u_0 = u_{start} \land \forall i \in I^n \backslash \{0\} : u_i = trans(u_{i-1}, r_{i-1})$$

Let $(u, r, u') \in U \times R \times U$, $u_0 \in U$. We define $(\boldsymbol{u, r, u'}) \gg \boldsymbol{\Psi(u_0)} \Leftrightarrow$

$$\exists x_r \in R^{I^{n-1}}, \exists x_u \in U^{I^n}, \exists i \in I^n \backslash \{0\} : \qquad (14.1)$$

$$(x_r, x_u) \in \Psi(u_0) \land u_i \succ x_u \land u_{i+1} \succ x_u \land r_i \succ x_r \land \qquad (14.2)$$

$$(u, r, u') = (u_{i-1}, r_{i-1}, u_i). \qquad (14.3)$$

This means, that (u, r, u') is part of a system if a sequence of requests and states (14.1) exists, of which u, r and u' are part of (14.2) and a transition from state u to u' by request r (14.3) exists.

Next, we define a *safe state* and a *safe system* that consists only of *safe state sequences*.

Definition 15. $u \in U$ is a **safe state** $\Leftrightarrow u$ satisfies the CFP. $(u_0, ..., u_n) \in U^{I^n}$ is a **safe state sequence** $\Leftrightarrow \forall i \in I^n : u_i$ is a safe state. A system $\Psi(u_0) \subset U^{I^n} \times R^{I^n}$ with $x_r \in R^{I^{n-1}}$ and $x_u = (u_0, ..., u_n) \in U^{I^n}$ is a **safe system** $\Leftrightarrow \forall(x_r, x_u) \in \Psi(u_0) : x_u$ is a safe sequence.

By using the definition of a *safe system* we prove in the next section that the CFP defined in Sect. 4 is always satisfied if the initial state satisfies CFP.

5.3   Proof

Since the states and transitions of our model consist of mathematical formulations, we define a proposition that corresponds to the CFP defined in Sect. 4 and helps us to prove the safety of our model. Let $u, u', u_0 \in U$; $u' = (cons', ctx')$; $u = (cons, ctx)$; $r \in R$.

Proposition 1. All sequences in $\Psi(u_0)$ satisfy CFP for all u_0 that satisfy CFP $\Leftrightarrow$ $\forall (u, r, u') \in U \times R \times U : (u, r, u') \gg \Psi(u_0) \Rightarrow u, u' \in U$ satisfy CFP.

Proposition 1 says that all sequences in a system $\Psi(u_0)$ satisfy CFP if, and only if, for all states u' which can be directly generated from any state u with one request, the respective states u and u' also satisfy CFP. If this proposition holds, every system $\Psi(u_0)$ is a safe system if state u_0 satisfies the CFP in Sect. 4.

To prove the correctness of Proposition 1. We define a lemma to prove the proposition using complete induction over the states of the system. The following Lemma CFP states that a transition from a state which satisfies the CFP will always end in a state which also satisfies the CFP.

Lemma. CFP: All sequences in $\Psi(u_0)$ satisfy CFP for all u_0 which satisfy CFP $\Leftrightarrow \forall (u, r, u') \in U \times R \times U : (u, r, u') \gg \Psi(u_0) \Rightarrow u, u' \in U$ satisfy CFP.

Proof: According to Sect. 5, a request $r \in R$ is either in RP or in RC. The case $r \in RC$ is trivial, since Rule 3 (Sect. 5) does not change the set of constrained-permissions $cons$ and therefore is not relevant for Lemma CFP. In case $r = (ra, s, s', cp) \in RP$, we have to consider the following three sub-cases:

(R1): Let $ra = append$ and the condition $cond_1$ be fulfilled. We follow that the transition $trans(u, r) = (add_{cp}(cons, s, s', cp), ctx)$ leads to the set of received constrained-permissions $received_{cp}(cons', s') = received_{cp}(cons, s') \cup \{(s, cp)\}$.

We first show that cp is conflict-free with all granted constrained-permissions of s. Then, we show that cp is conflict-free with all constrained-permissions which do not depend on s. Finally, we follow that state u' satisfies the CFP. In detail, since u satisfies CFP and condition $cond_1$ is fulfilled, we follow $\forall (\tilde{s}, \tilde{cp}) \in granted_{cp}(cons, s) : cp \sqcap \tilde{cp} = \emptyset$ with cp granted by s. In addition, we know that $(s, cp) \notin received_{cp}(cons, s')$ due to $cond_1$. We follow in state u' that cp is conflict-free with all granted constrained-permissions of s.

In addition, $cond_1$ implies $\exists \hat{s} \in S$ with $(\hat{s}, \hat{cp}) \in received_{cp}(cons, s)$: $cp \sqsubseteq \hat{cp}$. Since state u satisfies CFP, we know that $\hat{cp}$ is conflict-free for all applications and constrained-permissions in the state u. We follow with $cp \sqsubseteq \hat{cp}$ and $(s, cp) \in received_{cp}(cons', s')$ that cp is conflict-free with all constrained-permissions which do not depend on s in state u'. Finally, due to $\forall cp'' \in CP, \forall s, s_1, s_2 \in S''$: $(s_1, cp'') \in received_{cp}(cons', s'')$ and $(s_2, cp) \in received_{cp}(cons', s')$, it follows $cp \sqcap cp'' = \emptyset$ since $s' \neq_{cp} s''$ and $s' \neq_{cp''} s$.

(R2): Let $ra = discard$ and $cond_2$ be fulfilled. Then it follows $trans(u, r) = (del_{cp}(cons, s, s', cp), ctx)$.

Since u satisfies CFP we know $\forall(\tilde{s}, \tilde{cp}) \in granted_{cp}(cons, s) : cp \sqcap \tilde{cp} = \emptyset$. Moreover, we know that in the state u the constrained-permission cp received by the application s' $((s, cp) \in received_{cp}(cons, s'))$ is conflict-free to all other constrained-permissions, i.e.,

$$\forall s, s', s_1, s_2 \in S; \forall cp, cp' \in CP : cp \neq cp' \wedge (s_1, cp) \in received_{cp}(cons, s) \wedge$$
$$(s_2, cp') \in received_{cp}(cons, s') \wedge s' \neq_{cp} s \wedge s' \neq_{cp'} s \Rightarrow cp \sqcap cp' = \emptyset$$

We know that all constrained-permissions in the set of received constrained-permissions are conflict-free in state u and therefore cp is also conflict-free. After the transition we know that the function $del_{cp}(cons, s, s', cp)$ leads to $(s, cp) \notin received_{cp}(cons, s')$ and additionally removes all constrained-permissions that depend on the constrained-permission cp, i.e., $\forall s_1 \in S : s_1 <_{cp} s \Rightarrow received_{cp}(cons', s_1) = received_{cp}(cons, s_1) \setminus \{(s_2, cp') \in S \times CP | s_2 <_{cp'} s_1 \wedge cp' \sqsubseteq cp\}$. Hence, in state u' the constrained-permission cp and all depending constrained-permissions are removed from the set of received and granted constrained-permissions of all applications, whereas all the other constrained-permissions are not changed, i.e., $\forall s_3 \in S \setminus \{s', s\}; \forall cp' \in CP : cp' \sqsubseteq cp \wedge s \neq_{cp'} s_3 \vee s <_{cp'} s_3 \Rightarrow cons'(s_3) = cons(s_3)$. We follow, that in state u' all remaining constrained-permissions are also conflict-free and state u' satisfies the CFP.

(otherwise): We know that $u' = u$. Since u satisfies the CFP, it follows that u' also satisfies CFP.

Finally, we prove Proposition 1 by complete induction.

Let $(x_r, x_v) \in \Psi(u_{start})$ with $x_r = (r_0, ..., r_{n-1}) \in R^{I^{n-1}}$, $x_u = (u_0, ..., u_n) \in U^{I^n}$. We define $u_0 = u_{start}$ as initial state and generate the states in x_u by using our transition: $\forall i \in I^n \setminus \{0\} : u_i = trans(u_{i-1}, r_{i-1})$. The state u_0 satisfies the CFP (induction base). Let $\forall i \in I^n \setminus \{0\} : (v_{i-1}, r_{i-1}, v_i) \gg \Psi(v_0)$, cf. Eq. 14.3.

Base: u_0 satisfies the CFP. With $u_1 = trans(u_0, u_0)$ we conclude u_1 satisfies the CFP, according to Lemma CFP.

Induction Hypothesis: u_i satisfies the CFP.

Induction Step: Let u_i satisfy the CFP. From the Lemma CFP follows $u_{i+1} = trans(u_i, r_i)$ satisfies the CFP. $\qquad\square$

We follow that all systems $\Psi(u_0)$ are safe systems if the state u_0 satisfies the CFP. This means, that our transitions do not violate the CFP. Hence, implementing our access control model by initially assigning all available display area for a certain context to a single application—which is a state that satisfies the CFP—leads to a safe system.

6   Implementation

In this section we describe the proof-of-concept implementation of our access control model for an automotive HMI system. Basically, an application that wants to display content on the screen, first needs to obtain a permission which then is used to create a window. Our compositor copies the content of the windows to the screen-buffer which makes them appear on the displays.

Traditionally, compositors operate on rectangular windows. In contrast, our compositor operates on (typically) non-rectangular windows, since the set of pixels (atomic objects) in a constrained-permission (CP) might not be rectangular. To this end, our implementation uses windows with a bitmap attached that represents the subset of pixels of the windows, the application is actually allowed to access. In Fig. 7, we depict a typical **Automotive Scenario** for a given set of CPs and active contexts, using applications like speedometer, tachometer, indicators, trip, car status, and menu. In Fig. 8, we depict the bitmasks used in the active CPs of Fig. 7. All CPs are conflict-free and hierarchically granted in the order of their criticality. Besides this depicted scenario, our implementation includes many more scenarios for IC and HU. For instance, we implemented CPs that allow to display half of the speedometer and the tachometer in the left and the right corner, respectively, in favor of a bigger display area for the presentation of the navigation system in the middle of the screen.

Fig. 7. Automotive Scenario using typical IC applications

Fig. 8. Bitmasks of the **Automotive Scenario**

The implementation consists of the software components depicted in Fig. 9. To isolate the safety-critical applications (e.g., brake failure warning) from the non-safety-critical applications (e.g., media playback) traditionally running physically isolated on IC and HU, we use different virtual machines (VM) running on the virtualization solution PikeOS from Sysgo. We use a dedicated VM—called *Virtualization Manager*—which provides access control and has exclusive access to the hardware components GPU, displays, and input devices.

The *Isolated Communication Channel* provides session-based FIFO communication between the applications in the VMs and the system components of the *Virtualization Manager* by using shared memory. The applications communicate via *Communication Channel* with the Virtualization Manager to get access to the hardware components. The *Communication Manager* stores the certificates of the applications, forwards them to the *Authentication Manager (AM)*, and creates a dedicated communication channel to the system components for each authenticated application. The AM restricts the communication between applications and system components based on their identification. The context-based

Virtualization Manager		Instrument cluster (VM1)		Head unit (VM2)		Custom apps (VM3)
Authentication Man.(AM)	Context Man.(CM)	Speedometer	Indicators	Radio	Navi	Games
Constrained-Permission Manager (CPM)		Tachometer	Warnings	Media player		
Context-based access control layer		Trip Computer				
Compositing	Window Manager					
	Communication Manager	Communication Client		Comm. Client		Comm. Client
Isolated Communication Channel						
Virtualization layer (microkernel based hypervisor)						
Input Devices	GPU	Display 1	Display 2	Hardware		

Fig. 9. Implemented architecture

access control layer performs access decisions using contexts. The *Context Manager* (CM) provides context handling for applications which can set the status of contexts by using the API call *setContext(CTX c, CA a)* (cf. Rule 3 in Sect. 3) with context c and status a. The CPM handles granting and revoking of CPs and provides access decisions for the *Window Manager* (WM) which is responsible for creating, destroying, and positioning of windows. Applications can grant or revoke CPs by calling *grantConsPerm(CTX[(c_1, a_1), (c_2, a_2), ...], uuid_A, o)* (cf. Rule 1 in Sect. 3) with the list of contexts $[(c_1, a_1), (c_2, a_2), ...]$, the targeting application $uuid_A$, and the display area o or *revokeConsPerm(ID cp_{id})* (cf. Rule 2 in Sect. 3) with the id cp_{id} of the CP. Access control is enforced through pixel-exact CPs which are implemented using rectangular areas in combination with bitmasks that restrict operations to the allowed pixels. Applications can create, modify, or move a window within the bounds of a received CP. We created a *Compositing Layer* that provides an API for resizing and mapping of windows. Applications directly render into the off-screen buffers of their windows, and the compositing takes care of pixel-exact copying of the window contents to the screen buffers of the two displays. Due to the exclusive access property of our system, the compositing does not need to care about the layering of windows.

We use a cockpit demonstrator (cf. Fig. 10) with two automotive 12" displays each with a resolution of 1440×540 pixels and common input devices like steering wheel buttons and the central control knob to control the applications. The hardware platform is a Freescale i.MX6 SABRE for Automotive Infotainment quad core embedded board with three GPUs, namely, the GC2000 3D GPU providing OpenGL ES 2.0 support, the GC355 which supports vector graphics with OpenVG 1.1, and the GC320 which provides compositing of framebuffers with a 2D API. We use the OpenGL ES 2.0 API for the rendering of the graphical content into the applications' backbuffers. The compositing layer uses the 2D API of the Image Processing Unit (IPU) for copy operations in framebuffers.

7 Performance Evaluation

We evaluated the performance of our access control model implementation. To this end, we measured the latency introduced by our access control. Since some context changes are safety-critical the time required to change the access to

Fig. 10. Cockpit demonstrator

display areas delays the visibility of safety-critical applications. As described in [11], important information shall be visible within given time constraints. The time constraint is not a fixed value, but determined by the OEM based on automotive guidelines, ISO standards, and legal requirements. However, the required maximum latency for graphical output does not exceed 2 s. For instance, the image of the rear view camera shall be visible in no more than 2 s after shifting into reverse (as demanded by US National Highway Traffic Safety Administration). Thus, 2 s can be considered as generic upper bound. On the other hand, for time-critical user interaction, typically latency shall not exceed 250 ms [11]. More precisely, the time delay required to change the access to display areas and to allow applications to request new windows is crucial since it delays the visibility of safety-critical applications. Next, we describe the evaluation setup and present the results.

7.1   Setup

The latency introduced by our access control system primarily depends on the number of permissions that need to be changed. A permission can change either by being disabled, so that the application window is no longer visible, or by being enabled, making an application window visible. The latency to *get* a new permission, is denoted as Δt_{get}, i.e., the time between sending the command $setContext(CTX\ c, A\ a)$ to set a context c and receiving the command $confirmWindow(WinID\ id)$ which returns the id of the created window. The latency to *cede* an owned permission, is denoted as Δt_{cede}, i.e., the time between sending $setContext(CTX\ c, A\ a)$ and revoking access by using the command $revoke(o_x)$. Figure 11 depicts the messages sent between the components of our model, for a scenario where the permissions of two applications (B and C) are affected. In more detail, application A sets the context $c_1 = (A, 1)$ to status a by sending $setContext(c_1, a)$ to the CM. The CM changes the context status and notifies the CPM. The CPM determines the affected permissions and notifies the WM ($nofify(o_x, B)$, where o_x is the new bitmap) and the affected applications. Application C is notified ($revoke(o_x)$), that it has no longer access to o_x. Application B is granted a new permission ($grant(o_x)$) and creates windows

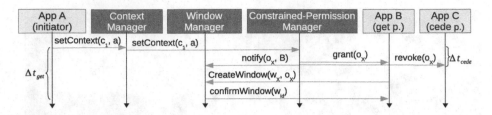

Fig. 11. Scenario, measuring access control latencies

w_x with $createWindow(w_x, o_x)$ using the bitmap o_x. Finally, the WM sends $confirmWindow(w_{id})$ to B.

We evaluated two different scenarios consisting of up to 16 applications. In the **first scenario** one application provides up to 15 constraint-permissions to 15 separate display areas, as depicted in Fig. 12. By setting a context, access to these dedicated display areas is granted to up to 15 different applications at once. After each applications successfully created a window the application revokes the granted permissions by setting back the context status. We call this *flat-granting* of permissions.

In the **second scenario**, each of the 15 applications provides one constraint-permission to part of its display area. The constrained-permissions are derived from one display area where (except for the last) each application grants exactly one application access to a subset of its display area, as depicted in Fig. 13. All granted constrained-permissions depend on the same context, i.e., if this context is changed, all applications eventually need to get or cede their respective window. We call this scenarios *deep-granting* of permissions.

7.2   Results

We measured the latencies Δt_{get} and Δt_{cede} for different numbers of affected applications. The average latencies over 100 runs of the *flat-granting* and of the

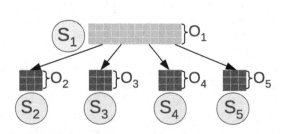

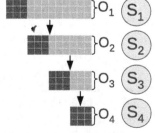

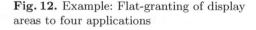

Fig. 12. Example: Flat-granting of display areas to four applications

Fig. 13. Example: Deep-granting of display areas

deep-granting of permissions are depicted in Figs. 14 and 15. In addition, the minimal and maximal latencies are depicted.

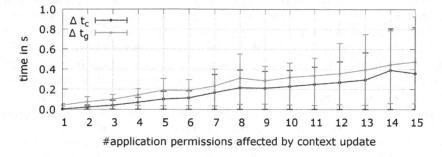

Fig. 14. Latencies of context changes affecting flatly granted permissions

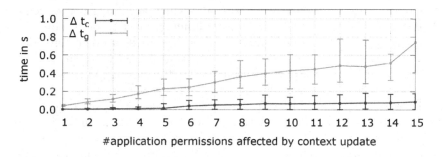

Fig. 15. Latencies of context changes affecting in deeply granted permissions

We observe, that the latency Δt_{get} linearly depends on the number of affected applications that get a new permission and create new windows. Even with 15 new application windows, the latency did not exceed 1 s in both evaluations. Situations where many new windows are created occur only in mode changes of big screen areas, e.g., if the rear-view camera needs to be switched off, or the IC display switches from full-screen video playback back to driving mode. Thus, the upper bound of 2 s (cf., [11]) applies and our implementation is always fast enough. For situations of time-critical user interaction, typically only one application gets a new permission which takes in our implementation up to 58 ms at worst. This is below the 250 ms threshold. In case of sequential granting, the upper bound of ceded permissions Δt_{cede} did not exceed 200 ms, thus staying below the 250 ms threshold. Although flatly granted permissions exceed the 250 ms in case of more than 10 applications, but still stay below 1 s. Thus, our measurement results indicate, that it is fast enough to fulfill automotive requirements for a sufficient amount of applications.

8   Related Work

In [10] we presented an access control concept, a formal model for defining and controlling the access to display areas to guarantee the safe and secure sharing of displays. However, this concept is not aware of contexts, which leaves the applications the complex task to detect combinations of distributed contexts and change the access rights accordingly within tight latency constraints. Window compositing for virtual machines is target of some works (e.g., [8,9,12]). However, they do not provide fine-grained access control and assume that the user has full control over window placement which incompatible with automotive requirements. Epstein addresses security issues in the X-server and proposes mechanisms [6] to prevent them. Again, the user controls compositing without restrictions. For context-aware access control, there exists a plethora of work. Schilit and Theimer [18] first introduced *context-awareness* and used *context* as location, identities of nearby people and objects, and changes to those objects. They focus on providing clients with information about located-objects and how those objects change over time. However, they do not consider any access control. The focus of [2,14,17,19] is on role-based access control (RBAC) using contexts to decide which roles are currently active and which according permissions are valid. But either do they consider a system administrator to be responsible for defining the applicable set of permissions for each context or do not provide delegation of access rights. Context-aware access control models which do not rely on RBAC are using context information similar to roles in the access decision process (e.g., [4,5]). Since they do not provide hierarchically depending permissions the access control prioritized usage of resources is not possible. Herges et al. [13] introduced a generic access control framework which uses an access control model based on context information, a trust model, and the concept of isolation domains to cope with automotive related requirements for infotainment applications. However, they focus on the communication between the components using messages. Our models are state-based systems similar to the Bell and LaPadula model (BLP) [1] which also defines a state machine for enforcing access control. BLP focuses on confidentiality of information and uses an access control matrix for restricting access to data. However, the BLP does neither prevent concurrent access nor allow flexible granting of permission by subjects.

9   Summary and Future Work

Sharing the available screen area between an increasing number of automotive applications becomes more and more important. Due to automotive safety requirements an appropriate access control system is required. Since the context of the car or applications often determines whether the automotive requirements are fulfilled or not it is an obvious evolution to use the context in the access decisions of automotive HMI. In this paper, we present a context-aware access control model that targets safety-critical automotive HMI systems. Our model provides the ability to hierarchically grant access to display areas depending on the contexts of the car and applications and offers dynamic flexibility without compromising on safety. This allows for guaranteed displaying of safety-critical applications and prevents intended or unintended presentation of driver-distracting content while the vehicle is in motion. Our fully formalized model meets the automotive safety requirements which can be formally proved using our defined safety property. To demonstrate the feasibility of our concept we presented a proof-of-concept implementation and evaluated it using an automotive scenario. Our next steps will be the optimization of the graphics forwarding between virtual machines to improve the rendering performance and a GPU scheduler that meets the timing requirements of the safety-critical applications. Additionally, we want to add a virtualized Android VM.

Acknowledgement. This paper has been supported in part by the ARAMiS project of the German Federal Ministry for Education and Research with funding ID 01IS11035.

References

1. Bell, D.E., Lapadula, L.J.: Secure computer system: unified exposition and MULTICS interpretation. Technical report ESD-TR-75-306 (1976)
2. Bhatti, R., et al.: A trust-based context-aware access control model for web-services. In: Proceedings, International Conference on Web Services (2004)
3. Broy, M., Kruger, I., Pretschner, A., Salzmann, C.: Engineering automotive software. Proc. IEEE **95**(2), 356–373 (2007)
4. Corradi, A., et al.: Context-based access control for ubiquitous service provisioning. In: Proceedings of the 28th COMPSAC (2004)
5. Corradi, A., et al.: Context-based access control management in ubiquitous environments. In: Proceedings of the 3rd NCA (2004)
6. Epstein, J., et al.: A prototype B3 trusted X window system. In: Proceedings of the 7th Annual Computer Security Applications Conference (1991)
7. ESOP: on safe and efficient in vehicle information and communication systems: update of the European statement of principles on human-machine interface. Commission of the European Communities (2008)
8. Feske, N., Helmuth, C.: Overlay window management: user interaction with multiple security domains (2004)
9. Feske, N., Helmuth, C.: A nitpicker's guide to a minimal-complexity secure GUI. In: Proceedings of the 21st ACSAC, December 2005
10. Gansel, S., et al.: An access control concept for novel automotive HMI systems. In: Proceedings of the 19th SACMAT (2014)
11. Gansel, S., Schnitzer, S., Dürr, F., Rothermel, K., Maihöfer, C.: Towards virtualization concepts for novel automotive HMI systems. In: Schirner, G., Götz, M., Rettberg, A., Zanella, M.C., Rammig, F.J. (eds.) IESS 2013. IFIP AICT, vol. 403, pp. 193–204. Springer, Heidelberg (2013)
12. Hansen, J.G.: Blink: advanced display multiplexing for virtualized applications. In: Proceedings of the 17th NOSSDAV (2007)
13. Herges, D., et al.: Ginger: an access control framework for telematics applications. In: Processing of the 11th TrustCom (2012)
14. Hong-Yue, L., Miao-Lei, D., Wei-Dong, Y.: A context-aware fine-grained access control model. In: Computer Science Service System (CSSS) (2012)

15. ISO 26262: Road vehicles - functional safety. ISO, Geneva, CH, November 2011
16. Janker, H.: Straßenverkehrsrecht: StVG, StVO, StVZO, Fahrzeug-ZulassungsVO, Fahrerlaubnis-VO, Verkehrszeichen. Bußgeldkatalog, Beck (2011)
17. Kouadri Mostéfaoui, G., Brézillon, P.: A generic framework for context-based distributed authorizations. In: Blackburn, P., Ghidini, C., Turner, R.M., Giunchiglia, F. (eds.) CONTEXT 2003. LNCS, vol. 2680, pp. 204–217. Springer, Heidelberg (2003)
18. Schilit, B., Theimer, M.: Disseminating active map information to mobile hosts. IEEE Netw. 8(5), 22–32 (1994)
19. Strembeck, M., et al.: An integrated approach to engineer and enforce context constraints in RBAC environments. ACM Trans. Inf. Syst. Secur. 7(3), 392–427 (2004)

Introducing Dynamic Identity and Access Management in Organizations

Michael Kunz[1]([✉]), Ludwig Fuchs[2], Matthias Hummer[2], and Günther Pernul[1]

[1] Department of Information Systems, University of Regensburg,
Regensburg, Germany
{michael.kunz,guenther.pernul}@ur.de
[2] Nexis GmbH, Regensburg, Germany
{ludwig.fuchs,matthias.hummer}@nexis-secure.com

Abstract. Efficient and secure management of access to resources is a crucial challenge in today's corporate IT environments. During the last years, introducing company-wide Identity and Access Management (IAM) infrastructures building on the Role-based Access Control (RBAC) paradigm has become the de facto standard for granting and revoking access to resources. Due to its static nature, the management of role-based IAM structures, however, leads to increased administrative efforts and is not able to model dynamic business structures. As a result, introducing dynamic attribute-based access privilege provisioning and revocation is currently seen as the next maturity level of IAM. Nevertheless, up to now no structured process for incorporating Attribute-based Access Control (ABAC) policies into static IAM has been proposed. This paper closes the existing research gap by introducing a novel migration guide for extending static IAM systems with dynamic ABAC policies. By means of conducting structured and tool-supported attribute and policy management activities, the migration guide supports organizations to distribute privilege assignments in an application-independent and flexible manner. In order to show its feasibility, we provide a naturalistic evaluation based on two real-world industry use cases.

Keywords: Identity and Access Management · IAM · ABAC · Policies

1 Motivation

The effective and secure management of employees' access to sensitive applications and data is one of the biggest security challenges for today's organizations [19]. A variety of national and international regulations or certifications like Basel III [3], the Sarbanes-Oxley-Act of 2002 [45], or the ISO 27000 family [23] together with internal guidelines force enterprises to audit and control actions within their systems. At the same time developments like the application of cloud-based services in corporate environments further underline the need for secure user management.

© Springer International Publishing Switzerland 2015
S. Jajodia and C. Mazumdar (Eds.): ICISS 2015, LNCS 9478, pp. 139–158, 2015.
DOI: 10.1007/978-3-319-26961-0_9

As a result, centralized Identity and Access Management (IAM) relying on the Role-based Access Control (RBAC) [43] paradigm became the core element for increasing user management efficiency and reduce related IT security risks over the last years. However, due to its static nature, the application of RBAC leads to a considerable amount of administrative overhead. Growing numbers of outdated roles stemming from organizational changes together with the need of manually administrating user role assignments as well as role permission assignments result in complex and outdated RBAC structures. Even disregarding the fact that it takes an average of 18 months for its initial implementation, RBAC consumes an average of 2,410,000\$ for a firm of 10,000 employees [34]. As a result, researchers and practitioners recently started to point out the need for dynamic access privilege management IAM infrastructures [14,27,42].

Using Attribute-based Access Control (ABAC) policies [20] for dynamically granting and revoking access based on employees' and privileges' attributes (from hereinafter referred to as dynamic Identity and Access Management (dIAM)) is seen as the next maturity level of company-wide IAM. The ABAC paradigm in general is based on the presumption that using a subject's, object's, and their shared context's attributes an authorization decision can be made. ABAC research traditionally focused on aspects like expressing ABAC rules (e.g. using XACML as standardized language) while only little attention has been paid to its adoption in company-wide IAM environments. This adaptation requires the definition of a potentially high number of policies within the central IAM system, the enforcement of policy decisions within the legacy applications depending on their underlying access control models, as well as the continuous policy maintenance. In order to complete these tasks, companies require a guided approach which is able to manage organizational project complexity as well es the technical heterogeneity of involved applications and protocols. To the best of our knowledge, no such structured approach has been provided up to now.

In this paper we are closing the existing research gap by firstly investigating the main building blocks required for dIAM infrastructures (Sect. 3). Secondly we propose a migration guide for implementing dIAM which serves as a project guideline dividing the necessary steps into manageable activities (Sect. 4). We thirdly evaluate our work within two real world use cases in the insurance and research industry. Besides the theoretical structuring of activities we identified the need for automation and thus additionally provided a prototypical software implementation for executing single activities of our migration guide. In order to achieve this we extended an existing IAM-tool proposed in [10] with attribute management and policy generation functionality. This allowed us to facilitate available functionality (e.g. data import or data visualization) and further evaluate our migration guide within real-life projects (see Sect. 5).

2   Related Work

Traditionally, Identity and Access Management in organizations has been associated with storing user data, maintaining user accounts, and controlling users' access to applications [11]. In today's medium to large-sized companies a centralized management of users following the RBAC paradigm has become the de facto standard approach for handling the challenges imposed by a steadily growing number of digital identities as well as access privileges. Recent surveys underline this growing importance of roles in information security in general and in IAM environments in particular [13]. However, over time and without proper controls such as de-provisioning processes, the number of roles is steadily growing, contradicting the benefits of administrative cost reduction [9]. In order to keep role systems up to date, methodologies and metrics for the ongoing optimization of role-based IAM infrastructures are required [10,26]. Nonetheless, the static concept of roles in general lacks the ability to adopt to company changes and struggles with situational adaptivity [42]. Both requirements, however, are main challenges of modern IAM infrastructures.

As a result, companies aim at enhancing their existing IAM systems with dynamic ABAC policies in order to increase provisioning capabilities, strategically reduce administrative tasks, and keep IAM infrastructures manageable [21]. While standard ABAC protocols like the eXtensible Access Control Markup Language (XACML) [33] have been around since 2003, Priebe et al. [36] and Yuan et al. [52] were the first to formally define ABAC as an access control model. However, their focus was on formalizing the model and did not consider an application-independent IAM scenario. Jin et al. suggest an attribute-based architecture for IAM focusing on attribute correlation and attribute importance in different IAM-related domains [25]. Their work, however, does not aim at supporting organizations during the set up of a dIAM system. Recently, Hu et al. [20] were amongst the first to provide generalized definitions and best practices while also giving recommendations on deploying ABAC in cross-application settings. They, however, neither provide the structured guidance nor an overview on how to adopt ABAC in an organization-wide IAM system.

Up to now, to the best of our knowledge, no approach constituting the single building blocks of ABAC-based company-wide IAM and aligning them into a structured process model exists. We close this gap in the remainder by firstly gathering the aforementioned building blocks on the basis of a thorough research review (Sect. 3). Secondly, we structure them in the form of a migration guide which can be employed by organizations that aim at extending their static identity- or role-based IAM towards the integration of ABAC policies (Sect. 4).

3 Building Blocks of Dynamic Identity and Access Management

In the following we present the core elements of dIAM systems derived from ABAC literature (e.g. building on the findings of [20]) as well as literature from related areas, such as data and information quality management or policy management. Even though most works do not consider their application for company-wide IAM in particular, researchers in general already identified attribute management as well as policy management as the two main aspects of any ABAC implementation. Attribute management [6,8,16,20,35,37,52] in general deals with requirements related to the attributes used within ABAC policies, ranging from the aggregation of attributes up to their ongoing maintenance. Policy management [4, 15, 20, 22, 24, 30, 37] deals with the development and continuous improvement of access policies.

3.1   Policy Management

While policies and their life-cycle in general have been studied in various research areas (e.g. [7]), researchers recently stated the need for a structured approach for policy management in IAM. Building on the generic policy life-cycle model proposed by Buecker et al. ([7], see Fig. 1) we outline relevant aspects of policy management in IAM in the following.

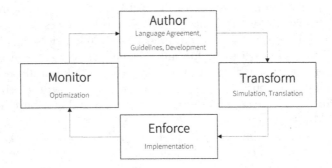

Fig. 1. Policy management based on [7] including corresponding dIAM aspects

Language Agreement. The first challenge prior to defining policies is the agreement upon a common expression language providing the syntax for depicting the semantics of policies interpreted by an IAM infrastructure. Looking at the research area, language requirements have been investigated [44] and comparisons of the suitability of policy languages (e.g. [17]) such as XACML [33] or EPAL [1] have been provided. Other authors like Strembeck [48] rather suggest generating a customized policy language tailored to the specific needs of a certain scenario. Within the area of IAM, however, a standardized approach seems more promising due to the high number of different applications and stakeholders involved.

Guidelines. Besides a common policy language, the establishment of policy guidelines plays an important role during the development as well as maintenance of dIAM systems. Policy guidelines are representing general rules on how policies are to be developed within a specific context. Note that in complex scenarios contradicting policies could potentially be defined. As a result, the establishment of design guidelines is mandatory in order to avoid semantically correct but inefficiently modeled and contradicting policies. Beckerle and Martucci [4] were the first to formally define security and manageability goals for policies.

They exclusively examined general goals for security and authorization rules. However, their results also can be applied in the context of IAM. Examples include the following goals provided in [4]:

- *Rule sets have to grant authorized access.*
- *Redundant rules need to be removed.*
- *Contradicting rules need to be removed.*
- *Concise rule sets are better than large rule sets.*

By means of such exemplary guidelines organizations can increase policy homogeneity and ease policy maintenance.

Development. Policy Development deals with the actual creation of policies. Choosing an appropriate policy development methodology within a given scenario (i.e. an IAM project) is crucial for project success. Available methodologies can be divided into policy engineering and policy mining approaches (see Fig. 2). Policy engineering deals with the top-down extraction of policies from business processes or workflows [2,5], optionally based on security policy templates as shown in [41]. Authors agree that the policy notation used during policy development [47] and the provided tool-support [46] are critical success factors for policy engineering. Policy mining, in contrast, applies data mining technologies for extracting policies from Natural Language Policies [29,49], currently assigned access privileges [50], or access logs [22,51]. While providing an increased level of automation, policy mining lacks the integration of business know-how and struggles with low-quality attribute values - above all in the context of company-wide IAM involving numerous stakeholders and policies. Research results from related areas [11] underline that in such scenarios a hybrid approach building on both, an increased level of automation as well as the integration of expert knowledge, is the most promising method for policy modeling.

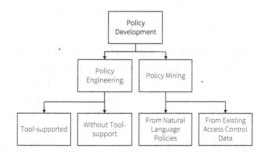

Fig. 2. Policy development methods

Simulation, Translation and Implementation. In company-wide IAM systems a potentially large number of ABAC policies affecting thousands of access privilege assignments might be required. As a result, a tool-supported simulation for anticipating the consequences of newly introduced policies becomes a central step during the setup of a policy base. Simulation tools can support the integration of policy owner feedback prior to policy activation as well as depict the future state of access within systems managed by an IAM infrastructure (e.g. using visual investigations as proposed in [31]). After simulation the policies need to be mapped onto the access control models of the legacy applications connected to an IAM. Those applications commonly are based on static access control models (e.g. SAP based on static roles or the Microsoft Active Directory (AD) based on groups). As a result, the IAM system in place has to carry out the required translations, i.e. the provisioning of dynamically calculated access privileges using static access control concepts (e.g. SAP roles).

Optimization. Once simulated and implemented, policies require the continuous monitoring of their correctness and validity by applying automated analytical methods. Note that due to the high number of expected policies a manual analysis is not feasible in the context of IAM. Lu et al., for instance, provide an approach for discovering inconsistencies and errors within policies at design-time [28]. Recently, Hummer et al. [22] proposed an approach that allows for a structured optimization of policies without interfering with a running IAM system. They apply anomaly detection methods in order to highlight deviations of normal policy patterns and visually present them to human policy engineers.

3.2 Attribute Management

Besides policy-related activities, attributes and their management form the foundation of any ABAC implementation. Attribute management is of great importance for company-wide IAM Despite its importance for company-wide IAM where employees are managed based upon master data attributes and access privileges are handled using attributes. However, attribute management in IAM has not attracted researchers' attention to a great extent up to now.

System and Attribute Selection. The initial selection and definition of application systems as well as related attributes managed within the ABAC policies [20] is the foundation for structured attribute management for dIAM. Note that in case an organization already has a deployed IAM system, basic attribute selection already took place during the initial system setup. Nevertheless, a reinvestigation and potential extension of attribute sets commonly needs to be executed. Several master data attributes stored within a personnel management system might, for instance, be unused up to now but needed during later policy definition (e.g. an employee's job position or cost center).

Constraints and Data Types. After selecting required attributes, a definition of their data types, values and constraints needs to be carried out. Data types commonly range from boolean to single-valued and multi-valued attributes [6]. Researchers recently analyzed the effects of policy evaluation performance and highlighted its relation to the used attributes and attribute values [32]. Regarding attribute constraints, Bijon et al., for instance, introduce constraints on attribute assignments and values [6]. As further examples, Jin et al. provide a methodology for the classification of attributes according to their criticality and importance for access [25], while there also exists an overview of data and systems that are typically involved in an IAM environment [22].

Data Integration. As aforementioned, company-wide IAM commonly handles large amounts of data stemming from numerous applications, databases, or directory services. Organizations already operating an IAM hence need to review and extend existing integration processes to reflect the needs of future dynamic ABAC policies. IAM systems in general differentiate between source and target systems whereas a source system for certain attributes can act as target system for other attributes at the same time. An example could be an HR system providing master data of employees while at the same time receiving employees' email addresses from a mail application. Note that the definition of master sources for attributes has implications on attribute ownership. It is e.g. likely that human resources representatives are responsible for reviewing and validating attributes stemming from the personnel system.

Cleansing and Quality Controls. Policies created on the basis of erroneous attribute values essentially lead to security vulnerabilities, compliance violations, and administrative overhead. As a result, a structured review and cleansing of incorporated attribute values is a mandatory building block of dIAM prior to policy development. For an overview of potential data quality problems, cf. [39]. Hummer et al. recently argued that for optimizing policies, a centralized view on available and utilizable attributes spanning all involved systems is necessary in order to detect data errors and inconsistencies [22]. Data cleansing additionally builds on available attribute quality controls (e.g. rules for valid attribute values). Such quality controls, e.g., support the automated monitoring of attribute value changes and the advent of new attribute values and attribute types. We suggest to apply measures and metrics (for an overview cf. [18]) as well as best practices [40] from the field of data and information quality management to address these challenges.

4 Migration Guide

After describing the building blocks of an ABAC-based IAM, this Section of the paper introduces our tool-supported migration guide supporting a step-by-step migration from an existing static towards a dynamic IAM solution. It consists of three phases, namely a preparatory phase, an implementation phase and a maintenance phase (see Fig. 3). The goal of the preparatory phase is to achieve

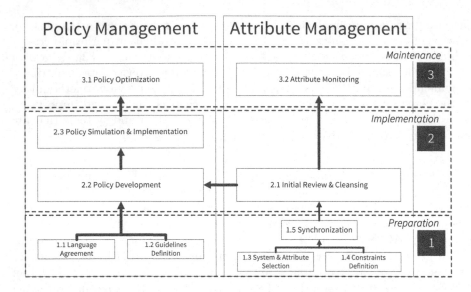

Fig. 3. Process model for migrating towards dIAM

a common understanding of policies and provide an attribute base used during later process phases. The subsequent implementation phase covers the cleansing of attributes and actual development of policies while the maintenance phase provides measures for continuous monitoring and improvement of the policy system. Note that due to space restrictions we cannot provide a detailed presentation of all involved sub-activities but rather aim at giving an overview of required tasks. In order to increase automation, we implemented a prototypical software for supporting the execution of attribute and policy management activities (Phase 2 of our migration guide). It is able to exchange data with an existing IAM system supporting the respective ABAC implementation process.

4.1   Preparation Phase

Due to the complexity and heterogeneity of static IAM environments, several preparatory activities have to be completed before ABAC policies can be defined. Relevant systems, attributes, responsibilities, and guidelines have to be reviewed and defined in order to foster a common understanding on a technical as well as organizational level among involved stakeholders.

Attribute Management. During system and attribute selection source systems for attribute data (e.g. personnel management systems) need to be investigated for attributes required during policy definition (Activity 1.3). Additional sources like IAM systems themselves or other applications providing information about user accounts or access privileges (e.g. ownership, criticality) might be identified. Note that organizations having basic attribute synchronization processes in place commonly have not dealt with the facilitation of extended attributes for complex access control decisions. By investigating system documentation or conducting expert interviews they hence need to review and extend the currently used attribute types in order to reflect ABAC requirements.

At the same time, data types need to be defined and constraint definitions for the attributes need to be established (Activity 1.4, cf. Sect. 3, *Constraints & Data Types*). This, amongst others, includes the definition of data types, master data sources, data ownerships, valid attribute values, or attribute ranges, i.e. intervals (if the data type is a numeric type) of validity. This way, erroneous attribute values can be identified during the subsequent cleansing activities.

After successfully completing the system and attribute selection and definition of constraints and data types, the attribute synchronization (Activity 1.5) takes place. Attribute values are imported into the IAM during this phase. At the same time conflicts like different encodings or granularity issues (e.g. *address* vs. *street* and *zip code*) can be detected.

Policy Management. Regarding policy management, a general language agreement (Activity 1.1) for policy expression as well as the definition of policy guidelines need to be established prior to policy creation. Most of the currently available IAM implementations, for instance, are able to foster XACML as standardized policy language. Additionally, a shared understanding among project stakeholders on an organizational level needs to be established in the form of a company-wide glossary with definitions for important terminology. Available policy types like grant or denial policies should, for instance, be described. Furthermore, guidelines for policies (Activity 1.2, cf. Sect. 3, *Policy Guidelines*) can act as sources on how the human policy engineers are requested to model policies. Imagine a scenario in which only grant policies are allowed. Policy engineers should hence not have the option to design denial policies throughout a tool-supported policy creation process at all. Additionally, guidelines for the strategic maintenance of policies (Phase 3 of our migration guide) need to be defined. By introducing policy and attribute ownerships and requiring a periodic certification process, companies can essentially increase long-term policy quality.

4.2   Implementation Phase

After the preparatory activities have been completed, organizations enter the implementation phase (Phase 2) of our migration guide, i.e. the initial development and setup of a dIAM based on ABAC policies. Concerning attribute management, a systematic initial review and cleansing (Activity 2.1) of attribute data is required before the initial creation of policies as well as their subsequent simulation and implementation (Activities 2.2 and 2.3) can be carried out (cf. Sect. 3, *Policy Development; Simulation, Translation and Implementation*).

Attribute Management. Medium and large-sized organizations commonly struggle with data quality issues regarding their digital identities and access privileges. As a result, a dedicated cleansing process for improving attribute data quality is a crucial success factor for implementing dIAM. Following an initial assessment of attribute data (e.g. the identification of empty or invalid attribute values) the manual or automated cleansing of attributes needs to take place. We argue that a tool-based detection and cleansing process fosters user adoption by reducing the overall project complexity. Automated error identification can, for instance, be carried out by means of data mining or data quality metrics. Data mining, for instance, can be applied to detect outliers and unusual attribute values (see [12]). Based on predefined quality metrics (e.g. general rules like the currency [18] of an attribute value or a list of valid location attribute values) it leads to an overall higher quality of defined policies. Figure 4 (left side) gives a simple attribute cleansing example by grouping current location attribute values from a personnel system within our prototype after the attribute synchronization took place. Existing data errors such as typos, different language codings, or misspellings can be identified easily. The right side of Fig. 4 displays the attribute values after cleansing by human experts in collaboration with attribute owners.

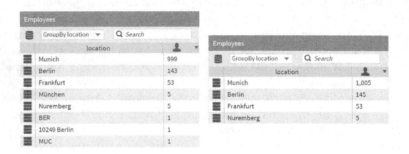

Fig. 4. Before and after manual cleansing by grouping of attribute *location* and its various occurrences

Policy Management. As aforementioned, a potentially high number of policies bundling a wide range of access privileges or responsibilities are managed in corporate IAM environments. As a result, a manual policy generation by human policy engineers is not feasible. Organizations thus aim at employing automation techniques for creating policies and reviewing them in a hybrid manner (e.g. by experts who provide business knowledge and semantics, see Sect. 3). As one example of a potential role development approach in large IAM environments, we thus implemented policy mining algorithms that are able to automatically generate candidates for grant policies based on given attribute information. In order to support human review processes we additionally developed a simple representation of policies using a wizard-based graphical interface within our prototype (see Fig. 5).

Using this approach, a human policy engineer can select combinations of available attributes (left side of Fig. 5, e.g. *function* and *location*) and option-ally merge semantically or syntactically equivalent attribute values (right side of

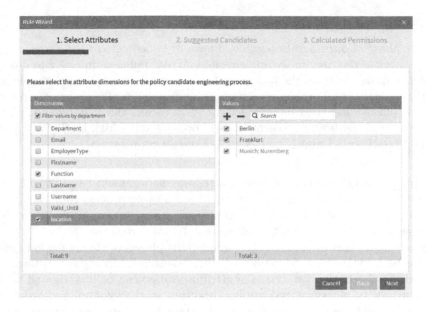

Fig. 5. Automated tool-based policy mining and review

Fig. 5, bundling the attribute values *Munich* and *Nuremberg*). In a second review step, suggested policy candidates are then displayed to the policy engineer. Continuing our example above, access is granted on the basis of the combination of employees' *location* and *function*. As a result, three policies for each function attribute value are generated, e.g. one policy for *sales representatives* in *Berlin*, *Frankfurt*, and *Munich/Nuremberg* each. During review, a human policy engineer can alter or remove unneeded policies (e.g. in case no *sales representatives* are located in *Frankfurt*). During a third step our prototype calculates the access rights shared by policy members based on customizable data mining algorithms. This way, a policy engineer could, for instance, enforce that only access rights that are not yet included in other policies are considered during the access privilege calculation or that critical access privileges are in general excluded from policy generation.

Completing the third step of our policy development wizard, policy owners are assigned and the policy candidates can be saved and exported to an IAM system. Ownership assignment can take place either based on rules (e.g. line managers are responsible for policies that affect their department) or manually.

After agreeing upon policy definitions, their simulation and implementation within an IAM test environment takes place. Due to the high number of organizational changes (e.g. restructuring organizational hierarchies, ownerships, and responsibilities) such policy simulation is a cornerstone of every policy modeling initiative. After final approval, the implementation of policies in the productive system occurs.

4.3   Maintenance Phase

The last phase of our migration guide (Phase 3) is dedicated to the continuous improvement of the previously implemented ABAC policies. In order to ensure long-term applicability of the defined rule set and minimize system complexity over time, a structured process for a periodic assessment and re-design of existing and new policies needs to be established. As a result, the maintenance phase deals with ensuring both, the correctness of policies and a high level of attribute quality (Activities 3.1 and 3.2, cf. Sect. 3, *Policy Optimization*).

Attribute Management. Regarding attribute management (Activity 3.2), we recommend the introduction of a structured monitoring process comprising two main activities, namely the periodic identification and review of quality metric violations as well as the definition of organizational agreements.

Quality measures defined during the previous phases of the migration guide form the basis for continuous attribute quality assurance. Throughout automated and periodic checks the correctness of attribute values can be investigated based on given quality measures and outlier detection methodologies. Examples for such checks can be periodic certifications of attributes by attribute owners or the detection of wrong attribute values using valid value lists. Besides such technical measures organizational agreements have to be made, e.g. in order to handle scenarios when new applications are connected to an IAM. In such cases, the IAM team has to decide whether the provided attributes fulfill the initially established constraints and attribute quality levels.

Policy Management. Besides the strategic management of attribute types and their values, the long-term maintenance of ABAC policies together with the potentially automated proposal of newly required but not yet defined policies need to be ensured. Note that both maintenance activities are highly dependent on each other. In contrast to attribute monitoring, discovering erroneous and outdated policies requires an increased level of automation. While single-valued attribute errors might be easily identified, a misconfiguration of policies granting critical access privileges can hardly be identified without tool-support. For addressing this challenge, Hummer et al. recently suggested measures and processes for strategic policy maintenance [22]. They, for instance, introduce tool-supported outlier and anomaly detection for identifying unused or outdated policies into the field of IAM.

5   Evaluation

After proposing our migration guide we now execute a naturalistic ex post evaluation covering two industry use cases based on the evaluation framework by Pries-Heje et al. [38]. The used real-life data-sets originate from companies operating in the health insurance in Switzerland (from hereinafter refereed to as 'Insucomp') as well as the research sector in Germany (from hereinafter refereed to as 'Rescomp'). All attribute values have been anonymized accordingly. While Rescomp already had a working IAM system in place, Insucomp conducted a policy development project as part of their initiative to initially implement an IAM system. The project duration was six months (Rescomp) and nine months (Insucomp) respectively, with both projects sharing the same overall goals:

1. Automatically providing new employees with correct basic access.
2. Increasing the amount of automatically distributed privileges by using dynamic provisioning policies.

In order to achieve these goals, both companies executed Phases 1 and 2 of our migration guide and facilitated our prototypical tool implementation during policy development. Insucomp additionally implemented basic measures for policy and attribute maintenance (Phase 3) while Rescomp plans to do so in future. Note that even though both use cases only aimed at policy definition based on subject attributes, our model can also be applied during the general development of policies comprising subject, object, and environmental attributes.

5.1   Insucomp

Insucomp is employing 349 external and 866 internal employees which in total own 7,777 accounts in 13 different application systems, including one AD and one SAP instance. In total, 2,297 different access rights are directly assigned to the user accounts resulting in 54,059 access rights assignments. Insucomp's variety of applications using static access privilege assignments in combination with manual provisioning processes resulted in large administrative efforts over the last years. As a result, a new IAM system based on dynamic access control policies had to be introduced between 2014 and 2015.

Preparation Phase. Throughout a kick-off workshop, Insucomp initially taught policy engineers guidelines on how to semi-automatically construct policies (Activity 1.2) while the IAM software implemented during the overall IAM project pre-defined the applied policy language (Activity 1.1). In the specific case the proprietary modeling capabilities of the Dell One Identity Manager were employed due to the reduced expected technical implementation efforts required. The system and attribute selection (Activity 1.3) took place in an iterative manner. Firstly, the HR system was defined as source for employee master data. The available attributes together with access privileges from all 13 applications were imported into our prototype. Consecutively, policy engineers and the responsible line officers agreed upon the exclusion of certain access rights from the Microsoft AD, the SAP, and the Customer Relationship Management system from further consideration. This decision was based on several reasons: Firstly, granting certain access rights in an automated manner would have resulted in an increase of license costs. Secondly, selected access privileges from the Customer Relationship Management system were classified as critical from an IT security perspective and hence excluded from automated provisioning processes.

Regarding the attributes for policy development, the domain experts and IAM team selected an employee's *position* as the main HR attribute for the policy construction. Constraints and data types were defined accordingly:

- C1: The German value for the *position* is used in policies.
- C2: A *code* is introduced for each value, referring to exactly one *position*.
- C3: A policy definition needs to contain both, a human-readable *position* as well as its respective machine-readable 4-digit *code*.
- C4: The *position* is a string value.

During attribute synchronization (Activity 1.5), violations of those constraints were identified. As an example, several languages were originally used to express an employee's position. In coordination with the HR department, the German *position* attribute value (C1) was selected as the defining attribute for later policy evaluations. Other languages were excluded from the data import and from now on are represented as translation of the main value (i.e. the German value) within a new attribute field in the HR system.

Implementation Phase. Following our migration guide a subsequent data cleansing process was conducted. Inspecting all attribute values within our prototype (Activity 2.1), Insucomp was, amongst others, able to discover ten erroneously defined *positions*. Additionally, *positions* with an inappropriate semantic granularity level were detected. For instance, initially one *position* for *Clerk Insurance Processing* existed within the HR system. However, for representing two semantically distinct insurance levels, Insucomp had to model two additional types of clerks with different access rights. As a result, the IAM team enforced the creation of more detailed *positions* and *codes* within the HR system. In the given example, two new *positions* were created in the HR system and employees were assigned accordingly (see Fig. 6). Finishing the data cleansing activities a total of 253 *positions* have been available in the final attribute base.

After successful attribute cleansing, the actual detection of policy candidates within our prototype and the respective review together with domain experts took place (Activity 2.2). As a side effect, Insucomp was able to discard 3,600 excessive assignments (i.e. 6.7 % of all access privilege assignments) during the policy review process as our prototype highlighted additional (potentially excessive) privileges of employees assigned to a certain policy. This had a large impact

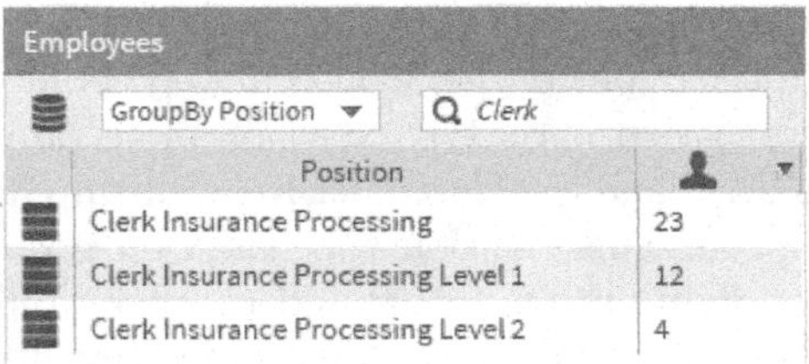

Fig. 6. Example for refactoring of employee *positions*

on the overall project, further underlining the importance of secure provisioning and de-provisioning processes based on dynamic policies.

Finally, Insucomp exported the defined policies from our prototype and imported them within their newly set-up IAM system (Activity 2.3). They randomly selected sample policies in order to simulate correct functionality throughout various identity lifecycle processes (i.e. onboarding, change, and offboarding of employees). As a result, a total of 253 policies were put into operation. This led to the dynamic provisioning of 32 % of all access rights among Insucomp's 13 connected application systems, essentially reducing the manual administrative workload while at the same time increasing the level of IT security.

Maintenance Phase. At the end of the migration project, Insucomp defined measures and quality controls in order to ensure the correctness of policies and attributes (Phase 3 of our migration guide). For conducting structured attribute management (Activity 3.2) newly introduced or changed attributes or attribute values have to be reported by the HR department to the IAM team in the future in order to adapt policies accordingly. Policy optimization has not been carried out up to now but is one element of the Insucomp IAM roadmap within the next year.

5.2   Rescomp

Rescomp already employed a working IAM system prior to the beginning of their policy definition project. Nonetheless, user management still was executed manually to a large extent for the 473 employees and the 761 different access rights (5,774 user privilege assignments in total). Rescomp's dynamic research environment requires automated and flexible access privilege provisioning in the future (e.g. for external employees like students needing temporary access to critical company data while undergoing regular organizational changes at the same time). As a result, a dIAM migration project was initiated in 2014. Similar to Insucomp, Rescomp executed the first two phases of our migration guide. Even though they have not executed maintenance activities up to now, they recently defined policy optimization as one element of their future IAM roadmap.

Preparation Phase. As a preparatory activity, Rescomp defined general guidelines for policy modeling (Activity 1.2). They introduced three types of valid policies, namely location-based policies, department and type-based policies, as well as function-based policies. Location-based policies represent the *physical location* of employees e.g. for granting physical access to buildings. *Department-* and *type-*based polices, in contrast, are defined based on the departmental assignment of employees in combination with their type, essentially granting access to departmental file shares for *internals, trainees, students*, or *externals*. In addition, function-based policies were defined to further refine employee's access rights according to their *job function*. Besides the three policy types, the IAM team defined a guideline regarding the definition of empty policies, i.e. policies that currently no employee is matching. In accordance with their project goals they decided to prepare such policies prior to an initial match of an employee (Activity 1.2). They, for instance, created a policy for all members of the technical service *department* whose *type of contract* is student. Students might only work within the department during their term holidays and thus the according policy might be unused for certain periods of the year but still is required during other months.

Following the migration guide, they selected two installations of their Microsoft AD for inclusion of access rights and provided the employee attributes from the HR system in place. During Activity 1.4 *department, type of contract, function, project* and *location* were selected as attribute base for policy definition. Similarly to Insucomp, Rescomp defined constraints and data types for these attributes. They, for instance, decided that regarding the *types of contract internals, apprentices,* and *students* should be treated equally in terms of their access rights.

Implementation Phase. Due to an already high attribute quality provided by the HR system, attribute cleansing was not required as no errors were identified during the attribute investigation. As a result, the IAM team subsequently conducted the policy development (Activity 2.2) in cooperation with business representatives. They started with the definition of basic *location* policies and continued with the creation of *department* and *employee type*-based policies as

```xml
<accesspolicy>
  <name>Controlling;trainee;intern;student</name>
  <accessrights>
    <accessright>
      <uid>CN=student_share,OU=student,OU=controlling,OU=rescomp_inc,DC=res,DC=loc</uid>
      <application>AD</application>
    </accessright>
    ...
  </accessrights>
  <rule>
    <operator value="AND">
      <attr>
        <attributename>department</attributename>
        <attributevalue>controlling(</attributevalue>
        <id>28822277221</id>
      </attr>
      <operator value="OR">
        <attr>
          <attributename>employeeType</attributename>
          <attributevalue>trainee</attributevalue>
        </attr>
        <attr>
          <attributename>employeeType</attributename>
          <attributevalue>intern</attributevalue>
        </attr>
        <attr>
          <attributename>employeeType</attributename>
          <attributevalue>student</attributevalue>
        </attr>
      </operator>
    </operator>
  </rule>
</accesspolicy>
```

Fig. 7. Example policy export using XML notation

well as policies for employees' *function* attributes. Business representatives were asked to review the policy candidates using our prototype. In total, this process lead to the definition of 449 policies for automatic access privilege assignments, covering a total of 34.8 % of all managed access privileges. Regarding the access rights, 45.9 % of all initially existing privileges can now be assigned in an automatic way, i.e. they are included in at least one policy. All policies were exported from our prototype using the XML-notation and consecutively transferred into the existing LDAP-based IAM system of Rescomp using custom Python scripts (Activity 2.3). Figure 7 presents a short XML export example of one department and employee type-based policy bundling students, trainees, and internships within a controlling department.

6   Conclusion

Dynamically assigning and revoking access privileges in company-wide IAM infrastructures has gained significant importance when it comes to automated and secure user management. Migrating to a dynamic IAM infrastructure based on ABAC policies can decrease manual administrative efforts while at the same time increasing the overall IT security level within companies. In order to support organizations during their required migration efforts, we proposed a novel three-step migration guide for implementing dynamic IAM based on ABAC policies in a structured manner. Up to now, no such structured process model highlighting and coordinating the respective migration tasks has been proposed. Our migration guide covers the required preparation, setup, as well as maintenance tasks and additionally offers tool-support in order to automate attribute and policy management activities. By doing so it increases the flexibility of policy engineers, reduces errors during policy modeling, and speeds-up the overall process of policy creation. Evaluating our migration guide throughout two real-life use cases we have further underlined its practical applicability.

In the future, we plan to extend our software prototype by implementing automated identity attribute monitoring activities that support companies during long-term attribute maintenance. In contrast to organizational guidelines this would support the enforcement of quality rules for attribute management. Additionally, we plan to expand policy development and policy maintenance capabilities in order to allow for a better cooperation between the responsible domain experts and the policy engineers.

Acknowledgment. The research leading to these results was supported by the "Bavarian State Ministry of Education, Science and the Arts" as part of the FORSEC research association.

References

1. Ashley, P., Hada, S., Karjoth, G., Powers, C., Schunter, M.: Enterprise Privacy Authorization Language (EPAL 1.2). Submission to W3C (2003)

2. Aubert, J., Gateau, B., Incoul, C., Feltus, C.: SIM: an innovative business-oriented approach for a distributed access management. In: Proceedings of the 3rd International Conference on Information and Communication Technologies: From Theory to Applications (ICTTA), pp. 1–6 (2008)
3. Basel Committee on Banking Supervision: Basel III - A Global Regulatory Framework for More Resilient Banks and Banking Systems (2011)
4. Beckerle, M., Martucci, L.A.: Formal definitions for usable access control rule sets from goals to metrics. In: Proceedings of the 9th Symposium on Usable Privacy and Security (SOUPS), p. 2 (2013)
5. Bhatti, R., Bertino, E., Ghafoor, A.: X-FEDERATE: a policy engineering framework for federated access management. IEEE Trans. Softw. Eng. **32**(5), 330–346 (2006)
6. Bijon, K.Z., Krishman, R., Sandhu, R.: Constraints specification in attribute based access control. Science **2**(3), 131 (2013)
7. Buecker, A., Andrews, S., Forster, C., Harlow, N., Lu, M., Muppidi, S., Norvill, T., Nye, P., Waller, G., White, E.T.: IT Security Policy Management Usage Patterns Using IBM Tivoli Security Policy Manager. IBM Redbooks (2011)
8. Chadwick, D.W., Inman, G.: Attribute aggregation in federated identity management. IEEE Comput. **42**(5), 33–40 (2009)
9. Elliott, A., Knight, S.: Role explosion: acknowledging the problem. In: Proceedings of the International Conference on Software Engineering Research and Practice (SERP), pp. 349–355 (2010)
10. Fuchs, L., Kunz, M., Pernul, G.: Role model optimization for secure role-based identity management. In: Proceedings of the 22nd European Conference on Information Systems (ECIS) (2014)
11. Fuchs, L., Pernul, G.: HyDRo – hybrid development of roles. In: Sekar, R., Pujari, A.K. (eds.) ICISS 2008. LNCS, vol. 5352, pp. 287–302. Springer, Heidelberg (2008)
12. Fuchs, L., Pernul, G.: Qualitätssicherung im Identity- und Access Management. HMD Praxi. Wirtschaftsinformatik **50**(1), 88–97 (2013)
13. Fuchs, L., Pernul, G., Sandhu, R.: Roles in information security - a survey and classification of the research area. Comput. Secur. **30**(8), 748–769 (2011)
14. Gartner: Gartner IAM 2020 Predictions. http://www.avatier.com/products/identity-management/resources/gartner-iam-2020-predictions/
15. Gupta, P., Stoller, S.D., Xu, Z.: Abductive analysis of administrative policies in rule-based access control. IEEE Trans. Dependable Secure Comput. **11**(5), 412–424 (2014)
16. Hamlen, K., Liu, P., Kantarcioglu, M., Thuraisingham, B., Yu, T.: Identity management for cloud computing: developments and directions. In: Proceedings of the 7th Annual Workshop on Cyber Security and Information Intelligence Research (CSIIRW), p. 32 (2011)
17. Han, W., Lei, C.: A survey on policy languages in network and security management. Comput. Netw. **56**(1), 477–489 (2012)
18. Heinrich, B., Kaiser, M., Klier, M.: How to measure data quality? a metric-based approach. In: Proceedings of the 6th International Conference on Computer and Information Science (ICIS) (2007)
19. Hovav, A., Berger, R.: Tutorial: identity management systems and secured access control. Commun. Assoc. Inf. Syst. **25**(1), 42 (2009)
20. Hu, V.C., Ferraiolo, D., Kuhn, R., Schnitzer, A., Sandlin, K., Miller, R., Scarfone, K.: Guide to Attribute Based Access Control (ABAC) Definition and Considerations. Technical report NIST SP 800–162 (2014)

21. Huang, J., Nicol, D.M., Bobba, R., Huh, J.H.: A framework integrating attribute-based policies into role-based access control. In: Proceedings of the 17th ACM Symposium on Access Control Models and Technologies (SACMAT), pp. 187–196 (2012)
22. Hummer, M., Kunz, M., Netter, M., Fuchs, L., Pernul, G.: Advanced identity and access policy management using contextual data. In: Proceedings of the 11th Internatinal Conference on Availability, Reliability and Security (ARES) (2015)
23. Iso: ISO/IEC 27000 Information Technology – Security Techniques – Information Security Management Systems – Overview and Vocabulary (2009)
24. Jin, X., Krishnan, R., Sandhu, R.: A unified attribute-based access control model covering DAC, MAC and RBAC. In: Cuppens-Boulahia, N., Cuppens, F., Garcia-Alfaro, J. (eds.) DBSec 2012. LNCS, vol. 7371, pp. 41–55. Springer, Heidelberg (2012)
25. Jin, Z., Xu, J., Xu, M., Zheng, N.: An attribute-oriented model for identity management. In: Proceedings of the International Conference on E-Education, E-Business, E-Management and E-Learning (IC4E), pp. 440–444 (2010)
26. Kunz, M., Fuchs, L., Netter, M., Pernul, G.: Analyzing quality criteria in role-based identity and access management. In: Proceedings of the 1st International Conference on Information Systems Security and Privacy (ICISSP) (2015)
27. Kunz, M., Hummer, M., Fuchs, L., Netter, M., Pernul, G.: Analyzing recent trends in enterprise identity management. In: Proceedings of the 25th International Workshop on Database and Expert Systems Applications (DEXA), pp. 273–277 (2014)
28. Lu, J., Li, R., Hu, J., Xu, D.: Inconsistency resolving of safety and utility in access control. J. Wirel. Commun. Networking 1, 1–12 (2011)
29. Marfia, F.: Using abductive and inductive inference to generate policy explanations. In: Proceedings of the International Conference on Security and Cryptography (SECRYPT) (2014)
30. Medvet, E., Bartoli, A., Carminati, B., Ferrari, E.: Evolutionary inference of attribute-based access control policies. In: Gaspar-Cunha, A., Henggeler Antunes, C., Coello, C.C. (eds.) EMO 2015. LNCS, vol. 9018, pp. 351–365. Springer, Heidelberg (2015)
31. Meier, S., Fuchs, L., Pernul, G.: Managing the access grid-a process view to minimize insider misuse risks. In: Proceedings of the 11th International Tagung Wirtschaftsinformatik (WI) (2013)
32. Ngo, C., Makkes, M.X., Demchenko, Y., De Laat, C.: Multi-data-types interval decision diagrams for XACML evaluation engine. In: Proceedings of the 11th Annual International Conference on Privacy, Security and Trust (PST), pp. 257–266 (2013)
33. OASIS: eXtensible Access Control Markup Language (XACML) Version 3.0 (2013)
34. O'Connor, A.C., Loomis, R.J.: 2010 Economic Analysis of Role-Based Access Control. Technical report (2010)
35. Park, J., Zhang, X., Sandhu, R.: Attribute mutability in usage control. In: Farkas, C., Samarati, P. (eds.) Research Directions in Data and Applications Security XVIII, pp. 15–29. Springer, US (2004)
36. Priebe, T., Dobmeier, W., Muschall, B., Pernul, G.: ABAC-Ein Referenzmodell für attributbasierte Zugriffskontrolle. In: Sicherheit, vol. 62, pp. 285–296 (2005)
37. Priebe, T., Dobmeier, W., Schläger, C., Kamprath, N.: Supporting attribute-based access control in authorization and authentication infrastructures with ontologies. J. Softw. 2(1), 27–38 (2007)

38. Pries-Heje, J., Baskerville, R., Venable, J.: Strategies for design science research evaluation. In: Proceedings of the 16th European Conference on Information Systems (ECIS), pp. 1–12 (2008)
39. Rahm, E., Do, H.H.: Data cleaning: problems and current approaches. IEEE Database Eng. Bull. **23**(4), 3–13 (2000)
40. Redman, T.C.: Data Quality for the Information Age, 1st edn. Artech House Inc., Norwood (1997)
41. Rudolph, M., Schwarz, R., Jung, C.: Security policy specification templates for critical infrastructure services in the cloud. In: Proceedings of the 9th International Conference for Internet Technology and Secured Transactions (ICITST), pp. 61–66 (2014)
42. Sandhu, R.: The authorization leap from rights to attributes: maturation or chaos? In: Proceedings of the 17th ACM Symposium on Access Control Models and Technologies (SACMAT), pp. 69–70 (2012)
43. Sandhu, R.S., Coyne, E.J., Feinstein, H.L., Youman, C.E.: Role-based access control models. Computer **2**, 38–47 (1996)
44. Seamons, K., Winslett, M., Yu, T., Smith, B., Child, E., Jacobson, J., Mills, H., Yu, L.: Requirements for policy languages for trust negotiation. In: Proceedings of the 3rd International Workshop on Policies for Distributed Systems and Networks (POLICY), pp. 68–79 (2002)
45. SOX: Sarbanes-Oxley Act of 2002, PL 107–204, 116 Stat 745 (2002)
46. Stepien, B., Felty, A., Matwin, S.: A non-technical XACML target editor for dynamic access control systems. In: Proceedings of the International Conference on Collaboration Technologies and Systems (CTS), pp. 150–157 (2014)
47. Stepien, B., Matwin, S., Felty, A.: An algorithm for compression of XACML access control policy sets by recursive subsumption. In: Proceedings of the 7th International Conference on Availability, Reliability and Security (ARES), pp. 161–167 (2012)
48. Strembeck, M.: Engineering of Dynamic Policy-Based Systems: A Policy Engineering of Dynamic Policy-Based Systems: Language Based Approach. Hab. Th. (2008)
49. Xiao, X., Paradkar, A., Thummalapenta, S., Xie, T.: Automated extraction of security policies from natural-language software documents. In: Proceedings of the 20th International Symposium on the Foundations of Software Engineering (SIGSOFT), p. 12 (2012)
50. Xu, Z., Stoller, S.D.: Mining attribute-based access control policies from RBAC policies. In: Proceedings of the 10th International Conference and Expo on Emerging Technologies for a Smarter World (CEWIT), pp. 1–6 (2013)
51. Xu, Z., Stoller, S.D.: Mining attribute-based access control policies from logs. In: Atluri, V., Pernul, G. (eds.) DBSec 2014. LNCS, vol. 8566, pp. 276–291. Springer, Heidelberg (2014)
52. Yuan, E., Tong, J.: Attributed based access control (ABAC) for web services. In: Proceedings of the International Conference on Web Services (ICWS), p. 569 (2005)

Attacks and Mitigation

Revisiting Democratic Mining in Bitcoins: Its Weakness and Possible Remedies

Goutam Paul[(⊠)]

Cryptology and Security Research Unit,
R. C. Bose Centre for Cryptology and Security,
Indian Statistical Institute, Kolkata 700 108, India
goutam.paul@isical.ac.in

Abstract. In ICISS 2014, Paul et al. identified several problems in the existing Proof-of-Work protocol for Bitcoin mining and proposed an alternative solution to generate blocks containing valid transactions. In their scheme, each miner generates a hash value locally and then the miners engage in a distributed computation of the minimum of the hashes to select the winner. The authors claimed that this will eliminate the advantage of the miners with more computational resources and therefore would be more democratic. However, in this paper we show that the new scheme is also subject to the same weakness in the sense that a miner with more computational resources can do some local computation in order to increase its winning probability. We also discuss possible remedies to this problem and their implications.

Keywords: Bitcoins · Cryptocurrency · Democratic mining · Electronic cash system · Miners · Proof-of-work

1 Introduction

Popularity of Bitcoins [15] as an electronic cash system is increasing day by day. In Bitcoins, the users are identified with virtual pseudonyms referred to as Bitcoin addresses, where each address corresponds to a unique public/private key pair. Transfer of coins from one address to the other is referred to as a transaction [7]. A transaction is formed by digitally signing a hash of the previous transaction where the coin was last spent along with the public key of the future owner and finally incorporating the signature in the transaction. Blocks [6] are used to store these transactions and they maintain a synchronization among all nodes in the network.

Any peer can verify the authenticity of a BTC transaction by checking the chain of signatures. A block of valid transactions contains a hash that takes as input only the transactions in the current block, but also the hash of the previous block and a nonce. This helps to prevent double-spending [1].

Before the transactions are verified, they are stored in a transaction pool. Each miner tries to create a hash less than a specified target by changing the

© Springer International Publishing Switzerland 2015
S. Jajodia and C. Mazumdar (Eds.): ICISS 2015, LNCS 9478, pp. 161–170, 2015.
DOI: 10.1007/978-3-319-26961-0_10

nonce and the winner creates a block of valid transactions and appends it to the existing block-chain. This is called the Proof-of-Work [3] (PoW) protocol. Upon successful generation of a block, a miner is granted a fixed amount of BTCs, known as coin-based transaction, plus the transaction fees from all the transactions that have been included in the block. This provides an incentive for users to continuously mine Bitcoins. The target is changed by the system from time and time and this helps to keep the Bitcoin generation rate under control.

1.1   Motivation and Contributions

In a recent work [16], the authors identified many weaknesses in the Pow protocol in Bitcoins. We summarize them below.

– A group of miners having 'rich' computational resource may set up a mining pool in such a way that it may control more than 50 % of the network's computing power. They can modify the ordering or exclude the occurrence of transactions by launching a 51 % attack [14]. The pool may indulge in double spending by simply reversing transactions that they send. It may also prevent other valid transactions from being confirmed or reject every block found by competing miners. The mining pool keeps on earning maximum profit and as pointed out in [16], this leads to the socially undesirable problem of "*rich gets richer*".
– The PoW protocol requires time (on an average 10 min) to verify a block [11]. So within the verification time a Bitcoin exchange might be completed. An attacker can simultaneously send an illicit transaction log to the seller and another log to the rest of the peers in the Bitcoin network, where the original owner gets back his currency. But by the time the seller realizes that he has received a fraudulent amount, the transaction may have already been carried out. This is called race-attack.
– When a miner solves the PoW puzzle and verifies a new block, he may keep it with himself and start working on the next puzzle for verifying the block which would follow his unreleased block. Thus if a mining pool is set up, they might use their overall computational power to keep verifying blocks. Finally, when other miners find a new block, the selfish miners releases their verified chain of blocks. Their blocks would automatically be added to the main Bitcoin chain and the selfish miners would always gain, since the longer chain always wins. This is called 'Selfish Mining' [9].
– Attackers may illegally infect a huge number of machines [10] in the network with malware, thus building a malicious botnet, that would be able to mine Bitcoins. There are several examples of such attacks [4,18,19].
– Each PoW problem generally requires 10^8 GH/s (Gigahashes/second) to be solved. According to "Bitcoin Watch" [12], the whole Bitcoin network hit a record-breaking high of 1 exaFLOPS a year earlier. The world's top 10 supercomputers can muster 5 percent of that total, and even the top 500 can only muster a mere 12.8 percent. The new ASIC machines used by the miners are built from scratch and are only used to mine Bitcoins. Thus they can't serve any other purpose. So the total power spent on Bitcoin mining could

theoretically be spent on something else, like real world problems that exist naturally.
- As discussed in [16], the time required for confirmation of a transaction usually takes around 5–20 minutes, which is against the policy where each transaction verification should take on an average 10 min. If more miners join in the race to find the puzzle for verifying the block, more hashes would be generated and tested within the same time-span. But according to the Bitcoin protocol, the network self-regulates the speed of generation of Bitcoins after a certain time-span (after every 2016 blocks) by checking the number of days required to generate x many hashes. If the time-span is found out to be too short, then the difficulty level of PoW puzzle is increased and so it becomes harder to find out the required hash in the next round. Thus, there is no guarantee of fixed generation rate of Bitcoins.

In [16], a new alternative of PoW was proposed with a view to mitigate the above problems. They called their mining method to be "democratic" in the sense that each miner has equal probability of winning. In this paper, we theoretically prove that the above claim is correct only when each miner generates only one hash and submits it as an input to the winner-finding algorithm. However, if the miners are allowed to compute multiple hashes by changing the nonce's, then one can submit a suitable function of those local hashes as one's input to the winner-finding algorithm and thereby increase one's winning probability. Thus, the problem of 'rich gets richer' and the associated issues like selfish mining and illegal use of computation-intensive machines still remain. As a remedy, we discuss several possible alternatives. However, none of the remedies suggested are perfect and it appears that achieving true democracy in Bitcoin mining in practice is indeed a very difficult open problem.

2   Analysis of Weakness of the Proposal in [16]

The idea behind the approach of [16] was that each user generates a hash, based on which the miner of the next block is decided. The hash H is generated from the 7 fields mentioned in Table 1. The work [16] suggested to use the following hash function

$$H = \text{SHA256}(\text{SHA256}(V||H_p||T||U_p||H_t||R||P)). \tag{1}$$

in tandem with the originally proposed one by Nakamoto [2,15].

Table 1. Items used by the user to generate the hash.

Version (V)	Previous block hash (H_p)	Timestamp (T)	Bitcoin address (U_p)	Hash of merkle tree of verified transactions (H_t)	Nonce (R)	Padding (P)

The user whose hash is of minimum value amongst all the users in the system, is the winner and generates the next block. This user receives the transaction fees for all the transactions that are verified in his/her block and it is added to the block-chain as the next block. The winner also initiates a coin-base transaction to his/her public address and awards himself/herself with a specified amount of Bitcoins. This serves an additional incentive for verifying the blocks.

The work [16] suggested a distributed algorithm for the minimum hash computation, divided into 3 phases: hash generation phase, hash broadcast phase and hash verification stage. These 3 phases together run for 10 min and give the true minimum hash of the system. This duration is called the *time frame* which should be maintained by the Bitcoin system time.

The time for hash generation is specified as the first 2 min of the *time frame*. This time is maintained by the Timestamp T in the hash message. Any message that has been generated after this 2 min will be discarded.

In this section, we show that if a miner generates hashes with different nonce's and reports the minimum of these locally generated ones as the input to the distributed algorithm, then he/she increases his/her winning probability over the scenario if he/she would have just tried with one nonce and sent the single generated hash. In order to formally prove our claim, we need to study the order statistics of the hashes.

2.1 Preliminaries

In this section, we revisit the order statistics of discrete random variables for the special case of the minimum. In the next section, we apply this theoretical framework to establish our claim. Detailed treatise of order statistics can be found in any standard textbook on probability and statistics such as [20]. However, for the sake of completeness and for ease of reference, we mention only the key results that we would need.

The cumulative distribution function $F(x)$ of any discrete random variable X is the probability that the random variable takes a value less than or equal to x. In other words,

$$F(x) = \Pr(X \leq x) = \sum_{a \leq x} \Pr(X = a). \tag{2}$$

Naturally,

$$\Pr(X \geq x) = 1 - \Pr(X \leq x - 1) = 1 - F(x - 1). \tag{3}$$

Now consider n independently and identically distributed (i.i.d.) discrete random variables $X_1, X_2, \ldots, X_n$. Let $X_{\min}$ denote the minimum of these n quantities. From Eq. (3), we can write

$$\Pr(X_{\min} \geq x) = \prod_{i=1}^{n} \Pr(X_i \geq x) = (1 - F(x - 1))^n. \tag{4}$$

Hence, from Eq. (4), we can get

$$\Pr(X_{\min} = x) = \Pr(X_{\min} \geq x) - \Pr(X_{\min} \geq x + 1)$$
$$= (1 - F(x - 1))^n - (1 - F(x))^n. \tag{5}$$

In particular, when the random variables denote a random sample $(X_1, \ldots, X_n)$ from a uniform distribution over $\{0, \ldots, k - 1\}$ for some fixed integer k, then we can substitute $F(x)$ by $\frac{x+1}{k}$ in all the above expressions.

2.2   How Local Power Can Affect Global Democracy

Here we show that if a miner or a mining pool has a large computational resource, then they can increase their winning probability by generating many hashes by changing the nonce's and reporting the minimum of the hashes as the input to the distributed algorithm.

Suppose the range of the hash function family is $\{0, 1\}^b$ and let $k = 2^b$. In Bitcoins, typical value of b is 256; however, our analysis works in general and hence we do not assume any concrete values of the variables used in our analysis. Since H serves as a random function, we can model n independent hashes as a random sample of size n from a uniform distribution over $\{0, \ldots, k - 1\}$.

Suppose there are n miners and let $X_1, \ldots, X_n$ be their respective inputs to the minimum-finding algorithm $\mathcal{D}$. When no miner does local computation and submits the first hash that he/she obtains, $(X_1, \ldots, X_n)$ may be considered a random sample of size n from the uniform distribution over $\{0, \ldots, k - 1\}$. Without loss of generality, let us analyze the winning probability of the first miner.

$$\Pr(X_1 = X_{\min})$$
$$= \Pr(X_1 \leq \min\{X_2, \ldots, X_n\})$$
$$= \sum_{x=0}^{k-1} \Pr(\min\{X_2, \ldots, X_n\} = x \ \& \ X_1 \leq x)$$
$$= \sum_{x=0}^{k-1} \Pr(\min\{X_2, \ldots, X_n\} = x) \cdot \Pr(X_1 \leq x) \quad [\text{since } X_i\text{'s are independent}]$$
$$= \sum_{x=0}^{k-1} \left((1 - F(x - 1))^{n-1} - (1 - F(x))^{n-1}\right) \cdot F(x) \quad [\text{from Eq. (5)}]$$
$$= \sum_{x=0}^{k-1} \alpha(x)\beta_1(x) = P_1 \ (\text{say}), \tag{6}$$

where $\alpha(x) = (1 - F(x - 1))^{n-1} - (1 - F(x))^{n-1}$ and $\beta_1(x) = F(x)$.

Now, suppose that the first miner performs local generation of the m hashes $Y_1, \ldots, Y_m$ and submits their minimum $Y_{\min}$ as his/her input to $\mathcal{D}$, while each of others follow the honest strategy of generating only hash and submitting it to $\mathcal{D}$. Then

$$X_1 = Y_{\min} = \min\{Y_1, \ldots, Y_m\}.$$

Note that $(X_2, \ldots, X_n)$ can be treated as an independent random sample of size $n - 1$ from the uniform distribution over $\{0, \ldots, k - 1\}$. In this case,

$$
\begin{aligned}
&\Pr(X_1 = X_{\min}) \\
&= \Pr(X_1 \leq \min\{X_2, \ldots, X_n\}) \\
&= \sum_{x=0}^{k-1} \Pr(\min\{X_2, \ldots, X_n\} = x \ \& \ X_1 \leq x) \\
&= \sum_{x=0}^{k-1} \Pr(\min\{X_2, \ldots, X_n\} = x) \cdot \Pr(X_1 \leq x) \quad [\text{since } X_i\text{'s are independent}] \\
&= \sum_{x=0}^{k-1} \Pr(\min\{X_2, \ldots, X_n\} = x) \cdot \Pr(Y_{\min} \leq x) \quad [\text{since } X_1 = Y_{\min}] \\
&= \sum_{x=0}^{k-1} \Pr(\min\{X_2, \ldots, X_n\} = x) \cdot \left(\sum_{y=0}^{x} \Pr(\min\{Y_1, \ldots, Y_m\} = y) \right) \\
&= \sum_{x=0}^{k-1} \left((1 - F(x-1))^{n-1} - (1 - F(x))^{n-1} \right) \cdot
\end{aligned}
$$

$$
\left(\sum_{y=0}^{x} (1 - F(y-1))^m - (1 - F(y))^m \right) \quad [\text{from Eq. (5)}] \tag{7}
$$

$$
= \sum_{x=0}^{k-1} \left((1 - F(x-1))^{n-1} - (1 - F(x))^{n-1} \right) \cdot (1 - (1 - F(x))^m) \tag{8}
$$

$$
= \sum_{x=0}^{k-1} \alpha(x) \beta_m(x) = P_m \ (\text{say}), \tag{9}
$$

where $\alpha(x) = (1 - F(x-1))^{n-1} - (1 - F(x))^{n-1}$ is the same as before and $\beta_m(x) = 1 - (1 - F(x))^m$. Note that the second argument of the product in Eq. (7) is a telescoping sum and only the first and the last term in this sum remains after intermediate cancellations, yielding the second argument of the product in Eq. (8).

By comparing the expressions of the probabilities in Eqs. (6) and (9), we can state the following result.

Theorem 1. *Suppose there are n miners and P_m denotes the winning probability of a miner who first computes $m \geq 1$ hashes locally and submits their minimum as input to the minimum-finding algorithm, and all the other $n - 1$ miners generate only one hash for submission as input. Then $P_m \geq P_1$ and $\lim_{m \to \infty} P_m = 1$.*

Proof. Note that $\beta_2(x) \geq \beta_1(x)$ iff $1 - (1 - F(x))^m \geq F(x)$, or in other words, iff $1 - F(x) \geq (1 - F(x))^m$, which holds for all $m \geq 1$. This proves the first part of the Theorem.

As $m \longrightarrow \infty$, $(1 - F(x))^m \longrightarrow 0$, and hence $\beta_m(x) \longrightarrow 1$. Then from Eq. (9), the limiting value of P_m becomes

$$\sum_{x=0}^{k-1} \alpha(x) = \sum_{x=0}^{k-1} \left((1 - F(x - 1))^{n-1} - (1 - F(x))^{n-1} \right).$$

This is again a telescoping sum. After cancellation of the intermediate terms, only the first term, wich is 1, minus the last term, which is 0, remains, yielding the value of the sum as 1.   □

Thus, the miners can arbitrarily increase their winning probabilities by generating more and more local hashes. This leads to the same problems as PoW. Note that our result does not depend on the uniformity assumption. As long as the hashes are independently and identically distributed, the result still holds.

3   Possible Remedies and Their Implications

It is easy to see that using similar analysis as in Sect. 2, one can prove that replacing the minimum by the maximum or the median does not serve as the remedy of the problem of democracy. In all these functions, local computation helps the miners and hence the one with more computational resource has more advantage. In this section, we discuss what are the possible counter-measures to mitigate this problem.

3.1   A Statistical Solution

This solution is surprisingly simple and yet it recovers the democracy of mining. We replace the winning condition from *minimum* of the submitted hash values to the *mode* of these values. In other words, suppose that there are m users who submits the hash values as $H_1, \ldots, H_m$. Let $h_1, \ldots, h_\ell$ be the distinct values among $\{H_1, \ldots, H_m\}$. Let f_i be the frequency of h_i in all the inputs, $1 \leq i \leq \ell$. If f_t is the maximum of these frequencies, $1 \leq t \leq \ell$, then h_t is the mode. Suppose there are a total of r users who submitted the value h_t. Then amongst these r users, the one with the minimum timestamp is chosen as the winner.

The question is why the mode works, but not any other function of the submitted hashes? We have already discussed why the individual hashes can be thought to follow uniform distribution over $\{0, \ldots, k-1\}$. Note that the uniform distribution of a discrete random variable is special in the sense that any value in the domain of the random variable can be the mode. This automatically removes any possibility of acquiring any advantage by repeated local sampling by the miners. Naturally, if the mode exists, there will be multiple users whose submitted hash values will be equal to the mode. One can then resolve the ties by the timestamp; whoever has the minimum timestamp wins.

We keep the rest of the parameters same as in [16]. This includes the modified format of the block header, the inputs to the hash function as described in Table 1, the hash generation time limit of 2 mins, and the hash verification stage as the last phase of the distributed algorithm.

3.2   The Problem of Distributed Mode Computation

The work [16] suggested to use the algorithm described in [17] to find the minimum hash in distributed manner. We suggest to use the distributed algorithm of [13] for finding the mode. The work [13] describes one deterministic and another randomized algorithm for distributed mode computation. We suggest to use the deterministic one and it has the time complexity of $O(D + \ell)$, where D is the diameter of the network and ℓ is the number of distinct elements (hashes). If the edges are unweighted, a trivial upper-bound of the diameter of the network is the number of nodes (users) in the network.

3.3   A Cryptographic Problem

While the above solution is theoretically sound, in practice it has its own limitation. The range of the hash function used in Bitcoins is $\{0, 1, \ldots, 2^{256} - 1\}$. However, the number of Bitcoin users is only a few million. Since the hash function output is assumed to be uniformly distributed, the probability of two hash outputs to collide would be vanishingly small. This implies that the frequency of each distinct hash output will be 1 most of the time and so all the hash values generated are modes. This is a case of multiple modes and for this situation, the behaviour of the distributed algorithm of [13] is not specified. If all the values are determined to be modes, which is natural in case of the current standards of hash functions, the only solution is to arbitrarily pick up a winner or use the minimum timestamp criteria.

3.4   Reducing Hash Output Size

One may think that shrinking the range of the hash function to the same order as the number of users will solve the problem. It is more likely that a mode will exist in this case. But again, reducing hash output size will cause easy attacks on collision resistance, pre-image resistance and second pre-image resistance. This may lead to forging a valid transaction or other kinds of attacks.

3.5   Purely Timestamp-Based Solution

Other possible solutions may be to select a winner based solely on the timestamp. In order to restrict the rate of the number of blocks added, the system can set a minimum threshold for each timestamp. This forces the users to wait for certain period of time before they can submit their data. After they submit, a distributed algorithm can be used to find the user with the minimum timestamp as the winner. While this solves the problems associated with mode computation or hash size reduction, in order to have only legitimate transactions in the block-chain, one must ensure that the timestamps cannot be manipulated.

4 Conclusion and Future Work

In this paper, we have analyzed the weaknesses of the recently proposed alternative [16] of the existing Proof-of-Work protocol of Bitcoins. The PoW protocol has the problem of selfish mining and illegal use of computational resources, that are associated with non-democratic Bitcoin mining. We showed in this paper that the alternative proposal of [16] claims to avoid these problems, but in practice this proposal fails to meet this claim.

We also discussed possible remedies of the above problem and their limitations. Though none of the remedies are perfect, still it opens up new directions of research. As part of our future work, we plan to investigate the feasibility of designing a truly democratic mining. The motivation for searching a democratic mining strategy is not only to establish equanimity between computationally rich and poor, but also to minimize power consumption and pave the way for greener Bitcoins.

References

1. Bitcoin-Wiki. Bitcoin Wikipedia. https://en.bitcoin.it/wiki/Main_Page
2. Bitcoin-Wiki. Block hashing algorithm. https://en.bitcoin.it/wiki/Block_hashing_algorithm
3. Bitcoin-Wiki. Proof of Work Protocol. https://en.bitcoin.it/wiki/Proof_of_work
4. Bitcoin Magazine. Government bans Professor mining bitcoin supercomputer. http://bitcoinmagazine.com/13774/government-bans-professor-mining-bitcoin-supercomputer/
5. Blockchain. Average Transaction Confirmation Time. http://blockchain.info/charts/avg-confirmation-time?timespan=2year&showDataPoints=false&daysAverageString=1&show_header=true&scale=0&address=
6. Blockchain. Blocks. https://en.bitcoin.it/wiki/Block
7. Blockchain. Transactions. https://en.bitcoin.it/wiki/Transaction
8. CoinDesk. Under the Microscope: Economic and Environmental Costs of Bitcoin Mining. http://www.coindesk.com/microscope-economic-environmental-costs-bitcoin-mining/
9. Eyal, Ittay and Sirer, Emin Gün Sirer. Majority is not enough: Bitcoin mining is vulnerable. CoRR, abs/1311.0243 (2013)
10. Forbes. Brilliant But Evil: Gaming Company Fined $1 Million For Secretly Using Players' Computers To Mine Bitcoin. http://www.forbes.com/sites/kashmirhill/2013/11/19/brilliant-but-evil-gaming-company-turned-players-computers-into-unwitting-bitcoin-mining-slaves/
11. Frequently Asked Questions. Transactions. https://bitcoin.org/en/faq#why-do-i-have-to-wait-10-minutes
12. Gizmodo. The World's Most Powerful Computer Network Is Being Wasted on Bitcoin. http://gizmodo.com/the-worlds-most-powerful-computer-network-is-being-was-504503726

13. Kuhn, F., Locher, T., Schmid,S.: Distributed computation of the mode. In: Bazzi, R.A., Patt-Shamir, B. (eds.) Proceedings of the Twenty-Seventh Annual ACM Symposium on Principles of Distributed Computing, PODC 2008, Toronto, Canada, 18–21 August 2008, pp. 15–24. ACM (2008)
14. Learn Cryptography. 51% Attack. http://learncryptography.com/51-attack/
15. Nakamoto, S.: Bitcoin: A peer-to-peer electronic cash system. May 2009
16. Paul, G., Sarkar, P., Mukherjee, S.: Towards a more democratic mining in bitcoins. In: Prakash, A., Shyamasundar, R. (eds.) ICISS 2014. LNCS, vol. 8880, pp. 185–203. Springer, Heidelberg (2014)
17. Santoro, N.: Design and Analysis of Distributed Algorithms. Wiley Series on Parallel and Distributed Computing, pp. 71–76. Wiley-Interscience, Hoboken (2006)
18. The Guardian. Student uses university computers to mine Dogecoin. http://www.theguardian.com/technology/2014/mar/04/dogecoin-bitcoin-imperial-college-student-mine
19. The Harvard Crimson. Harvard Research Computing Resources Misused for Dogecoin Mining Operation. http://www.thecrimson.com/article/2014/2/20/harvard-odyssey-dogecoin/
20. Wackerly, D.D., Mendenhall III, W., Scheaffer, R.L.: Mathematical Statistics with Applications. Duxbury Advanced Series, sixth edition (2002)
21. Wikipedia. Proof-of-stake – Wikipedia, The Free Encyclopedia. http://en.wikipedia.org/w/index.php?title=Proof-of-stake&oldid=615023202

FlowMiner: Automatic Summarization of Library Data-Flow for Malware Analysis

Tom Deering[1], Ganesh Ram Santhanam[2], and Suresh Kothari[2(✉)]

[1] Workiva, 2900 Unversity Blvd, Ames, IA 50010, USA
tomdeering7@gmail.com
[2] Department of Electrical and Computer Engineering,
Iowa State University, Ames, IA 50011, USA
{gsanthan,kothari}@iastate.edu

Abstract. Malware often conceal their malicious behavior by making unscrupulous use of library APIs. Hence any accurate malware analysis must track data-flows not only through the application but also through the library. Libraries like Android (2 mLOC) are too large to be analyzed repeatedly with each application, hence we need to compute data-flow summaries of libraries that are expressive enough to reveal possible malicious flows, and compact to be included in malware analysis along with each application.

We present FlowMiner, a novel approach to automatically extract the data-flow summary of a Java library, given its source or bytecode. FlowMiner's summaries are **fine-grained**, i.e., preserve key artifacts from the original library to enable accurate context, object, field, flow and type-sensitive malware analysis of applications in conjunction with the library. Unlike prior summarization techniques, FlowMiner resolves method calls to **anonymous classes** *to a single target*, making it more precise. FlowMiner's summaries are **compact**, e.g., contain only about a third (fourth) of the nodes (edges, resp.) in the data-flow semantics of recent versions of Android. FlowMiner's summaries are stored in XML, allowing any analysis tool to use them for analysis.

1 Introduction

Modern software is increasingly built on top of reusable libraries, and when such libraries are large, the static analysis of an application together with its libraries becomes prohibitively expensive. An alternative is to analyze an application

http://powerofpi.github.io/FlowMiner/.

This material is based on research sponsored by DARPA under agreement numbers FA8750-15-2-0080 and FA8750-12-2-0126. The U.S. Government is authorized to reproduce and distribute reprints for Governmental purposes notwithstanding any copyright notation thereon. The views and conclusions contained herein are those of the authors and should not be interpreted as necessarily representing the official policies or endorsements, either expressed or implied, of DARPA or the U.S. Government.

© Springer International Publishing Switzerland 2015
S. Jajodia and C. Mazumdar (Eds.): ICISS 2015, LNCS 9478, pp. 171–191, 2015.
DOI: 10.1007/978-3-319-26961-0_11

without its libraries. However, for security-critical analyses, this is inaccurate because it discounts data flow through the libraries. In particular for malware detection [14,17,20,26], such inaccuracies are unacceptable because the data flows through the library may provide the critical piece of missing evidence to reveal the malicious behavior of an application.

For example, Android [7,19] applications (apps) are often significantly smaller than the Android framework itself. While a typical app may have of the order of 100 k LOC, Android 4.4.4 (KitKat) [2] contains over 2 million LOC. Further, Android allows many mechanisms for information flows that pass back and forth between the app (many of which are asynchronous), all of which must necessarily be incorporated into an analysis to uncover possible malicious behaviors. This is not specific to Android however; in most malware analysis and other security audit use cases, it is essential to account for data flows through the library in order to avoid missed detections.

Library Summaries for Malware Detection. This paper focuses on the creation of the data flow summary of a Java library, which is a subset of the original data flow semantics of the library. It is desirable that the summary is (a) *compact*, i.e., is smaller than the library, and (b) *fine-grained*, i.e., preserves enough information so that it can be used (instead of the entire library) when analyzing an application to allow accurate detection of malicious flows. Summaries are application-agnostic, and once created be reused for analyzing any application.

Prior work on summarizing libraries are inadequate as their summaries are too *coarse* to be used accurately in a future analysis. For example, in [11], flows to or from a field in a class are counted as flow to or from the object, and the summary of a method is represented as simple mappings between its input parameters and return values. These preclude the summary from being used in a subsequent sensitive analysis accurately. Similarly, [22] does not resolve calls to anonymous classes as monomorphic, although such calls only have a single target. Hence, there is a need for algorithms and tools that compute fine-grained, compact and application-agnostic summaries of a library's semantics with enough information to be reused accurately in any future analyses of an application that uses the library.

FLOWMINER. In this work we present FLOWMINER, a novel approach to automatically extract *fine-grained* yet *compact* data-flow summaries of a Java library. We employ a *graphical summarization* paradigm wherein the library summary is expressed as a multi-attributed directed graph, which is more expressive than coarse, binary relationships between inputs and outputs. FLOWMINER extracts application-agnostic summary data-flow graph semantics through a one-time analysis of library bytecode. This summary is stored in a portable format, and can be reused by other analysis tools to accurately, scalably analyze applications.

FLOWMINER's summaries are **fine-grained** because they preserve *key artifacts* in the library that provide crucial information about its data-flow semantics. For example, individual field definitions must be present if a summary is to be used in a field-sensitive way, and individual call sites must be preserved if library callbacks are to be captured. We found that more than 90 % of summarized field flows will be false positives if field definitions are not retained (we present empirical results of our experiments that support this claim in Sect. 6). Consequently, FLOWMINER preserves fields, method call sites, literal values, and formal and informal method parameters and return values as *key* artifacts in the summary data-flow.

FLOWMINER's summaries are **compact** because FLOWMINER removes from the summary non-key features (e.g., irrelevant def-use chains of assignments that do not contribute flow information), which are of value to subsequent analyses. FLOWMINER also resolves method calls to **anonymous classes** *to a single target*, making it more precise. FLOWMINER *elides* (replaces paths with edges) these uninteresting flow details to arrive at a compact data-flow graph containing only the key artifacts crucial to the data-flow and reachability information between them (e.g., FLOWMINER's Android summary contains only about a third of the nodes and a fifth of the edges of the original program graph). Arguably, this makes subsequent analyses to be more scalable when using our summary versus the original library. Importantly, FLOWMINER is **sound** in the following sense – each flow preserved in FLOWMINER's summary is *actually possible* at runtime in the context of some application.

Contributions. In summary, the following are the contributions of this paper.

- A static analysis technique to automatically generate *fine-grained, expressive* data flow summary given the source or bytecode of any Java library that
  - Preserves *key artifacts* of the program semantics needed *to allow subsequent context, object, flow, field, and type-sensitive data-flow analyses*
  - Uses a *rich, multi-attributed graph as the mathematical abstraction* to encode fine-grained summaries
  - Extracts *compact* summaries much smaller than the original library by eliding *non-key features* in the flows of the original library into key paths.
- FLOWMINER, *an open-source reference implementation* [12] of our algorithms that extracts summaries given the source or bytecode of a library and exports them to a portable, tool-agnostic format.
- Evaluation of FLOWMINER's compactness and expressiveness on the recent versions of Android, and a comparison with the state-of-the-art.

Organization. The rest of the paper is organized as follows. Section 2 provides a motivating example of an Android application whose malicious behavior cannot be detected without data-flow semantics for the Android library. Section 3 outlines our approach, Sects. 4 and 5 provide algorithmic and implementation details of FLOWMINER. We evaluate our work in Sect. 6, compare it with prior work in Sect. 7, and conclude in Sect. 8.

2 Motivating Example

We put forward a motivating example of an Android application with a malicious behavior that cannot be detected without including the data-flow semantics of

```
 1  public class MainActivity extends Activity {
 2    private String deviceID;
 3    private String simSerial;
 4    private AsyncTask<String,Void,Void> at;
 5    @Override
 6    protected void onCreate(Bundle savedInstanceState) {
 7    TelephonyManager tm = (TelephonyManager) getSystemService(Context.
          TELEPHONY_SERVICE);
 8    deviceID = tm.getDeviceId();
 9    simSerial = tm.getSimSerialNumber();
10    at = new AsyncTask<String,Void,Void>(){
11      @Override
12      protected Void doInBackground(String... params) {
13        try {  String url = "http://evil.com/";
14               for(String s : params){ url += "&" + s; }
15               new URL(url).openConnection();
16        } catch (IOException e) {}
17        return null;
18        }
19    };
20    }
21    @Override
22    protected void onPause(){at.execute(deviceID, simSerial);}
23  }
```

Listing 1.1. Malicious Android app that uses Android's AsyncTask library class to leak data

the library (Android) or its summary in an analysis. While we illustrate the need to summarize data-flow semantics of libraries using an Android example, it arises in many applications not limited to malware detection, Android, or even the Java programming language. The techniques we propose in this paper for data-flow summarization are generic and widely-applicable.

Malicious App. Let us see the difficulty an analyst would encounter in detecting malware in an app without including the Android library or its appropriate summary. In the Android app shown in Listing 1.1, MainActivity is a subclass of Activity, so it defines an application screen. It overrides two lifecycle methods; the Android framework will call onCreate when MainActivity is initialized for the first time, and it will call onPause when MainActivity loses user focus. Therefore, at some point when this app is run, there will be a call to onCreate followed by a call to onPause. This triggers a latent malicious behavior.

Consider the onCreate method. On lines 8–9, the app retrieves the device ID and SIM card serial number, writing them to member fields. Lines 10–20 define and instantiate an anonymous AsyncTask, which is a threading mechanism defined by the Android library. A call to AsyncTask.execute(params) causes Android to run the object's doInBackground(params) method in a new thread, passing along the same arguments. Line 10 writes this anonymous AsyncTask object to a member field.

If we examine onPause(), we see that the AsyncTask is asynchronously executed with the device ID and SIM card serial number as arguments. The doIn Background method constructs a shady URL for a server operated by an attacker on lines 13–16, appending the sensitive information to the URL. Line 15 opens a connection, causing an HTTP GET request to be issued to the malicious server. This application behavior clearly will leak sensitive device data to http://evil.com.

Analysis Without Summaries. Consider how an analyst would hope to detect the malicious flow using a state-of-the-art static analysis tool without including the entire Android framework in the analysis. The analyst would first define `TelephonyManager.getDeviceId` and `TelephonyManager.getSimSerialNumber` to be sensitive information *sources*, and any constructor of `URL` to be a sensitive information *sink*. The analyst would then run a static analysis tool, hoping to detect data-flows from any of the sources to any of the sinks. Observe that static analysis tools can follow the data-flows from Android's `TelephonyManager` into the `onCreate` method, then through member field definitions, leading to the parameters of a call to `AsyncTask.execute` (defined by Android). The analyzer can follow the flow no further, as it has no information about the internal (private) implementation of `AsyncTask`. Thus static analysis fails to detect the malicious data-flow because data-flow semantics for the Android library are unavailable.

To solve this problem and identify the malicious flow via static analysis, we either have to (a) resort to whole-program analysis by including the entire Android implementation along with the app as input to the static analyzer, which is prohibitively expensive; or (b) include *summary data-flow semantics* for Android that precisely define the data-flow information between Android components necessary to track data-flow through Android. In this example, we require a summary of how data passed to `AsyncTask.execute` flows through the private implementation of Android and back into the app via asynchronous callback.

In Sect. 3, we provide an overview of our solution for computing precise summaries of a library. We perform an automatic, one-time extraction of summary data-flow semantics within a given library (such as Android). We demonstrate how these summaries can be grafted into the partial program analysis context, enabling us to detect the malicious program behavior presented in the example above. The resolution of this example is described in Sect. 5.

2.1 Background: Graph Schema to Represent Program Semantics

We use the graph paradigm for representing and reasoning with a program's structure and semantics. In this paradigm, the structure and semantics of a program $\mathfrak{P}$ is represented as a rich multi-attributed software graph called *program graph*, denoted $G(\mathfrak{P})$. The nodes of $G(\mathfrak{P})$ correspond to artifacts of $\mathfrak{P}$ such as variables, parameters to a method, call sites, classes, methods, etc., and the edges correspond to structural (e.g., contains, overrides, extends, etc.) and semantic (e.g., data-flow, call, control flow, etc.) relationships between those artifacts. We use the Atlas[13] platform to generate $G(\mathfrak{P})$ given $\mathfrak{P}$[1]. Atlas stores $G(\mathfrak{P})$ in an XML format following the eXtensible Common Software Graph (XCSG) [3]

---

[1] We omit details of the Atlas platform; the interested reader can refer [13].

schema, an open XML standard, and provides a language to query $G(\mathfrak{P})$. We use this query language in our implementation to extract relevant information needed for constructing the data-flow summary of $\mathfrak{P}$.

The artifacts in $G(\mathfrak{P})$ that serve as raw material for our summary extraction approach include:

- Program declarative structure
- Type hierarchy relationships (type points to a type it extends or implements)
- Method override relationships (method points to a method definition that it overrides)
- Static type relationships (variable points to its declared type)
- Call site information: Method signature, Type to search, Informal parameters
- Pre-computed data-flow relationships (variable points to its flow destination): Field reads and writes, Local def-use chains, Local array accesses.

3   Approach

In this section we provide a high-level overview of our novel approach to automatically-extract summary library data-flow semantics. Our approach has the following desirable attributes:

- Targets JVM bytecode for wide applicability
- Automatically extracts summaries without manual effort
- Retains enough details to enable context, object, field, flow and type-sensitive analysis of applications using the library
- Uses portable encoding to allow use by any analysis tool
- Summaries are much smaller than a library itself.

Notation. We begin by introducing the notation and concepts needed to explain the algorithmic aspects of our approach. Let $\mathfrak{P}$ be a program, and $G(\mathfrak{P})$ be its corresponding program graph. Let M be the set of methods defined in $\mathfrak{P}$. For each method $m_i \in M$ let the set $P_i = \{p_1^i, p_2^i \dots p_{|P_i|}^i\}$ denote the formal parameters to m_i, and r_i its return. We denote a method call site by $c := \langle m_j, t^c, P^c, r^c \rangle$ with P^c denoting the set of arguments (parameters passed) from the call site c to m_j and r^c denoting the returned type from m_j. t^c denotes either the `Class` where m_j is defined (if c is a static dispatch), or else the stated type of the reference on which m_j is invoked (if c is a dynamic dispatch). Statically-dispatched call sites do not require runtime information to calculate the target of the call. These include calls to static methods and constructors. Dynamically-dispatched call sites *do* require runtime information to calculate the destination, as is the case for calls to general member methods.

Remark 1. An interesting case arises when an application defines a subtype of a library type – this may introduce new potential runtime targets in the application for dynamic dispatch call sites in the library (callbacks). For example, an application may define implementations of the `java.util.List` interface and

```
1  static int average(List<Integer> l)
2  {   int lSum = sum(l); int lLength = l.size(); return lSum/lLength; }
3  static int sum(List<Integer> l)
4  { int s = 0;   for(Integer i : l)  s += i;   return s; }
```

Listing 1.2. Computing the average and sum of a set of Integers.

pass instances of these types as parameters of calls to the library. Hence, in order for the computed data-flow summaries of the library to be strictly application-agnostic and complete, they cannot pre-resolve a dynamically-dispatched callsite a priori. Our approach to computing data-flow summaries adheres to this principle, which we call the **open world assumption** for computing summaries.

Illustration of Approach. To illustrate the approach taken to extract summaries from $G(\mathfrak{P})$, consider the two methods, sum and average, defined in Listing 1.2. A subset of the program graph $G(\mathfrak{P})$ for the corresponding code is shown in Fig. 1. Our goal is to arrive at the data-flow summaries in Fig. 2. Observe that the summary graph is derived from the original program graph $G(\mathfrak{P})$; undistinguished nodes from $G(\mathfrak{P})$ are removed to simplify the summary flow semantics. However, the summary graph retains critical features of the flows such as literal values, call sites, method signature elements, which we identify as *key* nodes in the program graph, and the flows between them.

To get from $G(\mathfrak{P})$ in Fig. 1 to $G^S(\mathfrak{P})$ in Fig. 2, we perform the following high-level steps:

1. Compute the program graph $G(\mathfrak{P})$
2. Identify key nodes in $G(\mathfrak{P})$ (colored cyan in Fig. 1)
3. Compute flows between key nodes, eliding paths through non-key nodes into simple edges (details in Sect. 4.1)
4. Compute inter-procedural summary flows by analyzing callsites (in Sect. 4.2).

We note important differences between the program graph $G(\mathfrak{P})$ and the summary graph $G^S(\mathfrak{P})$ obtained. Nodes in $G(\mathfrak{P})$ that are important or *key* features of a data-flow, such as formal method parameters, method return nodes, and literal values, are all retained in $G^S(\mathfrak{P})$. On the other hand, intermediate nodes and edges in the program graph between *key* nodes are *elided* in the summary. For Listing 1.2, the *key* nodes in $G(\mathfrak{P})$ are colored cyan in Fig. 1; these are the only nodes retained in the summary graph (Fig. 2).

When intermediate nodes along a flow from key node k_1 to k_2 are removed from the program graph, a summary edge is introduced between k_1 to k_2 to convey the existence of a summary data-flow. For example, in the summary of the average method, the nodes corresponding to the variables lSum, lLength, and the operator / are intermediate nodes in Fig. 1 that are *elided* in the summary in Fig. 2. In their place are direct summary flow edges from the callsites of sum and List.size to the return value of the method.

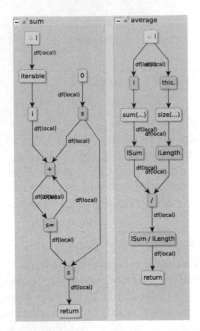

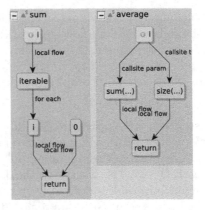

Fig. 1. Partial program graph for Listing 1.2 with key nodes colored cyan (Color figure online)

Fig. 2. Elided local flow summary $G^S(\mathfrak{P})$ for Fig. 1 (Color figure online)

In the next section, we describe algorithms for each high-level step listed above to automatically compute $G^S(\mathfrak{P})$ from $G(\mathfrak{P})$.

4   Automatic Summary Extraction

Given a Java library program $\mathfrak{P}$, we perform a one-time analysis of $\mathfrak{P}$ to construct the program graph $G(\mathfrak{P})$ (see Sect. 2.1). We explain our technique for summary computation in two parts. Section 4.1 describes in detail our algorithm to compute summaries of (local) data-flows within each method. Section 4.2 describes the corresponding algorithms to compute interprocedural data-flows.

4.1   Mining Local Flows

Before describing the algorithm to mine summary data-flows local to a method, we first identify *key* nodes in $G(\mathfrak{P})$.

Key Nodes. We define *key* nodes as precisely those nodes in the $G(\mathfrak{P})$ that must be preserved in the summary graph $G^S(\mathfrak{P})$. For the language of Java, the nodes we consider key include: (i) *method signature elements* (formal parameters, formal implicit identity parameter, return node), (ii) *call sites* (informal parameters, informal implicit identity parameter, return value), (iii) *fields*, (iv) *literal* *values*, (v) *definitions written to and read from fields*, (vi) *array access operators and operands* (array reference operand, array index operand), (vii) *for-each loop iterables and receivers*, (viii) *array components*.

Remark 2. The key nodes in $G(\mathfrak{P})$ will differ based on the language of the library, and hence the notion of key nodes must be well defined for the library's language prior to using our approach. For example, $G(\mathfrak{P})$ for a library written in the C language may contain other key nodes such as pointers to fields and functions.

The algorithm for extracting a summary of local data-flows (i.e., within a method) is based on the idea of *eliding pre-processed def-use chains with respect to the set of* key *nodes* in the method. Given the program graph $G(\mathfrak{P})$, we begin by identifying the set K of *key* nodes in the graph, and then reduce $G(\mathfrak{P})$ by preserving only the nodes in K and the reachability information among them. As a result, all intermediate data-flow nodes and edges that occur on paths between key nodes are *elided* for each method, resulting in a summary graph $G^S(\mathfrak{P})$ that is much smaller than $G(\mathfrak{P})$. Def-use paths occurring between key nodes in a method are merged into simple edges, but key nodes are never elided.

Extracting Summary Flows. Given the set K and the *pre-processed* data-flow graph of def-use chains that can be derived from $G(\mathfrak{P})$, Algorithm 1 computes elided summary data-flows with respect to K. The procedure MineFlow iterates over the key nodes in K. For each $k \in K$, MineFlow finds the set $K' \subseteq K$ of other key nodes that are reachable along data-flow paths that *do not include other key nodes as intermediates*, using procedure ElidedFlow (Line 3). For each key node $k' \in K'$, MineFlow introduces a summary flow edge from k to k' (Lines 4–5).

Eliding Intermediate Nodes. The procedure ElidedFlow computes the set of nearest-reachable key nodes K' for a given key node k by exploring the data-flow graph breadth-first starting from k. The procedure maintains a frontier containing the set of nodes that have to be processed, initialized to $\{k\}$. In each iteration, it adds each node f' in the frontier that has a key node successor to the return value (Lines 14–16); and otherwise, it is added to the frontier so that further key nodes potentially reachable from k via f' can be searched in a future iteration (Lines 14,17–18). ElidedFlow terminates when all nodes in the frontier have been processed (Line 12); since there are clearly finite number of nodes in a frontier, ElidedFlow always terminates. The set of nodes returned by ElidedFlow is exactly the set of key nodes reachable from k via non-key intermediate nodes.

Remark 3. The attributes labeling each summary edge are determined based on the kind of summary relationship being represented. For instance, if the origin or destination is a field definition, then the edge will be labeled with attributes indicating that it is a data-flow from or to a field.

Our summary also stores other kinds of relationships including array accesses, dynamic callsite information, for-each iteration, and resolved flows to methods. These relationships from $G(\mathfrak{P})$ are included in $G^S(\mathfrak{P})$.

Algorithm 1. Mining summary data-flows

procedure MINEFLOW(K, $G(\mathfrak{P})$)
2:      **for all** $k \in K$ **do**
            $K' \leftarrow$ ElidedFlow(k, K, $G(\mathfrak{P})$)
4:          **for all** $k' \in K'$ **do**
                Add summary flow edge from k to k'
6:          **end for**
        end for
8: **end procedure**

procedure ELIDEDFLOW(k, K, $G(\mathfrak{P})$)
10:     frontier $\leftarrow \{k\}$
        result $\leftarrow \{\emptyset\}$
12:     **for all** $f \in$ frontier **do**
            frontier $\leftarrow$ frontier - f
14:         **for all** f' s.t. (f, f') is a data-flow edge in $G(\mathfrak{P})$ **do**
                if $f' \in K$ **then**
16:                 result $\leftarrow$ result $\cup f'$
                else if $f' \notin$ frontier **then**
18:                 frontier $\leftarrow$ frontier $\cup f'$
                end if
20:         **end for**
        end for
            return result
22: **end procedure**

4.2   Mining Interprocedural Flows

The task of mining interprocedural flows involved in method calls, as well as dynamic call site information, is somewhat more complex. First, we must decide which call sites to resolve at present (during summary generation) and which cannot be resolved until summaries are applied in the context of an analysis. If a potential target of a call site may lay outside of the library after an application is introduced into the analysis context, then we *must not* resolve targets of the call site at this time. Clearly static dispatches can be resolved during summary generation, because the targets are unambiguous even with an open-world assumption about future analysis contexts (see Remark 1).

Resolvable and Unresolvable Call Sites. It is important to distinguish between call sites that can be statically-resolved and those which cannot at the time of summary generation. By pre-resolving those which are statically-resolvable to their targets, we generate *sound* data-flow relationships that a client can use, and prevent future rework by clients. Additionally, direct interprocedural flows are more compact to express than leaving a callsite description in the summaries. Thus, it is preferable to identify and resolve statically-dispatchable callsites at the time of summary generation.

```
1 public final class Integer extends Number implements Comparable<Integer> {
2     private final int value;
3     public Integer(int value) { this.value = value; }
4     public byte byteValue() { return (byte) value; }
5     public int compareTo(Integer object) { return compare(value,object.
          value);  }
6     public static int compare(int lhs, int rhs) {
7       return lhs < rhs ? -1 : (lhs == rhs ? 0 : 1); }  ...
8 }
```

Listing 1.3. Partial implementation of Integer from the Java standard library

Although dynamic dispatches are not statically-resolvable in general, they become so under certain circumstances. For instance, a call to a member method marked `final` or `private` cannot possibly have polymorphic behavior, even under an open-world assumption. Similarly, a call to a member method within a type that is marked `final` or `anonymous` is also unable to result in polymorphism.

The algorithm to mine interprocedural summary flows is shown in Algorithm 2. The procedure `MineCallsiteSummaries` in Algorithm 2 calls the procedure `ClassifyCallsites` to partition the set C of call sites as described above and returns (a) R^+ containing call sites for which targets may be unambiguously resolved even in the face of an open-world assumption at the time of summary generation, and (b) R^- containing call sites for which multiple targets (presently, or in a future analysis context), may be resolved.

Next, the procedure `MineMethodFlows` is called for R^+. For each call site, this procedure resolves the target using a dispatch calculation[2] (line 23) and adds summary flow edges in $G^S(\mathfrak{P})$ connecting the informal call site parameters Pc to the corresponding formal parameters P_j in the (resolved) target method m_j's definition (lines 24–27). `MineMethodFlows` concludes by connecting the return flows from the return value in the resolved method m_j to the receiving variable at the call site (line 29). Finally, `MineDynamicDispatch` is called on R^-, wherein the dynamic dispatch information for each call site in the $G(\mathfrak{P})$ is retained in the summary $G^S(\mathfrak{P})$ (lines 34–37) so that a client can resolve them in a future analysis context. `MineCallsiteSummaries` terminates despite the presence of recursive calls, as it iterates over the (finite number of) callsites only once.

4.3 Summary Extraction Example

Consider the `Integer` class from the Java standard library, a subset of which we show in Listing 1.3. Its summaries are shown in Fig. 3, where elements of $G^S(\mathfrak{P})$ are colored magenta. Note that due to Algorithm 1, e.g., the conditional operators and intermediate definitions in the `compare` method have been elided; and due to Algorithm 2 `compareTo` method has a statically-resolvable call to `compare`. FLOWMINER has resolved the call automatically, showing the flow of the two informal parameters in `compareTo` to the formal parameter and identity

---

[2] Recall that each call site in R^+ can be resolved to a single target.

Algorithm 2. Mining method flows and dynamic callsite information relationships

---

     procedure MINECALLSITESUMMARIES($\mathcal{C}$)

2:     $\langle R^+, R^- \rangle$ = CLASSIFYCALLSITES($\mathcal{C}$)

     MINEMETHODFLOWS(R^+)

4:     MINEDYNAMICDISPATCH(R^-)

     end procedure

6: **procedure** CLASSIFYCALLSITES($\mathcal{C}$)

     $R^+ \leftarrow \emptyset$

8:     $R^- \leftarrow \emptyset$

     for all $c \in \mathcal{C}$ **do**

10:         **if** c is a static dispatch **then**

             $R^+ \leftarrow R^+ \cup c$

12:         **else if** m_i is **final** $\vee$ **private** $\vee$ **constructor** **then**

             $R^+ \leftarrow R^+ \cup c$

14:         **else if** t is **final** $\vee$ **private** $\vee$ **anonymous** $\vee$ **array** **then**

             $R^+ = R^+ \cup c$

16:         **else**

             $R^- = R^- \cup c$

18:         **end if**

     end for

       return $\langle R^+, R^- \rangle$

20: **end procedure**

     procedure MINEMETHODFLOWS($\mathcal{C}$)

22:     **for all** $c := \langle m_i, Pc, r^c, t^c \rangle \in \mathcal{C}$ **do**

         $m_j \leftarrow$ dispatch(c)   ▷ *Unambiguous resolution of c to m_j*

24:         $P^c \leftarrow \{p_1^c, p_2^c \ldots p_{|Pc|}^c\}$ ▷ *Arguments passed at callsite c*

         $P_j \leftarrow \{p_1^j, p_2^j \ldots p_{|P_j|}^j\}$ ▷ *Formal parameters to m_j*

26:         **for all** $p_k^c \in P^c$ **do**

             Add method flow summary edge (p_k^c, p_k^j) to $G^S(\mathfrak{P})$

28:         **end for**

         Add return flow summary edge (r_j, r^c) to $G^S(\mathfrak{P})$

30:     **end for**

     end procedure

32: **procedure** MINEDYNAMICDISPATCH($\mathcal{C}$)

     for all $c := \langle m_i, Pc, r^c, t^c \rangle \in \mathcal{C}$ **do**

34:         Add dynamic callsite method edge (c, m_i) to $G^S(\mathfrak{P})$

         Add dynamic callsite type edge (c, t) to $G^S(\mathfrak{P})$

36:         **for all** $p_k^c \in P^c$ **do**

             Add dynamic callsite param edge (p_k^c, c) to $G^S(\mathfrak{P})$

38:         **end for**

     end for

40: **end procedure**

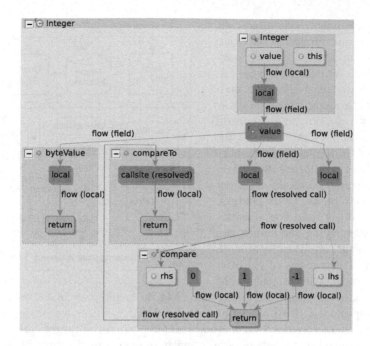

Fig. 3. Summary extraction results for the `Integer` class (Color figure online)

parameters of `compare`, and the corresponding flow of the return value back to `compareTo`. This example also illustrates field reads and writes, which were imported directly to $G^S(\mathfrak{P})$ from $G(\mathfrak{P})$ during mining. This summary graph enables accurate tracking of flows through the `Integer` class.

5   Implementation

Architecture. FLOWMINER is implemented as a plugin for the popular Eclipse IDE. As shown in the architectural diagram of Fig. 4, FLOWMINER takes Java library bytecode as input, typically in the form of a JAR archive. This is passed to Atlas that constructs an XCSG representation of the program graph (see Sect. 2.1) for the library. FLOWMINER then runs the algorithms described in Sect. 4 to extract a summarized version of the library's data-flow semantics from the library's program graph. This summary data-flow graph is packaged into a portable XML format according to a schema that extends the XCSG schema [3] that can be used to parse and import summaries into existing tools.

An XML schema definition (XSD) for expressing summary graphs in XML is provided with the open source reference implementation of FLOWMINER [12]. This can be used by other static analysis tools to parse and import the data-flow summary of a library for analysis of an application that uses the library.

It is worth noting two important features of our summary schema. *First*, our summaries pertain only to data-flow. While a flow edge (A, B) implies the existence of a control flow path along which this flow happens, we do not retain control flow nodes and edges from $G(\mathfrak{P})$. This allows $G^S(\mathfrak{P})$ to be much more compact than the library itself. *Second*, our summaries retain sufficient information to be used with context, type, field, object, and flow sensitivity. The client using the summaries for subsequent analysis is able to decide which categories of sensitivity to employ in order to achieve the desired level of accuracy and speed. One consequence of this philosophy

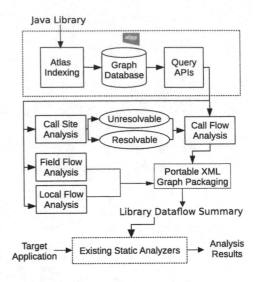

Fig. 4. Architecture of FLOWMINER

is that we only resolve flows for method call sites when the target can be unambiguously resolved to a single possibility with an open-world assumption, i.e., no matter what other types and methods are introduced into an analysis context by an application, the resolution decision for the call site cannot be changed. We leave dynamic dispatch call sites to be resolved when summaries are applied to an analysis context, since we cannot know ahead of time if that context may introduce new possibilities for the target of the call site. However, we do provide the signature of the call site, as well as the informal stack parameters involved in the call, so that clients may resolve it later.

Using Summaries. Existing static analyzers can apply summaries generated by FLOWMINER to perform a complete and accurate program analysis. What it means to *apply* summaries will differ based on the tooling used by the analyzer. For instance, an analyzer implemented on top of the Atlas platform would 'apply' summaries by translating the portable XML summary document into additional nodes and edges from $G^S(\mathfrak{P})$ for insertion into the program graph $G(\mathfrak{P})$ of an application. Once inserted, these supplementary data-flow semantics will be included in any subsequent analysis.

Recall the example malicious Android app from Sect. 2, for which a static analyzer was unable to detect the malicious behavior. The application asynchronously leaks the user's device ID and SIM card number to an attacker. We defined the values returned by `TelephonyManager.getSimSerialNumber` and `TelephonyManager.getDeviceId` to be sensitive information, and asked our analyzer to track forward data-flows from these artifacts. The result ran into a dead end as soon as the flow disappeared into the private implementation of Android's `AsyncTask.execute` API.

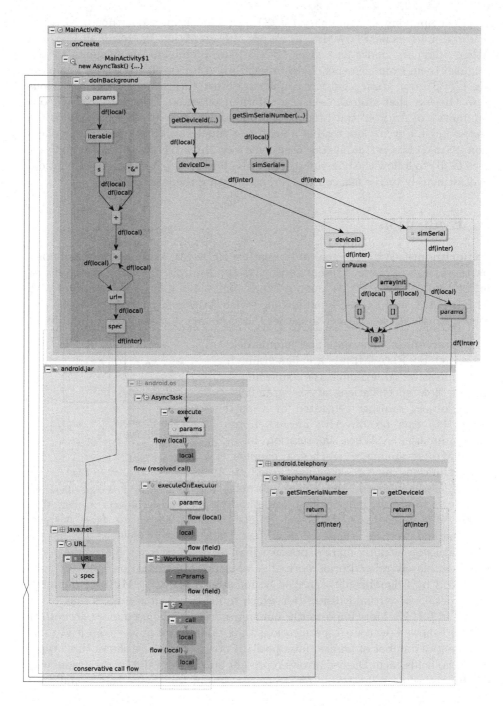

Fig. 5. Partial program analysis of malicious app from Listing 1.1 *with* FLOWMINER *summaries of Android* (Color figure online)

After applying the summary $G^S(\mathfrak{P})$ extracted from a one-time analysis of Android 4.4.4 using FLOWMINER, we are able to obtain the result in Fig. 5 on Atlas. Summary nodes and edges ($G^S(\mathfrak{P})$) are highlighted in magenta to distinguish them from elements of the original program graph ($G(\mathfrak{P})$). By employing $G^S(\mathfrak{P})$, our static analyzer is able to detect the entirety of the malicious flow. Observe that after the sensitive information enters AsyncTask.execute, our summaries of Android track the asynchronous data-flow involving local flows, a method call, a write and read of a field, and finally a callback into the application (MainActivity$1.doInBackground) on a new thread. From there, our analyzer uses $G(\mathfrak{P})$ to follow the flow through an enhanced for loop, string concatenation, and ultimately to the URL constructor, completing the leak.

6   Evaluation

Experiments. With the goal of evaluating FLOWMINER's accuracy and compactness, we summarized recent versions of the Android operating system listed in column 1 of Table 1[3]. We ran our experiments on a multi-core computer with 64 GB RAM, and Eclipse Luna installed with Atlas and FLOWMINER. We created a simple Atlas analyzer to gather the summary statistics listed in Table 1.

Expressiveness. The data-flow summaries extracted by FLOWMINER are fine-grained and expressive. For example, the coarse information flow specifications at the granularity of object tainting generated by Clapp et al. [11] can be directly inferred from our summaries – When information in a FLOWMINER summary reaches a member field definition, the corresponding "taint" on the object is implied; and when information flows from a member field to a method return, it is implied that the object "taints" the method return. Hence, FLOWMINER summaries are strictly more expressive than

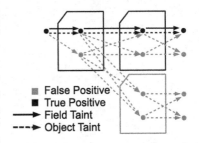

Fig. 6. Coarse flow specifications taint entire objects rather than fields, leading to false positives (Color figure online).

the most closely-related prior work. The presence of registration/callback pairs identified by EdgeMiner [9] can also be inferred from FLOWMINER summaries using details of virtual callsites (for which multiple runtime targets may exist) stored in $G^S(\mathfrak{P})$. More importantly, our summaries can be used more *accurately*. Figure 6 shows how coarse specifications that taint entire objects can lead to an exponential number of implied false positive flows. The figure shows three types with two fields each. Dashed arrows represent transfer of taint at the granularity of objects, while solid arrows represent transfer of taint with field granularity.

---

[3] For each version, we downloaded the Android framework from the build for the *aosp_arm-user* device configuration and then generated corresponding JVM bytecode that can be analyzed with Atlas.

While a subset of the flows implied by object granularity are true positives (black), the majority of flows will be false positives (red). In general, a flow involving object-granularity summaries that traverses through N classes (with K unrelated fields each) will produce on the order of K^N false positive flows!

Table 1 shows the number of data-flow edges induced in the summary by FLOWMINER in column 6 (fine-grained approach that tracks data-flows at field level granularity), which is about 8 % of that induced by the coarse-grained approach that tracks data-flows at object level granularity (shown in column 7). This means that over 92 % of the flows induced by coarse-grained approach are false positives compared to those produced by FLOWMINER.

Soundness and Completeness. We observe that FLOWMINER is *sound* in the following sense – each flow preserved in FLOWMINER's summary is *actually possible* at runtime in the context of some application. In other words, the removal of any summary flow edge would remove critical information needed later to compute a data-flow in some partial program analysis context. This follows from the way in which our summaries are generated (see Sect. 3 for details). FLOWMINER provides *complete* summaries of data-flow semantics, i.e., does not miss any true flows, except those induced (i) as side effects of reflective calls, and (ii) by mixed-language library code (e.g., Java library calling native C code). This follows from the facts that (i) Atlas fully supports the features of the Java 7 programming language, and hence captures all local, field, and method flows between Java program elements in the program graph it constructs; and (ii) the program graph that is used by FLOWMINER for extracting summary information contains all the possible edges from call sites to potential targets for dynamic dispatches (see Sect. 2.1).

We also empirically verified the correctness of our FLOWMINER implementation for the Android versions via an Atlas script as follows. We first computed both the program graph $G(\mathfrak{P})$ and the summary graph $G^S(\mathfrak{P})$, and then successfully verified the property that there is a data-flow path from one key node k to another k' in $G^S(\mathfrak{P})$ if and only if there is a corresponding data-flow path from k to k' in $G(\mathfrak{P})$.

Compactness. The compactness of extracted summary artifacts is important for practical use. As shown in Table 1, $G^S(\mathfrak{P})$ produced by FLOWMINER for Android 4.4.4 contains only 36.98 % of the nodes and 20.06 % of the edges of $G(\mathfrak{P})$ (other versions follow this trend). Hence, our summaries provide significant savings versus a fully-detailed program graph of a library, and yet retain the critical details for use in a partial-program data-flow analysis.

Scalability. We tested FLOWMINER's scalability on the Android framework. For example, Android 4.4.4 (KitKat) contains roughly 2 million lines of Java code, omitting comments and white space. At this scale, FLOWMINER completes its one-time analysis and export of data-flow summary semantics within an additional 45 min after constructing the original program graph.

Table 1. Experimental results showing the compactness and accuracy of FLOWMINER on recent versions of Android. $|V|$, $|E|$ denote the number of nodes and edges in the original program graph; $|V|^S$, $|E|^S$ denote the same for the summary graph. Column 6 represents the number of data-flow edges in FLOWMINER's summary that tracks flows at field level granularity, and column 7 shows the corresponding number of edges when flows are tracked at the object level granularity

Library	$|V|$	$|E|$	$|V^S|/|V|$ (%)	$|E^S|/|E|$ (%)	Field Flows	Object Flows	% False Positives[a] avoided
Android 4.2.2	6651277	33964070	37.11%	22.57%	1129523	16053060	92.96%
Android 4.3.1	6867245	35165616	37.10%	22.51%	1206542	16816490	92.83%
Android 4.4.4	7707688	44150241	36.98%	20.06%	1216178	17069468	92.88%
Android 5.0.2	8684208	45649066	37.05%	21.93%	1556027	21874691	92.89%

([a]Percentage of object-granularity flows that are avoided due to the field-sensitive flow summarization performed by FLOWMINER)

7 Related Work

Summarizing Call Graphs. There has been a lot of interest in summarizing control flow transitions within a software library. Such control-flow summaries are useful for routine static analysis tasks such as call graph generation [4,15, 24,25], tracking of non-trivial calling relationships between application and the library (e.g., asynchronous callbacks in Android) [9] and visualization of control flows from the application to the library and vice-versa [16].

Summarizing Data Flow Graphs. Mining data flows from object-oriented software libraries is an important problem, and is particularly crucial for security-critical analyses. Malware detection in Android apps [1], for example, requires tracking the flow of sensitive information (source, e.g., IMEI number) from the mobile device to potentially harmful destinations (sinks, e.g., a location on the internet).

Callahan first proposed the program summary graph as implemented in PTOOL [8] as a way to compactly represent the inter-procedural call and data flow semantics of the whole program. Rountev et al. [21] pointed out the need to use summaries of data flow semantics when analyzing applications that are dependent on large libraries. They proposed a general theoretical framework for summarizing data flow semantics of large libraries, using pre-computed summary functions per library component and building on the work of Pnueli [23].

Similarly to Rountev et al., Chatterjee et al. [10] summarize each procedure in the bottom up traversal order of the call graph such that the summary of a caller is expressed in terms of the summary of the callee component(s). More recently, Rountev et al. [22] described an approach called interprocedural distributive environment (IDE) data-flow analysis for summarizing object-oriented libraries (that subsumes the class of interprocedural, finite, distributive subset (IFDS) problems [18] which is used by FlowDroid [6]) by using a graph representation of the data-flow summary functions; their approach abstracts away redundant data-flow facts that are internal to the library, in a similar vein to our concept of *eliding* flows. Our summaries differ from that computed by Rountev et al. in that when mining inter-procedural flows, we resolve calls to a member method within an anonymous type to single target, because such calls can only have one possible runtime target, whereas Rountev et al. do not consider such calls to be monomorphic. Malicious applications often use custom anonymous classes to camouflage malicious behavior, and hence our approach of resolving calls to methods in anonymous classes to a single target is particularly useful to a security analyst or a subsequent analysis detect malicious flows by presenting more accurate and precise flow information. Secondly, the scalability of our approach has been validated on the Android framework, which is significantly larger in size (of the nodes and edges in the original and summary graphs) compared to the Java libraries evaluated by Rountev et al.

Some approaches summarize a software component independently of its callers and callees. For example, AVERROES [5] generates a placeholder that over-approximates the behavior of a given library. Their over-approximation may be too coarse to be useful in malware detection scenarios where we need summaries to retain enough information for various kinds of sensitive analyses.

Summarizing Android Flows. To the best of our knowledge, the most closely related work in summarizing libraries in the context of Android is by Clapp et al. [11], who employ a dynamic analysis approach to mine information flows from Android. Their approach successfully recovers 96 % of a set of hand-written information flow specifications. In contrast, FLOWMINER uses static analysis instead of dynamic analysis to identify possible flows within the library, hence avoiding the possibility that some execution paths are not covered. Furthermore, the flow specifications extracted by FLOWMINER track and preserve data flows at the granularity of individual variables and definitions (rather objects) within methods and objects, so we avoid falsely merging unrelated flows. Also, our flow specifications express flows among program elements that are not necessarily on the library API. This allows subsequent analyses to be context, field, type, object, and flow-sensitive. We retain the details of virtual call sites so that flows involving potential callbacks into an application are captured.

8   Conclusion

We presented FLOWMINER [12], a novel solution that uses static analysis techniques to automatically generate an expressive, fine-grained summary of a Java library that is particularly useful for accurate detection of malicious data-flows in applications that use the library. FLOWMINER identifies and retains key artifacts of the program semantics in the summary that are necessary to allow context, object, flow, field, and type-sensitive data-flow analyses of programs using the summarized library. FLOWMINER uses a rich, multi-attributed graph as the mathematical abstraction to store summaries. FLOWMINER's summaries are compact, containing only about a third of the nodes and a fifth of the edges of the original program graph when tested on recent versions of Android, as non-key features in the flows of the original library are elided into key paths. Because FLOWMINER retains individual flows through individual field definitions in contrast to existing coarse-grained methods that taint entire objects, over 92 % of the false positive flows indicated by tainting entire objects are avoided (for the Android framework). FLOWMINER extracts summaries given the bytecode of a library and exports them to a portable, tool-agnostic format. We demonstrated how FLOWMINER's summary can be used in the malware analysis of an Android app. Validation of FLOWMINER on recent versions of Android show that our summaries of are *significantly smaller than the original library*, yet more expressive and accurate than other state-of-the-art techniques. In the future, we plan to summarize Java libraries other than Android, and study the impact of using our summaries on specific data-flow analyses for malware detection.

Acknowledgements. We would like to thank the team at EnSoft Corp who developed the Atlas platform, including Jeremias Sauceda, Jon Matthews, and Nikhil Ranade; and ISU APAC team members who contributed to the malware detection tooling.

References

1. Automated program analysis for cybersecurity (apac), July 2011. https://www.fbo.gov/index?s=opportunity&mode=form&id=a14e4533c2a44c3288b6a29fa6fc5841&tab=core&_cview=1
2. Android 4.4.4 (kitkat), May 2015. http://www.android.com/versions/kit-kat-4-4/
3. Extensible common software graph, March 2015. http://ensoftatlas.com/wiki/Extensible_Common_Software_Graph
4. Ali, K., Lhoták, O.: Application-only call graph construction. In: Noble, J. (ed.) ECOOP 2012. LNCS, vol. 7313, pp. 688–712. Springer, Heidelberg (2012)
5. Ali, K., Lhoták, O.: AVERROES: whole-program analysis without the whole program. In: Castagna, G. (ed.) ECOOP 2013. LNCS, vol. 7920, pp. 378–400. Springer, Heidelberg (2013)
6. Arzt, S., Rasthofer, S., Fritz, C., Bodden, E., Bartel, A., Klein, J., Le Traon, Y., Octeau, D., McDaniel, P.: Flowdroid: Precise context, flow, field, object-sensitive and lifecycle-aware taint analysis for android apps. SIGPLAN Not. **49**(6), 259–269 (2014)
7. Burnette, E.: Hello, Android: introducing Google's mobile development platform. Pragmatic Bookshelf (2009)
8. Callahan, D.: The program summary graph and flow-sensitive interprocedual data flow analysis, vol. 23. ACM (1988)
9. Cao, Y., Fratantonio, Y., Bianchi, A., Egele, M., Kruegel, C., Vigna, G., Chen, Y.: Edgeminer: Automatically detecting implicit control flow transitions through the android framework. 22nd Annual Network and Distributed System Security Symposium, NDSS San Diego, California, USA (2015)
10. Chatterjee, R., Ryder, B.G., Landi, W.A.: Relevant context inference. In: ACM Symposium on Principles of Programming Languages, pp. 133–146. ACM (1999)
11. Clapp, L., Anand, S., Aiken, A.: Modelgen: mining explicit information flow specifications from concrete executions. In: International Symposium on Software Testing and Analysis, pp. 129–140. ACM (2015)

12. Deering, T.: April 2015. http://powerofpi.github.io/FlowMiner/
13. Deering, T., Kothari, S., Sauceda, J., Mathews, J.: Atlas: a new way to explore software, build analysis tools. In: Companion Proceedings of the International Conference on Software Engineering, pp. 588–591. ACM (2014)
14. Felt, A.P., Finifter, M., Chin, E., Hanna, S., Wagner, D.: A survey of mobile malware in the wild. In: Proceedings of the 1st ACM Workshop on Security and Privacy in Smartphones and Mobile Devices, SPSM 2011, pp. 3–14. ACM (2011)
15. Grove, D., Chambers, C.: A framework for call graph construction algorithms. ACM Trans. Prog. Lang. Syst. (TOPLAS) **23**(6), 685–746 (2001)
16. LaToza, T., Myers, B.: Visualizing call graphs. In: Visual Languages and Human-Centric Computing (VL/HCC), Symposium on, pp. 117–124. IEEE (2011)
17. Moser, A., Kruegel, C., Kirda, E.: Limits of static analysis for malware detection. In: Computer security applications conference, pp. 421–430. IEEE (2007)
18. Reps, T., Horwitz, S., Sagiv, M.: Precise interprocedural dataflow analysis via graph reachability. In: Proceedings of the 22nd ACM SIGPLAN-SIGACT symposium on Principles of programming languages, pp. 49–61. ACM (1995)
19. Rogers, R., Lombardo, J., Mednieks, Z., Meike, B.: Android Application Development: Programming with the Google SDK. O'Reilly Media, Inc., Sebastopol (2009)
20. Rosen, S., Qian, Z., Mao, Z.M.: Appprofiler: a flexible method of exposing privacy-related behavior in android applications to end users. In: Proceedings of the ACM conference on Data and application security and privacy, pp. 221–232. ACM (2013)
21. Rountev, A., Kagan, S., Marlowe, T.: Interprocedural dataflow analysis in the presence of large libraries. In: Mycroft, A., Zeller, A. (eds.) CC 2006. LNCS, vol. 3923, pp. 2–16. Springer, Heidelberg (2006)
22. Rountev, A., Sharp, M., Xu, G.: IDE dataflow analysis in the presence of large object-oriented libraries. In: Hendren, L. (ed.) CC 2008. LNCS, vol. 4959, pp. 53–68. Springer, Heidelberg (2008)
23. Sharir, M., Pnueli, A.: Two approaches to interprocedural data flow analysis. In: Muchnick, S.S., Jones, N.D. (eds.) Program Flow Analysis: Theory and Applications, pp. 189–234. Prentice Hall, New York (1981)
24. Yan, D., Xu, G., Rountev, A.: Rethinking soot for summary-based whole-program analysis. In: Proceedings of the ACM SIGPLAN International Workshop on State of the Art in Java Program analysis, pp. 9–14. ACM (2012)
25. Zhang, W., Ryder, B.: Constructing accurate application call graphs for java to model library callbacks. In: Sixth IEEE International Workshop on Source Code Analysis and Manipulation, SCAM 2006, pp. 63–74. IEEE (2006)
26. Zhou, Y., Jiang, X.: Dissecting android malware: Characterization and evolution. In: 2012 IEEE Symposium on Security and Privacy (SP), pp. 95–109. IEEE (2012)

SQLshield: Preventing SQL Injection Attacks by Modifying User Input Data

Punit Mehta, Jigar Sharda, and Manik Lal Das[(✉)]

DA-IICT, Gandhinagar, India
{punit9462,jigar.shar24}@gmail.com, maniklal_das@daiict.ac.in

Abstract. SQL injection attacks, a class of code injection attacks, pose a serious threat to web applications. A web server allows users to perform a query in order to get the intended service where the SQL queries containing user inputs are executed by the database server. An attacker can take advantage of this query-response mechanism to inject some characters into the user input based on the attack strategy. This may lead to an SQL injection attack. If an attacker can bypass the SQL injection defense put at the web server, then the attacker can obtain some sensitive information from the database. In this paper, we present a scheme, SQLshield that prevents SQL injection attacks in web applications. SQLshield uses a randomization technique that modifies the user input data before the SQL query is executed at the database server. The randomization technique used in SQLshield modifies the user input data in such a way that the execution of the resultant SQL query does not divert from its programmer-intended execution. We compare SQLshield with other schemes and show that SQLshield performs better than the other approaches used to detect and prevent SQL injection attacks.

Keywords: Web security · SQL injection attacks · SQL parse tree · Randomization

1 Introduction

World wide web consists of millions of web applications which are run with the power of internet for a variety of services such as financial, healthcare, research, entertainment, educational and so on. Most of the web applications' services require frequent access to the database while interacting with the users. These applications provide mechanisms by which a user is allowed to submit a query that aims to retrieve intended data or provide service with the help of the database server. If such applications do not handle the malicious queries appropriately, then the database's response to such queries would reveal some sensitive information to the malicious party. SQL injection attack [1,8,11] is one such attack which poses some serious threats (primarily authentication bypass and leakage of private information [17]) to web applications. Web application that uses SQL statement for query-response mechanism between the server and a

© Springer International Publishing Switzerland 2015
S. Jajodia and C. Mazumdar (Eds.): ICISS 2015, LNCS 9478, pp. 192–206, 2015.
DOI: 10.1007/978-3-319-26961-0_12

client may potentially be vulnerable to SQL injection attacks. By injecting malicious SQL statements into input fields, the attacker may execute malicious SQL queries in the database server. Such unintended execution of the SQL queries can reveal some sensitive information about the users as well as the server [15]. As a result, validating user-linked data is necessary in order to defend the web applications from SQL injection attacks. We give a simple example below which would help a naive reader to understand how a typical SQL injection attack works on a web application.

Actual Query:

SELECT password FROM users WHERE name = '$username'

Attacker Query:

SELECT password FROM users WHERE name = 'A' OR 1=1 #'

Consider the Attacker Query. The attacker's input to the query is *A' OR 1=1 #*. Here, *1=1* always results in true. Since the operation between the two operands **name = 'A'** and **1=1** is an **OR operation**, the entire "WHERE clause" is evaluated as TRUE. This would lead to the exposure of all the passwords from the users' table and a successful attempt at an SQL injection attack.

Several approaches [2–6, 25] have been proposed in literature for detecting (and/or preventing) SQL injection attacks. The techniques used in these approaches include the use of aliases for table and field names, **prepared** statement, stored procedures, limiting user input length, escaping string delimiters, filtering the error messages and a learning based approach [24] to detect SQL injection attack by measuring the anomaly score for a given query. Subsequently, string constraint solving [22], dynamic runtime monitoring of untrusted strings, training on trusted strings, automating the filtering and training mechanisms [9,10] can work to some extent for detecting and preventing SQL injection attacks. But, the training set and runtime monitoring downgrade the system's performance. The prevention mechanism can be effective if it detects malicious input and allows only legitimate input. Sometimes it may so happen that the user's input contains legitimate data, but the security mechanism used for detecting an SQL injection attack triggers it as a potential injection attack which deprives the legitimate users from getting the intended services.

Our Contributions. We present a scheme, SQLshield, which can detect and prevent SQL injection attacks on web applications. Whenever a user (possibly malicious) gives input through the web-interface, SQLshield appends a random key to the *selected* sub-strings of the user input (not to the underlined SQL query's keywords). Then, SQLshield forms the parse tree of a query and removes the random key from the user input. Here, the parse tree of the SQL query remains benign due to the randomization on user input. Therefore, the attacker cannot execute an SQL injection attack as the intended behaviour of the SQL query cannot be altered. We discuss some recently proposed techniques [2–4, 6] on defending SQL injection attacks and observe some limitations of them. Our proposed scheme, SQLshield, mitigates such limitations. The following limitations of SQLrand [2] and CANDID [3] are mitigated by SQLshield.

- Unlike SQLshield, SQLrand uses a secret key to prevent SQL injection attacks. Therefore, there is no threat of getting the key revealed while using SQLshield as a defence mechanism. In the case of handling exceptions and type-errors, the secret key may be revealed from the proxy functioning on SQLrand. This is due to the bad implementation of CGI scripts which ultimately exposes the underlined randomized queries [2].
- CANDID detects SQL injection attacks when candidate query's parse tree does not match the actual query's parse tree. If a benign user input contains *SQL keywords*, CANDID detects it as an SQL injection attack due to the mismatch occurring between the parse tree of the candidate query and user query. As SQLshield randomizes user inputs, the underlined structure of SQL query's parse tree does not alter even if the user inputs are part of the SQL keyword set.

The remainder of the paper is organized as follows. Section 2 reviews related approaches on preventing SQL injection attacks. Section 3 presents our scheme, SQLshield. Sections 4 and 5 provide implementation and performance details of SQLshield. We conclude the paper in Sect. 6.

2   Related Work

Over the years many approaches [2–6,21,23] have been proposed for mitigating SQL injection attacks on web applications. There exist several testing tools [26, 27] for the detection of code injection attacks including SQL injection. Overall, none of these approaches prevent SQL injection attacks completely. Each of these approaches has its merits and limitations towards the same security objective. We review some of these approaches in order to compare our proposed approach with them.

2.1   SQLrand

SQLrand [2] randomizes the SQL keywords used in a query statement. A secret keyword is shared between the web server and the proxy server. The web server appends this secret keyword to all the SQL keywords present in a query (containing user inputs), forms a randomized SQL and passes it to the proxy server. The secret keyword is removed from the randomized SQL query by the proxy which then produces the result set and forwards it to the web server. The architecture of SQLrand is shown in Fig. 1.

SQLrand protects the web server from SQL injection assuming that the attacker cannot steal the secret keyword (shared between web server and proxy) that is used to randomize the SQL keywords in the query statement. One of the advantages of choosing SQLrand to prevent SQL injection attacks is that it is relatively easy to implement. A major drawback of SQLrand is its dependence on a secret keyword. If the attacker manages to get the secret keyword, then he can bypass the prevention mechanism [2]. We briefly illustrate SQLrand with the secret keyword 123.

Actual Query:
SELECT password FROM users WHERE name = '$username'

Randomized Query:
SELECT123 .. FROM123 .. WHERE123 name = '$username'

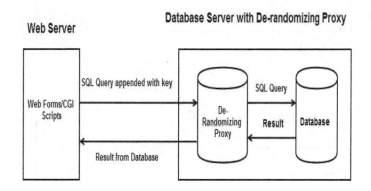

Fig. 1. Architecture of SQLrand [2]

Now, if the attacker successfully gets the secret keyword (i.e. 123), then he can append this keyword to all the SQL keywords in the (malicious) query (as shown below) and then try to bypass the web server's randomization process. If the attacker succeeds in bypassing the web server with the correct choice of the secret keyword, then the (malicious) query will get de-randomized by the proxy followed by the (malicious) query's successful execution by the database server.

Attacker Query:
SELECT123 .. FROM123 .. WHERE123 name = 'A' OR123 1=1 #

2.2   CANDID

CANDID (Candidate Evaluation for Discovering Intent Dynamically) [3] is also used to prevent SQL injection attacks in web applications. CANDID adds a benign query (known as *candidate query*) along the control path in the source code and compares the structure of the candidate query's parse tree with the structure of the actual query (containing possibly malicious user inputs) during runtime. CANDID detects an SQL injection attack when the structure of the actual query's parse tree (executed during the user's interaction with the database) differs from the structure of the benign query's parse tree. The architecture of CANDID is shown in Fig. 2.

Benign Query:
SELECT .. FROM .. WHERE name = 'ABC'

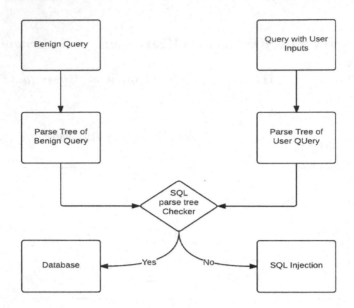

Fig. 2. Architecture of CANDID [3]

Attacker Query:
SELECT .. FROM .. WHERE name = 'A' OR 1=1 #'

Here, the structure of the attacker query's parse tree does not match to the structure of the benign query's parse tree. For example, the attacker query's parse tree has a node corresponding to the SQL keyword-OR which is not present in the benign query's parse tree. Therefore, CANDID detects such attempt at an SQL injection attack and does not allow the attacker query to execute. One major advantage of CANDID is that it considers special characters (e.g. #, ×, % etc.) as inputs to the query and detects SQL injection if the candidate query's parse tree structure does not match with the intended structure. One of the drawbacks of CANDID is that if the user input consists any of the SQL keywords or special characters, it may be treated as a malicious query even if the input is benign. Therefore, it cannot distinguish between the benign and the malicious inputs when the input itself is a *legitimate SQL token*. The query execution fails if the input itself is an SQL token due to the structural mismatch between the parse trees of the candidate query and actual query. Although there is no malicious input, CANDID considers the SQL tokens as malicious inputs and stops the execution of the query.

2.3   SDriver

SDriver (Secure Driver: location specific signatures) [6] keeps track of the stack frame of all the active function calls which are used to distinguish between legitimate and malicious query. SDriver is not easy to bypass as it does not depend on the source code of the application. However, the training phase's dependence on application is a major limitation of SDriver. For every application, it goes through the training process which results into a significant overhead in the entire execution. The architecture of SDriver is shown in Fig. 3.

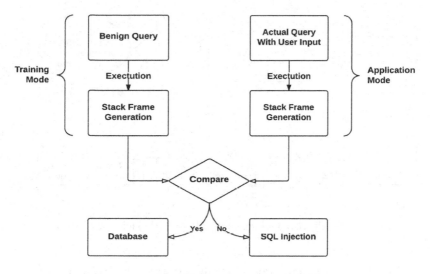

Fig. 3. Architecture of SDriver [6]

2.4 TAPS

TAPS (Tool for Automatically Preparing SQL statements) [4] transforms the original query into its corresponding *prepare* statement. It uses the parse tree of an SQL query to identify data place-holder. TAPS removes the burden of manual transformation of each query into its *prepared* statement. The limitation of TAPS is that it may malfunction depending on the source code of the web application. Furthermore, the queries need to be verified manually on the occurrence of errors once the transformation is performed. There also exist other defensive coding practices which include the use of prepared statements and stored procedures. Such techniques need a lot of software-development care [11] and some minor bug may potentially lead to the vulnerability to SQL injection attacks. Readers are encouraged to go through [11–14, 16, 20] to understand SQL injection attacks' defences and their limitations.

3   SQLshield - An Improved Scheme

We present a scheme, SQLshield, to prevent SQL injection attacks on web applications. SQLshield has the merits of SQLrand and CANDID. At the same time, it also mitigates their limitations. SQLshield uses a keyword to randomize user

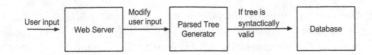

Fig. 4. Architecture of SQLshield

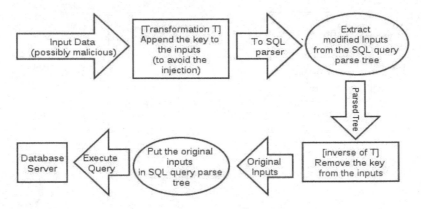

Fig. 5. Working principle of SQLshield

inputs (but not the SQL keywords). Initially, all the sub-strings of a user input are enumerated.

Then, the keyword is appended to a sub-string which belongs to the set of the standard SQL tokens and special characters. After this randomization on user inputs, the final structure of an SQL query's parse tree is generated, the user inputs are de-randomized and the query is executed. If the user inputs are benign, appropriate result sets are returned to the web-server after the safe access to the database. We note that the random keyword used for randomization process in SQLshield does not necessarily have to be secret. The architecture of SQLshield and the working principl e are presented in Figs. 4 and 5, respectively. We illustrate SQLshield with the following example.

SELECT *password* **FROM** *users* **WHERE** *name* $=$ *'$username'*

Suppose the attacker enters *' OR 1=1 #* as input, then SQLshield converts the input *' OR 1=1 #* to *'999 OR999 1=9991 #999'* by choosing a random key 999. Note that the random key is to be appended to the tokens (e.g., OR, AND, =, #, ', etc.) which are present in a user input. The modified query or newly formed query is as follows.

SELECT .. FROM .. WHERE *name* $=$ *''999 OR999 1=9991 #999'*

Now the modified query (i.e., a query with modified inputs) is fed into the SQL parser. The SQL parser generates the parse tree of the modified query (as shown in Fig. 6).

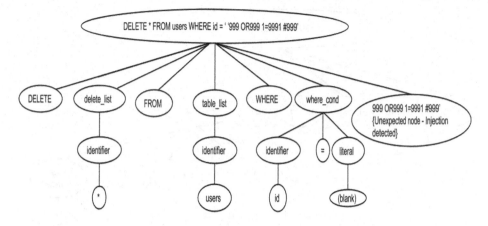

Fig. 6. SQLshield - Parse tree of SQL query with a modified (malicious) input

Since the parse tree contains an unexpected leaf node (i.e., *999 OR999 1=9991 #999'*, the SQL parser would report a syntactic error and does not proceed further for the execution. In this way, SQLshield blocks an attempt at SQL injection attack. If the user input is benign, the parse tree structure created after randomization process will be syntactically valid. Therefore, after the creation of the parse tree, SQLshield extracts the modified user input, de-randomizes it with the random key 999 and gets the actual input. Then, the parser places the actual input in appropriate places in the query's parse tree and sends the query to the database for execution.

The parse tree of the programmer intended query is shown in Fig. 7. If an attacker injects a malicious input, the modified parse tree of the query is shown in Fig. 8. Note that it has two unexpected nodes at the end due to the SQL injection attack. It can be seen from Fig. 7 that these nodes are not supposed to be present in this SQL query's parse tree. SQLshield focuses on eliminating such unintended structural change in SQL query's parse trees to avoid SQL injection attacks.

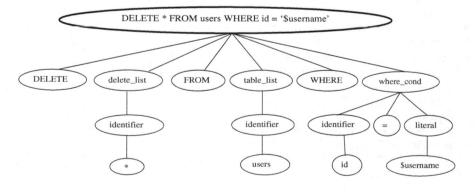

Fig. 7. Parse tree of SQL query containing a benign input

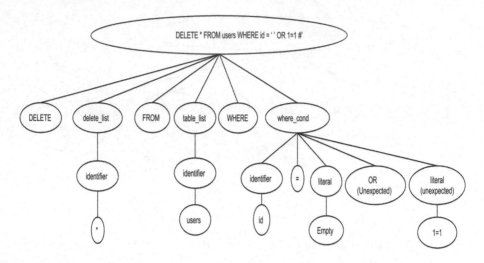

Fig. 8. Parse tree of SQL query with a malicious input

Algorithm 1. SQLshield
_____

1: **procedure** modifyQuery(*original_query*)
2: *sql_set* ← set of *SQL keywords and characters*
3: *parse-tree* ← original_query.getParseTree()
4: *parse-tree-valid* ← parse-tree.isValid()
5: *top*:
6: **if** !*(parse-tree-valid)* **then**
7:     **return** "ERROR"
8: **end if**
9: */* Main Operation of SQLshield */*
10: *map¡pos,str¿ extract-input* ← parse-tree.InputsPos()
11: **for all** input positions *pos* in *extract-input* **do**
12:     *user_input* ← *extract-input[pos]*
13:     **for all** sub-strings *substr* in *user_input* **do**
14:         **if** *substr* in *sql_set* **then**
15:             appendRandomKey(*user_input*, *substr*)
16:         **end if**
17:     **end for**
18:     *extract-input[pos]* ← *user_input*
19: **end for**
20: parse-tree.putInputs(*extract-input*)
21: *parse-tree-valid* ← parse-tree.isValid()
22: **if** !*(parse-tree-valid)* **then**
23:     **return** "ERROR"
24: **end if**
25: *modified_query* ← parse-tree.formQuery()
26: **return** *modified_query*
_____

SQLshield randomizes the user input by appending a random key to specific tokens of the user input, which belong to a pre-defined set of SQL tokens and special characters, and forwards the query to the parse tree generator which will generate the parse tree as shown in Fig. 6. Once this structure has been decided and validated syntactically, the randomized input is removed from the parse tree and it is replaced by the original input. In this way, our scheme does not completely alter the inputs and also it does not allow the attacker to change the parse tree structure of the query. As the actual cause of SQL injection attack lies in the malicious input, the initial procedure of SQLshield makes sure that the user inputs participating in the generation of the SQL query's parse tree are not malicious. To achieve this, SQLshield appends a random key to only those sub-strings of the user input which belong to a pre-defined set of SQL tokens and special characters. Even if the attacker knows the random key, he cannot execute any malicious query and exploit the system because SQLshield appends the random key (even the attacker has already appended the random key to any SQL token) to the user input. Therefore, after de-randomization, the query will have syntactically invalid *SQL tokens* which cannot be executed successfully as per the attacker's intention. The core idea of SQLshield is given in Algorithm 1.

4   Implementation of SQLshield

We implemented SQLshield using SQL Parser v1.5.1.8 written in JAVA [7]. The SQL query is parsed and the place-holder for user inputs are located. Randomized inputs are placed in the SQL query and fed to the parser. After the query's parse tree is finalized, the random key appended in the initial randomization stage is removed from the inputs. We evaluated SQLshield on a 64-bit Linux Machine running on quad-core Intel Core i3 CPU M 370 @ 2.40 GHz with a RAM of 5.6 GB. We have tested the following SQL queries (including malicious ones) in our experiments on SQLshield.

Test Case 1
Input SQL: SELECT * FROM products WHERE price BETWEEN 10 AND 20
Input Data: 10,20
Output SQL: SELECT * FROM products WHERE price BETWEEN 10 AND 20

Test Case 2
Input SQL: SELECT * FROM customers WHERE state='oregon' AND city='remand'
Input Data: oregon, remand
Output SQL: SELECT * FROM customers WHERE state='or999egon' AND city='remand999'

Test Case 3
Input SQL: INSERT INTO .. VALUES ('+1','test#')
Input Data: +1,test#
Output SQL: INSERT INTO .. VALUES ('+9991','test#999')

Test Case 4
Input SQL: UPDATE .. SET name='John Morr' WHERE age = '%1%'
Input Data: John Morr,%1%
Output SQL: UPDATE .. SET name='John Mor999r' WHERE age = '%9991%999'

The above four SQL queries have benign inputs. Since the user input contains SQL keywords and special characters, SQLshield modifies them by appending the random key 999 to each of such tokens (e.g., keywords, special characters). Now, the parse tree structure is constructed and the modified inputs in the parse tree are de-randomized by the same random key 999, which brings back the original inputs into the programmer desired query's parse tree.

Test Case 5
Input SQL: DELETE FROM .. WHERE id = '' OR 1=1 #'
Input Data: ' OR 1=1 #
Output SQL: DELETE FROM .. WHERE id = ''999 OR999 1=9991 #999'

The Test case 5 has malicious inputs. In this case, the user input contains an SQL keyword (e.g., OR) and special characters (e.g., ', =, #). Upon receiving these inputs, SQLshield modifies them by appending the random key 999 to each of such tokens (e.g., OR, ', =, #). Then, the parse tree structure is constructed. Based on the flow of the SQL parse tree construction, the parse tree has an input node without any text (shown as a blank node in Fig. 6) and an unexpected node with the value 999 OR999 1=9991 #999'. After randomizing the malicious user inputs, the modified inputs are no longer malicious. As the modified inputs are benign, the finalized parse-tree structure would be either the programmer's intended structure which will not have any malicious input or it will be syntactically invalid. As a result, even if the attacker injects malicious inputs, SQLshield will make sure that the underlying structure of the SQL query's parse tree which is sent to database for execution cannot be altered by the attacker.

4.1 Remarks

If the application developer wants to use any tool to strengthen the security (e.g. JDBC Checker [18,19]), then such type-validations have to be performed before SQLshield is executed. Therefore, the initial assumption while implementing the proposed Algorithm 1 is that the algorithm starts executing after all the necessary input validations and modifications such as input's format validation, are performed. The reason for this assumption is that if the randomization on inputs is performed before the validations, the input format might be changed and the application may misbehave. It is evident from the discussion that such an assumption does not violate the generality of SQLshield's security objectives.

5   Performance

We have executed 100 input queries and measured the starting and ending time of the program. We found that our JAVA code's average execution time is 2 s for processing 100 queries on NetBeans IDE 8.0 leading to an average execution time equal to 20ms per query which is in the same order of SQLrand [2]. This shows that the execution time of SQLshield is not significantly higher than what is normally observed. However, the additional cost in SQLshield is due to the parsing of an SQL query and it seems to be practical to fulfil the objective of preventing the application against SQL injection attacks.

SQLshield performs better than CANDID (and also others mentioned in Table 1) to prevent SQL injection attacks as SQLshield allows to have user inputs which belong to the set of SQL tokens and special characters. CANDID considers such inputs as SQL tokens and qualifies even a benign query as a malicious query and invalidates it. SQLshield overcomes this limitation as it allows SQL tokens as inputs by appending a random key to the input's sub-strings which match exactly to the SQL tokens. SQLshield appends a random key to every SQL token and special characters contained in the user input. If the attacker knows the random key (999 in our example) and tries to inject any malicious input, the attacker will not succeed in executing the query, because the SQL tokens in the input will lose their actual interpretation due to the randomization as explained in the previous section.

Table 1. Comparison of SQLshield with other schemes

Feature → Scheme ↓	Intermediate manipulation	Key dependency	Debugging cost[a]
SQLrand [2]	Yes	Yes (must be secret)	High
CANDID [3]	No	No	Moderate
SDriver [6]	Yes	No	Moderate
TAPS [4]	Yes	No	High
SQLshield	Yes	Yes (need not be secret)	Low

[a]Debugging cost denotes the amount of time and effort required by the developers to identify bugs and fix them

5.1   Limitations of SQLshield

Even though SQLshield effectively prevents SQL injection attacks and mitigates the limitations of SQLrand and CANDID, it has the following issues.

− Since SQLshield uses a string matching algorithm to identify SQL tokens and delimiters' presence in user input, the execution time of the program is a function of the length of the input. Therefore, it may take more time if the underlined string matching algorithm used is not efficient.

– The web application may have several user inputs. It may happen that not all these inputs contribute to SQL queries. Therefore, the programmer has to identify the inputs which go into an SQL query in order to determine which inputs have to be randomized. We do not want to randomize and de-randomize the user inputs which do not correspond to SQL query and do not cause SQL injection. If the application programmer wants this task to be automated, it requires development care and some extra effort in the implementation.

6   Conclusion

Preventing SQL injection attacks is an important requirement for smooth customer service in web-based applications. The main cause of SQL injection attacks lies in the malicious inputs submitted to a web application that allows the attacker to execute the malicious query and thereby, obtain some sensitive information of user or database. We proposed a scheme, SQLshield, to prevent SQL injection attacks on web applications. SQLshield inserts a random key in user inputs. After the parse tree of an SQL query is formed, the inputs are brought back from the tree and transformed to its original version by removing the random key. Then, SQLshield puts this original data in the respective place-holders in the query's parse tree and sends it for execution to the database server. We note that even if the attacker knows the random key, he cannot succeed in executing a malicious query because the malicious inputs are randomized again and the injected tokens are treated as invalid at the database server. Unlike other schemes, SQLshield allows a legitimate user input containing any SQL command. We compared SQLshield with SQLrand, CANDID, SDriver and TAPS, and showed that SQLshield performs better than others due to its strong defence against SQL injection attacks.

References

1. The Open Web Application Security Project (OWASP), OWASP top 10 web application security risks in year (2013). https://www.owasp.org/index.php/Top_10_2013-Top_10

2. Boyd, S.W., Keromytis, A.D.: SQLrand: preventing SQL injection attacks. In: Jakobsson, M., Yung, M., Zhou, J. (eds.) ACNS 2004. LNCS, vol. 3089, pp. 292–302. Springer, Heidelberg (2004)

3. Bisht, P., Madhusudan, P., Venkatakrishnan, V.N.: CANDID: Dynamic candidate evaluations for automatic prevention of SQL injection attacks. ACM Trans. Inf. Syst. Secur. **13**(2), 1–39 (2010)

4. Bisht, P., Sistla, A.P., Venkatakrishnan, V.N.: TAPS: automatically preparing safe SQL queries. In: Proceedings of the International Conference on Financial Cryptography and Data Security, pp. 272–288 (2010)

5. Buehrer, G., Weide, B.W., Sivilotti, P.A.: Using parse tree validation to prevent SQL injection attacks. In: Proceedings of the International Workshop on Software Engineering and Middleware, pp. 106–113 (2005)

6. Mitropoulos, D., Spinellis, D.: SDriver: Location-specific signatures prevent SQL injection attacks. J. Comput. Secur. **28**(3–4), 121–129 (2009)
7. General SQL parser implemented in JAVA. http://www.sqlparser.com/products.php
8. Clarke, J.: SQL Injection Attacks and Defense, vol. 2. Elsevier publisher, USA (2012)
9. Halfond, W.G., Orso, A.: Combining static analysis and runtime monitoring to counter SQL-injection attacks. In: Proceedings of the Third International Workshop on Dynamic Analysis, pp. 22–28 (2005)
10. Martin, M., Lan, M.S.: Automatic generation of XSS and SQL injection attacks with goal-directed model checking. In: Proceedings of the Conference on Security Symposium, pp. 31–43 (2008)
11. Halfond, W.G., Viegas, J., Orso, A.: A classification of SQL-injection attacks and countermeasures. In: Proceedings of the IEEE International Symposium on Secure Software Engineering (2006)
12. McClure, R., Kruger, I.: SQL DOM: compile time checking of dynamic SQL statements. In: Proceedings of the International Conference on Software Engineering (ICSE 05), pp 88–96 (2005)
13. McDonald, S.: SQL Injection: Modes of attack, defense, and why it matters. White paper (2002). GovernmentSecurity.org
14. Anley, C.: Advanced SQL Injection In SQL Server Applications. Next Generation Security Software Ltd., White paper (2002)
15. McDonald, S.: SQL Injection Walkthrough. White paper, SecuriTeam, May 2002. http://www.securiteam.com/securityreviews/5DP0N1P76E.html
16. Antunes, N., Laranjeiro, N., Vieira, M., Madeira, H.: Effective detection of SQL/XPath injection vulnerabilities in web services. In: Proceedings of IEEE International Conference on Services Computing (SCC 2009), pp. 260–267. IEEE (2009)
17. Shahriar, H., Zulkernine, M.: Mitigating program security vulnerabilities: approaches and challenges. ACM Comput. Surv. **44**(3), 1–46 (2012). Article 11
18. Gould, C., Su, Z., Devanbu, P.: JDBC Checker: a static analysis tool for SQL/JDBC applications. In: Proceedings of the International Conference on Software Engineering (ICSE 2004) - Formal Demos, pp. 697–698 (2004)
19. Gould, C., Su, Z., Devanbu, P.: Static checking of dynamically generated queries in database applications. In: Proceedings of the International Conference on Software Engineering (ICSE 2004), pp. 645–654 (2004)
20. Maor, O., Shulman, A.: SQL injection signatures evasion. White paper, Imperva (2002)
21. Xie, Y., Aiken, A.: Static detection of security vulnerabilities in scripting languages. In: Proceedings of the USENIX Security Symposium, pp. 179–192 (2006)
22. Kiezun, A., Ganesh, V., Guo, P.J., Hooimeijer, P., Ernst, M.D.: Hampi: a solver for string constraints. In: Proceedings of the International Symposium on Software Testing and Analysis, pp. 105–116 (2009)
23. Halfond, W.G., Orso, A.: AMNESIA: analysis and monitoring for neutralizing SQL-injection. In: Proceedings of the IEEE/ACM International Conference on Automated Software Engineering, pp. 174–183 (2005)
24. Valeur, F., Mutz, D., Vigna, G.: A learning-based approach to the detection of SQL attacks. In: Proceedings of the Conference on Detection of Intrusions and Malware Vulnerability Assessment, pp. 123–140 (2005)

25. Baranwal, A.K.: Approaches to detect SQL injection and XSS in web applications. Term Survey paper-EECE 571b, University of British Columbia (2012)
26. Security Compass. SQL Inject Me. https://addons.mozilla.org/en-US/firefox/addon/sql-inject-me/
27. Larouche, F.: SQL Power Injector. http://www.sqlpowerinjector.com/

Assessment of an Automatic Correlation Rules Generator

E. Godefroy[1,2,3]($\boxtimes$), E. Totel[3], M. Hurfin[2], and F. Majorczyk[1]

[1] DGA-MI, Bruz, France
erwan.godefroy@supelec.fr, frederic.majorczyk@intradef.gouv.fr
[2] Inria, Rennes, France
michel.hurfin@inria.fr
[3] CentraleSupélec, Rennes, France
eric.totel@supelec.fr

Abstract. Information systems are prone to attacks. Those attacks can take different forms, from an obvious DDOS to a complex attack scenario involving a step by step stealthy compromise of key nodes in the target system. In order to detect those multi-steps attack scenarios, alert correlation systems are required. Those systems rely on explicit or implicit correlation rules in order to detect complex links between various events or alerts produced by IDSes. Explicit and accurate correlation rules strongly linked with the system are difficult to build and maintain manually. However this process can be partially automated when enough information on the attack scenario and the target system are available. In this paper, we focus on the evaluation of correlation rules produced by an automatic process. In a first place, the method is evaluated on a representative system. In this realistic evaluation context, when the knowledge of both the attack scenario and the targeted system is precise enough, the generated rules allow to have a perfect detection rate (no false positive and no false negative). Then stress tests are conducted in order to measure the robustness of the approach when the generation of rules relies on a provided knowledge which is either partially incorrect or incomplete.

Keywords: Alert correlation evaluation · Attack scenario · Attack tree

1 Introduction

In order to handle the detection of multi-steps attack scenarios, it is necessary to produce correlation rules strongly linked to the target system. Most of the phases leading to the generation of the correlation rules can be automated with a generic process (provided that a description of the system is available and up to date). In order to produce realistic correlation rules, this process relies on suitable inputs: the knowledge base that describes the environment and an attack scenario

This work was partially funded by the European project Panoptesec (FP7-GA 610416).

S. Jajodia and C. Mazumdar (Eds.): ICISS 2015, LNCS 9478, pp. 207–224, 2015.
DOI: 10.1007/978-3-319-26961-0_13

specified with a suitable level of details. The main benefit of this approach is that once the system is defined in a knowledge base, it is easy to modify it to take into account small changes in the system or generate correlation rules for new attack scenarios without having to build or rebuild each rule manually. However, even if the process builds correct correlation rules if its inputs are complete and correct, no assumption can be made once these inputs are slightly faulty. These faults can be caused by a bad specification of the attack scenarios or outdated information about the target system. Thus, this paper proposes in a first part to test the accuracy and applicability of these generated correlation rules in a real environment. Then, the focus is on the evaluation of the accuracy of the correlation rules given faulty inputs parameters. This second evaluation is performed in a simulated environment. The generation process is explained in Sect. 2 and correlation rules built with this system are evaluated in a real case scenario in Sect. 3. The different factors that can hinder the generation of accurate correlation rules are exposed in Sect. 4 and used in Sect. 5 to put the system under stress in order to measure the impact of these factors on the detection. Section 6 introduces related works in alert correlation systems and their evaluation process and Sect. 7 concludes the paper.

2   Correlation Rule Generation Framework

The reference [3] describes a framework for generating correlation rules. The generation process consists in successive transformations of an attack tree to correlation rules given specific context information extracted from a knowledge base. Inputs are (1) an attack tree [2] built with three types of operators, *Or*, *And* and *Sand* (a sequential *And*), (2) a knowledge base referencing the target system topology, the system cartography (installed softwares and services) and the system supervision (sensors and detection devices information). The process is divided in five steps. Among them, the first one is manual and the others are automated. Those steps are illustrated in Fig. 1. In this toy example, the structure of the starting attack tree is composed of an operator *Sand* that links two leaves *A* and *B*. Informally, these leaves describe respectively a scan followed by an attack leading to a code execution on one of the scanned machine.

The first step aims at specifying each elementary attacker action in the attack tree. During this step, the attack tree is used to construct a more formal and structured representation of the attack scenario called an action tree. The use of an action language allows to specify elementary actions by defining a name (which defines the functional visibility of the action) and attributes (which define the topological visibility). The name of the action is extracted from a taxonomy. More precisely, depending on the nature of the action (explicit attack action or standard action), the name is taken from the CAPEC or CEE taxonomy. Attributes can be expressed by constants or by two types of variables. The first type of variable is called static variable. It is meant as a generalisation variable and represents a value that can be determined statically thanks to the

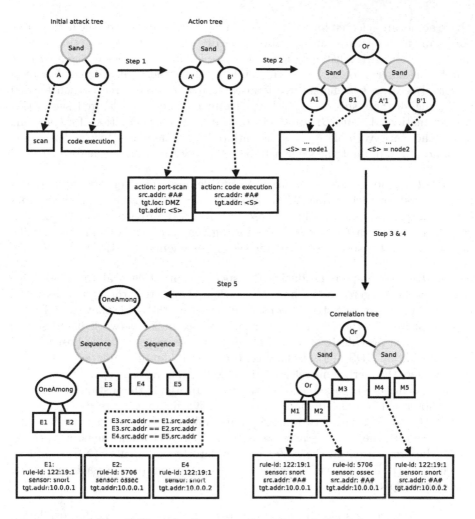

Fig. 1. Steps for the generation of correlation rules

information present in the knowledge base (e.g. the IP of a machine hosting a web server). The second type is called dynamic variable and represents data for which a value can only be specified at run time (e.g. the IP of an attacker). In Fig. 1, the action tree has a similar structure as the initial attack tree but the leaves *A'* and *B'* are actions specified with the action language. The scan action is named port-scan in the CAPEC taxonomy and the attacker machine (source address attribute) is modelled by a dynamic variable (#A#). On the other hand, the target attribute is a static variable (named <S>) that models any machine present in a subnetwork called DMZ.

The second step consists in the identification of the attack scenario actors (that means all nodes, services, user accounts that could be targeted by the attack).

Those actors are selected based on the specifications expressed by the action tree. For example, an action can describe a specific type of attack targeting a node in a given area with a listening network service. Then all nodes in the area that match this description and are vulnerable to the attack are selected. For each potential actor, a specific subtree is instantiated. A single tree is then formed by linking all these subtrees together with an *Or* operator. Figure 1 shows this transformation. *A1* and *B1* are the instantiated *A'* and *B'* actions for a specific actor (the static variable <S> is instantiated and references now *node1*) while *A'1* and *B'1* represent the same actions relatively to a different actor.

The third step focuses on selecting the suitable observers (sensors and supervision devices) for each action. These observers are selected based on their topological and functional visibility. Those visibilities are expressed in the knowledge base and characterize the ability for a given observer to monitor a specific perimeter of the system and a specific set of behaviours or actions.

The fourth step aims at producing the specification of each alarm or message that could be triggered by each observer when they detect the actions assigned to them in the previous step. It consists in selecting the fields that should actually be present in the generated alert. As an example, network based sensor cannot always provide information about software or users while host sensors can. In addition, IDS alerts usually contain a rule identifier related to the rule that triggers the alert. This reference is added to the message specification. The resulting structure is called a correlation tree. In Fig. 1, the instantiated action *A1* is observable by two distinct observers that can generate respectively messages *M1* and *M2*. These two messages are linked by an *Or* operator in order to express that the two messages are potentially raised when the action occurs. Thus, the first action on the *node1* can be detected by a snort (NIDS) and an Ossec agent (HIDS), each of these two devices can generate a message containing fields and a specific rule identifier.

The fifth step consists in translating the correlation tree to a specific correlation language syntax (which is related to a specific correlator). In our case, the target correlation language is ADeLe [6,10]. The transformations involve the translation of the constant fields of correlation tree leaves into event filters, the structure of logical operator into *Sequence*, *OneAmong* and *NonOrdered* temporal operator, and the binding between dynamic variables into inter-event constraints. Figure 1 shows the logical operator translation, some of the event filters ($E1,E2$) and the constraints between the different events.

3   Evaluation in a Real Environment

The different goals of this section are: (1) showing that the method is applicable in a real complex environment (2) testing that the generated correlation rules are able to detect real attacks performed during a pentest (no false negatives) (3) verifying that no false positives are introduced by the generation process.

3.1 System Topology and Cartography

The system is illustrated in Fig. 2. It consists in zones with dedicated roles. The main zones are the DMZ, the server zone and the client network. Each machine (in the DMZ and the server zone) has two interfaces: the first is connected to the production network, the second to the administration network. These zones are delimited by three firewalls: the frontal firewall between the Internet and the DMZ, the production firewall between the client network, the server zone and the DMZ, and the administrator firewall between the administrator network and the DMZ and the server zone. The DMZ hosts a Proxy that enables clients to access the outside, a mail server, two web servers (*Web1*, the main web server and *Web2*, a blog under construction), a FTP server, a DNS server and a VPN server, which allows remote user to connect to the server zone. The server zone contains an Active Directory server, a mail server, a Web server hosting an Intranet web service and a sensitive server, which hosts sensitive files. Several clients are present in the client network. They can access their mail accounts in the server zone, the web servers and the Internet via the proxy. Only a specific number of clients are allowed to connect to the sensitive server.

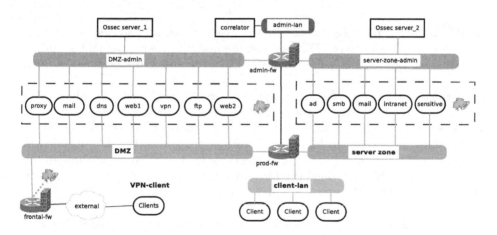

Fig. 2. Topology of the target system

3.2 Supervision

The system is supervised by several sensors and IDSes.

HIDS: Ossec HIDS are deployed in each server and client. They perform integrity checks on sensitive directories and analyse local logs generated by the operating system or the deployed services. All alerts raised by these sensors are collected by Ossec servers (located in the suitable administrator subnetwork). In addition, the availability of the different services deployed for each server is monitored with Nagios so that alerts could be triggered when a service stops unexpectedly. Ossec servers collect information provided by Arpwatch sensors as well.

NIDS: Four machines running the Snort NIDS are deployed respectively in the DMZ, in the server zone, in the client network and in front of the external firewall. To ensure that an IDS raises an alert only when the corresponding action really occurs, each of them has been accurately tuned: only reliable and relevant built-in rules are enabled and new custom rules are added to describe the security policy of the system (for example, some servers must not connect to each others in the DMZ or in the server zone) and to detect the exploitation of known vulnerabilities in the system.

3.3   Attack Steps

In this system, information present in the sensitive server could be disclosed by an external attacker. The details of a possible attack scenario is exposed in two parts. They focus respectively on the compromise of the DMZ and of the server zone.

DMZ Attack Path. The DMZ has a restrictive firewall allowing only access from external entities to two Web servers: the main Web server and a blog under construction. Consequently these nodes are the first target of an external attack.

Compromise of the web server: The main Web server is vulnerable to information disclosure through a directory traversal. A successful attack can lead the attacker to gather some username/password tuples. On the second Web server which hosts a blog, attackers can find the administrator password hash embedded in the sources of a specific page and then use these credentials to login through the administrator interfaces. With the blog administrator's rights, it is possible to upload a malicious PHP script to build a first attack relay in the DMZ.

Compromise of the FTP Server: The FTP server runs a vulnerable distributed compilation service accessible only from the DMZ. The successful exploitation of this vulnerability provides local access to this machine. Root privileges can then be obtained by running a local root exploit.

Server Zone Attack Path. The firewall that separates the DMZ and the server zone (prod-fw) forbids all direct connections from the DMZ except those incoming from VPN clients. As a consequence, this can be the next entry point. By usurping an IP address of a VPN client, an attacker can access some machines on the server zone and gather information on the mail server or on the Samba server by using credentials previously stolen. It is also possible to access to the intranet Web server.

Compromise of the intranet server: This server is vulnerable to an SQL injection or credential reuse to access administrator interface. It is then possible for attackers to escalate their privileges with a local root exploit kernel. Then, a man in the middle attack can disclose the IP address of a client machine that can access the protected server. A spoofing of this IP and the use of stolen credentials allow attackers to access the sensitive server.

3.4   Test Methodology

A set of attack scenarios is built without knowledge of the collected alerts. The attack scenarios are relatively small (4 actions in average). Indeed, various reasons make this choice viable. First small scenarios are more likely to match a real attack than a long complex scenario. Moreover, long scenarios can be cut into more elementary logical units (such as a fingerprinting followed by a successful privilege escalation followed by a scan on other machines from this compromised one).

Action Tree Example. Figure 3 illustrates the following scenario, which consists in a sequence of actions: the first action expected is a code injection attack from an attacker located in the DMZ network (we suppose that he manages to compromise a machine) to a server running a ftp service in the same network. Then two concurrent actions should be realized: the installation of a backdoor in the attacked server and the creation of a communication channel between this server and the attacker machine. Then, the attacker performs a privilege escalation and can shutdown some services with its administrator rights. In this picture, static variables are represented between signs "<>" and dynamic variables between signs "# #".

A second shorter attack scenario (see Fig. 4) introduces three actions. The first describes an attack from the external network to a web server located in the public DMZ. Then two actions are possible (as they are linked with an *Or* operator). These actions specify footprinting activities (it could be a port scan or any other recognition action) from the previous compromised web server to a second server in the DMZ or in the server zone.

The set of scenarios tested is composed of 15 different attack scenarios containing in average four actions (smallest and largest scenario contain respectively 2 and 8 actions). The scenarios expresses phases of recognition followed by exploitations and new recognitions from the compromised hosts, fishing attacks on the clients, compromises of a server and attacks to use the compromised machine against other servers on the internet.

Results. The attack scenarios tested were not all represented during the pentest (for example no attacks on clients were performed). In the other hand we know exactly which machines were compromised. This allows to classify each detection result. 7 (among 15) correlation rules trigger alerts that detect real multi-steps attacks (no false positive). Correlation rules that trigger no alarm

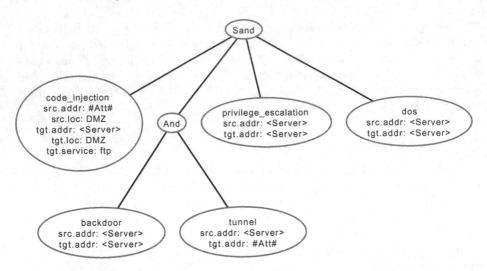

Fig. 3. Action tree: taking control of a machine and shutting down services

were representing multi-steps attacks that were not performed or performed only partially (no false negative). The detailed of the detected actions for each of the attack scenarios described in Figs. 3 and 4 are summarized in Fig. 6. A subset of this second correlation tree is illustrated in Fig. 5.

4   Introducing Faults in the Correlation Rule Generation Process

The Sect. 3 emphasises that with a knowledge base describing accurately the defended system and well described attack scenario, the generated correlation rules permit to correlate attack steps. False positives and false negative produced by IDSes can hinder the correlation process. Indeed, false positives can in some cases trigger the recognition of some attack scenario. False negatives can also hinder the recognition, but some methods can be used for taking into account missed attack in an attack chain [1]. In addition, the process can be altered in different ways, leading to altered correlation rules that could generate false positives or miss attacks. The goal of this section is to list the different ways the rules can be impacted. An experimental analysis of some of these faults is developed in Sect. 5

4.1   Faults in the Knowledge Base

Obsolete entries in the knowledge base lead to the generation of a correlation rule referencing irrelevant attack paths or irrelevant alerts. Consequences can be (1) generation of false positives triggered by the irrelevant messages present in the correlation rule, (2) false negatives in the case where irrelevant messages are

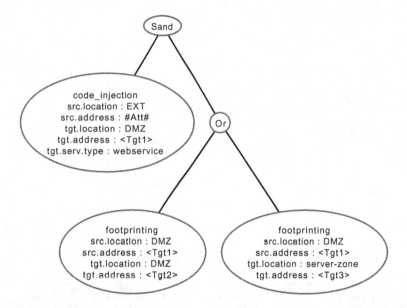

Fig. 4. Attack scenario: compromise

added to Sand or And operators. However, the presence of obsolete attack paths referencing host or services not present in the system can probably lead to very few false positives given that no alerts or messages concerning the services should be produced. These obsolete attack path should not trigger false negatives, as the correlation rule is a superset of the reference correlation rule.

Missing entries in the knowledge base can lead to false positives or false negatives depending on the data missing and the attack scenario involved. In general, a lack of information about devices in the knowledge base leads to false negatives. If some information concerning sensors are missing and the attack scenario consists in a sequence of unordered set of actions (Sand or And), the lack of suitable observers for an action can lead to the deletion of some important messages, leading to have less restrictive correlation rules that can trigger false positives.

Figure 7 illustrates the effects of two specific missing entries and one obsolete entry. The reference correlation tree (*T0*) is composed of messages that can be generated by a network IDS (*N1*) and local sensors (*L1* and *L2*). If we suppose that the knowledge base is outdated and references only one node (among two) or the network IDS is not present (or incorrectly referenced), we obtain respectively the correlation trees *T1* and *T2*. *T1* consists in the left branch of the reference tree and the correlation tree *T2* is not referencing any message produced by the NIDS *N1* (*N1_1* and *N1_2*). On the other hand, *T3* can result from a knowledge base containing a second network IDS *N0* that does not exist any more in the real system.

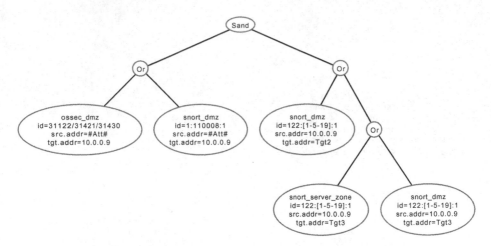

Fig. 5. Correlation tree

First attack scenario		Second attack scenario	
Attacker action	**Detected by**	**Attacker action**	**Detected by**
DISTCC vulnerability exploitation	Custom rule	code injection	snort rule 119:19:1
Backdoor	netstat result changes	dns zone transfert denied	Ossec rule 12145
tunnel between FTP and web server	ssh protocol detection		
perf_event local to root exploit	Custom rule		
Ossec agent stop	Nagios rule		

Fig. 6. Details of two attack scenarios and the related actions. Each elementary action is detected by a specific IDS rule

System size impact on fault consequences: The impact of the faults presented in Subsect. 4.1 can be modified by the size of the target system. Indeed, in a big system, a mistake in the knowledge base can lead to a correlation tree in which a relatively small part is false. As a consequence, is it less probable that an attack targets specifically only the nodes of the system that are not correctly represented in the knowledge base. Thus the rate of false negatives should be lower in this case than for smaller system.

4.2   Faults in Action Tree Specification

Some faults can be made during the process of transformation of an attack tree to an action tree (step 1).

Lack of details in the specification is characterized by a poor translation of an attack tree subgoal into elementary actions. If those actions are described too generically or are not all specified, the resulting correlation tree can be too generic and could generate potentially a lot of false positives.

Specifying too many elementary actions can have the opposite effect. Indeed, if a sequence contains actions that are not correctly ordered or an additional action

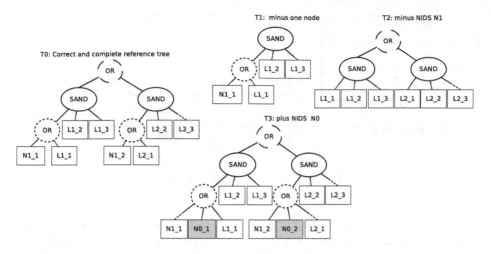

Fig. 7. Influence of some faults on the correlation tree

that is not going to be realized by the attacker, then the process generates correlation rules unable to detect the attack scenario, leading to false negatives.

5 Evaluating the Impact of Faults in the Correlation Process

Section 4 describes the theoretical consequences of different faults on the correlation tree. In this section, we propose to conduct an experimentation in order to evaluate the influence of different faults on the detection process. We focus on faults that affect the knowledge base because it seems to be the more common case. The evaluation consists in injecting known type of faults in an up to date knowledge base. The detection capability of the resulting rules is compared with the fault-free correlation rules.

5.1 System and Scenarios Tested

We start with an initial knowledge base that models properly the target system. This system is shown in Fig. 8. From this initial base, different faults are injected in the knowledge base. Then, correlation rules are generated based on the modified knowledge base. The detection capabilities of theses rules are then compared to those of the initial correlation rule. The injected faults are divided in two categories: Addition of an element that are not present in the reference knowledge base and deletion of elements. For this specific system, 13 attack scenarios are tested. In order to evaluate short scenarios and long and more complex scenarios, two types of scenarios are built: (1) attack scenarios consisting in two to four actions. (2) scenarios composed of the assembly of two simple scenarios joined together with the *Or* or the *Sand* logical operator.

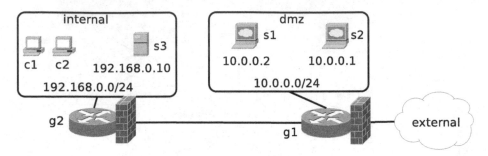

Fig. 8. Reference system topology

The first three scenarios (s0, s1, s2: see Fig. 9) focuse on actions that are mainly detectable by network sensors. The three ones that follow (s3, s4, s5) are built from the previous by replacing the root operator *sand* by an *and* operator. The next three (s6, s7, s8) are composed mostly of actions observable by host sensors. The last four consist in combinaison of the previous ones: s9 and s10 are respectively scenario built from linking the scenario s0 and s6 (resp. s0 and s3) with an *sand* operator. s11 and s12 are built in the same way as s9 and s10 but with an *or* operator instead of a *sand.*

5.2   Evaluation Mechanisms

Figures 10 and 11 explicit the way the influence of faults is evaluated. The reference knowledge base is the starting point. A fault is injected in the reference knowledge base and leads to the creation of an altered knowledge base. Given a specific attack scenario, it is possible to generate a correlation tree associated with each of these two knowledge bases. This process is illustrated in Fig. 10. Once the two correlations tree are built, they are feed to a correlator in order to process different logs. Some logs contain attack traces related to the initial attack scenario. False positives are evaluated for logs that contain no attack trace. Each such log can generate one false alarm. Thus, for a given attack scenario, the maximum number of false positives matches the number of logs with no attack traces. False negative are counted similarly: for each log containing an attack trace, each time no alert is raised, one false negative is counted. This method allows us to compare the number of false negatives and positives among the different scenarios. False positives and negatives are then compared to those produced by the reference output (This reference output produces no false positive and no false negatives by construction). This process is illustrated in Fig. 11.

Log generation: The logs used to test the generated correlation rules are semi randomly generated based on specific set of possibles fields values (IP addresses, Sensor Rule Id, ports). For each attack scenario, 200 samples of logs are generated. Each sample contains 1000 lines of logs. Initially, the log samples do not contain any trace matching the reference attack scenario. Traces of the attack is

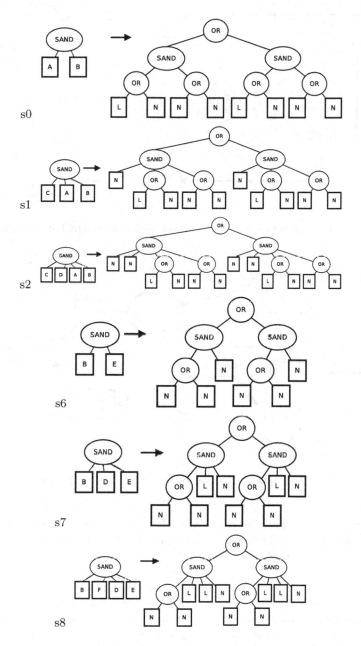

Fig. 9. Action trees and their matching correlation trees. In action trees (left of each arrow), letters denote different types of actions. In correlation trees (right), L and N stand respectively for an action visible by a local observer and a network observer.

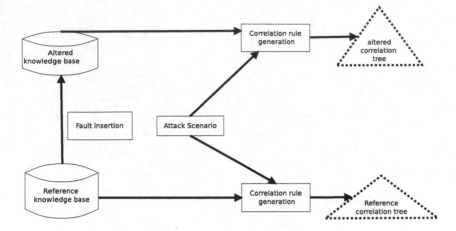

Fig. 10. Fault injection and faulty correlation rule generation procedure

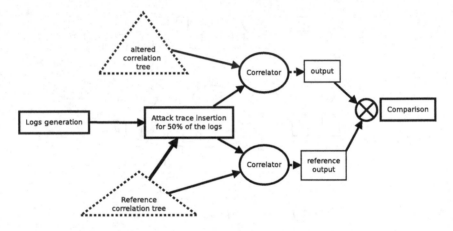

Fig. 11. Faulty correlation rule performances evaluation

included in half of the samples. These attack traces are generated by selecting a random attack path in the reference correlation tree (the details are explained in the following paragraph).

Attack insertion algorithm: The correlation tree contains all messages that could be generated when an attacker performs the attack scenario on the system. This tree contains several attack paths and each action could be monitored potentially by different sensors that may be complementary. In order to choose a realistic sequence of logs, an attack path (a branch among the root OR) is randomly chosen. Each time the branch contains an OR (which matches a choice in the attack scenario or a potential detection by several sensors), a random number of branches among the possible OR children are chosen. Thus, this process builds an attack sequence observable from a subpart of the possible observers.

5.3   Results

The results are shown in Table 1. Each line represents an attack scenario and each column a knowledge base configuration. The column labelled *ref* is the reference case. Other columns are labelled with the type of fault involved. The O prefix stands for the obsolete entries and the M prefix for the missing entries in the knowledge base. The added or removed elements include nodes, network sensor, local sensors and sensors rules. The recall and precision are used to measure the efficiency of the detection. Those values are defined as follows:

(TP : True Positives, TN : True Negatives, FP : False Positives, FN : False Negatives)

$$Recall = \frac{TP}{TP + FN}$$

$$Precision = \frac{TP}{TP + FP}$$

The results show that 50 % of the tested faults have an impact on the detection (this impact could be false negatives, false positives or both). Among all the tested faults, the most critical impact is observed for a missing network sensor. It can be explained by the wide visibility of this category of detecting device.

Test results show that additions of some types of elements (obsolete entries) in the knowledge base are not affecting the results. This can be explained by the way the rules are generated. Adding irrelevant items to the base will not change the output rules because these objects are not considered. On the other hand, the addition of potentially relevant facts (sensors or rules) makes altered correlation rules containing references to messages that can not be generated by any observer in the system. This case is discussed in the next paragraph and does not occur in our example because at least one observer can detect each action for each attack scenario. The explanation of the different scores depends greatly on the attack scenarios specific features. For example, scenarios 6 to 8 are composed of actions that are mostly only locally observable. Thus, the absence of a local sensor in the knowledge base (*M_local_sensor*) leads to correlation rules that generate false positives and no false negatives, contrary to the other scenarios for this fault. This can be explained by the correlation rule structure that is reduced to only one network sensor event and no local sensor events. Thus, each time this event occurs, an alarm is raised. On the other hand, these scenarios are less prone to false negatives than the others when a network sensor is missing in the knowledge base.

From the figure, we should conclude that superfluous information never impacts the correlation rule efficiency. This is false in theory, but three conditions have to be met in order to impact the detection. It supposed that: (1) the attack scenario contains at least one action that cannot be monitored by at least one observer (2) this action is directly part of a sequence of actions or a conjunction of actions (Sand or And) (3) there is a superfluous observer or detection rule in the knowledge base and this observer/rule can monitor the specific action. Given those prerequisites, the generated correlation rule includes the

Table 1. Recall (Rec.) and precision (Pre.) for each tested faults types

Fault	ref		O_node		O_sig_net_sensor		O_node_loc_sensor		O_sig_loc_sensor		M_node		M_net_sensor		M_local_sensor		M_net_sig	
Scenario	Rec.	Pre.	Rec.	Pre.	Rec.	Pre.	Rec.	Pre.	Rec.	Pre.	Rec.	Pre.	Rec.	Pre.	Rec.	Pre.	Rec.	Pre.
S0	100	100	100	100	100	100	100	100	100	100	50	100	92	52	76	100	50	100
S1	100	100	100	100	100	100	100	100	100	100	57	100	90	52	80	100	61	100
S2	100	100	100	100	100	100	100	100	100	100	50	100	91	51	71	100	55	100
S3	100	100	100	100	100	100	100	100	100	100	47	100	90	51	81	100	57	100
S4	100	100	100	100	100	100	100	100	100	100	47	100	94	52	68	100	40	100
S5	100	100	100	100	100	100	100	100	100	100	49	100	91	52	69	100	49	100
S6	100	100	100	100	100	100	100	100	100	100	45	100	100	56	100	90	53	100
S7	100	100	100	100	100	100	100	100	100	100	49	100	100	97	100	92	47	100
S8	100	100	100	100	100	100	100	100	100	100	57	100	100	95	100	85	63	100
S9	100	100	100	100	100	100	100	100	100	100	51	100	82	64	71	100	31	100
S10	100	100	100	100	100	100	100	100	100	100	51	100	33	83	67	100	22	100
S11	100	100	100	100	100	100	100	100	100	100	49	100	99	50	79	100	68	100
S12	100	100	100	100	100	100	100	100	100	100	49	100	91	51	73	100	49	100

messages that should be raised by the non existent observer. As a consequence, it acts as a blocking event in the attack scenario recognition (false negative).

6   Related Work

One of the main prerequisite of the alert correlation rule generation is the knowledge base that models the environment. Such an environment model is an important feature in the field of alert correlation. The approaches [13] and [7] use an environment model describing the different hosts, services, vulnerabilities and access control lists present in the system in order to classify the received alerts based on their accuracy and reliability.

Moreover, some works [4,8] rely on attack graphs, a structure sharing some similarities with attack trees. The main difference is that attack graphs are often automatically generated from known vulnerabilities or possible elementary attacks on a given system. As a consequence, the attack correlation method relying on automatically generated attack graph are only accurate for the detection of attack paths exploiting known and identified vulnerabilities.

Evaluating correlation system is a complex task. Indeed, the dataset used to test the correlation system has to be representative of a real system and should not introduce biases while containing interesting complex attack traces. Famous datasets have been studied and used by the intrusion detection and alert correlation community. These datasets include the DARPA[1] intrusion dataset, the Defcon 9 dataset, the honeynet project scan of the month 17 and the Treasure Hunt dataset [12]. DARPA dataset are criticised in [5] and [11]: the main problem is related to the fact that these datasets are not real and include bare attack traces synthetically injected in a background noise. This noise alone should normally never produce false positives, which could be a problem (because some normal traffic are created by poor implementations of protocols that can behave like abnormal behaviour). In addition, these datasets include only events (and no alerts). As a consequence, it is difficult to evaluate the efficiency of the correlation system alone because of the dependencies with the IDSses choices and

---

[1] MIT Lincoln Laboratory, DARPA Intrusion Detection Evaluation, http://www.ll.mit.edu/ideval/.

configurations. The problem with the Defcon 9 dataset is the lack of realistic background traffic and amount of attacks compared to legitimate traffic. The honeynet logs are limited to an infrastructure consisting in a single web server. Moreover, normal and representative traffic is not expected on a honeypot. The treasure Hunt is more interesting from the system complexity and attack scenario point of view but it provides only raw data and no alerts. As explained in [11], running IDSes on those data can generate bias because the quality and number of alarms generated depends highly on the IDSses configurations. In other works [9] logs from university network are used. This can provide more realistic data but some sensible information must be removed prior to the detection, which can bias the results.

7   Conclusion and Future Work

In this article, we show that, with ideal conditions, the process that creates correlation rules neither create malformed rules nor introduce false positives in those rules. Then, we show that this process is applicable in a real case scenario including a medium size system. Finally, we take into account the fact that the generation process relies on a knowledge base that may not be properly synchronised with the real environment. As a consequence, the reliability of the generated correlation rules has been tested after some controlled fault injections in the knowledge base. It resulted that some types of faults have a great impact on false positives and false negatives while other types have no easily noticeable impacts. These results show that if the knowledge base describes a superset of the real system, the detection is not hindered in most case scenarios. On the contrary, a knowledge base describing a subset of the actual system causes detection capabilities deterioration. However, it is important to notice that the impact of the faults is also determined by the features of each attack scenario (size, action visibility). It could be then interesting to consider a study on possible attack scenario structures for which the different faults only slightly alter the detection process.

References

1. Ahmadinejad, S.H., Jalili, S., Abadi, M.: A hybrid model for correlating alerts of known and unknown attack scenarios and updating attack graphs. Comput. Netw. **55**(9), 2221–2240 (2011)
2. Çamtepe, S.A., Yener, B.: Modeling and detection of complex attacks. In: Proceedings of the 3rd International Conference on Security and Privacy in Communications Networks, pp. 234–243. IEEE (2007)
3. Godefroy, E., Totel, E., Hurfin, M., Majorczyk, F.: Automatic generation of correlation rules to detect complex attack scenarios. In: 2014 10th International Conference on Information Assurance and Security (IAS), pp. 23–28. IEEE (2014)
4. Jajodia, S., Noel, S.: Topological vulnerability analysis: A powerful new approach for network attack prevention, detection, and response. Indian Statistical Institute Monograph Series (2007)

5. McHugh, J.: Testing intrusion detection systems: a critique of the 1998 and 1999 darpa intrusion detection system evaluations as performed by lincoln laboratory. ACM Trans. Inf. Syst. Secur. **3**(4), 262–294 (2000)

6. Michel, C., Mé, L.: ADeLe: an attack description language for knowledge-based intrusion detection. In: Dupuy, M., Paradinas, P. (eds.) SEC 2001. IFIP AICT, vol. 65, pp. 353–365. Springer, Heidelberg (2001)

7. Noel, S., Robertson, E., Jajodia, S.: Correlating intrusion events and building attack scenarios through attack graph distances. In: ACSAC, pp. 350–359 (2004)

8. Roschke, S., Cheng, F., Meinel, C.: A new alert correlation algorithm based on attack graph. In: Herrero, A., Corchado, E. (eds.) CISIS 2011. LNCS, vol. 6694, pp. 58–67. Springer, Heidelberg (2011)

9. Tjhai, G.C., Papadaki, M., Furnell, S., Clarke, N.L.: Investigating the problem of ids false alarms: An experimental study using snort. In: Jajodia, S., Samarati, P., Cimato, S. (eds.) Proceedings of the IFIP TC 11 23rd International Information Security Conference. IFIP AICT, vol. 278, pp. 253–267. Springer, Boston (2008)

10. Totel, E., Vivinis, B., Mé, L.: A language driven intrusion detection system for event and alert correlation. In: Proceedings ot the 19th IFIP International Information Security Conference, pp. 209–224. Kluwer Academic (2004)

11. Valdes, A., Skinner, K.: Probabilistic alert correlation. In: Lee, W., Mé, L., Wespi, A. (eds.) RAID 2001. LNCS, vol. 2212, pp. 54–68. Springer, Heidelberg (2001)

12. Vigna, G.: Teaching hands-on network security: Testbeds and live exercises. J. Inf. Warfare **3**(2), 8–25 (2003)

13. Xu, D., Ning, P.: Alert correlation through triggering events and common resources. In: 20th Annual Computer Security Applications Conference, pp. 360–369. IEEE (2004)

Cloud Security

Similarity Measure for Security Policies in Service Provider Selection

Yanhuang Li[1,2(✉)], Nora Cuppens-Boulahia[2], Jean-Michel Crom[1],
Frédéric Cuppens[2], Vincent Frey[1], and Xiaoshu Ji[1]

[1] Orange Labs, 4 Rue du Clos Courtel, 35510 Cesson-Sévigné, France
{yanhuang.li,jeanmichel.crom,vincent.frey,xiaoshu.ji}@orange.com
[2] Télécom Bretagne, 2 Rue de la Châtaigneraie, 35510 Cesson-Sévigné, France
{nora.cuppens,frederic.cuppens}@telecom-bretagne.eu

Abstract. The interaction between different applications and services requires expressing their security properties. This is typically defined as security policies, which aim at specifying the diverse privileges of different actors. Today similarity measure for comparing security policies becomes a crucial technique in a variety of scenarios, such as finding the cloud service providers which satisfy client's security concerns. Existing approaches cover from semantic to numerical dimensions and the main work focuses mainly on XACML policies. However, few efforts have been made to extend the measure approach to multiple policy models and apply it to concrete scenarios. In this paper, we propose a generic and light-weight method to compare and evaluate security policies belonging to different models. Our technique enables client to quickly locate service providers with potentially similar policies. Comparing with other works, our approach takes policy elements' logic relationships into account and the experiment and implementation demonstrate the efficiency and accuracy of our approach.

Keywords: IT security · Access control · Policy evaluation · Similarity measure

1 Introduction

Nowadays, data and service exchange across multiple actors becomes an emerging demand to provide dynamic ecosystems. This process involves a large number of actors such as cloud service provider (SP) and client. From customer's point of view, it is always difficult to decide whose service should be chosen so they use a broker to rank and select the suitable SPs based on user's requirement. However, most of the current service ranking technologies [1] do not consider the security aspect or they only measure security parameters such as encryption method [2] and security level [3,4]. Among various criteria that need to be considered for the service selection, security policy is a critical concern. Before a collaboration takes place between different actors, an actor A may need to know

© Springer International Publishing Switzerland 2015
S. Jajodia and C. Mazumdar (Eds.): ICISS 2015, LNCS 9478, pp. 227–242, 2015.
DOI: 10.1007/978-3-319-26961-0_14

if the other actor guarantees a similar level of A's security policies. Policy comparison is one of the main mechanisms to that end. It consists in measuring the similarity between two security policies and giving an evaluation score. A higher score between policies p_1 and p_2 indicates that they are more likely to share an equivalent security level and yield the same decisions. Unlike other measure criteria, security policies are usually based on first-order logic. For example, an access control policy consists of multiple elements and they collectively determine whether a user is allowed to take some actions on certain objects. Thus, the existing brokering technologies are difficult to apply on security policies.

In this paper, we propose a new algorithm to calculate the similarity score between two policies. The contribution is twofold. On one hand, our method is policy-agnostic and can be applied on various types of security policies. On the other hand, we propose integrating our policy similarity measure algorithm in SP selection process and the implementation proves that this integration can enrich the services offered with efficiency.

The rest of the paper is organized as follows: Sect. 2 reviews existing proposals on security policy models and policy similarity measure techniques. Section 3 proposes the policy similarity measure algorithm with an exhaustive calculation example. Section 4 illustrates an experiment in which the accuracy of our algorithm is demonstrated. Section 5 gives an implementation integrated with our algorithm. Section 6 concludes the paper and outlines future work.

2   Related Work

To present our policy evaluation method, we suggest, as a first step, to specify security policies which describe and control different exchanges within a dynamic environment of diverse applications. In this context, the administrator of these applications has to define what is permitted and what is prohibited during the execution in order to secure the use of the proposed services. To do that, he should specify the security policy to be implemented. Access control policy is one kind of such policies. An access policy governs access to protected resources by specifying which subjects can access which resources by which operations and under which circumstances. The specification of access control policy depends on different policy models. One widely used model is RBAC (Role-Based Access Control) [5]. In the RBAC model, access permissions are not assigned directly to the users but are abstracted as roles which correspond to different task descriptions. To apply RBAC, users should be assigned to different roles thus they possess indirectly the relevant permissions. The OrBAC (Organization Based Access Control) model [6] is an extension of the RBAC model. It defines a conceptual and industrial framework to meet the needs of information security and sensitive communications and allows the policy designer to define a security policy independently. With the development of web service, ABAC (Attribute Based Access Control) model [7] brings flexibility and interoperability for policy definition. The ABAC model defines permissions based on security-relevant attributes such as subject attributes, resource attributes and environment attributes.

To the best of our knowledge, most approaches to evaluate policy similarity are based on XACML [8] policies. Lin et al. [9] propose an algorithm to evaluate policy similarity by calculating the similarity score between two XACML policies. This is indeed a pioneering work and it effectively distinguishes the categorical predicate and numerical predicate cases. The second version of the algorithm [10] advances the measure algorithm for numerical predicate and integrates ontology matching. However, the work has two limitations. Firstly, the algorithm only focuses on the literal level but not logic aspect of security policy. As a result, the similarity score computed may have a large difference with the test value in real cases (presented in Appendix A). Secondly, the former algorithm contains 9 weight parameters which need to be configured and choosing the proper values is not easy to users. In addition, there are two variants of the former work. Bei et al. [11] investigate the contrary of the similarity: dissimilarity. In order to address the rule relationship comparison, they apply fuzzy theory to compute rule dissimilarity. Pham et al. [12] improve the similarity computing approach specified by Lin et al. [9] and also propose a mechanism to calculate a dissimilarity score by identifying related policies which are likely to produce different access decisions. Based on policy similarity measure, there exist some applications. Lin et al. [13] present a novel data protection framework in which policy similarity comparison approach is applied on policy ranking model. Cho et al. [14] propose a technique that allows similarity evaluation of encrypted policies. Shaikh et al. [15] suggest using similarity measure to select services in a distributed and heterogeneous environment. Bertolino et al. [16] put forward a new approach for access control test prioritization based on similarity.

3   Policy Similarity Measure (PSM)

The PSM assigns a similarity score S_{policy} for any two given policies, which approximates the percentage of the rule pairs having the same decision. The formal definition is given in Eq. (1), where $Num(sameDecision(r_{1i}, r_{2j}))$ denotes the quantity of the rule pairs having the same decision and $Num(allDecision(r_{1i}, r_{2j}))$ denotes the amount of the total decision pairs.

$$S_{policy}(p_1, p_2) \approx \frac{Num(sameDecision(r_{1i}, r_{2j}))}{Num(allDecision(r_{1i}, r_{2j}))}, \qquad r_{1i} \in p_1, \ r_{2j} \in p_2 \quad (1)$$

The similarity score is a value between 0 and 1. Two equivalent policies are expected to obtain a similarity score which equals 1. We mention that the definition of policy similarity score in [10] focuses on the percentage of the requests obtaining the same decisions. Comparing with the former work, our definition for PSM is more fine-grained because the same decision from two policies can be derived from one or multiple rule pairs. Consequently, by considering decisions of rule pairs but not final policy decisions, our PSM is more accurate from both calculation and test aspects. More details are shown in Sect. 4.

3.1 Policy Structure

As a generic algorithm, our PSM can be applied on different policy models and this compatibility requires a transformation process before calculation. Policies are firstly split into different rules and each rule is expressed in the form of:

$$decision\_effect(attr\_name_1 \oplus attr\_value_1, ..., attr\_name_n \oplus attr\_value_n) \quad (2)$$

where *decision_effect* is a decision effect such as permit and deny; *attr_name* denotes the name of an attribute; $\oplus$ indicates a comparison operator and *attr_value* represents an attribute value. We define $(attr\_name_i \oplus attr\_value_i)$ as a policy element and it can be broadly classified into the following five categories [17,18]:

Category 1: One Variable Equality Constraints. $x = c$, where x is a variable and c is a constant.

Category 2: One Variable Inequality Constraints. $x \triangleright c$, where x is a variable, c is a constant and $\triangleright \in \{<, \leq, >, \geq\}$.

Category 3: Real Valued Linear Constraints. $\sum_{i=1}^{n} a_i x_i \triangleright c_i$, where x_i is a variable, a_i, c_i are constants and $\triangleright \in \{=, <, \leq, >, \geq\}$. This category contains conjunctions of atomic boolean expressions defined by linear constraints in m-dimensional real space.

Category 4: Regular Expression Constraints. The general form of boolean expression in this category is any element formed using $\wedge$ and $\vee$ with expressions of the form either $s \in L(r)$ or $s \notin L(r)$, where s is a *string* variable and $L(r)$ is the language generated by regular expression r.

Category 5: Compound Boolean Expression Constraints. This category includes constraints obtained by combining elements belonging to the categories listed above. The combination operators can be $\wedge, \vee$ and $\neg$.

It is worth noting that elements in most security policies usually belong to category 1 2 and 3. In this paper, we are not going to address how to deal with category 4 because expressing security policy by generated language is out of scope of basic security policy definition. We would also like to mention that the categories listed above are not mutually exclusive. For example, the expression "$8:00 \leq Time \leq 18:00$" which belongs to category 3 can be also expressed by category 5: "$(8:00 \leq Time) \wedge (Time \leq 18:00)$". In our formalization, in order to minimize the expected computational burden, we avoid the use of category 5 by transforming the policy elements with Boolean combinations into category 3.

We would also like to note that each element in Form 2 after transformation should be atomic. An element is atomic if it does not contain explicitly compound logical operator $(\wedge, \vee, \neg)$. By this definition, an atomic element can belong to category 1, 2 and just one dimension of category 3. In category 5, an element whose attribute values are connected by "$\vee$" operator can be expressed by a set. Here we don't consider "$\neg$" operator for the reason that "$\neg$" relation can be converted into rules having contrary effects. Having different types of attribute values, atomic elements in security policies can be divided into the following two types:

- **Categorical element**: The operator is "=" and the attribute value belongs to the *string* data type or be a set of *string*. For example "Role=admin" and "Action=[read,write,create]" are categorical atomic elements.
- **Numerical element**: The operator can be "=","<","≤",">","≥" and the attribute value can be integer, real, date/time data types. Operators and values can be combined into a set or an interval. For example, elements "time={3 pm, 4 pm, 5 pm}", *"FileSize* > 5 GB", "8 : 00 ≤ *Time* ≤ 18 : 00" are numerical atomic elements.

In an example that we will use throughout the paper, we consider three XACML policies illustrated in [10]. These policies are defined for managing an information system of a research laboratory. The policies after transformation are:

Policy1 (p_1)
r_{11} : $Permit(Role = \{professor, postDoc, student, techStaff\},$
$Resource = \{source, documentation, executable\}, Action = \{read, write\})$
r_{12} : $Deny(Role = \{student, postDoc, techStaff\},$
$Resource = \{source, documentation, executable\}, Action = write,$
$19 : 00 \leq Time \leq 21 : 00)$

Policy2 (p_2)
r_{21} : $Permit(Role = \{student, faculty, techStaff\}, Action = \{read, write\},$
$FileSize \leq 120 \text{ MB})$
r_{22} : $Permit(Role = techStaff, Action = \{read, write\}, 19 : 00 \leq Time \leq 22 : 00)$
r_{23} : $Deny(Role = student, Action = write, 19 : 00 \leq Time \leq 22 : 00)$
r_{24} : $Deny(Role = \{student, faculty, staff\}, Action = \{read, write\},$
$Resource = media)$

Policy3 (p_3)
r_{31} : $Permit(Role = businessStaff, Resource = xls, Action = \{read, write\},$
$8 : 00 \leq Time \leq 17 : 00, FileSize \leq 10 \text{ MB})$
r_{32} : $Deny(Role = student, Action = \{read, write\})$

From a user's perspective, p_1 is more similar to p_2 than p_3 because most activities described by p_1 for the data owner are allowed by p_2. Our motivation is to quickly compute similarity scores $S_{policy}(p_1, p_2)$ and $S_{policy}(p_1, p_3)$ with expectation that the former is higher than the latter. The expected result is to indicate that the similarity between p_1 and p_2 is much higher than the similarity between p_1 and p_3.

3.2 Overview of PSM Algorithm

Shown in Fig. 1, the PSM algorithm takes two policies as input and generates a similarity score as output. The calculation process can be divided into four steps.

Step 1: Policy Transformation. Two policies to be computed are split into rules in Form 2 which consist of atomic elements as follows.

$$r_{1i} : Permit(e_{1i\_1}, e_{1i\_2}, ...), \ r_{2j} : Permit(e_{2j\_1}, e_{2j\_2}, ...), \ ...$$

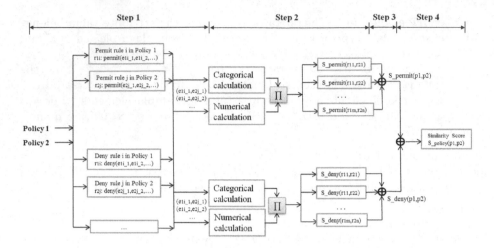

Fig. 1. The process of similarity score calculation

Step 2: Rule Pair Calculation. Scores of each rule pair in the same decision effect (d) between two policies are calculated. In Eq. (3), the score for each rule pair is the product of the scores of all the element pairs. Product operation is chosen because any mismatch of element pair results different replies from two policies. Details for element pair calculation are shown in Sect. 3.3.

$$S_d(r_{1i}, r_{2j}) = \prod_k S(e_{1i\_k}, e_{2j\_k}), \qquad r_{1i} \in p_1,\ r_{2j} \in p_2,\ e_{1i\_k} \in r_{1i},\ e_{2j\_k} \in r_{2j} \quad (3)$$

Step 3: Decision Effect Calculation. Each $S_d(p_1, p_2)$ equals the sum of all the similarity scores of rule pairs in one decision effect (Eq. (4)).

$$S_d(p_1, p_2) = \sum_i \sum_j S_d(r_{1i}, r_{2j}), \qquad r_{1i} \in p_1,\ r_{2j} \in p_2 \quad (4)$$

Step 4: Total Score Calculation. Shown in Eq. (5), the total score is based on the scores from different decision effects $S_d(p_1, p_2)$ and the total amount of rule pairs from all the decision effects.

$$S_{policy}(p_1, p_2) = \frac{\sum_d S_d(p_1, p_2)}{\sum_d Num(d)}, \qquad d \in (permit, deny, ...). \quad (5)$$

3.3   Similarity Score of Rule Elements

The score of an element pair can be calculated when they share the same attribute name and in the same decision effect. In step 2 above, the score of a rule pair is based on the rule elements having the same attribute name. When an element's attribute name does not appear in another rule, the access decisions from the two rules are not affected due to this difference. For this reason, we consider that the score of such element is 1. The calculation for similarity score of rule elements differs in element type.

Similarity Score for Categorical Elements. For categorical elements, we measure the exact match of two values. A higher score indicates that the two elements share more common attribute values. The formula for two elements e_1 and e_2 is defined as follows:

$$S_c(e_1, e_2) = \frac{num(v_1 \cap v_2)}{num(v_1 \cup v_2 \cup v_3 ... \cup v_n)} \tag{6}$$

$S_c(e_1, e_2)$ presents the exact percentage of the same decision for one element pair. $num(v_1 \cap v_2)$ denotes the quantity of common attribute values between element e_1 and e_2; $num(v_1 \cup v_2 \cup v_3 ... \cup v_n)$ is the quantity of common attribute values among all the elements in two policies and these elements should (1) have the same attribute name (2) belong to the rules of the same decision effect. Equation (6) is an extension of Jaccard similarity coefficient [19]. The difference is that the denominator in our equation covers two policies but not two rules because the aggregation of element scores in decision effect calculation (Eq. 4) requires the same attribute space shared by different rule pairs.

Some policy models may use abstract element to represent a set of concrete values. For example, in RBAC, *Role* element is an abstraction of *Subjects*; in OrBAC, a *Role* is a set of *Subjects*, an *Activity* is a set of *Actions* and a *View* is a set of *Objects*. In this case, the abstract values should be transformed to their related concrete values. For example, abstraction trees for *Role* and *Resource* elements of p_1, p_2, p_3 are shown in Figs. 2 and 3.

Fig. 2. Abstraction tree for Role element.

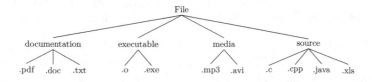

Fig. 3. Abstraction tree for Resource element.

To calculate the score of *Role* elements between r_{11} and r_{21}, as *student* and *faculty* are two abstract values, they should be translated into concrete values which are leaves: $\{undergraduate, graduate\}$ and $\{postDoc, professor, professorEmeritus, instructor\}$. After the transformation, we find that the two elements share 5 common attribute values. The disjunction of all the *Role* elements from policy 1 and policy 2 contains 8 attribute values. Applying Eq. (6), $S_c(e_{r\_11(Role)}, e_{r\_21(Role)}) = 5/8 = 0.625$.

Another application of tree architecture is to represent the inheritance relation. The inheritance mechanism is defined in object-oriented programming as an efficient way to design an application. In Java, a class which is derived from another class is called a subclass. A similar mechanism for roles is used in RBAC [5] and the hierarchy of roles is associated with inheritance of permission. The role inheritance mechanism is extended in OrBAC model [20]: hierarchies of roles, views and activities are formally defined associated with inheritance relationships. In an inheritance tree, child elements can inherit the privileges of their parent elements. For example, the *Role* elements of a research laboratory may possess an inheritance tree for permission (Fig. 4). When applying Eq. (6), all the attribute values having inheritance relationship in the same inheritance tree should be treated as identical ones.

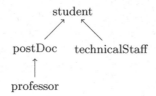

Fig. 4. Inheritance tree for *Role* element

Similarity Score for Numerical Elements. The calculation for numerical elements is more complex because numerical attribute values may have different forms such as single value, set, bounded interval and unbounded interval. Here we propose a unified method defined in Algorithm 1 for computing the similarity score between two numerical elements. The algorithm takes two numerical elements as input. Firstly, if two elements have the same attribute name, operator(s) and attribute value(s), the score is 1 (lines 1,2). Secondly, the two elements should be checked if their intersection is empty. An empty intersection returns 0 as similarity score (lines 4,5). Otherwise, there are three cases:

- **Bounded interval (lines 7,8):** Two elements' values are both bounded interval. Length of an interval equals the difference between its endpoints. To compute the score, we divide the length of the conjunction of two intervals by the length of their disjunction. For example, the score for time elements in r_{12} and r_{23} is: $S_n(r\_12(time), r\_23(time)) = Len(21 - 19)/Len(22 - 19) = 0.67$.

Algorithm 1. $S_n(e_1, e_2)$: numerical similarity score calculation
Input: two numerical elements e_1 and e_2
Output: numerical similarity score

1: **if** $e_1 = e_2$ **then**
2:     return 1
3: **end if**
4: **if** $e_1 \cap e_2 = \phi$ **then**
5:     return 0
6: **else**
7:     **if** both e_1 and e_2 are bounded intervals **then**
8:        **return** $\frac{Len(e_1 \cap e_2)}{Len(e_1 \cup e_2)}$
9:     **else if** both e_1 and e_2 are sets **then**
10:        **return** $\frac{Num(e_1 \cap e_2)}{Num(e_1 \cup e_2)}$
11:     **else**
12:        return 0.5
13:     **end if**
14: **end if**

- **Set (lines 9,10)**: Two elements' values are both sets. To compute the score, we divide the cardinality of the conjunction of two sets by the cardinality of their disjunction. For example, $Time_1 = [3\ am, 4\ am, 5\ am]$, $Time_2 = [4\ am, 5\ am, 6\ am]$, $S_n(Time_1, Time_2) = 2/4 = 0.5$.
- **Other cases**: As calculation between two different forms is difficult, we assign a fuzzy value 0.5 as the similarity score. 0.5 is chosen because it is the average value of similarity score.

3.4 Example of Calculation

Here we present an exhaustive example to illustrate how the PSM works. Continuing with the three policies p_1, p_2, p_3 defined in Sect. 3.1 and their abstraction trees introduced in Sect. 3.3, we illustrate the four steps of calculation.

1. **Policy transformation:** Shown in Sect. 3.1, the three policies have already been transformed from XACML policies to rules composed of atomic elements.
2. **Rule pair calculation:** Applying Eqs. (3), (6) and Algorithm 1, we calculate scores for different rule pairs in each decision effect:

$$Permit:$$
$$S_{rule}(r_{11}, r_{21}) = 0.625 \times 1 \times 1 \times 1 = 0.625$$
$$S_{rule}(r_{11}, r_{22}) = 0.125 \times 1 \times 1 \times 1 = 0.125$$
$$Deny:$$
$$S_{rule}(r_{12}, r_{23}) = 0.25 \times 1 \times 0.5 \times 0.67 = 0.084$$
$$S_{rule}(r_{12}, r_{24}) = 0.5 \times 0 \times 0.5 \times 1 = 0$$

3. **Decision effect calculation:** By Eq. (4), scores of each decision effect are:

$$S_{permit} = S_{rule}(r_{11}, r_{21}) + S_{rule}(r_{11}, r_{22}) = 0.75$$
$$S_{deny} = S_{rule}(r_{12}, r_{23}) + S_{rule}(r_{12}, r_{24}) = 0.084$$

4. **Total score calculation:** The final score between two policies is calculated by Eq. (5):

$$S_{policy}(p_1, p_2) = \frac{S_{permit} + S_{deny}}{Num(permit) + Num(deny)} = \frac{0.75 + 0.084}{2 + 2} = 0.209$$

Applying the same process, we can also calculate the similarity score between policies p_1 and p_3: $S_{policy}(p_1, p_3) = 0.083$. The two scores $S_{policy}(p_1, p_2)$ and $S_{policy}(p_1, p_3)$ indicates that policy p_1 is more similar to p_2 than p_3 in terms of the percentage of rule pairs having the same decision.

4   Experimental Results

In order to verify if our algorithm is applicable to real cases, we compare the percentage of the same decision pairs with the PSM score. Firstly, we implement a random policy generator which takes policy elements as input then generates access control policies in Form 2. Secondly, we extract policy elements from four policies with different models and each of them is related to a real scenario: RBAC for project management [21], Net-RBAC for firewall configuration [22], OrBAC for hospital management [23], ABAC for administration of research laboratory [10]. Thirdly, these policy elements are inputted to the policy generator and each policy pair generated obtains a similarity score by our algorithm. Finally, we input various combinations of elements as access control requests into the four policies and count the percentage of the same decision pair between rules from output. We mention that the test method which we used are brute-force based: for categorical element, we take all the combination of *string* values; for numerical element, enumerating all the numerical based attribute value in an interval (For example $19 : 00 \leq Time \leq 21 : 00$) is impossible. Without loss of generalization, we make equidistant sampling for bounded interval and bilateral sampling for unbounded interval. For example, inputs are all the integers from 1 to 24 for $0 : 00 \leq Time \leq 24 : 00$; for $FileSize > 10$ MB, inputs are $FileSize = 9$ MB and $FileSize = 11$ MB.

Figures 5 and 6 show the policy similarity score (y-axis) and the same decision percentage for rule pairs (x-axis) in *set*-4 and *set*-8. Each test set contains 1000 pairs of policies. In *set*-4, each policy has four rules and in *set*-8 each policy has eight rules. The configurations of elements for each policy model are shown in Table 1. For example, laboratory administration policies are written by ABAC model and these policies contain 19 categorical elements with permit and deny effects. We observe that the score increases when the similarity between two policies increases. At the same time, the experimental values approach to the scores calculated and the quantity of test rules has no impact on the variation of curves. These data enable us to conclude that the PSM score well approximates the similarity between policies.

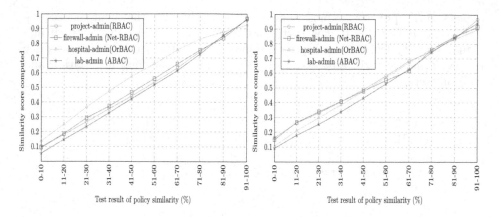

Fig. 5. Experiment of similarity score (*set*-4).

Fig. 6. Experiment of similarity score (*set*-8).

Table 1. Policies tested

Policy	Model	Categorical element	Numerical element	Effect
project-admin	RBAC	15	0	permit
firewall-admin	Net-RBAC	4	28	permit
hospital-admin	OrBAC	15	6	permit,deny
lab-admin	ABAC	19	0	permit,deny

5 Application

Our PSM algorithm can be applied to different SP selection use cases such as network configuration, compute allocation and cloud storage. This section presents a concrete scenario.

5.1 Scenario Description

SUPERCLOUD [24] is a European project which aims to support user-centric deployments across multi-clouds and enables the composition of innovative trustworthy services. SUPERCLOUD will build a security management architecture and infrastructure to fulfill the vision of user-centric secure and dependable clouds of clouds. One use case is to build a middle-ware layer between cloud customer and cloud SPs and this middle-ware could select SP(s) according to the security requirement of client. Here we implement a scenario of cloud storage. The subjects involved in the scenario are cloud client, cloud broker and SP. A cloud client wants to use the cloud storage service(s) provided by one or multiple SPs. At the same time, the client wishes that the security policies of SP meet his requirement. Otherwise, he may launch a negotiation process with SP(s) whose security policies are most approximate. To this end, the client chooses the SUPERCLOUD solution. It is worth noting that discovering SP(s) with client's similar security level is just a pre-selection phase. Other criteria such as price and performance will be taken into consideration in the final negotiation and decision steps.

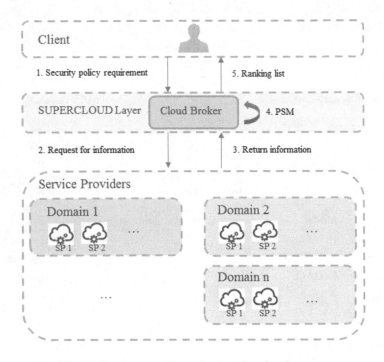

Fig. 7. Service provider selection for cloud storage

The implementation is based on CloudSim [22] simulation framework. Figure 7 illustrates the architecture of our implementation. Firstly, client expresses his requirement on cloud storage by security policies. For example, client may wish that he could have a space of 100 GB and he is allowed to upload files between 8:00 and 22:00. Then the client sends his requirement to the SUPERCLOUD layer where a cloud broker is deployed. The cloud broker obtains the information and security policy templates from SPs. Applying our PSM algorithm, the broker proposes a ranking list of SPs which meet client's requirement from storage space to security policies. PSM scores from SPs are ranked from high to low. When one SP's storage space is less than the requirement, broker may also propose a composition of two SPs in the same domain[1]. In this case, two SPs' security policies should be combined and the policy after composition is also calculated by PSM and ranked. The composition operation depends on concrete use

---

[1] We suppose that SPs in a cloud federation share the same domain and two SPs in the same domain can be composed as a virtual SP.

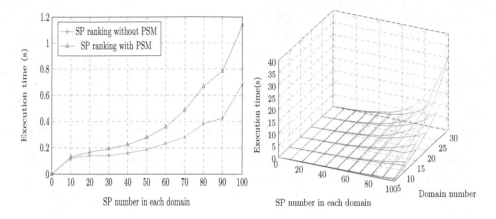

Fig. 8. Execution time of SP ranking (domain number=5)

Fig. 9. Execution time of SP ranking (domain number=5~30)

cases. Here we apply *Conjunction* (&) operation proposed in [25] for cloud storage policies. Consequently, there is more storage space and the security policy is stricter after composition. An example is as follows:

SP$_1$: 50 GB, *Permit*(*Action* : [*upload, download*], 8 : 00 ≤ *Time* ≤ 23 : 00)

SP$_2$: 50 GB, *Permit*(*Action* : [*upload, download, delete*], 7 : 00 ≤ *Time* ≤ 22 : 00)

SP$_1$&SP$_2$: 100 GB, *Permit*(*Action* : [*upload, download*], 8 : 00 ≤ *Time* ≤ 22 : 00).

5.2   Performance

The implementation is programmed in JAVA and is executed on an Intel machine having configuration: 2.2 GHz with 4 GB of RAM running Windows 8 and JDK 1.8. We measure the execution time needed until the client receives a SP ranking list. Figure 8 shows the execution time with the increase of SP quantity from 0 to 100 in each domain and there exist five domains. Blue line with triangles presents the execution time with the PSM and red line with stars shows the execution time without the PSM. In Fig. 9, the domain number varies from 5 to 30. The higher surface presents the execution time with the PSM and the lower surface shows the execution time without the PSM. From the two figures, we remark that the introduction of the PSM does not cause much of performance loss and it proves that our PSM algorithm is light-weight.

6   Conclusion and Future Work

The main objective of this paper is to expose our proposition to show how to measure the similarity between two security policies. The proposition gives mainly a generic and light-weight algorithm with which we can calculate a similarity score between two access control policies. After introducing the categorical measure and numerical measure, output of our algorithm approximates to the test result. In addition, our algorithm can be applied on policies with different models such as ABAC, RBAC and OrBAC.

We are planning to extend our work along the following directions. The first direction is related to policy negotiation between SP and client in a real distributed environment such as Grid'5000 [26]. The similarity evaluation may serve as a filter step to find out the SPs with similar security level. The second direction is to integrate our algorithm in some security policy negotiation frameworks [27]. The similarity score will be helpful in the negotiation process such as counter offer generation and decision making.

Acknowledgments. The work reported in this paper has been supported by ANRT (Association Nationale de la Recherche et de la Technologie) and Orange as CIFRE (Conventions Industrielles de Formation par la REcherche) thesis and the work of Nora Cuppens-Boulahia and Frédéric Cuppens has been partially carried out in the SUPERCLOUD project, funded by the European Union's Horizon 2020 research and innovation programme under grant agreement No 643964.

Appendix

A   Brute-force based test for existing work

Figure 10 shows the brute-force test result of policy similarity score by using the same test environment illustrated in Sect. 4. The y-axis represents the PSM score computed by the algorithm proposed in [10]; the x-axis shows the test result of policy similarity defined by Eq. (7) [10], where $Sreq$ denotes the set of the requests with the same decisions from p_1 and p_2 and Req is the set of the requests applicable to either p_1 or p_2:

$$S_{policy}(p_1, p_2) = |Sreq|/|Req| \tag{7}$$

We remark that the similarity score computed does not approximate to the test result. The main reason is that, firstly, as a brute-force based test method, our input requests are more exhaustive than ones generated by other test tools such as MTBDD [18]. Secondly, the PSM algorithm defined in [10] focuses only on the literal level but not logic aspect of security policy. As a result, two security rules sharing the majority of common elements are considered to hold a higher similarity score. However, the rest of elements may cause totally different decisions which indicates that the two rules are not similar in terms of output.

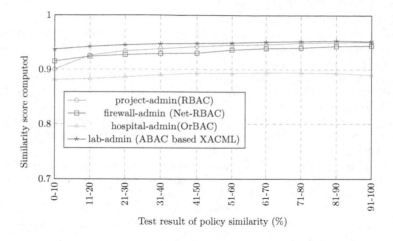

Fig. 10. Experiment of similarity score (*set*-4).

References

1. Li, A., Yang, X., Kandula, S., Zhang, M.: Cloudcmp: comparing public cloud providers. In: Proceedings of the 10th ACM SIGCOMM Conference on Internet Measurement, pp. 1–14. ACM (2010)
2. Yau, S.S., Yin, Y.: Qos-based service ranking and selection for service-based systems. In: 2011 IEEE International Conference on Services Computing (SCC), pp. 56–63. IEEE (2011)
3. Luna, J., Ghani, H., Germanus, D., Suri, N.: A security metrics framework for the cloud. In: 2011 Proceedings of the International Conference on Security and Cryptography (SECRYPT), pp. 245–250. IEEE (2011)
4. Taha, A., Trapero, R., Luna, J., Suri, N.: Ahp-based quantitative approach for assessing and comparing cloud security. In: 2014 IEEE 13th International Conference on Trust, Security and Privacy in Computing and Communications (Trust-Com), pp. 284–291. IEEE (2014)
5. Sandhu, R.S., Coyne, E.J., Feinstein, H.L., Youman, C.E.: Role-based access control models. Computer **29**(2), 38–47 (1996)
6. Kalam, A.A.E., Baida, R., Balbiani, P., Benferhat, S., Cuppens, F., Deswarte, Y., Miege, A., Saurel, C., Trouessin, G.: Organization based access control. In: IEEE 4th International Workshop on Policies for Distributed Systems and Networks, 2003, Proceedings, POLICY 2003, pp. 120–131. IEEE (2003)
7. Yuan, E., Tong, J.: Attributed based access control (abac) for web services. In: 2005 IEEE International Conference on Web Services, 2005, ICWS 2005, Proceedings. IEEE (2005)
8. Standard, O.: extensible access control markup language (xacml) version 2.0 (2005)
9. Lin, D., Rao, P., Bertino, E., Lobo, J.: An approach to evaluate policy similarity. In: Proceedings of the 12th ACM Symposium on Access Control Models and Technologies, pp. 1–10. ACM (2007)
10. Lin, D., Rao, P., Ferrini, R., Bertino, E., Lobo, J.: A similarity measure for comparing xacml policies. IEEE Trans. Knowl.Data Eng. **25**(9), 1946–1959 (2013)

11. Bei, W., Xing-yuan, C., Yong-fu, Z.: A policy rule dissimilarity evaluation approach based on fuzzy theory. In: International Conference on Computational Intelligence and Software Engineering, 2009, CiSE 2009, pp. 1–6. IEEE (2009)
12. Pham, Q., Reid, J., Dawson, E.: Policy filtering with xacml (2011)
13. Lin, D., Squicciarini, A.: Data protection models for service provisioning in the cloud. In: Proceedings of the 15th ACM Symposium on Access Control Models and Technologies, pp. 183–192. ACM (2010)
14. Cho, E., Ghinita, G., Bertino, E.: Privacy-preserving similarity measurement for access control policies. In: Proceedings of the 6th ACM Workshop on Digital Identity Management, pp. 3–12. ACM (2010)
15. Shaikh, R.A., Sasikumar, M.: Dynamic parameter for selecting a cloud service. In: 2014 International Conference on Computation of Power, Energy, Information and Communication (ICCPEIC), pp. 32–35. IEEE (2014)
16. Bertolino, A., Daoudagh, S., El Kateb, D., Henard, C., Le Traon, Y., Lonetti, F., Marchetti, E., Mouelhi, T., Papadakis, M.: Similarity testing for access control. Inf. Softw. Technol. **58**, 355–372 (2015)
17. Agrawal, D., Giles, J., Lee, K.W., Lobo, J.: Policy ratification. In: Sixth IEEE International Workshop on Policies for Distributed Systems and Networks, 2005, pp. 223–232. IEEE (2005)
18. Lin, D., Rao, P., Bertino, E., Li, N., Lobo, J.: Exam: a comprehensive environment for the analysis of access control policies. Int. J. Inf. Secur. **9**(4), 253–273 (2010)
19. Jaccard, P.: Nouvelles recherches sur la distribution florale. Bulletin de la Société Vaudoise des Sciences Naturelles **44**, 223–270 (1908)
20. Cuppens, F., Cuppens-Boulahia, N., Miège, A.: Inheritance hierarchies in the orbac model and application in a network environment. In: Proceedings of the Foundations of Computer Security (FCS04), pp.41–60 (2004)
21. http://docs.openstack.org/developer/keystone/configuration.html
22. Hachana, S., Cuppens-Boulahia, N., Cuppens, F.: Mining a high level access control policy in a network with multiple firewalls. J. Inf. Secur. Appl. **20**, 61–73 (2015)
23. Autrel, F., Cuppens, F., Cuppens-Boulahia, N., Coma, C.: Motorbac 2: a security policy tool. In: 3rd Conference on Security in Network Architectures and Information Systems (SAR-SSI 2008), Loctudy, France, pp.273–288 (2008)
24. http://www.supercloud-project.eu
25. Bonatti, P., De Capitani di Vimercati, S., Samarati, P.: An algebra for composing access control policies. ACM Trans. Inf. Syst. Secur. (TISSEC) **5**(1), 1–35 (2002)
26. Bolze, R., Cappello, F., Caron, E., Daydé, M., Desprez, F., Jeannot, E., Jégou, Y., Lanteri, S., Leduc, J., Melab, N., et al.: Grid'5000: a large scale and highly reconfigurable experimental grid testbed. Int. J. High Perform. Comput. Appl. **20**(4), 481–494 (2006)
27. Li, Y., Cuppens-Boulahia, N., Crom, J.M., Cuppens, F., Frey, V.: Reaching agreement in security policy negotiation. In: 2014 IEEE 13th International Conference on Trust, Security and Privacy in Computing and Communications (TrustCom), pp. 98–105. IEEE (2014)

A Statistical Approach to Detect Anomalous User Requests in SaaS Cloud-Centric Collaborations

Anant Pushkar[1], Nirnay Ghosh[2], and Soumya K. Ghosh[2(✉)]

[1] Department of Computer Science and Engineering,
Indian Institute of Technology, Kharagpur 721302, India
anantpushkar009@gmail.com
[2] School of Information Technology,
Indian Institute of Technology,
Kharagpur 721302, India
nirnay.ghosh@gmail.com, skg@iitkgp.ac.in

Abstract. Cloud-centric collaboration enables participating domains to dynamically interoperate through sharing and accessing of information. Owing to the loosely-coupled nature of such collaborations, access requests from remote users are made in the form of set of permissions. The collaboration service provider maps the requested permissions into appropriate local roles to allow resource accesses. Access request are made either by applications or human users, and may be either pre-registered, or anonymous. Authentication in cloud-based collaborations is done using web-based tokens which do not consider the properties of the requester. Access permission is given strictly on the basis of the validity of the issued tokens for a particular session. But there is no provision to determine if any user with the valid tokens will cause any security breach with the shared resources. The human element involved in these collaborations becomes a single point of failure, exploiting which, a malicious user can gain control over a cloud-based account. Thus, there is a need to learn and identify the requesters' behaviors from the history of their access patterns and subsequently use that knowledge, at runtime, to flag certain requests that are anomalous with respect to the normal behavior profile. In this paper, we propose a parametric statistical based approach which enables a resource providing domain to detect request anomalies made by a given user. Finally, we validate our methodology using publicly available datasets and present a performance evaluation in terms of accuracy of the proposed mechanism.

Keywords: Cloud computing · Access tokens · Collaboration service · Anomaly detection · Statistical testing

1 Introduction

Cloud computing supports three prominent service delivery models: (i) *Infrastructure-as-a-Service (IaaS)*, (ii) *Platform-as-a-Service (PaaS)*, and

© Springer International Publishing Switzerland 2015
S. Jajodia and C. Mazumdar (Eds.): ICISS 2015, LNCS 9478, pp. 243–262, 2015.
DOI: 10.1007/978-3-319-26961-0_15

(iii) *Software-as-a-Service (SaaS)*. One of the popular offerings of the SaaS cloud is the *online collaboration service* [4,21]. In this service, the cloud vendor provides online collaboration tools which facilitate faster sharing and accessing of information. Examples of cloud-based collaboration include document-centric collaboration, project management, blogs, micro blogging, wikipages, feeds from social networks, file sharing and synchronization, and so on. A recent Forrester[1] survey reveals that cloud-centric collaboration has become valuable and essential, and that more than 56 % of software decision-makers are using or will use SaaS offerings to replace or complement their existing collaboration technology. Cloud providers, such as, Google Cloud Storage, Microsoft Azure, and so on offers online collaboration service which is essentially loosely-coupled in nature. In such collaborations, independent domains dynamically interoperate and reveal only limited information about their services and policies, relevant to collaboration [3]. We define the scope of this paper as: *detecting anomalous access requests from users to secure collaborations among multiple autonomous domains in the SaaS cloud environment.*

Authorization of requests in cloud-based collaborations is done through web-based access tokens (e.g., OAuth 2.0), eliminating the need for furnishing sensitive credential information, as is done in the trust management systems, like PolicyMaker [7,8], KeyNote [9], Cassandra [6], Traust [20], and so on. These systems use certificates issued by a trusted Certification Authority (CA) or a public key infrastructure (PKI) to map unknown subjects to predefined roles. For cloud-based collaborations, the participating domains have to strictly use vendor provided APIs to model the access policies in form of access control lists (ACL). The cloud authentication server issues access tokens on behalf of the collaborating domains to the requesting user applications. The requesting application can be either pre-registered, or anonymous. These tokens contain the allowed scopes of access modes (e.g., read, write, execute, etc.) on the shared objects. To initiate collaborative activities, the querying application attaches this token with the hashed code of the object. On receiving the request, the cloud authentication server reads the user-defined access control list (ACL) on the object and determines whether to allow or reject the request. If the ACL grants permission for the requested operation, the access is granted until the token is timed out. Otherwise, the request fails and a *403 Forbidden Error (Access Denied)* is returned.

As token-based cloud authentication is not based on the properties of the requesting entity, it does not bind a user to its purported behavior or actions. It does not convey any information about the behavior of the bearer between the time the token was issued and its use. Access permission is given strictly on the basis of the validity of the issued token for a particular session. Either the requester's token is accepted and required privileges are allowed, or the token is rejected and access is denied. But there is no provision to determine if any user with valid token will cause any security breach with the shared information. Therefore, to prevent unauthorized disclosure of the shared resources and possi-

---

[1] http://www.informationweek.com/cloud-computing/software/cloud-collaboration-tools-big-hopes-big/240143787.

ble misappropriation, there is a need to learn and identify the normal behavior of the users from the history of access requests. Then, at runtime, if some requests are observed to deviate from this normal behavior, they will be flagged as "anomalous". The work in this paper proposes an approach to detect anomalous access requests at runtime. We have used parametric statistical technique to implement our anomalous request detection mechanism.

To the best of our knowledge, the anomalous access request detection in cloud-based collaborations through parametric statistical technique has not been studied in earlier works. The contributions of this work are highlighted as follows:

- We propose a mathematical framework for evaluating our anomaly indicator.
- An algorithm has been proposed to detect anomalous user requests using statistical confidence interval testing.
- Validation of the approach done using publicly available datasets.
- Simulation-based experiments have been done to evaluate the performances (with respect to accuracy) of the proposed algorithm in terms of the following parameters: *false-positive, false-negative, precision,* and *recall.*

The rest of the paper is organized as follows. In Sect. 2, related work in the areas of fraud detection and anomaly detection based on the parametric statistical techniques have been discussed. Section 3 describes the proposed approach through mathematical formulations and statistical modeling. In Sect. 4 experimental study and performance analysis have been done. Finally, conclusions are drawn in Sect. 5.

2   Related Work

In this paper, our area of focus is to detect anomalous (fraudulent) access requests in cloud-centric collaborations based on parametric statistical techniques. Therefore, as the current work is a blend of *fraud detection* and *parametric statistical techniques,* we present the reviews of the reported works on these two aspects.

A fraud occurs when a malicious user utilizes the resources provided by an organization in an unauthorized manner. In such cases, the malicious user can either be the actual customer of the organization or might be impersonating a legitimate user of the system. A typical approach to detect frauds in financial organizations is activity monitoring [16]. In this approach, a usage profile for each customer is maintained and monitored to detect any deviations. Few areas where activity monitoring have been extensively used are:

- *Credit-card and banking fraud detection:* Profiling and clustering based approaches are used in this type of fraud detection [18]. Two approaches which are usually adopted are *detection by-owner,* and *detection by-operation.* In [10], the authors propose a decision support system for online banking fraud analysis and investigation, termed as *BankSealer.* The proposed model builds three-fold user profile, such as: (i) local profile, (ii) global profile, and (iii) temporal profile. At runtime, *BankSealer* supports analysts by ranking new transactions that deviate from the learned profiles.

- *Insurance claim fraud detection* [16]*:* Detection of such fraud has been very important for the associated companies to avoid financial losses. Neural network based techniques [19] have been applied to identify anomalous insurance claims.
- *Insider trading detection:* Insider trading can be detected by dynamically identifying anomalous trading activities in the market. In [2], temporal and streaming data has been used for such anomaly detection.

Statistical technique assumes that normal data instances occur in higher probability region of a stochastic model, while anomalies occur in the low probability region [11]. In such technique, a statistical model (usually for normal behavior) is fit to the given data and then inference tests are applied to determine if an unseen instance belongs to this model or not. Both *parametric* as well as *nonparametric* techniques have been applied to fit a statistical model.

Parametric techniques assume the knowledge of the underlying distribution and estimate the parameters from the given data. It performs a statistical hypothesis testing, where the *null hypothesis* implies that the data instance is generated by the estimated distribution [5]. If the statistical test rejects the null hypothesis, the data point is an anomaly. The literature on parametric techniques can be classified into the following categories:

- *Gaussian model-based* [15]*:* It assumes that the data is generated from a Gaussian distribution. The general approach is to declare all data beyond 3σ anomalous. However, some of the sophisticated techniques used in this category are: *box plot rule, Grubb's test, student's t-test,* and χ^2*-test.*
- *Regression model-based:* This technique consists of two steps: In the first step, a regression model is fitted on the data. In the second step, for each test instance, the residual for the test instance is used to determine the anomaly score. In [1], the authors have done anomaly detection on time-series data using regression.

As evident from the above review, the state-of-the-art literature on fraud detection does not address detection of anomalous requests in a cloud environment. Such requests, if not detected, can compromise a legitimate user's account leading to unauthorized disclosure of the shared information. Similarly, researchers have used the parametric statistical techniques in different domains, however, no work which has used it in securing cloud-based collaborations is reported. Thus, these limitations in the state-of-the-art literatures have motivated the authors to address this problem.

3   Anomalous Request Detection in Cloud-based Collaborations

As discussed in Sect. 1, token-based authentication in cloud systems does not bind a user to its purported behavior or actions. Neither does it convey any information about the behavior of the bearer between the time the token was issued and its use. Hence, to secure collaborations among the participating domains, there is a need to learn the normal behavior profile of the users and flag the requests which deviate from this profile. This section presents our approach of detecting anomalous access requests in cloud-based collaborations.

3.1 Parametric Statistical Approach for Anomalous Request Detection

As mentioned in Sect. 1, the nature of collaborations prevalent in the cloud environment is loosely-coupled, and the requests from the remote users are made in form of set of permissions. Formally a collaborative access request is defined as follows:

Definition 1 *(Collaborative access request). A collaborative access request, car, is defined as a tuple $\langle d_r, T_{ID}^{d_r}, P_{req} \rangle$, where d_r is the requesting (remote) domain, $T_{ID}^{d_r}$ is the identity of a requesting user from d_r, and P_{req} is a set of permissions requested by $T_{ID}^{d_r}$ to accomplish specific task(s).*

Here, P_{req} either consists of one or a set of permissions $p_1, p_2, \ldots$ where each p_i is defined as follows:

Definition 2 *(Permission). A permission, p_i, is defined as a tuple $\langle o_i, a_i \rangle$, where o_i is an object or resource and a_i is the privilege to access o_i.*

Here, the privilege indicates read, write, execute, and so on. These permissions are mapped into a set of roles, which need to be activated by the user to perform the desired collaborative actions. Traditionally, this assignment of mapping the requested permissions into a set of roles is known as the *inter-domain role mapping (IDRM)* problem [12]. An important requirement of the IDRM problem is to generate a *minimal* set of roles that match the requested set of permissions [13]. This ensures that the *principle of least privilege* [22] is not violated during cross-domain interoperations. IDRM belongs to the NP-complete class, as there is no polynomial time solution to find the minimal set of roles that exactly cover the requested set of permissions. In [17], the authors have proposed a heuristic to perform this mapping in polynomial time, which have been used in the present work.

Irrespective of how we map a set of permissions to a minimal set of roles, the stream of requests from a user provides the source of learning the access pattern. Hence, if we are able to quantify the set of requests into a stationary parameter, anomaly detection techniques can be used to mark atypical behavior of a user which could potentially be an intrusion. The basic idea of this work is to learn the behavior of the user within a look-back window (L), quantify it, and detect the anomalies. We formally define the look-back window as follows:

Definition 3 *(Look-back window). Look-back window (L) is the size of the set of historical user requests (U) for learning a given requester's behavior.*

Hence, if $P_{req}^1, P_{req}^2, \ldots P_{req}^i \ldots$ are the requests made over different intervals of time by user u, then the historical user request is given as: $U = \{P_{req}^1, P_{req}^2, \ldots P_{req}^i \ldots\}$. The maximum look-back window size is: $L = \sum_j |P_{req}^j|$.

For learning the user behavior, we adopt the "semi-supervised" technique, in which all the requests in the set U are labeled to be non-anomalous (or, belonging to normal class). A model representing the class of normal behavior will be build using the historical request set (training data), and at runtime, any request (test data) which does not belong to the normal class will be marked as fraudulent. In any collaborative system, multiple domains with a large number of shared resources are involved. Owing to the complexity of such systems, the access policies of the participating domains do not change frequently. Also, the users have access to a fixed set of objects/resources predefined by the policies designed by the collaborators. Based on this notion, the following two assumptions have been adopted by our approach:

1. Request size from a non-fraudulent user is constant.
2. User shows a stationary (normal) behavior in the given look-back window.

Generally, in any organization, there exists two types of permissions: (i) generic, and (ii) specific. The generic permissions are the most commonly used ones and are required for the most basic actions. For instance, the read permission in a user's profile is expected to be activated most often. Conversely, the specific permissions are those which are activated only for a certain set of activities. For example, the write permission in a user's profile will be activated only when a request for profile edit is made. This notion has been validated in Sect. 4.1 using some publicly available datasets.

Let at a given session, a registered user requests for any permission $p_k \in P_Q$, where P_Q is the current requested set. If E_k be the event that p_k does not belong to a request set randomly chosen from the user's historical requests (U) within a given look-back window (i.e., $p_k \notin P_{req}^j$, P_{req}^j being a random element of U), we can use $Pr(E_k)$ to quantify the probability of deviation of p_k from the user's recent behavior. Now, if none of the requests in P_Q belongs to a randomly chosen element in U, then deviation of the request set P_Q from the user's recent behavior, assuming that each E_k is independent, becomes:

$$\delta(P_Q) = \prod_{\forall p_k \in P_Q} Pr(E_k) \tag{1}$$

where, $\delta(P_Q)$ denotes that the degree of deviation of the request set P_Q from the recent behavior. If at least one of the permissions, say p_k, belongs to a randomly chosen set $P_{req}^k \in U$, then deviation of the request set P_Q becomes:

$$\delta(P_Q) = \prod_{\forall p_k \in P_Q} 1 - Pr(\overline{E_k}) \tag{2}$$

where, $\overline{E_k}$ is the event where at least one permission, say p_k, belongs to the user's recent behavior. If N be the set of requests which contains p_k ($N \subseteq U$), then the probability that p_k will belong to the given look-back window will be given as:

$$Pr(\overline{E_k}) = \frac{|N|}{L} \tag{3}$$

Substituting Eq. (3) in Eq. (2) we get the following:

$$\delta(P_Q) = \prod_{\forall p_k \in P_Q} 1 - \frac{|N|}{L} \tag{4}$$

Taking logarithm on both sides of the Eq. (4):

$$\delta'(P_Q) = \sum_{\forall p_k \in P_Q} \log(1 - \frac{|N|}{L}) \tag{5}$$

Where, $\delta'(P_Q)$ is the logarithm of our deviation function $\delta(P_Q)$. However, as $\log \delta(P_Q)$ will generate another constant (real) value, we do not change the notation for the degree of deviation in the above equation.

Generic permissions, due to their common usage, will occur more often in different request sets in the given look-back window. In contrast, the specific permissions will have rare occurrences and thus have the value $\frac{|N|}{L} \ll 1$.

Let $\zeta \subseteq P_Q$ is the set of specific permissions from the requested set. The amount of activity that a single request accounts for is constant. Assuming that specific permissions account for specific activities, we can assume that the number of specific permissions in a non-fraudulent request is constant. Thus, without loss of generality, we can term ζ to be a *stationary time series* process.

Now, using *Taylor's expansion* of $\log(1 + x)$ and neglecting the higher order terms in the Eq. (5), we define the probabilistic deviation of P_Q from the recent behavior as:

$$\delta(P_Q) = \sum_{\forall p_k \in \zeta} \log(1 - \frac{|N|}{L})$$

$$= \sum_{\forall p_k \in \zeta} -\frac{|N|}{L} \tag{6}$$

Assuming that a user deviates from his current behavior at every request only be a constant probability, we can say that $\delta(U)$ is also a *stationary time series* process. Adding two stationary time series gives us another stationary time series conditioned upon a stable behavior of a user:

$$|\zeta| + \delta(U) = \sum_{\forall p_k \in \zeta} 1 - \sum_{p_k \in \zeta} \frac{|N|}{L}$$

$$= \sum_{\forall p_k \in \zeta} 1 - \frac{|N|}{L} \tag{7}$$

Therefore, Eq. (7) expresses a stationary property and can be used to detect the deviation from a user's stable behavior.

As discussed earlier, for specific permissions in a request set, the probability of occurrences will be on the lower side. Hence, to estimate the "specificity" of a particular permission, we define the following:

Definition 4 *(Specificity of a permission). If $N \subseteq U$ be the set of requests which contains permission p observed over the given look-back window of L, then the specificity of p is defined as:*

$$\pi(p) = 1 - \frac{|N|}{L}$$

Thus, specificity will be low for frequently requested (activated) permissions, and vice-versa for the rare ones. From the perspective of role-based access control (RBAC) model [23], we know that a role consists of a set of permissions. Therefore, if a particular role is not often activated, it can be assumed to be a administrative one containing specific or critical privileges. Formally, we define the specificity of a role as follows:

Definition 5 *(Specificity of a role). If $Perm$ is the set of permissions constituting any role r, then the specificity of r observed over the given look-back window of L is defined as:*

$$\pi(r) = \sum_{\forall p \in Perm} \pi(p)$$

Similarly, specificity of a set of roles R will be given by the sum of the specificities of individual roles: $\pi(R) = \sum_{\forall r \in R} \pi(r)$

Choice of the above entities (permission or role or role-set) for anomaly detection is an implementation issue and depends upon the number of roles/permissions in the domain. However, it is always preferable to work with the entity with higher cardinality. This gives more granularity and the lesser likelihood of information loss.

Based on Definition 4, we modify the Eq. (7) as:

$$|\zeta| + \delta(U) = \sum_{\forall p_k \in \zeta} \pi(p_k) \tag{8}$$

Thus, specificity of request entities forms the indicator (parameter) in the proposed anomaly detection approach. As we have assumed that the user shows stationary behavior, the distribution parameters (mean, standard deviation) at any time instant t is same as (and hence independent of) the parameters at time instant $(t + 1)$. Additionally, if we consider a look-back window of significant size, both the properties (viz., *independence* and *sample size/skewness*) of central limit theorem (normal distribution) are satisfied.

In the next section, we discuss about our anomalous request detection algorithm using the concept of specificity.

3.2   Anomalous Request Detection Algorithm

Specificity (π), in general, is the measure of how the given entity (permission or role or role-set) is likely to deviate from the user's normal behavior. Entities regularly requested by a user will have a low specificity and vice-versa. Suppose access to an entity becomes unexpectedly high due to certain constraints. The administrator can control that by artificially increasing the specificity of that entity to a very high value. For instance, consider a scenario where an online examination is being conducted using cloud-based collaboration service. After the examination is over we would want the access to the answer scripts to be frozen. One way to do this is to keep the role-permissions assignments to be dynamic. Another more subtle way is to artificially increase the specificity of write permissions to the answer scripts to a very high value after the test is over. Therefore, the relationship between a user's behavior and the specificity of an entity (permission or role or role-set) can be proposed as:

Proposition 1. *The more regular the user's behavior with respect to an entity, the lesser is its specificity.*

To explain a user's regular behavior, we present the following use case: Consider a generic role *Employee* that a user has to activate every time he accesses the system. In contrast, the user activates the role *Project Head* only for a particular purpose, and during a predefined time of the day. Thus, in terms of access pattern, the user's behavior is more regular and frequent with respect to the generic role than the specific role. So, the *Employee* role will have a lower specificity than that of *Project Head* role.

Algorithm 1 describes our technique to detect anomalous requests made by a particular user during accessing the resources through cloud-based collaboration service. We determine if a particular request is anomalous or not through estimation of the confidence intervals. The input to the algorithm are the current request (permission) set P_{req}, historical request set U relevant to the given user,

---

Input: Requested permission set (P_{req}), Historical user request set (U),
Confidence level (z^*)
Output: Confidence value (c)
Initialize: $R \leftarrow \Phi$;
Initialize: μ, σ;
$R \leftarrow mapPermissionsToRoles(P_{req})$;
$\mu \leftarrow U.getMeanSpecificity()$;
$\sigma \leftarrow U.getStandardDeviation()$;
$F \leftarrow \pi(R)$;
if $F > \mu + z^*\sigma$ **then**
  | mark P_{req} as anomalous;
end
else
  | $U.update(P_{req})$;
end
$c \leftarrow Pr(\mu, \sigma, F)$;
Return: c;

Algorithm 1. Anomalous Request Detection

and a confidence boundary z^*. The confidence boundary may vary with different users, however, it can be regulated by the security administrators of the collaborating domains. The requested permission set is mapped into a set of roles R using the heuristic presented in [17]. For all the roles in U, the mean specificity (μ) and the standard deviation (σ) are computed. Specificity of the generated role set R is computed and the value is stored in a variable F. Then we perform a confidence interval testing to determine if the observed specificity of the role set R can be entailed as anomalous or not. If the observed value falls beyond the confidence boundary, we mark the request to be anomalous. Conversely, if the observed specificity is found to be within the confidence interval, the requested permission set P_{req} is added to the historical user request. For both cases, the algorithm returns the probability by which F belongs to the normal distribution with mean μ and standard deviation σ.

In Sect. 3.1, we derived the mathematical formula for specificity, assuming that $\frac{|N|}{L} \ll 1$. However, in Algorithm 1 we have not filtered out the generic permissions for which the assumption is not valid. Experimentally it was found that there has been a slight improvement in the performance of the algorithm after explicitly removing generic permissions. But the task of marking a permission generic or specific has to be done manually, which increases the possibility of over fitting the historical data. Moreover, the specificity for such permissions will be very close to 0. Hence, their contribution to the mean and standard deviation remains insignificant even if we consider them.

4   Results and Discussion

In this section, we first validate our approach of estimating the specificity of entities (permissions, roles, role-sets) which forms an integral part of our approach to detect anomalous requests. Next, performances of the proposed algorithm (refer to Algorithm 1) in terms of *precision* and *recall* for different sizes of the look-back window have been evaluated and analyzed.

4.1   Validation of the Proposed Approach

We have discussed in Sect. 3.1 that in any domain there exists two types of entities: generic and specific. Generic entities are the ones which are requested/activated frequently and are available to most of the users in the system. While, the specific ones are those which are restricted by imposing spatio-temporal constraints, and are also available only to the privileged users. Based on this heuristic, we have defined the "specificity" parameter for estimating the degree of deviation from the user's recent access behavior. To validate the abovementioned concept we have attempted to study this pattern in some of the datasets from [14]. These datasets are the network access control rules used in Hewlett Packard (HP) to manage external business partner connectivity. They include two matrices: (i) permission assignments (PA), and (ii) role assignments (RA) for nine different domains. PA contains the role to permissions mapping, and

RA has the user to role mapping. Each row in the *RA* matrix corresponds to a request, that may or may not come from the same user.

Table 1 gives the details about the sizes of different entities available in those nine domains [14].

In the first step, we study the role to permission assignments using bipartite graphs which capture the degree distribution of different roles. Due to brevity of space, we present only the degree distribution obtained for two smaller domains (Domino and Healthcare (HC)), and one larger domain (Americas Large) in Fig. 1. It is evident from the degree distributions, that there are a few permissions that are associated with a large number of roles and the rest are limited to only a few, which attribute to our designated generic and specific permissions,

Table 1. Test datasets

Domain	Roles	Permissions	Role-sets
Americas Large	421	10127	3485
Americas Small	1587	211	3477
Apj	1164	456	2044
Customer	284	276	10961
Domino	231	20	79
Emea	3046	34	35
Firewall1	709	69	365
Firewall2	590	10	325
Healthcare	46	15	46

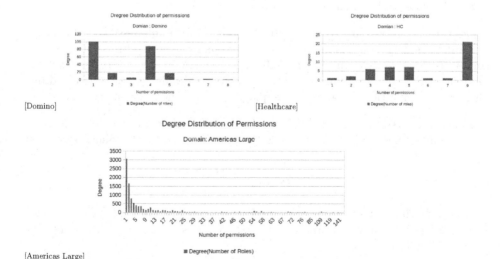

[Domino]   [Healthcare]

[Americas Large]

Fig. 1. Degree distribution of permissions

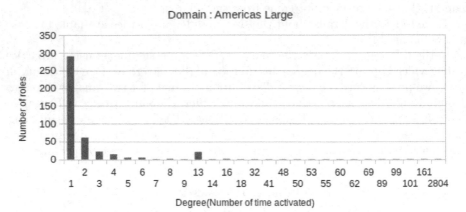

Fig. 2. Degree Distribution of roles in Americas Large

respectively. Hence, it can be inferred that for all reasonable-sized domains, there exists a set of generic and a set of specific permissions. Similar observation in case of roles is also available in Fig. 2.

From Fig. 2 it is clear that only a few roles are frequently activated (generic), while a large proportion of the roles are restricted from regular accesses (specific). Thus, our notions of generic and specific entities in a given domain are validated through the analysis on degree distribution.

4.2 Experimental Study

As mentioned in Sect. 3.2, the proposed algorithm for anomalous request detection takes the following as inputs: (i) current requested set of permissions, (ii) historical user request set, and (iii) a confidence level. As real-time request streams in cloud-based collaborations are not available, we simulate requests to feed our algorithm. Simulation of permission requests requires the following types of data:

- *Permission assignment matrix:* This matrix (PA) gives the role to permission mapping for a domain. Each entry in the matrix can have the following values:

$$PA_{i,j} = \begin{cases} 1 & \text{If } role_i \text{ contains } permission_j \\ 0 & \text{Otherwise} \end{cases}$$

- *Role activation history:* This gives the series of roles-sets activated in a domain. These role-sets may have been activated by the same or different users. Let us denote it as H_{act}.

The different steps for evaluating the performance of our algorithm have been described below.

Table 2. Role-permission assignment in provider domain d_j

Role ID	Permissions ($Perm$)
0	19
1	21
2	20
3	0
4	1
5	8
6	89
7	23
8	9
9	30
10	22
11	0 4 6 8 12 20 22 23 28 29 56 81 85 150 229 230
12	3 5 7 9 11 13 14 16 19 21 24 27 30 32 33 34 35
13	0 3 5 7 9 10 11 12 13 14 16 18 19 21 23 24 25
14	0 1 3 5 7 8 9 11 12 13 14 16 19 20 21 23 24 25
15	1 19 23 25 98 121 122
16	3 5 7 9 11 13 14 16 18 19 21 24 27 30 32 33 34
17	0 1 8 9 19 20 21 24 25 26 27 28 29 30 31
18	2 3 4 5 6 7 8 9 10 11 12 13 14 15 16 21
19	2 10

User Profile Generation. For generating user profiles, we begin with a series of role-sets, that may or may not have come from the same user. We create an average user, parameterized by these role-sets. Let $F_q(r)$ be the number of times role r was activated in the role activation history (H_{act}). Let $\rho()$ be the reverse map from a permission to role, i.e. $\rho(p) = \{r : p, r \in PA\}$. For every permission p we can define count as below:

$$count(p) = \sum_{r \in \rho(p)} F_q(r)$$

In other words, $count(p)$ gives the number of times the permission p was requested/ accessed in H_{act}. This is an approximate frequency of use of the permission. Permissions used very regularly will have a higher count value and vice-versa. Therefore, an estimate of the probability that the permission p will be accessed is given as follows:

$$Pr(p \in P_Q) = \frac{count(p)}{|H_{act}|}$$

Input: Role activation history H_{act}, Request size (M)
Output: Simulated request set (R_Q)
Initialize: $R \leftarrow \Phi$;
Initialize: $P \leftarrow \Phi$;
Initialize: $rand$;
for $\forall r \in domain.roles$ **do**
   | $rand \leftarrow randInt(0, |H_{act}|)$;
   | **if** $rand < F(r)$ **then**
   | | $R \leftarrow R \cup r$;
   | **end**
end
for $\forall r \in R$ **do**
   | **for** $\forall p \in Perm(r)$ **do**
   | | $P \leftarrow P \cup p$;
   | **end**
end
$R_Q \leftarrow random.choice(P, M)$;
Return: R_Q;

Algorithm 2. Request Generator for an Average User

where, P_Q being a randomly chosen request set from the history.

We can similarly define the probability that a role is activated in response to a request as:

$$Pr(r \in R_Q) = \frac{F_q(r)}{|H_{act}|}$$

where, R_Q is the set of roles activated in response to P_Q. This pair of probability values for every permission/role constitutes the user profile.

Request Generation. Once the user profile is created, we generate a request to simulate the average user's behavior using Algorithm 2. The above procedure selects roles that are frequently activated with high probabilities and generates a series of requests, considered to be normal. To simulate anomalous behavior, the first *if-clause* after random number generation is changed to $rand < F(r)$, which will select roles that are less likely to be activated/requested. For testing our algorithm, a small set of anomalous requests are inserted in the generated series of normal requests with frequencies of one in 4, 8, 16, and 32 requests.

Application of the Anomalous Request Detection Algorithm. In this section, we demonstrate an example scenario where the proposed mechanism of anomalous request detection has been applied to secure collaborations among participating domains in the cloud. We consider a cloud provider C which provides an online collaboration tool as service. Multiple domains $d_1, d_2, \ldots, d_n$ share their resources in C and manage access to them through the available APIs.

Table 3. Estimates generated by the proposed algorithm

ID	Request set	Generated role set (R)	$\pi(R)$	Profile (μ, σ)
1	19 0 4 6 8	3 18 19	16	18.5, 4.092
2	122 0 4 6 8	3 15 18 19#	21.5	18.5, 4.092
3	1 0 4 6 8	3 4 18 19	16.5	18.5, 4.555
4	19 0 4 6 8	3 18 19	16	17.25, 3.73
5	122 1 19 0 4 6 8	3 15 18 19	20	18.25, 3.799
6	122 0 4 6 8	3 15 18 19 #	21.2222	18.25, 3.381
7	122 1 19 0 4 6 8	3 15 18 19	20	19.25, 2.43
8	122 0 4 6 8	3 15 18 19	21.1	20.5, 1.870
9	1 0 4 6 8	3 4 18 19	16.4545	19.5, 3.316
10	122 0 4 6 8	3 15 18 19 #	21.0769	19.5, 3.082
11	19 0 4 6 8	3 18 19	16	18.25, 3.072
12	1 0 4 6 8	3 4 18 19	16.4286	18.25, 3.031
13	19 0 4 6 8	3 18 19	16	17.25, 2.947
14	122 1 19 0 4 6 8	3 15 18 19 #	20	17, 2.5
15	122 0 4 6 8	3 15 18 19 #	21.0625	18.25, 2.989
16	1 0 4 6 8	3 4 18 19	16.4375	18.25, 3.031
17	19 0 4 6 8	3 4 18 19	16.4444	17.25, 3.491
18	122 1 19 0 4 6 8	3 15 18 19 #	21.0769	19.5, 3.082
19	19 0 4 6 8	3 18 19	16	18.25, 3.072

We assume that the vendor provides the APIs for proposed anomaly detection approach, which are used by the domains to determine if the current collaboration request is conforming to the user's normal behavior.

Let there be two domains, d_i and d_j, which will collaborate using the cloud vendor's APIs, d_i being the requesting domain and d_j the providing domain. The role-permission assignment in d_j is given in Table 2. Now consider a user $u_i \in d_i$ who mostly requests for the permissions $\{0, 1, 4, 6, 8, 19\}$. We introduce a few requests with an anomalous permission 122 in order to make the algorithm to activate role 15. The moving average and standard deviation for a look-back window of $L = 5$ have been used to demonstrate how the algorithm updates itself with any change in the user behavior. A sample run of the algorithm with a confidence level of 0.5 on a simulated set of requests has been shown in Table 3. We have used # to indicate the flagged (anomalous) requests. The observed specificity (π) of the generated role set (R), the mean specificity, and the standard deviation characterizing a user behavior are computed by Algorithm 1. From the role-permission assignment in Table 2, it is clear that permissions like 122 are critical, as in order to access them a large number of extra permissions must be activated. The estimations (given in Table 3) illustrate that the algorithm is able to recognize this risk when a request for 122 comes as an isolated request,

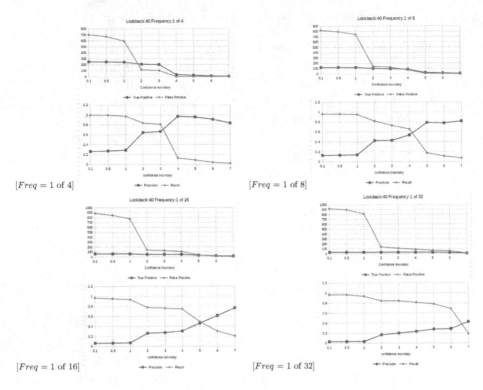

[$Freq = 1$ of 4]   [$Freq = 1$ of 8]

[$Freq = 1$ of 16]   [$Freq = 1$ of 32]

Fig. 3. Parameter estimation with look-back window size = 40

for instance, in IDs 2, 10, and 18. However, when these requests come one after the other, they become a part of the user's behavior and hence are not flagged (as observed in IDs 5, 7, and 8), showing the adaptive nature of the algorithm.

4.3   Performance Analysis

In this section, we evaluate the performance of our algorithm in terms of the following well accepted parameters:

- *False Positive:* Normal request wrongly detected as anomalous.
- *False Negative:* Anomalous request not detected, but marked as normal.
- *Precision:* It measures the probability that a request is actually anomalous, in situation where it has been flagged to be anomalous. Mathematically, precision is expressed as:

$$Precision = \frac{TruePositive}{TruePositive + FalsePositive}$$

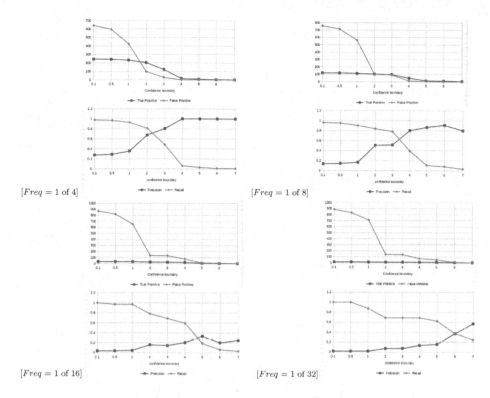

[*Freq* = 1 of 4]

[*Freq* = 1 of 8]

[*Freq* = 1 of 16]

[*Freq* = 1 of 32]

Fig. 4. Parameter estimation with look-back window size = 80

- *Recall:* It computes the percentage of actual anomalous requests which has been flagged. Mathematically, recall is given as:

$$Recall = \frac{TruePositive}{TruePositive + FalseNegative}$$

Another parameter that has been adjusted for performance evaluation of the algorithm is the look-back window. As discussed in Sect. 3.1, the look-back window is the size of the set of previous requests made by a particular user. We study the performances of the algorithm for different sizes of the look-back window (consisting of 40, 80, and 120 historical requests) and for different frequencies of occurrences of the anomalous requests viz., 1 out of 4, 8, 16, and 32. Figure 3 gives the plots of the abovementioned parameters (for $L = 40$) with respect to the dataset given for the *Domino* domain. Similarly, in Figs. 4 and 5, the performances of the algorithm in terms of the specified parameters have been depicted.

Observations from the Performance Analysis. The performance of the anomaly detection algorithm greatly depends upon the value of the confidence level z^* to be set by the security expert in the collaborating domains. Based on the experimentation done, the optimal value depends upon the expected

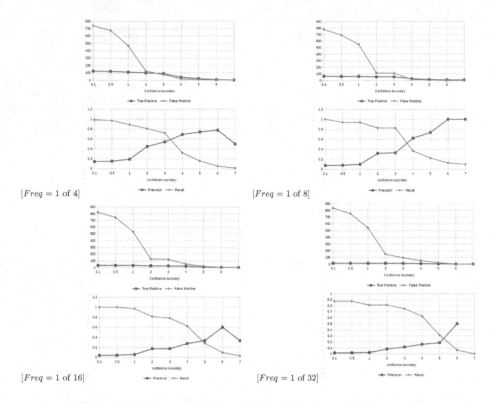

[*Freq* = 1 of 4]

[*Freq* = 1 of 8]

[*Freq* = 1 of 16]

[*Freq* = 1 of 32]

Fig. 5. Parameter estimation with look-back window size = 120

frequency of the anomalous requests. As expected, smaller the frequency, larger is the optimal confidence level. In fact, confidence level seems to be logarithmic upon the frequency of anomaly.

Look-back window is a function of the stability of a user's behavior. However, if the user is expected to change his behavior very frequently, a smaller look-back window will work better so that the system may be able to adapt well to the changes in behavior with a lesser number of false alarms. Keeping the stability factor of behavior stationary, no significant effect of look-back window was observed on performance as is demonstrated by the given plots. Thus, we have the following observations with respect to the performance of the proposed anomaly detection algorithm:

- If the frequency is low, there will be a high percentage of false positives.
- For stationary behavior, the look-back window size does not significantly change the experimental parameters.
- Look-back window size depends on the expected frequency of anomaly, but is not correlated to the performance.
- Performance of the proposed approach depends upon the confidence level. For narrower confidence intervals, recall is close to 1 and precision is very low, and vice-versa for the wider intervals.

- If the security expert of a domain is not aware of the users and the typical requests they make, it is safe to maintain a moderate confidence boundary between 2 and 3.
- Performance degrades if the frequency of anomaly decreases, as there are not enough data points to flag.

5 Conclusion

Online collaboration has become one of the popular services provided by the present day SaaS clouds. Through such services, customers are given a loosely-coupled environment where they can share and access resources remotely. In the state-of-the-art clouds, authorizing accesses to shared resources is done based on the validity of tokens, which do not have any mechanism to determine if a valid user will cause security breach with the shared information. The human element involved in these collaborations becomes a single point of failure, which may be exploited by a malicious user to gain control over a genuine user account. Thus, there is a need to learn and identify the requesters' behaviors from the history of their access patterns and subsequently use that knowledge, at runtime, to flag certain requests that are anomalous with respect to the normal behavior profile. In this paper, we propose an algorithm based on parametric statistical technique to detect request anomalies made by a given user. The frequency of activation of an entity (permission or role or role-set) forms the anomaly indicator for this work. We validate our methodology using publicly available datasets and present a detail experimental study for performance evaluation based on accuracy. The results suggest that the proposed algorithm will perform better if the confidence boundary is set between 2 and 3, and the occurrence of anomalous requests is frequent. As a part of the future work, we will attempt to implement our algorithm in a cloud system such that real-time request feeds can be analyzed. Further, we plan to evaluate the performance analysis of the algorithm in terms of the anomaly detection latency to address the following scenarios: (i) size of policy set in the collaborating domains change frequently, and (ii) low occurrence of anomaly in the requested entities.

References

1. Abraham, B., Chuang, A.: Outlier detection and time series modeling. Technometrics **31**(2), 241–248 (1989)
2. Aggarwal, C.C.: On abnormality detection in spuriously populated data streams. In: SDM, pp. 80–91. SIAM (2005)
3. Almutairi, A., Sarfraz, M., Basalamah, S., Aref, W., Ghafoor, A.: A distributed access control architecture for cloud computing. IEEE Softw. **29**(2), 36–44 (2012). doi:10.1109/MS.2011.153
4. Banks, D., Erickson, J.S., Rhodes, M.: Toward cloud-based collaboration services. In: Usenix Workshop HotCloud (2009)
5. Barnett, V., Lewis, T.: Outliers in Statistical Data, vol. 3. Wiley, New York (1994)

6. Becker, M.Y., Sewell, P.: Cassandra: distributed access control policies with tunable expressiveness. In: Proceedings of the Fifth IEEE International Workshop on Policies for Distributed Systems and Networks (POLICY 2004), pp. 159–168. IEEE (2004)
7. Blaze, M., Feigenbaum, J., Lacy, J.: Decentralized trust management. In: Proceedings of the IEEE Symposium on Security and Privacy, pp. 164–173. IEEE (1996)
8. Blaze, M., Feigenbaum, J., Strauss, M.: Compliance checking in the PolicyMaker trust management system. In: Hirschfeld, R. (ed.) FC 1998. LNCS, vol. 1465, pp. 254–274. Springer, Heidelberg (1998)
9. Blaze, M., Keromytis, A.D.: The KeyNote trust-management system version 2. RFC 2704 (Informational) (1999)
10. Carminati, M., Caron, R., Maggi, F., Epifani, I., Zanero, S.: BankSealer: A decision support system for online banking fraud analysis and investigation. Comput. Secur. **53**, 175–186 (2015)
11. Chandola, V., Banerjee, A., Kumar, V.: Anomaly detection: a survey. ACM Comput. Surv. (CSUR) **41**(3), 15 (2009)
12. Chen, L., Crampton, J.: Inter-domain role mapping and least privilege. In: Proceedings of the 12th ACM Symposium on Access Control Models and Technologies, pp. 157–162. ACM (2007)
13. Du, S., Joshi, J.B.: Supporting authorization query and inter-domain role mapping in presence of hybrid role hierarchy. In: Proceedings of the 11th ACM Symposium on Access Control Models and Technologies (SACMAT 2006), pp. 228–236. ACM (2006)
14. Ene, A., Horne, W., Milosavljevic, N., Rao, P., Schreiber, R., Tarjan, R.E.: Fast exact and heuristic methods for role minimization problems. In: Proceedings of the 13th ACM Symposium on Access Control Models and Technologies, pp. 1–10. ACM (2008)
15. Eskin, E.: Anomaly detection over noisy data using learned probability distributions. In: Proceedings of the 17th International Conference on Machine Learning, pp. 255–262. Morgan Kaufmann Publishers Inc. (2005)
16. Fawcett, T., Provost, F.: Activity monitoring: Noticing interesting changes in behavior. In: Proceedings of the Fifth ACM SIGKDD International Conference on Knowledge Discovery and Data Mining, pp. 53–62. ACM (1999)
17. Ghosh, N., Ghosh, S.K., Das, S.K.: SelCSP: a framework to facilitate selection of cloud service providers. IEEE Trans. Cloud Comput. **3**(1), 66–79 (2015)
18. Ghosh, S., Reilly, D.L.: Credit card fraud detection with a neural-network. In: Proceedings of the Twenty-Seventh Hawaii International Conference on System Sciences, vol. 3, pp. 621–630. IEEE (1994)
19. He, Z., Deng, S., Xu, X.: An optimization model for outlier detection in categorical data. In: Huang, D.-S., Zhang, X.-P., Huang, G.-B. (eds.) ICIC 2005. LNCS, vol. 3644, pp. 400–409. Springer, Heidelberg (2005)
20. Lee, A.J., Winslett, M., Basney, J., Welch, V.: Traust: a trust negotiation-based authorization service for open systems. In: Proceedings of the 11th ACM Symposium on Access Control Models and Technologies (SACMAT 2006), pp. 39–48. ACM (2006)
21. Liu, F., Tong, J., Mao, J., Bohn, R., Messina, J., Badger, L., Leaf, D.: NIST Cloud Computing Reference Architecture. NIST special publication 500, 292 (2011)
22. Nyanchama, M., Osborn, S.: The role graph model and conflict of interest. ACM Trans. Inf. Syst. Secur. (TISSEC) **2**(1), 3–33 (1999)
23. Sandhu, R.S., Coyne, E.J., Feinstein, H.L., Youman, C.E.: Role-based access control models. Computer **29**(2), 38–47 (1996)

DARAC: DDoS Mitigation Using DDoS Aware Resource Allocation in Cloud

Gaurav Somani[1,2]([✉]), Abhinav Johri[3], Mohit Taneja[3], Utkarsh Pyne[3],
Manoj Singh Gaur[2], and Dheeraj Sanghi[4]

[1] Central University of Rajasthan, Ajmer, India
gaurav@curaj.ac.in
[2] Malaviya National Institute of Technology, Jaipur, India
[3] LNM Institute of Information Technology, Jaipur, India
[4] Indian Institute of Technology, Kanpur, India

Abstract. Internet-based computing has lead to an emergence of a large number of threats. One of the major threat is DDoS (Distributed Denial of Service) attack. Recent incidents have shown that DDoS attacks have the capability of shutting a business not for a day but weeks. DDoS attacks have a greater impact on multi-tenant clouds than traditional infrastructure. DDoS attacks in the cloud, take the shape of EDoS (Economic denial of sustainability) attacks. In EDoS, instead of "Service Denial", economic harms occur due to fake resource usage and subsequent addition or buying of resources using on-demand provisioning. To detect and mitigate DDoS attacks in the cloud, we argue that on-demand resource allocation (known as auto-scaling) should also be looked, in addition to network or application layer mitigation. We have proposed a novel mitigation strategy, DARAC, which makes auto-scaling decisions by accurately differentiating between legitimate requests and attacker traffic. Attacker traffic is detected and dropped based on human behavior analysis based detection. We also argue that most of the solutions in the literature, do not pay much attention to the service quality to legitimate requests during an attack. We calculate the share of legitimate clients in resource addition/buying and make subsequent accurate auto-scaling decisions. Experimental results show that DARAC mitigates various DDoS attack sets and take accurate and quick auto-scaling decisions for various legitimate and attacker traffic combinations saving from EDoS. We also show how proposed mechanism could make "arms-race" very difficult for the attackers as the resource need to defeat DARAC mechanism on a very small capacity server is huge. Results also show significant improvements in the average response time of the web-service under attack, in addition to infrastructure cost savings up to 50 % in heavy attack cases.

1 Introduction

DDoS attacks are on the rise, with attackers being supported by mass exploitation of web vulnerabilities, millions of exploitable internet-abled devices, successful botnet building and the monetization of these resources in the DDoS-for-Hire

© Springer International Publishing Switzerland 2015
S. Jajodia and C. Mazumdar (Eds.): ICISS 2015, LNCS 9478, pp. 263–282, 2015.
DOI: 10.1007/978-3-319-26961-0_16

strategies [14]. Attackers have continued renting these botnets, mainly to perform volumetric attacks. Affordable but fatal services like these, can create sufficient traffic to take down a business infrastructure, which lacks DDoS protection. Targeting businesses without DDoS protection have made attackers successful and earned them a huge profit. There are multiple attack impact studies which are published by many DDoS mitigation solution providers [33,37,42]. According to a quarterly report by Akamai (Q4) [42] 2014, DDoS attacks are increased by 90 % as compared to their Q3 report in 2013. Recent reports give interesting and awakening facts about the economic harms due to DDoS attacks [34]. There is 400 % rise in economic losses per hour at peak times than the last year. Our work is also motivated by the recent DDoS attacks (Q1 2015) on cloud services. Attacks on Microsoft and Sony gaming servers by Lizard Squad and similar attacks on Amazon EC2 and Rackspace servers are alarming events for the whole security community. This gives a rise to the attack motives and its shift from service denial to economic harms and massive cloud service denial [32,39]. Similarly, Greatfire.org faced a DDoS attack in March 2015 with a heavy costs as large as $30 K/day on Amazon EC2 cloud [29]. Reports by [19], states that the economic losses due to DDoS on the average is near $400 K.

One of the important characteristic of cloud is elasticity of resources, which enables cloud based services to be scaled horizontally to a large magnitude. It is visible that DDoS attack could be successful on cloud services as they dynamically scale their servers in magnitude. DDoS attacks have a different behavior when targeted to cloud. They do not disrupt the services but affect the consumer's monetary strength. This has been attributed as fraudulent resource consumption in [11]. Cloud consumer, in anticipation that the resource utilization activity as genuine, may scale the server and would be trapped in this catch. These types of attacks were first coined by Christopher Hoff in 2008 with the term Economic Denial of Sustainability (EDoS) attacks. Subsequently, DDoS attacks on cloud was picked up in [11] where the authors explains the fraudulent resource consumption as a threat to cloud consumers.

Through this paper, we are putting up an argument that DDoS attack on cloud should be treated differently. They cannot be detected and mitigated as they were being addressed in fixed and dedicated server infrastructure. We propose that economic and performance aspect are quite essential parameters in detecting and mitigating such type of attacks. We have proposed a novel mitigation scheme, which takes auto-scaling decisions wisely on the basis of real requirement of legitimate traffic by falsifying the attacker traffic. This has been achieved by identifying legitimate requests and their share in auto-scaling decisions.

The rest of the paper is organized as follows, Sect. 2 discusses DDoS attacks in cloud and initial experiment to show the convergence and difference between EDoS to DDoS. Section 3 details various requirements of an effective solution to DDoS in cloud computing. Section 4 discusses, DARAC, our proposed strategy towards DDoS mitigation. Results to various experiments are shown and discussed in Sect. 6. Various related contributions in this area are described in Sect. 7. Conclusion and future work are described in Sect. 8.

2   DDoS Attack in Cloud: Impact

Services in cloud can be scaled up or down using auto-scaling utility. This utility is the main target of EDoS attackers, who may send huge no. of requests, which will result in scaling resources up and causing huge losses to the cloud consumers. This is explained as fraudulent resource consumption (FRC) in [10], where authors call such kind of resource consumption as fraudulent. On demand cloud will scale virtual servers by looking at the demand. However, these fake resource claims will force cloud consumers to pay for the traffic which was not genuine. In cloud environment, EDoS may culminate to DDoS. Initially when the servers are under attack, the billing usage of the cloud consumers rise. When the service level agreement is saturated for the maximum allowed resources, it transforms to DDoS (Fig. 1).

We performed certain experiments which illustrates this effect in detail. A virtual machine(VM) is created on a server running a hypervisor. VM under

Table 1. DDoS Impact: configuration

Item	Configuration
Physical server	i5 3330 S 2.70 GHz
Total CPUs	(4 Cores, 8 VCPus)
Total memory	8 GB
Hypervisor	XenServer 6.2
Guest/Attacker OS	Ubuntu 14.04 Server
Guest configuration	Specified in Table 2
Guest application	Apache2
Attackers	Dual Core (4 GB)
Attacker application	ApacheBench2

Table 2. SLA for Auto-scaling

Item	Configuration
Initial resources (Static server)	VCPUs=1 and Memory=256 MB
Initial resources (Dynamic server)	VCPUs=1 and Memory=1 GB
Min to max memory (Static server)	256 MB and 1024 MB
Min to max memory (Dynamic server)	1024 MB and 4096 MB
Min to max VCPUs	1 and 4 VCPUs
Monitoring period	3 min
Condition for overload	70 % Utilization
Condition for underload	30 % Utilization
Increase-Decrease factor	128 MB and 1 VCPU (Static)
	256 MB and 1 VCPU (Dynamic)

attack is running a webserver. For characterising the impact, both static and dynamic webservers are tested against a DDoS attack. Whenever a cloud consumer deploys a VM, it's performance is bounded by a fixed SLA (Service Level Agreement). Auto-scaling policy [21,41,44] is one of the most important point in SLA, which is used in our discussion. There are many auto-scaling policies which are used in literature and in production environments [2]. Few providers use customized policies where user can decide underload and overload conditions. Subsequently, auto-scaling will increase new or remove idle resources from the VM. We are using one such policy which is simple and has set these thresholds to 70 % ("Overload") and 30 % ("Underload"). This algorithm runs in background and monitors the VM. If the memory utilization exceeds the threshold of 70 % for 3 min ("Overload" State) than an additional chunk of memory is added to the VM. Similarly, if the CPU utilization exceeds the threshold of "Overload" State, which is of 70 %, one addiitional VCPU is hot plugged to support the load. This resource addition/expansion continues till the SLA is not breached, keeping cost and resource caps in consideration. Same is true for idle resource removal, where utilization threshold of "Underload" state is 30 %. If utilization below this level, is observerd for 3 min, some fixed amount of memory or one VCPU is removed. Auto-scaling will account and bill only for the resources which are used to follow the principles of "Pay-as-you-Go" accounting. This is important to note that this policy may not be optimal in terms of resource usage and cost consideration. However, for the purpose of our work, we wanted to have a basic auto-scaling policy which can help us in analysing the impact of DDoS. Any other policy of auto-scaling, would ideally not change the impact much.

Other important parameters of this policy is listed in Table 2. Various configuration and parameters related to attack scenario, are listed in Table 1.

2.1   Static Webserver

This web server had one static page of size 2 MB. The web server was flooded by four attackers with 200 concurrent requests for a total of 200 K requests from each one of them. The web server received 800 concurrent connections in total and served 800 K (200 K × 4 attackers) requests. Figure 2c and d show the effects of the attack on Memory. Due to the persistent attack, the memory utilization always peaked above 70 %. This resulted into multiple triggers of auto-scaling and has recieved regular addition of memory chunks in the form of 128 MB each. Finally, it becomes stable at 1024 MB because of maximum limit posed by the SLA. Once Memory allocation reaches 1024 MB, auto-scaling would not assign any more memory resource and EDoS culminates to DDoS which is evident by large number of failed requests and timeouts. For the case of VCPUs, there is not much effect (Fig. 2a and b). This is mostly due to the static nature of the application. As the major stress in this attack is towards memory and disk transfer, there are no visible effets on CPUs.

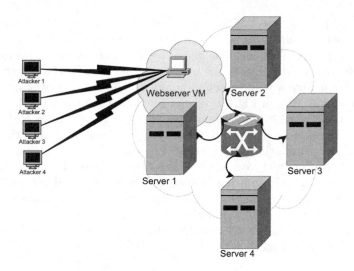

Fig. 1. DDoS Scenario: experimental design

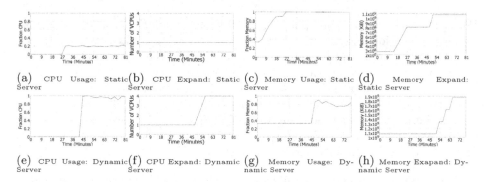

(a) CPU Usage: Static Server (b) CPU Expand: Static Server (c) Memory Usage: Static Server (d) Memory Expand: Static Server

(e) CPU Usage: Dynamic Server (f) CPU Expand: Dynamic Server (g) Memory Usage: Dynamic Server (h) Memory Exapand: Dynamic Server

Fig. 2. Behavior of auto-scaling during attack

2.2 Dynamic Webserver

Dynamic web server is a WikiBook Dump and was configured with mysql at the backend to serve wiki pages. This VM was given an initial RAM of 1024 MB and one VCPU. Attack was performed with 1500 transactions, each transaction with 6 requests in each one of them. This way it makes 1500×6, 9000 requests with a concurrency of 4. The results of the attack is shown in Fig. 2e, f, g, and h, which show the behavior of auto-scaling towards a dynamic server. The CPU usage which started from values close to 0 % but due to attack, the utilization reached around 100 % (at 45th minute). This usage remained 100 % for the whole duration of the attack there after. We can see that despite providing extra resources in the form of VCPUs, the usage didn't fall. The pattern could be appreciated more vividly in Fig. 2f, VM was hot plugged with an extra VCPU at 51st minute, once again as CPU usage was higher than 70 % for 3 min, one more VCPU was hot plugged. Likewise, the VM was provided with all 4 the VCPUs but still the utilization was around 90%. As the SLA didn't specify more VCPUs, attack turned into a DDoS. This is visible due to request failures and timeouts.

Similarly, due to the attack, the memory usage exceeds the threshold of 70 percent and memory was incrementally added. The memory was incremented by a factor of 256 MB. In Fig. 2h, we can see, how the memory is being added to the VM during attack. This is now clear that the EDoS attack had adversely affected the cloud consumer to buy more and more resources and the sustainability of utility computing was affected. For the infrastrcture limitations, we have limited the maximum resources allowed to a VM in the SLAs. In case, if the SLA has "unlimited" addition of resources with horizontal scaling [2], where instead of adding more resources on the same server, cloud may start more VM clones/instances on other servers or even migrate the server to a "spacious" server. This will be economically disastrous for the cloud consumer to pay heavy bills of these extra instances.

3   Needs of Effective Mitigation

We argue that the real problem behind the success of EDoS in cloud is fake resource allocation and consumption. If "auto-scaling" can differentiate between the malicious traffic and benign traffic and calculate their individual shares in triggering the resource allocation, we can stop such attacks. Solutions based on Turing tests [28,40], traditional rate based [1,5], threshold based [10] and anomaly detection methods [8,11], may not be solely apt to mitigate these attacks. In addition to these methods, we argue that few very important features are needed in an ideal solution for the context of cloud. Following are requirements of an effective solution for cloud environments.

1. **Segregation:** Mitigation should ideally be able to segregate good and benign traffic and drop attack traffic.
2. **Real Requirement:** Addition of resource should only be allowed, if there is a real requirement of benign traffic.
3. **Service to Benign users:** Benign users should be given a timely and quality response as if there was no attack.

Point no. 1 has been a key idea, among many of the solutions, presented in the past. Point no. 2 is specifically needed for the utility computing models to tackle the consequences of EDoS. Point no. 3 is an aspect which has not been addressed by the state of the art solutions. As the server under attack, gets busy in attack mitigation, it does not really find resources and time to take care of legitimate customers. Though, mitigation solutions actually work towards keep serving legitimate customers, however, there is no specific work towards this problem in the literature.

4 DARAC: DDoS Aware Resource Allocation in Cloud

We propose a novel mitigation system which helps in mitigating DDoS flavored attacks in cloud computing. This solution incorporates all three features into account.

1. Segregation between attacker traffic and benign traffic is done on the basis of human behavior analysis [22,35,46]. By this, we are successful in identifying attackers on the basis of the total no. of unique page requests from each unique source in a minute. Many contributions have worked in this area and identified that a real human user would not request more than a specific number of requests (n) for a webpage (a page on a website) in a minute. For our experiments, we have considered this to be 25 requests/minute for a webpage. This number can be easily calculated and decided by an usability survey in which the maximum number of times a real user can request a page can be calculated in real setting. Requests having more than these many requests, would be considered as attack traffic and dropped [38]. This number may vary depending upon the application a site is running. In particular, the detection would be much effective if this number is decided based on a specific webpage. For example, a user might have opened 20 tabs on the same ecommerce website but his target webpage (complete url) in all these tabs may be different. As novelty of our idea, contributes towards point no. 2 and 3 for an effective solution (Sect. 3), we are not providing other detailed methods for this purpose. However, any other method can be used to perform the traffic segragation activity.
2. DARAC provides a mechanism by which "auto-scaling" mechanism of cloud will always ask DARAC, whether to add resources or not. This is supported by the whole mechanism mentioned in point 1 above. In particular, once the attacker traffic is dropped, the features of legitmate traffic recorded in last 3 min are used to decide whether the additional resources are needed. This intelligent auto-scaling mechanism is supported by "Capacity Planner".
3. Capacity Planner module keeps a track of required quality of service to users and needed resources. This is very important to serve legitimate customers well. Required QoS and corresponding resources (in terms of CPU, memory and bandwidth) can be stored using a dry stress run or can learned using machine learning techniques [26].

4.1 DARAC Approach

Figure 3 shows the detailed step-by-step process of DARAC. Detailed steps are as follows.

1. An auto-scaling trigger, which is discussed in Sect. 2, is an event in which auto-scaling has to either increase/decrease resources. This may be due to an attack or may be due to the real need.

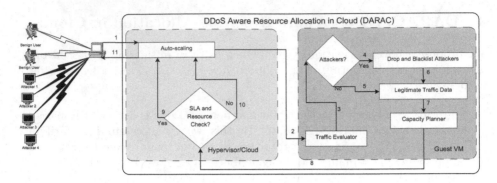

Fig. 3. DARAC: mitigation mechanism

2. Auto-scaling asks DARAC to evaluate the situation. Specifically, auto-scaling triggers, "Traffic Evaluator" module in DARAC.
3. Traffic Evaluator checks whether there is an attack. This is done on the basis of segregation based on human behavior analysis and blacklisted IPs collected in step 4.
4. If there are attacker IPs available in the traffic analysis, they are deropped and added to the blacklist.
5. In case if there is no attack, DARAC directly goes to see the legitimate traffic statistics.
6. Remaning traffic which is actually legitimate traffic is used to calculate the frequency at which the real traffic is coming in.
7. The calculated legitimate traffic is then sent to "Capacity Planner" module.
8. "Capacity Planner" module sees the traffic and consults its capacity plan to get the resources required to support the service quality. The resulted resource capacity is then sent to auto-scaling algorithm in Hypervisor/cloud manager.
9. Here, SLA compatibility is checked whether the required resource change can be made. Additionally, resource availability is also checked whether required amount of resources are available on the same server (Vertical Scaling). In case if it is not the situation, migration or another VM instance creation (Horizontal Scaling) needed. In case of resource removal, the same can be performed by the auto-scaling.
10. The required resource change is made by auto-scaling.
11. The required resource change becomes effective.

Step 2 to 8 are performed by the VM itself and step no. 1, 9 and 10 are performed by the cloud/hypervisor. This is a solution which harness both the levels of control into account. This is also important from the perspective that the VM owner's right to decide the resource requirement and privacy of traffic statistics. The VM owner may want to have different QoS levels, resource needs and cost constraints while planning capacity specific to their application requirements. Based on these reasons, the separation has been made. Following are the detailed descriptions of two most important modules of DARAC.

4.2 Traffic Evaluator

Traffic Evaluator sees the traffic of last 3 min and segregates the legitimate traffic from the attacker traffic. If the rate of traffic originated from each unique IP address to a unique webpage (complete url) is more than n requests per minute (25 requests/minute for our experimental setup) it is considered as a non-human behaviour and IP is tagged as illegitimate and gets blocked. After packets arriving from these IP address are dropped, this module calculates the frequency of legitimate traffic that has arrived in the time frame under consideration. Traffic is captured using libpcap libraries. One of the most important contribution of our work is that the traffic is always recorded consistently but the evaluation and drop is not a continous process. It is purely a trigger based approach where auto-scaling flags the resource addition to trigger "Traffic Evaluator" module.

4.3 Capacity Planner

Capacity planning module takes the frequency of legitimate arriving traffic as input and tells minimum number of resources required to cater to incoming traffic so that quality of service is maintained at a particular threshold. If the present number of resources is less than what it should be as suggested by the capacity planning algorithm, then the resource hot plug request is genuine and should be catered. On the other hand, if present number of resources are sufficient to cater the present incoming traffic then the resource hot plug request was mainly because of illegitimate traffic and resources should not be increased in this case. Therefore, this module returns "No Change" in this case. A web server with a response time not more than 1 s is considered as an ideal web server [30,43]. We benchmark our web server and try to find out the maximum requests per second that can be served by the web server with the given amount of resources such that the response time of the service, remains within the required threshold. We start with a unit resource and find the volume of the traffic (request per second) beyond which QoS of service would start degrading. We repeat this step several times incrementally increasing the number of resources each time. Initial capacity plan is given in Table 3. Similar detailed plans can be evaluated for all the resource combinations like CPU, memory, disk and bandwidth and using other QoS parameters [26].

Table 3. Capacity planning table

Request/s	VCPUs	Memory	Disk
5	1	1 GB	10 GB
10	2	1 GB	10 GB
15	3	1 GB	10 GB
20	4	1 GB	10 GB

5   Evaluation of DARAC

Evaluation of DARAC is conducted by multiple attack experiments. For this purpose a scenario as shown in Fig. 3 has been used. Auto-scaling is only considered for the CPU resources for simplicity in analyzing the cost considerations. Computational power is what the costliest utility in cloud pricing models. The experimental setup and configuration is similar to the preliminary experiments shown in Tables 1 and 2 except the fact the auto-scaling is only enabled for VCPUs and memory is fixed at 1GB. The webserver under attack is dynamic webserver presented in Sect. 2.2 for its applicability to real environment. We will discuss the attack and legitimate traffic generation and various experiments in the following sections.

5.1   Traffic Design

For the effectiveness of the evaluation we have mixed the normal traffic, which is the representative of benign users, and the attacker traffic, which is representative of attackers, who want to fraudulently consume the resources of the cloud based service. For this purpose, we used different methods for traffic generation. There are no attack datasets available, which give the vast coverages of various attack scenarios, therefore, we have generated our own traffic sets combining attack and benign request frequecies.

Legitimate Traffic. It is established that the benign user traffic follows the poisson distribution [47].

$$P(k) = \frac{e^{\lambda.t}.(\lambda.t)^k}{k!} \tag{1}$$

λ is the average rate of arrival of request, t is the time. For our experiment we have taken k from 0 to 100 and t = 60 s. Data generated using the distribution has been used to plan and send the legitimate traffic.

Attacker Traffic. We performed a total of nine experiments. For an a affective attack scenario we have taken a very low attack of frequency 1 requests/second, Medium which is of 100 requests/second and 200 requests/second. Attack of 1 requests per second could be from a case when attacker rents huge botnets and attacks from myriad IPs in that case even a request of 1 req/second is to be characterized as an attack as it will be scale up. There are attack instances where even 1 request per minute attack costed a cloud consumer on Amazon AWS [11]. Moderate and high level traffic is chosen as per the discussions in the classical paper [27]. Four attacker machines are used to send concurrent attack traffic.

5.2 Experimental Design

To try out all possibilities of an attack on server we have taken 9 combinations of attack and benign traffic. This has helped us in covering almost all the attack scenarios. We took benign traffic to be 10 (low benign), 20 (Moderate benign), 50 (Heavy benign) requests per second. Similary, attacker traffic was designed to have 1 (Very low attack), 100 (Moderate attack), 200 (heavy attack) requests per second. This resulted into nine traffic sets as shwon in Table 4.

Table 4. Traffic sets

Traffic set	Attack frequency	Benign frequency	Traffic set	Attack frequency	Benign frequency	Traffic set	Attack frequency	Benign frequency
1	1	10	4	100	10	7	200	10
2	1	20	5	100	20	8	200	20
3	1	50	6	100	50	9	200	50

6 Results and Discussion

Figures 4 and 5 shows various result graphs. These graphs show the behavior of auto-scaling and webserver responses in both scenarios ("No DARAC" and "With DARAC"). Once the attack starts, the resource utilization (CPU Utilization) reaches the auto-scaling "overload" threshold for the duration specified by the auto-scaling algorithm, which is three minutes in this case. This triggers the "auto-scaling", which in turn triggers, DARAC to see if it is real resource surge. DARAC, in its traffic evaluator module, checks the traffic and tries to get insight into the traffic data of each unique source to each unique webpage. Human behavior for each specific website is different but finite. This finite number is based upon usability surveys conducted on muliple users and their behavior on each specific website and page. This has helped us in segregating the traffic in good and bad traffic. This results into blocking and dropping any subsequent requests from the attackers. This is quite visible in each plot ("With DARAC" plots in Figs. 4 and 5.), where after dropping the attack traffic, the resource utilization changes. At the same time, the capacity planner module, decides about the required resource change by looking at the quality of service. After changing (adding/removing) the resources, the response time pattern and auto-scaling resource addition pattern settles to a attack free point. By doing this, DARAC achieves all the requirements of an effective solution, which are mentioned in Sect. 3. Following are some specific inferences into the results.

1. **Impact on auto-scaling and costs:** Impact on auto-scaling is quite visible in Figs. 4 and 5. Additionally, considering flat pricing of the infrastructure cloud resources, cost of resources with and without DARAC has been shown in Table 5. A representative saving of upto 50 % has been achieved using

DARAC. This cost saving consequently allows the cloud provider to allocate resources to needy VMs which have a real requirements and also saves on unnecessary migrations which would have been there in case of total resource outage on the server.

2. **Impact on response time:** It is quite evident that the page response time is the most important quality of a web-server. As shown in Table 6, average response time without any mitigation, with DARAC and "post-attack mitigation" have reasonable difference. There is a significant decrease in response times after the mitigation has been applied. Though, it could not reach the ideal (1 s) but it was quite near to it while the attack effects were gone. Response time with the combinations, where benign frequency is 50, are not providing the expected benefit. This is due to the fact that the server under consideration only provide required QoS till benign request frequency of 20 requests/second. However, this could be decreased by giving more VCPUs or alternative horizontal scaling methods like migration and VM instance creation.

With this, we showcase how our proposed mitigation mechanism, DARAC, is able to detect and mitigate DDoS traffic. Whether it is a myriad attack with intensity as low as 4 requests per second (1 request/second from each attacker) or as high as 800 requests per second (200 requests/second from each attacker), DARAC was able to mitigate the attack. DARAC tries to segregate the good and the bad IP and the allocation of the resources is done by a capacity planner based on requirement and quality of service to benign users. DARAC is also very cost effective (refer Table 5) as it saves resources and does not need any additional resources due to its simple segregation method. DARAC can successfully mitigate the attacks without any downtime and take a quick decision over whether there is real need to increase the resources or not. The time required to mitigate and take a decision is around 10–15 s in most of the cases, which is less than what is considered as the ideal time period for resource hot plug. Now let us see two most specific and important aspects which make DARAC an important direction and contribution to defeat DDoS attacks in cloud.

1. **Defense against well planned DDoS attacks**

> *Q.1. What would happen if an attacker plans a DDoS attack on this server by intelligently sending requests just one less than the detection threshold n? Would attacker be successful if she sends requests from multiple different machines or spoofed IPs?*

DDoS attacks which are planned intelligently in a manner such that if the attacker comes to know the detection threshold, it may plan an attack from large number of distributed nodes (or spoofed IPs) sending (just one request less than the threshold). Though knowing this would not help an individual attacker but as a group they may be successful. However, in order to plan this attack the resource requirement at the attacker side would be huge. For a quick calculation based on the present attack scenario:

Attack frequency A_f in the test is 200 requests/sec * 4 attackers which would result into 800 requests/seconds. As the detection method is minute based, the total number of requests which should be sent in a minute would be 48000 requests/minute (800*60 s). Now in order to plan an attack which would send requests lesser than the threshold, attacker may choose to send just 24 requests/minute from each unique source (one less than the threshhold n). In order to plan a successful attack, this would require at least 2000 nodes to send $n-1$ requests/minute to the victim server for 1000 s. This is an estimate for a server of capacity as detailed in Table 1. For a production level cloud VM with large amount of resources, the required number to attackers/bots would be much greater. This would even remain true for attackers with IP spoofing. Even if the attacker are able to spoof IPs quickly they would need 800 nodes where at least half of them would need to spoof IPs at least once in a minute and other half of them would need to spoof/change their IPs twice in the same one minute duration. This is required to have 2000 unique source IPs in one minute to send $n - 1$ requests.

2. **Winning the resource race**

> Q.2. DDoS attacks are like "arms race" between the victim and attack-ers [25]. How do we win this race?

DDoS attacks boils down to the fact that the one who will have more active resources will win the DDoS race. We argue that this aspect should be seen from a different perspective in cloud. *DDoS race will be won by the side which sustains the attack with minimum resources (costs) and motivates (insti-gates) the other side to acquire more and more resources (again more costs).* This aspect is quite visible in DARAC, where attacker side, instead of only 4 attackers requires at least 2000 attackers to get the attack succesful. DDoS attacks with large botnets using exhaustive IP spoofing without any visi-ble coordination for attack among themselves are near impossible to detect. There are large number of surveys and contributions supoorting this argu-ment. This is a strong statement to make but in the past there has been no ful-proof solutions against these types of DDoS attacks, which is going to become the biggest cyber hurdle for cloud operations.

7   Related Work

Most of the state of the art solutions for DDoS detection and mitigation are based on three key ideas. Turing tests [9,40] and Crypto puzzles [4], Anomaly detection [8,24] and threshold based detection [1,5,18]. There are few solutions in the literature which are specifically proposed for cloud but use one or more of these three ideas [12,40]. This is evident that the solutions pertaining to DDoS in cloud require a treatment covering resource allocation in cloud. As that is the main hit and gain attraction point for the attackers. We are only listing contributions which have worked towards the DDoS mitigation in cloud with a

Table 5. Impact on auto-scaling and savings

Traffic set	Attack frequency	Benign frequency	No DARAC (VCPUs)	With DARAC (VCPUs)	Savings (%)
1	1	10	3	2	33 %
2	1	20	3	2	33 %
3	1	50	3	2	33 %
4	100	10	4	3	25 %
5	100	20	4	3	25 %
6	100	50	4	3	25 %
7	200	10	4	2	50 %
8	200	20	4	2	50 %
9	200	50	4	3	25 %

Table 6. Impact on response time

Traffic set	Attack frequency	Benign frequency	No DARAC average response time(s)	With DARAC average response time(s)	Post-mitigation average response time(s)
1	1	10	6.55	2.86	1.5
2	1	20	7.67	5.60	3.36
3	1	50	11.93	4.94	3.27
4	100	10	8.80	5.49	1.63
5	100	20	11.72	5.83	2.10
6	100	50	14.72	14.71	14.78
7	200	10	7.95	3.31	2.73
8	200	20	12.35	2.49	2.42
9	200	50	15.03	15.52	13.35

special interest towards utility computing. However, we acknowledge large no. of key works solving DDoS in non-cloud or fixed infrastrucure server environments [6,36].

Idziorek et al. in [10,11] have termed these attacks as "Fraudulent Resource Consumption". They provided solutions based on anomaly detection using features like session length and volume of the requests by using a machine learning system trained against legitimate web traffic. In [15], authors describe sPoW, which is a unilaterally deployable "Pay-as-you-Go" cloud-based EDDoS (Distributed EDoS) mitigation mechanism that offers network-level and application level EDDoS protection to servers deployed in clouds. By mediating connectivity to servers and varying the channel identities used to reach the servers frequently, sPoW transforms network-level EDDoS into traffic that can be filtered.

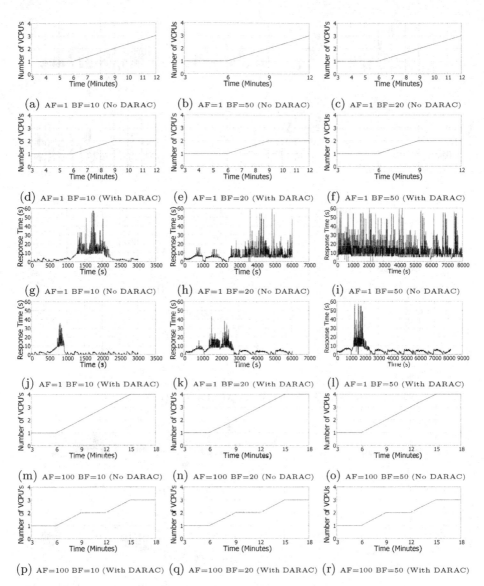

Fig. 4. Effects of DARAC, AF=Attacker Frequency, BF= Benign Frequency

In another work, authors proposed EDoS-armour, a two fold solution based on admission control and congestion control [23]. In admission control, a limit is put on number of clients (that can simultaneously send requests), thus allowing only enough clients that can be served easily within available resources of the web server. In congestion control, priority of allowed client is done based on the type of resources they visit and type of activities they perform.

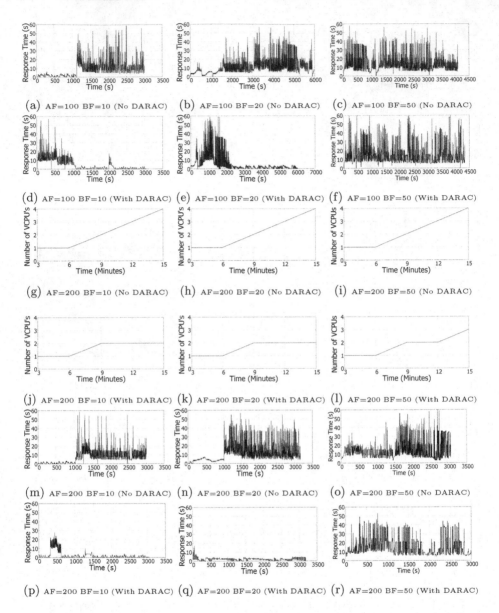

Fig. 5. Effects of DARAC, AF=Attacker Frequency, BF= Benign Frequency

Authors in [31] give in-cloud EDDoS mitigation service (Scrubber Service), which is used on demand and is charged according to pay-per-use basis. As the Puzzle generation and Verification is done by the Scrubber Service, the burden on Service Provider server can be achieved by reducing cloud bills to the service provider and guaranteed availability of service. There are other approaches, where the authors propose a moving-target based defense that dynamically obscures network-layer and transport-layer addresses [13,45]. By constantly moving the logical location of a host on a network, this technique prevents targeted attacks, host tracking, and eavesdropping. Authors in [20,48] have proposed solutions which follow a recovery based approach by doing migration of webserver under attack. This allows serving legitimate customers and saving the server in getting into a severe attack. Backup resources in the form of replicated attack mitigation servers have also been proposed in [20].

In an another work, Shui et al. in [47] have proposed a dynamic resource allocation based DDoS mitigation solution. Authors proposed that reserved or idle resources should be used in quick attack mitigation. One important concern is about the overhead of the reserved resources cost. Additionally, prediction about the amount of needed reserved resources is also difficult. There are other DDoS mitigation solutions based on third party mitigation using cloud resources [7,16,17]. Other fixes like CloudWatch API [3] have been proposed to keep a track of resource usage and scaling, in addition to resource caps/limits. With this discussion, this is evident that there are very few solutions which have used the direction of resource allocation based mitigation in clouds. DARAC is one such solution which works in this direction by only allocating resources to legitmate requests with service quality.

8   Conclusion and Future Work

DDoS attacks are well studied in the literature, but their impact is different in the emerging cloud computing environments. The difference is mostly due to utility computing based "Pay-as-you-Go" model. There is a high need to devise solutions that are capable of solving the cloud version of DDoS, which is EDoS. We have shown through preliminary experiments that the fake resource utilization and subsequent resource addition due to the attack resuls into EDoS, which ultimately converges to DDoS.

This has motivated us to design our proposed mitigation system, DARAC, which is DDoS aware resource allocation in the cloud. There are three important aspects of DARAC which make it quick and effective DDoS mitigation solution for cloud computing. The attacker and benign traffic segregation based on human behavior analysis, intelligent auto-scaling for real users and quality services to benign users during the attack, are three significant contributions of our work. The novelty of our work lies in the wise auto-scaling strategy with capacity planning for the services. Experiments are shown with wide coverage of attacker and benign traffic sets. Results show significance of DARAC in the detection and blocking attacker traffic, stopping EDoS culmination. Importantly, DARAC achieved significant achievement in response time improvement and infrastructure cost savings up to 50 %.

Through this, we have started a new direction of DDoS mitigation in the cloud where instead of only working on the application level, we show that multi-level mitigation is useful. Extending the "arms race" to instigate the attackers to spend more and more resources, makes it difficult for the attackers to defeat such a small capacity server using DARAC. The present solution in its stage, requires improvements in some directions. We plan to extend DARAC to support dynamic thresholds based on the requirement and resource availability. We also plan to devise and test dynamic auto-scaling algorithms having migration and VM instance creation support. Detailed production level capacity planning methods with variety of QoS parameters are also needed to have effective service quality.

References

1. Chen, Q., Lin, W., Dou, W., Yu, S.: Cbf: a packet filtering method for ddos attack defense in cloud environment. In: IEEE Ninth International Conference on Dependable, Autonomic and Secure Computing (DASC), pp. 427–434. IEEE (2011)
2. Clemente, L.: Auto scaling on aws: an overview (2013). http://www.luigiclemente.com/scalable-websites-on-aws-an-overview/
3. Amazon CloudWatch (2014). https://aws.amazon.com/cloudwatch/
4. Dean, D., Stubblefield, A.: Using client puzzles to protect tls. In: USENIX Security Symposium, vol. 42 (2001)
5. Dou, W., Chen, Q., Chen, J.: A confidence-based filtering method for ddos attack defense in cloud environment. Future Gener. Comput. Syst. **29**(7), 1838–1850 (2013)
6. Douligeris, C., Mitrokotsa, A.: DDoS attacks and defense mechanisms: classification and state-of-the-art. Comput. Netw. **44**(5), 643–666 (2004)
7. Du, P., Nakao, A.: Ddos defense as a network service. In: Network Operations and Management Symposium (NOMS), pp. 894–897. IEEE (2010)
8. Ismail, M.N., et al.: Detecting flooding based doS attack in cloud computing environment using covariance matrix approach. In: ICUIMC, p. 36. ACM (2013)
9. Huang, V.S., Huang, R., Chiang, M.: A ddos mitigation system with multi-stage detection and text-based turing testing in cloud computing. In: 2013 27th International Conference on Advanced Information Networking and Applications Workshops (WAINA), pp. 655–662. IEEE (2013)
10. Idziorek, J., Tannian, M., Jacobson, D.: Detecting fraudulent use of cloud resources. In: Proceedings of the 3rd ACM Workshop on Cloud Computing Security, pp. 61–72. ACM (2011)
11. Idziorek, J., Tannian, M., Jacobson, D.: Attribution of fraudulent resource consumption in the cloud. In: 2012 IEEE 5th International Conference on Cloud Computing (CLOUD), pp. 99–106. IEEE (2012)
12. Jeyanthi, N., Iyengar, N.C.S.N., Mogan Kumar, P.C., Kannammal, A.: An enhanced entropy approach to detect and prevent ddos in cloud environment. Int. J. Commun. Netw. Inf. Secur. (IJCNIS) **5**(2), 110–119 (2013)
13. Jia, Q., Wang, H., Fleck, D., Li, F., Stavrou, A., Powell, W.: Catch me if you can: a cloud-enabled ddos defense. In: 44th Annual IEEE/IFIP International Conference on Dependable Systems and Networks (DSN), pp. 264–275. IEEE (2014)
14. Kandula, S., Katabi, D., Jacob, M., Berger, A.: Botz-4-sale: Surviving organized DDoS attacks that mimic flash crowds (awarded best student paper). In: NSDI, USENIX (2005)
15. Khor, S.H., Nakao, A.: spow: On-demand cloud-based eddos mitigation mechanism. In: HotDep (2009)

16. Khor, S.H., Nakao, A.: Daas: Ddos mitigation-as-a-service. In: 11th International Symposium on Applications and the Internet (SAINT), pp. 160–171. IEEE (2011)
17. Kim, S.H., Kim, J.H.: Method for detecting and preventing a ddos attack using cloud computing, and server, 12 July 2010. US Patent App. 13/386,516
18. Koduru, A., Neelakantam, T., Saira Bhanu, S.M.: Detection of economic denial of sustainability using time spent on a web page in cloud. In: 2013 IEEE International Conference on Cloud Computing in Emerging Markets (CCEM), pp. 1–4, October 2013
19. Kaspersky Labs. Global it security risks survey 2014 distributed denial of service (ddos) attacks (2014). http://media.kaspersky.com/en/B2B-International-2014-Survey-DDoS-Summary-Report.pdf
20. Latanicki, J., Massonet, P., Naqvi, S., Rochwerger, B., Villari, M.: Scalable cloud defenses for detection, analysis and mitigation of ddos attacks, In: Future Internet, Assembly, pp. 127–137 (2010)
21. Mao, M., Li, J., Humphrey, M.: Cloud auto-scaling with deadline and budget constraints. In: 2010 11th IEEE/ACM International Conference on Grid Computing (GRID), pp. 41–48. IEEE (2010)
22. Marck, S.J., Lyon, J.A., Smith, R.C.: System and method for mitigating application layer distributed denial of service attacks using human behavior analysis, 31 October 2013. US Patent App. 13/458,129
23. Masood, M., Anwar, Z., Raza, S.A., Hur, M.A.: Edos armor: a cost effective economic denial of sustainability attack mitigation framework for e-commerce applications in cloud environments. In: 2013 16th International Multi Topic Conference (INMIC), pp. 37–42, December 2013
24. Mirkovic, J., Reiher, P.: A taxonomy of ddos attack and ddos defense mechanisms. SIGCOMM Comput. Commun. Rev. **34**(2), 39–53 (2004)
25. Mirkovic, J., Robinson, M., Reiher, P.: Alliance formation for ddos defense. In: Proceedings of the 2003 Workshop on New Security Paradigms, pp. 11–18. ACM (2003)
26. Mohan, S., Alam, F.M., Fowler, J.W., Gopalakrishnan, M., Printezis, A.: Capacity planning and allocation for web-based applications. Decis. Sci. **45**(3), 535–567 (2014)
27. Moore, D., Shannon, C., Brown, D.J., Voelker, G.M., Savage, S.: Inferring internet denial-of-service activity. ACM Trans. Comput. Syst. (TOCS) **24**(2), 115–139 (2006)
28. Morein, W.G., Stavrou, A., Cook, D.L., Keromytis, A.D., Misra, V., Rubenstein, D.: Using graphic turing tests to counter automated ddos attacks against web servers. In: Proceedings of the 10th ACM Conference on Computer and Communications Security, CCS 2003, pp. 8–19. ACM, New York (2003)
29. Munson, L.: Greatfire.org faces daily $30,000 bill from ddos attack (2015). https://nakedsecurity.sophos.com/2015/03/20/greatfire-org-faces-daily-30000-bill-from-ddos-attack/
30. Nah, F.F.-H.: A study on tolerable waiting time: how long are web users willing to wait? Behav. Inf. Technol. **23**, 153–163 (2004)
31. Naresh Kumar, M., Sujatha, P., Kalva, V., Nagori, R., Katukojwala, A.K., Kumar, M.: Mitigating economic denial of sustainability (edos) in cloud computing using in-cloud scrubber service. In: Fourth International Conference on CICN, pp. 535–539. IEEE (2012)
32. Nelson, P.: Cybercriminals moving into cloud big time, report says (2015). http://www.networkworld.com/article/2900125/malware-cybercrime/criminals-moving-into-cloud-big-time-says-report.html

33. Arbor Networks. Understanding the nature of ddos attacks (2014). http://www.arbornetworks.com/asert/2012/09/understanding-the-nature-of-ddos-attacks/
34. SPAMfighter News. Survey - with ddos attacks companies lose around 100k/hr (2015). http://www.spamfighter.com/News-19554-Survey-With-DDoS-Attacks-Companies-Lose-around-100kHr.htm
35. Oikonomou, G., Mirkovic, J.: Modeling human behavior for defense against flash-crowd attacks. In: IEEE International Conference on Communications, 2009, ICC 2009, pp. 1–6. IEEE (2009)
36. Peng, T., Leckie, C., Ramamohanarao, K.: Survey of network-based defense mechanisms countering the dos and ddos problems. ACM Comput. Surv. **39**(1) (2007)
37. Prolexic (2014). http://www.prolexic.com/
38. Saini, B., Somani, G.: Index page based EDoS attacks in infrastructure cloud. In: Martínez Pérez, G., Thampi, S.M., Ko, R., Shu, L. (eds.) SNDS 2014. CCIS, vol. 420, pp. 382–395. Springer, Heidelberg (2014)
39. Seals, T.: Q1 2015 ddos attacks spike, targeting cloud (2015). http://www.infosecurity-magazine.com/news/q1-2015-ddos-attacks-spike/
40. Sqalli, M.H., Al-Haidari, F., Salah, K.: EDoS-shield - A two-steps mitigation technique against EDoS attacks in cloud computing. In: UCC, pp. 49–56. IEEE Computer Society (2011)
41. Stillwell, M., Schanzenbach, D., Vivien, F., Casanova, H.: Resource allocation algorithms for virtualized service hosting platforms. J. Parallel Distrib. Comp. **70**(9), 962–974 (2010)
42. Akamai Technologies. Akamai's state of the internet q4 2013 executive summary vol. 6(4) (2013). http://www.akamai.com/dl/akamai/akamai-soti-q413-exec-summary.pdf
43. WAPT Load Testing Tool. Response time (2015). http://www.loadtestingtool.com/help/response-time.shtml
44. Vaquero, L.M., Rodero-Merino, L., Buyya, R.: Dynamically scaling applications in the cloud. SIGCOMM Comp. Comm. Rev. **41**(1), 45–52 (2011)
45. Wang, H., Jia, Q., Fleck, D., Powell, W., Li, F., Stavrou, A.: A moving target ddos defense mechanism. Comput. Commun. **46**, 10–21 (2014)
46. Wang, J., Yang, X., Long, K.: Web ddos detection schemes based on measuring user's access behavior with large deviation. In: Global Telecommunications Conference (GLOBECOM 2011), 2011 IEEE, pp. 1–5. IEEE (2011)
47. Yu, S., Tian, Y., Guo, S., Wu, D.: Can we beat ddos attacks in clouds? IEEE Trans. Parallel Distrib. Syst. **25**(9), 2245–2254 (2013)
48. Zhao, S., Chen, K., Zheng, W.: Defend against denial of service attack with vmm. In: Eighth International Conference on Grid and Cooperative Computing, 2009, GCC 2009, pp. 91–96. IEEE (2009)

Crypto Systems and Protocols

New HMAC Message Patches: Secret Patch and CrOw Patch

Donghoon Chang[1], Somitra Kumar Sanadhya[1], and Nishant Sharma[2]([✉])

[1] IIIT-Delhi, New Delhi, India
{donghoon,somitra}@iiitd.ac.in
[2] Airtight Networks, Pune, India
nishant.sharma@airtightnetworks.com

Abstract. At Asiacrypt 2012, Peyrin *et al.* showed generic attacks against the HMAC design. They utilized a pair of related keys where only the relation between the keys is known to the attacker but not the keys themselves (the secret key model). On similar lines, at Crypto 2012, Dodis *et al.* showed differentiability attacks based on ambiguous and colliding keys on HMAC in known/chosen key model. Peyrin *et al.* also proposed a patching scheme for HMAC and claimed that the proposed patch thwarts their attacks.

In this work, we first show that the patch proposed by Peyrin *et al.* will not prevent their attacks for the HMAC construction for certain "good" cryptographic hash functions. Specifically, we show that no public and reversible patch will prevent their attack on HMAC instantiated with a weakly collision resistant hash function. Following this, we propose two different patches, called the *secret* patch and the *collision resistant one way (CrOw)* patch, to thwart the attacks of Peyrin *et al.* and Dodis *et al.* Our work is theoretical in nature, and does not threaten the security of HMAC used with standard hash functions. Further, both our patches are designed to be used as wrappers and do not affect the underlying HMAC construction. This property is similar to Peyrin *et al.*'s patch.

Keywords: HMAC · Patch · Related key attack · Colliding keys · Ambiguous keys · Indifferentiability

1 Introduction

HMAC (designed by Bellare, Canetti and Krawczyk in 1996 [4]) is a MAC algorithm based on a cryptographic hash function. It was subsequently adopted by IETF working group as RFC 2104 [9] and made a standard for authentication in secure internet protocols. It is widely used in banking industry and secure web connections via its use in TLS and IPSEC (i.e. HMAC-SHA-1 which uses SHA-1 [1] as the underlying hash).

The HMAC construction [4], using a hash function H, is defined as HMAC $(K,M) = H(K \oplus opad \,||H(K \oplus ipad \,||M))$, where ipad and opad are constants

© Springer International Publishing Switzerland 2015
S. Jajodia and C. Mazumdar (Eds.): ICISS 2015, LNCS 9478, pp. 285–302, 2015.
DOI: 10.1007/978-3-319-26961-0_17

defined as ipad = 0x3636...36 and opad = 0x5C5C...5C. H is any cryptographically secure hash function which takes an arbitrary sized input message M and produces an n bit output after finalization of l bit internal state. K is the message authentication secret key shared between the two communicating parties. Let d be the block length of underlying compression function h of hash H in HMAC. In HMAC scheme the key size $|K|$ should be equal to block size d of underlying compression function h. If $|K| < d$ then we have to pad the key with zero bits to make it equal to d and if $|K| > d$ then the key K is fed to the hash function H and its output is used as key i.e. $K = H(K)$. For this purpose key padding schemes are used. However if $|K| = d$ then no padding is done.

Pad$^{0^*}(x)$ padding scheme or 0^* or zero padding, defined as $pad^{0^*}(x) = x||0^v$ where $v = d - |x|$ when $|x| < d$, $pad^{0^*}(x) = H(x)$ when $|x| > d$ and $pad^{0^*}(x) = x$ when $|x| = d$.

Pad$^{10^*}(x)$ padding scheme or 10^* padding, defined as $pad^{10^*}(x) = x||10^{v-1}$ where $v = d - |x|$ when $|x| < d$ and $pad^{10^*}(x) = H(x)$ when $|x| \geq d$.

$\overline{K}$ be the zero padded (pad^{0^*}) version of the key K i.e. $\overline{K} = K \parallel 0000....$ For sake of simplicity, we will denote padded key $\overline{K}$ with K for the rest of the paper. The HMAC or HMAC-H(K, M) construction is explained in Fig. 1.

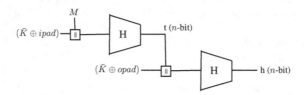

Fig. 1. The HMAC construction

Mihir Bellare [3] showed that the MAC is pseudo-random if the underlying keyed compression function is pseudo random. Leurent *et al.* [8] proposed attacks on HMAC based on cycle detection technique discussed in [11] with a little higher complexity than birthday bound $2^{l/2}$ where l is the size of internal state i.e. output size of its underlying compression function h. They suggested that in order to prevent this attack the parameter l should be increased. For example, the size l is recommended to be at least 256 bits in order to achieve 128-bit security. Note that they considered standard secret key attack model but not related secret/known/chosen key attack models. Related secret key attack model is one where some relation between the two keys is known but keys themselves are not known. On the other hand, in related chosen/known key attack models, both the relation and the keys are chosen/known. Peyrin *et al.* [11] and Dodis *et al.* [6] introduced two types of related keys, namely ambiguous keys and colliding keys, defined below.

Type I Related Key: Ambiguous keys are key pair (K_1, K_2) such that $K_1 \neq K_2$ but $pad(K_2) = pad(K_1) \oplus ipad \oplus opad$.

Type II Related Key: Colliding keys are key pair (K_1, K_2) such that $K_1 \neq K_2$ but $pad(K_1) = pad(K_2)$.

In [11], Peyrin *et al.* showed that ambiguous keys can lead to cycle detection based Distinguishing-R (complexity: $2^{n/2+1}$), Distinguishing-H (complexity: $2^{n/2+1}$ for narrow-pipe and $2^{n/2+2}+2^{l-n+1}$ for wide pipe), internal state recovery (complexity: $2^{n/2+2}+2^{l-n+1}$) and forgery attacks (complexity: $2^{n/2+2}+2^{l-n+1}$) on HMAC in secret related key model. These attacks are briefly discussed in Sect. 2. Here n is the output size of its underlying hash function and l is the output size of the compression function h of hash function H. Note that complexity of Distinguishing-R and Distinguishing-H attacks depends only on n (in order to give 128 bit security, the n is recommended to be at least 256 bit and l does not make any impact). Thus these attacks can't be prevented even if we increase l. This is in contrast with the attacks of Leurent *et al.* [8]. Especially in case of $l/2 \leq n \leq l$, the complexity of internal recovery and forgery attacks is less than $2^{l/2}$, so in order to give 128 bit security against these attacks the recommended sizes of l and n are such that $l - n \geq 128$ or $n \geq 256$. Peyrin *et al.* [11] then proposed a patch for HMAC to prevent the same attacks based on cycle detection using ambiguous keys in secret key attack model. On similar lines, Dodis *et al.* [6] showed differentiability attacks against HMAC using colliding keys and ambiguous keys in known/chosen key model. In [7], authors have presented selective forgery attacks and improved universal forgery attacks. It uses the functional graph properties discussed in [8] to improve attacks but differs from our approach.

Our contributions

1. We show a weakness in the patch proposed by Peyrin *et al.* [11] and explain how the patch proposed by them may not work, even when the hash function H of HMAC is collision, preimage and second preimage resistant.
2. As discussed above these attacks can be prevented by choosing large n and l, which will hamper the efficiency. Hence, instead of increasing n and l, we propose to use two new message patches, namely (i) secret patch and (ii) collision resistant one way (CrOw) patch. These patches efficiently prevent attacks of Peyrin *et al.* using ambiguous keys in secret key attack model and differentiability attacks of Dodis *et al.* using ambiguous keys in chosen/known key attack model.
3. We propose 10^* key padding for HMAC to prevent differentiability attack of Dodis *et al.* based on colliding keys in chosen/known key attack model.
4. SP and CrOw patches thwart the attacks by Peyrin *et al.* Also, both patches are supposed to be applied as a wrapper over HMAC construction. Hence, the HMAC construction remains intact as in the earlier work.
5. SP and CrOw can be combined with 10^* key padding without losing the effects described in item 3 and 4.
6. Our work is essentially a theoretical study of HMAC patches without affecting the real HMAC construction. We understand that our attack may not be possible in real world deployments but it help us improve our understanding of such constructions.

Table 1 shows the attack complexities of various generic attacks in single and related key model (cycle based). The explanation for complexities provided is given in Appendix A.

Table 1. Attack complexities of generic attacks under various scenarios.

Generic attacks	Single key	Related key (cycle based attacks)			
		Without patch	Peyrin's patch	Secret patch	CrOw patch
Distinguishing R	$2^{l/2}$	$2^{n/2+1}$	$2^{l/2}$	$2^{n/2+1}+2^k$	$2^{n/2+2+u}$
Distinguishing H	2^l	$2^{n/2+2}+2^{l-n+1}$	2^l	$2^{n/2+2}+2^k+2^{l-n+1}$	$2^{n/2+2+u}+2^{l-n+1}$
Existential foregry	$2^{l/2}$	$2^{n/2+2}+2^{l-n+1}$	$2^{l/2}$	$2^{n/2+2}+2^k+2^{l-n+1}$	$2^{n/2+2+u}+2^{l-n+1}$
Internal state recovery	2^n	$2^{n/2+2}+2^{l-n+1}$	2^n	$2^{n/2+2}+2^k+2^{l-n+1}$	$2^{n/2+2+u}+2^{l-n+1}$

Table 2 clearly indicates that HMAC scheme patched with our patches is secure from cycle detection based attacks discussed by Peyrin *et al.* [11].

2   Previous Work

In [11], Peyrin *et al.* state that the "choice of ipad and opad is not anecdotal". If any other random pair of constants is used as ipad and opad then the attacks may work for all key sizes. They show that related key pairs which allow distinguishing attacks only exist for keys of length $\geq (d-1)$, where d is the block length of compression function h of hash function H. They showed four different types of attacks on HMAC, namely, Distinguishing-R, Internal State Recovery, Distinguishing-H and forgery attack. These attacks are described briefly below,

Distinguishing R Attack: The attacker can query two oracles, FK and FK', that are instantiated either with $HMAC$ or with a random function R. He must obtain non-negligible advantage in distinguishing the two cases:

$$Adv(A) = |Pr[A(HMAC(K,M), HMAC(K',M)) = 1]$$
$$- Pr[A(R(K,M), R(K',M)) = 1]|$$

Distinguishing H Attack: The attacker can query oracles, HMAC(K,M) and HMAC(K,M) based on H where H is a known dedicated hash function instantiated either with known underlying compression function h or with random compression function r. He must obtain non-negligible advantage in distinguishing the two cases:

$$Adv(A) = |Pr[A(HMAC^{H(h)}(K,M), HMAC^{H(h)}(K',M)) = 1]$$
$$- Pr[A(HMAC^{H(r)}(K,M), HMAC^{H(r)}(K',M)) = 1]|$$

Table 2. Summary of feasibility of cycle detection based attacks based on ambiguous keys when HMAC is used with our patches i.e. $SP(K, M)$ and $CrOw(M)$, and padding schemes i.e. pad^{0*} and pad^{10*}. $|K|$ is length of the key K, d is the block size of H. HMAC-H($pad^x(K), M$) is HMAC-H(K, M) with pad^x (either pad^{0*} or pad^{10*}). Similarly HMAC-H($pad^x(K), P0(M)$) is for HMAC-H(K, M) patched with patch $P0$ and padding scheme pad^x, HMAC-H($pad^x(K), SP(K, M)$) is for HMAC-H(K, M) patched with patch $SP(K, M)$ and padding scheme pad^x and HMAC-H($pad^x(K), CrOw(M)$) is for HMAC-H(K, M) patched with patch $CrOw(M)$ and padding scheme pad^x. Each O entry represent that respective scheme is secure against that attack whereas X entry represent that respective construction is not secure against that attack. We have considered two overlapping range sets of key sizes (i.e. $0 < |K| < d-2$, $d-2 \le |K| < d$ and $0 < |K| < d-1$, $d-1 \le |K| < d$). This is done to show that when pad^{10*} is used with key sizes of $d-2 \le |K| < d$ ambiguous pairs occurs due to xor of key K with $ipad$ and $opad$ i.e. $pad(K_1) = pad(K_2) = pad(K) \oplus ipad \oplus opad$.

Construction	Key Size $|K|$	Cycle Detection attack based on ambiguous pairs	Construction	Key Size $|K|$	Cycle Detection attack based on ambiguous pairs
HMAC-H($pad^{0*}(K), M$) [3]	$0 < |K| < d-1$	X	HMAC-H($pad^{10*}(K), M$) [our contribution]	$0 < |K| < d-1$	O
	$d-1 \le |K| < d$	O		$d-1 \le |K| < d$	O
	$0 < |K| < d-2$	X		$0 < |K| < d-2$	X
	$d-2 \le |K| < d$	O		$d-2 \le |K| < d$	O
	$|K| = d$	O		$|K| = d$	O
HMAC-H($pad^{0*}(K), P0(M)$) [11]	$0 < |K| < d-1$	X	HMAC-H($pad^{10*}(K), P0(M)$) [our contribution]	$0 < |K| < d-1$	O
	$d-1 \le |K| < d$	O		$d-1 \le |K| < d$	O
	$0 < |K| < d-2$	X		$0 < |K| < d-2$	X
	$d-2 \le |K| < d$	O		$d-2 \le |K| < d$	O
	$|K| = d$	O		$|K| = d$	O
HMAC-H($pad^{0*}(K), SP(K, M)$) [our contribution]	$0 < |K| < d-1$	X	HMAC-H($pad^{10*}(K), SP(K, M)$) [our contribution]	$0 < |K| < d-1$	X
	$d-1 \le |K| < d$	X		$d-1 \le |K| < d$	X
	$0 < |K| < d-2$	X		$0 < |K| < d-2$	X
	$d-2 \le |K| < d$	X		$d-2 \le |K| < d$	X
	$|K| = d$	X		$|K| = d$	X
HMAC-H($pad^{0*}(K), CrOw(M)$) [our contribution]	$0 < |K| < d-1$	X	HMAC-H($pad^{10*}(K), CrOw(M)$) [our contribution]	$0 < |K| < d-1$	X
	$d-1 \le |K| < d$	X		$d-1 \le |K| < d$	X
	$0 < |K| < d-2$	X		$0 < |K| < d-2$	X
	$d-2 \le |K| < d$	X		$d-2 \le |K| < d$	X
	$|K| = d$	X		$|K| = d$	X

Internal State Recovery: Internal State Recovery is said to be done success-fully if attacker can recover the l-bit internal state of underlying hash H from n-bit output.

Forgery: Forgery is said to be done successfully when attacker can generate a valid tag t for a message m, which it never queried to HMAC.
The forgery is classified into two broad categories:

– If the message is chosen by attacker then it is *Existential* Forgery.
– If the message is chosen by challenger the it is *Universal* Forgery.

We omit the description of these attacks due to space limitations and refer the reader to [11] for details of these attacks. The main idea behind all these attacks is to obtain a cycle or a synchronized cycle by generating long query paths. If we can prevent the adversary from obtaining a cycle then all these attacks will be thwarted.

2.1   Patch Proposed by Peyrin *et al.*

The authors then proposed few patching schemes which can avoid these attacks by preventing the formation of cycles and comment about shortcomings of each of these schemes. The schemes are as follows:

1. Use of different IVs in inner and outer instances of HMAC. It was rejected as it requires modification of the HMAC implementation.
2. Truncating the output of HMAC. It was also rejected as the expected generic security of MAC algorithm reduces due to this change.
3. XORing some distinct constants to inner and/or outer hash calls. As explained in [11], this patch does not work since the attacker can suitably modify its query strategy and can still get synchronized chains.
4. Adding an extra bit to the input of outer hash call. It was also rejected since the attacker can still get synchronized chains by modifying his query strategy.
5. To prepend a 0 bit (byte) to the input message before feeding it to HMAC.

After analyzing all possible schemes they proposed to prepend 0 bit (or byte) to the input message before passing it to the HMAC construction. They claimed that this patch successfully prevents an adversary from generating cycles and the additional overhead of adding 1 bit (or byte) to the message is insignifi-cant. This patch has the additional advantage of the feasibility of being imple-mented by means of a message wrapper while keeping the HMAC implementation unchanged. Therefore, this patching scheme was claimed as the best for patching HMAC against such attacks. For our analysis, we will refer to this patch as the patch $P0$. Note that no proof of security of the patch has been provided.

Patch $P0$ is defined as $P0(M) = 0||M$ where M is a message of any length and resulting $\text{HMAC}^{P0}\text{-H}(K, M)$ (also denoted as $\text{HMAC-}\text{H}(pad^{0^*}(K), P0(M))$) is defined as follows.

$$\text{HMAC}^{P0}\text{-H}(K, M) = \text{HMAC-H}(K, P0(M)),$$
$$= \text{HMAC-H}(K, 0 \parallel M).$$

This construction is defined in Fig. 2.

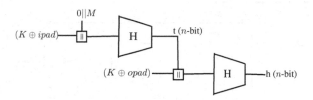

Fig. 2. $\text{HMAC}^{P0}\text{-H}(K, M)$ construction.

3 Insecurity of Patch $P0$

To analyse patch $P0$, we may modify underlying primitives but not the fundamental HMAC construction. We emphasize that we allow the attacker to tamper the output of oracle HMAC-H(K,M) (or HMAC-H(K',M)) before the next call to the same or a different oracle. However, the attacker can't tamper within the HMAC construction (he can only tamper between two calls to the HMAC oracle). In Fig. 3 we have depicted the attack/modification area. By introducing changes at the place marked as "attack" in this figure, we analyse the patch $P0$.

3.1 MAC Security

The security of a Message Authentication Code (MAC) is defined in terms of unforgeability i.e. MAC scheme is said to be (A^f, q) secure if no adversary A can produce a valid message-tag pair (m_v, t_v) after asking q queries $((m_1, t_1),(m_2, t_2),\ldots(m_q, t_q))$ with non negligible advantage A^f. Such that $(m_v, t_v) \notin ((m_1, t_1),(m_2, t_2),\ldots(m_q, t_q))$.

Hash construction$\mathbf{H}^{P0}$: Let H^{P0} be a collision resistant function H. The H^{P0} outputs $H(M)$ prepended with 0. Patch $P0$ is defined as

$$P0(M) = 0 \parallel M,$$

where M is a message of arbitrary length. H^{P0} is defined as

$$H^{P0}(M) = P0(H(M)) = 0 \parallel H(M) = 0 \parallel h.$$

The HMAC construction which is patched with patch $P0$ and uses H^{P0} as underlying hash function will be denoted as $\text{HMAC}^{P0}\text{-H}^{P0}(K, M)$.

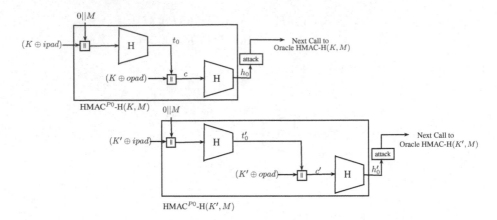

Fig. 3. HMAC^{P0}-H(K, M) and HMAC^{P0}-H(K', M) behave like black boxes, hence an attacker can only modify the sequence between two consecutive calls to the oracles.

Security of H^{P0}: Note that the hash function H^{P0} is not a PRF due to an trivial distinguisher against it. The distinguisher only looks at the first bit of the hash output and concludes that it is a random function if the first bit of the hash output is 1, and a hash function otherwise. This may lead one to believe that the hash function H^{P0} is not suitable for use inside the HMAC construction, as the security proof of HMAC is expected to hold only when the underlying hash function is a PRF. However, it was shown in [3] that HMAC instantiated with a hash function H is secure as a keyed MAC if the following two conditions hold:

1. the hash function H is "computational almost universal" (cAU).
2. the compression function h used inside the hash function H is "Privacy Preserving MAC" (PP-MAC).

We now discuss these two properties with respect to the hash function H^{P0} assuming that H is a random oracle. H$^{P0}(K, M)$ is said to be PP-MAC if no adversary A with multiple queries (q_0, q_1) can distinguish H$^{P0}(K||q_0)$ and H$^{P_0}(K||q_1)$, where all queries (q_0, q_1) are distinct. There is no way to distinguish H$^{P0}(K, M)$ in this setting since H is taken to be a random oracle and the first bit of output (which is always 0) is useless for the distinguishing attack. Now we show that H$^{P0}(K, M)$ is also a cAU hash function. If an adversary chooses two *different* messages M_1 and M_2 without knowing the secret key then H$^{P0}(K||M_1)$ $\neq$ H$^{P0}(K||M_2)$ with overwhelming probability. Since H is assumed to be random oracle the matching probability will be 2^{-n}, where the output size of H^{P0} is $n + 1$ bits. Therefore, H^{P0} is PP-MAC and cAU.

3.2 Security of HMAC^{P0}-H$^{P0}(K, M)$

Let adversary A guesses a valid message-tag pair (m_v, t_v) and perform forgery. Now, forgery is only be successful if $(m_v, t_v) \notin ((m_1, t_1), (m_2, t_2), \ldots (m_q, t_q))$. We will denote the internal state of HMAC-H(K, M) i.e. output of H$(K \oplus ipad||M)$ by z and output size by n. The probability of successful forgery will be given by summation of probabilities of the following cases:

1. $m_v \neq m_i$ and $t_v \neq t_i$, $\forall\, i$ in $\{1, 2 \ldots q\}$:
   In this case both m_v and t_v are $\notin \{(m_1, t_1),(m_2, t_2),\ldots (m_q, t_q)\}$. Hence, the probability of happening this event $\approx 1/2^n$.
2. $m_v = m_i$ and $t_v \neq t_i$, $\forall\, i$ in $\{1, 2 \ldots q\}$:
   (a) $m_v = m_i$, $z_v \neq z_i$ and $t_v \neq t_i$, $\forall\, i$ in $\{1, 2 \ldots q\}$:
       In this case $m_v \in \{m_1, m_2, \ldots m_q\}, z_v \notin \{z_1, z_2, \ldots z_q\}$ and $t_v \notin \{t_1, t_2, \ldots t_q\}$.
       Hence, the probability of happening this event $\approx q$ queries $*1/2^n = q/2^n$.
   (b) $m_v = m_i$, $z_v = z_i$ and $t_v \neq t_i$, $\forall\, i$ in $\{1, 2 \ldots q\}$:
       In this case $m_v \in \{m_1, m_2, \ldots m_q\}, z_v \in \{z_1, z_2, \ldots z_q\}$ and $t_v \notin \{t_1, t_2, \ldots t_q\}$.
       Hence, the probability of happening this event $\approx q$ queries $*1/2^n = q/2^n$.
3. $m_v \neq m_i$ and $t_v = t_i$, $\forall\, i$ in $\{1, 2 \ldots q\}$:
   (a) $m_v \neq m_i$, $z_v \neq z_i$ and $t_v = t_i$, $\forall\, i$ in $\{1, 2 \ldots q\}$:
       In this case $m_v \notin \{m_1, m_2, \ldots m_q\}, z_v \notin \{z_1, z_2, \ldots z_q\}$ and $t_v \in \{t_1, t_2, \ldots t_q\}$.
       Hence, the probability of happening this event $\approx q$ queries $*1/2^n = q/2^n$.
   (b) $m_v \neq m_i$, $z_v = z_i$ and $t_v = t_i$, $\forall\, i$ in $\{1, 2 \ldots q\}$:
       In this case $m_v \notin \{m_1, m_2, \ldots m_q\}, z_v \in \{z_1, z_2, \ldots z_q\}$ and $t_v \in \{t_1, t_2, \ldots t_q\}$.
       Hence, the probability of happening this event $\approx q$ queries $*1/2^n = q/2^n$.

The total probability of successful forgery $(1 + 2 + 3) \approx 1/2^n + 2q/2^n + 2q/2^n = (1 + 4q)/2^n$. In practice $q <<< 2^n$, therefore the probability is negligible and construction HMAC^{P0}-H$^{P0}(K, M)$ is secure from forgery.

3.3   HMAC^{P0}-H$^{P0}(K, M)$ is not Secure

The attack described in [11] relies on the fact that given large numbers of queries on oracles HMAC-H(K, M) and HMAC-H(K', M), a collision will occur at some instance. After the collision same input will be forwarded to identical stages in both the cases and this trend (collisions) will continue. The term walk refers to output chains which can be generated by selecting a random input at first and then using its output as input to next stage. Figure 4 illustrates the walk generation using HMAC^{P0}-H$^{P0}(K, M)$ and HMAC^{P0}-H$^{P0}(K', M)$. To avoid the attacker from getting a cycle, occurrence of the same consccutive outputs (either intermediate or final) of HMAC^{P0}-H$^{P0}(K, M)$ and HMAC^{P0}-H$^{P0}(K', M)$ must be prevented. By prepending an extra 0 bit (or byte) in every call to HMAC-H(K, M), the authors of [11] tried to make the internal states different. So that even if the outputs of $H_{K_{out}}$ or $H_{K_{in}}$ collide in HMAC^{P0}-H$^{P0}(K, M)$ and HMAC^{P0}-H$^{P0}(K', M)$, the outputs of next stage will never collide. This is because inputs to the next stage are different for both calls due to the prepended extra 0 (If at some point h_0 and t'_1 collides then 0 is prepended to h_0). So the values at b and c' (used in Fig. 4) are not same hence outputs t_1 and h'_1 also differ. If we manage to keep the inputs same in both cases then collision will propagate, resulting in cycles. In Fig. 4, we can observe that in this scenario if

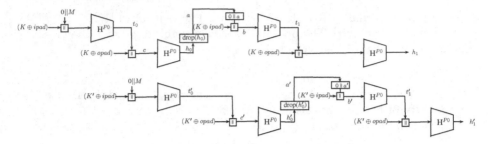

Fig. 4. Walk Generation using oracle $\text{HMAC}^{P0} - H^{P0}(K, M)$ and $\text{HMAC}^{P0} - H^{P0}(K', M)$.

the collision takes place at any point, then the probability of a collision taking place at the next step is 1.

In Fig. 4, $\text{HMAC}^{P0}\text{-}H^{P0}(K, M)$ and $\text{HMAC}^{P0}\text{-}H^{P0}(K', M)$ are used as oracles, both of which use H^{P0} as hash function. The message M is prepended with 0 in both the cases. The output given by H^{P0} hash is prepended with 0. In the same figure we can observe that due to this step, if a collision occurs at h_0 and t_0' (i.e. $0||h_0 = 0||t_0'$) then it will not propagate to the next step. As all calls to H^{P0} provide 0 prepended to the output of the actual hash function H, due to which at the beginning of next call of $\text{HMAC}^{P0}\text{-}H^{P0}(K, M)$ or $\text{HMAC}^{P0}\text{-}H^{P0}(K', M)$, there will be two extra 0 bits (one from the hash function H^{P0} and another one prepended according to the patching scheme $P0$). To tackle this, we have to deploy *drop(x)* function block which will remove this extra zero. If this extra zero is not removed then the length of b will become 1 bit longer than c' and hence the hash value will differ completely.

The dropping of this extra 0 bit makes the value at b and c' same (i.e. $h_0 = t_0'$). As a result of this, t_1 and h_0' will also collide (i.e. $t_1 = h_0'$). This chain will continue and hence cycles will be obtained by the attacker. Therefore, the patching scheme proposed in [11] is completely broken even when a hash function which is collision resistant, preimage resistant and 2nd preimage resistant, but is not a random oracle.

3.4 $\text{HMAC}^{P0}\text{-}H(K, M)$ is Secure

The patching scheme proposed by Peyrin *et al.* [11] suggests prepending a 0 bit (or byte) and thwarts synchronized computation chain (i.e. cycle). Even if the values collide i.e. $h_0 = t_1'$, since the function H is a random oracle, the probability of having $t_1 = h_1'$ is negligible. The prepended extra 0 increases the length of the message hence altering the output significantly. As a first try, we would like to bring this probability to some measurable bounds.

We propose function *modify(x)* to do some modifications to x. Suppose that a collision happens at some point in the path i.e. $h_0 = t_0'$, as shown in Fig. 5. After the *modify(x)* function is applied to h_0, the probability of having a collision in each subsequent step is at most $1/2$.

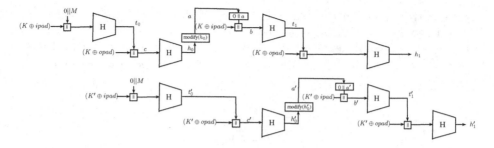

Fig. 5. Walk Generation using oracles HMAC^{P0}-H(K, M) and HMAC^{P0}-H(K, M).

As at least $2^{n/2}$ elements are needed in a computational chain, the probability of getting a chain will be $\leq 2^{-2^{n/2}}$. This probability is very low and infeasible in real world scenario i.e. for HMAC-SHA1(K, M) it is $2^{-2^{80}}$. Hence HMAC-H(K, M) is secure when a collision resistant, preimage resistant and second preimage resistant hash H is used which behaves like a random oracle.

4   Insecurity of Any Public and Reversible Patch

In Sect. 3 we observed that the attack is possible due to $drop(x)$ function which is the inverse of the patch (Patching scheme prepends 0 to message whereas $drop(x)$ drops the prepended 0). Hence the attack is only possible when attacker knows the patching scheme and can find its inverse. In this section we will demonstrate how HMAC^P-H$^P(K, M)$ scheme is insecure for any public and reversible patch P.

Hash construction H^P. To demonstrate attacks on generic design, hash function H^P is defined such that it is based on a good hash function H. H^P is a random oracle or not depends on the function P which applies on the output of function H. Let P be a public and reversible function. The hash function H^P is defined as

$$H^P(M) = P(H(M)) = P(h).$$

4.1   HMAC^P-H$^P(K, M)$ is not Secure

To analyse the security of HMAC^P-H$^P(K, M)$, we consider two oracles HMAC^P-H$^P(K, M)$ and HMAC^P-H$^P(K', M)$ depicted in Fig. 6. From previous sections we know that *patch* part changes the input before feeding it to HMAC-H(K, M) hence thwarting the attack. Even by using custom hash function H^P which outputs $P(h)$ we are not able to get a computational chain. Suppose collision happened at $h_0 = t'_0$, still $t_1 \neq h'_0$. This is due to the fact that b differs from c', because in case of oracle HMAC^P-H$^P(K, M)$, patch P is applied. Therefore to carry the attack we have to get rid of this extra padding (applied to h_0 in case of HMAC^P-H$^P(K, M)$). As we know P is public and reversible so we can easily construct function P^{-1} which is inverse of P. In Fig. 6, the attacker uses P^{-1} to remove extra patching of h_0 such that $h_0 = P(a)$ where $a = P^{-1}(h_0)$. So inputs b and c' become same and hence adversary can get computational chains. Hence HMAC^P-H$^P(K, M)$ construction is not safe if the patch P is public and reversible.

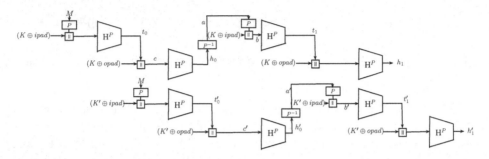

Fig. 6. Path generation using oracle HMAC^P-H$^P(K, M)$ and HMAC^P-H$^P(K', M)$.

5   Our Two New Patch Proposals

In previous sections we discussed the patching scheme proposed by Peyrin et al. [11] and showed that it is not secure against cycle detection based attacks described by them. We observed that if one wants to patch the HMAC-H(K, M) scheme then patching scheme should satisfy some minimum conditions. Such a patching scheme should be either secret or one way. We will discuss such patches and then compare them.

5.1   Secret Patch SP(K, M)

A secret patch is one which is unknown to the attacker, i.e., either the attacker is unaware of the patching scheme or unaware of the patch applied despite knowing the patching scheme. Secret patching scheme SP(K, M) is defined as

$$SP(K, M) = M[1] \oplus K || M[2]M[3] \ldots M[s]$$

where message M is divided into s blocks of block length d, say $M[1]M[2]\ldots M[s]$. If $|M| < d$ then $M[1]$ is padded with 0's such that $|M[1]00\ldots0| = d$, otherwise it is used as it is. K is a secret key of length $|K|$-bit. If $|K| < d$ then K is padded with 0's such that $|K00\ldots0| = d$, if $|K| > d$ then $H(K)$ is used as key where H is a hash function with output length n. We will consider K as the padded secret key from now on. In the case of a secret patch we don't bother about the randomness of underlying hash function H, i.e. we need H to be collision resistant, preimage and second preimage resistant but we don't care about its randomness.

Lemma 1. *The HMAC scheme is secure with respect to related key attacks using cycle detection described by Peyrin et al. [11] and Dodis et al. [6] if a secret patch is used. Secret patch refers to a patching scheme which is applied to the message M before passing it into HMAC and the attacker can't predict patch with more than negligible probability.*

The explanation is given in Appendix B. We propose $HMAC^{SP_K}$-$H(K, M)$ as the secret patch, shown in Fig. 7 and defined as

$$\begin{aligned} HMAC^{SP_K} - H(K, M) &= HMAC(K, SP(K, M)), \\ &= H_{K_{out}}(H_{K_{in}}(SP(K, M))), \\ &= H_{K_{out}}(H_{K_{in}}(K \oplus M[1]\|M[2]M[3]\ldots M[s]))). \end{aligned}$$

We emphasize to use the same key K in secret patch SP and HMAC. Explanation for this is provided in appendix C. $HMAC^{SP_K}$-$H(K, M)$ (also denoted as HMAC- $H(pad^{0^*}(K), SP(K, M)))$ is secure against cycle detection based related key attacks shown in [11].

5.2   Collision Resistant One Way Patch CrOw(M)

A good collision resistant one way function is one in which computation in one direction is easy and fast whereas it is very hard (or may be impossible) to go in the other direction and is resistant to collision, preimage and 2nd preimage attacks. This will be applied to message M before passing it into HMAC-$H(K, M)$ scheme, though it is public but no adversary can efficiently invert its output to obtain the correct input. Collision Resistant One way patching scheme $CrOw(M)$ is defined as

$$CrOw(M) = f'(M[1])\|M[2]M[3]\ldots M[s]$$

here message M is divided into s blocks of block length d say $M[1]M[2]M[3]\ldots M[s]$ and f' is a one way function with output length d.

$HMAC^{CrOw}$-$H(K, M)$ or HMAC-$H(pad^{0^*}(K), CrOw(M)))$ is HMAC-$H(K, M)$ construction which is using one way patch $CrOw(K, M)$ as the patching scheme, and any collision resistant, preimage and second preimage resistant hash

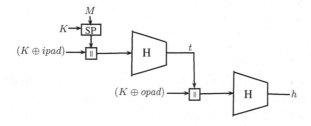

Fig. 7. The $HMAC^{SP_K}$-$H(K, M)$ construction

function H (not necessarily a random oracle) internally. To analyse the security of HMAC^{CrOw}-H(K, M), in Fig. 8 we show the path generation by using oracles HMAC^{CrOw}-H(K, M) and HMAC^{CrOw}-H(K', M).

As we discussed earlier, HMAC^{CrOw}-H(K, M) will behave like a black box. The attacker will be left with only one choice for mounting the attack, i.e., between two calls to oracle HMAC^{CrOw}-H(K, M) (or HMAC^{CrOw}-H(K', M)). If h_0 and t'_0 collides then for a successful attack b and c' should also collide, so that the collision chain can propagate. In case of HMAC^{CrOw}-H(K, M), the value h_0 will be patched by patch CrOw(M). Therefore, the only way to make b and h_0 same is to apply CrOw$^{-1}(M)$ on h_0 so that when CrOw is applied on it, it remains h_0 i.e. $h_0 = $ CrOw$(a) = f'(a[1])||a[2]a[3].....a[s]$.

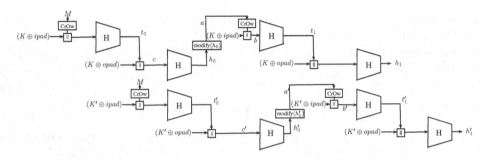

Fig. 8. Path generation using oracle HMAC^{CrOw}-H(K, M) and HMAC^{CrOw}-H(K', M)

As the patch is a one way function f'. Hence, no attacker can design an inverse function f'^{-1} for it. To carry out the attack we need to find preimage of the given $f'(M)$ for each step. Let the average complexity to do this be 2^{avg}. Since H is a n bit output hash function and the attacker has to do this for all the steps, a total of $2^{n/2}$ steps are needed to get synchronized cycle. Our CrOw patch is similar to construction proposed in [2], however the motive is different. As a result, the total complexity of this attack will be around

$$\text{Total Complexity} \equiv 2^{avg} * 2^{n/2} = 2^{avg+n/2}.$$

Therefore, if a good collision resistant one way function f' is used then the complexity is very high. Hence HMAC^{CrOw}-H(K, M) is very difficult to attack by using cycle detection based attacks discussed in [11].

5.3 Comparison

We have proposed two patches for HMAC. Both patches are individually capable of securing the HMAC scheme. The security of collision resistant one way patch depends on choice of function $f'(x)$ which can be any good function, we can't provide concrete complexity bounds. Also patch SP(K, M) uses XOR operation on first block of message $M[1]$ and key K whereas the patch CrOw(M) calculates function f' on first block of message $M[1]$, so from efficiency point of view the patch $SP(K, M)$ is better because the XOR operation is lightweight as compared to any good one way function f' where many XOR/other operations may be required to be implemented to achieve randomness and preimage resistance (here we may use a good hash function like SHA-1 as function f').

$\Rightarrow$ Secret Patch $SP(K, M)$ is a more efficient choice for preventing cycle detection based related key attacks described in [11] on HMAC-H(K, M).

6   Preventing Differentiablilty Attacks

In [6], Dodis *et al.* described two kinds of weak keys i.e. related/ambiguous keys and colliding keys discussed in previous sections, which when used with HMAC can allow an attacker to mount differentiablilty attacks exploiting structure of HMAC on the scheme. They suggested that the only way to avoid such attacks is not to use these weak keys. These keys can be avoided by using keys of fixed length $|K|$ such that key length $|K| < d - 1$, where d is block length of compression function h of hash function H. In [5], Coron *et al.* suggested that a hash function should behave like a random oracle, so such attacks raise a serious issue for scheme. To prevent differentiability attacks based on colliding keys, we propose a new padding scheme pad^{10^*}.

Lemma 2. *In case of padding pad^{10^*}, there exists no colliding keys but ambiguous keys may exist for key of size $|K| < d - 2$ is used.*

6.1   Security Against Attacks

Table 2 shows the feasibility of attacks when HMAC is used with different patches and paddings. We have discussed the following two attacks in the table.

1. Related key attacks based on ambiguous keys. Related key attacks comprises of distinguishing-R, distinguishing-H, internal state recovery and forgery attacks on HMAC scheme. The Table 2 shows that HMAC when used with our patches is secure from cycle detection and differentiability attacks based on ambiguous keys.

2. Indifferentiability attacks based on colliding keys. As described in [6], indifferentiability attack on HMAC is said to be performed successfully if the attacker can distinguish between pair of oracles consisting of HMAC with underlying hash H and a random oracle with a simulator based on the random oracle. In [10], the authors show that if a component S is indifferentiable from T, then the security of any crypto system $C(T)$ based on T is not affected when T is replaced by S.

For HMAC scheme collision keys based attacks is not possible for $|K| = d$ whereas for all other possible keys it is feasible. Further, ambiguous keys based attacks will only be prevented when $|K| < d - 1$. On the other hand, HMAC when used with $pad^{10^*}(K)$, collision keys based attacks are not possible for any case and ambiguous keys based attacks will work for all keys of size except $|K| < d - 2$. Results are similar for HMAC-H($pad^x(K), P0(M)$). For HMAC patched with our patching schemes i.e. HMAC-H($pad^x(K), SP(K, M)$) and HMAC-H($pad^x(K), CrOw(M)$), when $pad^{0^*}(K)$ is used, colliding keys based attack is feasible for all keys of size except $|K| = d$. On the other hand, when padding scheme $pad^{10^*}(K)$ is used, colliding keys based indifferentiability attacks are not feasible for any key size.

7   Conclusion

In this work, we have shown that HMAC-H(K, M) patched with the patching scheme proposed by Peyrin *et al.* in [11] fails when a collision, preimage and 2nd preimage resistant but not a random oracle function is used as the underlying hash function. We provided the explanation of failure for their patching scheme and showed that the use of secret or collision resistant one way patching scheme (i.e. SP(K, M) and CrOw(M)) can secure HMAC-H(K, M). We proposed that HMAC patched with any one of our two patches with pad^{10} or $10\ldots0$ padding, is resistant to cycle detection based generic related key attacks due to ambiguous keys discussed by Peyrin *et al.* [11] and indifferentiability attacks based on colliding keys discussed by Dodis *et al.* [6].

A   Explanation of Complexities in Table 1

The generic attack complexities in single key model and for related key model (cycle attack) is provided in [11] by Peyrin et al., but they didn't provide any calculations of complexities after applying their patch. In our views, as the patch prevents the cycle formation, the attack is not possible hence the complexity will be that is in single key setting. However in secret patch the attacker can guess the key in 2^k efforts where k is length of unpadded key. So, the efforts for getting cycle will be $2^{n/2} + 2^k$. The point to note here is that adversary has to guess the key only once for whole cycle but if he can find key, the security of HMAC is completely broken (now the key is known to adversary) and it needs very high effort. For CrOw patch in order to crack patch attacker needs to find the preimage of output of CrOw patch, which will require 2^u efforts where u is output length of CrOw patch. Unlike secret patch, here it has to be done for all $2^{n/2}$ steps so the complexity will be $2^{n/2+2+u}$.

B   Explanation for Secret Patch SP

HMAC^{SP_K}-H(K, M) is HMAC-H(K, M) which is using secret patch $SP(K, M)$ as the patching scheme, any collision resistant, preimage resistant and second preimage resistant hash function H (not necessarily a random oracle). Here $\overline{K} = K00\ldots$ whereas $|\overline{K}| = d$ and M is the message. For subsequent sections, we will consider $K = \overline{K}$. To analyse the security of HMAC^{SP_K}-H(K, M), in Fig. 9, we have path generation by using oracles HMAC^{SP_K}-$H(K, M)$ and $\text{HMAC}^{SP_{K'}}$-$H(K', M)$.

As discussed earlier, HMAC^{SP_K}-$H(K, M)$ will behave like a black box. So an attacker can only mount attack between two calls to oracle HMAC^{SP_K}-$H(K, M)$ (or $\text{HMAC}^{SP_{K'}}$-$H(K', M)$). If h_0 and t_0' collide then for a successful attack b and c' should also collide, so that the collision chain can propagate. In case of HMAC^{SP_K}-$H(K, M)$, h_0 will be applied upon by patch $SP(K, M)$. Therefore, the only way to make b and h_0 same is to apply $SP^{-1}(K, M)$ on h_0 so that when $SP(K, M)$ is applied on it, it remains h_0 i.e. $h_0 = SP(K, a) = K \oplus a[1]||a[2]a[3].....a[s]$.

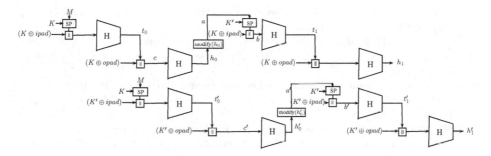

Fig. 9. Path generation using oracle HMAC^{SP_K}-$H(K, M)$ and $\text{HMAC}^{SP_{K'}}$-$H(K', M)$.

Hence the attacker needs the secret key K to carve such a out of h_0. The attacker attempt to guess the key and guesses K. The probability of guessing the right key is

$$\text{Prob}\,[K = h_0 \oplus a] \leq 2^{-d} \leq \text{Negligible}$$

where the total effort required is $2^d + 2^{n/2}$. Note that 2^d is the effort of getting the key K and $2^{n/2}$ is number of consecutive rounds needed to construct a cycle. As

$$\text{Total Complexity } = 2^d + 2^{n/2}$$

which is very high, so the probability of getting a synchronized cycle in this case is negligible. We emphasize the use of same key K for secret patch as well as for HMAC. Use of two different keys for secret patch and HMAC leads to forgery attack explained in Appendix C.

C $\text{HMAC}^{SP_{K_2}}$-$H(K_1, M)$ is not Secure

If secret patch is used with two different keys K_1, K_2 are used i.e. $\text{HMAC}^{SP_{K_2}}$-$H(K_1, M)$, then the construction prevents related key attacks based on cycle detection techniques but it allows forgery attack on $\text{HMAC}(K, M)$. If we use two different keys K_1, K_2 when calculating secure tag of message M then tag can be forged by using keys K_1, K_2' on a crafted message M' such that $K_2 \oplus M =$

$K'_2 \oplus M'$. When such message, key pair is fed to the construction it will produce the same secure tag h in both the cases. Therefore, by using this attack, an adversary can forge secure tags. If single key K is used and the attacker tries to forge a secure tag on HMAC^{SP_K}-H(K, M). It is impossible to have two messages M, M' such that $K \oplus M = K \oplus M'$. If the attacker chooses different K for two separate HMAC^{SP_K}-H(K, M) calls then the inner and the outer keys will be different in both the cases. This will prevent forgery attacks on the scheme. Therefore we can not use two different keys for this purpose.

References

1. Request For Comments: 3174, US Secure Hash Algorithm 1 (SHA1). IETF Working group (2001)
2. Andreeva, E., Preneel, B.: A three-property-secure hash function. In: Avanzi, R.M., Keliher, L., Sica, F. (eds.) SAC 2008. LNCS, vol. 5381, pp. 228–244. Springer, Heidelberg (2009)
3. Bellare, M.: New proofs for NMAC and HMAC: security without collision-resistance. In: Dwork, C. (ed.) CRYPTO 2006. LNCS, vol. 4117, pp. 602–619. Springer, Heidelberg (2006)
4. Bellare, M., Canetti, R., Krawczyk, H.: Keying hash functions for message authentication. In: Koblitz, N. (ed.) CRYPTO 1996. LNCS, vol. 1109, pp. 1–15. Springer, Heidelberg (1996)
5. Coron, J.-S., Dodis, Y., Malinaud, C., Puniya, P.: Merkle-Damgård revisited: how to construct a hash function. In: Shoup, V. (ed.) CRYPTO 2005. LNCS, vol. 3621, pp. 430–448. Springer, Heidelberg (2005)
6. Dodis, Y., Ristenpart, T., Steinberger, J., Tessaro, S.: To hash or not to hash again? (In)differentiability results for H^2 and HMAC. In: Safavi-Naini, R., Canetti, R. (eds.) CRYPTO 2012. LNCS, vol. 7417, pp. 348–366. Springer, Heidelberg (2012)
7. Guo, J., Peyrin, T., Sasaki, Y., Wang, L.: Updates on generic attacks against HMAC and NMAC. In: Garay, J.A., Gennaro, R. (eds.) CRYPTO 2014, Part I. LNCS, vol. 8616, pp. 131–148. Springer, Heidelberg (2014)
8. Leurent, G., Peyrin, T., Wang, L.: New generic attacks against hash-based MACs. In: Sako, K., Sarkar, P. (eds.) ASIACRYPT 2013, Part II. LNCS, vol. 8270, pp. 1–20. Springer, Heidelberg (2013)
9. Canetti, R., Bellare, M., Krawczyk, H.: Request For Comments: 2104, HMAC: Keyed-Hashing for Message Authentication. IETF Working group (1997)
10. Maurer, U.M., Renner, R.S., Holenstein, C.: Indifferentiability, impossibility results on reductions, and applications to the random oracle methodology. In: Naor, M. (ed.) TCC 2004. LNCS, vol. 2951, pp. 21–39. Springer, Heidelberg (2004)
11. Peyrin, T., Sasaki, Y., Wang, L.: Generic related-key attacks for HMAC. In: Wang, X., Sako, K. (eds.) ASIACRYPT 2012. LNCS, vol. 7658, pp. 580–597. Springer, Heidelberg (2012)

Search Algorithm of Precise Integral Distinguisher of Byte-Based Block Cipher

Haruhisa Kosuge$^{(\boxtimes)}$, Keisuke Iwai, Hidema Tanaka, and Takakazu Kurokawa

National Defence Academy of Japan, Yokosuka, Japan
{em53036,iwai,hidema,kuro}@nda.ac.jp

Abstract. Integral distinguisher is the main factor of integral attack. Conventionally, first order integral distinguisher is obtained and higher order integral distinguisher is derived from extension of first order (conventional algorithm). The algorithm was applied to many byte-based block ciphers, and such application was thought to be established. Even in such application, however, we find that the conventional algorithm is imprecise. We discovered integral distinguisher of byte-based block ciphers, TWINE and LBlock, which are different from results of the conventional evaluation. As a substitute for the imprecise algorithm, we propose a new algorithm to search higher order integral distinguisher. The point of the proposal algorithm is exploitation of bijective and injective components of cipher functions. We focus on injective components for the first time, in addition to bijective components which are already exploited. We demonstrate the proposal algorithm by TWINE and LBlock. As a result, we confirm the result of the proposal algorithm is consistent with our result which was conjectured from computer experiment. Obtaining more precise integral distinguisher allows designers to select stronger cipher structures and key schedules, and the proposal algorithm contributes to it.

Keywords: Chosen plaintext attack · Light-weight block cipher · Integral attack · Saturation attack

1 Introduction

1.1 Background

When we consider secret keys as constant values, cipher functions are considered as bijective function of $\mathbb{F}_2^L \to \mathbb{F}_2^L$, where L is the block length. Also, bijective component exists in block ciphers, and integral attack exploit these bijective component. Integral attack was originally proposed as SQUARE attack [1]. SQUARE attack was given different names such as saturation attack [6], and Knudsen et al. formalized it as integral attack [3].

We define *byte-based block cipher* as a block cipher in which operation unit can be defined as m-bit ($m > 1$), and we call the operation unit as *sub block*. Note that a block is divided into N sub blocks ($L = N \times m$). Also we define *bit-based block cipher* as a block cipher in which we can not define any sub block ($m = 1$).

© Springer International Publishing Switzerland 2015
S. Jajodia and C. Mazumdar (Eds.): ICISS 2015, LNCS 9478, pp. 303–323, 2015.
DOI: 10.1007/978-3-319-26961-0_18

Integral distinguisher is the main factor of integral attack. We construct integral distinguisher from 2^{mn} chosen plaintexts, where n is the order of integral. Basically, we need to know whether a summation of all 2^{mn} sub block values is 0 or not. Knudsen et al. studied integral distinguisher as first order initially, and considered higher order integral distinguisher as extension of first order one [3]. We call this algorithm as *conventional algorithm*. In the conventional algorithm, they search higher order integral distinguisher with two steps. In the first step, they obtain first order integral distinguisher. In the second step, they extend first order integral distinguisher by increasing the order.

Integral attack was applied to many byte-based block ciphers, and these attacks were based on integral distinguisher obtained by the conventional algorithm [1,2,5,6,8]. However, the conventional algorithm is imprecise even in evaluation of byte-based block ciphers. We point out it is problematic to apply the algorithm for Feistel ciphers whose N is large such as TWINE [7] and LBlock [8] ($N = 16$). We found new fifteenth order integral distinguisher of TWINE and LBlock which contradicts results of the conventional algorithm in our previous work [4,5,7,8]. Also, we point out there is a restriction of input integrals in the conventional algorithm. Note that we define *input integral* as a condition of chosen plaintexts. Input integrals in the scope of the conventional algorithm are only ones of first order and their extensions.

1.2 Contribution

In this paper, we propose a new algorithm to search higher order integral distinguisher. We search higher order integral property from input to output (from top to down). In other word, we do not use *extension* which is used in the conventional algorithm. From this, we can search all of input integrals, and this is a solution for restriction of input integrals.

As for a solution for the problem of preciseness, we exploit bijective and injective component of cipher functions. We focus on injective components for the first time, in addition to bijective components which are already exploited. We divide the proposal algorithm into two algorithms. One is Algorithm A which exploits bijective component, an we use new idea, *bijective path*, to analyze it. The other is Algorithm B which exploits injective component, and we use new idea, *independent* to analyze it.

As an application of the proposal algorithm, we search precise integral distinguisher of TWINE and LBlock. As a result, we confirm that the result of the proposal algorithm is consistent with one which is conjectured from computer experiment, and they are the most precise distinguisher until now.

More precise integral distinguisher is always more advantageous for the attacker. If distinguisher of more rounds is constructed, the number of rounds to be attacked can be extended. Even if only the number of balanced sub blocks increases, it is also advantageous for the attacker. As the number of balanced sub blocks increases, the number of sub keys the attacker can guess from single integral distinguisher increases. In other word, the attacker needs less chosen plaintexts to guess all of the secret keys. From designers' viewpoint, they need to select stronger cipher algorithm and key schedule by considering such vulnerabilities, and the proposal algorithm contributes to it.

2   Preliminaries

2.1   Notations

Throughout the paper, we use the notations shown in Table 1.

Table 1. Notation of variables.

N	the number of sub blocks
m	bit-length of a sub block $(m > 1)$
n	the order of integral distinguisher $(1 \leq n \leq N - 1)$
x_b^r	bth sub block of r-th round $(0 \leq b \leq N - 1, 0 \leq r)$.
$\tilde{x}_b^r$	sequence (ordered collection of values) of values of x_b^r.
v	variable sub block.
c	constant sub block.
RK_k^r	sub key inputed in F functions of r-th round $(0 \leq k, 1 \leq r)$.
$\alpha_{\{a_0,a_1,...,a_{n-1}\}}$	input integral; condition of chosen plaintexts, and $a_0, a_1, ..., a_{n-1}$ indicates the position of variable sub blocks.
$\beta_{\{b_0,b_1,...,b_{n-1}\}}$	output integral of γ-th round; summation of all γ-th round block values, and $b_0, b_1, ..., b_{n-1}$ indicates the position of balanced sub blocks.
$\alpha \rightarrow^\gamma \beta$	integral distinguisher; output integral β is obtained after γ-th round encryption by input integral α.

2.2   Integral Attack

Based on integral distinguisher, an attacker guess some sub keys. To construct integral distinguisher, he prepares a set of chosen plaintexts and encrypt them. The attacker chooses one or several sub blocks of plaintext as *variable sub blocks*. When n sub blocks are chosen, he needs to prepares 2^{mn} plaintexts, where m is bit-length of a sub block. In 2^{mn} plaintexts, a concatenation of variable sub blocks takes every possible element of $\mathbb{F}_2^{mn}$ and one of the other sub blocks takes a constant value. Let $v_0||v_1||...||v_{n-1}$ be a concatenation of variable sub blocks of plaintext, and $c_0||c_1||...||c_{N-n-1}$ a concatenation of constant sub blocks, where N is the number of sub blocks. In short, we prepare a set of 2^{mn} plaintexts which satisfies

$$v_0||v_1||...||v_{n-1} = \{0, 1, ..., 2^{mn} - 1\},$$
$$c_0||c_1||...||c_{N-n-1} = const. \tag{1}$$

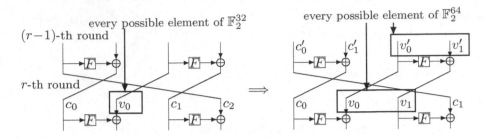

Fig. 1. Outline of extension from first order integral to second order integral.

We call a condition of chosen plaintexts as *input integral*, and we denote it by α.

A set of 2^{mn} plaintexts and block values of intermediate rounds are analyzed in sub block unit. Let $x^r_{b,i} \in \mathbb{F}^m_2$ be i-th element of 2^{mn} values of a sub block x^r_b. The summation of all values has following property.

$$\sum_{i=0}^{2^{nm}-1} x^r_{b,i} = \begin{cases} 0 \\ random \end{cases} \qquad (2)$$

If the summation is always 0, we say it is *balanced*, otherwise *unbalanced*. We call balanced sub blocks of γ-th round as *output integral*, and we denote it by β. We denote integral distinguisher by input and output integral. Let $\alpha \rightarrow^\gamma \beta$ be integral distinguisher that output property β is obtained after γ-th round encryption when we set chosen plaintexts according to input condition α. We call integral distinguisher gained by choosing n variable bits as n-th order integral distinguisher.

3   Conventional Algorithm

The conventional algorithm is divided into two steps. In the first step, they obtain first order integral distinguisher. In the second step, they extend first order integral distinguisher to higher order integral distinguisher. Mathematical validity of extension of integral distinguisher is proven [3]. However, we disagree with the usage as *extension of first order integral distinguisher*.

We use the idea of first order integral in the proposal algorithm, however, we do not use extension of integral distinguisher in it. Therefore, we only explain extension of integral distinguisher in this section, and explain the way to obtain first order integral distinguisher in Sect. 5.3. A typical extension of integral distinguisher is shown in the evaluation of CLEFIA [6]. The designers of CLEFIA extend first order integral distinguisher to second one. Figure 1 shows the outline.

At first, following first order integral distinguisher is obtained.

$$\alpha_{\{1\}} \rightarrow^6 \beta_{\{1\}} \qquad (3)$$

We regard $\alpha_{\{1\}}$ as integral of r-th round. We let v be variable sub blocks and c constant sub blocks. Sub blocks $\{x^r_0, x^r_1, x^r_2, x^r_3\}$ is written as $\{c_0, v_0, c_1, c_2\}$ and

x_1^r takes every possible element of $\mathbb{F}_2^{32}$. Considering an input integral which can be extended to one of $(r-1)$-th round, we assign x_2^r as a variable sub block to make $x_1^r\|x_2^r$ take every possible element of $\mathbb{F}_2^{64}$. From this, sub blocks of r-th round becomes $\{c_0, v_0, v_1, c_2\}$, i.e., $\alpha_{\{1,2\}}$.

Calculating back $(r-1)$-th round, x_2^{r-1} and x_3^{r-1} must be variable. Suppose we write $\{x_0^{r-1}, x_1^{r-1}, x_2^{r-1}, x_3^{r-1}\}$ as $\{c_0', c_1', v_0', v_1'\}$. Since a mapping from $x_1^r\|x_2^r$ to $x_2^{r-1}\|x_3^{r-1}$ is bijective, $x_2^{r-1}\|x_3^{r-1}$ takes every possible element of $\mathbb{F}_2^{64}$. Therefore, $\{c_0', c_1', v_0', v_1'\}$ denotes the same state as $\alpha_{\{2,3\}}$. Hence, $\alpha_{\{1,2\}}$ of $(r-1)$-th round results in $\alpha_{\{2,3\}}$ of r-th round.

For these reason, integral distinguisher of $\alpha_{\{1\}}$ can be extended to integral distinguisher of $\alpha_{\{2,3\}}$ as follows.

$$\begin{cases} \alpha_{\{1\}} \to^6 \beta_{\{1\}} \\ \alpha_{\{2,3\}} \overset{1}{\leftarrow} \alpha_{\{1\}} \end{cases} \Rightarrow \quad \alpha_{\{2,3\}} \to^7 \beta_{\{1\}} \tag{4}$$

In the second step of the conventional algorithm, we extend first order integral such as Eq. (3) round by round, exploiting bijective components.

4 Problems of Conventional Algorithm

In Feistel ciphers whose number of sub blocks N is small such as CLEFIA ($N = 4$), the conventional algorithm is still effective and precise. However, we find it is problematic to apply the algorithm for Feistel ciphers whose N is large such as TWINE and LBlock ($N = 16$). In evaluation of such ciphers, the results of the algorithm become imprecise. We discovered following integral distinguisher of TWINE and LBlock in our previous work [4]. We used computer experiment to discover them. Note that computer experiment is an experiment to compute a summation of intermediate values such as Eq. (2). We executed computer experiment for 10 times to verify each integral distinguisher. Due to limitations of space, we can not show the detail of these ciphers, see the details in [7,8].

TWINE [7]: We discovered following first order integral distinguisher of TWINE by computer experiment.

$$\alpha_{\{1\}} \to^9 \beta_{\{1,3,13,15\}} \tag{5}$$

This integral distinguisher can be extended to fifteenth order integral distinguisher as follows.

$$\alpha_{\{0,1,2,3,4,5,6,7,8,9,10,11,12,13,15\}} \to^{15} \beta_{\{1,3,13,15\}} \tag{6}$$

Note that integral distinguisher shown by the designers of TWINE is different from Eq. (6) [7]. In our previous work [4], we discovered following eleventh order integral distinguisher of TWINE by computer experiment.

$$\alpha_{\{0,2,3,5,6,7,8,9,10,12,15\}} \to^{11} \beta_{\{1,3,5,7,9,11,13,15\}} \tag{7}$$

This integral distinguisher can be extended to fifteenth order integral distinguisher as follows.

$$\alpha_{\{1,2,3,4,5,6,7,8,9,10,11,12,13,14,15\}} \rightarrow^{15} \beta_{\{1,3,5,7,9,11,13,15\}} \tag{8}$$

LBlock [8]: Following fifteenth order integral distinguisher of LBlock obtained by the conventional algorithm is known [5,8].

$$\begin{cases} \alpha_{\{8\}} \rightarrow^9 \beta_{\{9,11,13,15\}} \\ \alpha_{\{0,1,2,4,5,6,7,8,9,10,11,12,13,14,15\}} \xleftarrow{6} \alpha_{\{8\}} \end{cases} \tag{9}$$

$$\Rightarrow \quad \alpha_{\{0,1,2,4,5,6,7,8,9,10,11,12,13,14,15\}} \rightarrow^{15} \beta_{\{9,11,13,15\}} \tag{10}$$

We discovered following fifteenth order integral distinguisher by computer experiment and its extension [4].

$$\begin{cases} \alpha_{\{0,2,3,4,5,6,8,10,12,13,15\}} \rightarrow^{11} \beta_{\{8,9,10,11,12,13,14,15\}} \\ \alpha_{\{0,1,2,4,5,6,7,8,9,10,11,12,13,14,15\}} \xleftarrow{4} \alpha_{\{0,2,3,4,5,6,8,10,12,13,15\}} \end{cases} \tag{11}$$

$$\Rightarrow \quad \alpha_{\{0,1,2,4,5,6,7,8,9,10,11,12,13,14,15\}} \rightarrow^{15} \beta_{\{8,9,10,11,12,13,14,15\}} \tag{12}$$

We point out following two problems of the conventional algorithm; preciseness and restriction of input integrals. As for preciseness, it is obvious from above results of TWINE and LBlock.

We define *input integral* as a condition of chosen plaintexts such as Eq. (1). The number of possible input integral is $2^N - 2$, where N is the number of sub blocks. Subtraction denotes a full code book and single chosen plaintext which are out of scope of integral attack. On the other hand, input integrals in the scope of the conventional algorithm are only ones of first order and their extensions. The number of input integral in the scope of the conventional algorithm is calculated as

$$\sum_{i=0}^{N-1} (\Gamma_i + 1), \tag{13}$$

where Γ_i is the number of rounds that i-th first order integral distinguisher can be extended at most. Note that there are overlaps among extensions of first order integral, so that the number of different input integrals is always less than Eq. (13). In CLEFIA ($N = 4$), the number of input integrals in the conventional algorithm is 8, and the actual number is 14. When N is large, differential between $2^N - 2$ and Eq. (13) becomes large. As for TWINE ($N = 16$), the number of input integrals in the scope of the conventional algorithm is 56, and the actual number is $2^{16} - 2$.

From these two problems, we disagree with application of the conventional algorithm to Feistel ciphers whose N is large.

5   Fundamentals of Proposal Search Algorithm

5.1   Byte-Based Block Cipher

In this paper, we limit the scope of target cipher function to byte-based block cipher. To define such cipher exactly, we suppose a block cipher which composes of bijective functions and addition on $\mathbb{F}_2^m$. With respect to bijective functions, we denote L and F be linear and nonlinear function, s.t., $\mathbb{F}_2^m \to \mathbb{F}_2^m$.

For example, we consider a nonlinear function F which contains key addition as follows.

$$F(x; RK) = S(x \oplus RK),$$
$$x, RK \in \mathbb{F}_2^m, \tag{14}$$

where S is a S-box of $\mathbb{F}_2^m \to \mathbb{F}_2^m$. Suppose RK is random constant, F is regarded as $\mathbb{F}_2^m \to \mathbb{F}_2^m$ random functions chosen by RK. Although a cipher function includes 2^m possible random functions, we ignore the detail of functions and denote them by F, since our interest is only in their bijection and nonlinearity. With respect to addition, we denote $\oplus$ and $\boxplus$ as XOR(eXclusive OR) and addition mod 2^m, respectively.

In the following sections, we use partial functions of byte-based block cipher as follows.

$$G : \mathbb{F}_2^{mn} \to \mathbb{F}_2^{mn}$$
$$H : \mathbb{F}_2^{mn} \to \mathbb{F}_2^m \tag{15}$$

We suppose G and H are composed of L, F, $\oplus$ and $\boxplus$.

5.2   Sequence of Sub Blocks

We analyze higher order integral distinguisher in sub block unit. For analyzing sub blocks, multiset was adopted to denote them in the previous work [3]. However, sequence allows us to analyze more precise properties of sub blocks, since it represent actual cipher states. We denote a sequence of a sub block λ as follows.

$$\tilde{\lambda} = (\lambda_i)_{i=0}^{2^{mn}-1} , \ \lambda_i \in \mathbb{F}_2^m \tag{16}$$

Also, a sequence of a concatenation of l sub blocks Λ is written as

$$\tilde{\Lambda} = (\Lambda_i)_{i=0}^{2^{mn}-1} = (\lambda_{0,i}||\lambda_{1,i}||...||\lambda_{l-1,i})_{i=0}^{2^{mn}-1}, \ (1 \leq l \leq N), \tag{17}$$

where $\Lambda = \lambda_0||\lambda_1||...||\lambda_{l-1}$.

In construction of integral distinguisher, sequential order to input each plaintexts does not affect output integral. In other word, we can sort chosen plaintexts optionally. Therefore, we can define a mapping to sort a sequence of Λ, s.t.,

$$\mathfrak{S} : (\Lambda_i)_{i=0}^{2^{mn}-1} \to (\Lambda_{\sigma(i)})_{i=0}^{2^{mn}-1}, \tag{18}$$

where σ is any permutation function.

5.3   First Order Integral Property

First order integral distinguisher is easily obtained by symbolization of sequences of sub block values. We call symbols to denote the property of each sequence of a sub block as *integral property*. Especially we call integral property of first order integral as *first order integral property*. We introduce a definition of first order integral property used in the evaluation of CLEFIA [6].

Definition 1. *Let $\tilde{x}_b^r = (x_{b,i}^r)_{i=0}^{2^m-1}(x_{b,i}^r \in \mathbb{F}_2^m)$ be a sequence of sub block x_b^r and X_b^r be a first order integral property of $\tilde{x}_b^r$. First order integral property X_b^r is categorized as follows.*

$$Constant(C) : {}^\forall i, i', \; x_{b,i}^r = x_{b,i'}^r \tag{19}$$

$$All(A) : {}^\forall i, i'(i \neq i'), \; x_{b,i}^r \neq x_{b,i'}^r \tag{20}$$

$$Balance(B) : \sum_{i=0}^{2^m-1} x_{b,i}^r = 0 \tag{21}$$

$$Random(R) : Others \tag{22}$$

For example, when first order integral property of $\tilde{x}_b^r$ is $All(A)$, we denote $X_b^r = A$. To show the usage of Definition 1, we exemplify determination of first order integral property when two sequences are XORed. Suppose $X_b^r = A$ and $X_{b'}^r = A$, and a sequence of another sub block $\tilde{z}$ is calculated as $(x_{b,i}^r \oplus x_{b',i}^r)_{i=0}^{2^m-1}$. We only consider X_b^r and $X_{b'}^r$ to determine first order integral property of $\tilde{z}$ without considering operations of each element such as $x_{b,i}^r \oplus x_{b',i}^r$. In this case, we can determine first order integral property of $\tilde{z}$ as B from previous works [6,8]. In this way, we only consider their properties, and we do not need to consider each element of sequences of sub blocks.

Focusing on first order integral property C, there is an important characteristic. From previous works [1,2,6,8,9] and validation of computer experiment, following is derived as an obvious proposition.

Proposition 1. *First order integral distinguisher holds for any values of constant sub blocks and sub keys.*

5.4   Higher Order Integral Property

We call integral property whose order n equals to or greater than 2 as *higher order integral property*. To analyze higher order integral property, we define new symbolization as follows.

Definition 2. *Let $\tilde{x}_b^r = (x_{b,i}^r)_{i=0}^{2^{mn}-1}(x_{b,i}^r \in \mathbb{F}_2^m)$ be a sequence of a sub block x_b^r, and $y_b^r(k)$ multiplicity of $x_{b,i}^r = k$ in the sequence. We denote $\mathcal{X}_b^r$ as higher order integral property of $\tilde{x}_b^r$. Higher order integral property $\mathcal{X}_b^r$ is categorized as follows.*

$$Constant(\mathcal{C}) : {}^{\forall}i, i', \quad x_{b,i}^r = x_{b,i'}^r \tag{23}$$

$$Uniform(\mathcal{U}) : {}^{\forall}k, \quad y_b^r(k) = 2^{n(m-1)} \tag{24}$$

$$Even(\mathcal{E}) : {}^{\forall}k, \quad y_b^r(k) \bmod 2 \equiv 0 \tag{25}$$

$$Balance(\mathcal{B}) : \sum_{i=0}^{2^{mn}-1} x_{b,i}^r = 0 \tag{26}$$

$$Random(\mathcal{R}) : Others \tag{27}$$

Each element $x_{b,i}^r$ is in $\mathbb{F}_2^m$. On the other hand, $\tilde{x}_b^r$ must have multiplicity, since the length of $\tilde{x}_b^r$ is 2^{mn}. Therefore, we define $\mathcal{U}$ instead of A of first order integral, and $\mathcal{U}$ has different property from $\mathcal{B}$. Also, we define special property $\mathcal{E}$ which is the intermediate property between $\mathcal{U}$ and $\mathcal{B}$. If an input sequence is $\mathcal{U}$ or $\mathcal{E}$, an output sequence of nonlinear bijective function F has the same property as input.

From definition of higher order integral properties, we have following inclusion relation among properties.

$$\mathcal{B} \supset \mathcal{E} \supset \mathcal{U} \tag{28}$$

There is a case that analysis of one sub block results in multiple properties. If it is analyzed to be $\mathcal{B}$ and $\mathcal{E}$, we determine higher order integral property of the sub block is $\mathcal{E}$, since it does not contradict the analysis of $\mathcal{B}$. In the same way, we choose $\mathcal{U}$, if it is analyzed to be $\mathcal{B}$, $\mathcal{E}$ and $\mathcal{U}$.

5.5 Search Algorithm Using Bijection

We can say that integral distinguisher is mainly dependent of bijection between input variable sub blocks and output sub blocks of intermediate rounds. Using bijection, we can predict higher order integral distinguisher. In n-th order integral, the number of input variable sub blocks V is n. Considering intermediate variable sub blocks V', there are some combinations of n variable sub blocks, s.t., $V \rightarrow V'$ is bijective. To analyze bijective characteristics, we define *bijective path* P which consists of such sub blocks (V and V') as follows.

Definition 3. *Let V be a set of input variable sub blocks (start point), and E a temporary end point of bijective path ($|V| = |E| = n$). We denote G as a function of $\mathbb{F}_2^{mn} \rightarrow \mathbb{F}_2^{mn}$ supposed in Eq. (15). We define bijective path P and end point of bijective path E as following recursive conditions.*

(i) Input variable sub blocks V is added to P and V is substituted for E at first.

(ii) If E and n sub blocks E', s.t., $E' = G(E)$, satisfies that $E \rightarrow E'$ is bijective, E' is added to P and E' is substituted for E. Note that any sub blocks outside E' and P must not be codomain of any mapping from E.

(iii) If $E \rightarrow E'$ is not bijective for any n combinations of E', E is a final end point of bijective path.

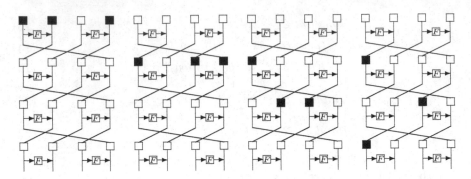

Fig. 2. Trail of temporary end point of bijective path E in CLEFIA.

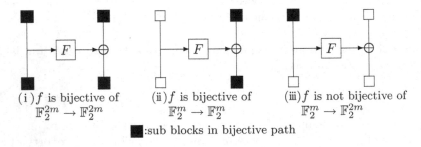

(i) f is bijective of   (ii) f is bijective of   (iii) f is not bijective of
$\mathbb{F}_2^{2m} \to \mathbb{F}_2^{2m}$ $\mathbb{F}_2^m \to \mathbb{F}_2^m$ $\mathbb{F}_2^m \to \mathbb{F}_2^{2m}$

■ :sub blocks in bijective path

Fig. 3. Bijective characteristics of f function.

We use recursive conditions of Definition 3 as algorithm to search bijective path (see Algorithm A). We update positions of temporary end point of bijective path, and add all of them to bijective path P. We demonstrate it in CLEFIA as toy example. We show the trail of temporary end point of bijective path E when we set input integral $\alpha_{\{0,1,3\}}$ in Fig. 2. Filled squares indicate positions of sub blocks in E. From left to right, E is updated and the rightmost one shows final end point of bijective path. We use a function f as follows.

$$\{x_0', x_1'\} = f(x_0, x_1) = \{x_0, F(x_0, \oplus RK) \oplus x_1\},$$
$$x_0, x_1, RK \in \mathbb{F}_2^{32}, \tag{29}$$

where RK is a constant value. The function f has following characteristics.

(i) If $x_0, x_1 \in E$, f is bijective of $\mathbb{F}_2^{2m} \to \mathbb{F}_2^{2m}$.
(ii) If $x_1 \in E$ and $x_0 \notin E$, f is bijective of $\mathbb{F}_2^m \to \mathbb{F}_2^m$.
(iii) If $x_0 \in E$ and $x_1 \notin E$, f is not bijective, since it is $\mathbb{F}_2^m \to \mathbb{F}_2^{2m}$.
    We show these characteristics in Fig. 3.

Using bijective path and end point of bijective path, we determine higher order integral property of sub blocks is $\mathcal{U}$ or $\mathcal{E}$ from following propositions.

Proposition 2. *If a sub block x_b^r is in bijective path P ($x_b^r \in P$), higher order integral property of $\tilde{x}_b^r$ is $\mathcal{U}$ ($\mathcal{X}_b^r = \mathcal{U}$).*

Proof. Suppose $V \rightarrow V'$ is bijective. From Definition 3, at least one combination of n variable sub blocks V' exists in P. From condition of chosen plaintexts, i.e., Eq. (1), $\tilde{V}$ contains all elements of $\mathbb{F}_2^{mn}$ without multiplicity. Therefore, all sequences in $\tilde{V}$ satisfy the definition of $\mathcal{U}$ (Eq. (24)). Since $V \rightarrow V'$ is bijective, $\tilde{V}'$ also contains all elements of $\mathbb{F}_2^{mn}$ without multiplicity. Therefore, all sequences in $\tilde{V}'$ satisfy the definition of $\mathcal{U}$. All sub blocks in P are also in V or V'. Hence, higher order integral properties of sequences of all sub blocks in P are $\mathcal{U}$.   □

Proposition 3. *Let V be a set of input variable sub blocks, and $E = \{e_0, e_1, ..., e_{n-1}\}$ end point of bijective path. Let $\{X_b^r(e_0), X_b^r(e_1), ..., X_b^r(e_{n-1})\}$ be a set of first order integral properties of sub sequences, s.t., $E \backslash e_t$ ($0 \le t \le n-1$) are constant. If following condition holds, higher order integral property $\mathcal{X}_b^r$ is $\mathcal{U}$.*

$$^\exists e_t \in E, \ X_b^r(e_t) = A \ \Rightarrow \ \mathcal{X}_b^r = \mathcal{U} \tag{30}$$

Proof. Let H be a function of $\mathbb{F}_2^{mn} \rightarrow \mathbb{F}_2^m$ supposed in Eq. (15). Suppose a sub block value is expressed as

$$x_b^r = H(e_0, e_1, ..., e_{n-1}). \tag{31}$$

A sequence $\tilde{x}_b^r$ is written as

$$\tilde{x}_b^r = (H(e_{0,i}, e_{1,i}, ..., e_{n-1,i}))_{i=0}^{2^{mn}-1}$$
$$= (H(e_{t,i}, E_i \backslash e_{t,i}))_{i=0}^{2^{mn}-1}. \tag{32}$$

where $e_{t,i}$ is i-th element of $\tilde{e}_t$ and E_i is a set of i-th elements of sequences of sub blocks in $\tilde{E} = \{\tilde{e}_0, \tilde{e}_1, ..., \tilde{e}_{n-1}\}$. We substitute $i = 2^m k + l$ ($0 \le k \le 2^{m(n-1)} - 1$,

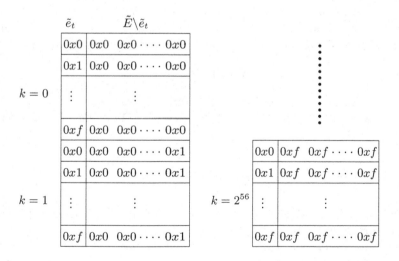

Fig. 4. Example of sorted sequence.

$0 \leq l \leq 2^m - 1$). We rewrite Eq. (32) as

$$\tilde{x}_b^r = \left(\left(H(e_{t,2^m k+l}, E_{2^m k+l} \backslash e_{t,2^m k+l}) \right)_{l=0}^{2^m-1} \right)_{k=0}^{2^{m(n-1)}-1}. \tag{33}$$

From an assumption that $V \to \tilde{E}$ is bijective (see Definition 3), the number of distinct combinations of $\tilde{E}$ is 2^{mn} and one of $\tilde{E} \backslash \tilde{e}_t$ is $2^{m(n-1)}$. The multiplicity of each combination in $\tilde{E} \backslash \tilde{e}_t$ is 2^m, and $\tilde{e}_t$ takes 2^m distinct values for every possible combination of $\tilde{E} \backslash \tilde{e}_t$. Therefore, it is possible to sort $\tilde{x}_b^r$ which satisfies following two conditions in Eq. (33).

(i) $^\forall k, l, l'(l \neq l')$, $e_{t,2^m k+l} \neq e_{t,2^m k+l'}$
(ii) $^\forall k, l, l'(l \neq l')$, $E_{2^m k+l} \backslash e_{t,2^m k+l} = E_{2^m k+l'} \backslash e_{t,2^m k+l'}$

We show an example sorted sequence, s.t., each element is in $\mathbb{F}_2^4$ and $n = 15$, in Fig. 4.

Let $\tilde{x}_b'^r$ be a sub sequence of sorted $\tilde{x}_b^r$ for given k, and $\tilde{x}_b'^r$ is written as

$$\tilde{x}_b'^r = \left(\left(H(v'_{t,2^m k+l}, V'_{2^m k+l} \backslash v'_{t,2^m k+l}) \right)_{l=0}^{2^m-1} \right)_{k=const}. \tag{34}$$

We can regard integral property of $\tilde{x}_b'^r$ as first order, and $X_b^r(e_t)$ holds for any values of constant sequences from Proposition 1. Suppose a first order integral property of $\tilde{x}_b'^r$ is A ($X_b^r(e_t) = A$), $\tilde{x}_b'^r$ contains every possible element of $\mathbb{F}_2^m$ for any k in Eq. (42). In addition, $\tilde{x}_b^r$ is a summation of individual sub sequences $\tilde{x}_b'^r$ which is respectively chosen by k. Therefore, $\tilde{x}_b^r$ contains $2^{m(n-1)}$ sub sequences which contains every possible element of $\mathbb{F}_2^m$, and this satisfies the definition of $\mathcal{U}$ (Eq. (24)). $\qquad \square$

Proposition 4. Let V be a set of input variable sub blocks and $E = \{e_0, e_1, ..., e_{n-1}\}$ end point of bijective path. Let $\{X_b^r(e_0), X_b^r(e_1), ..., X_b^r(e_{n-1})\}$ be a set of first order integral properties of sub sequences, s.t., $E \backslash e_t (0 \leq t \leq n - 1)$ are constant. If following condition holds, higher order integral property $\mathcal{X}_b^r$ is $\mathcal{E}$.

$$^\exists e_t \in E, \ X_b^r(e_t) = C \ \Rightarrow \ \mathcal{X}_b^r = \mathcal{E} \tag{35}$$

Proof. Since $X_b^r(e_t) = C$, there is not any mapping, s.t., $e_t \to x_b^r$. We substitute $i = 2^{m(n-1)}k + l$ ($0 \leq k \leq 2^m - 1$, $0 \leq l \leq 2^{m(n-1)} - 1$) of Eq. (32). We rewrite Eq. (32) as

$$\tilde{x}_b^r = \left(\left(H(E_{2^{m(n-1)}k+l} \backslash e_{t,2^{m(n-1)}k+l}) \right)_{l=0}^{2^{m(n-1)}-1} \right)_{k=0}^{2^m-1}, \tag{36}$$

where E_i is a set of i-th elements of sequences of sub blocks in $\tilde{E} = \{\tilde{e}_0, \tilde{e}_1, ..., \tilde{e}_{n-1}\}$, and H be a function of $\mathbb{F}_2^{mn} \to \mathbb{F}_2^m$ supposed in Eq. (15). Since $V \to E$ is bijective, $\tilde{E} \backslash \tilde{e}_t$ contains $2^{m(n-1)}$ distinct combinations, and multiplicity of $\tilde{E} \backslash \tilde{e}_t$ is 2^m. Therefore, we can sort x_b^r as $E_{2^{m(n-1)}k+l} \backslash e_{t,2^{m(n-1)}k+l}$ whose multiplicity of each element of $\mathbb{F}_2^m$ is the same for any k in Eq. (36). Therefore, $\tilde{x}_b^r$ is regarded *as a summation of 2^m sub sequences which has the same multiplicity for any element of $\mathbb{F}_2^m$. Hence, multiplicity of each element of $\mathbb{F}_2^m$ in the sequence $\tilde{x}_b^r$ is the product of 2^m (even number) and this multiplicity satisfies the definition of $\mathcal{E}$ (Eq. (25)).* $\square$

From Propositions 2, 3 and 4, we search $\mathcal{U}$ and $\mathcal{E}$ sub blocks among all sub blocks of a cipher function. Thereafter, we search $\mathcal{B}$ sub blocks in the same manner of first order integral property. Note that $\mathcal{B}$ or $\mathcal{E}$ sub blocks has probability to be analyzed as $\mathcal{U}$ by using injection (see Proposition 5).

5.6 Search Algorithm Using Injection

Since we can exploit similar property of Proposition 3 from injection among sub blocks, integral distinguisher obtained by bijective path is not sufficiently precise. In actual, we can obtain precise distinguisher only by an algorithm using injection, since property obtained by bijection is also obtained by injection. However, the algorithm using bijection is more efficient than one of injection. Therefore, we execute the former at first, and execute the latter as supplement.

To analyze injection, we use new idea, *independent*. This idea resembles to linear independent. We define independent as follows.

Definition 4. *Let $H_i(0 \leq i \leq n' - 1, n \leq n')$ be nonlinear functions of $\mathbb{F}_2^{n'm} \mapsto \mathbb{F}_2^m$ which are supposed in Eq. (15). We denote $E = \{e_0, e_1, ..., e_{n-1}\}$ as end point of bijective path. Suppose a set of n' intermediate variable sub blocks $V' = \{v_0', v_1', ..., v_{n'-1}'\}$ are expressed as*

$$H_0(e_0, e_1, ..., e_{n-1}) = v_0',$$
$$H_1(e_0, e_1, ..., e_{n-1}) = v_1',$$
$$\vdots$$
$$H_{n'-1}(e_0, e_1, ..., e_{n-1}) = v_{n'-1}'. \tag{37}$$

If V' satisfies following conditions, a sub block $v_t' \in V'(0 \leq t \leq n' - 1)$ is independent of V'.

(i) $E \to V'$ is injective ($|E| \leq |V'|$).
(ii) $\exists e_s \in E(0 \leq s \leq n - 1)$, $E \backslash e_s \to V' \backslash v_t'$ is injective.

Proposition 5. *Let H be a function of $\mathbb{F}_2^{mn'} \to \mathbb{F}_2^m$ supposed in Eq. (15). Let $V' = \{v_0', v_1', ..., v_{n'-1}'\}$ be a set of intermediate variable sub blocks, and a sub block x_b^r and V' satisfy*

$$x_b^r = H(v_0', v_1', ..., v_{n'-1}'). \tag{38}$$

Suppose $v_t' \in V'$ is independent of V' (see Definition 4). If following condition holds, higher order integral property $\mathcal{X}_b^r$ is $\mathcal{U}$.

$$X_b^r(v_t') = A \Rightarrow \mathcal{X}_b^r = \mathcal{U} \tag{39}$$

Proof. A sequence $\tilde{x}_b^r$ can be written as

$$\tilde{x}_b^r = \left(H(v_{t,i}', V_i'\backslash v_{t,i}')\right)_{i=0}^{2^{mn}-1}. \tag{40}$$

where $v_{t,i}'$ is i-th element of $\tilde{v}_t'$ and $V_{t,i}'$ is a set of i-th elements of sequences of sub blocks in $\tilde{V}' = \{\tilde{v}_0', \tilde{v}_1', ..., \tilde{v}_{n'-1}'\}$. We substitute $i = 2^m k + l$ $(0 \le k \le 2^m - 1,$ $0 \le l \le 2^{m(n-1)} - 1)$ of Eq. (40). We rewrite Eq. (40) as

$$\tilde{x}_b^r = \left(\left(H(v_{t,2^m k+l}', V_{2^m k+l}'\backslash v_{t,2^m k+l}')\right)_{l=0}^{2^m-1}\right)_{k=0}^{2^{m(n-1)}-1}. \tag{41}$$

From condition (ä) of Definition 4, $\tilde{V}'\backslash\tilde{v}_t'$ contains $2^{m(n-1)}$ distinct combinations, and multiplicity of each distinct combinations is 2^m. From condition (i) of Definition 4, $\tilde{V}'$ contains 2^{mn} distinct combinations, and there is no multiplicity. Therefore, $\tilde{v}_t'$ takes 2^m distinct values for every possible combination of $\tilde{V}'\backslash\tilde{v}_t'$. We sort $\tilde{x}_b^r$ as following two conditions in Eq. (41).

(i) $^\forall k, l, l'(l \ne l')$, $v_{t,2^m k+l}' \ne v_{t,2^m k+l'}'$
(ii) $^\forall k, l, l'(l \ne l')$, $V_{2^m k+l}'\backslash v_{t,2^m k+l}' = V_{2^m k+l'}'\backslash v_{t,2^m k+l'}'$

Let $\tilde{x}_b'^r$ be a sub sequence of sorted sequence $\tilde{x}_b^r$ for given k, and $\tilde{x}_b'^r$ is written as

$$\tilde{x}_b'^r = \left(\left(H(v_{t,2^m k+k'}', V_{2^m k+k'}'\backslash v_{t,2^m k+k'}')\right)_{k'=0}^{2^m-1}\right)_{k=const}. \tag{42}$$

Therefore, we can regard integral property of sub sequence $\tilde{x}_b'^r$ as first order, and $X_b^r(v_t')$ holds for any values of constant sequences from Proposition 1. Suppose a first order integral property of $\tilde{x}_b'^r$ is A $(X_b'^r(v_t') = A)$, $\tilde{x}_b'^r$ contains every possible element of $\mathbb{F}_2^m$ for any k in Eq. (42). In addition, $\tilde{x}_b^r$ is a summation of individual sub sequences $\tilde{x}_b'^r$ which is respectively chosen by k. Therefore, $\tilde{x}_b^r$ contains $2^{m(n-1)}$ sub sequences which contains every possible element of $\mathbb{F}_2^m$, and this satisfies the definition of $\mathcal{U}$ (Eq. (24)). □

6   Procedure of Proposal Algorithm

We divide search algorithm into two algorithms, Algorithm A and B. Algorithm A is based on Sect. 5.5 and Algorithm B is based on Sect. 5.6. In addition, we propose Algorithm B′ for Algorithm B. We test injection by Algorithm B′.

Algorithm A: We divide search scope into two domains, inside and outside of bijective path. Inside bijective path, higher order integral properties of sub blocks are obviously $\mathcal{U}$ from Proposition 2. Outside bijective path, we analyze relation between end point of bijective path and each output sub blocks to determine their higher order integral property. After $\mathcal{U}$ and $\mathcal{E}$ sub blocks are specified, we search for $\mathcal{B}$ sub blocks.

Algorithm A has following six steps.

Step-1. Choose n sub blocks as input variable sub blocks V ($|V| = n$). Add V to bijective path P and substitute V for temporary end point of bijective path E.

Step-2. For every possible combination of n sub blocks $E' = G(E)$, test if $E \rightarrow E'$ is bijective or not. If $E \rightarrow E'$ is bijective, go to Step-3. Otherwise, E is end point of bijective path, go to Step-4.

Step-3. Add E' to P and substitute E' for E. Return to Step-2.

Step-4. Determine higher order integral property of sub blocks inside P as $\mathcal{U}$. For every possible combination of $\{e_t, x_b^r\}(e_t \in E, x_b^r \notin P)$, calculate first order integral properties $X_b^r(e_t)$ and preserve them.

Step-5. Using every set of $X_b^r(e_t)(e_t \in E, x_b^r \notin P)$, determine whether higher order integral property of every sub block outside P is $\mathcal{U}$ or $\mathcal{E}$ from Propositions 2, 3 and 4.

Step-6. Search sub blocks which are calculated as $\mathcal{B}$. End algorithm.

Higher order integral properties of $\mathcal{B}$ or $\mathcal{E}$ sub blocks are temporary. Their higher order integral properties can be changed in Algorithm B.

Algorithm B: In Algorithm B, we reanalyze higher order integral properties of sub blocks which were determined as $\mathcal{B}$ or $\mathcal{E}$ in Algorithm A. We call these sub blocks as *undetermined* $\mathcal{B}$ or $\mathcal{E}$ sub blocks. They can be $\mathcal{U}$ from Proposition 5. Let $V' = \{x_0^{r_0}, x_1^{r_0}, ..., x_{n'}^{r_0}\}$ be sub blocks in r_0-th round which satisfies

$$x_b^r = H(x_0^{r_0}, x_1^{r_0}, ..., x_{n'}^{r_0}), 0 \leq r_0 \leq r - 1, \tag{43}$$

where x_b^r is a target sub block to determine higher order integral property. We test injection of $E \rightarrow V'$ for each r_0-th round. Note that $n' = |V'|$ must be equal to or greater than $n = |V| = |E|$ from definition of injection. When we find V', s.t., $E \rightarrow V'$ is injective, we search a combination of $\{v_t', e_s\}$ which satisfies the definition of independent (see Definition 4). If we find at least one combination of $\{v_t', e_s\}$ which satisfies the definition of independent, we obtain $X_b^r = \mathcal{U}$. We execute above procedure for every undetermined $\mathcal{B}$ or $\mathcal{E}$ sub block.

Algorithm B has following four steps.

Step-1. Find an undetermined $\mathcal{B}$ or $\mathcal{E}$ sub block, and let the sub block be target sub block x_b^r. If it is found, go to Step-2, and substitute $r_0 = r-1$. Otherwise, end algorithm.

Step-2. Test injection of $E \rightarrow V'$, where V' is sub blocks in r_0-th round, s.t., Eq. (43). If $E \rightarrow V'$ is injective, go to Step-3. Otherwise, repeat Step-2 by decrementing r_0 ($r_0 = r_0 - 1$). If r_0 is less than 0 ($r_0 < 0$), X_b^r is determined $\mathcal{B}$ or $\mathcal{E}$, and return to Step-1.

Step-3. For every possible combination of $\{v_t', e_s\}$, test whether they satisfies $X_b^r(v_t') = A$ and injection of $E\backslash e_s \rightarrow V'\backslash v_t'$. If at least one combination is found, $X_b^r = \mathcal{U}$, and go to Step-4. Otherwise, substitute $r_0 - 1$ for r_0 ($r_0 = r_0 - 1$), and return to Step-2 and.

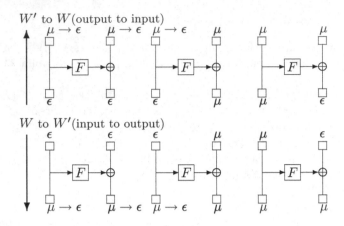

Fig. 5. Characteristics of f function in terms of μ to ϵ.

Step-4. Update higher order integral properties which can be changed by the fact that $\mathcal{X}_b^r = \mathcal{U}$ ($\mathcal{B}$ sub blocks increase). Return to Step-1.

Integral distinguisher obtained by Algorithm A increases preciseness by Algorithm B. We show a detailed algorithm of Step-2 and 3 in Algorithm B′.

Algorithm B′: Let W be output sub blocks of intermediate rounds, and $\mathcal{G}$ a function of $\mathbb{F}_2^{mn} \to \mathbb{F}_2^{mn'}$ such as Eq. (37). To generalize situation to test injection, we suppose that injection of $W \to W'(= \mathcal{G}(W), |W'| = n')$ is tested. Note that we substitute $W = E$ or $W = E \backslash e_s$ in Algorithm B. Here, we assume $W = E$ ($|W| = n$).

To test injection, we use contraposition of definition of injection. Suppose we input two plaintexts into cipher function. Let w and Δw be values of concatenation of every sub block in W, and they are element of $\mathbb{F}_2^{mn}$. Let w' and $\Delta w'$ be values of concatenation of every sub block in $W' = \mathcal{G}(W)$, and they are element of $\mathbb{F}_2^{mn'}$. When we have $w' = \Delta w'$, we test whether we can obtain $w = \Delta w$. If $w = \Delta w$ is obtained, $W \to W'$ is injective.

We regard output sub blocks of intermediate rounds as variable term used in Eq. (37). We define two states of such sub blocks as *equal* (ϵ) and *unequal* (μ) as follows. Suppose a sub blocks are derive from $x_b^r = G(W)$, where G is a function of $\mathbb{F}_2^{mn} \to \mathbb{F}_2^m$ supposed in Eq. (15). As same as w and Δw, we consider two actual values of x_b^r. Let χ_b^r and $\Delta \chi_b^r$ be actual values of x_b^r, and they are element of $\mathbb{F}_2^m$. If $\chi_b^r = \Delta \chi_b^r$, x_b^r is ϵ and we write $x_b^r = \epsilon$. Otherwise, x_b^r is μ and we write $x_b^r = \mu$.

At first, ϵ is substituted for sub blocks in W' and constant sub blocks and μ is for the others.

$$(x_b^r \in W') \lor (\mathcal{X}_b^r = \mathcal{C}) \Rightarrow x_b^r = \epsilon$$
$$(x_b^r \notin W') \land (\mathcal{X}_b^r \neq \mathcal{C}) \Rightarrow x_b^r = \mu \tag{44}$$

Regarding current ϵ sub blocks as start point, we consider the diffusion of ϵ sub blocks. In other words, we search sub blocks which is changed from μ to ϵ. Considering input-output relation of each functions such as f function (see Eq. (29)), we can determine whether each sub block is μ or ϵ. For example, f function has following three characteristics in terms of μ to ϵ.

(i) $\{x_0, x_1\} = \{\epsilon, \epsilon\} \Rightarrow \{x_0', x_1'\} = \{\epsilon, \epsilon\}$.
(ii) $\{x_0, x_1\} = \{\epsilon, \mu\} \Rightarrow \{x_0', x_1'\} = \{\epsilon, \mu\}$.
(iii) $\{x_0, x_1\} = \{\mu, \epsilon\} \Rightarrow \{x_0', x_1'\} = \{\mu, \mu\}$.

These characteristics holds if we replace $\{x_0, x_1\}$ as $\{x_0', x_1'\}$. We show six characteristics in Fig. 5. We search sub blocks which is changed from μ to ϵ in two direction. One is direction from W' to W (output to input). The other is direction from W to W' (input to output). After repetition of these two steps, if all sub blocks in W are equal, $W \rightarrow W'$ is injective from contraposition of definition of injection.

Algorithm B′ has following five steps.

Step-1. Set input variable sub blocks W and output variable sub blocks W'. If $|W| > |W'|$ holds, output "$W \rightarrow W'$ is not injective", and end Algorithm. Otherwise, substitute ϵ or μ for every sub block by using Eq. (44).
Step-2. From W' to W, search μ sub blocks to be ϵ and substitute ϵ for them.
Step-3. From W to W', search μ sub blocks to be ϵ and substitute ϵ for them.
Step-4. If there are not any change from μ to ϵ in Step-2 and 3, go to Step-5. Otherwise, return to Step-2.
Step-5. If all sub blocks in W are ϵ, output "$W \rightarrow W'$ is injective". Otherwise output "$W \rightarrow W'$ is not injective". End algorithm.

7 Application of Proposal Algorithm

As an application of the proposal algorithm shown in Sect. 6, we search integral distinguisher of TWINE and LBlock, and compare the results with ones of previous work [4]. Since the number of sub blocks N is 16, we analyze fifteenth order integral distinguisher of TWINE and LBlock. As an example, we show fifteenth order integral distinguisher of TWINE in Fig. 6 and demonstrate the proposal algorithm in it. In Algorithm Λ, we search bijective path at first. Underlined sub blocks are in bijective path P and ones squared with solid line are end point of bijective path E in Fig. 6. Higher order integral properties of these sub blocks are $\mathcal{U}$ from Proposition 2. Sub blocks without any lines or squares are sub blocks whose higher order integral properties are determined in Algorithm A.

In Algorithm B, we search independent sub blocks to change higher order integral property of $\mathcal{B}$ to $\mathcal{U}$. $\mathcal{U}$ sub blocks squared with broken line are sub blocks whose higher order integral property are changed from $\mathcal{B}$ to $\mathcal{U}$ or $\mathcal{R}$ to $\mathcal{B}$. All of independent sub blocks to change these properties are in 7-th round.

We show the way to change higher order integral property of x_0^{13} as example. Let $V_{r=7}'$ be a set of sub blocks of 7-th round. The sub block x_0^{13} is written as

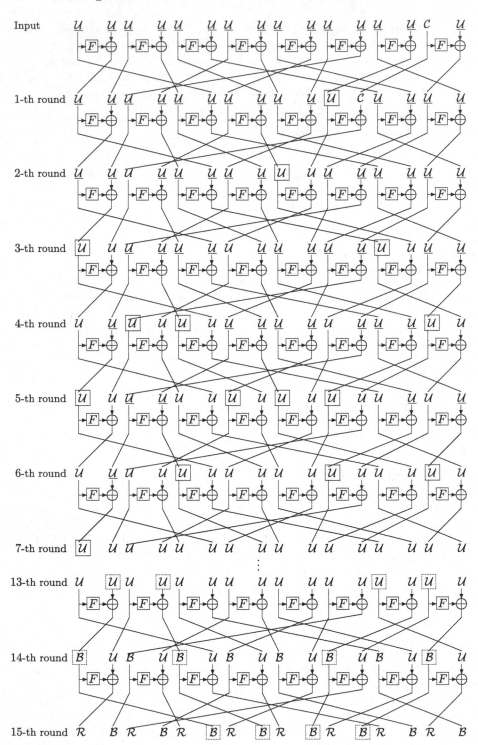

Fig. 6. Fifteenth order integral distinguisher of TWINE obtained by the proposal algorithm.

$x_0^{13} = H(V')$, s.t., $V' = V'_{r=7} \backslash x_9^7$. We choose x_{11}^7 as v'_t, since first order integral property $X_0^{13}(x_{11}^7) = A$. Also, we choose x_{10}^6 as $e_s \in E$. Using Algorithm B', we confirm $E \to V'$ and $E \backslash x_{10}^6 \to V' \backslash x_{11}^7$ are injective. Therefore, higher order integral property of $\tilde{x}_0^{13}$ is changed from $\mathcal{B}$ to $\mathcal{U}$. In the same way, higher order integral properties of $\tilde{x}_2^{13}$, $\tilde{x}_{12}^{13}$ and $\tilde{x}_{14}^{13}$ are changed from $\mathcal{B}$ to $\mathcal{U}$. Higher order-integral properties of sub blocks which are output of $\oplus$ operation of two $\mathcal{U}$ sub blocks are $\mathcal{B}$. Therefore, higher order integral properties of $\tilde{x}_0^{14}$, $\tilde{x}_4^{14}$, $\tilde{x}_{10}^{14}$ and $\tilde{x}_{14}^{14}$ are changed from $\mathcal{R}$ to $\mathcal{B}$. Hence, we find output integral is $\mathcal{B}_{\{1,3,5,7,9,11,13,15\}}$, and this is the same as the result which is discovered from computer experiment shown in Eq. (8). Also, we find the same output integrals are obtained if we choose a constant sub block whose index is even in fifteenth order integral of TWINE. These results are also consistent with the result which is discovered from computer experiment. In addition to TWINE, we search fifteenth order integral distinguisher of LBlock, and obtain results which are consistent with the results discovered by computer experiment such as Eq. (12).

Since integral distinguisher discovered in previous work [4] is the most precise distinguisher of TWINE and LBlock, we confirm preciseness of the proposal algorithm.

8   Discussion

8.1   Comparison with Conventional Search Algorithm

There are two major differences between the proposal algorithm and the conventional one. One is an approach to search higher order integral property from input to output (from top to down). From this, the proposal algorithm is feasible independent of the order and the selection of input variable sub blocks. Therefore, all input integrals are in the scope of the proposal algorithm. Also, integral properties of all sub blocks are obtained. In the conventional algorithm, unsearched domain inevitably exists, since they only extend first order integral.

The other is an approach to elucidate higher order integral property. Only property as first order integral is elucidated in the conventional algorithm. Since the number of plaintexts is 2^{mn}, the definition of first order integral property does not represent actual properties. Our definition of higher order integral property represent actual properties.

In addition to above theoretical superiority, we have shown preciseness of the proposal algorithm in Sect. 7. In Sect. 8.2, we consider computational complexity of the proposal search algorithm.

8.2   Computational Complexity of Proposal Algorithm

Suppose a cipher function has N sub blocks and consists of R-th round iteration, and we try to gain $(N - 1)$-th order integral distinguisher. We calculate computational complexity of each algorithm respectively.

Algorithm A: Algorithm A has two major steps, search of bijective path and determination of higher-order integral property. With respect to search of bijective path, we look up small tables such as Fig. 3 to determine temporary end point of bijective path E is changed from current one. Let T_{A_1} be a table size of bijective characteristics of every function such as f (Eq. (29)). Even if we lookup table in every sub block, computational complexity is $N \times R$ times lookup table(LUT) and the table size is T_{A_1}.

With respect to determination of higher-order integral property, we calculate first-order integral property of every sub blocks in terms of each sub block in end point of bijective path E ($|E| = N - 1$). We prepare a table of calculation of each first-order integral property such as $A \oplus A = B$. Let T_{A_2} be a table size of such calculations. Even if we lookup table in every sub blocks, computational complexity is $N^2 \times R$ times LUT and the table size is T_{A_2}.

Algorithm B: Suppose we test every $N \times R$ sub blocks is $\mathcal{U}$. For every R round and possible combination of $\{v'_t, e_s\}$, we test injection of $E \to V'$ and $E \backslash e_s \to V' \backslash v'_t$. Therefore, computational complexity of Algorithm B is $N^3 \times R^2$ times computational complexity of Algorithm B'.

Algorithm B': We lookup small tables such as Fig. 5 to determine whether sub blocks are changed from μ and ϵ. Let $T_{B'}$ be table size of characteristics in terms of μ and ϵ of every function such as f. Even if we repeat Step-2 and 3 for $N \times R$ times(maximum times), computational complexity is $N^2 \times R^2$ times LUT and the table size is $T_{B'}$. Therefore, computational complexity of Algorithm B is $N^5 \times R^4$ times LUT and the table size is $T_{B'}$.

From these computational complexity, we can execute the proposal algorithm even in general-purpose computers.

9   Conclusion

When a cipher is byte-based, the proposal algorithm is applicable to not only Feistel type but also SPN type ciphers. For example, AES is in the scope, since Mixcolums is decomposed of L and $\oplus$ in sub block unit which is element of $\mathbb{F}_2^8$. As for fastness, we can execute it even in personal computers. Therefore, we recommend the proposal algorithm instead of the conventional one.

Designers of block ciphers must consider precise integral distinguisher obtained by the proposal algorithm. There is a possibility that the number of rounds to be attacked increases from the precise integral distinguisher. Even if it is not, it can be less difficult to guess all of the secret keys from increased balanced sub blocks. Therefore, the designers need to consider such vulnerabilities and select stronger cipher algorithm and key schedule.

References

1. Daemen, J., Knudsen, L.R., Rijmen, V.: The block cipher SQUARE. In: Biham, E. (ed.) FSE 1997. LNCS, vol. 1267, pp. 149–165. Springer, Heidelberg (1997). http://dx.doi.org/10.1007/BFb0052343

2. Ferguson, N., Kelsey, J., Lucks, S., Schneier, B., Stay, M., Wagner, D., Whiting, D.: Improved cryptanalysis of Rijndael. In: Schneier, B. (ed.) FSE 2000. LNCS, vol. 1978, pp. 213–230. Springer, Heidelberg (2001). http://dx.doi.org/10.1007/3-540-44706-7_15

3. Knudsen, L., Wagner, D.: Integral cryptanalysis. In: Daemen, J., Rijmen, V. (eds.) FSE 2002. LNCS, vol. 2365, pp. 112–127. Springer, Heidelberg (2002). http://dx.doi.org/10.1007/3-540-45661-9_9

4. Kosuge, H., Tanaka, H., Iwai, K., Kurokawa, T.: Computational security evaluation of light-weight block cipher against integral attack by gpgpu. In: The 2nd IEEE International Conference on Cyber Security and Cloud Computing

5. Sasaki, Y., Wang, L.: Comprehensive study of integral analysis on 22-round LBlock. In: Kwon, T., Lee, M.-K., Kwon, D. (eds.) ICISC 2012. LNCS, vol. 7839, pp. 156–169. Springer, Heidelberg (2013). http://dx.doi.org/10.1007/978-3-642-37682-5_12

6. Sony Corporation: The 128-bit blockcipher CLEFIA security and performance evaluations revision 1.0 (2007). http://www.sony.net/Products/cryptography/clefia/download/data/clefia-eval-1.0.pdf

7. Suzaki, T., Minematsu, K., Morioka, S., Kobayashi, E.: TWINE: a lightweight block cipher for multiple platforms. In: Knudsen, L.R., Wu, H. (eds.) SAC 2012. LNCS, vol. 7707, pp. 339–354. Springer, Heidelberg (2013). http://dx.doi.org/10.1007/978-3-642-35999-6_22

8. Wu, W., Zhang, L.: LBlock: a lightweight block cipher. In: Lopez, J., Tsudik, G. (eds.) ACNS 2011. LNCS, vol. 6715, pp. 327–344. Springer, Heidelberg (2011). http://dx.doi.org/10.1007/978-3-642-21554-4_19

9. Zhang, W., Su, B., Wu, W., Feng, D., Wu, C.: Extending higher-order integral: an efficient unified algorithm of constructing integral distinguishers for block ciphers. In: Bao, F., Samarati, P., Zhou, J. (eds.) ACNS 2012. LNCS, vol. 7341, pp. 117–134. Springer, Heidelberg (2012). http://dx.doi.org/10.1007/978-3-642-31284-7_8

Plaintext Checkable Signcryption

Angsuman Das[1] and Avishek Adhikari[2] (✉)

[1] Department of Mathematics, St. Xavier's College, Kolkata, India
angsumandas@sxccal.edu
[2] Department of Pure Mathematics, University of Calcutta, Kolkata, India
avishek.adh@gmail.com

Abstract. Digital signature guarantees the authenticity and encryption ensures the confidentiality of a transmitted message. Signcryption, as the name indicates, is a primitive which serves both these purpose with added efficiency and features. In this paper, we introduce a variant of signcryption called Plaintext Checkable Signcryption (PCSC), which extends signcryption by the following functionality: given a signcryptext c, a plaintext m and the corresponding public values, it is universally possible to check whether c is a signcryption of m. The security requirements of such a primitive is studied and a suitable model of security is proposed. Moreover, we provide efficient generic model construction for PCSC based on "Encrypt-then-Sign" paradigm using an arbitrary partially trapdoor one-way function and a signature scheme. Finally, the construction is shown to be secure in the proposed model.

Keywords: Plaintext checkability · Signcryption · Random oracle model

1 Introduction

Signcryption, introduced by Zheng [16] and formalized in [1,2], has been an area of active research from the day of its inception. Signcryption is a primitive which encrypts as well as authenticates a message. The main objective in the study of signcryption scheme was two-fold: to reduce the cost of signcryption than naive combination of encryption and signature and to achieve better security than the components: encryption and signature scheme. Till then, depending upon their applicability in various requirements, various signcryption schemes along with several variants like, identity-based signcryption [14], proxy signcryption, aggregate signcryption [9], signcryption with delayed identification [7], threshold signcryption [13], heterogeneous signcryption [12] etc., various techniques for constructing these schemes like [6] and their corresponding security notions have evolved.

In this paper, we propose a new signcryption variant, called *plaintext checkable signcryption* (PCSC). A plaintext checkable signcryption scheme is a signcryption scheme with the additional functionality that anyone can test whether a ciphertext c is the signcryption of a given plaintext message m. To clarify the applicability of such a primitive, we give one potential application of this primitive PCSC as follows:

© Springer International Publishing Switzerland 2015
S. Jajodia and C. Mazumdar (Eds.): ICISS 2015, LNCS 9478, pp. 324–333, 2015.
DOI: 10.1007/978-3-319-26961-0_19

Suppose there are many doctors in a hospital. The patients may send their messages, such as seeking an appointment for a particular doctor at certain time, the reports or even their emergencies, to the drop-box of the doctors in a signcrypted way.[1] But due to the busy schedules, the doctors are unable to go through each of the signcrypted messages from the patients. Thus, the hospital management appoints several secretaries (who work in shifts) for all the doctors. Each secretary should have access to the drop-box of all the doctors and each of them should be able to sort all the signcrypted messages of each doctor depending on the instructions for sorting from the doctors. A trivial solution could be to provide the secret keys of all the doctors to each secretary. However, the patients or even the management of the hospital may not want to do that. Instead, the management wants the secretaries to have only the power to search any message (for the convenience of the doctors so that a particular secretary may be asked for any message to search) but must not have the power to decrypt the encrypted messages. For example, a doctor D, who is now on vacation, requests secretary S to redirect only the messages containing the phrase "emergency" in it to his smart phone. Once the drop-box of D receives those particular messages having "emergency" as a plaintext, the secretary S sorts the encrypted messages to redirect to the corresponding doctor for necessary actions.

Note that a PCSC scheme cannot achieve even the standard notion of indistinguishability of signcryptions under chosen-plaintext attack: an adversary choosing two messages and receiving the signcryption of one of them can simply test which message was signcrypted using the plaintext checking functionality. However, we want that the signcryptext to leak as little information as possible about the plaintext.

1.1 Related Work

The problem of searching an encrypted database [4, 10, 11] etc. has been well studied under the name of *searchable encryption* in the last decade. However, searchable versions of signcryption schemes are not yet explored. As a matter of fact, a searchable signcryption scheme built using techniques from any of [4, 10] will not suffice, as for each individual message to be searched by the secretary, a separate trapdoor (message-specific trapdoor) must be generated and sent to her by each doctor through a secure channel. Thus, for each request to search a plaintext, each doctor needs to issue a separate trapdoor to be sent to the secretary, making the scheme impractical in the proposed scenario. For signcryption schemes built using delegated searchable encryption [11], the secretaries will have to store multiple master trapdoors, one for each of the doctors. Moreover, all the existing constructions of delegated searchable encryption [11] are pairing-based, thereby restricting the constructions only to a specific tool. In *publicly verifiable signcryption schemes*, though the validity of the signcryption can be checked publicly without revealing the message in question, it does not allow for plaintext checkability.

---

[1] Note that authentication of the message is important in this scenario to avoid spam messages.

The only work closely related to this scenario, is *Plaintext Checkable Encryption* (PCE) [5]. A plaintext checkable encryption scheme is a probabilistic public-key encryption scheme with the additional functionality that *anyone* can test whether a ciphertext c is the encryption of a given plaintext m under a public encryption key pk. Thus, an obvious solution is to carefully combine a PCE and a standard signature scheme to construct a PCSC. However, this method restricts the choice of building blocks of the proposed primitive. In fact, our generic construction can be securely designed using encryption schemes with weaker security than that used in generic constructions of PCE in [5].

1.2   Our Contribution

In this paper, we introduce a new signcryption variant, Plaintext Checkable Signcryption (PCSC), and carefully formalize its security notion based on the scenario stated above. As stated earlier, indistinguishability against chosen plaintext attack can not be achieved by a PCSC scheme and mere one-wayness of the signcryption may not be acceptable as it may leak some information about the underlying plaintext. Although the plaintext checkability itself leaks some information about the plaintext, we want it to leak the bare minimum. To frame a proper notion of minimal information leakage, we introduce the notion of *unlinkability of signcryptions*. Informally speaking, a signcryption scheme is said to have unlinkable signcryptions if no probabilistic polynomial time adversary is able to distinguish two signcryptions of the same message from signcryptions of different messages. We also provide an efficient generic construction of PCSC using partially trapdoor one-way function and a signature scheme. Finally, we prove its security along the proposed model.

Organisation of the Paper. The rest of the paper is organised as follows: In Sect. 2, some definitions of existing cryptographic primitives and their security notions are discussed. In Sect. 3, we propose the formal definition and security notion of PCSC. The main construction is given in Sect. 4 and its security analysis is done in Sect. 5. Finally we conclude with some open issues in Sect. 6.

2   Preliminaries and Definitions

We begin by formally defining the notions of *Public-Key Encryption* (PKE) and Signature Scheme (SS) and their corresponding security notions.

2.1   Public-Key Encryption (PKE)

A Public-Key Encryption (PKE) is a tuple of probabilistic polynomial-time (ppt.) algorithms (Gen, Enc, Dec) such that:

1. The key generation algorithm, Gen, takes as input a security parameter 1^n and outputs a public-key/private-key pair (pk, sk).

2. The encryption algorithm Enc takes as input a public key pk, a message m from the underlying plaintext space $\mathcal{M}$ and an ephemeral key r from the randomness space $\mathcal{R}$ to output a ciphertext $c := \mathsf{Enc}(pk, m, r)$ belonging to the ciphertext space $\mathcal{C}$.
3. The decryption algorithm Dec takes as input a private key sk and a ciphertext c to output a plaintext m or a special reject symbol "$\perp$".

It is required that there exists a negligible function negl such that for every n, every (pk, sk) and every message m in the corresponding plaintext space, it holds that $\Pr[\mathsf{Dec}(sk, \mathsf{Enc}(pk, m, r)) \neq m] \leq \mathsf{negl}(n)$.

Security Notion for Public-Key Encryption (PKE): Though there are various notions of security for public-key encryption scheme, one of the weakest one, partially trapdoor one-wayness, is discussed here as it suffices for our construction.

Partially Trapdoor One-wayness (PTOW): A PKE scheme is said to be partially trapdoor one-way (PTOW) if its encryption function $\mathsf{Enc}_{pk} : \mathcal{M} \times \mathcal{R} \rightarrow \mathcal{C}$ is partially trapdoor one-way, i.e.,

– for any given $c = \mathsf{Enc}_{pk}(m, r)$ and pk, it is computationally infeasible to get back m. In this case, m is said to be a partial pre-image of c. Formally speaking, for any probabilistic polynomial time adversary $\mathcal{A}$, its success, defined by $\mathsf{Succ}_{\mathcal{A}} = \Pr[\mathcal{A}(pk, c) \rightarrow m : \exists r \in \mathcal{R} \text{ such that } \mathsf{Enc}_{pk}(m, r) = c]$ is negligible.
– given a secret trapdoor sk, for any $c \in \mathsf{Enc}_{pk}(\mathcal{M} \times \mathcal{R})$, it is easily possible to get back $m \in \mathcal{M}$ such that there exists an $r \in \mathcal{R}$ such that $c = \mathsf{Enc}_{pk}(m, r)$. The secret trapdoor sk is called a partial trapdoor as it enables a partial pre-image (i.e., m) recovery.

Remark 1. It is to be noted that a partially trapdoor one-wayness of encryption is a strictly weaker security notion than indistinguishability of encryption against chosen plaintext attack.

If we wish to analyse a scheme PKE in the random oracle model [3], the hash functions are replaced by random oracle queries as appropriate, and $\mathcal{A}$ is given access to the random oracle in the above attack game.

2.2   Signature Scheme (SS)

A Signature Scheme is a tuple of ppt. algorithms (Gen, Sign, Ver) such that:

1. The key generation algorithm, Gen, takes as input a security parameter 1^n and outputs a signing-key/verification-key pair (sk, pk).
2. The signing algorithm Sign takes as input a signing-key sk, a message m from the underlying plaintext space to output a signature $s := \mathsf{Sign}(sk, m)$.
3. The verification algorithm Ver takes as input a verification-key pk and a message-signature pair (m, s) to output 0 or 1.

It is required that there exists a negligible function negl such that for every n, every (pk, sk) and every message m in the corresponding plaintext space, it holds that $\Pr[\mathsf{Ver}(pk, m, \mathsf{Sign}(sk, m)) \neq 1] \leq \mathsf{negl}(n)$.

Security Notion for Signature Scheme (SS): A Signature Scheme $SS =$ (Gen, Sign, Ver) is said to achieve *existential unforgeability against chosen message attack* (UF-CMA) if any probabilistic polynomial-time adversary $\mathcal{A}$ has negligible chance of winning against a challenger $\mathcal{C}$ in the following game:

1. Given the security parameter, $\mathcal{C}$ generates a key pair (pk, sk) and returns pk to $\mathcal{A}$.
2. $\mathcal{A}$ is given oracle access to the signing oracle.
3. $\mathcal{A}$ outputs a message-signature pair (m^*, s^*).

$\mathcal{A}$ wins the game if s^* is a valid signature on m^* and if m^* was never queried to the signing oracle.

3   Plaintext Checkable Signcryption (PCSC)

In this section, we formally define *Plaintext Checkable Signcryption* (PCSC) and frame its security notions based on the requirements of the proposed scenario.

Plaintext Checkable Signcryption (PCSC) consists of five-tuple of ppt. algorithms (Setup, Keygen$_A$, Keygen$_B$, Signcrypt, Unsigncrypt, PCheck) such that

1. The setup algorithm Setup, takes as input a security parameter 1^n and returns common parameter *par* required by the PCSC scheme.
2. The key generation algorithm for the sender A, Keygen$_A$, takes as input the common parameters *par* and outputs a public-key/private-key pair (pk_A, sk_A).
3. The key generation algorithm for the receiver B, Keygen$_B$, takes as input the common parameters *par* and outputs a public-key/private-key pair (pk_B, sk_B).
4. The signcryption algorithm Signcrypt takes as input common parameters *par*, sender's secret key sk_A, receiver's public key pk_B and a message m to output a signcryptext $c := $ Signcrypt(par, sk_A, pk_B, m).
5. The unsigncryption algorithm Unsigncrypt takes as input common parameter *par*, sender's public key pk_A, receiver's secret key sk_B, a signcryptext c to output a message $m := $ Unsigncrypt(par, pk_A, sk_B, c) or an error symbol $\bot$.
6. The plaintext checking algorithm, PCheck, takes as input common parameter *par*, sender's public key pk_A, receiver's public key pk_B, a plaintext m and a signcryptext c to output 1 or 0, i.e.,

$$\mathsf{PCheck}(par, pk_A, pk_B, m, c) = 1 \text{ or } 0.$$

Correctness: It is required that for every n, every (pk_A, sk_A), (pk_B, sk_B), every message m in the corresponding plaintext space, it hold that

$$\mathsf{Unsigncrypt}(sk_B, pk_A, \mathsf{Signcrypt}(par, sk_A, pk_B, m)) = m \text{ and}$$

$$\mathsf{PCheck}(par, pk_A, pk_B, m, \mathsf{Signcrypt}(sk_A, pk_B, m)) = 1.$$

3.1   Security Notions for PCSC

As mentioned earlier in Sect. 1.2, PCSC can not achieve indistinguishability of signcryption even against chosen plaintext attack. Thus, as an alternative, we define unlinkability of signcryptions through the following game between an adversary and a challenger. The game combines both the features of insider security of (ordinary) signcryption scheme as well as unlinkability of encryptions of a plaintext checkable encryption scheme [5].

Unlinkability: A Plaintext Checkable Signcryption Scheme (PCSC) is said to achieve unlinkability (UNLINK-PCSC) if any probabilistic polynomial-time adversary $\mathcal{A} = (A_f, A_g)$ has negligible advantage against a challenger $\mathcal{C}$ in the following game:

1. Given the security parameter, $\mathcal{C}$ generates common parameter par and then with that generates a sender's key-pair (pk_A, sk_A) using $\mathsf{KeyGen_A}$ and a receiver's key-pair (pk_B, sk_B) using $\mathsf{KeyGen_B}$.
2. A_f is given par, sk_A, pk_A, pk_B. A_f outputs a pair of distinct messages m_0, m_1 from the associated plaintext space.
3. $\mathcal{C}$ chooses $b \in_R \{0,1\}$, computes and sends the challenge signcryptexts $c_0 = \mathsf{Signcrypt}(par, sk_A, pk_B, m_b)$ and $c_1 = \mathsf{Signcrypt}(par, sk_A, pk_B, m_1)$ to A_g;
4. A_g outputs a bit b'.

The advantage $\mathbf{Adv}^{unlink}_{A,PCSC}(n)$ is defined to be $|Pr[b' = b] - 1/2|$.

It is assumed that A_f and A_g share neither coins nor state (e.g., the messages m_0, m_1 chosen by A_f in the find stage are not known to A_g in the guess stage), and the messages are to be drawn from a high min-entropy space, as otherwise the notion is not satisfiable by a PCSC scheme, since the adversary could simply check all messages.

Unforgeability: A Plaintext Checkable Signcryption Scheme (PCSC) is said to achieve existential signcryptext unforgeability against chosen message attack in UF-PCSC-CMA sense if any probabilistic polynomial-time adversary $\mathcal{A}$ has negligible chance of winning against a challenger $\mathcal{C}$ in the following game:

1. Given the security parameter, $\mathcal{C}$ generates common parameter par and then with that generates a sender's key-pair (pk_A, sk_A) using $\mathsf{KeyGen_A}$ and a receiver's key-pair (pk_B, sk_B) using $\mathsf{KeyGen_B}$.
2. $\mathcal{A}$ is given par, pk_A, pk_B, sk_B as well as access to the signcryption oracle $\mathsf{Signcrypt}(par, sk_A, pk_B, \cdot)$. For each signcryption query m, the oracle answers it with $c = \mathsf{Signcrypt}(par, sk_A, pk_B, m)$.
3. $\mathcal{A}$ outputs a signcryptext c^*.

$\mathcal{A}$ wins the game if $m^* \leftarrow \mathsf{Unsigncrypt}(par, pk_A, sk_B, c^*)$ satisfies $m^* \neq \perp$ and if its underlying plaintext m^* was never submitted to the signcryption oracle $\mathsf{Signcrypt}(par, sk_A, pk_B, \cdot)$.

4   The Proposed Generic Construction

In this section, we propose a generic construction of a plaintext checkable signcryption scheme (PCSC) from a public-key encryption scheme (PKE) and a signature scheme (SS). The construction is based on "Encrypt-then-Sign" paradigm.

Let $\Pi=(\mathsf{Gen}, \mathsf{Enc}, \mathsf{Dec})$ be a probabilistic PKE scheme with message space $\{0,1\}^{k_1}$ and randomness space $\{0,1\}^k$, and $\mathcal{SS}=(\mathsf{Gen}', \mathsf{Sign}, \mathsf{Ver})$ be a signature scheme. We construct a PCSC scheme given by (Setup, KeygenA, KeygenB, Signcrypt, Decrypt, PCheck) as follows:

1. Setup: $\mathsf{Setup}(1^n) \to par$.
2. KeyGenA: $\mathsf{Gen}'(par) \to (pk_A, sk_A)$.
3. KeyGenB:
   (a) $\mathsf{Gen}(par) \to (pk_B, sk_B)$.
   (b) Choose a hash function $H : \{0,1\}^{k_1+k_2} \to \{0,1\}^k$.
   (c) The receiver B publishes pk_B, H and keeps sk_B as his decryption key.
4. Signcrypt: For a given message $m \in \{0,1\}^{k_1}$,
   (a) Choose $r \in_R \{0,1\}^{k_2}$.
   (b) Compute $\rho = H(m||r)$.
   (c) Set $c = \mathsf{Enc}(pk_B, m, \rho)$ and $\sigma = \mathsf{Sign}(sk_A, c||r)$.
   (d) Output signcryptext $\bar{c} = (c, \sigma, r)$.
5. Unsigncrypt: For a given signcryptext $\bar{c} = (c, \sigma, r)$,
   (a) If $\mathsf{Ver}(pk_A, c||r, \sigma) = 0$ or $\mathsf{Dec}(sk_B, c) = \perp$, return $\perp$.
   (b) Else compute $\mathsf{Dec}(sk_B, c) = m'$ and $\rho' = H(m'||r)$.
   (c) If $\mathsf{Enc}(pk_B, m', \rho') = c$, return m', else return $\perp$.
6. PCheck: For a given $\bar{c} = (c, \sigma, r)$ and a message m',
   (a) Compute $\rho' = H(m'||r)$
   (b) If $c = \mathsf{Enc}(pk_B, m', \rho')$ and $\mathsf{Ver}(pk_A, c||r, \sigma) = 1$, return 1, else return 0.

Remark 2. The proposed construction is almost as efficient as the standard encrypt-then-sign approach of constructing signcryption schemes, only computational overhead being evaluation of one hash value and the need of the transmitting the value r along with the signcryptext obtained by standard encrypt-then-sign approach. However, as PCSC is a signcryption scheme with an additional feature of plaintext checkability, its computational overhead and ciphertext expansion factor can not be better than the typical generic constructions of signcryption schemes.

Remark 3. From the point of view of size of the signcryptext $\bar{c}$, we would like to minimize the size of r, i.e., k_2. But, it should be done in accordance with the constraint that there should be an efficient hash function compressing $k_1 + k_2$ bit strings to k bit strings.

5   Security Analysis of Construction

In this section, we provide the security analysis of the proposed construction along the security model described in Sect. 3.1.

Theorem 1. *The proposed* $PCSC$ *is UNLINK in random oracle model if* Π *is PTOW.*

Proof. We will construct an algorithm $\mathcal{B}$ which finds a partial pre-image of Enc_Π using an UNLINK adversary $\mathcal{A} = (A_f, A_g)$ against $PCSC$. As an input, B is fed with pk_R of Π and a challenge ciphertext c^* generated by Enc_Π, whose partial pre-image is sought. $\mathcal{B}$ runs KeyGen_A to output (pk_A, sk_A). Finally, $\mathcal{B}$ simulates A_f with pk_R, pk_A, sk_A and answers the H oracle queries of A_f as follows:

Simulation of H-oracle: When A_f submits a H-query $m_i \| r_i$, $\mathcal{B}$ chooses a random $\rho_i \in \{0,1\}^k$ and returns ρ_i to $\mathcal{A}$. For each returned value, $\mathcal{B}$ maintains a list called H-list containing (m_i, r_i, ρ_i). For subsequent queries, $\mathcal{B}$ checks the H-list whether the query has been previously answered or not. For repeated queries, same value of ρ_i is returned whereas new queries are recorded in H-list.

  Once the first query phase is over, A_f returns two plaintexts $m_0, m_1 \in \{0,1\}^{k_1}$ to $\mathcal{B}$. $\mathcal{B}$ randomly chooses $b \in_R \{0,1\}, r_0, r_1 \in_R \{0,1\}^{k_2}, \rho_1 \in_R \{0,1\}^k$, sets $c_0 = c^*$ and computes $c_1 = \mathsf{Enc}(m_1, \rho_1), \sigma_0 = \mathsf{Sign}(sk_A, c_0 \| r_0), \sigma_1 = \mathsf{Sign}(sk_A, c_1 \| r_1)$. Finally, $\mathcal{B}$ simulates A_g with $\bar{c}_0 = (c_0, \sigma_0, r_0)$ and $\bar{c}_1 = (c_1, \sigma_1, r_1)$.

  In the second query phase, A_g is allowed to make H-queries as before. After the second query phase is over, A_g outputs a guess b' to $\mathcal{B}$ and $\mathcal{B}$ returns the set S consisting of the first coordinates of all the entries in the H-list.

  The theorem now follows immediately from the following lemma.

Lemma 1. *If ϵ be the advantage that given a valid signcryptext, A_g can correctly guess the bit b, then a partial pre-image of c^* is in S with probability greater than $\epsilon/2$.*

Proof. Let us assume that $c^* = \mathsf{Enc}(pk_B, m^*, \rho^*)$ for some (m^*, ρ^*). Because of injectivity of Enc, if such a pair exists, it is unique. In view of the simulated game, we define AskH to be the event that $m^* \| r_0$ is queried to the H-oracle, where r_0 is randomly chosen while simulating $\bar{c}_0 = (c_0, \sigma_0, r_0)$ and $\mathsf{Ask'H}$ to be the event that $m^* \| r'$ is queried to the H-oracle for some $r' \in \{0,1\}^{k_2}$.

  We say that the attacker wins the simulated game if AskH occurs or $b = b'$. With above simulation of H-oracle, it is clear that the above game perfectly simulates the real UNLINK game unless AskH occurs. Thus, $\mathsf{Adv}_\mathcal{A}^{\mathsf{sim}} \geq \mathsf{Adv}_\mathcal{A}^{\mathsf{real}} = \epsilon$. However, as no advantage can be gained without AskH, $\Pr[\mathsf{Wins}^{\mathsf{sim}}] = \Pr[b' = b] + \Pr[\mathsf{AskH}]$. As $\bar{c}_0$ is independent of the hidden bit b, $\Pr[b' = b] = \frac{1}{2}$. Thus, $\Pr[\mathsf{Wins}^{\mathsf{sim}}] = \frac{1}{2} + \Pr[\mathsf{AskH}]$. Therefore,

$$\epsilon \leq \mathsf{Adv}_\mathcal{A}^{\mathsf{sim}} = 2\Pr[\mathsf{Wins}^{\mathsf{sim}}] - 1 = 2\Pr[\mathsf{AskH}] < 2\Pr[\mathsf{Ask'H}]$$

$$\text{i.e., } \Pr[\mathsf{Ask'H}] > \frac{\epsilon}{2}.$$

  This means that with probability greater than $\frac{\epsilon}{2}$, m^* lies in the set S consisting of all first coordinate entries in the H-list.   □

Remark 4. The proposed $PCSC$ can also be shown to satisfy UNLINK in random oracle model if Π is taken to be IND-CPA secure. The proof technique is almost similar to that of Theorem 1 in [5].

Theorem 2. *PCSC is insider existential signcryptext unforgeable against chosen message attack in UF-PCSC-CMA sense in standard model if the underlying signature scheme SS is UF-CMA secure.*

Proof. We construct an UF-CMA adversary $\mathcal{B}$ against SS using an UF-PCSC-CMA adversary $\mathcal{A}$ against $PCSC$. $\mathcal{B}$ takes as input the common parameter par, a sender's public-key pk_A and a signing oracle $\mathcal{O}\mathsf{Sign}(sk_A, \cdot)$. $\mathcal{B}$ runs KeyGen_B $(par) \rightarrow (pk_B, sk_B)$ and chooses a hash function H of the form $H : \{0,1\}^{k_1+k_2} \rightarrow \{0,1\}^k$ and feeds $\mathcal{A}$ with par, pk_A, sk_B, pk_B and H. In the query phase, when $\mathcal{A}$ submits a signcryption query for m_i, $\mathcal{B}$ chooses $r_i \in_R \{0,1\}^{k_2}$ and computes $\rho_i = H(m_i||r_i)$ and $c_i = \mathsf{Enc}(pk_B, m_i, \rho_i)$. Then $\mathcal{B}$ queries the $\mathcal{O}\mathsf{Sign}(sk_A, \cdot)$ with $c_i||r_i$ to get a response σ_i and finally returns (c_i, σ_i, r_i) to $\mathcal{A}$. $\mathcal{B}$ also maintains a list, S-list, consisting of the queried messages, m_i's. Once the query phase is over, $\mathcal{A}$ outputs a signcryptext (c^*, σ^*, r^*) to $\mathcal{B}$. $\mathcal{B}$ returns $(c^*||r^*, \sigma^*)$ to the UF-CMA challenger $\mathcal{C}$.

Let U be the event that σ^* is a valid signature on $c^*||r^*$ i.e., $\mathsf{Ver}(pk_A, c^*||r^*, \sigma^*) = 1$ and $c^*||r^*$ has not been queried to the signing oracle $\mathcal{O}\mathsf{Sign}$ and V be the event that (c^*, σ^*, r^*) is a valid signcryptext i.e., $\mathsf{Unsigncrypt}(pk_A, sk_B, (c^*, \sigma^*, r^*)) = m^* \neq \perp$ and m^* has not been queried to the signcryption oracle $\mathcal{O}\mathsf{Signcrypt}$. Note that, if m^*, the underlying message of c^*, has not been submitted to the signcryption oracle $\mathcal{O}\mathsf{Signcrypt}(sk_A, pk_B, \cdot)$, then, as Enc is an injection, $c^*||r^*$ has not been queried to the signing oracle $\mathcal{O}\mathsf{Sign}(sk_A, \cdot)$, i.e., as per the simulation, the event U occurs only if the event V occurs. Hence, we have $Pr[\mathcal{B} \; wins] = Pr[U] \geq Pr[V] = Pr[\mathcal{A} \; wins]$.   □

6   Conclusion

In this paper, we have introduced a new primitive called Plaintext Checkable Signcryption (PCSC) and discussed its applications in certain functionalities. It was also noted that the proposed generic construction is almost as efficient as the standard encrypt-then-sign approach of constructing signcryption schemes, only overhead being evaluation of one hash value. A challenging issue for further research in this direction could be to construct a designated checker version of the above primitive, as in [8] along with its appropriate security notions.

Acknowledgement. The authors would like to thank Partha Sarathi Roy and Sabyasachi Dutta of University of Calcutta, India for several fruitful discussions during the work. The research is supported in part by NBHM, DAE, Government of India (No 2/48(10)/2013/NBHM(R.P.)/R&D II/695).

References

1. An, J.H., Dodis, Y., Rabin, T.: On the security of joint signature and encryption. In: Knudsen, L.R. (ed.) EUROCRYPT 2002. LNCS, vol. 2332, pp. 83–107. Springer, Heidelberg (2002)

2. Baek, J., Steinfeld, R., Zheng, Y.: Formal proofs for the security of signcryption. J. Cryptology **20**(2), 203–235 (2007)
3. Bellare, M., Rogaway, P.: Random oracles are practical: a paradigm for designing efficient protocols. In: Proceedings of the 1st CCS, 62–73. ACM Press, New York (1993)
4. Boneh, D., Di Crescenzo, G., Ostrovsky, R., Persiano, G.: Public Key Encryption with Keyword Search. In: Cachin, C., Camenisch, J.L. (eds.) EUROCRYPT 2004. LNCS, vol. 3027, pp. 506–522. Springer, Heidelberg (2004)
5. Canard, S., Fuchsbauer, G., Gouget, A., Laguillaumie, F.: Plaintext-Checkable Encryption. In: Dunkelman, O. (ed.) CT-RSA 2012. LNCS, vol. 7178, pp. 332–348. Springer, Heidelberg (2012)
6. Das, A., Adhikari, A.: Signcryption from randomness recoverable PKE revisited. In: Bagchi, A., Ray, I. (eds.) ICISS 2013. LNCS, vol. 8303, pp. 78–90. Springer, Heidelberg (2013)
7. Das, A., Adhikari, A.: Signcryption with delayed identification, ICMC 2013. Springer Proc. Math. Stat. **91**, 23–40 (2014)
8. Das, A., Adhikari, A., Sakurai, K.: Plaintext checkable encryption with designated checker. Adv. Math. Commun. **9**(1), 37–53 (2015)
9. Selvi, S.S.D., Vivek, S.S., Shriram, J., Kalaivani, S., Rangan, C.P.: Identity based aggregate signcryption schemes. In: Roy, B., Sendrier, N. (eds.) INDOCRYPT 2009. LNCS, vol. 5922, pp. 378–397. Springer, Heidelberg (2009)
10. Fuhr, T., Paillier, P.: Decryptable searchable encryption. In: Susilo, W., Liu, J.K., Mu, Y. (eds.) ProvSec 2007. LNCS, vol. 4784, pp. 228–236. Springer, Heidelberg (2007)
11. Ibraimi, L., Nikova, S., Hartel, P., Jonker, W.: Public-Key encryption with delegated search. In: Lopez, J., Tsudik, G. (eds.) ACNS 2011. LNCS, vol. 6715, pp. 532–549. Springer, Heidelberg (2011)
12. Hang, Q., Wong, D.S., Yang, G.: Heterogeneous signcryption with key privacy. Comput. J. **54**(4), 525–536 (2011)
13. Ma, C., Chen, K., Zheng, D., Liu, S.: Efficient and proactive threshold signcryption. In: Zhou, J., López, J., Deng, R.H., Bao, F. (eds.) ISC 2005. LNCS, vol. 3650, pp. 233–243. Springer, Heidelberg (2005)
14. Malone-Lee, J.: Identity-Based Signcryption, Cryptology ePrint Archive, Report 2002/098. http://eprint.iacr.org/2002/098
15. Pointcheval, D.: Chosen-ciphertext security for any one-way cryptosystem. In: Imai, H., Zheng, Y. (eds.) PKC 2000. LNCS, vol. 1751, pp. 129–146. Springer, Heidelberg (2000)
16. Zheng, Y.: Digital signcryption or how to achieve cost (signature & encryption) << cost(signature) + cost(encryption. In: Kaliski Jr, B.S. (ed.) CRYPTO 1997. Lecture Notes in Computer Science, vol. 1294, pp. 165–179. Springer, Heidelberg (1997)

A New Distinguisher on Grain
v1 for 106 Rounds

Santanu Sarkar[✉]

Department of Mathematics, Indian Institute of Technology,
Sardar Patel Road, Chennai 600036, India
sarkar.santanu.bir@gmail.com

Abstract. In Asiacrypt 2010, Knellwolf, Meier and Naya-Plasencia proposed distinguishing attacks on Grain v1 when (i) Key Scheduling process is reduced to 97 rounds using 2^{27} chosen IVs and (ii) Key Scheduling process is reduced to 104 rounds using 2^{35} chosen IVs. Using similar idea, Banik obtained a new distinguisher for 105 rounds. In this paper, we show similar approach can work for 106 rounds. We present a new distinguisher on Grain v1 for 106 rounds with success probability 63 %.

Keywords: Differential cryptanalysis · Distinguisher · Grain v1 · Stream cipher

1 Introduction

The Grain v1 is a well-known hardware-efficient, synchronous and bit oriented stream cipher. Designed in 2005 by Hell, Johansson and Meier [18], it has been widely studied for nearly a decade mostly because of its simplistic structure and selection in the eStream hardware profile (profile 2) portfolio [14]. In order to prevent the correlation attacks [6] on Grain v0, the modified versions Grain v1 [18] was proposed after incorporating certain changes. Grain 128 and Grain 128a are inspired from Grain v1, and use a similar structure.

Küçük et al. [9] proposed related key-IV attack on Grain v1. They observed that for any (K, IV) pair, there exist related (K', IV') pair with probability 0.25 that generates 1-bit shifted keystream. Bjørstad [7] showed that Grain v1 has a low resistance to BWS sampling. Other cryptanalytic results related to this cipher have been presented in [15,16,19,24,25,27,28].

In [8], an attack on nonlinear filter generators with linear resynchronization and filter function with few inputs is presented. To avoid such attacks, the initialization of stream ciphers should be designed carefully. The common design paradigm (including the Grain family) of stream ciphers is as follows. The key K and initialization vector IV are loaded into the state along with some padding bits. Next, state update function is applied to the internal state iteratively for a number of rounds without producing any output (key-stream). Hence, the number of rounds is important for both security and efficiency of the cipher, since increasing the number of rounds will slow down the cipher, but at the same time

© Springer International Publishing Switzerland 2015
S. Jajodia and C. Mazumdar (Eds.): ICISS 2015, LNCS 9478, pp. 334–344, 2015.
DOI: 10.1007/978-3-319-26961-0_20

likely to increase the security. Hence, finding the minimal number of rounds that would ensure the conjectured security level is a critical task, and studying the ciphers in its reduced variant (i.e., treating as if the key-streams are available just after the key & IV are loaded to the register).

Trivium [10], another candidate in the hardware profile of eStream, has been cryptanlysed for reduced round by many researchers. Englund et al. [15] showed statistical weaknesses on Trivium for 736 rounds. Aumasson et al. [1] were able to build a distinguisher on Trivium after 790 round. Independently Knellwolf et al. [21] built a distinguisher up to 806 rounds.

Grain v1 is studied extensively for reduced round. In [2], a non-randomness for 81 round has been reported. In [20], Knellwolf et al. proposed a distinguisher for 97 rounds and 104 rounds. However results of [20] were based on experiments only. Later, Banik [3] proved a theoretical result for 97 rounds. Recently a distinguisher for 105 round has been proposed in [4]. These attacks on Grain v1 are known as *Conditional Differential Cryptanalysis* (CDC), which was first introduced by Ben-Aroya and Biham [5] for block cipher cryptanalysis. It studies the output frequency of derivatives of output bit on specifically chosen IV.

However, in recent terminology, CDC on stream cipher can be described as dynamic cube attack. Cube attacks, introduced by Dinur and Shamir [12], have been used in cryptanalysis. Although cube attack works [11,13] successfully on Grain 128, its performance on Grain v1 is not that effective. Using CDC, Knellwolf et al., in their Asiacrypt 2010 paper [20] obtained a practical distinguisher on Grain 128 for 215 rounds. Higher order conditional differential attacks on Trivium and Grain 128 have been studied in [22]. CDC has been applied successfully in [23] on Grain 128a. In this paper, we show that one can attack Grain v1 up to 106 rounds using CDC method.

The paper is organized as follows. In Sect. 2, we describe the design of Grain v1. We present our experimental results in Sect. 3. Section 4 gives a new distinguisher on Grain v1 up to 106 rounds. Conclusion is presented in Sect. 5.

2   Brief Description of Grain v1

Grain v1 has 80 bit key K and 64 bit initialization vector IV. The structure of the Grain v1 is depicted in Fig. 1. The state consists an 80-bit LFSR and an 80-bit NFSR. The update function of the LFSR is given by: $y_{t+80} = f(Y_t)$, where $Y_t = [y_t, y_{t+1}, \ldots, y_{t+79}]$ is an 80-bit vector that denotes the LFSR state at the tth clock interval and f is a linear function on the LFSR state bits obtained from a primitive polynomial in $GF(2)$ of degree 80. The NFSR state is updated as $x_{t+80} = y_t \oplus g(X_t)$. Here, $X_t = [x_t, x_{t+1}, \ldots, x_{t+79}]$ is an 80-bit vector that denotes the NFSR state at the tth clock interval and g is a non-linear function of the NFSR state bits.

The output keystream is produced by combining the LFSR and NFSR bits as $z_t = h'(X_t, Y_t) = \bigoplus_{a \in A} x_{t+a} \oplus h(X_t, Y_t)$, where A is some fixed subset of $\{0, 1, 2, \ldots, n-1\}$. Below we present the detailed description.

As stated, the key-stream generation of Grain v1 consists of three phases. In the first phase, the key & IV bits are loaded to the state register in the *Key Loading Algorithm* routine; then the state bits are updated during the *Key Scheduling Algorithm* routine; and next the *Pesudo-Random Generation Algorithm* routine produces the key-streams. These routines are described as follows.

Key Loading Algorithm (KLA). The key (80-bits) is loaded in the NFSR and the IV(64-bits) is loaded in the 0th to the 63th bits of the LFSR. The remaining 64th to 79th bits of the LFSR are loaded with 1.

Key Scheduling Algorithm (KSA). After the KLA, for the first 160 clocks, the keystream produced at the output point of the function h' is XOR-ed to both the LFSR and NFSR update functions. So during the first 160 clock intervals, the LFSR and the NFSR bits are updated as $y_{t+80} = z_t \oplus f(Y_t)$, $x_{t+80} = y_t \oplus z_t \oplus g(X_t)$.

Pseudo-Random Keystream Generation Algorithm (PRGA). After the completion of the KSA, z_t is no longer XOR-ed to the LFSR and the NFSR but it is used as the Pseudo-Random keystream bit. Hence in this phase, the LFSR and NFSR are updated as $y_{t+80} = f(Y_t), x_{t+80} = y_t \oplus g(X_t)$.

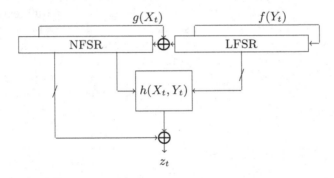

Fig. 1. Structure of stream cipher in grain family

The LFSR update rule is given by $y_{t+80} = y_{t+62} \oplus y_{t+51} \oplus y_{t+38} \oplus y_{t+23} \oplus y_{t+13} \oplus y_t$. The NFSR state is updated as $x_{t+80} = y_t \oplus g(x_{t+63}, x_{t+62}, x_{t+60}, x_{t+52}, x_{t+45}, x_{t+37}, x_{t+33}, x_{t+28}, x_{t+21}, x_{t+15}, x_{t+14}, x_{t+9}, x_t)$, where,

$$g(x_{t+63}, x_{t+62}, x_{t+60}, x_{t+52}, x_{t+45}, x_{t+37}, x_{t+33}, x_{t+28}, x_{t+21}, x_{t+15}, x_{t+14}, x_{t+9}, x_t)$$
$$= x_{t+62} \oplus x_{t+60} \oplus x_{t+52} \oplus x_{t+45} \oplus x_{t+37} \oplus x_{t+33} \oplus x_{t+28}$$
$$\oplus x_{t+21} \oplus x_{t+14} \oplus x_{t+9} \oplus x_t \oplus x_{t+63}x_{t+60} \oplus x_{t+37}x_{t+33} \oplus x_{t+15}x_{t+9}$$
$$\oplus x_{t+60}x_{t+52}x_{t+45} \oplus x_{t+33}x_{t+28}x_{t+21} \oplus x_{t+63}x_{t+45}x_{t+28}x_{t+9}$$

$$+ x_{t+60}x_{t+52}x_{t+37}x_{t+33} \oplus x_{t+63}x_{t+60}x_{t+21}x_{t+15}$$

$$\oplus x_{t+63}x_{t+60}x_{t+52}x_{t+45}x_{t+37} \oplus x_{t+33}x_{t+28}x_{t+21}x_{t+15}x_{t+9}$$

$$\oplus x_{t+52}x_{t+45}x_{t+37}x_{t+33}x_{t+28}x_{t+21}.$$

The key-stream is produced by combining the LFSR and NFSR bits as:

$$z_t = \bigoplus_{a \in A} x_{t+a} \oplus h(y_{t+3}, y_{t+25}, y_{t+46}, y_{t+64}, x_{t+63}),$$

where, $A = \{1, 2, 4, 10, 31, 43, 56\}$ and $h(s_0, s_1, s_2, s_3, s_4) = s_1 \oplus s_4 \oplus s_0 s_3 \oplus s_2 s_3 \oplus s_3 s_4 \oplus s_0 s_1 s_2 \oplus s_0 s_2 s_3 \oplus s_0 s_2 s_4 \oplus s_1 s_2 s_4 \oplus s_2 s_3 s_4$.

3   Biases Beyond 105 Rounds of KSA

As evident from the description, the NFSR update function used in Grain v1 is of degree 6. So symbolic expressions (treating the key & IV as symbolic variables and then doing the state update operation) of Grain v1 grow very fast. In Fig. 2, we show the number of monomials in key-stream expression of Grain v1 over some initial rounds.

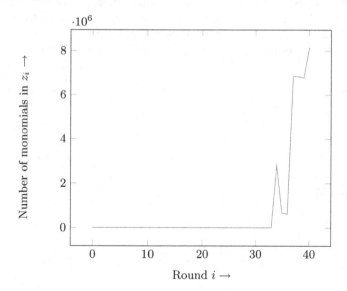

Fig. 2. Growth of key-stream expression of Grain v1

As mentioned, Knellwolf et al. [20] observed a new distinguisher on Grain v1. Now we briefly explain how one can interpret the idea of [20] as a dynamic cube attack. Recall from Sect. 2 that Grain v1 contains 80-bit key $k_0, \ldots, k_{79}$ and 64-bit IV $v_0, \ldots, v_{63}$. Grain v1 is initially loaded with $X_0 = [k_0, \ldots, k_{79}]$ and

$Y_0 = [v_0, \ldots, v_{63}, \overbrace{1, \ldots, 1}^{16}]$ (here X_0 corresponds to NFSR and Y_0 corresponds to LFSR).

Next start with NFSR $X_0' = [k_0, \ldots, k_{79}]$ but different LFSR $Y_0' = [v_0, \ldots, 1 \oplus v_{37}, v_{63}, \overbrace{1, \ldots, 1}^{16}]$. That is, in cube attack terminologies, v_{37} is chosen as cube. Thus two states S_0 and S_0' initialized by (X_0, Y_0) and (X_0', Y_0') are different only at one position. Suppose z_i and z_i' are the key stream bits for S_0 and S_0' respectively at i-th round of KSA. They observed experimentally that if $z_{12} = z_{12}', z_{34} = z_{34}', z_{40} = z_{40}'$ in KSA and KSA is reduced to 97 rounds, the first output bit in PRGA will be same with probability more than 0.5. In ACISP 2014, Banik [3] gave the theoretical justification for this result.

Recently, Banik [4] showed a distinguishing attack for 105 round. Instead of 37-th bit of IV, he chose 61-bit of IV for the differential. In his work, it is considered the equality of $z_{15} = z_{15}', z_{36} = z_{36}', z_{39} = z_{39}'$ and $z_{42} = z_{42}'$ in KSA.

In this paper, we experiment for all single IV differential. Thus we have a total of 64 differentials. For any such differential, in the initial rounds of KSA, it is highly likely that $z_i = z_i'$ is satisfied. We load symbolically with $X_0 = [k_0, \ldots, k_{79}]$ in NFSR and $Y_0 = [v_0, \ldots, v_{63}, \overbrace{1, \ldots, 1}^{16}]$ in Sage [26]. Next we run KSA for few rounds, and find z_i as a polynomial of $k_0, \ldots, k_{79}, v_0, \ldots, v_{63}$. For each v_j, we identify first four rounds where coefficient of v_j in z_i is not constant for $0 \le j \le 63$. We identify these rounds using Algorithm 1. In step 3 of the algorithm, $\mathcal{I}_A$ corresponds to the ideal generated by a set of polynomials in A.

Input: v_j, z_i and an empty array A
Output: An array A

1 $i = 0$;

2 **while** $\Big(\text{Coefficient } c_{ij} \text{ of } v_j \text{ in } z_i \text{ is nonconstant } \& |A| < 4\Big)$ **do**

3   **if** $c_{i,j} \notin \mathcal{I}_A$ **then**

4 | Include $c_{i,j}$ in A ;

      end

5      $i = i + 1$;

   end

Algorithm 1. Generating polynomial equations in KSA

Conditions for each differential are presented in Appendix A. We find the probability of the equality of the first output keystream bits for each KSA round 105 to 128. Our probability is taken over 2^{30} random key-IV.

Our experimental values have been presented in Fig. 3 for rounds 105 to 110. Here x axis corresponds to the rounds of KSA, y corresponds to each differential and z corresponds the equality of output keystream bits. From the Fig. 3, it is

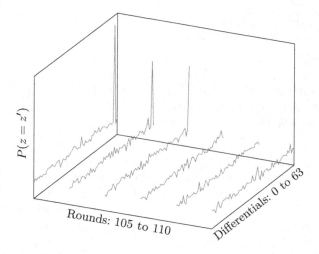

Fig. 3. Basies from 105 to 110 rounds of KSA for each single bit differential on IV

clear we may get distinguisher using the similar idea of [20] for 106 and 107 rounds. In fact, we observe

$$P\big(z_{105} = z'_{105} \mid z_{15} = z'_{15} \ \& \ z_{36} = z'_{36} \ \& \ z_{39} = z'_{39} \ \& \ z_{42} = z'_{42}\big) = 0.500365,$$

$$P\big(z_{106} = z'_{106} \mid z_{16} = z'_{16} \ \& \ z_{34} = z'_{34} \ \& \ z_{37} = z'_{37} \ \& \ z_{40} = z'_{40}\big) = 0.500245,$$

$$P\big(z_{107} = z'_{107} \mid z_{17} = z'_{17} \ \& \ z_{35} = z'_{35} \ \& \ z_{38} = z'_{38} \ \& \ z_{41} = z'_{41}\big) = 0.500246,$$

when differentials are given on v_{61}, v_{62} and v_{63} respectively.

After 107 rounds, all curves become almost flat. Thus it seems beyond 107 rounds, it might not be possible to attack Grain v1 using single differentiable.

4 New Result on Grain v1: Distinguisher upto 106 Rounds

Grain v1 is first intialised with $X_0 = [k_0, \ldots, k_{79}]$ and $Y_0 = [v_0, \ldots, v_{63}, \overbrace{1, \ldots, 1}^{16}]$. Here X_0 corresponds to NFSR and Y_0 corresponds to LFSR.

Now choose v_{62} as cube. Hence start with NFSR $X'_0 = [k_0, \ldots, k_{79}]$ but different LFSR $Y'_0 = [v_0, \ldots, 1 \oplus v_{62}, v_{63}, \overbrace{1, \ldots, 1}^{16}]$.

Thus two states S_0 and S'_0 initialized by (X_0, Y_0) and (X'_0, Y'_0) different only at one position. But when more and more KSA rounds are completed, more and more positions of the states will differ. The idea is to delay the diffusion of the differential for as many KSA rounds as possible, by imposing many algebraic conditions over key and IV. We find algebraic expressions using Sage [26]. The conditions may be classified in to two types:

- **Type 1:** Conditions only on IV
- **Type 2:** Conditions on both Key and IV.

Let z_t and z'_t be the bit produced in the t-th KSA round when states are loaded by (X_0, Y_0) and (X'_0, Y'_0). Recall for r-th reduced version of Grain v1, all bits z_i, z'_i are unknown to the attacker for $i < r$. But giving Type 1 and Type 2 conditions, attacker can guarantee that $z_i \oplus z'_i = 0$ for few initial rounds. The attack idea is as follows:

1. For $i = 0, \ldots, 15$, it is not difficult to show that $z_i = z'_i$. Hence we do not need any condition to make $z_i \oplus z'_i = 0$ for $0 \leq i \leq 15$.
2. When $i = 16$, $z_i \oplus z'_i$ is polynomial degree 2 over Key and IV. Now we set $v_{19} = v_{41} = 1, v_{46} = 0$ and $v_0 = k_1 \oplus k_2 \oplus k_4 \oplus k_{10} \oplus k_{31} \oplus k_{43} \oplus k_{56} \oplus v_3 \oplus v_{13} \oplus v_{23} \oplus v_{25} \oplus v_{38} \oplus v_{51}$. Then $z_{16} = z'_{16}$. Thus we have three Type 1 conditions $v_{19} = v_{41} = 1, v_{46} = 0$ and one Type 2 condition $C_1 : v_0 = k_1 \oplus k_2 \oplus k_4 \oplus k_{10} \oplus k_{31} \oplus k_{43} \oplus k_{56} \oplus v_3 \oplus v_{13} \oplus v_{23} \oplus v_{25} \oplus v_{38} \oplus v_{51}$.
3. For $i = 17, \ldots, 26$, z_i will be always equal to z'_i.
4. When $i = 27$, z_{27} will be always different from z'_{27}. So by imposing any conditions, we can not make $z_{27} \oplus z'_{27} = 0$.
5. z_i will be always equal to z'_i for $i = 28, \ldots, 33$.
6. When $i = 34$, $z_{34} \oplus z'_{34}$ will be an algebraic expression on Key and IV. However if attacker sets 17 Type 1 conditions $v_2 = v_{15} \oplus v_{18} \oplus v_{25} \oplus v_{31} \oplus v_{40} \oplus v_{53} \oplus v_{56} \oplus v_{59}, v_{63} = 0, v_{14} = v_{24} \oplus v_{39} \oplus v_{52}, v_{13} = v_{23} \oplus v_{38} \oplus v_{51}, v_{17} = v_{42}, v_{43} = 0, v_{47} = 0, v_{38} = 0, v_4 = 0, v_1 = 0, v_5 = 0, v_{20} = 0, v_{21} = 0, v_{26} = 0, v_{27} = 0, v_{37} = 0, v_{48} = 0$ and one Type 2 condition

$$C_2 : v_{59} = f_1(K),$$

where $f_1(K)$ is a polynomial over Key of degree 16 and 9108 monomials, $z_{34} = z'_{34}$.

7. We have $z_i = z'_i$ for $i = 35, 36$.
8. When $i = 37$, again $z_{37} \oplus z'_{37}$ will be an algebraic expression on Key and IV. Now attacker sets 7 Type 1 conditions $v_{15} = v_{18} \oplus v_{25} \oplus v_{31} \oplus v_{53} \oplus v_{55} \oplus v_{56} \oplus v_{59}, v_{16} = v_{54}, v_{49} = 1, v_{28} = 0, v_6 = 0, v_{50} = 0, v_{23} = v_{45}$ and two Type 2 conditions

$$C_3 : v_3 = k_4 \oplus k_5 \oplus k_7 \oplus k_{13} \oplus k_{34} \oplus k_{46} \oplus k_{59} \oplus k_{66}$$
$$C_4 : v_7 = v_{29} \oplus f_2(K),$$

where $f_2(K)$ is a polynomial over Key of degree 15 and 1535 monomials. Then we have $z_{37} = z'_{37}$.

9. We have $z_i = z'_i$ for $i = 38, 39$.
10. If we set 7 Type 1 conditions $v_{58} = v_7, v_{57} = v_{44} \oplus v_{29}, v_{51} = 0, v_{52} = 0, v_{10} = 0, v_{32} = 0, v_{53} = 0$ and 2 Type 2 conditions

$$C_5 : v_9 = k_7 \oplus k_8 \oplus k_{10} \oplus k_{16} \oplus k_{37} \oplus k_{49} \oplus k_{62} \oplus v_{31}$$
$$C_6 : v_8 = f_3(K),$$

where $f_3(K)$ is a polynomial over Key of degree 15 and 1572 monomials, $z_{40} = z'_{40}$.

Thus we have a total of 34 Type 1 conditions and 6 Type 2 conditions $C_1, \ldots, C_6$. We can rewrite the Type 2 conditions as

$$C_1 : v_0 = K_1 \oplus v_3 \oplus v_{13} \oplus v_{23} \oplus v_{25} \oplus v_{38} \oplus v_{51},$$
$$C_2 : v_{59} = K_2,$$
$$C_3 : v_3 = K_3,$$
$$C_4 : v_7 = K_4 \oplus v_{29},$$
$$C_5 : v_9 = K_5 \oplus v_{31},$$
$$C_6 : v_8 = K_6,$$

where K_is are function of Key only for $1 \le i \le 6$. Hence for fixed Key, K_is are fixed.

Now since attacker does not know the values $K_1, \ldots, K_6$, he has to consider all combinations. Let $U = [K_1, K_2, K_3, K_4, K_5, K_6]$. Then for each $U \in \{0,1\}^6$, attacker chooses such that

$$\left\{ v_{19} = v_{41} = 1, v_{46} = 0, v_{63} = 0, v_{14} = v_{24} \oplus v_{39} \oplus v_{52}, \right.$$

$$v_{13} = v_{23} \oplus v_{38} \oplus v_{51}, v_{17} = v_{42}, v_{43} = 0, v_{47} = 0, v_{38} = 0,$$
$$v_4 = 0, v_1 = 0, v_5 = 0, v_{20} = 0, v_{21} = 0, v_{26} = 0, v_{27} = 0,$$
$$v_{37} = 0, v_{48} = 0, v_{49} = 1, v_{28} = 0, v_6 = 0, v_{50} = 0,$$
$$v_{23} = v_{45}, v_{51} = 0, v_{52} = 0, v_{10} = 0, v_{32} = 0, v_{53} = 0,$$
$$v_0 = K_1 \oplus v_3 \oplus v_{13} \oplus v_{23} \oplus v_{25} \oplus v_{38} \oplus v_{51}$$

$$\left. v_{59} = K_2, v_3 = K_3, v_7 = K_4 \oplus v_{29}, v_9 = K_5 \oplus v_{31}, v_8 = K_6 \right\}$$

Hence for the correct choice of $K_1, \ldots, K_6$, we have $z_{16} = z'_{16}, z_{34} = z'_{34}, z_{37} = z'_{37}$ and $z_{40} = z'_{40}$.

Note that due to Type 1 conditions, IV space is reduced to $\{0,1\}^{64-34} - \{0,1\}^{30}$. Corresponding to 6 Type 2 conditions, attacker divides this space into $2^6 = 64$ partitions. Here free IV variables are: $v_{11}, v_{12}, v_{18}, v_{22}, v_{24}, v_{25}, v_{29}, v_{30}, v_{31}, v_{33}, v_{34}, v_{35}, v_{36}, v_{39}, v_{40}, v_{42}, v_{44}, v_{45}, v_{54}, v_{55}, v_{56}, v_{60}, v_{61}$.

Since there are 6 expressions on the unknown key, the attacker chooses all 64 options. Among these 64 options, one must be correct. For each option, attacker takes the dynamic variables $v_0, v_{59}, v_3, v_7, v_9, v_8$ accordingly. So for fixed key, we have 64 values corresponds to the probability $P(z_{106} = z'_{106})$ for each Type 2 condition. We use the idea as follows.

We consider only those probabilities for which $P(z_{106} = z'_{106}) > 0.5$, and we add all such probabilities. Let the sum of these probabilities be S. For the random case, this sum will be

$$S_R = 64 \times \frac{1}{\sqrt{2\pi}\sigma} \int_{Np}^{N} e^{-\frac{(x-\mu)^2}{2\sigma^2}} \left(\frac{x}{N} - p \right) dx, \tag{1}$$

where N is the size of sample space, $\mu = \frac{N}{2}, \sigma^2 = \frac{N}{4}$ and $p = 0.5$. For $N = 2^{23}$, value of S_R will be 0.0044.

From our experiment with 1000 random keys, we observe that for 63 % situations, the sum in Eq. (1) for Grain v1 is greater than 0.0044 when we are using all 23 free IV variables. Thus we can distinguish Grain v1 from random source up to 106 rounds with success probability 0.63.

We try similar idea for 107 rounds. But the algebraic expressions for 107 rounds are much more complicated. Hence getting constraints on Key and IV i.e., Type 1 and Type 2 conditions would be very difficult for this case.

5   Conclusion

In this paper, we have first presented experimental results for all single bit differential on IV. From these experiments, it seems that one may find a distinguisher on Grain v1 for 106 and 107 rounds. Then we have presented our result Grain v1 for 106 rounds. We have shown that it is possible to divide the search space into 64 partitions so that for one partition of IV values the differential of key stream bits at certain positions will be zero. Experiments show that one can distinguish Grain v1 for 106 rounds with 63 % success probability.

From our experiments, it seems one may attack Grain v1 up to 107 rounds. However, in this case the conditions are much more complicated. We leave this as an open problem.

Appendix A: Condition on Key-Stream for Different Locations

Shaded conditions for 37 and 61 are previously explored by others [4, 20]. In this paper, we consider the conditions for 62 (Table 1).

Table 1. Different KSA round numbers for different IV locations.

Location	Rounds	Location	Rounds	Location	Rounds	Location	Rounds
0	16 17 34 35	16	13 33 35 36	32	7 29 35 41	48	2 23 41 42
1	17 18 35 36	17	14 34 36 37	33	8 30 36 42	49	3 24 42 43
2	19 34 35 36	18	15 34 35 37	34	9 31 37 43	50	4 25 43 44
3	0 20 35 36	19	16 35 36 38	35	10 32 38 44	51	5 16 26 34
4	1 21 36 37	20	17 36 37 39	36	11 33 39 45	52	6 17 27 35
5	2 22 37 38	21	18 37 38 40	37	12 34 40 46	53	7 28 34 35
6	3 23 38 39	22	19 38 39 41	38	13 16 34 35	54	8 29 35 36
7	4 24 39 40	23	16 20 34 39	39	14 17 35 36	55	9 30 36 37
8	5 25 40 41	24	17 21 35 40	40	15 34 35 36	56	10 31 34 37
9	6 26 41 42	25	0 22 34 35	41	16 34 35 36	57	11 32 35 38
10	7 27 42 43	26	1 23 35 36	42	17 35 36 37	58	12 33 36 39
11	8 28 43 44	27	2 24 36 37	43	18 36 37 38	59	13 34 37 40
12	9 29 44 45	28	3 25 37 38	44	19 37 38 39	60	14 35 38 41
13	10 16 30 34	29	4 26 38 39	45	20 38 39 40	61	15 36 39 42
14	11 17 31 35	30	5 27 39 40	46	0 21 39 40	62	16 34 37 40
15	12 32 34 35	31	6 28 34 40	47	1 22 40 41	63	17 35 38 41

References

1. Aumasson, J.-P., Dinur, I., Meier, W., Shamir, A.: Cube testers and key recovery attacks on reduced-round MD6 and trivium. In: Dunkelman, O. (ed.) FSE 2009. LNCS, vol. 5665, pp. 1–22. Springer, Heidelberg (2009)
2. Aumasson, J.P., Dinur, I., Henzen, L., Meier, W., Shamir, A.: Efficient FPGA implementations of high-dimensional cube testers on the stream cipher Grain-128. In: SHARCS - Special-Purpose Hardware for Attacking Cryptographic Systems (2009)
3. Banik, S.: Some insights into differential cryptanalysis of grain v1. In: Susilo, W., Mu, Y. (eds.) ACISP 2014. LNCS, vol. 8544, pp. 34–49. Springer, Heidelberg (2014)
4. Banik, S.: A Dynamic Cube Attack on 105 round Grain v1. IACR Cryptology ePrint Archive 2014: 652. http://eprint.iacr.org/2014/652
5. Ben-Aroya, I., Biham, E.: Differential cryptanalysis of lucifer. In: Stinson, D.R. (ed.) CRYPTO 1993. LNCS, vol. 773, pp. 187–199. Springer, Heidelberg (1994)
6. Berbain, C., Gilbert, H., Maximov, A.: Cryptanalysis of grain. In: Robshaw, M. (ed.) FSE 2006. LNCS, vol. 4047, pp. 15–29. Springer, Heidelberg (2006)
7. Bjørstad, T.E.: Cryptanalysis of Grain using Time/Memory/Data tradeoffs (v1.0/2008–02-25). http://www.ecrypt.eu.org/stream
8. Daemen, J., Govaerts, R., Vandewalle, J.: Resynchronization weaknesses in synchronous stream ciphers. In: Helleseth, T. (ed.) EUROCRYPT 1993. LNCS, vol. 765, pp. 159–167. Springer, Heidelberg (1994)
9. De Cannière, C., Küçük, Ö., Preneel, B.: Analysis of grain's initialization algorithm. In: Vaudenay, S. (ed.) AFRICACRYPT 2008. LNCS, vol. 5023, pp. 276–289. Springer, Heidelberg (2008)
10. De Cannière, C., Preneel, B.: Trivium. http://www.ecrypt.eu.org/stream/p3ciphers/trivium/trivium_p3.pdf
11. Dinur, I., Güneysu, T., Paar, C., Shamir, A., Zimmermann, R.: An experimentally verified attack on full grain-128 using dedicated reconfigurable hardware. In: Lee, D.H., Wang, X. (eds.) ASIACRYPT 2011. LNCS, vol. 7073, pp. 327–343. Springer, Heidelberg (2011)
12. Dinur, I., Shamir, A.: Cube attacks on tweakable black box polynomials. In: Joux, A. (ed.) EUROCRYPT 2009. LNCS, vol. 5479, pp. 278–299. Springer, Heidelberg (2009)
13. Dinur, I., Shamir, A.: Breaking grain-128 with dynamic cube attacks. In: Joux, A. (ed.) FSE 2011. LNCS, vol. 6733, pp. 167–187. Springer, Heidelberg (2011)
14. The ECRYPT Stream Cipher Project. eSTREAM Portfolio of Stream Ciphers. Accepted 8 September 2008
15. Englund, H., Johansson, T., Sönmez Turan, M.: A framework for chosen IV statistical analysis of stream ciphers. In: Srinathan, K., Rangan, C.P., Yung, M. (eds.) INDOCRYPT 2007. LNCS, vol. 4859, pp. 268–281. Springer, Heidelberg (2007)
16. Fischer, S., Khazaei, S., Meier, W.: Chosen IV statistical analysis for key recovery attacks on stream ciphers. In: Vaudenay, S. (ed.) AFRICACRYPT 2008. LNCS, vol. 5023, pp. 236–245. Springer, Heidelberg (2008)
17. Fredricksen, H.: A survey of full length nonlinear shift register cycle algorithms. SIAM Rev. **24**(1982), 195–221 (1982)
18. Hell, M., Johansson, T., Meier, W.: Grain - A Stream Cipher for Constrained Environments. ECRYPT Stream Cipher Project Report 2005/001 (2005). http://www.ecrypt.eu.org/stream

19. Khazaei, S., Hassanzadeh, M., Kiaei, M.: Distinguishing Attack on Grain. ECRYPT Stream Cipher Project Report 2005/071 (2005). http://www.ecrypt.eu. org/stream
20. Knellwolf, S., Meier, W., Naya-Plasencia, M.: Conditional differential cryptanalysis of NLFSR-based cryptosystems. In: Abe, M. (ed.) ASIACRYPT 2010. LNCS, vol. 6477, pp. 130–145. Springer, Heidelberg (2010)
21. Knellwolf, S., Meier, W., Naya-Plasencia, M.: Conditional differential cryptanalysis of trivium and KATAN. In: Miri, A., Vaudenay, S. (eds.) SAC 2011. LNCS, vol. 7118, pp. 200–212. Springer, Heidelberg (2012)
22. Knellwolf, S., Meier, W.: High order differential attacks on stream ciphers. Crypt. Commun. 4(3–4), 203–215 (2012)
23. Lehmann, M., Meier, W.: Conditional differential cryptanalysis of grain-128a. In: Pieprzyk, J., Sadeghi, A.-R., Manulis, M. (eds.) CANS 2012. LNCS, vol. 7712, pp. 1–11. Springer, Heidelberg (2012)
24. Lee, Y., Jeong, K., Sung, J., Hong, S.H.: Related-key chosen IV attacks on grain-v1 and grain-128. In: Mu, Y., Susilo, W., Seberry, J. (eds.) ACISP 2008. LNCS, vol. 5107, pp. 321–335. Springer, Heidelberg (2008)
25. Mihaljevic, M.J., Gangopadhyay, S., Paul, G., Imai, H.: Internal state recovery of grain-v1 employing normality order of the filter function. IET Inf. Secur. 6(2), 55–64 (2012)
26. Stein, W.: Sage Mathematics Software. Free Software Foundation Inc. (2009). http://www.sagemath.org. (Open source project initiated by W. Stein and contributed by many)
27. Stankovski, P.: Greedy distinguishers and nonrandomness detectors. In: Gong, G., Gupta, K.C. (eds.) INDOCRYPT 2010. LNCS, vol. 6498, pp. 210–226. Springer, Heidelberg (2010)
28. Zhang, H., Wang, X.: Cryptanalysis of Stream Cipher Grain Family. IACR Cryptology ePrint Archive 2009: 109. http://eprint.iacr.org/2009/109

Functional Encryption in IoT E-Health Care System

Dhruti Sharma[1][✉] and Devesh Jinwala[2]

[1] Sarvajanik College of Engineering and Technology, Surat, Gujarat, India
dhruti.sharma@scet.ac.in
[2] S.V. National Institute of Technology, Surat, Gujarat, India
dcj@svnit.ac.in

Abstract. In Internet of Things (IoT), several smart devices (accompanied with sensors) integrate real world information at central server. Providing security and privacy, the collected information can be used for various analytical tasks like mining of data, taking intelligent decision to control machines, issuing alerts/notifications etc. In this paper, we present a framework for efficient utilization of centralized data while protecting data confidentiality and data privacy in IoT infrastructure. We have combined the concept of attribute based cryptography and functional encryption to process data with efficient access control. To show theoretical and empirical analysis, we have used a candidate area of IoT application viz. E-Health care system.

Keywords: Internet of Things (IoT) · Security Architecture of IoT · Functional encryption

1 Introduction

Internet of Things (IoT) is the interconnection of uniquely identifiable smart objects (an object with an associated sensor) through Internet. Each object in IoT is considered as virtual entity which produces or consumes data. The objective of an IoT infrastructure is to provide an environment for easy collaboration among objects towards common goal [1,22,26]. The major application areas of IoT involve ubiquitous computing where information collected from various sources are integrated at centralized location for further processing. Since all objects in IoT are interconnected through global communication network (i.e. Internet), security of collected data as well as communication among devices is crucial aspect in IoT. The security challenges are ranging from deployment of smart objects to maintaining users' privacy and data privacy. Moreover, confidentiality of communicated information, authenticity of users, integrity of exchanged data and access control are most obvious security requirements in an IoT system [15,17,20].

Having vast data collection, a central system is indeed an information repository in IoT infrastructure. This information can be used for various statistical

© Springer International Publishing Switzerland 2015
S. Jajodia and C. Mazumdar (Eds.): ICISS 2015, LNCS 9478, pp. 345–363, 2015.
DOI: 10.1007/978-3-319-26961-0_21

analysis and performing different activities. For example; in smart city system, traffic related data are continuously being sent to central system and based on their analysis, a traffic control authority can make necessary traffic plan for next hour. In health-monitoring system, a patient's body information (blood pressure, pulse rate, temperature etc.) is periodically sent to central system for caring out analysis; medical staff can provide treatment or send notifications to that patient. To perform such analysis, IoT system requires an automation tool or a service at central site which processes collected data without compromising data security and privacy. In this paper, we have designed a framework which provides such services at central system. Our system processes centralized data in secure manner and thus be useful for diversified IoT applications.

1.1 Background

As IoT is a network of smart objects, it involves varieties of devices and communication technologies. To precisely describe security issues, authors of [12,23–25] divided IoT infrastructure into three layers (i) Physical Layer, (ii) Network Layer, (iii) Application layer as shown in Fig. 1.

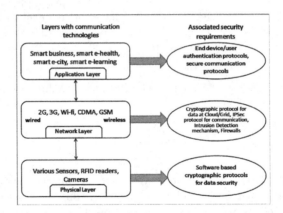

Fig. 1. IoT Security Architecture

The physical layer is comprised of various data collector devices viz. sensors, RFID readers, cameras etc. The common threats at this layer are device capturing, malicious substitution of a device, cloning of a device, device abnormalities, radio interference etc. [14,23,24]. Different cryptographic software protocols [10,11,27,30] can be used for basic security service like confidentiality, integrity, authentication. The collected data from physical layer are available at network layer through diverse communication networks like wired/wireless network, mobile network etc. This layer is generally formed by cloud or grid computing technology and responsible for data processing, classification, broadcasting/multicasting etc. [12,24]. Application layer is the topmost layer which directly deals with end users (may be persons or machines) and provides different services based on the various applications. A device authentication and users' authentication are some of the key concerns at this layer.

Numerous works have been proposed to improve security of IoT systems. In 2009, Mayer [17] had analyzed security and privacy sensitivity by categorizing various technologies (like sensors, storages, actuators, processes, devices etc.). The protocol given in [20] demonstrates the use of secure multiparty computation to preserve privacy in several ubiquitous applications of IoT. Various protocols [13,15,19,29] for secure authentication and access control system in IoT exist. The schemes described in [13,15,19] are based on access control using elliptic curve cryptography and mutual authentication while the other [29] is based on attribute based access control [18,28]. A notable point is that all these schemes are designed for devices at physical layer of IoT infrastructure.

1.2   Motivation

The existing methods for secure IoT infrastructure allow legitimate users to access resources and information as well as decline malicious persons or an attacker. But they neither provide any mechanism to protect integrated data at network layer nor even any technique to process the collected data. Our main objective is to propose a framework for network layer of IoT infrastructure to secure centralized data as well as utilize them for various analytical processing. To accomplish this, we use a combine approach of an ciphertext policy attribute Based Encryption (CPABE) [3] and a Functional Encryption (FE) [5,21]. With the use of CPABE, we propose privacy preservation with access control of centralized data and with FE, we are able to execute various analytical functions on an encrypted data. To explain our system, we use an effective application of IoT i.e. E-Health system which is an online health monitoring and analyzing system. To the best of our knowledge, ours is the first attempt to propose such approach.

1.3   Organization

The sequel of this paper is as follows: Sect. 2 gives brief overview of some preliminary technologies. In Sect. 3, we have described the detailed architecture of our proposed approach with security model. Section 4 shows working of our system with the help of an illustration. Finally, Sect. 5 includes performance evaluation with results and analysis followed by conclusion.

2   Preliminaries

Before discussing the detailed architecture of our proposed framework, some preliminary concepts of Attribute Based Encryption (ABE) and Functional Encryption (FE) are required. This section describes the brief synopsis of both these concepts.

2.1 Attribute Based Encryption (ABE)

Attribute Based Encryption is a refined version of public key cryptography (PKC). In ABE, a public key is formed by various attributes (in terms of string) related to user instead of a long random integer as in traditional PKC. ABE provides fine grained access control where a sender can define an access policy for receiver and thus could control accessibility of data. ABE comes in either forms: Key Policy ABE (KPABE) or Cipher text Policy ABE (CPABE). In CPABE [3], a policy is associated with ciphertext and a list of attributes is associated with a secret key whereas in KPABE [9], a reverse concept is used. The entire ABE system is defined by four algorithms: (i) *Setup*: To initiate system, generate system wide public key P_k and master secret key M_k. (ii) *Extract*: To extract private key S_k for the requesting user, it uses master secret key M_k in addition to policy *Pol* (in case of KPABE)/a list l of attributes (in case of CPABE). (iii) *Encrypt*: Generate ciphertext C from an input message M using P_k and a list l of attributes (in case of KPABE)/*Pol* (in case of CPABE). (iv) *Decrypt*: By decrypting available C using S_k, a receiver could get plaintext message M.

2.2 Functional Encryption (FE)

Functional Encryption (FE) [5,6,8,21] is a generalization of existing public key encryption technologies like Identity based encryption (IBE), Attribute based encryption (ABE), Homomorphic encryption (HE), Predicate Encryption (PE), Searchable Encryption (SE) etc. In FE, original data are encrypted and then predefined functions can run on encrypted data. Instead of generating plaintext as output, the decryption phase runs a function on ciphertext and returns the result. The functional encryption can be defined by four algorithms: (i) *Setup*: By taking security parameters, it generates system public key P_k and master private key P_r. (ii) *Encrypt*: To encrypt a message M, this algorithm uses P_k and generates functional ciphertext FC. (iii) *GenTok*: This algorithm constructs a token T_{f_i} for a function f_i using P_r. (iv) *Execute*: To run a function f_i, this algorithm applies token T_{f_i} onto ciphertext FC. The output is just the result of function f_i and neither ciphertext nor plaintext.

2.3 Bilinear Map

To formally define our system (given in Sect. 3.5), we use groups with efficiently computable bilinear maps [3]. Let we have two multiplicative cyclic groups G_1 and G_2 of prime order p. Let g is the generator of G_1. The pairing among elements of these groups can be performed using a bilinear map $e: G_1 \times G_1 \to G_2$ which has following properties:

1. *Computable:* Given $g, h \in G_1$, there is a polynomial time algorithms to compute $e(g, h) \in G_2$.
2. *Bilinear:* For any integers $x, y \in [1, p]$ we have $e(g^x, g^y) = e(g, g)^{xy}$.
3. *Non-degenerate:* if g is a generator of G_1 then $e(g, g)$ is a generator of G_2.

3   Proposed Approach

3.1   Problem Formulation

The main objective of proposed framework is to design a dynamic central system at network layer of IoT infrastructure, that collects data from various sources, stores them with impregnable security and processes them to perform numerous intelligent tasks. Moreover, it provides fine-grained access control of centrally integrated data.

Generally, security of data is provided by central service provider at network layer but it is not trust worthy. A most common approach is to forward already encrypted information to server and thus the server would be the repository of huge amount of encrypted information. These information can be used for various analytical approaches i.e. generate reports and charts, statistical computations, forecasting etc.

The idea behind our scheme is to work with encrypted data by running different functions on them and generate desired results. The outcome of our approach is that an end user would be able to perform various tasks without bothering about processing. This will be aiding to users who possess resource constrained devices i.e. mobile, tablet etc. Moreover, all data at central system are in encrypted form and only authorized users can access them so data privacy can be preserved.

3.2   Basic Idea

In IoT infrastructure, a central system contains large amount of critical information. Apart from an individual usage, these data can be used for various analytical processing. The main purpose of our approach is to efficiently utilize vast collection of data available at the central server. In this paper, we define a framework which stores encrypted data on server and do further processing on them to generate necessary results. Although our system runs numerous analytical functions on data, it preserves data privacy as well as owners privacy.

To represent our framework, we use an effective IoT application i.e. E-Health system which is an online health monitoring and analyzing system. An E-Health system collects data and stores them to central servers. These data are then utilized by research centers, government offices, hospitals, doctors, patients or any other user. In detail, E-Health system gathers records from various sources like sensors attached with patient's body, mobile devices used by patients, desktop machines used by hospitals or doctors etc. These assembled data may then be used either by medical staff (nurse, doctor, ward boy etc.) to provide necessary treatment to any patient or by analyst at research centre to generate various kinds of analytical reports. In the former usage of data, a doctor may require to see detailed history of any patient while in the later case, an analyst would perform statistical computations on a bunch of data without seeing internal detail of any record. The integrated data at centralized system may contain critical private information about patients and thus security and privacy of data are key concerns.

Here, we design a dynamic central system which is facilitated by Functional Virtual Machine (FVM). An FVM is a software process responsible for execution of different functions on encrypted data. Apart from this, FVM supports fined grained access control by providing ciphertexts which could be accessible only by authorized users. To implement this scheme, we combine the concept of CPABE and FE systems. In our system, data owner creates FE ciphertext by applying functional encryption on CPABE ciphertext. An FVM supports two different queries: (i) query for function execution, (ii) query for CPABE ciphertext. A user queries FVM by presenting a token for function or data; and gets corresponding response. These tokens can be issued to authenticate user by trusted authority. In response of function execution query, FVM runs a requested function and forwards the result to requester while in case of CPABE ciphertext query, FVM separates out CPABE ciphertext from FE ciphertext and send it to requester. To get plaintext from a CPABE ciphertext, one can use CPABE secret key.

A vital property of our proposed idea is our system provides relevant information according to users' requirements. Also an FE ciphertext available on server serves multiple functions and uploading of new FE ciphertexts doesn't affect existing functions. Moreover, inclusion of a new function in system is completely independent from available ciphertexts. This proves the dynamic nature of our framework. All data at central system are in encrypted form and so our scheme maintains confidentiality and data owners' privacy. The functions supported by FVM are based on a set of keywords defined at the time of system setup. So any new function must be based on this set of available keywords. The following are examples of some functions:

- Count the number of patients taking treatment in 'Apollo' hospital in month of February 2015. Here an analyst will keep his focus on count without being keen to know patients name or his decease.
- How many hospitals are being visited by 'Dr. Desai'? Here, analyst will only be interested in number of hospitals and not in internal detail of a doctor or of any hospital.
- Count the number of hospitals available in city 'Delhi'.
- Find out the number of patients suffering with 'Cancer' and taking consultation from Dr. Shah.
- How many 'Cancer Specialist' are available in 'Mumbai'.
- So on..

Assumptions: (i) We have resource rich central system accompanying with several processing servers and storage servers. (ii) All data owners as well as data users are authentic entities. (iii) All key materials are transmitted using secure channel among trusted authorities and authorized users.

3.3 Strengths and Limitations

The major strengths of our proposed framework are

- **Fine grained access control:** As data at central system are encrypted using CPABE technique, only authorized users (who satisfy the policy for CPABE ciphertext) can access corresponding plaintexts.
- **Privacy preservation:** All data available at central server are in encrypted form and so neither an unauthorized user nor an authorized central server would be able to access plaintext for any ciphertext. Thus, privacy of data is preserved.
- **Functional system:** As our centralized system can process integrated data by running various functions on them, we achieve a functional system at network layer of IOT. Our system runs heavy weight processes (i.e. functions) on a central server only and generates functions' output without revealing plaintexts. Such system is beneficial to end users (like doctor, nurse etc.) who possess resource constraint devices.
- **Dynamic environment:** As there is no dependency of any ciphertext to any function, dynamic insertion of new ciphertexts as well as new functions is possible.

The main limitation of our proposed framework is the use of double encryption. To create FE ciphertext, we use already encrypted data (i.e. CPABE ciphertext) as payload. But this issue will be suppressed by the benefits and usefulness of our system.

3.4   Architecture

The general architecture of our proposed system is shown in Fig. 2. The owners of data can be patients(P), doctors(D), hospitals(H) or any other entity who owns data. The data/function requesters are the people who make request either

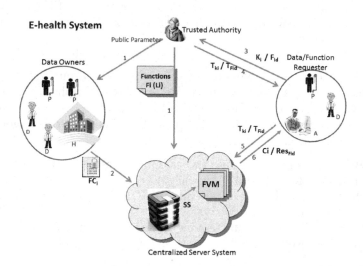

Fig. 2. Architecture of proposed framework

for plaintext data or for function execution. Normally, data can be requested by doctors(D) or patients(P) while analyst(A) makes request for function execution. The centralized server system contains two main entities: Storage Servers (SS) and Functional Virtual Machine (FVM). Our system involves a trusted authority (TA) who is responsible for entire system setup. The general flow of our approach is as follows (as shown in Fig. 2):

1. TA sets up the system by publishing public parameters.
2. Data owners create functional ciphertexts (FC_i) and forward them to the central storage server.
3. A Data/Function requester asks TA for a token by presenting single keyword (K_i) or function id (F_{id}).
4. TA issues a token $(T_{ki}$ or $T_{Fid})$ to a the requester.
5. A Data/Function requester presents an available token to the FVM.
6. FVM either runs a function F_{id} and returns the result Res_{Fid} or extracts C_i from FC_i and sends it to the requester.

To perform above steps, our proposed E-Health system works in 5 phases: (1) System Setup, (2) User Registration, (3) Data Encryption, (4) Function Execution, (5) CPABE Decryption. The notations used in defining our system is given in Table 1.

System Setup. A trusted authority TA generates system-wide parameters to setup CPABE and FE system using following algorithms:

– SET_ABE(): With this algorithm, TA defines M and AL and generates CPABE public-private key pair (A_{pk}, A_s).
– SET_FE(): Using this algorithm, TA defines a universe of keywords UF. For each keyword $W_i \in UF$, TA creates a public-private key pair (W_{ip}, W_{ir}). Moreover, it defines a list of functions FL and prepares an FVM for all available functions. Moreover, TA periodically resets an FVM with new timestamp T_{FVM} to prevent reuse of same token multiple times.

User Registration. Three types of users are supported by our system: (i) *Data owner:* One who owns plaintext data and creates FE ciphertexts (ii) *Data requester:* One who queries for plaintext, (iii) *Function requester:* One who queries for execution of any available function. Based on a user's category, three types of registrations are supported by our system:

– REG_OW(): Registration as data owner. Once registration is confirmed, TA returns (M, AL, A_{pk}, UF, $\{W_{ip}$ for each $W_i \in UF\}$).
– REG_DR(): Registration as data requester. Once registration is confirmed, TA returns (AL, UF).
– REG_FR(): Registration as function requester. Once registration is confirmed, TA returns (AL, FL).

For all types of registration, TA can use any authentication protocol to check the validity of users.

Table 1. Notations

Entity	Description
TA	Trusted authority for CPABE and FE system setup
SS	Storage Server
FVM	Functional Virtual Machine
(A_{pk}, A_s)	CPABE master (public, private) key pair
M	Message Space for defining input message
m_i	Message from patient P_i
AL	List of attributes to define policy for CPABE encryption
Pol_i	Policy used for CPABE encryption of message m_i
A_{pri}	CPABE decryption key for user i
UF	List of keywords to express functions
(W_{ip}, W_{ir})	(Public, Private) key pair for the keyword W_i
$FL = \{F_{id}(L_{id})\}$	Set of functions supported by FVM where each function F_{id} is defined by a list of keywords $L_{id} \subseteq UF$
WL_i	List of keywords used for functional encryption for C_i and $WL_i \subseteq UF$
WL_{ip}	List of public keys for keywords in WL_i
T_{Fid}	A token for function F_{id}
C_i	CPABE cipher text for message m_i
Res_{Fi}	Result of a function F_i
nAL	Total number of attributes available in AL
$nFun$	Total number of functions available in FL
nUF	Total number of keywords available in UF
nL_{id}	Total number of keywords used for defining F_{id}
nFC_i	Number of keywords used for functional encryption
T_s	Timestamp associated with T_{Fid}
T_{FVM}	Timestamp associated with FVM
T_w	Token for plaintext data

Data Encryption. After data collection, an owner creates functional ciphertext using combined approach of ciphertext policy attribute based encryption and functional encryption. The followings are the algorithms.

- ABE_ENC(A_{pk}, m_i, Pol_i): The plaintext message m_i gets encrypted using master public key A_{pk} and CPABE policy Pol_i with the encryption technique given in [3]. This algorithm generates CPABE ciphertext C_i.
- FE_ENC(C_i, WL_i, WL_{ip}): A functional ciphertext FC_i is created by associating encrypted keyword(s) with C_i. Each keyword $W_i \in WL_i$ is encrypted with its public key $W_{ip} \in WL_{ip}$ using public key searchable encryption (PEKS) technique [4].

At the end, a functional ciphertext FC_i is uploaded to central server system.

Function Execution. A function requester can execute any function using following algorithms.

- TOK_GEN(F_{id}): TA issues a token T_{Fid} for a function (F_{id}) to a function requester. T_{Fid} is created based on the keywords list L_{id} defining function F_{id}. With each T_{Fid}, a timestamp T_s is associated, so a token can be reused within fix time period.
- FUN_EXE(T_{Fid}): FVM first checks the freshness of a given T_{Fid} against his timestamp T_{FVM}. For a fresh T_{Fid}, FVM runs a function F_{id} and forwards the result Res_{Fi} to the function requester. FVM is facilitated by definition of different functions at system setup time. The code for each function includes search over encrypted keywords available in functional ciphertexts using T_{Fid} and also some analytical processing. Finally, the result Res_{Fi} is available to an end user.

CPABE Decryption. A data requester can access plaintext message m_i from FC_i using following algorithms:

- TOK_GEN(W'): A data requester asks TA for data token by sending W'. If TA finds W' $\in$ UF, a data token T_w is issued to data requester.
- CIP_RET(T_w): For a given T_w, FVM do single keyword search over each FC_i. It returns C = {C_i for all FC_i where it found match for T_w}
- ABE_DEC(C, A_{pri}): A data user can access only those plaintext from available C for which he has secret key A_{pri}. TA issues a secret key A_{pri} to data requester only if requester satisfies the policy associated with that ciphertext. Once A_{pri} is available, a requester could get plaintext from C_i by CPABE decryption algorithm [3].

3.5   Security Model

In this section, we describe a security model for proposed framework. Like ciphertext policy attribute based encryption [3], our security model allows an attacker to query for tokens of available functions with the restriction that any issued token can not be used to run a function over challenge ciphertext.

We claim that our proposed approach is semantically secure against an active attacker $\mathcal{A}$ who is able to obtain token T_{Fid} for any function F_{id} of his choice.

We prove this by ensuring that our scheme doesn't reveal any information about function F_i unless T_{Fid} is available to him. Moreover, with our functional encryption scheme, an attacker wouldn't be able to distinguish a ciphertext FC_i with the list of keywords S_i from a ciphertext FC_j with the list of keywords S_j. The formal definition of security for our approach is given by the following game between an active attacker $\mathcal{A}$ and a challenger.

1. The challenger runs the $SET\_FE()$ algorithm and provides a public key for each keyword $W_i \in UF$ and all available functions F_{id} to an attacker $\mathcal{A}$.
2. An attacker $\mathcal{A}$ adaptively asks for token T_{Fid} of function F_{id} to challenger. A token T_{Fid} contains a set of token values of all keywords used for function F_{id}.
3. At some point in between, an attacker $\mathcal{A}$ asks the challenger for functional encryption using a set of keywords S_0 and S_1 as a challenge for which he doesn't know any token T_{Fid}. In response, the challenger randomly selects i and gives an FC_i using set S_i.
4. An attacker $\mathcal{A}$ applies T_{Fid} on FC_i and finds the result. He can continue to ask for available token T_{Fid} of keywords S until $S \neq \{S_0, S_1\}$
5. At the end, the attacker $\mathcal{A}$ outputs $S' \in \{0, 1\}$ and wins the game if $S = S'$.

Our proposed approach is semantically secure, if the attacker $\mathcal{A}$ could correctly guess whether the given S is for S_0 or S_1 and wins the game. To break our system, the advantage for an attacker $\mathcal{A}$ can be defined as follows.

$$Adv_{\mathcal{A}}(s) = |Pr[S' = S] - \frac{1}{2}|$$

We say that our proposed approach is semantically secure against an adaptive chosen keyword attack if for any polynomial time attacker $\mathcal{A}$ we have that $Adv_{\mathcal{A}}(s)$ is a negligible function.

3.6 Formal Definition

To define functional encryption concept, we combine two cryptographic schemes CPABE and FE. To implement FE, we have modified the existing public key encryption for keyword search (PEKS) [4] which is a method for single keyword search over encrypted data. We have extended it for multiple keywords search. Though we use CPABE algorithms [3] directly in our scheme, we just skip their internal details. We use bilinear pairing (as discussed in Sect. 2.3) to formally define our framework. Our framework supports the following algorithms:

System Setup

– SET_ABE(): Select $AL = \{a_i | 1 \leq i \leq nAL\}$ and run original Setup() algorithm of CPABE [3].
– SET_FE(): Select $UF = \{W_i | W_i \in AL, 1 \leq i \leq nUF\}$. Take generator g of G_1 and for each W_i take a random $\alpha_i \in Z_p^*$. Create a public key h_i for each W_i as $h_i = g^{\alpha_i}$.

Also define a list of functions $FL = \{F_{id}$ where $1 \leq id \leq nFun\}$ where each function F_{id} is defined with a list of keywords $L_{id} \subseteq UF$. Prepare FVM available on server with definition of each function F_{id}.

User Registration. As discussed in Sect. 3.4, different types of users make registration with TA based on their role. TA uses any authentication algorithm for validity of a user. As our main purpose is to create functional virtual machine, the selection of authentication protocol is out of focus for this paper.

Data Encryption

- ABE_ENC(A_{pk}, m_i, Pol_i): Run *Encrypt()* algorithm of CPABE [3]. As a result, for a message m_i, we get CPABE ciphertext C_i.
- FE_ENC(C_i, WL_i, WL_{ip}): Take a random $r \in Z_p^*$. For each keyword $W_j \in WL_i$, compute $t_j = e(H_1(W_j), h_j^r)$ where $h_j = WL_{ip}$. Then, output $FC_i = (A, (B_1, \ldots, B_{nFCi})) \parallel C_i$ where $A = g^r$ and $B_j = H_2(t_j)$ and $1 \leq j \leq nFC_i$. The $\parallel$ denotes concatenation symbol.

Function Execution

- TOK_GEN(F_{id}): For each $W_i \in L_{id}$ of F_{id}, create $s_i = H_1(W_i)^{\alpha_i}$. Then output a token $T_{Fid} = ((s_1, s_2.., s_{nLi}), T_s)$.
- FUN_EXE(T_{Fid}): For given T_{Fid}, FVM checks whether $T_s \geq T_{FVM}$. If 'Yes' then T_{Fid} is fresh. For a fresh T_{Fid}, for each available FC_i, FVM performs the following test:
  For each s_j in T_{Fid}, (where $1 \leq j \leq nLi$)
      For each B_k in FC_i (where $1 \leq k \leq nFC_i$)
          If ($H_2(e(s_j, A)) = B_k$) is true, Then do analytical processing corresponding to function F_{id}.

CPABE Decryption

- *TOK_GEN(W′)*: Instead of F_{id}, if TA finds single keyword in token generation request, he takes α (from available set of α) for that W' and outputs $W_{id} = H_1(W')^{\alpha}$.
- *CIP_RET(W_{id})*: For each available FC_i, FVM performs the following test:
  For each B_k in FC_i (where $1 \leq k \leq nFC_i$)
      If ($H_2(e(W_{id}, A) = B_k$) is true,
          then extract payload C_i from FC_i and compute $C = C \parallel C_i$.
  Return C.
- *ABE_DEC(C)*: Run KeyGen() algorithm [3] to get CPABE secret key A_{pri}.
  For each $C_i \in C$
      Apply CPABE decryption() algorithm [3] to get plaintext message m_i.
  A data requester can access plaintext from only those C_i for which he has A_{pri}.

4   An Illustration

To precisely describe our framework, we have taken an example and showed working of each phase of our proposed approach in the following section.

4.1 Setup

In setup phase, message space M, attributes list AL for policy definition and keywords list UF for functions' definitions are defined.

Let our system supports 3 different types of entities (Data Owners): Patients(P), Doctors(D) and Hospitals(H). The message space M is a generalized set of attributes of data owner and $AL, UF \subseteq M$. For our discussion, we have selected AL and UF as given in Table 2. The capitalized word in bracket with each attribute shows the keyword we use for functional encryption and decryption.

4.2 User Registration

Our system supports different types of data owners. An owner may be the data requester or the functions requester. So each user does registration in a suitable category as per his requirements.

Table 2. Example: Entities and associated AL,UF

Patient (P)	AL	Doctor Name (PDN), Doctors Registration (DREG), Doctors Specialization (DSP1), Patient Name (PN), Patient Mobile No (PMN)
	UF	Ow_type (OT), Patient City (PC), Patient State (PS), Patient Hospital (PH), Descease1 (PD1), Desease2 PD2), Consulting Doc1 (PDoc1), Consulting Doc2 (PDoc2)
Doctor (D)	AL	Head of Medical Council (HMC), Member of Doctor's Association (MDA), Doctor Name (DN), Doctor Mobile No (DMN)
	UF	Ow_type (OT), Doctor Name (DN), Visiting Hospital1 (DH1), Visiting Hospital2 (DH2), Specialization1 (DSP1), Specialization2 (DSP2)
Hospital (H)	AL	Doctor Name (DN), Hospital RegNo. (HREG)
	UF	Ow_type (OT), Hospital Name (HN), Hospital City (HC), Hospital State (HS), ACRooms (HACR), DlRooms (HDLR), Number of Doctors (HNoD)

4.3 Encryption

Let's we work for 5 patients $(P_1, P_2, P_3, P_4, P_5)$, 2 Doctors (D_1, D_2) and 2 Hospitals (H_1, H_2). First we perform CPABE encryption on plaintext message m_i from patient P_i with associated policy Pol_i given in Table 3. The result of encryption of m_i is C_i.

Table 3. Example: CPABE policies

Patients	Policies (Pol_i)
P_1	(DN = 'Dr. Shah' AND DREG = 'D101010' AND DSP1 = 'Cancer')
P_2	(DN = 'Dr. Desai' AND DREG = 'D208990')
P_3	(DSP1 = 'Cancer' OR DSP1 = 'LungSpecialist')
P_4	(DN = 'Dr. Mark' OR DN = 'Dr. Desai')
P_5	(DN = 'Dr. Desai' AND DREG = 'D20899')

Once C_i is generated, we apply functional encryption using keywords from UF. The Table 4 shows list of keywords WL_i used for each C_i for performing functional encryption.

As a result of functional encryption, we get functional ciphertext FC_i which is uploaded to server.

4.4   Function Execution

Now suppose our FVM supports a set $FL = \{F_1, F_2, F_3\}$ where each F_{id} is associated with L_{id} as shown in Table 5.

To run any function, FVM checks L_{id} against WL of each ciphertext. The following Table 6 shows the output of each of the above listed function.

4.5   CPABE Decryption

For the above example, details about patient P_1 can be seen only by 'Dr.Shah' whose registration number is 'D101010' and who is specialist for 'Cancer' diseases. Same way, detail case of P_2 can be studied by 'Dr. Desai' with Registration

Table 4. Example: Keywords used for functional encryption

Patients	Keywords (WL_i)
P_1	OT = Patient, PC = Surat, PS = Gujarat, PH = Apollo, PD1 = Cancer, PDoc1 = Dr.Shah
P_2	OT = Patient, PC = Surat, PS = Gujarat, PH = Apollo, PD1 = Cancer, PD2 = Brain, PDOC1 = Dr.Desai, PDOC2 = Dr.Shah
P_3	OT = Patient, PC = Madras, PS = TN, PH = Apple, PD1 = Cancer, PD2 = Eye, PDOC1 = Dr.Mark
P_4	OT = Patient, PC = Kolkata, PS = WB, PH = Apollo, PD1 = Heart, PDOC1 = Dr.Mark
P_5	OT = Patient, PC = Surat, PS = Gujarat, PH = Apollo, PD1 = Cancer, PDOC1 = Dr.Desai, PDOC2 = Dr.Shah

number 'D208990'. Though P_1, P_2 be the part of execution of functions F_1 and F_2, their internal details are hidden from function requester.

Table 5. Example: Functions with associated Lists

F_{id}		L_{id}	
Functions	Description	List	Description
F_1	Count all patients suffering with 'Cancer'	L_1	PD1 = 'Cancer'
F_2	How many patients are currently admitted in hospital 'Apollo' located in city 'Surat'	L_2	PH = 'Apollo', PC = 'Surat'
F_3	Find out number of patients consulted by 'Dr. Mark' in city 'Madras'	L_3	PDOC1 = 'Dr.Mark', PC = 'Madras'

Table 6. Example: Results of Functions

Function (Fi)	ResFi	Remark
F_1	$Res_{F_1} = 4$	Match found for Patients P1, P2, P3, P5
F_2	$Res_{F_2} = 3$	Match found for Patients P1, P2, P5
F_3	$Res_{F_3} = 1$	Match found for Patient P3

5   Performance Evaluation and Analysis

To evaluate the performance of our approach, we have used the cpabe toolkit [2] and Pairing-Based Cryptography (PBC) Library [16]. We run the experiments on a server running Linux with a 32-bit, 2.10 GHz Pentium Core 2 Duo CPU. To perform group operations, we use type A curve supported by PBC Library. The type A curve has group order r = 160 bits which provides 80-bit security strength.

5.1   Experimental Setup

To create CPABE ciphertext, we use cpabe toolkit [2] directly. The concept of FVM is implemented using PBC library [16] with gcc compiler. To generate functional ciphertext using various keywords, we have worked with Nursery data set from the UCI Machine Learning Repository [7]. The Nursery data set has 8 categorical attributes with 27 different values and we consider these values as keywords for functions supported by FVM.

To define our system for nursery data set, the setup phase generates 27 pairs (one pair per value) of public/private keys. For performance evaluation of proposed approach, we have implemented 9 different functions F_{id} (where $1 \leq id \leq 9$). Also to define a function F_{id}, we have used id number of keywords.

5.2   Results

We have given time analysis of three important phases of our scheme i.e. *Functional encryption* and *Function token generation* and *Function execution* in Figs. 3, 4 and 5 respectively.

The results in Fig. 3 depict that time taken by functional encryption is $\mathbf{O(nm)}$ where $n =$ total number of plaintext records and $m = nFC_i$. Here, the encryption time includes the time required for CPABE encryption also. The most important point here is the encryption time is completely independent from all available functions in system.

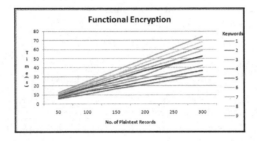

Fig. 3. Timing analysis for functional encryption

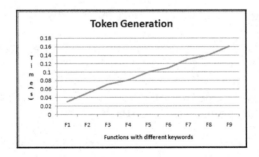

Fig. 4. Timing analysis for token generation

The results in Fig. 4 proves that time required to generate token for a function $F_{id} = \mathbf{O(nL_{id})}$. This shows that time is increasing linearly with increase in number of keywords in L_{id}. The timing analysis for execution of different functions in system is shown in Fig. 5. These results shows that for a function F_{id}, execution time $= \mathbf{O(pq)}$ where p = total number of functional ciphertexts available in system and q = nL_{id}.

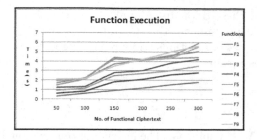

Fig. 5. Timing analysis for functional execution

5.3 Analysis

Data Privacy. As per data encryption phase, each functional ciphertexts is blinded by user's secret value r. As r is completely random, collusion attack becomes impossible. Also, a payload of functional ciphertext is CPABE ciphertext and so a malicious user will not be able to access plaintext by getting functional ciphertext.

User Privacy. By making proper choice of keywords to define UF, we could achieve user privacy. In the other words, the field related to more sensitive information should not be the part of UF, rather can be used for defining policies for CPABE ciphertexts. As per our scheme, we allow data owner to choose a set of keywords from UF to create functional ciphertext and thus based on his privacy requirements, an owner selects different set of keywords for different functional encryption.

Function Privacy. As per Sect. 3.4, all available functions' identity are issued to valid function requester, so no unauthorized user can make query to run any function. A user possessing a function token can run that function for fix time period as with each token a time stamp is associated. Moreover, at function definition time, each keyword $w_i \in L_{id}$ is blinded by random secret value α_i. So even by knowing a single keyword w_i, an attacker would not be able to get the knowledge of entire L_{id} for a function F_{id}.

As our proposed approach allows multiple functions with different definitions and insertion of a new function (based on available UF) into system at any time, we claim that our system has versatile and flexible architecture. In addition, entire processing task (function execution) is done at central system, our scheme is more beneficial to an end user having resource constrained devices.

6 Conclusion

An E-Health online medical system is one of the biggest application areas of IoT where critical medical information of patient(s) is available at centralized system.

To securely process these data, functional encryption is an ideal mechanism. With this paper we propose an idea to build a secure E-Health IoT system which supports varieties of functions while providing data confidentiality as well as data privacy preservation.

References

1. Atzori, L., Iera, A., Morabito, G.: The internet of things: a survey. Comput. Netw. **54**(15), 2787–2805 (2010)
2. Bethencourt, J., Sahai, A., Waters, B.: Advanced crypto software collection: the cpabe toolkit (2011)
3. Bethencourt, J., Sahai, A., Waters, B.: Ciphertext-policy attribute-based encryption. In: IEEE Symposium on Security and Privacy, SP 2007, pp. 321–334. IEEE (2007)
4. Boneh, D., Di Crescenzo, G., Ostrovsky, R., Persiano, G.: Public key encryption with keyword search. In: Cachin, C., Camenisch, J.L. (eds.) EUROCRYPT 2004. LNCS, vol. 3027, pp. 506–522. Springer, Heidelberg (2004)
5. Boneh, D., Sahai, A., Waters, B.: Functional encryption: definitions and challenges. In: Ishai, Y. (ed.) TCC 2011. LNCS, vol. 6597, pp. 253–273. Springer, Heidelberg (2011)
6. Boneh, D., Sahai, A., Waters, B.: Functional encryption: a new vision for public-key cryptography. Commun. ACM **55**(11), 56–64 (2012)
7. Frank, A., Asuncion, A., et al.: Uci machine learning repository (2010)
8. Goldwasser, S., Kalai, Y.T., Popa, R.A., Vaikuntanathan, V., Zeldovich, N.: Succinct functional encryption and applications: reusable garbled circuits and beyond. IACR Cryptology ePrint Archive 2012, 733 (2012)
9. Goyal, V., Pandey, O., Sahai, A., Waters, B.: Attribute-based encryption for fine-grained access control of encrypted data. In: Proceedings of the 13th ACM Conference on Computer and Communications Security, pp. 89–98. ACM (2006)
10. Huan, W., et al.: Studying on internet of things based on fingerprint identification. In: 2010 International Conference on Computer Application and System Modeling (ICCASM 2010), vol. 14 (2010)
11. Juels, A.: Rfid security and privacy: a research survey. IEEE J. Sel. Areas Commun. **24**(2), 381–394 (2006)
12. Kumar, J.S., Patel, D.R.: A survey on internet of things: security and privacy issues. Int. J. Comput. Appl. **90**(11), 20–26 (2014)
13. Le, X.H., Khalid, M., Sankar, R., Lee, S.: An efficient mutual authentication and access control scheme for wireless sensor networks in healthcare. J. Netw. **6**(3), 355–364 (2011)
14. Li, X., Xuan, Z., Wen, L.: Research on the architecture of trusted security system based on the internet of things. In: 2011 International Conference on Intelligent Computation Technology and Automation (ICICTA), vol. 2, pp. 1172–1175. IEEE (2011)
15. Liu, J., Xiao, Y., Chen, C.P.: Authentication and access control in the internet of things. In: 2012 32nd International Conference on Distributed Computing Systems Workshops, pp. 588–592. IEEE (2012)
16. Lynn, B., et al.: The pairing-based cryptography library. Internet: crypto. stanford. edu/pbc/[27 March 2013] (2006)

17. Mayer, C.P.: Security and privacy challenges in the internet of things. Electron. Commun. EASST **17** (2009)
18. Mon, E.E., Naing, T.T.: The privacy-aware access control system using attribute- and role-based access control in private cloud. In: 2011 4th IEEE International Conference on Broadband Network and Multimedia Technology (IC-BNMT), pp. 447–451. IEEE (2011)
19. Ndibanje, B., Lee, H.J., Lee, S.G.: Security analysis and improvements of authentication and access control in the internet of things. Sensors **14**(8), 14786–14805 (2014)
20. Oleshchuk, V.: Internet of things and privacy preserving technologies. In: 2009 1st International Conference on Wireless Communication, Vehicular Technology, Information Theory and Aerospace & Electronic Systems Technology (2009)
21. O'Neill, A.: Definitional issues in functional encryption. IACR Cryptology ePrint Archive 2010, 556 (2010)
22. Roman, R., Najera, P., Lopez, J.: Securing the internet of things. Computer **44**(9), 51–58 (2011)
23. Said, O.: Development of an innovative internet of things security system. Int. J. Comput. Sci. Issues (IJCSI) **10**(6), 155–161 (2013)
24. Suo, H., Wan, J., Zou, C., Liu, J.: Security in the internet of things: a review. In: 2012 International Conference on Computer Science and Electronics Engineering (ICCSEE), vol. 3, pp. 648–651. IEEE (2012)
25. Wang, K., Bao, J., Wu, M., Lu, W.: Research on security management for internet of things. In: 2010 International Conference on Computer Application and System Modeling (ICCASM 2010), vol. 15 (2010)
26. Weber, R.H.: Internet of things-new security and privacy challenges. Comput. Law Secur. Rev. **26**(1), 23–30 (2010)
27. Wong, K.H., Zheng, Y., Cao, J., Wang, S.: A dynamic user authentication scheme for wireless sensor networks. In: IEEE International Conference on Sensor Networks, Ubiquitous, and Trustworthy Computing, vol. 1, p. 8. IEEE (2006)
28. Xin-fang, S., Xiao-hua, H.: A new access control scheme based on protection of sensitive attributes. In: 2012 7th International Conference on Computer Science & Education (ICCSE), pp. 1021–1024. IEEE (2012)
29. Ye, N., Zhu, Y., Wang, R.C., Malekian, R., Min, L.: An efficient authentication and access control scheme for perception layer of internet of things. Int. J. Appl. Math. Inf. Sci. **8**, 1617–1624 (2014)
30. Zhu, S., Setia, S., Jajodia, S.: Leap+: efficient security mechanisms for large-scale distributed sensor networks. ACM Trans. Sens. Netw. (TOSN) **2**(4), 500–528 (2006)

Asynchronous Error-Decodable Secret-Sharing and Its Application

Ashish Choudhury[✉]

International Institute of Information Technology, Bangalore, India
ashish.choudhury@iiitb.ac.in

Abstract. In this paper, we study error-decodable secret-sharing schemes against general adversaries in the asynchronous communication setting. Previously, such schemes were designed in the synchronous communication setting. As an application of our scheme, we present the *first* single round asynchronous perfectly-secure message transmission protocol against general adversaries.

1 Introduction

Secret sharing [Sha79, Bla79] is one of the fundamental problems in distributed cryptography. In its simplest form, it allows a special party D called *dealer* to share a secret among a set $\mathcal{P} = \{P_1, \ldots, P_n\}$ of n parties. The sharing is done in such a way that certain designated subsets of parties called *access sets* can reconstruct the secret by pooling their shares; on the other hand, subsets of parties which does not constitute an access set get no information about the shared secret. The latter condition holds even if the parties in the non-access sets are computationally unbounded. The set of access sets and non-access sets are represented by Σ and Γ respectively; these sets are called *access structure* and *adversary structure* respectively. It is assumed that there exists a *computationally unbounded* adversary $\mathcal{A}$, who selects a set from Γ for corruption and *passively* corrupts the parties in that set.

Error-decodable secret-sharing (EDSS) is a special type of secret sharing, which allows *robust* reconstruction of the secret, even in the presence of a malicious $\mathcal{A}$. More specifically, it ensures that the honest parties reconstruct the correct secret even if the corrupted parties produce incorrect shares during the reconstruction process. Such schemes are more practically relevant because in practice it is a very strong assumption that adversary will do only passive corruption. A popular adversary structure which is widely studied in the literature is the *threshold* adversary structure, where it is assumed that $\mathcal{A}$ can corrupt at most t parties out of the n parties; for such an $\mathcal{A}$, the set Γ is the set of all possible $\binom{n}{t}$ subsets of t parties. It is well known that EDSS against a threshold adversary is possible if and only if $t < n/3$ [MS81].

A non-threshold adversary is a generalizatiob of threshold adversary, where Γ consists of subsets of arbitrary size. The motivation for studying non-threshold adversaries is that in certain scenarios, threshold adversaries may be un-realistic.

© Springer International Publishing Switzerland 2015
S. Jajodia and C. Mazumdar (Eds.): ICISS 2015, LNCS 9478, pp. 364–377, 2015.
DOI: 10.1007/978-3-319-26961-0_22

For example, certain computer viruses, such as the ILOVEYOU [Mis00] virus and the Internet virus/worm [ER89] spreads only to Windows and Unix respectively. An attacker who can exploit a weakness in one platform, can with al most the same ease attack many computers, if not all, on that same platform. Such a scenario is more naturally captured by a non-threshold adversary instead of a threshold adversary.

EDSS against non-threshold adversaries are first studied in [Kur11], where it is shown that EDSS is possible if and only if $\mathcal{P}$ satisfies $\mathcal{Q}^{(3)}$ condition with respect to Γ (see Definition 4); informally this means that the union of every *three* sets from Γ is a proper subset[1] of $\mathcal{P}$. The sufficiency is shown by designing an efficient EDSS scheme for $\mathcal{Q}^{(3)}$ adversary structures, whose complexity is polynomial in n and the size of the underlying monotone span program (MSP) realizing Γ (see the next section for the definition of MSP).

Our Motivation and Results: All the results discussed above are in the synchronous communication setting, where it is assumed that the parties are synchronized via a global clock and hence there exists strict upper bound on message delays. Unfortunately, real-world networks like the Internet does not provide such synchronization and the messages can be arbitrarily delayed. Motivated by this, [BCG93] introduced the asynchronous communication setting, where the messages can be arbitrarily delayed. Compared to the protocols in the synchronous setting, asynchronous protocol are highly complex. This stems from the fact that in a completely asynchronous protocol, it is impossible to distinguish between a slow but *honest* sender, whose messages are delayed arbitrarily and a *corrupted* sender, who does not send any message at all. As a result, at any stage of the protocol, no party can afford to listen from all the n parties, as this may turn out to be endless. Hence as soon as a party receives communication from "sufficient" number of parties[2], it has to proceed to the next stage, ignoring the communication from the rest of the parties. However, the ignored parties may be potentially honest parties.

Even though the asynchronous communication model is practically relevant, to the best of our knowledge nothing is known in the literature about EDSS in the asynchronous setting. Motivated by this, in this work we initiate the study of asynchronous EDSS (AEDSS). Specifically, we design an AEDSS scheme for $\mathcal{Q}^{(3)}$ adversary structures. The scheme is obtained by modifying the EDSS scheme of [Kur11] to adapt it to the asynchronous setting. Interestingly, the adaptation is not straight forward and requires the parties to iteratively perform certain steps in an "online" fashion upon the disclosure of every share, to deal with the asynchronous nature of the communication (more on this later).

EDSS is very closely related to one round *perfectly-secure message transmission* (PSMT) [Kur11]. On a high level, a PSMT protocol allows a distributed sender and a receiver to carry out reliable and secure communication

---

[1] Note that this is a generalization of the condition $t < n/3$ for the threshold setting.

[2] For example, in the threshold setting, a party has to proceed to the next step after listening from $n - t$ parties, as t corrupted parties may decide not to send any communication.

over n channels, some of which may be under the control of a computationally unbounded malicious adversary [DDWY93]. Given an EDSS scheme, one can easily design a one round PSMT protocol. As an application of our AEDSS, we present the first one round asynchronous PSMT (APSMT) protocol tolerating a generalized adversary. This significantly improves upon the previous best APSMT protocol against non-threshold adversary [SKR02], which requires $\mathcal{O}(|\mathcal{A}|)$ rounds of interaction between the sender and the receiver; here $|\mathcal{A}|$ denotes the cardinality of the set of channels corrupted by the adversary in the protocol.

Overview of Our AEDSS: We follow [Kur11] and first design a weaker primitive called *weak secret sharing* (WSS). Informally a WSS scheme is similar to EDSS, where sharing is done with respect to a designated party, say P_i, who is given the shared secret as well as the randomness used to compute the shares of the secret. The reconstruction protocol is now invoked by this designated P_i, who publicly reveals the assigned secret and the randomness, which is then compared with the shares disclosed by the individual share holders. If P_i is honest, then it correctly discloses the secret and the randomness. And this will be "consistent" with the individual shares of all but the parties belonging to an access set. Based on this observation, the parties can accordingly decide to accept or reject the secret disclosed by the designated P_i. It is ensured that a secret is accepted if and only if the secret (and the associated randomness) are revealed correctly by the designated P_i [Kur11]. Given a WSS scheme, [Kur11] designed their EDSS as follows: the dealer first computes the shares of the secret and the shares are distributed to the respective share holders. In addition, each individual share is further shared via WSS, where the randomness used for WSS is assigned to the corresponding share holder. Later during the reconstruction phase, each share holder reveals its share via the reconstruction algorithm of the WSS. The properties of WSS ensure that only the correctly revealed shares are accepted, which ensures robust reconstruction.

To design our AEDSS, we first extend the WSS of [Kur11] to the asynchronous setting. Here we need to deal with two issues due to the asynchronous nature of the communication. First, the designated P_i with respect to which WSS is executed may not invoke the reconstruction algorithm if P_i is *corrupted*. As a result, the reconstruction protocol of WSS may not terminate for a corrupted P_i. Second, even if the designated P_i invokes the reconstruction protocol by revealing the secret and the randomness, the individual shares of the share holders will be revealed asynchronously and hence may not be available simultaneously. As a result, each time a new share is revealed, the parties need to verify the consistency of the revealed secret and the corresponding shares in an online fashion. So unlike the synchronous setting, the reconstruction protocol of the asynchronous WSS will no longer be a single step process, but rather an iterative process. Once we have an asynchronous WSS, we obtain AEDSS as follows: the dealer first computes the shares of the secret and each share is further shared via our AWSS. During the reconstruction phase, each share holder reveals its share by executing the reconstruction protocol of the AWSS. However due to the asynchronous nature of the communication, the parties cannot afford to terminate the reconstruction of all the AWSS instances. Hence as soon as the parties terminate the AWSS instances of a set of parties belonging to an access set, they reconstruct the secret by using the shares revealed in those instances.

2   Preliminaries

We assume a set $\mathcal{P} = \{P_1, \ldots, P_n\}$ of n parties and an *external* dealer $\mathsf{D} \notin \mathcal{P}$. The parties are connected by pair-wise private and authentic channels. There exists a finite field $\mathbb{F}$ and all computation are assumed to be performed over $\mathbb{F}$. We denote by $\mathbf{S}$ the set of all possible secrets that can be shared. The distrust among the parties is modeled by a centralized adversary $\mathcal{A}$, who can corrupt a subset of parties from $\mathcal{P}$. The set of potential subsets of corruptible parties is denoted by an *adversary structure* Γ, where $\Gamma \subseteq 2^{\mathcal{P}}$. Adversary $\mathcal{A}$ is assumed to be *static*, who decides the subset of parties to corrupt at the beginning of the execution of a protocol; the corrupted subset is one of the elements of Γ. The adversary is computationally unbounded and can force the corrupted parties to deviate from the protocol instructions in any arbitrary fashion. The dealer D is always assumed to be honest. Let $\Sigma = \Gamma^c$, where Γ^c denotes the complement of Γ; we call the set Σ *access structure* and the elements in Σ are called *access sets*. We next define secret-sharing scheme.

Secret-Sharing Scheme: In a secret-sharing scheme, D has a secret which it wants to share among $\mathcal{P}$. The sharing needs to be done in a way that the parties in any access set can reconstruct the secret by combining their shares, while the parties in any set belonging to the adversary structure gets no information about the secret. More formally:

Definition 1 (Secret-Sharing Scheme [Kur11]). *A secret-sharing scheme over the adversary structure Γ and access structure $\Sigma = \Gamma^c$ is a pair of algorithms* $(\mathsf{Sh}, \mathsf{Rec})$ *where:*

- $(\mathsf{Share}_1, \ldots, \mathsf{Share}_n) \leftarrow \mathsf{Sh}(s, r)$: *the sharing algorithm Sh takes the secret s to be shared along with some randomness r and computes the shares $\mathsf{Share}_1, \ldots,$ Share_n, with Share_i designated for the party P_i, for $i = 1, \ldots, n$.*
- Rec *is the reconstruction algorithm such that:*

$$\mathsf{Rec}(A, \mathsf{Share}_A) = \begin{cases} s, & if \quad A \subset \Sigma \\ \perp, & if \quad A \in \Gamma \end{cases}$$

where $\mathsf{Share}_A = \{\mathsf{Share}_i | P_i \in A\}$.
- *The following holds:*

$$H(S|SHARE_A) = \begin{cases} 0, & if \quad A \in \Sigma \\ H(S), & if \quad A \in \Gamma \end{cases}$$

where H is the entropy function [CT06], S is a random variable induced by s and $SHARE_A$ is a random variable induced by Share_A.

We next define monotone access structures.

Definition 2 (Monotone Access Structure). *An access structure Σ is called monotone provided the following holds:*

$$if \ \ A \in \Sigma \ \ and \ \ A' \supseteq A, \ \ then \ \ A' \in \Sigma.$$

In [CDM00] it is shown how to design a secret-sharing scheme for any given monotone access structure Σ using monotone span programs (MSP); we briefly recall the same in the sequel.

Linear Secret-Sharing Scheme (LSSS) and MSP [CDM00]: On a very high level, an MSP M is an $\ell \times d$ matrix over $\mathbb{F}$, with $\ell \geq d$ and $\ell \geq n$, where

$$M = \begin{pmatrix} m_1 \\ \vdots \\ m_\ell \end{pmatrix}.$$

There exists a labeling function $\psi : \{1, \ldots, \ell\} \to \mathcal{P}$ and we say row j is *associated* with party P_i if $\psi(j) = P_i$. For a subset of parties $A \subseteq \mathcal{P}$, let M_A be the sub-matrix of M consisting of the rows m_i such that $\psi(i) \in A$. Matrix M has the property that A is an access set if and only if the vector $(1, 0, \ldots, 0)$ is in the linear span of M_A. Given such an M, an LSSS can be designed as follows:

Algorithm Sh: To share a secret $s \in \mathbb{F}$, the dealer D does the following:

– Select a random vector $r \in \mathbb{F}^{d-1}$ and compute a vector

$$v = M \times \begin{pmatrix} s \\ r \end{pmatrix}$$

where $v = (v_1, \ldots, v_\ell)^T$.
– Let $\mathsf{LSSS}(s, r) \overset{def}{=} (\mathsf{Share}_1, \ldots, \mathsf{Share}_n)$, where $\mathsf{Share}_i = \{v_j | \psi(j) = P_i\}$. Dealer D gives Share_i to party P_i for $i = 1, \ldots, n$.

Algorithm Rec: Let $A \in \Sigma$ be an access set. To reconstruct s, the parties in A do the following:

– Let μ_A be a row vector such that $\mu_A \cdot M_A = (1, 0, \ldots, 0)$; such a μ_A is bound to exist as $(1, 0, \ldots, 0)$ is in the linear span of M_A. Given such a μ_A, the parties in A reconstruct s by computing:

$$s = \mu_A \cdot \mathsf{Share}_A, \ \ where \ \ \mathsf{Share}_A = \{\mathsf{Share}_i | P_i \in A\}.$$

We say that the above (M, ψ) is an MSP which realizes[3] Γ. In [CDM00] it is shown how to design an MSP realizing any monotone access structure. Moreover, it is also shown that the above pair of algorithms (Sh, Rec) indeed constitute a valid secret-sharing scheme.

---

[3] Readers familiar with the classical (n, t) Shamir secret-sharing scheme [Sha79] can see that M for the Shamir's scheme is the $n \times (t + 1)$ Vandermonde matrix. The vector $(s, r)^T$ constitutes the coefficients of the sharing polynomial of degree at most t, with s as the constant term. The reconstruction vector μ_A consists of the Lagrange's reconstruction coefficients.

In our protocols, we use the following metric to check the locations at which two vectors of shares match.

Definition 3. *Let* Share $=$ (Share$_1$, ..., Share$_n$) *and* Share* $=$ (Share$_1^\star$, ..., Share$_n^\star$) *be two vectors of shares, where* Share$_i$, Share$_i^\star$ *are associated with party* P_i, *for* $i = 1, \ldots, n$. *Then* Match(Share, Share*) $\stackrel{def}{=}$ $\{P_i|$Share$_i =$ Share$_i^\star\}$.

In our protocol, we will use the following property of LSSS, which simply follows from the property of MSP that the shares of the parties in an access set uniquely determine the shared secret.

Lemma 1 ([CDM00,Kur11]). *Let* Share *and* Share* *be two vectors of shares, where* Share $=$ LSSS(s, r), Share* $=$ LSSS$(s^\star, r^\star)$ *and* Σ *is the underlying access structure. If* Match(Share, Share*) $\in \Sigma$, *then* $s = s^\star$.

In our protocols, we often require to verify whether a given set of parties A is an access set. This can be done in time polynomial in the size of the underlying MSP by verifying whether the row vector $(1, 0, \ldots, 0)$ is in the linear span of M_A. We next present the following definition of $\mathcal{Q}^{(k)}$ condition from [HM97].

Definition 4 ($\mathcal{Q}^{(k)}$ **Condition** [HM97]). *Let* $\mathcal{S} \subseteq \mathcal{P}$ *be a set and* Γ *be an adversary structure over* $\mathcal{P}$. *We say that* $\mathcal{S}$ *satisfies* $\mathcal{Q}^{(k)}$ *condition with respect to* Γ *if there exists no* k *sets* $\mathcal{B}_1, \ldots, \mathcal{B}_k \in \Gamma$, *such that* $\mathcal{S} \subseteq \mathcal{B}_1 \cup \ldots \cup \mathcal{B}_k$.

Finally we note that like the standard secret-sharing schemes, we assume a fixed set of n parties. However it is well known in the literature how to deal with situations where the set of parties changes dynamically (see for example [NS13]); similar techniques are applicable even against generalized adversary.

2.1   The Asynchronous Model and Definitions

Our protocols are designed in the asynchronous communication setting, where there exists no global clock and the channels between the parties have arbitrary delays; thus there are no strict upper bounds within which messages reach to their destinations. The only guarantee in this model is that the messages sent by the honest parties will eventually reach to their destinations. The order of the message delivery is decided by a *scheduler*. To model the worst case scenario, we assume that the scheduler is under the control of the adversary. The scheduler can only schedule the messages exchanged between the honest parties, without having access to the "contents" of these messages. We consider a protocol execution in the asynchronous setting as a sequence of *atomic steps*, where a single party is *active* in each such step. A party is activated when it receives a message. On receiving a message, it performs an internal computation and then possibly sends messages on its outgoing channels. The order of the atomic steps are controlled by the scheduler. At the beginning of the computation, each party will be in a special *start* state. A party is said to *terminate/complete* the computation if it reaches a *halt* state, after which it does not perform any further computation. A protocol execution is said to be complete if all the honest parties terminate the computation. For an excellent introduction to the asynchronous protocols, see [Can95].

We next define asynchronous error-decodable secret-sharing scheme (AEDSS). Informally such a scheme consists of two protocols, a sharing protocol and a reconstruction protocol. The sharing protocol allows the dealer D to share a secret among $\mathcal{P}$. The reconstruction protocol allows the parties to reconstruct the shared secret, even if the corrupted parties provide incorrect shares. Both the protocols terminate for the honest parties. Formally:

Definition 5 (AEDSS). *Let* (AEDSS-Sh, AEDSS-Rec) *be a pair of asynchronous protocols for the dealer* D *and the set of parties* $\mathcal{P}$. *Dealer* D *has a private input* $s \in \mathbb{F}$ *for the protocol* AEDSS-Sh, *which it wants to share among* $\mathcal{P}$. *Then* (AEDSS-Sh, AEDSS-Rec) *is called an AEDS scheme for the adversary structure* Γ *if the following are satisfied for every possible* $\mathcal{A}$:

- **Termination.** *Every honest party eventually terminates* AEDSS-Sh, AEDSS-Rec.
- **Correctness.** *Every honest party upon terminating* AEDSS-Rec *outputs* s.
- **Privacy.** *No information about* s *is revealed to* $\mathcal{A}$ *during* AEDSS-Sh.

To design our AEDSS, we actually require a weaker primitive called *asynchronous weak secret-sharing* (AWSS). Like AEDSS, an AWSS scheme also consists of a sharing protocol and a reconstruction protocol. During the sharing protocol, D shares a secret s among $\mathcal{P}$; additionally the secret s is also handed over to a *designated* party $P_i \in \mathcal{P}$. The reconstruction protocol allows P_i to reveal s to a *designated* party $P_R \in \mathcal{P}$. The sharing protocol always terminate for the honest parties. But the reconstruction protocol need not always terminate for P_i and P_R; however it always terminates if P_i and P_R are *honest*. Moreover, it is required that if an *honest* P_R terminates the reconstruction protocol, then the reconstructed value is the same as distributed by D to P_i. More formally:

Definition 6 (AWSS). *Let* (AWSS-Sh, AWSS-Rec) *be a pair of asynchronous protocols for a pair of designated parties* $P_i, P_R \in \mathcal{P}$, *the dealer* D *and the set of parties* $\mathcal{P}$. *Dealer* D *has a private input* $s \in \mathbb{F}$ *for the protocol* AWSS-Sh, *which it wants to give to* P_i *and share it among* $\mathcal{P}$. *Party* P_i *has a private input* $s^\star$ *for* AWSS-Rec, *which it wants to reveal to party* P_R. *Then* (AWSS-Sh, AWSS-Rec) *is called an AWSS scheme for the adversary structure* Γ *if the following are satisfied for every possible* $\mathcal{A}$:

- **Termination.** *All the following should be satisfied:*
  - *Every honest party eventually terminates* AWSS-Sh.
  - *Every honest party in* $\mathcal{P} \setminus \{P_i, P_R\}$ *eventually terminates* AWSS-Rec. *Moreover, if* P_i *and* P_R *are honest then they also eventually terminate* AWSS-Rec.
- **Correctness.** *The following holds:*
  - *If* P_i *is honest then it obtains* s *at the end of* AWSS-Sh.
  - *If* P_R *is honest and terminates* AWSS-Rec, *then* $s^\star = s$.
- **Privacy.** *If* P_i *is honest then no information about* s *is revealed during* AWSS-Sh.
  - *If* P_R *is honest then no information about* s *is revealed during* AWSS-Rec.

3   Asynchronous Weak Secret-Sharing Scheme (AWSS)

Let $\mathcal{P}$ satisfies $\mathcal{Q}^{(3)}$ condition with respect to Γ. We present an AWSS scheme for Γ. The AWSS scheme consisting of protocols AWSS-Sh (for the sharing phase) and AWSS-Rec (for the reconstruction of the secret by a designated party) is presented in Fig. 1. Protocol AWSS-Sh is straight forward: let (M, ψ) be an MSP realizing Γ, where M is of size $\ell \times d$. The dealer then computes the shares according to the LSSS and distributes it among the parties. In addition, the secret along with the randomness used in the LSSS are handed to the designated party P_i. The protocol eventually terminates for every honest party.

During AWSS-Rec, party P_i first reveals the secret along with the randomness to the designated party P_R. Hence the participation of P_i is very crucial for the termination of AWSS-Rec; a corrupted P_i may choose not to participate in the protocol, in which case the protocol does not terminate for P_R. Independently, every party hands over their shares to P_R. Party P_R on receiving the secret and randomness from P_i, itself computes the shares of all the parties according to the LSSS. It then matches these shares with the ones it received from the corresponding parties. The comparison is performed till the matching occurs for all but a set of parties belonging to the adversary structure. This ensures that the matching occurs for a set of parties satisfying $\mathcal{Q}^{(2)}$ condition. Note that the shares of the parties reach asynchronously to P_R. Hence P_R needs to perform the comparison every time it receives a new share. The idea here is that the set of *honest* parties in $\mathcal{P}$ satisfy $\mathcal{Q}^{(2)}$ condition and their shares will eventually reach to P_R. Moreover, if P_i is *honest*, it correctly reveals the secret and randomness to P_R; so eventually the shares sent by the honest parties will match with the corresponding shares, computed by P_R itself from the revealed secret and the randomness. On the other hand, if P_i is *corrupted* and the matched set satisfies $\mathcal{Q}^{(2)}$ condition, then also it is ensured that P_i has revealed the correct secret. This is because among these matched set of parties, the set of honest parties will constitute an *access* set, whose shares uniquely determine the original secret.

The properties of AWSS-Sh and AWSS-Rec are stated in Theorem 1.

Theorem 1. *Let $\mathcal{A}$ be an adversary specified by an adversary structure Γ over $\mathcal{P}$, such that $\mathcal{P}$ satisfies $\mathcal{Q}^{(3)}$ condition with respect to Γ. Then (AWSS-Sh, AWSS-Rec) constitutes a valid AWSS scheme for Γ. Protocol AWSS-Sh runs in time polynomial in $|\mathbf{S}|$ and ℓ. Protocol AWSS-Rec runs in time polynomial in $|\mathbf{S}|$, ℓ and n.*

Proof **(Termination).** Since D is honest, protocol AWSS-Sh eventually terminates for every honest party. During AWSS-Rec, every honest party in the set $\mathcal{P} \backslash \{P_i, P_R\}$ terminates after sending its share to P_R. Next we consider an honest P_i and P_R. If P_i is honest, then P_R eventually receives (s, r) from P_i. Moreover, the set of honest parties in $\mathcal{P}$ satisfies $\mathcal{Q}^{(2)}$ condition with respect to Γ. Furthermore, the shares of each honest party eventually reaches P_R. Given this, it is easy to see that P_R eventually finds that the set $\mathcal{P} \setminus \mathsf{Match}(\mathbf{Y}, \mathbf{Y}') \in \Gamma$ and terminates.

Algorithm AWSS-Sh(D, P_i, s)

DISTRIBUTING THE SHARES, SECRET AND THE RANDOMNESS — Only D executes the following code:

- On having a secret $s \in \mathbb{F}$, D randomly selects $r \in \mathbb{F}^{d-1}$, computes LSSS(s, r) = (Share$_1$, ..., Share$_n$).
- D sends (s, r) to party P_i.
- D sends Share$_j$ to every party $P_j \in \mathcal{P}$ as its share and terminate.

RECEIVING THE SHARES — Every party $P_j \in \mathcal{P}$ executes the following code:

- Wait to receive the share Share$_j$ from D. If $P_j = P_i$ then additionally wait to receive (s, r). On receiving, terminate.

Algorithm AWSS-Rec(P_i, P_R, s)

DISCLOSING THE SECRET AND THE RANDOMNESS — Only P_i executes the following code:

- Send (s, r) to the party P_R.

DISCLOSING SHARES — Every $P_j \in \mathcal{P}$ (including P_i and P_R) executes the following code:

- Send the share Share$_j$ to the party P_R. If $P_j \neq P_R$ then terminate upon sending.

RECONSTRUCTING THE SECRET — Only party P_R executes the following code:

- Wait to receive (s, r) from P_i. Upon receiving, compute LSSS(s, r) = (Share$_1$, ..., Share$_n$). Let $\mathbf{Y}$ = (Share$_1$, ..., Share$_n$)
- Create a vector $\mathbf{Y}'$ of length n, initialize it to ($\perp$, ..., $\perp$(n times)); here $\perp$ is a special symbol not in $\mathbb{F}$. Repeat the following after receiving a share Share$_j$ from any party P_j such that $\mathbf{Y}'(j) = \perp$:
  - Set $\mathbf{Y}'(j) = $ Share$_j$.
  - Check if $\mathcal{P} \setminus \mathsf{Match}(\mathbf{Y}, \mathbf{Y}') \in \Gamma$.
  - If the above condition is satisfied then output s and terminate.

Fig. 1. Asynchronous weak secret-sharing scheme

Correctness. We have to consider an honest P_R. Since P_R terminates, it implies that $\mathcal{P} \setminus \mathsf{Match}(\mathbf{Y}, \mathbf{Y}') \in \Gamma$. This further implies that $\mathsf{Match}(\mathbf{Y}, \mathbf{Y}')$ satisfies $\mathcal{Q}^{(2)}$ condition with respect to Γ. If not, then the set $\mathsf{Match}(\mathbf{Y}, \mathbf{Y}') \cup \mathcal{P} \setminus \mathsf{Match}(\mathbf{Y}, \mathbf{Y}') = \mathcal{P}$ fails to satisfy $\mathcal{Q}^{(3)}$ condition, which is a contradiction. Let P_R receives ($s^\star, r^\star$) from P_i, implying $\mathbf{Y} = $ LSSS($s^\star, r^\star$). Note that if P_i is honest then ($s^\star, r^\star$) = (s, r). Let Com = $\mathsf{Match}(\mathbf{Y}, \mathbf{Y}')$ and let Com-Hon be the set of honest parties in the set Com. It is easy to see that Com-Hon is an access set, as otherwise this will contradict the fact that Com satisfies $\mathcal{Q}^{(2)}$. Now this implies that LSSS(s, r) and LSSS($s^\star, r^\star$) are the same, with respect to the parties in Com-Hon. This from Lemma 1 implies that $s^\star = s$.

Privacy. During AWSS-Sh, the dealer D just distributes the shares computed according to LSSS and there is no interaction among the parties. So it follows from the properties of LSSS that if P_i is honest, then no information about s is revealed to $\mathcal{A}$. During AWSS-Rec, all the shares are sent only to P_R, along with (s, r). So if P_R is honest, then the privacy of s is preserved.

Efficiency. During AWSS-Sh, computing the shares costs time polynomial in $|\mathbf{S}|$ and ℓ for D. During AWSS-Rec, party P_R has to verify if the set $\mathcal{P} \setminus \mathsf{Match}(\mathbf{Y}, \mathbf{Y}')$ $\in \Gamma$; moreover this verification may need to be performed n times in the worst case. So overall this costs time polynomial in n and ℓ for P_R.   □

4   Asynchronous Error-Decodable Secret-Sharing Scheme (AEDSS)

Let $\mathcal{P}$ satisfy $\mathcal{Q}^{(3)}$ condition with respect to Γ and let (M, ψ) be an MSP realizing Γ, where M is of size $\ell \times d$; we present an AEDSS tolerating $\mathcal{A}$. Note that $\mathcal{P}$ satisfying $\mathcal{Q}^{(3)}$ is a necessary condition for the existence of EDSS even in the synchronous communication setting. So obviously it is necessary even for AEDSS. The AEDSS scheme consisting of protocols AEDSS-Sh (for the sharing phase) and AEDSS-Rec (for the public reconstruction of the secret) is presented in Fig. 2. For simplicity and without loss of generality, we assume that $\ell = n$ and $\psi(i) = i$ for $i = 1, \ldots, n$.

During AEDSS-Sh, the dealer first computes the shares of the secret according to the LSSS and distributes the shares among the parties. In addition, for each share, it executes an instance of AWSS-Sh to further share the share; as a result, each party will have a share of each share. The protocol eventually terminates for the honest parties. During AEDSS-Rec, each share holder P_j executes an instance AWSS-Rec$_{ji}$ of AWSS-Rec to reveal its share to every other party P_i. Party P_i waits to terminate AWSS-Rec instances corresponding to the parties in an access set. Once it terminates those many instances, it reconstructs the secret using the shares revealed at the end of those instances. The idea here is that the instances AWSS-Rec$_{ji}$ executed by each *honest* P_j eventually terminates for each *honest* P_i and the set of honest parties constitute an access set. Moreover, for every instance AWSS-Rec$_{ji}$ terminated by P_i, the share revealed by P_j is the same as distributed by the dealer; this is true even if P_j is corrupted (follows from the properties of AWSS-Rec). So every honest P_i eventually terminates the protocol with the correct secret.

The properties of AEDSS-Sh and AEDSS-Rec are stated in Theorem 2.

Theorem 2. *Let $\mathcal{A}$ be an adversary specified by an adversary structure Γ over $\mathcal{P}$, such that $\mathcal{P}$ satisfies $\mathcal{Q}^{(3)}$ condition with respect to Γ. Then (AEDSS-Sh, AEDSS-Rec) constitutes a valid AEDSS for Γ. Both protocols run in time polynomial in $|\mathbf{S}|, n$ and ℓ.*

Proof (Termination). Since D is honest, the instances AWSS-Sh$_1, \ldots,$ AWSS-Sh$_n$ eventually terminates for every honest party and so every honest party eventually terminates AEDSS-Sh. We next claim that AEDSS-Rec also terminates eventually for every honest party P_i. This follows from the fact that the AWSS-Rec$_{ji}$ instances invoked by *honest* parties P_j corresponding to P_i eventually terminates (follows from Theorem 1) and the set of honest parties constitutes an access set.

Algorithm AEDSS-Sh(D, s)

DISTRIBUTING THE SHARES — Only D executes the following code:

- On having a secret $s \in \mathbb{F}$, D randomly selects $r \in \mathbb{F}^{d-1}$ and computes LSSS$(s, r) = (\text{Share}_1, \ldots, \text{Share}_n)$.
- For every $P_i \in \mathcal{P}$, D invokes an instance AWSS-Sh(D, P_i, Share$_i$) of AWSS-Sh. Denote this instance of AWSS-Sh as AWSS-Sh$_i$. Let r_i be the randomness used during AWSS-Sh$_i$ and Share$_{i1}, \ldots,$ Share$_{in}$ be the shares of the share Share$_i$ generated during AWSS-Sh$_i$.
- Terminate after terminating the instances AWSS-Sh$_1, \ldots,$ AWSS-Sh$_n$.

RECEIVING THE SHARE INFORMATION — Every party $P_j \in \mathcal{P}$ executes the following code:

- Corresponding to every $P_i \in \mathcal{P}$, participate in the instance AWSS-Sh$_i$ invoked by D.
- Terminate after terminating the instances AWSS-Sh$_1, \ldots,$ AWSS-Sh$_n$.

Let (Share$_j, r_j$), Share$_{jj}$ be obtained at the end of AWSS-Sh$_j$ and Share$_{ij}$ be obtained at the end of AWSS-Sh$_i$ for every $P_i \in \mathcal{P} \setminus P_j$.

Algorithm AEDSS-Rec(s)

DISCLOSING THE SHARES — Every party $P_j \in \mathcal{P}$ executes the following code:

- Corresponding to every $P_i \in \mathcal{P}$, invoke an instance AWSS-Rec(P_j, P_i, Share$_j$) of AWSS-Rec by sending (Share$_j, r_j$) to party P_j. Denote this instance of AWSS-Rec as AWSS-Rec$_{ji}$.
- Corresponding to every $P_k, P_i \in \mathcal{P}$, participate in the instance AWSS-Rec$_{ki}$ of AWSS-Rec by sending the share-share Share$_{kj}$ to the party P_i.

RECONSTRUCTING THE SECRET AND TERMINATION — Every party $P_i \in \mathcal{P}$ executes the following code:

- Create a set $\mathcal{C}_i$, which is initially $\emptyset$. Include party P_j to $\mathcal{C}_i$ if P_i terminates the instance AWSS-Rec$_{ji}$ with output Share$_j$.
- Wait till $\mathcal{C}_i \in \Sigma$. Once $\mathcal{C}_i \in \Sigma$, reconstruct s by applying the reconstruction algorithm of the LSSS to the shares $\{\text{Share}_j\}_{P_j \in \mathcal{C}_i}$ and terminate.

Fig. 2. Asynchronous error-decodable secret-sharing scheme

Correctness. Let P_i be an *honest* party. For correctness, we need to argue that if $P_j \in \mathcal{C}_i$ then Share$_j$ obtained at the end of the instance AWSS-Rec$_{ji}$ is indeed correct. However, this follows from the correctness property of AWSS-Rec (follows from Theorem 1).

Privacy. During AEDSS-Sh, the adversary gets no information about the shares of the honest parties, as they are shared via AWSS; this follows from the privacy property of AWSS. Given this, it is easy to see that s remains private during AEDSS-Sh.

Efficiency. In the protocol, n instances of AWSS-Sh and n^2 instances of AWSS-Rec are executed. It now follows easily that both AEDSS-Sh and AEDSS-Rec runs in time polynomial in $|\mathbf{S}|, n$ and ℓ. □

Notation 1. *In the next section, while using* AEDSS-Sh *and* AEDSS-Rec *we will use the following notation:*

- AEDSS-Sh$(s, r) = (\widehat{\text{Share}}_1, \ldots, \widehat{\text{Share}}_n)$: *this denotes* D *executing* AEDSS-Sh *with secret* s *and randomness* r *and computing all the information to be distributed among the parties. Here* $\widehat{\text{Share}}_j$ *denotes all the information distributed by* D *to the party* P_j. *Thus* $\widehat{\text{Share}}_j = (\text{Share}_j, r_j, \{\text{Share}_{ij}\}_{i=1}^n)$.
- AEDSS-Rec$_i(\cdot) = s$: *this denotes party* P_i *reconstructing* s *by executing its part of the code of* AEDSS-Rec(s). *This is an online process, where* P_i *asynchronously receives information from various parties and performs computation on them, till it receives sufficient information to reconstruct* s.

5   Application of AEDSS to Asynchronous Perfectly-Secure Message Transmission (APSMT)

In the model of *perfectly-secure message transmission* (PSMT), there exists a sender S and a receiver R connected by n channels $\mathcal{W} = \{w_1, \ldots, w_n\}$, some of which may be under the control of a computationally unbounded malicious adversary $\mathcal{A}$. There exists a message $m \in \mathbb{F}$, which S wants to reliably and privately communicate to R over the n channels, even in the presence of the adversary. In [SKR02], asynchronous PSMT (APSMT) is studied in the presence of a non-threshold adversary. In the asynchronous model, the channels are not synchronized and there can be arbitrary delays; the only guarantee is that information sent over honest channels reach to their destination eventually. The non-threshold adversary is characterized by an adversary structure Γ over $\mathcal{W}$, which denotes the set of possible subsets of channels which can be potentially corrupted by $\mathcal{A}$; during the execution of a protocol, adversary can select any subset of channels from Γ for corruption. In [SKR02] it is shown that APSMT tolerating $\mathcal{A}$ is possible if and only if $\mathcal{W}$ satisfies $\mathcal{Q}^{(3)}$ condition with respect to Γ. To prove the sufficiency of the $\mathcal{Q}^{(3)}$ condition, they presented a protocol, which requires $\mathcal{O}(|\mathcal{A}|)$ rounds of interaction between S and R, where $|\mathcal{A}|$ denotes the cardinality of the set of channels corrupted by $\mathcal{A}$ in the protocol. We present an APSMT protocol, which requires only one round of interaction between S and R, thus significantly improving the protocol of [SKR02].

Our APSMT protocol called APSMT (see Fig. 3) is adapted from our AEDSS, where S plays the role of the dealer and $\mathcal{W}$ is treated as $\mathcal{P}$, with w_i playing the "role" of party P_i. Specifically, S considers m as the secret to be shared among $\mathcal{P}$ and computes the information to be distributed among the parties as part of AEDSS-Sh; the information that needs to be given to party P_i is sent over the channel w_i. Receiver R asynchronously receives information over the channels and recovers m by executing the steps of AEDSS-Rec that an honest party would have executed to recover m.

The properties of APSMT are stated in Theorem 3, which simply follow from the protocol steps and the properties of AEDSS-Sh, AEDSS-Rec.

Protocol APSMT(S, m)

CODE FOR S — Only S executes the following code:

- On having the message m, S selects a random string r and computes AEDSS-Sh$(m, r) = (\widehat{\text{Share}_1}, \ldots, \widehat{\text{Share}_n})$.
- For $i = 1, \ldots, n$, S sends $\widehat{\text{Share}_i}$ over channel w_i and terminate.

CODE FOR R — Only R executes the following code:

- R asynchronously receives information over the channels, computes AEDSS-Rec$_i(\cdot) = m$ and terminates.

Fig. 3. Single round APSMT protocol

Theorem 3. *Let A be an adversary specified by an adversary structure Γ over W, such that W satisfies $Q^{(3)}$ condition with respect to Γ. Then* APSMT *constitutes a valid APSMT protocol. Protocol* APSMT *runs in polynomial time in $|\mathbf{M}|$, ℓ and n, where $\mathbf{M}$ is the set of all possible messages that can be communicated.*

6   Open Problems

Our AEDSS requires computation time polynomial in the size of the underlying MSP. In the worst case, the underlying MSP may be exponential in n. On the other hand, certain access structures like the threshold access structures have very efficient MSP and hence error-decoding mechanism, requiring computation time polynomial only in n. It is a very interesting open problem to design AEDSS for arbitrary access structures with running time polynomial in n.

Acknowledgement. The author would like to thank the anonymous referees for their useful feedback.

References

[BCG93] Ben-Or, M., Canetti, R., Goldreich, O.: Asynchronous secure computation. In: STOC, pp. 52–61. ACM (1993)

[Bla79] Blakley, G.R.: Safeguarding cryptographic keys. In: AFIPS National Computer Conference, pp. 313–317 (1979)

[Can95] Canetti, R.: Studies in secure multiparty computation and applications. Ph.D. thesis, Weizmann Institute, Israel (1995)

[CDM00] Cramer, R., Damgård, I.B., Maurer, U.M.: General secure multi-party computation from any linear secret-sharing scheme. In: Preneel, B. (ed.) EUROCRYPT 2000. LNCS, vol. 1807, pp. 316–334. Springer, Heidelberg (2000)

[CT06] Cover, T.M., Thomas, J.A.: Elements of Information Theory, 2nd edn. Wiley, New York (2006)

[DDWY93] Dolev, D., Dwork, C., Waarts, O., Yung, M.: Perfectly secure message transmission. J. ACM **40**(1), 17–47 (1993)

[ER89] Eichin, M.W., Rochlis, J.A.: With microscope and tweezers: an analysis of the internet virus of November 1988. In: IEEE Symposium on Security and Privacy, pp. 326–343. IEEE Computer Society (1989)

[HM97] Hirt, M., Maurer, U.M.: Complete characterization of adversaries tolerable in secure multi-party computation (extended abstract). In: PODC, pp. 25–34. ACM (1997)

[Kur11] Kurosawa, K.: General error decodable secret sharing scheme and its application. IEEE Trans. Inf. Theory **57**(9), 6304–6309 (2011)

[Mis00] Computer bug bites hard, spreads fast [online] (2000). http://www.cnn.com/2000/TECH/computing/05/04/iloveyou.01/index.html

[MS81] McEliece, R.J., Sarwate, D.V.: On sharing secrets and reed-solomon codes. Commun. ACM **24**(9), 583–584 (1981)

[NS13] Nojoumian, M., Stinson, D.R.: On dealer-free dynamic threshold schemes. Adv. Math. Commun. **7**(1), 39–56 (2013)

[Sha79] Shamir, A.: How to share a secret. Commun. ACM **22**(11), 612–613 (1979)

[SKR02] Srinathan, K., Kumar, M.V.N.A., Pandu Rangan, C.: Asynchronous secure communication tolerating mixed adversaries. In: Zheng, Y. (ed.) ASIACRYPT 2002. LNCS, vol. 2501, pp. 224–242. Springer, Heidelberg (2002)

On Anonymous Attribute Based Encryption

Payal Chaudhari[1,2], Manik Lal Das[2(✉)], and Anish Mathuria[2]

[1] LDRP-ITR, Gandhinagar, India
payal.ldrp@gmail.com
[2] DA-IICT, Gandhinagar, India
{maniklal_das,anish_mathuria}@daiict.ac.in

Abstract. Attribute Based Encryption (ABE) has found enormous scope in data confidentiality and fine-grained access control of shared data stored in public cloud. Classical ABE schemes require attaching the access policy along with the ciphertext, where the access policy describes required attribute values of a receiver. As attributes of a receiver (i.e., user) could relate to the identity of users, it could lead to reveal some sensitive information of the ciphertext (e.g. nature of plaintext, action sought from of receiver) for applications like healthcare, financial contract, bureaucracy, etc. Therefore, anonymizing attributes while sending ciphertext in use of ABE schemes, known as Anonymous ABE (AABE), is a promising primitive for enforcing fine-grained access control as well as preserving privacy of the receiver. In ASIACCS 2013, Zhang *et al.* proposed an AABE scheme using the *match-then-decrypt* [1] technique, where before performing decryption, the user performs a match operation that ensures a user whether he is the intended recipient for the ciphertext or not. We found that Zhang *et al.*'s scheme [1] is not secure, in particular, it fails to achieve receiver's anonymity. In this paper, we discuss the security weaknesses of Zhang *et al.*'s scheme. We show that an adversary can successfully check whether an attribute is required to decrypt a ciphertext, in turn, reveal the receiver's identity. We also suggest an improved scheme to overcome the security weakness of Zhang *et al.*'s scheme.

Keywords: Attribute based encryption · Anonymity · Bilinear pairing · Access structure

1 Introduction

Cloud infrastructure provides important features to service providers and consumers such as high data availability, reliability and low-cost maintainability of stored data in cloud server. While storing data in third party cloud server and accessing it over public channel security of users data and privacy of data access are become an active research problem in recent times. Attribute Based Encryption (ABE) [2–4] is a public-key cryptographic primitive suitable for data confidentiality and fine-grained access control enforced in public cloud. ABE is

© Springer International Publishing Switzerland 2015
S. Jajodia and C. Mazumdar (Eds.): ICISS 2015, LNCS 9478, pp. 378–392, 2015.
DOI: 10.1007/978-3-319-26961-0_23

more flexible than conventional public-key encryption, as ABE supports one-to-many encryption instead of one-to-one. With ABE, a data owner can share the data with multiple designated users by sending ciphertext, pertaining to target user's attributes. There are two kinds of ABE – (1) Key-Policy Attribute Based Encryption(KP-ABE) [2,4]; and (2) Ciphertext-Policy Attribute Based Encryption (CP-ABE) [3]. In KP-ABE, each ciphertext is labeled by the encryptor with a set of descriptive attributes and the private key of a user is associated with an access structure that specifies which type of ciphertext the user can decrypt. Whereas, in CP-ABE a user is identified by a set of attributes which are included in his private key, and a data owner can decide the access policy for decrypting ciphertext intended to the user. The encrypted message must specify an associated access policy over attributes. A user can only able to decrypt a ciphertext if the user's attributes pass through the ciphertext's access policy.

Although ABE scheme supports fine-grained access control, it discloses receiver's identity by which an adversary can guess the purpose of the message from the ciphertext by seeing receiver's attributes. For example, the adversary can guess that the receiver is a faculty if some of the attributes are *question paper*, *student*, *first year*, *discipline*, etc. Therefore, protecting receiver's identity while using ABE is a challenging research problem.

Anonymous ABE (AABE) is introduced in [5–8] as a promising public-key primitive that allows sender in achieving receiver anonymity in ABE. In anonymous CP-ABE, access policy is hidden in the ciphertext. A user requires to decrypt a ciphertext using secret key belongs to his attributes. If his secret key matches with the access policy, the user can successfully decrypt the ciphertext. If the attribute set associated with the secret key does not match with the access policy, then the user cannot get what access policy is specified by the encryptor. Therefore, the user in AABE schemes is required to perform the whole decryption procedure in order to verify if he is the intended receiver of the ciphertext or not, which results into a large overhead on the user when the ciphertext is not intended to him, but the user is engaged with the decryption procedure for the ciphertext.

In ASIACCS 2013, Zhang *et al.* [1] proposed an AABE scheme to address receiver anonymity by adding one matching phase before decryption of the ciphertext. The user performs the match-then-decrypt procedure using his secret key components and ciphertext components to check if he is the intended recipient of the ciphertext. The scheme of Zhang *et al.* is efficient than other AABE schemes in the sense that all receiver do not engage in full decryption procedure used in other schemes, instead after the partial decryption (i.e., match-then-decrypt phase) the intended receiver goes for the final decryption procedure in Zhang *et al.*' scheme. However, we found that Zhang *et al.*'s scheme is not secure, that is, it does not support receiver's anonymity. Any user of the system or an outsider (say, adversary) can successfully check whether an attribute is required to decrypt a ciphertext, in turn, reveal receiver's identity.

In this paper, we show the security weaknesses of Zhang *et al.*'s scheme. We propose an improved scheme to mitigate the security weakness of

Zhang *et al.*'s scheme. We show that the improved scheme is secure with respect to the security claim of the Zhang *et al.*'s scheme.

The remainder of the paper is organized as follows. Section 2 gives some preliminaries. Section 3 reviews Zhang *et al.*'s scheme [1]. Section 4 discusses the security flaws of Zhang *et al.*'s scheme [1]. Section 5 presents the improved scheme followed by its analysis in Sect. 6. Section 7 provides the performance analysis of the improved scheme. We conclude the paper in Sect. 8.

2   Preliminaries

In order to make the paper self-contained, we provide some preliminaries that have been used throughout the paper.

2.1   Bilinear Mapping

Let G and G_T be two multiplicative cyclic groups of prime order p. Let g be a generator of G and e be a bilinear map, $e : G \times G \to G_T$. The bilinear map e has the following properties:

- Bilinearity: for all $u, v \in G$ and $a, b \in \mathbb{Z}_p$, we have $e(u^a, v^b) = e(u, v)^{ab}$.
- Non-degeneracy: $e(g, g) \neq 1$.
- $e: G \times G \to G_T$ is efficiently computable.

2.2   Complexity Assumption

Decisional Linear (D-Linear) Assumption. Let z_1, z_2, z_3, z_4, $z \in \mathbb{Z}_p$ be chosen at random and g be a generator a cyclic group G. The decisional Linear assumption [9] is that no probabilistic polynomial-time algorithm $\mathcal{P}$ can distinguish the tuple $(Z_1 = g^{z_1}, Z_2 = g^{z_2}, Z_3 = g^{z_1 z_3}, Z_4 = g^{z_2 z_4}, Z = g^{z_3 + z_4})$ from the tuple $(Z_1 = g^{z_1}, Z_2 = g^{z_2}, Z_3 = g^{z_1 z_3}, Z_4 = g^{z_2 z_4}, Z = g^z)$ in G with more than a negligible advantage ϵ.

The advantage of $\mathcal{P}$ is $\Pr[\mathcal{P}(Z_1, Z_2, Z_3, g^{z_3 + z_4}) = 0]$ - $\Pr[\mathcal{P}(Z_1, Z_2, Z_3, g^z) = 0] = \epsilon$ where the probability is taken over the random choice of the generator g, the random choice of $z_1, z_2, z_3, z_4, z \in \mathbb{Z}_p$, and the random bits consumed by $\mathcal{P}$.

For the proof of our proposed improved scheme we consider a variant of D-Linear Assumption [7] which states that no probabilistic polynomial-time algorithm $\mathcal{P}$ can distinguish the tuple $(Z_1 = g^{z_1}, Z_2 = g^{z_2}, Z_3 = g^{z_3 + z_4}, Z_4 = g^{z_2 z_4}, Z = g^{z_1 z_3})$ from the tuple $(Z_1 = g^{z_1}, Z_2 = g^{z_2}, Z_3 = g^{z_3 + z_4}, Z_4 = g^{z_2 z_4}, Z = g^z)$ in G with more than a negligible advantage ϵ.

Decisional Diffie-Hellman (DDH) Assumption. Let $a, b, z \in \mathbb{Z}_p$ be chosen at random and g be a generator of a cyclic group G. The decisional Diffie Hellman assumption is that no probabilistic polynomial-time algorithm $\mathcal{B}$ can distinguish the tuple $(g, P = g^a, Q = g^b, R = g^{ab})$ from the tuple $(g, P = g^a, Q = g^b, R = g^z)$ with more than a negligible advantage ϵ.

The advantage of $\mathcal{P}$ is $\Pr[\mathcal{P}(g, g^a, g^b, g^{ab}) = 0]$ - $\Pr[\mathcal{P}(g, g^a, g^b, g^z) = 0] = \epsilon$ where the probability is taken over the random choice of the generator g, the random choice of a, b, $z \in \mathbb{Z}_p$, and the random bits consumed by $\mathcal{P}$.

2.3 Access Structure

Let there be n attributes in the universe and each attribute i (for all $1 \leq i \leq n$) has value set $V_i = \{v_{i,1}, v_{i,2}, \cdots, v_{i,n_i}\}$. $L = [L_1, L_2, \cdots, L_n]$ is an attribute list, where each L_i represents one value from the value set of attribute i. A ciphertext policy $W = [W_1, W_2, \cdots, W_n]$ where $W_i \subseteq V_i$ for $1 \leq i \leq n$. Each W_i represents the set of permissible values of an attribute i in order to decrypt the ciphertext. An access structure W is a rule that returns 1 when given a set L of attributes if L satisfies W, else, it returns 0. An attribute list L satisfies W, if $L_i \in W_i$ for all $1 \leq i \leq n$.

3 Zhang *et al.'s* Scheme

3.1 Scheme Definition

Zhang *et al.*'s scheme [1] consists of four algorithms – **Setup, KeyGen, Encrypt,** and **Decrypt**, which are defined as follows:

- Setup(1^l) $\rightarrow$ (PK,MK): The setup algorithm is run by the attribute center. On input a security parameter l it returns public key PK which is distributed to users, and the master key MK which is kept private.
- KeyGen(PK,MK,L) $\rightarrow$ SK_L: This algorithm is run by the attribute center. On input the public key PK, the master key MK and an attribute List L, it outputs SK_L as the attribute secret key associated with the attribute list L.
- Encrypt(PK, M, W) $\rightarrow$ CT_W: An encryptor runs this probabilistic algorithm. The input to the algorithm is public key PK, a message M, and a ciphertext policy W, and output is a ciphertext CT_W which is a encryption of M with respect to W.
- Decrypt(PK, CT_W, SK_L) $\rightarrow$ M or $\perp$: The decryption algorithm is deterministic and it involves two phases, attribute matching detection and decryption phase. When user provides as input the system public key PK, a ciphertext CT_W and a secret key SK_L associated with L, the algorithm proceeds as follows:
  1. Matching Phase: If the attribute list L associated with SK_L matches with the ciphertext policy W of CT_W then it initiates Decryption phase, else, it returns $\perp$ and terminates decryption.
  2. Decryption Phase: It returns message M.

3.2 Detailed Construction

- **Setup(1^l)**: Let G, G_T be cyclic multiplicative groups of prime order p, and $e : G \times G \rightarrow G_T$ be a bilinear map. $H : \{0,1\}^* \rightarrow G$ is a map-to-point function that takes a string as input and outputs a point on elliptic curve. The attribute center chooses $y \in_R \mathbb{Z}_p, g, g_1, g_2 \in_R G$, and computes $Y = e(g_1, g_2)^y$. The system public key is $PK = \langle g, g_1, g_2, Y \rangle$, and the master key is $\langle y \rangle$.

– **KeyGen**(*PK,MK,L*): Let $L = [L_1, L_2, \cdots, L_n]$ be the attribute list for the user who requires a secret key. The attribute center chooses $r_1, r_2, \cdots, r_{n-1} \in_R \mathbb{Z}_p$ and computes $r_n = y - \sum_{i=1}^{n-1} r_i \pmod{p}$. Then the attribute center chooses $r \in_R \mathbb{Z}_p$ and $\{\hat{r}_i, \lambda_i, \hat{\lambda}_i \in_R \mathbb{Z}_p\}_{1 \le i \le n}$, sets $\hat{r} = \sum_{i=1}^{n} \hat{r}_i$ and computes $[\hat{D}_0, D_{\Delta,0}] = [g_2^{y-\hat{r}}, g_1^r]$. For $1 \le i \le n$, the attribute center computes
$[D_{\Delta,i}, D_{i,0}, D_{i,1}, \hat{D}_{i,0}, \hat{D}_{i,1}] = [g_2^{\hat{r}_i} H(i||v_{i,k_i})^r, g_2^{\lambda_i}, g_1^{r_i} H(0||i||v_{i,k_i})^{\lambda_i}, g_1^{\hat{\lambda}_i}, g_2^{r_i} H(1||i||v_{i,k_i})^{\hat{\lambda}_i}]$ where $L_i = v_{i,k_i}$.
The secret key is $SK_L = \langle \hat{D}_0, D_{\Delta,0}, \{D_{\Delta,i}, D_{i,0}, D_{i,1}, \hat{D}_{i,0}, \hat{D}_{i,1}\}_{1 \le i \le n}\rangle$.

– **Encrypt**(*PK,M,W*): For encryption of a message M with respect to access control policy W, encryptor selects s, s' and, $s'' \in_R \mathbb{Z}_p$ and computes $\tilde{C} = MY^s, C_\Delta = e(g,g)^s Y^{s'}, C_0 = g^s, \hat{C}_0 = g_1^{s'}, C_1 = g_2^{s''}, \hat{C}_1 = g_1^{s-s''}$. Then for $1 \le i \le n$ and $1 \le j \le n_i$ the encryptor computes $[C_{i,j,\Delta}, C_{i,j,0}, \hat{C}_{i,j,0}]$ as follows: If $v_{i,j} \in W_i$ then $[C_{i,j,\Delta}, C_{i,j,0}, \hat{C}_{i,j,0}] = [H(i||v_{i,j})^s, H(0||i||v_{i,j})^s, H(1||i||v_{i,j})^{s-s''}]$ else if $v_{i,j} \notin W_i$ then $[C_{i,j,\Delta}, C_{i,j,0}, \hat{C}_{i,j,0}]$ are random elements.
The encryptor prepares $CT_W = \langle C_\Delta, C_0, \hat{C}_0, \tilde{C}, C_1, \hat{C}_1, \{\{C_{i,j,\Delta}, C_{i,j,0}, \hat{C}_{i,j,0}\}_{1 \le j \le n_i}\}_{1 \le i \le n}\rangle$.

– **Decrypt**(*PK,CT_W,SK_L*): A receiver of the ciphertext tests and decrypts the ciphertext CT_W using his secret key SK_L as follows:

1. Matching Phase: Receiver checks if his attributes L satisfies W or not by checking if following equality holds true. In the following equation the $C_{i,j}$ denotes the cipher component related to j^{th} value of an attribute i which a receiver possesses.

$$\frac{C_\Delta}{e(g, C_0)} = \frac{e(\hat{C}_0, \hat{D}_0 \prod_{i=1}^{n} D_{\Delta,i})}{e(\prod_{i=1}^{n} C_{i,j,\Delta}, D_{\Delta,0})}$$

If the equality holds false then decryption procedure is aborted; otherwise, the Decryption Phase is initiated.

2. Decryption Phase: The receiver recovers message M using following computation

$$M = \frac{\tilde{C} \prod_{i=1}^{n} e(C_{i,j,0}, D_{i,0}) e(\hat{C}_{i,j,0}, \hat{D}_{i,0})}{\prod_{i=1}^{n} e(C_1, D_{i,1}) e(\hat{C}_1, \hat{D}_{i,1})}.$$

4   Security Flaws in Zhang *et al.*'s Scheme

The authors of the scheme [1] proposed a cost-effective decryption procedure with a matching phase operation before the decryption procedure. The authors in [1] claimed that the scheme provides anonymity, and the ciphertext does not disclose the identity of the receiver. They have also stated that if any receiver succeeds in decryption of a message, he is not be able to identify who else can decrypt the same ciphertext. However, the authors did not provide the security proof for the matching phase elements and match operation. The security proof presented in their scheme primarily focused on the matter that the ciphertext is not distinguishable from any other random element, if the adversary does not possess the corresponding attribute secret key. We found that the cipher components for matching phase themselves discloses the underlying ciphertext access policy. In this section we show that the scheme [1] does not provide receiver's anonymity

We consider as an adversary, any user inside the system or any outsider, who has knowledge of universe of attributes. The adversary can successfully check if a particular attribute is included in ciphertext. In particular, the attributes which make the attack successful are $\hat{C}_0$ and $\{\{C_{i,j,\Delta}\}_{1\leq j\leq n_i}\}_{1\leq i\leq n}$. To check whether an attribute $v_{i,j}$ is included in ciphertext or not, the adversary calculates $D'_{\Delta,i,j} = H(i\|v_{i,j})$. Then, the adversary checks if following equation returns true for an attribute $v_{i,j}$.

$$e(\hat{C}_0, D'_{\Delta,i,j}) = e(C_{i,j,\Delta}, g_1)$$

If the above equality holds true, the adversary can conclude that the attribute used in the equation is included in ciphertext access policy. With this, the adversary now checks if a specific attribute which may be an identity of a user is integrated in access policy or not.

For example, suppose a University has three different departments *"Computer Science, Electrical Engineering, and Mechanical Engineering"*. The attribute categories and their corresponding value sets are as follows.

- For the attribute *"Role"* $W_{Role} = \{Dean, Teacher, Student, Administrative Staff\}$
- For the attribute *"Department"* $W_{Dept} = \{CS, EL, ME\}$
- For the attribute *"Course"* $W_{Course} = \{PhD, MS, BS\}$

When the Dean sends some confidential notice to all teachers in an encrypted form using the scheme [1], the Dean generates an encrypted message with following ciphertext components. For simplicity, we do not show all ciphertext components. Instead, we provide the ciphertext components for the attribute *"Role"*.

$$C_\Delta = e(g,g)^s Y^{s'}$$
$$C_0 = g^s$$
$$\hat{C}_0 = g_1^{s'}$$
$$\tilde{C} = MY^s$$
$$C_1 = g_2^{s''}$$
$$\hat{C}_1 = g_1^{s-s''}$$

$$\{C_{Role,Teacher,\Delta}, C_{Role,Teacher,0}, \hat{C}_{Role,Teacher,0}\}$$
$$= \{H(Role\|Teacher)^{s'}, H(0\|Role\|Teacher)^{s''}, H(1\|Role\|Teacher)^{s-s''}\}$$

Random values are provided for other attributes such as *Student, Dean* and *Administrative staff*.

The adversary now checks whether a *Teacher* is the intended recipient of the ciphertext with following equation.

$$e(\hat{C}_0, H(Role\|Teacher)) = e(C_{Role,Teacher,\Delta}, g_1).$$

The correctness of the equation is shown below.

$$e(\hat{C}_0, H(Role\|Teacher))$$
$$= e(g_1^{s'}, H(Role\|Teacher))$$
$$= e(H(Role\|Teacher)^{s'}, g_1)$$
$$= e(C_{Role,Teacher,\Delta}, g_1)$$

To recover the whole access policy the adversary requires $n_i \times n$ bilinear pairing operations. Let $m = \max (n_i)_{1 \leq i \leq n}$. Therefore, to disclose the receiver's identity the adversary requires at most $O(mn)$ bilinear pairing operations.

5   An Improved Scheme

The security weakness of the scheme in [1] occurs in the *matching phase*. The authors in [1] do not provide any security proof for the matching phase components. In the improved scheme we provide an improved matching phase that can be incorporated with any existing Anonymous ABE schemes. We do not include the cipher components and key components required for encryption and decryption of a message as it depends on the AABE scheme used for encryption and decryption of a message. The proposed modified scheme uses a set of parameters which is isolated from the parameters used for the encryption and decryption of a message. The underlying access structure for the improved scheme is as described in Sect. 2.3.

5.1   Scheme Definition

Like Zhang *et al.*'s scheme [1], the improved scheme consists of Setup, KeyGen, Encrypt, and Decrypt phases, which are defined as follows.

Setup(1^l): The Setup algorithm takes as input a security parameter l. The output of this phase is Master Secret Key MSK and Master Public Key MPK.

KeyGen(MSK,MPK,L): On input of an attribute list L, MSK and MPK, the algorithm outputs user's secret key SK_L.

Encrypt(MPK, W): The Encrypt algorithm takes as input the ciphertext access policy W required for decryption and MPK. The output of this algorithm is cipher components CT_W, which are used for matching phase.

Match(MPK,SK_L,CT_W): Match phase enables the receiver to check whether he is the intended receiver or not. It takes as input MPK, SK_L, CT_W, and returns whether the SK_L is matched with CT_W or not. The output of the algorithm will guide the receiver as he should perform the decryption of the received ciphertext or not.

5.2   Detailed Construction

The scheme works as follows.

- **Setup**(1^l): The Attribute Center (AC) performs the setup phase. It selects two groups G and G_T of prime order p whose bit-length is l and a bilinear mapping function $e : G \times G \to G_T$. The AC chooses two random generators g_1 and g_2 from group G and one hash function H is defined as H: $\{0,1\}^* \to G$. The master secret key MSK is chosen as $\langle \alpha, \beta \in_R \mathbb{Z}_p \rangle$. The corresponding master public key MPK $\langle g_1, g_2, g_1^\alpha, g_2^\beta, e(g_1, g_2)^\alpha \rangle$ is published.

- **KeyGen**(MSK,MPK,L): Let $L=[L_1, L_2, \cdots, L_n]$ be the attribute list for the user who requires a secret key. Here L_i represents a value $v_{i,j}$ that a user possess for attribute i. A user possess exactly one value $v_{i,j}$ for each attribute i where $1 \leq i \leq n$. For every user in the system the AC picks a random value ρ and generates a user's secret key SK_L for performing the matching phase operation as follows.

$$D = (g_2 \prod\nolimits_{i=1}^n H(i\|v_{i,j}))^\alpha \cdot g_2^\rho \text{ where } L_i = v_{i,j}.$$
$$\bar{D} = g_1^{\frac{\rho}{\beta}}$$

- **Encrypt**(MPK,W): We provide the construction of cipher components for matching phase only. Therefore, we have not included encryption of message. The algorithm takes the access policy W and public key MPK as input. Here, $W = \{W_1, W_2, \cdots W_n\}$ where W_i $\{1 \leq i \leq n\}$ is the set of values permissible for decryption. To prepare the cipher components for matching phase the encryptor takes secret values s and t from $\mathbb{Z}_p$ and makes n portions of t as t_i such that $\sum_{i=1}^n t_i = t$. For attribute values from each set W_i create the following cipher components.
  - If $v_{i,j} \in W_i$ $\tilde{C}_{i,j} = g_2^{t_i} H(i\|v_{i,j})^{st}$
  - If $v_{i,j} \notin W_i$ $\tilde{C}_{i,j}$ is a random value.
  The other cipher components are $\hat{C} = g_1^{st}, \bar{C} = g_2^{st\beta}$ and $C' = e(g_1, g_2)^{\alpha(s-1)t}$.

- **Match**(MPK, SK_L, CT_W): A user performs the match operation before going for decryption of an encrypted message. The user checks if his set of attribute values L satisfies access policy W or not by checking if following equality holds true. User collects the relevant $\tilde{C}_{i,j}$ cipher components. Here $\tilde{C}_{i,j}$ denotes cipher component related to value $v_{i,j}$ for an attribute i which a receiver possesses.

$$C' = \frac{e(\hat{C}, D)}{e(\prod_{i=1}^n \tilde{C}_{i,j}, g_1^\alpha)e(\bar{C}, \bar{D})}$$

If the equality does not hold true, the decryption procedure for a message is aborted, otherwise, the user initiates a decryption procedure related to encryption scheme used for encrypting a message.

Correctness: The correctness of the matching phase is as follows.

$$\frac{e(\hat{C}, D)}{e(\prod_{i=1}^{n} \tilde{C}_{i,j}, g_1^\alpha)e(\bar{C}, \bar{D})}$$

$$= \frac{e(g_1^{st}, (g_2 \prod_{i=1}^{n} H(i||v_{i,j}))^\alpha \cdot g_2^\rho)}{e(\prod_{i=1}^{n} (g_2^{t_i} H(i||v_{i,j})^{st}), g_1^\alpha)e(g_2^{st\beta}, g_1^{\frac{\rho}{\beta}})}$$

$$= e(g_1, g_2)^{(\alpha(s-1))t}$$

$$= C'$$

After the matching phase, the receiver goes for the final decryption procedure as in [1] to obtain the message.

6   Security Analysis

6.1   Security Model

We consider the IND-sCP (Indistinguishability against selective ciphertext policy) model to analyze the proposed improved scheme. In the analysis we exclude the encryption and decryption of a message as they are not part of the proposed matching scheme. The improved scheme is simulated with the following security game.

Init: The adversary $\mathcal{A}$ commits two ciphertext Policies W_0^* and W_1^* that he wishes to be challenged upon.

Setup: The challenger $\mathcal{B}$ chooses l as a security parameter and chooses α at random from $\mathbb{Z}_p$. $\mathcal{B}$ also defines a bilinear mapping function from $G \times G \to G_T$ and chooses two generators from G as g_1, g_2. The master private key is α. The public parameters g_1, g_2, g_1^α, g_2^β and $e(g_1, g_2)^\alpha$ are sent to $\mathcal{A}$.

The game has following four steps.

Step 1. **Preprocessing Phase.** With this phase $\mathcal{A}$ issues polynomially bounded number of queries and gathers following items from the challenger.
- Secret key SK_L for attribute set L such that L satisfies either both challenge ciphertext policies W_0^* and W_1^* or satisfies none of them.
- matching phase elements for different access policies W.

Step 2. **Challenge Phase.** The challenger $\mathcal{C}$ randomly picks a bit $\nu = 0$ or 1 and submits the ciphertext elements for matching phase related to W_ν^* using two random secret values s, t from $\mathbb{Z}_p$.

Step 3. **Post Processing Phase.** The adversary $\mathcal{A}$ is allowed to run a number of queries as done in preprocessing phase.

Step 4. **Guess:** The adversary $\mathcal{A}$ outputs a guess ν'. $\mathcal{A}$ wins the game if $\nu' = \nu$. The advantage of $\mathcal{A}$ in this game is defined as $Adv_{\mathcal{A}}(l) = |Pr[\nu' = \nu] - 1/2|$.

We show that the improved scheme is secure in the IND-sCP model. We prove the security of the scheme relies on the hardness of D-Linear Assumption and Decisional Diffie-Hellman assumption. We prove the security of proposed scheme in two theorems. In first theorem we prove that unless a valid decryption key is available, the adversary is not able to find a valid match. In the second theorem we prove that receiver anonymity is preserved in the improved scheme. We show that even if an adversary is able to get a valid key and find the match successfully, he can not find out the underlying access policy.

The security model consists of a Challenger $\mathcal{C}$, a Simulator $\mathcal{S}$ and an Adversary $\mathcal{A}$.

Theorem 1. *If an adversary can break the proposed improved scheme in the random oracle model, then a simulator can be constructed who can break the D-Linear assumption with a non-negligible advantage.*

Proof. We show that without a correct decryption key $\mathcal{A}$ is not able to compute any function of C'. If an adversary is able to succeed in doing so with non-negligible advantage ϵ_1, then we are able to design a simulator $\mathcal{S}$ that can play the D-Linear game with advantage $\frac{\epsilon_1}{2}$. For the proof we consider a variant of D-Linear assumption. The simulation proceeds as follows: We first let the challenger set the groups G and G_T of prime order p, with an efficient bilinear map, e and generator g. The challenger flip a fair binary coin μ, outside of $\mathcal{S}$'s view. If $\mu = 0$, the challenger sets $(g, Z_1, Z_2, Z_3, Z_4, Z) = (g, g^{z_1}, y^{z_2}, y^{z_2 z_4}, y^{z_3+z_4}, y^{z_1 z_3})$, otherwise it sets $(g, Z_1, Z_2, Z_3, Z_4, Z) = (g, g^{z_1}, g^{z_2}, g^{z_2 z_4}, g^{z_3+z_4}, g^z)$ for values z_1, z_2, z_3, z_4 and z chosen randomly from $\mathbb{Z}_p$.

Init: The simulator $\mathcal{S}$ runs $\mathcal{A}$. $\mathcal{A}$ commits two access policies W_0^* and W_1^* for which he wishes to be challenged upon.

Setup: $\mathcal{S}$ takes the following values: $g_1 = g^a$, $g_2 = g$, $g_1^\alpha = g^{a\alpha}$ with the assumption that $\alpha = z_1$. Here a is chosen randomly from $\mathbb{Z}_p$. With the selection of random value β from $\mathbb{Z}_p$, g_2^β is calculated as g^β. $H(i\|v_{i,j})$ is assumed as $g^{\frac{1}{n z_1}+H'(i\|v_{i,j})}$. Here n denotes the number of attribute categories and $H'(i\|v_{i,j})$ is computed from random oracle, producing an element of $\mathbb{Z}_p$ in output. The simulator $\mathcal{S}$ announces the public key as $g_1 = g^a$, $g_2 = g$, $g_1^\alpha = g^{a z_1}$, $g_2^\beta = g^\beta$, $e(g_1, g_2)^\alpha = e(g, g)^{a z_1}$.

Preprocessing Phase: The adversary $\mathcal{A}$ gathers following information from the simulator $\mathcal{S}$.

- Whenever $\mathcal{A}$ makes its kth key generation query for the set S_k of attributes such that S_k satisfies neither W_0^* nor W_1^*. The simulator $\mathcal{S}$ selects a random value $\rho \in \mathbb{Z}_p$ and the resultant key components are generated as follows.

$$D = (g_2 \prod_{i=1}^{n} H(i\|v_{i,j_i}))^\alpha \cdot g_2^\rho$$

$$= (g \prod_{i=1}^{n} g^{\frac{1}{n z_1}+H'(i\|v_{i,j_i})})^{z_1} \cdot g^\rho$$

$$= g^{z_1} \cdot g^{1+\sum_{i=1}^{n}(H'(i\|v_{i,j_i})z_1)} \cdot g^{\rho}$$

$$= Z_1 \cdot g \cdot Z_1^{\sum_{i=1}^{n}(H'(i\|v_{i,j_i}))} \cdot g^{\rho}$$

$$\bar{D} = g_1^{\frac{\rho}{\beta}} = g^{\frac{a\rho}{\beta}}$$

- When $\mathcal{A}$ issues queries for ciphertext elements related to any access policy W, then the simulator $\mathcal{S}$ chooses random values s and t from $\mathbb{Z}_p$ and provides the output of matching phase components incorporating access policy W.

Challenge: Let the two challenge ciphertext policies submitted by the adversary $\mathcal{A}$ are $W_0^* = [W_{0,1}, W_{0,2}, \cdots, W_{0,n}]$ and $W_1^* = [W_{1,1}, W_{1,2}, \cdots, W_{1,n}]$.

Now $\mathcal{S}$ does following. $\mathcal{S}$ flips a random coin ν, and computes the cipher components for W_ν^* as follows. $\mathcal{S}$ assumes $st=z_1z_3$, with the assumptions that $s = \frac{z_1z_3}{z_4(z_2+1)}$ and $t = z_4(z_2+1)$. For the values which are included in W_ν^*, $\mathcal{C}$ calculates $\tilde{C}_{i,j} = g_2^{t_i} H(i\|v_{i,j_i})^{st} = g^{\frac{z_2z_4+z_4}{n}} g^{(\frac{1}{nz_1}+H'(i\|v_{i,j_i}))z_1z_3} = Z_4^{\frac{1}{n}} Z_3^{\frac{1}{n}} Z^{H'(i\|v_{i,j_i})}$.

For other attribute values which are not included in W_ν^*, $\tilde{C}_{i,j}$ are random values. Subsequent cipher components are calculated by $\mathcal{S}$ as $\hat{C} = g_1^{st} = Z^a$, $\bar{C} = g_2^{st\beta} \doteq Z^\beta$ and $C' = \frac{e(Z_1^a,Z)e(g,Z)}{e(Z_1^a,Z_4)e(Z_1,Z_3)}$. C' is correct cipher component only if $Z = g^{z_1z_3}$. Else C' is a random element. Ciphertext components $\tilde{C}, \bar{C}, \hat{C}, C'$ are given to $\mathcal{A}$.

Post Processing Phase: $\mathcal{A}$ is allowed to run a number of queries for attribute keys and ciphertext components for matching phase with the same conditions as imposed in the preprocessing phase.

Guess: $\mathcal{A}$ submits a guess ν' of ν. If $\nu' = \nu$, then $\mathcal{S}$ outputs $\mu=1$ to indicate that it was given a valid D-Linear tuple, else it outputs $\mu=0$ to indicate that the ciphertext is a random element. Therefore, $\mathcal{A}$ gains no information about ν, in turn, $Pr[\nu \neq \nu'|\mu = 0]= \frac{1}{2}$. As the simulator guesses $\mu'=0$ when $\nu \neq \nu'$, $Pr[\mu = \mu'|\mu = 0] = \frac{1}{2}$. If $\mu = 1$, then the adversary $\mathcal{A}$ is able to view a valid matching phase components with advantage $\epsilon_1(l)$, a negligible quantity in security parameter in l. Therefore, $Pr[\nu = \nu'|\nu = 1] = \frac{1}{2} + \epsilon_1(l)$. Similarly, the simulator $\mathcal{S}$ guesses $\mu'=1$ when $\nu = \nu'$, in turn, $Pr[\mu' = \mu|\mu = 1] = \frac{1}{2} + \epsilon_1(l)$. The overall advantage of the simulator in D-Linear game is $\frac{1}{2} \times Pr[\mu = \mu'|\mu = 0] + \frac{1}{2} \times Pr[\mu = \mu'|\mu = 1] - \frac{1}{2} = \frac{1}{2} \times \frac{1}{2} + \frac{1}{2} \times (\frac{1}{2} + \epsilon_1(l)) - \frac{1}{2} = \frac{\epsilon_1(l)}{2}$.

Therefore, if the $\mathcal{A}$ has a non-negligible advantage $\epsilon_1(l)$ in the above game then we can build a simulator (S) which can break the D-Linear problem with non-negligible quantity $\frac{\epsilon_1(l)}{2}$. Hence, the theorem. $\square$

Theorem 2. *The proposed improved scheme provides receiver anonymity in IND-sCP game under the DDH assumption if there is no polynomial time adversary $\mathcal{A}$ who can distinguish a valid ciphertext and a random element with non-negligible advantage $Adv_{\mathcal{A}}(l)$ in security parameter l.*

Proof. In the second theorem we prove that the cipher components provides receiver anonymity. We prove in the following game that even if an attacker gains a valid decryption key, he is only able to find a correct match with C'. The attacker can not find out the underlying access policy. This proof strengthen our claim that even if any user is able to find himself as the intended recipient for a ciphertext, he is not able to find out who else are the other intended recipients for the same ciphertext. We show that the cipher components generated for an access policy are indistinguishable from an element chosen randomly from the group.

We first let the challenger set the groups G and G_T of prime order p, with an efficient bilinear map, e and generator g. The challenger flips a binary coin μ outside of S view and assigns a tuple $(g, A = g^a, B = g^b, Z)$ to $\mathcal{A}$. If $\mu = 1$ then the challenger sets Z as g^{ab} else a random value with equal probability.

Init: The simulator S runs $\mathcal{A}$. $\mathcal{A}$ commits two access policies W_0^* and W_1^* for which he wishes to be challenged upon.

In W_0^* and W_1^* for one attribute λ, $W_{0,\lambda}^* \neq W_{1,\lambda}^*$. There is at least one value $v_{\lambda,r}$ from value set of attribute λ, such that $v_{\lambda,r} \notin W_{0,\lambda}^*$ and $v_{\lambda,r} \in W_{1,\lambda}^*$. Here $1 \leq r \leq n_\lambda$. For rest of the attributes $W_{0,i}^* = W_{1,i}^*$ where $1 \leq i \leq n$ and $i \neq \lambda$.

Setup: S takes the following values: $g_1 = g$, $g_2 = g^{x_2}$. Here, x_2 is chosen randomly from $\mathbb{Z}_p$. $H(i\|v_{i,j})$ is computed as an output of an random oracle. Another two random secret values are chosen as α and β. The simulator S announces the public key as: $g_1 = g$, $g_2 = g^{x_2}$, $g_1^\alpha = g^\alpha$, $g_2^\beta = g^{x_2\beta}$, $e(g_1,g_2)^\alpha = e(g,g)^{x_2\alpha}$.

Preprocessing Phase: The attacker $\mathcal{A}$ collects following results in response of his queries made to simulator.

- Whenever $\mathcal{A}$ makes its kth key generation query for the set L_k of attributes such that $F(L_k, W_0^*) = F(L_k, W_1^*)$. That is, $\mathcal{A}$ is allowed to issue a valid secret key for which the match procedure returns true with the challenge ciphertext components. However the restriction is imposed as the key should match with both the challenge access structure W_0^* and W_1^*. The simulator S selects a random value ρ and the key components are generated as follows.

$$D = (g_2 \prod_{i=1}^{n} H(i\|v_{i,j_i}))^\alpha \cdot g_2^\rho = (g^{x_2} \cdot g^{H'(i\|v_{i,j})})^\alpha \cdot g^{x_2\rho}$$

$$\bar{D} = g_1^{\frac{\rho}{\beta}} = g^{\frac{\rho}{\beta}}$$

- For the matching phase, S chooses random values s, and t from $\mathbb{Z}_p$. Then S provides the output of matching phase components for access policies W.
- The attacker issues the query for $H(i\|v(i,j))$. For all the attribute values except $v_{\lambda,r}$, The simulator S runs the random oracle function and provides as output an element from G. The simulator S records the queries and its outputs. So that if any query is repeated by attacker then the same result as given for that query previously is repeated in output. For an query for $H(\lambda\|v_{\lambda,r})$ the output returned is $B = g^b$.

Challenge: Then $\mathcal{S}$ flips a random coin ν.

- $\mathcal{S}$ sets st as a and t is selected as any random value chosen from $\mathbb{Z}_p$. This results in $g_1^{st} = g^a = A$ and $g_2^{st\beta} = g^{x_2 a\beta} = A^{x_2\beta}$.
- The simulator $\mathcal{S}$ generates n shares of value t and use each share t_i for encrypting the values for attribute i. For all the cipher components $W_{\nu,i}^*$ where $1 \leq i \leq n$ and $i \neq \lambda$ the cipher components $\tilde{C}_{i,j}$ are generated as $g_2^{t_i} H(i\|v_{i,j})^{st} = g^{x_2 t_i} g^{H'(i\|v_{i,j})a}$.
- For values $v_{\lambda,j}$ of attribute $W_{\nu,\lambda}^*$ which are included in both $W_{0,\lambda}$ and $W_{1,\lambda}$, the cipher components $\tilde{C}_{\lambda,j}$ are generated as in the real scheme using the value of t_λ.
- For the value $v_{\lambda,r}$ which makes a differentiation between $W_{0,\lambda}$ and $W_{1,\lambda}$, the cipher component $\tilde{C}_{\lambda,r}$ is calculated as follows.
  - If $\nu = 0$ then $\tilde{C}_{\lambda,r}$ will be a random value. This is valid because $\tilde{C}_{\lambda,r}$ is not in $T_{0,\lambda}$ as per definition.
  - If $\nu = 1$ then $\tilde{C}_{\lambda,r}$ is set as $g^{x_2 t_\lambda} Z$. Here we have taken the output of $H(\lambda\|v(\lambda,j))$ from random oracle as g^b. If Z is a valid element with value g^{ab} then $\tilde{C}_{\lambda,r}$ will be a correct element else it will be a random element.
- C' is calculated as $e(g,g)^{ax_2\alpha}$.

The adversary will be given ciphertext components $\langle C', \hat{C}, \bar{C}, \{\{\tilde{C}_{i,j}\}_{1 \leq j \leq n_i}\}_{1 \leq i \leq n}\rangle$. At the end of the challenge phase the adversary uses following values $\langle\ g_1^{st} = g^a$, $H(\lambda\|v(\lambda,r)) = g^b$, $C_{\lambda,r}\ \rangle$ to find out the underlying access policy. If $C_{\lambda,r}$ is a correct cipher component then it represents the value $g_2^{t_\lambda} \cdot g^{ab}$ else it is a random value.

Postprocessing Phase: $\mathcal{A}$ is allowed to run a number of queries for attribute keys and ciphertext components for the matching phase with the same conditions as imposed in the preprocessing phase.

Guess: $\mathcal{A}$ submits a guess ν' of ν. If $\nu' = \nu$, then $\mathcal{S}$ outputs $\mu=1$ to indicate that it was given a valid DDH-tuple, else it outputs $\mu=0$ to indicate that the ciphertext is a random element. Therefore, $\mathcal{A}$ gains no information about ν, in turn, $Pr[\nu \neq \nu' \mid \mu=0] = \frac{1}{2}$. As the simulator guesses $\mu'=0$ when $\nu \neq \nu'$, $Pr[\mu = \mu' \mid \mu=0] = \frac{1}{2}$. If $\mu = 1$, then the adversary $\mathcal{A}$ is able to view a valid cipher components with advantage $\epsilon_2(l)$, a negligible quantity in security parameter in l. Therefore, $Pr[\nu = \nu'|\mu = 1] = \frac{1}{2} + \epsilon_2(l)$. Similarly, the simulator $\mathcal{S}$ guesses $\mu'=1$ when $\nu = \nu'$, in turn, $Pr[\mu' = \mu|\mu = 1] = \frac{1}{2} + \epsilon_2(l)$. The overall advantage of the simulator in DDH game is $\frac{1}{2} \times Pr[\mu = \mu'|\mu = 0] + \frac{1}{2} \times Pr[\mu = \mu'|\mu = 1] - \frac{1}{2} = \frac{1}{2} \times \frac{1}{2} + \frac{1}{2} \times (\frac{1}{2} + \epsilon_2(l)) - \frac{1}{2} = \frac{\epsilon_2(l)}{2}$.

Therefore, if the $\mathcal{A}$ has a non-negligible advantage $\epsilon_2(l)$ in the above game then we can build a simulator (S) which can break the DDH problem with non-negligible quantity $\frac{\epsilon_2(l)}{2}$. Hence, the theorem. $\qquad\square$

7   Performance Analysis

We have experimented the proposed scheme on a Linux system with Intel core-i3 processor running at 2.30 GHz and 3 GB RAM. Pairings are constructed on the curve $y^2 = x^3 + x$ over the field F_q for some prime q = 3 mod 4. The order p of the groups G and G_T is a prime number 160 bits, while the length of q is 512 bits. The resultant time required in matching phase operation is around 0.04 to 0.08 s with respect to total number of attributes values ranging from 10 to 100.

The improved scheme facilitates a receiver to find out whether he is the intended recipient or not with just n multiplication operations and three bilinear pairing operations. Here, n denotes the number of attribute categories. The operation complexity of matching phase is $O(n) + O(1) \approx O(n)$. While comparing the improved scheme with Zhang et al.'s scheme we found the following results with respect to matching phase operation (Table 1).

Table 1. Comparison of the matching phase

Parameters (Used for match operation)	Zhang et al.'s scheme [1]	Proposed scheme
Number of user key components	$n+2$	2
Number of cipher components	$n_i \cdot n + 3$	$n_i \cdot n + 3$
Number of bilinear mapping operations	3	3
Number of multiplication operations	$2 \cdot n$	n

Here, n denotes the attribute categories in the system and n_i denotes the number of attribute values in i^{th} category ($1 \leq i \leq$ n).

We note that the performance comparison is done for the matching operation of the Zhang et al.'s scheme and the proposed improvement. The other AABE schemes [5–8] do not provide matching operation, as a result, the decryption procedure of these schemes are not efficient. The proposed improved scheme can be used with any existing AABE scheme to make the decryption procedure efficient.

8   Conclusion

We discussed anonymous attribute based encryption (AABE) schemes and found security flaws in a recently proposed AABE scheme [1]. The security weakness of the scheme [1] occurs in its matching phase that discloses the identity of the user. We proposed an improved scheme for the matching phase that keeps the scheme's anonymity feature intact. The proposed improved scheme can be incorporated in any AABE scheme in order to improve the efficiency of decryption procedure. User accountability is another important concern in AABE scheme, which can also be integrated in the proposed improvement and we left this as an interesting future scope of the proposed work.

References

1. Zhang, Y., Chen, X., Li, J., Wong, D.S., Li, H.: Anonymous attribute-based encryption supporting efficient decryption test. In: Proceedings of the ACM SIGSAC Symposium on Information, Computer and Communications Security, pp. 511–516 (2013)
2. Sahai, A., Waters, B.: Fuzzy identity-based encryption. In: Cramer, R. (ed.) EURO-CRYPT 2005. LNCS, vol. 3494, pp. 457–473. Springer, Heidelberg (2005)
3. Bethencourt, J., Sahai, A., Waters, B.: Ciphertext-policy attribute-based encryption. In: Proceedings of IEEE Symposium on Security and Privacy, pp. 321–334 (2007)
4. Goyal, V., Pandey, O., Sahai, A., Waters, B.: Attribute-based encryption for fine-grained access control of encrypted data. In: Proceedings of the ACM Conference on Computer and Communications Security, pp. 89–98 (2006)
5. Kapadia, A., Tsang, P.P., Smith, S.W.: Attribute-based publishing with hidden credentials and hidden policies. In: Proceedings of Network and Distributed System Security Symposium, pp. 179–192 (2007)
6. Yu, S., Ren, K., Lou, W.: Attribute-based content distribution with hidden policy. In: Proceedings of Workshop on Secure Network Protocols, pp. 39–44 (2008)
7. Nishide, T., Yoneyama, K., Ohta, K.: Attribute-based encryption with partially hidden encryptor-specified access structures. In: Bellovin, S.M., Gennaro, R., Keromytis, A.D., Yung, M. (eds.) ACNS 2008. LNCS, vol. 5037, pp. 111–129. Springer, Heidelberg (2008)
8. Li, J., Ren, K., Zhu, B., Wan, Z.: Privacy-aware attribute-based encryption with user accountability. In: Samarati, P., Yung, M., Martinelli, F., Ardagna, C.A. (eds.) ISC 2009. LNCS, vol. 5735, pp. 347–362. Springer, Heidelberg (2009)
9. Boneh, D., Boyen, X., Shacham, H.: Short group signatures. In: Franklin, M. (ed.) CRYPTO 2004. LNCS, vol. 3152, pp. 41–55. Springer, Heidelberg (2004)

Information Flow Control

An Automatic Inference
of Minimal Security Types

Dominik Bollmann, Steffen Lortz, Heiko Mantel, and Artem Starostin$^{(\boxtimes)}$

Computer Science Department, TU Darmstadt, Darmstadt, Germany
{bollmann,lortz,mantel,starostin}@mais.informatik.tu-darmstadt.de

Abstract. Type-based information-flow analyses provide strong end-to-end confidentiality guarantees for programs. Yet, such analyses are not easy to use in practice, as they require all information containers in a program to be annotated with security types, which is a tedious and error-prone task — if done manually. In this article, we propose a new algorithm for inferring such security types automatically. We implement our algorithm as an Eclipse plug-in, which enables software engineers to use it for verifying confidentiality requirements in their programs. We experimentally show our implementation to be effective and efficient.

We also analyze theoretical properties of our security-type inference algorithm. In particular, we prove it to be sound, complete, minimal, and of linear time-complexity in the size of the program analyzed.

1 Introduction

We present a solution for verifying confidentiality requirements in Java programs. Our solution consists of a type system for verifying information-flow security, a language for annotating sources, sinks, and other information containers, and an algorithm for inferring such annotations. We implement our solution as an Eclipse plug-in, and our experimental evaluation shows that it significantly outperforms prior solutions. We prove that our solution is sound and minimal.

Our solution runs in $O(n)$ time, where n is the size of the input program. It requires annotations of sources to be fixed, while allowing annotations of sinks and all other information containers to be flexible. Other solutions that run in $O(n)$ time require either annotations of all information containers to be fixed (see, e.g., [30]), or at least annotations of all sources and sinks to be fixed (see, e.g., [10]). On the other side of the spectrum, principal types [12,13,29] provide enough information for verifying a program against arbitrary annotations of sources and sinks. A disadvantage of principal types is that their construction requires $O(nv^3)$ time, where n is the size of the input program and v is the number of its variables [13]. A conceptual novelty of our solution is that, despite it runs in $O(n)$ time, it achieves minimality, similarly to principal types.

The soundness of our security analysis might not be a distinctive feature because there are other information-flow analyses that have been proven sound (e.g., [1,2,12,29–31]), but it is an important one. However, there are also well-known information-flow analyses for which no soundness result exists

© Springer International Publishing Switzerland 2015
S. Jajodia and C. Mazumdar (Eds.): ICISS 2015, LNCS 9478, pp. 395–415, 2015.
DOI: 10.1007/978-3-319-26961-0_24

(e.g., [4,8,18]). We consider soundness a crucial attribute, because without it, the guarantees established by a security analysis are unclear.

We implemented our solution as an Eclipse plug-in ADELE (Assistant for Developing Leak-free Programs). It supports developers in writing Java programs with secure information flow. ADELE analyzes the source code in the background, fully automatically, and reports detected information leaks. Due to the minimality result, ADELE provides developers with an overview of all potential sinks to which the confidential information flows. This overview enables an informed navigation in the decision space for refactoring the program into a leak-free one.

We experimentally evaluated our solution at a spectrum of Java programs. We observed that for a single manually annotated information container, our algorithm infers security types for up to 128 other containers. Hence, our algorithm reduces the burden of manual security-type annotation by up to two orders of magnitude. Regarding performance, our experiments suggest that our solution needs, on average, less than 0.02 ms to analyze a line of source code. We also wanted to compare, in practice, the performance of our solution with that of principal types. Unfortunately, we did not find any implementation of principal types that we could have used in an experimental comparison. The other most flexible sound algorithm for inferring security types [27], that we are aware of, is implemented in SECJ [26]. Hence, we used it as a point of comparison. We experimentally compared the performance of our solution and SECJ, which revealed ours to be two orders of magnitude faster (in addition to being more flexible).

In summary, the novelties of this article are both conceptual and practical. Conceptually, we show how to achieve minimality without having to use principal types. Practically, we present a solution for the verification of confidentiality requirements in Java programs that is sound and flexible, and we experimentally demonstrate it to be effective and efficient.

The article is structured as follows. In Sect. 2, we define the Java subset that we focus on. In Sect. 3, we present our language for annotating information containers, our type system for verifying information-flow security, and a soundness result for the type system. In Sect. 4, we introduce our type-inference algorithm. In Sect. 5, we provide soundness, completeness, minimality, and complexity results for our algorithm. In Sect. 6, we present the implementation of our solution. In Sect. 7, we experimentally evaluate our solution. After a discussion of related work in Sect. 8, we conclude in Sect. 9.

ADELE, its source code, and our benchmark programs are available for download under the MIT license at www.mais.informatik.tu-darmstadt.de/adele.

2   Programming Language

We focus on a sequential object-oriented fragment of Java with recursive method calls. Let underspecified sets $\mathcal{C}$, $\mathcal{M}$, $\mathcal{F}$, and $\mathcal{X}$ denote the sets of class, method, field, and variable names, respectively. Let $\mathcal{M} \cap \mathcal{F} = \emptyset$, let $this, result \in \mathcal{X}$, and let $Object \in \mathcal{C}$. We define the sets of data types T, expressions E, statements

S, method definitions M, and class definitions C by the BNF in Fig. 1, where $C, D \in \mathcal{C}$, $x \in \mathcal{X}$, $f \in \mathcal{F}$, $m \in \mathcal{M}$, and overlined terms, e.g., $\overline{T\,x}$, denote arbitrarily but finitely many repetitions of the term. We define a program as $P \subseteq \mathsf{C}$.

A data type is the primitive type boolean or a class name from $\mathcal{C}$. An expression is a literal expression null, true, or false, a variable access x, a field access $e.f$, an equality check $e_1 == e_2$, a type check e instanceof C, or a cast $((C)\ e)$. A statement is a field assignment $e_1.f = e_2$, variable assignment $x = e$, instance creation

$$T ::= \textbf{boolean} \mid C$$

$$E ::= \textbf{null} \mid \textbf{true} \mid \textbf{false} \mid x \mid E.f \mid E == E$$
$$\mid E\ \textbf{instanceof}\ C \mid ((C)\ E)$$

$$S ::= E.f = E \mid x = E \mid x = \textbf{new}\ C() \mid x = E.m(\overline{E})$$
$$\mid T\ x = E;\ S \mid \textbf{if}\ (E)\ \{\ S;\ \}\ \textbf{else}\ \{\ S;\}\mid S;S$$

$$M ::= T\ m(\overline{T\ x})\ \{\ T\ result;\ S;\ \textbf{return}\ result;\ \}$$

$$C ::= \textbf{class}\ C\ \textbf{extends}\ D\ \{\ \overline{T\ f};\ \overline{M}\ \}$$

Fig. 1. Programming language syntax.

$x = \textbf{new}\ C()$, method call $x = e.m(e_1, \ldots, e_n)$, variable declaration $T\ x = e;\ S$, conditional branching $\textbf{if}\ (e)\ \{S_1;\}\ \textbf{else}\ \{S_2;\}$, or sequential composition $S_1; S_2$. In a method definition $T\ m(T_1\ x_1, \ldots, T_n\ x_n)\{T\ result;\ S;\ \textbf{return}\ result;\}$, m denotes the method name, $T_1\ x_1, \ldots, T_n\ x_n$ denote the formal parameters with their data types, S denotes the method body, and T denotes the data type of the return value. In a class definition $\textbf{class}\ C\ \textbf{extends}\ D\ \{T_1\ f_1; \ldots; T_i\ f_i;\ M_1 \ldots M_j\}$, C denotes the class name, D denotes the name of the immediate superclass of C, $T_1\ f_1, \ldots, T_i\ f_i$ denote the field declarations of C with their data types, and $M_1, \ldots, M_j$ denote the method definitions of C.

Class definitions specify the inheritance hierarchy: For all classes $C, D \in \mathcal{C}$ defined in a program P, C is a subclass of D, written $C \leq_P D$, if and only if $D = C$ or another class $D' \in \mathcal{C}$ is defined, such that D' is the immediate superclass of C and $D' \leq_P D$. A subclass C of a class D inherits all field declarations and method definitions from D. If C defines a method with the same name as in D, then the method is overridden by the new definition from C. We assume that $Object$ is the common superclass of all classes in a program, and that it does not declare any fields or define any methods.

We call a program *well-formed* if (1) it satisfies type-safety conditions commonly imposed by Java compilers, (2) each class has a unique name, fields and methods have unique names within each class, and local variables and formal parameters have unique names within each method, and (3) field names declared in a class are not reused in field declarations of its subclasses, and methods are only overridden by methods that declare the same formal parameters with the same data types. In this article, we assume all programs to be well-formed.

The uniqueness of names allows identifying classes within a program P by elements of $\mathcal{C}$, fields by elements of $\mathsf{FID} = \mathcal{F} \times \mathcal{C}$, methods by elements of $\mathsf{MID} = \mathcal{M} \times \mathcal{C}$, and variables by elements of $\mathsf{VID} = \mathcal{X} \times \mathcal{M} \times \mathcal{C}$. For all $C \in \mathcal{C}$ and $f \in \mathcal{F}$, the partial function $\mathsf{fieldsof}_P : \mathcal{C} \rightharpoonup \mathcal{P}(\mathcal{F})$ is defined, such that $C \in dom(\mathsf{fieldsof}_P)$ if and only if P contains a definition of class C, and $f \in \mathsf{fieldsof}_P(C)$ if and only if class C in P declares or inherits field f. For all $C \in \mathcal{C}$ and $m \in \mathcal{M}$, the partial function $\mathsf{methodsof}_P : \mathcal{C} \rightharpoonup \mathcal{P}(\mathcal{M})$ is defined, such that $C \in dom(\mathsf{methodsof}_P)$ if and only if P contains a definition of class C, and $m \in \mathsf{methodsof}_P(C)$ if and only if class C in P defines or inherits method m. For all $C \in \mathcal{C}$, $m \in \mathcal{M}$, and $x \in \mathcal{X}$, the partial function $\mathsf{varsof}_P : \mathsf{MID} \rightharpoonup \mathcal{P}(\mathcal{X})$ is defined, such that $(m, C) \in dom(\mathsf{varsof}_P)$ if and only if $m \in \mathsf{methodsof}_P(C)$, $x \in \mathsf{varsof}_P(m, C)$ if and only if formal parameter x is declared by method m defined or inherited by class C in P, or local variable x is declared by method m defined by class C in P. The set of *defined identifiers* in P is $\mathsf{names}_P = \{(x, m, C) \in \mathsf{VID} \mid x \in \mathsf{varsof}_P(m, C)\}$ $\cup \{(f, C) \in \mathsf{FID} \mid f \in \mathsf{fieldsof}_P(C)\} \cup \{(m, C) \in \mathsf{MID} \mid m \in \mathsf{methodsof}_P(C)\}$.

The semantics of the language in Fig. 1 corresponds to that of a syntactically equivalent Java subset.

3   A Type System for Verifying Information-Flow Security

We define a security type system in the spirit of [1] for the language from Sect. 2. This type system ensures that confidential information does not flow to untrusted sinks during a program execution. Which containers store confidential and which store public information is specified by security-type annotations.

3.1   An Annotation Language and Information-Flow Policy

To specify between which information containers information may flow, every information container in a program may be annotated with a security-type annotation @High or @Low. Such annotations induce an information-flow policy.

An information-flow policy (brief: policy) defines a set of security domains $\mathcal{D}$, an interference relation $\sqsubseteq \subseteq \mathcal{D} \times \mathcal{D}$, and a domain assignment $\mathsf{da} : \mathsf{VID} \cup \mathsf{FID} \rightharpoonup \mathcal{D}$. The security domains (brief: domains) from the set $\mathcal{D}$ denote abstract levels of confidentiality. The interference relation is a partial order on security domains that specifies between which domains information may flow. The domain assignment associates some information containers in a program with a security domain. A policy defines the permitted flows of information between the information containers: For any two containers $a, b \in \mathsf{VID} \cup \mathsf{FID}$ with $\mathsf{da}(a) = d$ and $\mathsf{da}(b) = d'$, information from a may be written into b if and only if $d \sqsubseteq d'$. We assume a two-level information-flow policy $(\mathcal{D}, \mathsf{da}, \sqsubseteq)$ with the security domains $\mathcal{D} = \{low, high\}$ and the interference relation $\sqsubseteq = \{(low, low), (low, high), (high, high)\}$. This policy allows expressing that confidential information must not leak to untrusted sinks of a program. While we focus on the two-level policy, an extension to arbitrary lattices is straightforward.

The domain assignment is induced from the security-type annotations of a concrete program as follows. For any program P with security-type annotations, the *annotation-induced domain assignment* $\mathsf{da} : \mathsf{VID} \cup \mathsf{FID} \rightharpoonup \mathcal{D}$ is defined, such that for all $x \in \mathcal{X}$, $m \in \mathcal{M}$, $C \in \mathcal{C}$, and $f \in \mathcal{F}$: (1) $\mathsf{da}(f, C)$ is defined if and only if program P contains class C that declares field f, and the declaration is annotated with either @High or @Low, (2) if $\mathsf{da}(f, C)$ is defined, $\mathsf{da}(f, C) = high$ if the declaration of field (f, C) in program P is annotated with @High, and $\mathsf{da}(f, C) = low$ otherwise, (3) $\mathsf{da}(x, m, C)$ is defined if and only if program P contains class C that defines method m, and in the definition, the declaration of variable x is annotated with either @High or @Low, (4) if $\mathsf{da}(x, m, C)$ is defined, $\mathsf{da}(x, m, C) = high$ if the declaration of variable (x, m, C) is annotated with @High, and $\mathsf{da}(x, m, C) = low$ otherwise. An information-flow policy $(\mathcal{D}, \mathsf{da}, \sqsubseteq)$ with an annotation-induced domain assignment intuitively requires for an annotated program that information obtained from information containers annotated with @High shall not flow to those annotated with @Low.

Due to inheritance and overriding, certain identifiers in names_P can be aliases of the same information container. To ensure that a domain assignment does not associate different security domains with such identifiers, we require any domain assignment for P to be *consistent for P*. For any set X, a partial function $g : \mathsf{names}_P \rightharpoonup X$ is consistent for P if and only if for all $C, D \in \mathcal{C}$ with $C \leq_P D$ it holds: (1) for all $f \in \mathsf{fieldsof}_P(D)$, if $(f, C) \in dom(g)$ and $(f, D) \in dom(g)$ then $g(f, C) = g(f, D)$, (2) for all $m \in \mathsf{methodsof}_P(D)$, if $(m, C) \in dom(g)$ and $(m, D) \in dom(g)$, then $g(m, C) = g(m, D)$, (3) for all $m \in \mathsf{methodsof}_P(D)$ and $x \in \{x \mid (x_1, \ldots, x_n) = \mathsf{pars}_P(m, D) \wedge \exists i \in \{1, \ldots, n\}.x = x_i\}$, if $(x, m, C) \in dom(g)$ and $(x, m, D) \in dom(g)$, then $g(x, m, C) = g(x, m, D)$, where the partial function $\mathsf{pars}_P : \mathsf{MID} \rightharpoonup \mathcal{X}^*$ is defined for $T \ m(T_1 \ x_1, \ldots, T_n \ x_n)\{\ldots\}$ in the definition of any class $C \in \mathcal{C}$ in P, such that $\mathsf{pars}_P(m, C) = (x_1, \ldots, x_n)$, and $\mathsf{pars}_P(m, C) = \mathsf{pars}_P(m, D)$ if C inherits m from superclass $D \in \mathcal{C}$.

3.2 A Security Type System

A domain assignment assigns security domains to a subset of fields and variables in a program. Our security type system requires the domain assignment to be extended, so that all defined identifiers of fields, methods, and variables are associated with a security domain. A *complete typing* (brief: typing) of a program P is a function $\mathsf{t} : \mathsf{names}_P \to \mathcal{D}$ that is consistent for P. Intuitively, a typing of a program associates all variables, fields, and methods of the program with security domains, such that all identifiers that could be aliases of the same field, method, or variable are assigned the same domain. We call typing t *compatible* with domain assignment da if and only if for all $a \in dom(\mathsf{da})$ it holds $\mathsf{t}(a) = \mathsf{da}(a)$.

Our type system uses a function type_P to determine data types of information containers and expressions in a given program P. The definition of type_P relies on the partial functions $\mathsf{ftype}_P : \mathsf{FID} \rightharpoonup \mathsf{T}$ and $\mathsf{vtype}_P : \mathsf{VID} \rightharpoonup \mathsf{T}$ to determine data types of fields and local variables, respectively. $\mathsf{ftype}_P(f, C)$ is defined if and only if $f \in \mathsf{fieldsof}_P(C)$, and $\mathsf{ftype}_P(f, C) = T$ if f is declared with data type T in C,

$$\mathsf{type}_P(x, m, C) = \mathsf{vtype}_P(x, m, C)$$
$$\mathsf{type}_P(e_1.f, m, C) = \mathsf{ftype}_P(f, \mathsf{type}_P(e_1, m, C))$$
$$\mathsf{type}_P(((T)\ e_1), m, C) = T$$
$$\mathsf{type}_P(\mathtt{null}, m, C) = Object$$
$$\mathsf{type}_P(e, m, C) = \mathtt{boolean}, \text{ for all other } e$$

Fig. 2. Data types of expressions.

and otherwise $\text{ftype}_P(f, C) = \text{ftype}_P(f, D)$, where D is the immediate super-class of C. $\text{vtype}_P(x, m, C)$ is defined if and only if $x \in \text{varsof}_P(m, C)$, and $\text{vtype}_P(x, m, C) = T$ if x is declared with data type T in method m defined by C, and otherwise $\text{vtype}_P(x, m, C) = \text{vtype}_P(x, m, D)$, where D is the immediate superclass of C. Finally, the partial function $\text{type}_P : \text{E} \times \text{MID} \rightharpoonup \text{T}$ is defined in Fig. 2, where $e, e_1, e_2 \in \text{E}$, $T \in \text{T}$, $x \in \mathcal{X}$, $f \in \mathcal{F}$, $m \in \mathcal{M}$, and $C \in \mathcal{C}$.

For a given program P and function $\gamma : \text{names}_P \rightarrow Y$, we use *method signatures* $\text{msig}_P^\gamma : \text{MID} \rightharpoonup Y^*$ to denote the values that γ associates with a method's formal parameters, return value, and heap effect, e.g., in the signature $\text{msig}_P^t(m, C) = \langle d_t, (d_1, \ldots, d_n) \xrightarrow{d_h} d_r \rangle$ of method (m, C) wrt. typing t, d_t and d_r denote the security domains associated with *this* and *result*, respectively, $d_1, \ldots, d_n$ denote the domains associated with the method's parameters, and d_h denotes the domain associated with the method's heap effect.

Whether a program is typable wrt. a typing is defined by a set of security typing rules. A selection of our security typing rules corresponding to object-oriented features is presented in Fig. 3. In these rules, the judgment for expressions is denoted by $m, C, P; t \vdash e : d$, where m, C, P denote the context in which the expression e is evaluated, and d denotes the security domain of the value the expression evaluates to wrt. typing t of P. The judgment for statements is denoted by $m, C, P; t \vdash S : (d', \kappa')$, where $S \in \text{S}$ denotes a statement and $d', \kappa' \in \mathcal{D}$ denote security domains. The judgment for method definitions is denoted by $C, P; t \vdash M$, where C denotes the class of program P in which the method is defined. The judgment for typing program P wrt. complete typing t of P is denoted by $t \vdash P$. It is derivable if the judgment for method definitions is derivable wrt. t, for all method definitions in all class definitions in P. We say that program P is *accepted* by our security type system wrt. complete typing $t : \text{names}_P \rightarrow \mathcal{D}$ for P if and only if the judgment $t \vdash P$ is derivable.

If a program is accepted by the type system wrt. a complete typing of the program, the typing is an approximation of the possible distribution of confidential

$$\frac{\begin{array}{c} m, C, P; t \vdash e_1 : d_1 \\ d = t(f, \text{type}_P(e_1, m, C)) \\ d_1 \sqsubseteq d' \qquad d \sqsubseteq d' \end{array}}{m, C, P; t \vdash e_1.f : d'} \qquad \frac{\begin{array}{c} m, C, P; t \vdash e_1 : d_1 \quad m, C, P; t \vdash e_2 : d_2 \\ d = t(f, \text{type}_P(e_1, m, C)) \\ d_1 \sqsubseteq d \qquad d_2 \sqsubseteq d \qquad \kappa' \sqsubseteq d \end{array}}{m, C, P; t \vdash e_1.f = e_2 : (d', \kappa')}$$

$$\frac{\begin{array}{c} m, C, P; t \vdash e_1 : d_1 \quad \ldots \quad m, C, P; t \vdash e_n : d_n \\ \text{msig}_P^t(m_2, \text{type}_P(e_1, m, C)) = \langle d_t', (d_2', \ldots, d_n') \xrightarrow{d_h'} d_r' \rangle \\ d_x = t(x, m, C) \qquad \forall i \in \{2, \ldots, n\}. d_i \sqsubseteq d_i' \\ d_r' \sqsubseteq d_x \quad d_1 \sqsubseteq d_t' \quad d_1 \sqsubseteq d_h' \quad d_1 \sqsubseteq d_x \quad d' \sqsubseteq d_x \quad \kappa' \sqsubseteq d_h' \end{array}}{m, C, P; t \vdash x = e_1.m_2(e_2, \ldots, e_n) : (d', \kappa')}$$

$$\frac{m, C, P; t \vdash S : (d', \kappa') \quad t(m, C) \sqsubseteq \kappa'}{C, P; t \vdash T_r \ m(\ldots) \ \{ \ T_r \ \textit{result}; \ S; \ \textbf{return } \textit{result}; \}}$$

Fig. 3. Selected security typing rules.

information during program's execution. Intuitively, (1) each security domain associated by the typing with an information container is an upper bound on the security domains of containers from which information may flow into this one, and (2) each security domain associated by the typing with a method is a lower bound on all security domains of fields that the method may write.

3.3 Soundness of the Security Type System

We prove the soundness of our security type system wrt. a security property in the style of Noninterference [9]. For an execution of a single method, our noninterference-like security property intuitively requires that the information stored in *low* return values and *low* object fields on the resulting heap is independent from the information stored in *high* formal parameters and *high* object fields on the initial heap. Which information containers are *low* or *high* is given by a typing. If all executions of a method respect our noninterference-like security property, we call such a method *noninterfering wrt. a typing*. A program is *noninterfering wrt. a typing*, if all its methods are noninterfering wrt. the typing.

Theorem 1 (Soundness of the Security Type System). Let $P \subseteq C$ be a program and $t : \mathsf{names}_P \to \mathcal{D}$ be a complete typing for P. If $t \vdash P$ is derivable, then P is noninterfering wrt. t.

4 Our Security-Type Inference Algorithm

The type system from Sect. 3 requires a complete typing of a program for verification of the program's information-flow security. In this section, we define our security type inference algorithm to automatically infer, for a given program and a domain assignment, a complete typing for the program that is compatible with the domain assignment. The algorithm consists of four steps: (1) *Assignment of security type variables:* Associate each information container and method in the program not associated with a security domain by the domain assignment with a type variable. (2) *Derivation of constraints:* Derive constraints from the program that an inferred typings has to satisfy, so that the program is accepted wrt. the inferred typing by the security type system. (3) *Constraint solving:* Assign a domain to each type variable, so that all constraints are satisfied. (4) *Inferring a typing:* If constraint solving was successful, output a typing, and an error value indicating failure, otherwise. Sections 4.1, 4.2, 4.3 and 4.4 present Step 1 to Step 4, respectively.

4.1 Assignment of Security Type Variables

Let $\mathcal{V}$ denote the infinite *set of type variables*. Each information container and method in a given program, not associated with a domain by a given domain assignment, is associated with a type variable by the security context of the program and domain assignment. Let typevar : $\mathsf{VID} \cup \mathsf{FID} \cup \mathsf{MID} \to \mathcal{V}$ be an arbitrary but fixed injective function assigning type variables to identifiers of variables, fields, and methods. A *security context* for program P and domain assignment da is a function $\sigma : \mathsf{names}_P \to \mathcal{D} \cup \mathcal{V}$, such that:

- for all $(f, C) \in \mathsf{FID} \cap \mathsf{names}_P$ it holds that (1) if $D \in \mathcal{C}$ exists, so that $(f, D) \in dom(\mathsf{da})$ and $C \leq_P D \vee D <_P C$, then $\sigma(f, C) = \mathsf{da}(f, D)$, else (2) if $D \in \mathcal{C}$ exists, so that $f \in \mathsf{fieldsof}_P(D)$ and $C <_P D$, then $\sigma(f, C) = \sigma(f, D)$, and (3) $\sigma(f, C) = \mathsf{typevar}(f, C)$, otherwise,
- for all $(m, C) \in \mathsf{MID} \cap \mathsf{names}_P$ it holds that (1) if $D \in \mathcal{C}$ exists, so that $m \in \mathsf{methodsof}_P(D)$ and $C <_P D$, then $\sigma(m, C) = \sigma(m, D)$, and (2) $\sigma(m, C) = \mathsf{typevar}(m, C)$, otherwise, and
- for all $(x, m, C) \in \mathsf{VID} \cap \mathsf{names}_P$ it holds that (1) if $(x, m, C) \in dom(\mathsf{da})$, then $\sigma(x, m, C) = \mathsf{da}(x, m, C)$, else (2) if $D \in \mathcal{C}$ exists, so that $(x, m, D) \in dom(\mathsf{da})$, $C <_P D \vee D <_P C$, and $x \in \{x \mid (x_1, \ldots, x_n) = \mathsf{pars}_P(m, D) \wedge \exists i \in \{1, \ldots, n\}.x = x_i\}$, then $\sigma(x, m, C) = \mathsf{da}(x, m, D)$, else (3) if $D \in \mathcal{C}$ exists, so that $m \in \mathsf{methodsof}_P(D)$, $C <_P D$, and $x \in \{x \mid (x_1, \ldots, x_n) = \mathsf{pars}_P(m, D) \wedge \exists i \in \{1, \ldots, n\}.x = x_i\}$, then $\sigma(x, m, C) = \sigma(x, m, D)$, and (4) $\sigma(x, m, C) = \mathsf{typevar}(x, m, C)$, otherwise.

The first condition requires the security context to assign to each field identifier (1) the same security domain that da assigns to an alias of the field, (2) the same security type variable the security context assigns to the same field in a super class, or (3) a unique security type variable if the field is declared in the class denoted by the identifier. The second and third conditions impose similar requirements for method identifiers and variable identifiers, respectively. The third condition distinguishes between formal parameters and local variables, since only parameters can be aliases of each other, whereas local variables are only accessible within the declaring method definition.

A security context agrees with the corresponding domain assignment for all field and variable identifiers, for which the domain assignment is defined, by construction. All identifiers that are not associated with a security domain based on the domain assignment are assigned a security type variable. The set of type variables in the range of σ is denoted by $\mathsf{typevars}_\sigma = \{\alpha \in \mathcal{V} \mid \alpha \in rng(\sigma)\}$. The set $\mathsf{typevars}_\sigma$ denotes the set of type variables for which constant security domains have to be inferred to obtain a complete typing of the program P.

4.2   Derivation of Constraints

In the second step of our security-type inference algorithm, constraints on type variables are derived that a typing of a program has to satisfy, so that the program is accepted wrt. the typing by the security type system from Sect. 3. We use the notation for constraints and derivations rules in the spirit of [27].

Constraints. We denote constraints on type variables by constraint formulas. A *constraint formula* (brief: constraint) is a term $\lambda \preceq \lambda'$, where $\preceq$ is a binary relation symbol and $\lambda, \lambda' \in \mathcal{D} \cup \mathcal{V}$ are either security domains or type variables. The set $\mathcal{K}_V$ of all constraint formulas over some set of type variables $V \subseteq \mathcal{V}$ is defined by $\mathcal{K}_V = \{\lambda \preceq \lambda' \mid \lambda, \lambda' \in \mathcal{D} \cup V\}$. Intuitively, a constraint formula $\lambda \preceq \lambda'$ requires that information is permitted to flow from the security domain denoted by λ to the security domain denoted by λ'. A *constraint scheme* is a pair (V, K) of a finite set of type variables $V \subseteq \mathcal{V}$ and a set of constraint formulas $K \subseteq \mathcal{K}_V$ over the type variables in V. The set $\mathcal{S}$ of all constraint schemes is defined by $\mathcal{S} = \{(V, K) \mid V \subseteq \mathcal{V} \wedge |V| \in \mathbb{N}_0 \wedge K \subseteq \mathcal{K}_V\}$.

Constraint Derivation Rules. We define a set of derivation rules that analyze the possible flow of information through the program and generate a constraint scheme with constraints imposed on an acceptable typing of the program. Most of the rules impose constraints on auxiliary type variables that are not in the security context. To ensure the uniqueness of these type variables, all rules, except the rule for programs take a set V_0 of already used type variables, to exclude when selecting a new auxiliary type variable. Selected constraint derivation rules for object-oriented features of our language are given in Fig. 4.

The judgment for deriving constraint schemes from expressions is of the form $m, C, P; \sigma; V_0 \vdash e : \alpha \rightsquigarrow (V, K)$. It denotes that expression e in method (m, C) of program P under security context σ is associated with type variable α, and constraint scheme (V, K) specifies requirements on the security domain that α denotes. Intuitively, the constraint scheme derived from an expression requires that the domain denoted by α is an upper bound on the domains of all information containers from which information flows into the expression's value.

The judgment for deriving constraint schemes from statements is of the form $m, C, P; \sigma; V_0 \vdash S : (\alpha, \beta) \rightsquigarrow (V, K)$. It denotes that statement S in method (m, C) of program P under security context σ is associated with type variables α and β, and imposes constraints specified by constraint scheme (V, K). Intuitively, the derived constraints require that the auxiliary type variable α denotes a lower bound on all security domains of variables that the statement may write, β denotes a lower bound on all security domains of fields that the statement may write, and all security domains of information containers that the statement may write denote upper bounds on the security domains of the information written into the respective information container.

The judgment for deriving constraint schemes from method definitions is of the form $C, P; \sigma; V_0 \vdash T\ m(\ldots)\ \{\ T\ result;\ S;\ \mathtt{return}\ result;\} \rightsquigarrow (V, K)$. It denotes that the definition of method (m, C) in program P under security context σ imposes the constraints specified by constraint scheme (V, K). This constraint scheme contains the constraints derived from the body of the method and one additional constraint $\lambda_h \preceq \beta_1$, requiring that the security domain of the method's heap effect is a lower bound on the domains of the fields the execution of the method's body may write.

The constraint scheme derived from the definition of a class is comprised of the constraints imposed by the definitions of the methods of this class. The constraint scheme derived from a program is the union of all constraints of all defined methods of all classes in the program.

$$\frac{m, C, P; \sigma; V_0 \vdash e_1 : \alpha_1 \rightsquigarrow (V_1, K_1) \quad \lambda = \sigma(f, \mathsf{type}_P(e_1, m, C))}{\alpha \in \mathcal{V} \setminus (V_0 \cup V_1) \quad V = V_1 \cup \{\alpha\} \quad K = K_1 \cup \{\alpha_1 \preceq \alpha, \lambda \preceq \alpha\}}{m, C, P; \sigma; V_0 \vdash e_1.f : \alpha \rightsquigarrow (V, K)}$$

$$\frac{\begin{array}{cc} m, C, P; \sigma; V_0 \vdash e_1 : \alpha_1 \rightsquigarrow (V_1, K_1) & m, C, P; \sigma; V_0 \cup V_1 \vdash e_2 : \alpha_2 \rightsquigarrow (V_2, K_2) \\ \alpha, \beta \in \mathcal{V} \setminus (V_0 \cup V_1 \cup V_2) & V = V_1 \cup V_2 \cup \{\alpha, \beta\} \\ \lambda = \sigma(f, \mathsf{type}_P(e_1, m, C)) & K = K_1 \cup K_2 \cup \{\alpha_1 \preceq \lambda, \alpha_2 \preceq \lambda, \beta \preceq \lambda\} \end{array}}{m, C, P; \sigma; V_0 \vdash e_1.f = e_2 : (\alpha, \beta) \rightsquigarrow (V, K)}$$

$$m_1, C, P; \sigma; V_0 \vdash e_1 : \alpha_1 \rightsquigarrow (V_1, K_1)$$

$$\vdots$$

$$\frac{\begin{array}{c} m_1, C, P; \sigma; \bigcup_{i \in \{0, \ldots, n-1\}} V_i \vdash e_n : \alpha_n \rightsquigarrow (V_n, K_n) \\ \langle \lambda_t, (\lambda_2, \ldots, \lambda_n) \xrightarrow{\lambda_h} \lambda_r \rangle = \mathsf{msig}_P^\sigma(m_2, \mathsf{type}_P(e_1, m_1, C)) \quad \lambda_x = \sigma(x, m_1, C) \\ \alpha, \beta \in \mathcal{V} \setminus (\bigcup_{i \in \{0, \ldots, n\}} V_i) \quad V = \bigcup_{i \in \{1, \ldots, n\}} V_i \cup \{\alpha, \beta\} \\ K = K_1 \cup \bigcup_{i \in \{2, \ldots, n\}} (K_i \cup \{\alpha_i \preceq \lambda_i\}) \cup \\ \{\alpha_1 \preceq \lambda_t, \alpha_1 \preceq \lambda_h, \alpha_1 \preceq \lambda_x, \alpha \preceq \lambda_x, \beta \preceq \lambda_h, \lambda_r \preceq \lambda_x\} \end{array}}{m_1, C, P; \sigma; V_0 \vdash x = e_1.m_2(e_2, \ldots, e_n) : (\alpha, \beta) \rightsquigarrow (V, K)}$$

$$\frac{m, C, P; \sigma; V_0 \vdash S : (\alpha_1, \beta_1) \rightsquigarrow (V_1, K_1) \quad \lambda_h = \sigma(m, C) \quad K = K_1 \cup \{\lambda_h \preceq \beta_1\}}{C, P; \sigma; V_0 \vdash T\ m(\ldots)\ \{\ T\ result;\ S;\ \mathbf{return}\ result;\ \} \rightsquigarrow (V_1, K)}$$

Fig. 4. Selected constraint derivation rules.

4.3   Constraint Solving

In the third step of our security-type inference algorithm, the constraints in a derived constraint scheme are solved. The objective is to determine a *variable valuation* associating the type variables in the constraints with security domains, so that all constraints are satisfied if interpreting the binary relation $\preceq$ as $\sqsubseteq$. A variable valuation is a total function $I : V \to \mathcal{D}$, where $V \subseteq \mathcal{V}$ and V is finite. We denote the set of all variable valuations by $\mathcal{I}$. A variable valuation I is lifted to $\widehat{I} : V \cup \mathcal{D} \to \mathcal{D}$ so that for all $\lambda \in V \cup \mathcal{D}$ that $\widehat{I}(\lambda) = \lambda$ if $\lambda \in \mathcal{D}$ and $\widehat{I}(\lambda) = I(\lambda)$, otherwise. Hence, $\widehat{I}$ associates all domains with themselves.

A constraint formula $\lambda \preceq \lambda' \in \mathcal{K}_V$ is satisfied by a variable valuation I, denoted by $I \models \lambda \preceq \lambda'$, if and only if $\widehat{I}(\lambda) \sqsubseteq \widehat{I}(\lambda')$. For a set of constraint formulas $K \subseteq \mathcal{K}_V$, we write $I \models K$ to denote that $I \models \lambda \preceq \lambda'$ for all $\lambda \preceq \lambda' \in K$. Intuitively, constraint formula $\lambda \preceq \lambda'$ is satisfied by variable valuation I, if the interference relation $\sqsubseteq$ permits flows from the domain that I associates with the left operand to the domain that I associates with the right operand. A variable valuation satisfies a set of constraints if it satisfies all constraints in the set.

To solve a constraint scheme, we adopt a constraint solving algorithm of Rehof and Mogensen [21]. The algorithm takes a constraint scheme and either computes variable valuation I satisfying all constraints, or it determines that the constraint set is not satisfiable and outputs an error value $\bot$. We model this algorithm by the function $\mathsf{solve} : \mathcal{S} \to \mathcal{I} \cup \{\bot\}$.

4.4   Inferring a Typing

In the fourth step of our security-type inference algorithm, the results from the other steps are combined to infer a typing based on a program and a domain assignment. Our security-type inference algorithm takes a program and a domain assignment for the program as input, and either outputs a complete typing of the program, or an error value denoting that no typing could be inferred. We model our algorithm by the function infer : $\mathcal{P}(\mathsf{C}) \times (\mathsf{VID} \cup \mathsf{FID} \rightharpoonup \mathcal{D}) \rightarrow (\mathsf{names}_P \rightharpoonup \mathcal{D}) \cup \{\bot\}$ that is defined for any $P \subseteq \mathsf{C}$ and da : $\mathsf{VID} \cup \mathsf{FID} \rightharpoonup \mathcal{D}$ for P by

(1) $\mathsf{infer}(P, \mathsf{da}) = \widehat{\mathrm{I}} \circ \sigma$ if $(V, K) \in \mathcal{S}$ and $\mathrm{I} : V \to \mathcal{D}$ exist so that $\mathsf{solve}(V, K) = \mathrm{I}$ and $\sigma \vdash P \rightsquigarrow (V, K)$ is derivable under the security context σ : $\mathsf{names}_P \rightharpoonup \mathcal{D} \cup V$ for P and da, and by

(2) $\mathsf{infer}(P, \mathsf{da}) = \bot$, otherwise.

5   Soundness, Completeness, Minimality, Complexity

In this section, we present the soundness, completeness, minimality and complexity results for our security-type inference algorithm.

5.1   Soundness

If our security-type inference algorithm infers a typing for a given program and domain assignment, then the program is accepted wrt. the inferred typing by the security type system from Sect. 3.

Lemma 1 (Correctness). Let $P \subseteq \mathsf{C}$ be a program, and da : $\mathsf{VID} \cup \mathsf{FID} \rightharpoonup \mathcal{D}$ be a domain assignment for P. If a complete typing t : $\mathsf{names}_P \to \mathcal{D}$ of P exists, such that $\mathsf{infer}(P, \mathsf{da}) = \mathsf{t}$, then $\mathsf{t} \vdash P$ is derivable.

In order to express the soundness of our security-type inference algorithm, we need to lift our notion of noninterference from Sect. 3 to one wrt. a domain assignment. For a program P and a domain assignment da : $\mathsf{VID} \cup \mathsf{FID} \rightharpoonup \mathcal{D}$ for P, P is *noninterfering* wrt. da if and only if a complete typing t : $\mathsf{names}_P \to \mathcal{D}$ exists, such that t is compatible with da and P is noninterfering wrt. t. If a program is noninterfering wrt. a typing t and t is compatible with a domain assignment da, then all outputs of the program into information containers that da associates with *low* are independent from information stored in containers that da associates with *high*. This holds because t agrees with da on all identifiers for which da is defined, and a noninterfering program wrt. t is guaranteed to have no flows of information from information containers that t associates with *high* to containers that t associates with *low*. If our algorithm infers a typing for a given program and domain assignment, then the program is noninterfering wrt. the domain assignment.

Theorem 2 (Soundness). Let $P \subseteq \mathsf{C}$ be a program, and da : $\mathsf{VID} \cup \mathsf{FID} \rightharpoonup \mathcal{D}$ be a domain assignment for P. If a complete typing t : $\mathsf{names}_P \to \mathcal{D}$ exists, such that $\mathsf{infer}(P, \mathsf{da}) = \mathsf{t}$, then P is noninterfering wrt. da.

5.2   Completeness

The completeness result guarantees that our security-type algorithm always outputs a typing for a program and domain assignment, if the domain assignment can be extended to a complete typing of the program, such that the program is accepted wrt. the typing by our security type system.

Theorem 3 (Completeness). Let $P \subseteq C$ be a program, and $\mathsf{da} : \mathsf{VID} \cup \mathsf{FID} \rightharpoonup \mathcal{D}$ be a domain assignment for P. If $\mathsf{t} : \mathsf{names}_P \to \mathcal{D}$ exists, so that t is a complete typing of P, t is compatible with da, and $\mathsf{t} \vdash P$ is derivable, then $\mathsf{infer}(P, \mathsf{da}) \neq \bot$.

5.3   Minimality

In order to define the minimality of typings, we first introduce the interference relation $\sqsubseteq_P \subseteq (\mathsf{names}_P \to \mathcal{D}) \times (\mathsf{names}_P \to \mathcal{D})$ on typings of a program P, that is defined, such that for all typings $\mathsf{t}, \mathsf{t}' : \mathsf{names}_P \to \mathcal{D}$, $\mathsf{t} \sqsubseteq_P \mathsf{t}'$ if and only if $\mathsf{t}(a) \sqsubseteq \mathsf{t}'(a)$ for all $a \in \mathsf{names}_P$. For program P and domain assignment $\mathsf{da} : \mathsf{VID} \cup \mathsf{FID} \rightharpoonup \mathcal{D}$ for P, a complete typing $\mathsf{t} : \mathsf{names}_P \to \mathcal{D}$ is *minimal* for P and da, if and only if for all typings $\mathsf{t}' : \mathsf{names}_P \to \mathcal{D}$, such that t' is a complete typing of P, t' is compatible with da, and $\mathsf{t}' \vdash P$ is derivable, it holds that $\mathsf{t} \sqsubseteq_P \mathsf{t}'$. Intuitively, a typing is minimal for a program and domain assignment, if it is a lower bound on all typings of the program that are compatible to the domain assignment and under which the program is accepted by our security type system. Our inference algorithm only infers typings that are minimal.

Theorem 4 (Minimality). Let $P \subseteq C$ be a program, and $\mathsf{da} : \mathsf{VID} \cup \mathsf{FID} \rightharpoonup \mathcal{D}$ be a domain assignment for P. If a typing $\mathsf{t} : \mathsf{names}_P \to \mathcal{D}$ exists such that $\mathsf{infer}(P, \mathsf{da}) = \mathsf{t}$, then t is minimal for P and da.

Intuitively, an inferred typing for a given program and domain assignment associates a domain with each information container that is a least upper bound on all domains of containers from which information may flow into this container. This offers two appealing opportunities for using our security-type inference algorithm (1) to explore where the confidential information in a program may flow, and (2) to verify a program against arbitrary annotations of sinks.

Exploring Flows of Confidential Information. To use our security-type inference algorithm for exploring where confidential information in a program may flow, one annotates sources of confidential information, i.e., information containers from which confidential information is read, in the program with @High. Then the security-type inference algorithm infers the security domain *high* for all information containers to which these confidential inputs may flow, and *low* for all other information containers.

Verifying a Program Against Arbitrary Annotations of Sinks. As long as the sources annotated with @High remain the same, one inferred typing for a program allows to verify the program against different annotations of sinks. Given an annotation-induced domain assignment $\mathsf{da} : \mathsf{VID} \cup \mathsf{FID} \rightharpoonup \mathcal{D}$ for a program P

and an inferred typing $t : \mathsf{names}_P \to \mathcal{D}$ for a domain assignment that associates the same identifiers of sources with $high$ as da, P is noninterfering wrt. da if $t(a) \sqsubseteq \mathsf{da}(a)$ for all identifiers $a \in dom(\mathsf{da})$.

5.4   Computational Complexity

Our security-type inference algorithm and security type system analyze a program with a worst case time-complexity that is linear in the size of the program. As the *size of a program*, we consider the number of nodes in the program's abstract syntax tree.

Theorem 5 (Complexity). For any program $P \subseteq \mathsf{C}$ and domain assignment $\mathsf{da} : \mathsf{VID} \cup \mathsf{FID} \rightharpoonup \mathcal{D}$ for P, given a precomputed security context $\sigma : \mathsf{names}_P \to \mathcal{D} \cup \mathcal{V}$ for P and da, the security-type inference and security type checking take $O(n)$ time, where n is the size of the program.

6   Implementation as an Eclipse Plug-In

We implemented our solution as an Eclipse plug-in ADELE (Assistant for Developing Leak-free Programs). It leverages our security-type inference algorithm and security type system for the development of Java programs with secure information flow. ADELE integrates into the Eclipse IDE, analyzes the source code in the background, fully-automatically, and reports detected information leaks.

User Interface: Input. ADELE allows its user to control two parameters of the analysis: the location of the source code to analyze and the information-flow policy. The location of the source code can be specified by selecting a source directory or a package containing Java source files within the current workspace of Eclipse. Selecting a package within a larger program allows focusing the analysis on a security-critical part of a given program. The information-flow policy is specified directly in the source code with Java annotations @High and @Low. The usage and semantics of these annotations are as described in Sect. 3.

User Interface: Output. The output of ADELE consists of (1) a report on detected information leaks, and (2) inferred security types for information containers. ADELE displays this information in the views "Information Flow Problems" and "Inferred Security Types", respectively. The view "Information Flow Problems" (see Fig. 5(a)) lists detected leaks together with information that could be helpful for mitigating them, e.g., the location of the leak in the code, and sources and sinks relevant for the leak. The detected leaks are also marked in the source code editor of Eclipse. In the view "Inferred Security Types" (see Fig. 5(b)), information containers are structured into categories "Sources", "Sinks", and "Transit Nodes". "Sources" groups information containers from which information is read but not written to. "Sinks" groups information containers to which flows within the program exist, but which are never read. "Transit Nodes" contains information containers that are read and written. Within these three categories, the identifiers are grouped by whether they are manually annotated or have an inferred security type, and by their security types.

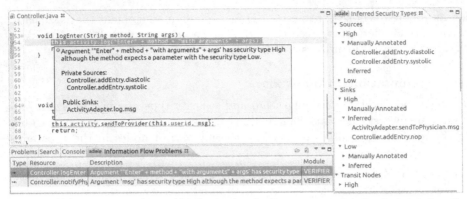

(a) Reporting detected information leaks.

(b) Exploring inferred
security types.

Fig. 5. User interface of ADELE.

7   Evaluation

The experimental evaluation of our solution has the goal of answering the following three questions: (i) What is the ratio between manually annotated and automatically inferred types, in practice? (ii) What is the performance of our solution, in practice? (iii) What is the relationship between the performance of our solution and that of SECJ [26], an implementation of a security-type inference algorithm [27] for a programming language similar to the one that we use?

Our Benchmark Applications. We conduct our evaluation on four conceptual Java applications that we developed ourselves, inspired by real-world applications with similar functionality. We decided to develop applications ourselves in order to introduce information leaks into some of them, purposely, and investigate how the implementation of our solutions detects these leaks. Application "Blood Pressure History" (short: BPH) allows its user to record blood pressure values and to view previously recorded values. The application automatically informs a physician if the measured values are critical. The security concern is that the user's blood pressure values leak to third parties. Application "Company Strategy" (short: CS) allows a company to send resource requests to a supplier in order to pursue an internal strategy with certain resource requirements. The security concern is that confidential details about the company's internal strategy leak to the supplier. Application "Job Finder" (short: JF) searches a database for jobs that match the user's keywords. The security concern is that the user's keywords leak to an employer. Application "Online Shop" (short: OS) allows its users to maintain a wish list that their friends can use for selecting gifts. The security concern is that confidential information about user's purchases leaks to friends. Applications BPH and CS are analyzed in three variants each with modifications of the code that affect their security.

Our Experimental Setup. We run all our experiments on a typical laptop with Intel Core i7 CPU at 2.50 GHz × 4 and 8 Gb of RAM. We use Ububtu 12.04 and Oracle Java Platform SDK in version 1.8.0_45 for 64-bit Linux.

7.1 Ratio Between Manually Annotated and Inferred Types

For evaluating the ratio between manually annotated and inferred security types, we annotated each of our benchmark applications with information-flow policies that reflect the aforementioned security concerns. This results in annotating one or several information containers that correspond to a source with @High, and one or several containers that correspond to a sink with @Low. Altogether the number of such manually annotated information containers ranges from 2 to 5 in our experiments. Our solution infers security types for all remaining information containers. Table 1 presents the results of our experiments.

Our solution successfully verifies the information-flow security of applications "Blood Pressure History 1" (BPH 1) and "Company Strategy 3" (CS 3). All remaining applications are insecure, and our solution successfully detects information leaks in them. In Table 1, we observe that the ratio between manually annotated information containers and those containers for which security types are inferred by our solution varies between 1:17 and 1:128 in our experiments. This suggests that our security-type inference algorithm reduces the burden of manual security-type annotation by up to two orders of magnitude.

Table 1. Number of security types in our benchmark applications: $\mathcal{M}$ denotes the number of manually annotated information containers, $\mathcal{I}$ denotes the number of inferred security types for other information containers.

#	Application	LoC	Leak	$\mathcal{M}$	$\mathcal{I}$	$\lfloor \mathcal{M} : \mathcal{I} \rfloor$
1	BPH 1	135	No	4	89	1:22
2	BPH 2	135	Yes, explicit	5	88	1:17
3	BPH 3	136	Yes, explicit	4	89	1:22
4	CS 1	147	Yes, explicit	4	89	1:22
5	CS 2	151	Yes, implicit	4	88	1:22
6	CS 3	307	No	4	190	1:47
7	JF	311	Yes, implicit	3	187	1:62
8	OS	410	Yes, implicit	2	256	1:128

7.2 Performance

For evaluating the performance of our solution we use the same benchmark applications and information-flow policies as in Subsect. 7.1. We collect 1000 samples of our solution's running time on each benchmark application, from which we compute the estimated mean running time. We measure the running time in the steady state of the JVM using `System.nanoTime()` timer. To reduce the interference of the garbage collection with the measurements, `System.gc()` is called before each run of the analysis. Table 2 presents the results of our performance evaluation (see section "ADELE" of the table).

Table 2. Estimated mean running time of ADELE and SECJ, in milliseconds.

#	Application	LoC	Estimated mean running time					
			Overall	Inference	Collecting	Solving	Overall per LoC	Inference per LoC
ADELE								
1	BPH 1	135	2.6600	1.0302	0.9526	0.0776	0.0197	0.0076
2	BPH 2	135	2.6865	0.8723	0.7833	0.0890	0.0199	0.0065
3	BPH 3	136	2.8716	1.0279	0.9318	0.0961	0.0211	0.0076
4	CS 1	147	2.8797	1.1081	0.9704	0.1376	0.0196	0.0075
5	CS 2	151	2.7458	1.0189	0.8581	0.1608	0.0182	0.0067
6	CS 3	307	4.6359	2.0526	1.9852	0.0674	0.0151	0.0067
7	JF	311	5.1064	2.5773	2.2175	0.3598	0.0164	0.0083
8	OS	410	6.8985	3.6433	3.2686	0.3748	0.0168	0.0089
SECJ								
1	BPH 1	135	775.9983	24.1443	20.7841	3.3602	5.7481	0.1788
2	BPH 2	135	736.9718	24.3384	21.3163	3.0221	5.4591	0.1803
3	BPH 3	136	801.3648	26.8502	23.1533	3.6968	5.8924	0.1974
4	CS 1	147	745.5113	27.7995	24.2680	3.5315	5.0715	0.1891
5	CS 2	151	757.0713	30.7687	26.6143	4.1543	5.0137	0.2038
6	CS 3	307	1169.3359	130.2044	118.6230	11.5814	3.8089	0.4241
7	JF	311	1279.5666	160.5022	140.3807	20.1215	4.1144	0.5161
8	OS	410	1655.0694	284.5710	249.6445	34.9265	4.0368	0.6941

The overall time corresponds to the running time of the analysis from parsing to reporting. It includes the time of the type inference, the sum of the times of constraint collecting and solving. By dividing the running times estimated during the analysis of each application by the corresponding number of the source code lines, we compute the running time per line of code for the overall analysis, and for the type inference. We observe: (1) the overall running time of our solution, averaged among the benchmark applications, lies below 0.02 ms per line of code, and (2) the running time required for the type inference, averaged among the benchmark applications, lies below 0.008 ms per line of code. Taking into account that our solution has a linear time-complexity in size of the analyzed program (see Theorem 5), our experimental results suggest that our solution shall also be efficient when analyzing significantly larger applications.

7.3   Relationship to SecJ wrt. Performance

For evaluating the relationship of our solution to SECJ wrt. performance, we run the experiments from Subsect. 7.2 also for SECJ [26]. Table 2 presents the results of this performance evaluation (see section "SECJ" of the table). By comparing the running time values observed in our experiments for ADELE and SECJ, we conclude: (1) overall, our solution is two order of magnitude faster than SECJ, and (2) the implementation of our security-type inference algorithm is an order of magnitude faster than the type inference in SECJ.

Leak Not Detected by SECJ. During our experiments, we found that the information leak in the application "Job Finder" is not detected by SECJ. In the code snippet, the con-

```
public JobRecord makeChoice(JobList jobs) {
    @High Element job = jobs.getFirst();
    @Low JobRecord choice = (JobRecord)job;
    return choice;
}
```

fidential result of a job search `job` is converted into an instance of `JobRecord` and written to untrusted sink `choice`. Hence, there is an information leak from `job` to `choice`. SECJ, however, accepts this example as secure. We inspected the implementation of SECJ and suspect an error in its constraint derivation for the type casting, which results in the undetected leak. It seems that the error is caused by a wrong type variable in the implementation.

8   Related Work

The certification of programs for secure information flow [6] is a long-standing line of research. Starting from the work of Volpano, Irvine, and Smith [30], security type systems have attracted a lot of attention for such certification. Sabelfeld and Myers provide in [22] a comprehensive overview of this area until the beginning of 2000s. Since then, a notable branch of this area focused on making security type systems applicable for realistic object-oriented languages, like Java. We limit this paragraph to security type systems for such languages, as we focus on a subset of Java in this article. Strecker [24] formalizes a security type system for MicroJava in Isabelle/HOL. Banerjee and Naumann [1] propose a security type system for a Java-like programming language extended with access-control features. We drew inspiration from their work when we were defining our programming language and our security type system. Barthe et al. [2] propose a security type system for a Java-like language that supports exceptions. Rafnsson et al. [20] propose a security type system that addresses dynamic class loading and the initialization of static fields. The aforementioned security type systems have been proven sound in [1,2,20,24], respectively. There are also type-based information-flow analyses [4,8,16,18] that target programs written in larger fragments of Java, some — even full Java. Yet, they are not accompanied by formal soundness proofs, to the best of our knowledge.

Security type systems require all information containers in a program to be annotated with security types. Doing such annotations manually is a tedious and error-prone task. Security-type inference algorithms have a goal of inferring such annotations automatically. Type inference, in general, has a long-standing tradition (see, e.g., [7,17,25]). Starting from Volpano and Smith's type inference algorithm [31] for the security type system from [30], there has been a growing interest for type-inference algorithms tailored to information-flow analyses [3,5,10–14,19,23,27,28,32]. In Table 3, we list attributes of twelve well-known security-type inference algorithms and compare them to our algorithm.

Table 3. Attributes of security-type inference algorithms. (A dash means that the respective article does not provide information on the attribute.)

Type-inference algorithm of	Imperative, object-oriented language	Soundness result	Completeness result	Minimality result	Time-complexity
Volpano/Smith [31]	No	Yes	Yes	No	–
Pottier/Simonet [19]	No	Yes	Yes	No	–
Sun et al. [27]	Yes	Yes	Yes	No	$O(n)$
Deng/Smith [5]	No	Yes	Yes	No	$O(n^2)$
Hristova et al. [10]	No	No	No	No	$O(n)$
Hunt/Sands [12,13]	No	Yes	Yes	Yes	$O(nv^3)$
Smith/Thober [23]	Yes	Yes	Yes	No	$O(n^{n^5})$
King et al. [14]	Yes	No	No	No	–
Terauchi [28]	No	Yes	No	No	Polynomial
Bedford et al. [3]	No	Yes	Yes	No	–
Weijers et al. [32]	No	No	No	No	–
Huang et al. [11]	Yes	No	No	No	$O(n^3)$
Our algorithm	Yes	Yes	Yes	Yes	$O(n)$

A conceptual novelty of our algorithm over other security-type inference algorithms is that it is accompanied by a formally proven minimality result without having to use principal types [12,13,29]. Hunt and Sands [12] show how to infer principal types for programs written in a simple while-language. Their principal types describe, for each variable, all possible flows of information through the variable. This description is so fine-grained that is provides enough information for checking a program's compliance with an arbitrary information-flow policy. In [13], Hunt and Sands provide an algorithm for computing principal types in $O(nv^3)$, where n is the size of an input program and v the number of its variables. In a recent work [29], their principal type system is lifted to support dynamic policies. Generally, the idea of extending principal types to support an object-oriented Java-like programming language seems rather appealing. Yet, at this time it is not clear how to achieve this at low computational costs.

The security-type inference algorithm of Sun et al. [27] is the closest to our algorithm, supporting a programming language with the same features. The algorithms differ, most notably, in the following two technical aspects: (1) The algorithm of Sun et al. [27] maintains a type environment to dynamically read and keep track of the security types of local variables and formal parameters. We use a predefined security context to access security types of all information containers. (2) The algorithm of Sun et al. [27] conducts data type inference for local variables and expressions in parallel to the derivation of constraints for security types. As a consequence, all constraint derivation rules for expressions have to capture also inference of data types, and the type environment has to store data types of local variables and formal parameters, in addition to their security types. In contrast, we use results of a separate data-type inference algorithm just in those rules that require it, i.e., rules for a field access, field assignment, and method call. Modelling both the type environment and the inference of data types by separate functions enables implementation of our algorithm in a clean, modular fashion.

Sun et al. [27] do not comment whether their algorithm infers minimal typings. We conjecture that it probably does, at least if no polymorphism is used. However, due to the additional complexity coming with polymorphic classes, we cannot intuitively assess the minimality of their full algorithm without having to conduct a formal proof.

9 Conclusion

We presented a new algorithm for inferring security types in Java programs. We proved it to be sound, complete, minimal, and of linear time-complexity in the size of the program analyzed. The minimality of our algorithm allows flexible security analyses, in the sense that programs can be analyzed wrt. information-flow policies that fix only the annotations of sources, while leaving the annotations of sinks flexible. Based on our algorithm, we developed a solution for verifying confidentiality requirements in Java programs. We implemented or solution as an Eclipse plug-in, and experimentally showed that it is effective and efficient.

As future work, we plan to deploy the presented algorithm, after necessary adaptations, in our information-flow analysis for Dalvik bytecode [15].

Acknowledgements. We thank the anonymous reviewers for their valuable comments. We thank Patrick Metzler for his help in the implementation of ADELE. This work has been partially funded by the BMBF within EC SPRIDE and by the DFG as part of project E2 within the CRC 1119 CROSSING.

References

1. Banerjee, A., Naumann, D.A.: Stack-based access control and secure information flow. J. Funct. Program. **15**(2), 131–177 (2005)
2. Barthe, G., Rezk, T., Naumann, D.A.: Deriving an information flow checker and certifying compiler for Java. In: Proceedings of the 27th IEEE Symposium on Security and Privacy (S&P), pp. 230–242. IEEE (2006)
3. Bedford, A., Desharnais, J., Godonou, T.G., Tawbi, N.: Enforcing information flow by combining static and dynamic analysis. In: Danger, J.-L., Debbabi, M., Marion, J.-Y., Garcia-Alfaro, J., Heywood, N.Z. (eds.) FPS 2013. LNCS, vol. 8352, pp. 83–101. Springer, Heidelberg (2014)

4. Broberg, N., van Delft, B., Sands, D.: Paragon for practical programming with information-flow control. In: Shan, C. (ed.) APLAS 2013. LNCS, vol. 8301, pp. 217–232. Springer, Heidelberg (2013)

5. Deng, Z., Smith, G.: Type inference and informative error reporting for secure information flow. In: Proceedings of the 44th Annual Southeast Regional Conference (ACM-SE), pp. 543–548. ACM (2006)

6. Denning, D.E., Denning, P.J.: Certification of programs for secure information flow. Commun. ACM **20**(7), 504–513 (1977)

7. Duggan, D., Bent, F.: Explaining type inference. Sci. Comput. Program. **27**(1), 37–83 (1996)

8. Ernst, M.D., Just, R., Millstein, S., Dietl, W.M., Pernsteiner, S., Roesner, F., Koscher, K., Barros, P., Bhoraskar, R., Han, S., Vines, P., Wu, E.X.: Collaborative verification of information flow for high-assurance app store. In: Proceedings of the 21st ACM Conference on Computer and Communications Security (CCS), pp. 1092–1104. ACM (2014)

9. Goguen, J.A., Meseguer, J.: Security policies and security models. In: Proceedings of the 3rd IEEE Symposium on Security and Privacy (S&P), pp. 11–20. IEEE (1982)

10. Hristova, K., Rothamel, T., Liu, Y.A., Stoller, S.D.: Efficient type inference for secure information flow. In: Proceedings of the 2006 Workshop on Programming Languages and Analysis for Security (PLAS), pp. 85–94. ACM (2006)

11. Huang, W., Dong, Y., Milanova, A.: Type-based taint analysis for Java web applications. In: Gnesi, S., Rensink, A. (eds.) FASE 2014 (ETAPS). LNCS, vol. 8411, pp. 140–154. Springer, Heidelberg (2014)

12. Hunt, S., Sands, D.: On flow-sensitive security types. In: Proceedings of the 33rd ACM Symposium on Principles of Programming Languages (POPL), pp. 79–90. ACM (2006)

13. Hunt, S., Sands, D.: From exponential to polynomial-time security typing via principal types. In: Barthe, G. (ed.) ESOP 2011. LNCS, vol. 6602, pp. 297–316. Springer, Heidelberg (2011)

14. King, D., Hicks, B., Hicks, M.W., Jaeger, T.: Implicit flows: can't live with 'em, can't live without 'em. In: Sekar, R., Pujari, A.K. (eds.) ICISS 2008. LNCS, vol. 5352, pp. 56–70. Springer, Heidelberg (2008)

15. Lortz, S., Mantel, H., Starostin, A., Bähr, T., Schneider, D., Weber, A.: Cassandra: towards a certifying app store for android. In: Proceedings of the 4th ACM Workshop on Security and Privacy in Smartphones and Mobile Devices (SPSM), pp. 93–104. ACM (2014)

16. Lux, A., Starostin, A.: A tool for static detection of timing channels in Java. J. Cryptographic Eng. **1**(4), 303–313 (2011)

17. Milner, R.: A theory of type polymorphism in programming. J. Comput. Syst. Sci. **17**(3), 348–375 (1978)

18. Myers, A.C.: JFlow: practical mostly-static information flow control. In: Proceedings of the 26th ACM Symposium on Principles of Programming Languages (POPL), pp. 228–241. ACM (1999)

19. Pottier, F., Simonet, V.: Information flow inference for ML. ACM Trans. Program. Lang. Syst. **25**(1), 117–158 (2003)

20. Rafnsson, W., Nakata, K., Sabelfeld, A.: Securing class initialization in Java-like languages. IEEE Trans. Dependable Secure Comput. **10**(1), 1–13 (2013)

21. Rehof, J., Mogensen, T.A.: Tractable constraints in finite semilattices. Sci. Comput. Program. **35**(2), 191–221 (1999)

22. Sabelfeld, A., Myers, A.C.: Language-based information-flow security. IEEE J. Sel. Areas Commun. **21**(1), 5–19 (2003)
23. Smith, S.F., Thober, M.: Improving usability of information flow security in Java. In: Proceedings of the 2007 Workshop on Programming Languages and Analysis for Security (PLAS), pp. 11–20. ACM (2007)
24. Strecker, M.: Formal Analysis of an Information Flow Type System for MicroJava. Technical report, Technische Universität München (2003)
25. Sulzmann, M.: A general type inference framework for Hindley/Milner style systems. In: Kuchen, H., Ueda, K. (eds.) FLOPS 2001. LNCS, vol. 2024, pp. 248–263. Springer, Heidelberg (2001)
26. Sun, Q.: Constraint-Based Modular Secure Information Flow Inference for Object-Oriented Programs. Ph.D. thesis, Stevens Institute of Technology (2008)
27. Sun, Q., Banerjee, A., Naumann, D.A.: Modular and constraint-based information flow inference for an object-oriented language. In: Giacobazzi, R. (ed.) SAS 2004. LNCS, vol. 3148, pp. 84–99. Springer, Heidelberg (2004)
28. Terauchi, T.: A type system for observational determinism. In: Proceedings of the 21st IEEE Computer Security Foundations Symposium (CSF), pp. 287–300. IEEE (2008)
29. van Delft, B., Hunt, S., Sands, D.: Very static enforcement of dynamic policies. In: Focardi, R., Myers, A. (eds.) POST 2015. LNCS, vol. 9036, pp. 32–52. Springer, Heidelberg (2015)
30. Volpano, D., Irvine, C., Smith, G.: A sound type system for secure flow analysis. J. Comput. Secur. **4**(2/3), 167–188 (1996)
31. Volpano, D., Smith, G.: A type-based approach to program security. In: Bidoit, M., Dauchet, M. (eds.) CAAP/FASE /TAPSOFT 1997. LNCS, vol. 1214, pp. 607–621. Springer, Heidelberg (1997)
32. Weijers, J., Hage, J., Holdermans, S.: Security type error diagnosis for higher-order polymorphic languages. Sci. Comput. Program. **95**(2), 200–218 (2014)

Sensor Networks and Cognitive Radio

Program Integrity Verification for Detecting Node Capture Attack in Wireless Sensor Network

Sarita Agrawal[✉], Manik Lal Das, Anish Mathuria, and Sanjay Srivastava

Dhirubhai Ambani Institute of Information and Communication Technology,
Gandhinagar, India
{sarita_agrawal,maniklal_das,anish_mathuria,
sanjay_srivastava}@daiict.ac.in

Abstract. Wireless Sensor Networks (WSNs) are used in various applications mostly in hostile and emergency environments e.g. battle field surveillance, monitoring of nuclear activities, etc. The unattended deployment of WSNs, unreliable wireless communication and inherent resource constraints necessitate addressing the security of the WSNs in an efficient and economical way. In this paper, a node program integrity verification protocol is proposed in which the cluster heads are equipped with Trusted Platform Module (TPM) and serve as the verifiers. The protocol aims to first ensure the authentication of the verifier by a node, thereby, only an authenticated verifier is allowed to verify the authenticity and the integrity of the program of a node within its cluster. The proposed protocol also ensures that capture of one node does not reveal the secret of any other node in the network to the adversary. In addition to this, the protocol is secured against node collusion, man-in-the-middle and impersonation attacks. Since, the proposed protocol considers TPMs only at the cluster heads, unlike fully TPM enabled WSN, the overall network deployment cost is reduced. The aim of the proposed protocol is to provide program integrity verification for detecting node capture attack in a WSN with reduced computational, communication and storage cost overhead compared to the existing protocols for program integrity verification. The performance analysis and the simulation results verify the performance improvement.

Keywords: Wireless sensor network · Node capture attack · Trusted platform module · Program integrity verification

1 Introduction

A Wireless Sensor Network (WSN) consists of a large number of sensor nodes which cooperatively monitor the physical or environmental conditions such as temperature, sound, vibrations, pressure and motion [2]. Sensor nodes have inherent constraints of memory, computation power, and energy. In a WSN,

© Springer International Publishing Switzerland 2015
S. Jajodia and C. Mazumdar (Eds.): ICISS 2015, LNCS 9478, pp. 419–440, 2015.
DOI: 10.1007/978-3-319-26961-0_25

there are usually one or more base stations, which are assumed to be more powerful in terms of storage capacity, computation and communication capabilities, as compared to sensor nodes and be physically protected. Base station acts as a central trusted authority and also serves as the data sink/processor and as the interface between sensor network and the external world. WSNs are usually deployed unattended in hostile terrains for applications such as military surveillance and disaster management and therefore, the security of wireless sensor network (WSN) has been a matter of concern.

The threat to security of WSN is influenced by various factors such as the underlying key management scheme used in WSN, the topology of the network and the density of the network [3], the level of tamper-resistance of a node and the capability of an attacker being the decisive factors.

Various aspects of WSN security have been dealt with in the literature. Over the years, the key management schemes have been improved in order to improve the security. However, the major security threat that is still of concern is the node capture attack because of unattended deployment of nodes in hostile environments. Node capture attack is the ability of an attacker to access (and eventually change) the program running on a sensor node [2]. An attacker gains full control over a sensor node through a direct physical access and then easily extracts cryptographic primitives, obtains unlimited access to the information stored on the memory chip of the captured node through a reverse engineering process, subsequently causing substantial damage to the entire WSN [3].

The node capture attack has different level of severity depending upon the adversary capability and the time available with an adversary to carry out an attack. Becher et al. [4] has given the classification of node capture attack based on severity and duration of attack. Starting from simply manipulating the radio communications, influencing sensor readings, reading out RAM or program memory in whole or in part, the severity of attack can go up to adversary gaining complete read/write access to the micro-controller. The attack may involve creating plug-in connections and transferring few data in less than 5 mins, termed as *short attacks* or some mechanical work such as soldering carried out within 30 min (*medium attack*). *Long attacks* are possible only in specialized labs by skilled personnel that may take hours or days depending on the intended damage.

The node capture attack in wireless sensor networks (WSNs) can be decomposed into three stages: physical capture of node, redeployment of compromised node, and rejoining the network for various insider attacks [12]. Although resilience to node capture threat has improved with the improved key management, addressing the threat of node capture still remains a major research challenge.

Motivation and Contribution. Typically, it is assumed that in physical attacks, attacker has unsupervised access to a node for an extended period of time. However, in normal WSN operation, nodes keep communicating with their neighboring nodes and if a node is continuously absent then it is an unusual condition that neighbors can notice and if time needed to perform an attack is known, the neighbors can monitor each other periodically. The existing protocols to detect the node capture [8–13] are based on monitoring of the nodes through base station, cluster head, group manager or peer nodes. Even with the continuous monitoring, it is possible that the malicious neighbors collude and the detection is bypassed, resulting in node capture. For example, consider a scenario in which a set of nodes are monitoring a neighbour node. Now, suppose two or more of the monitoring node goes malicious (a node may act malicious even without being capture) and the adversary captures the monitored node. The malicious nodes may report the captured node to be present in the network, though it is not there and the absence of the node in the threshold time may go unnoticed.

After the capture, a node may be reprogrammed by the adversary and later be used to launch various insider attacks. In order to prevent an attacker from deploying a reprogrammed node for carrying out insider attacks, various attestation and program integrity verification protocols have been proposed [14–19]. The protocols that rely completely on software attestation require strict time measurement and in multi-hop wireless networks, it is impractical to achieve the same. Software based program integrity verification such as [15] expose all node program codes to adversary on verifier compromise. The hardware based protocols, for example [19], require specialized hardware such as Trusted Platform Module (TPM) [5] at all the sensor nodes, which may not be desirable in large sensor networks where cost is a major constraint.

The need of efficiently and securely detecting the node capture attack by verifying the integrity of a node program while ensuring the optimal overall network cost is the motivating factor for proposing a cost effective secure program integrity verification protocol. In this paper, a protocol is proposed for verifying the integrity of a node program in a secure and cost-effective manner. In the proposed protocol, a clustered network is setup with TPM enabled cluster heads each having a set of sensor nodes within its cluster. A cluster head acts as a TPM enabled Verification Server (TVS) that verifies the integrity of the sensor node program to ensure the node program is not tampered with by an adversary.

Although, the main goal of the protocol is to verify the integrity of a sensor node program to detect if a node is a victim of node capture attack, there is a possibility that the verifier itself is compromised. Therefore, the cluster heads are equipped with the TPM [5]. Whenever a sensor node is asked to prove the integrity of its program, node first ensures that TVS itself is not tampered with and it is authentic. Once a node is assured of the authenticity of TVS, it presents itself to TVS that executes the program integrity verification protocol to ensure the integrity of the program residing in the node's program memory.

The analysis of the proposed protocol shows that it is secure and efficient in terms of communication, computation and storage cost as compared to the existing software based attestation protocols. The simulation results show that the average energy consumption and communication latency is reduced with the proposed protocol. Moreover, even though the protocol uses TPM enabled cluster heads, the network cost overhead is found lesser in comparison to the hardware based attestation protocols [19].

The rest of the paper is organized as follows: In Sect. 2, we reviewed the exiting protocols used to detect/prevent node capture attack. In Sect. 3, the details of the proposed protocol are presented. In Sect. 4, we analyze the protocol for the security and performance. In Sect. 5, the work is concluded.

2   Related Work

Seshadri et al. [16] created a SoftWare-based ATTestation technique (SWATT), a code attestation algorithm that is executed solely through software means to externally verify the code running on embedded devices. They also proposed a protocol called SCUBA [17] to recover the sensor nodes after compromise, which uses two-authenticated channel between a node and the base station. Both these protocols require the trusted verifier (in case of WSN, the base station) to continuously be in communication with the nodes. The verification procedure loaded in node memory can itself be corrupted, if a node is compromised. Also these protocols depend on accurate time measurements and optimal program code.

Park and Shin [14] proposed a software solution using randomized hash functions in which base station is needed to authorize the Program Integrity Verification Servers (PIVS). The communication between a PIVS and a node happens on public channel which may cause man-in-the-middle attack resulting in a valid node failing the verification. Later Chang and Shin [15] suggested using PIV with distributed authentication, called Distributed Authentication Protocol of PIVSs (DAPP), wherein a set of PIVSs authenticates a PIVS to node and then the node uses this authenticated PIVS to present its program code for verifying the integrity. All the PIVSs keep the entire program code of all nodes in the network to verify the integrity of node programs. In case a PIVS itself is compromised, all node programs are available to the adversary. In the DAPP protocol [15], a polynomial share is stored at node which is used to compute a pair-wise key with verification servers in the network. If a node is captured, the polynomial share is disclosed and the adversary can use the captured node to communicate with any other node/server in the network. Moreover, a prover node needs to compute a polynomial based pair-wise key with the verifying server as well as for all the PIVSs who have provided the authentication tickets to the verifying PIVS, resulting in computation and storage overhead for a resource constrained node.

Subsequently, many hardware attestation techniques have been proposed that use Trusted Platform Module (TPM) [6,7]. To make the paper self-sufficient, a brief overview of the TPM is given. A TPM is capable of protecting the system from malicious activities and unauthorized changes. The shielded memory of TPM can not be accessed by any other entity other than the TPM itself. Each TPM has a unique Endorsement Key (EK) used to identify the TPM. It is typically a pair of public-private keys and the private key is embedded into the TPM and never leaves it. TPM has a unique feature in terms of the Secure Platform Configuration Registers (PCR). PCRs store the integrity metrics that are used to measure the integrity of any code prior to its execution. This code may be BIOS or an application code.

TPM provides a unique capability of *Sealing* any data block with TPM's platform configuration. This feature can be used to secretly store the data in TPM and also verify the integrity of the device which is embedded with TPM. TPM provides *TPM_Seal()* and *TPM_Unseal()* commands for this purpose. The data is encrypted with the public key of the TPM. This encrypted data is bound with the current platform configuration (stored in PCR) of the same TPM. In order to retrieve this data block, not only the private key of the TPM is needed, but at the time of retrieval, TPM has to be in the same configuration using which the data was sealed. *TPM_Unseal()* command takes the sealed data block, TPM's private key and the current platform configuration and if the current configuration matches the initial configuration, it will unseal the data block.

A simple abstraction of *TPM_Seal()* and *TPM_Unseal()* is defined as [18]:

PSeal(Platform_Configuration_at_sealing_time, public_key_of_TPM, data_to_be_sealed)
PUnSeal(Platform_Configuration_at_unsealing_time, private_key_of_TPM, sealed_data)

Kraus et al. [18] had proposed two attestation protocols using which a cluster head can prove to a node, the validity of its platform configuration i.e. the software components including applications. The proposed protocols work in multi-hop WSNs as well. Recently, Tan et al. [19] suggested attaching TPM to

Table 1. Comparison of the existing proposals

Features → Scheme ↓	Resistance to node collusion	Resistance to Man-in-the-Middle attack	Works without reliance on node response time	Program integrity verification	Verifier secure	Works without central authority
Software attestation [16]	Yes	Yes	No	Yes	Yes	No
Soft tamper proofing [14]	No	No	No	Yes	No	Yes
Distributed program integrity verification [15]	Yes	Yes	No	Yes	No	Yes
TPM enabled server attestation [18]	Yes	Yes	Yes	No	Yes	Yes
TPM enabled mutual attestation [19]	Yes	Yes	Yes	Yes	Yes	No

all the sensor nodes, using which a node can verify the integrity of any peer node. However, [18] does not address the main objective of verifying the integrity of node program. For large WSNs, the proposal of [19] of equipping all the nodes with TPM will result in increased network cost. Moreover, Tan el al scheme [19] needs a node to interact with base station for each verification, which is a communication overhead.

Table 1 gives a comparison of the existing proposals.

3   Proposed Protocol

To detect node capture attack through verification of the integrity of a sensor node program in a distributed environment, the protocol proposes the verification using TPM enabled verification servers. A node can authenticate a verification server before its own program integrity verification by that server. In the subsequent subsections we discuss the details of the proposed protocol.

3.1   System Model

The WSN comprises of two types of nodes. One small set of nodes called cluster heads that act as node program integrity verification servers and the rest of the nodes are normal sensor nodes with limited resources (Fig. 1).

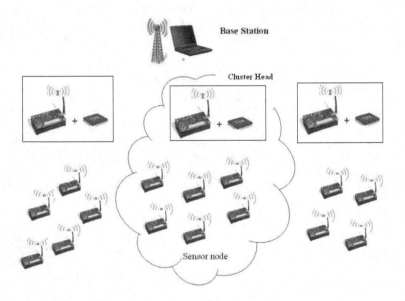

Fig. 1. Proposed network model

Each verification server is equipped with TPM chip (will be referred as TPM enabled Verification Server (TVS) in the rest of the paper). TVSs are more

BOOT CODE	BOOT CODE	BOOT CODE
MAIN APPLICATION CODE	MAIN APPLICATION CODE	MAIN APPLICATION CODE
FREE SPACE	(Incompressible bit string) S_{A1}	(Incompressible bit string) S_{B1}
MAC(), h()	MAC(), h()	MAC(), h()
FREE SPACE	(Incompressible bit string) S_{A2}	(Incompressible bit string) S_{B2}
FLASH DOWNLOADER	FLASH DOWNLOADER	FLASH DOWNLOADER
FREE SPACE	(Incompressible bit string) S_{A3}	(Incompressible bit string) S_{B3}
(a) Normal Sensor Node Program Memory Layout	(b) Sensor Node Program Memory of a Node **A** (Free space filled with Random incompressible bits unique for node A)	(c) Sensor Node Program Memory of another Node **B** (Free space filled with Random incompressible bits unique for node B)

Fig. 2. Program memory space

powerful in terms of storage, communication and computation, as compared to the normal cluster nodes. Overall control and interaction with outside world is done by a resourceful trustworthy central authority called Base Station.

The nodes are loaded with the program securely by the base station prior to deployment. The program memory's free space is filled with unique random incompressible bit strings for each node, thus making the program memory space unique for each node (Fig. 2).

Prior to deployment, the base station stores the copy of program memory contents of each node securely at each TVS in the network. Since, only the free space filled with unique random incompressible bit strings is different for each node, each TVS has only the free space contents for each node and one common copy of the rest of the program memory content. The program memory content of a node stored at TVS is sealed with the initial platform configuration of TPM embedded in that TVS. Immediately after deployment, the nodes associate themselves with a cluster head nearest within their transmission range.

A node moving away from its cluster informs its cluster head, who in turn informs the move to other nodes in its cluster as well as to the head of new cluster which the moving node decides to join. In DAPP [15], a bi-variate polynomial based secret key is used for communication between a node and a server. If a node is captured, the key is disclosed to the adversary. If a node is not captured by an adversary, then even the contents of its program memory remain secret. Therefore, in the proposed protocol, we have utilized the secrecy of the program memory content and the hash of program memory content of a node is used as initial secret between the node and its cluster head.

For example, as shown in Fig. 2, suppose there are two nodes A and B. Assume that the incompressible bit strings stored in the free space of node A are S_{A1}, S_{A2} and S_{A3}. Similarly, a different set of incompressible bit strings is stored in the free space of node B, These strings are S_{B1}, S_{B2} and S_{B3}. These bit strings are loaded in the respective nodes prior to deployment of the nodes and will not be known to the adversary.

The overall program memory content of node A will be different than the program memory content of node B. Therefore, the hash code computed over the entire memory content of node A will be different from the hash code for node B. In case, an adversary captures node A, it will certainly have access to the entire memory content of the node A. However, the adversary does not know the overall content of program memory of node B, since the incompressible bit strings S_{B1}, S_{B2} and S_{B3} are different than S_{A1}, S_{A2} and S_{A3} stored in node A. Hence, the secret hash code of node B is not revealed to adversary on capture of node A.

In our proposal, we assume that sensor nodes have separate user(or data) memory and program memory. The application related data is managed in user (or data) memory, program memory is fixed that contains boot code, main application code. (For details of the program memory structure, please refer Fig. 2). In order to update software in the node, the main application code needs to be changed. If the new code is bigger than the existing code, the free space is utilized and adjusted accordingly.

3.2 Goal and Assumptions

Goal. The goal of the proposed TPM enabled Program Integrity Verification (TPIV) protocol is to ensure:

- *TVS authentication by a node* - A node does not run the node authentication and program integrity verification protocol with a TVS that fails authentication.
- *Node authentication and program integrity verification by TVS* - A TVS declares a node to be captured, if the node fails the program integrity verification.
- *Resilience to node capture* - A captured node does not reveal the secret of other nodes.

Assumptions. The WSN is assumed to have a base station as the central trusted authority. The free space in the program memory of each node is filled with unique incompressible bit strings to avoid memory compression attack and have overall program memory content unique for each node. The cluster heads keep a copy of the program memory contents of nodes in a secured space sealed within their TPMs. We assume the presence of an adaptive adversary. The details of the capabilities of such an adversary is given in Sect. 4.1 as *Adversary Model*.

3.3   Preliminaries and Notations

The proposed protocol is based on one way hash function (OWHF) and message authentication code (MAC) [1]. A one-way hash function h converts an input x of an arbitrary finite bit-length into output $h(x)$ of fixed bit-length n such that $h()$ is easy to compute and for a given y, it is computationally infeasible to find any pre-image x' such that $h(x') = y$. Message authentication code (MAC) is used to ensure the integrity of the source of the message as well as the message itself. A MAC algorithm is a family of functions h_k with a secret key k as parameter. It is computationally infeasible to compute the MAC without knowing the secret key k. The notations used in the rest of the paper are given in Table 2 below.

The proposed protocol comprised of three phases: *System setup phase*, *Monitoring phase* and *Authentication and code verification phase*.

3.4   System Setup Phase

Prior to deployment, each node X in the network is assigned a unique identity, ID_X, by the base station. All the nodes are equipped to perform hash

Table 2. Notations used in the protocol

Notation	Description
Z_q	Finite field of order q, q is a large prime
ID_A	Unique identity of a node A
CH_i	Unique identity of a cluster head (TVS) i
t_A^{last}	Time of last transmission heard from node A
t_A^{new}	Time of latest new transmission heard from node A
T_t	Threshold time to decide the absence of a node from network
P_A	Program memory content of node A
$h()$	Public one-way function to compute hash
$N_i \in_R Z_q$	Nonce chosen at random by TVS i from Z_q
(x_i, y_i)	Public-private key pair for TPM of TVS i
PC_i^0	Initial platform configuration of TPM at TVS i
$PSeal()$	Abstraction of function $TPM\_Seal()$ for sealing
$PUnseal()$	Abstraction of function $TPM\_Unseal()$ for unsealing
PC_i^t	Platform configuration of TPM at TVS i during unsealing of P_A at time t
$MAC()$	Public function to compute Message Authentication Code - $MAC_{key}(\text{data})$
$PIV\_Challenge$	Message sent by TVS i to node A to challenge the integrity of A's program
$PIV\_Response$	Response of node A to TVS i for proving A's program integrity
$X \rightarrow Y : M$	Entity X sends message M to entity Y

operation $h()$ and MAC operation $MAC_k()$, where k is the MAC key. The base station also assigns a unique identity CH_i to TVS i and TVSs can also perform hash $h()$ and MAC operation $MAC_k()$. Each TVS shares a pair-wise secret with other TVSs in the network. A unique non-migratable public-private key pair (x_i, y_i) always resides in protected storage within TPM that is attached to each TVS i.

When TVS i is initially switched on, its initial platform configuration PC_i^0 (at time $t=0$) is stored in the PCRs of the TPM attached to i. The program memory content P_X for node X is stored by the base station in each TVS's memory where it is sealed within the associated TPM with the $PSeal()$ function using the initial platform configuration and the TPM's public key.

For example, within the TPM of TVS i, the program memory content P_X is stored as:

$$\{P_X\}_{PC_i}^{x_i} = PSeal(PC_i^0, x_i, P_X)$$

The unsealing of $\{P_X\}_{PC_i}^{x_i}$ can take place at any time t, if the platform configuration PC_i^t of TVS i at time t is same as PC_i^0 and can be done as:

$$P_X = PUnseal(PC_i^t, y_i, \{P_X\}_{PC_i}^{x_i}).$$

3.5   Monitoring Phase

In the proposed clustered network, a cluster head keeps track of the transmissions from the nodes of its own cluster. For this purpose, the cluster head maintains a record of the time of last transmission heard t_A^{last} from each node A within its cluster. If the cluster head hears next transmission from node A at time t_A^{new} which is at the time interval beyond the set threshold time T, $t_A^{new} - t_A^{last} \geq T$, then it is suspected to be captured and the cluster head requests the node to prove the integrity of its program space. If the program integrity verification fails or if the node is not heard again and cluster head does not get the intimation of its move to some other cluster, the node is considered to be captured and revoked.

3.6   Authentication and Code Verification

A TVS asks a node within its cluster to prove the integrity of its program at periodic intervals or whenever a TVS suspects a node to be a victim of node capture attack. On a verification query from the TVS, a sensor node needs to ensure that the TVS itself is valid, before the node can present its program for the integrity verification by the querying TVS. This process helps a sensor node ensuring the authenticity of a TVS. Once the TVS is authenticated, node can present itself for its program integrity verification.

Table 3 below gives the notations for intermediate terms obtained through computations in the protocol.

The protocol is explained in two sub phases: TVS Authentication by node and Node Authentication and Program Integrity Verification by TVS.

Table 3. Intermediate terms

Notation	Description
K	$= h(P_A)$, key used as an initial secret between node A and TVS i
PS_A	$= PSeal(PC_i^0, x_i, P_A)$, sealing of P_A using x_i and PC_i^0
P'_A	$= PUnseal(PC_i^t, y_i, PS_A)$, unsealing of PS_A using y_i and PC_i^t
	($P'_A = P_A$, if $PC_i^t = PC_i^0$, else unsealing operation fails)
n_0	$= N_i \oplus K$, Response nonce of TVS i XORed with the shared key K
m_0	$= MAC_K(N_i, ID_A, CH_i)$, MAC from TVS i, for node A to authenticate TVS i
K_A	$= h(P_A, N_i, ID_A, CH_i)$, new key computed by node A
m_1	$= MAC_K(N_i)$, MAC from A, to confirm correct receipt of nonce N_i
K_I	$= h(P'_A, N_i, ID_A, CH_i)$, new key computed by TVS i
M_A	$= MAC_{K_A}(ID_A, CH_i, N_i)$, MAC computed by node A using key K_A
M_I	$= MAC_{K_I}(ID_A, CH_i, N_i)$, MAC computed by TVS i using key K_I

TVS Authentication by Node. In this first phase of the protocol, node A authenticates the TVS i. The message exchange in this phase is as follows:

(PIV_Challenge) TVS $i \rightarrow$ Node A: CH_i, ID_A, n_0, m_0

In order to challenge a node A to prove the integrity of its program memory, TVS i unseals program memory block related to node A to retrieve the program memory content of node A as P'_A sealed within TPM. (A TVS can only retrieve a data block value if TVS's current platform configuration matches with its initial platform configuration which was used to seal that data block).

TVS i calculates the secret K by computing the hash of P'_A $(= P_A)$ i.e. $K = h(P_A)$. TVS randomly chooses a nonce N_i and computes program integrity verification challenge (PIV_Challenge) by XORing N_i with K. It also computes MAC of identities and nonce N_i using key K. TVS sends the "PIV_Challenge" message to node A. Node A retrieves TVS's nonce N_i and computes the MAC. It verifies the computed MAC with the received MAC to confirm the authenticity of TVS. Only if, TVS had access to K, it could have computed m_0 using the key K. If the TVS does not get any response from the challenged node A within the expected time period (round trip time plus the time needed to do the processing by node A), then TVS resends the challenge assuming the message is corrupted on the way and MAC verification has failed. If TVS does not get the response of PIV challenge message even after three trials and also does not get any intimation of node's move to another cluster, a link/node failure or an adversary's presence in the network is suspected and appropriate action is taken. The detailed protocol for TVS authentication by node is given in Fig. 3.

Node Authentication and Program Integrity Verification by TVS. After the node has authenticated the TVS, the node considers that TVS to

Cluster Head i (TVS)   **Sensor Node** A

1. Unseals program memory content for node A:

   $P'_A \; (=P_A)$

   If Unsealing fails then

   "TVS itself is Invalid", EXIT

2. Sets round $= 1$

3. Computes secret K

4. Selects a nonce $N_i \in_R Z_q$

5. Computes n_0 and MAC m_0

6. PIV_Challenge:

$\overrightarrow{CH_i, ID_A, n_0, m_0}$

       7. Computes secret K

       8. Extracts nonce of TVS as:

          $N_i = n_0 \oplus K$

       9. Computes MAC to compare with m_0:

       if $m_0 \neq MAC_K(N_i, ID_A, CH_i)$ then

          "Msg Corrupted/TVS Invalid" EXIT

       else "TVS Authentication Successful"

Fig. 3. TVS authentication protocol

be a valid TVS to communicate with. In this phase, TVS i authenticates and verifies the program integrity of node A. The communication between TVS i and node A in this phase is as below:

(PIV_Response) Node $A \rightarrow$ TVS i: ID_A, CH_i, m_1, M_A

Node A takes the nonce N_i just received from TVS during TVS authentication. Node A computes a new hash value of its program memory content (P_A) using the nonce N_i i.e. $K_A = h(P_A, N_i, ID_A, CH_i)$ and computes the MAC of IDs using this new key. It also computes MAC of N_i using the old key K which was used in the "PIVS_Challenge" message. This is to ensure that node had received the correct N_i that it used to compute the new key. Node A sends "PIV_Response" (program integrity verification response) to TVS i.

On receiving "PIV_Response", TVS i first constructs the MAC of N_i using K and compares it with the corresponding MAC received. After ensuring the correct receipt of N_i by node A, TVS i computes the new key as K_I by calculating new hash at its end, computes the MAC using K_I and checks the integrity of the received values by comparing this computed MAC with the corresponding received MAC. If MAC verification succeeds, TVS CH_i considers the node to be authenticated and its program integrity verification to be successful.

| **Cluster Head** i **(TVS)** | **Sensor Node** A |

$\qquad\qquad\qquad\qquad\qquad\qquad$ 1. Picks the nonce N_i received from CH_i

$\qquad\qquad\qquad\qquad\qquad\qquad$ 2. Computes new key K_A

$\qquad\qquad\qquad\qquad\qquad\qquad$ 3. Computes MACs M_A and m_1

$\qquad\qquad\qquad\qquad$ 4. PIV_Response:
$\qquad\qquad\qquad\qquad\overleftarrow{\quad ID_A,\ CH_i,\ m_1,\ M_A \quad}$

5. Unseals program block P'_A $(=P_A)$

$\quad$ if Unsealing fails then

$\qquad$ "TVS becomes invalid", EXIT

6. Computes MAC to compare with m_1:

$\quad$ if($m_1 = MAC_K(N_i)$) then Go To Step 7

$\quad$ else "Nonce N_i received incorrectly"

$\qquad$ if round ≤ 3 then

$\qquad\quad$ Increment round by 1

$\qquad\quad$ Repeat "PIV_Request"

7. Sets round $=1$

8. Computes new secret K_I

9. Computes MAC M_I

10. Compares M_I with M_A:

$\quad$ if($M_A = M_I$) then

$\qquad$ "Program Integrity Verification Successful"

$\quad$ else "Message corrupted"

$\qquad$ if round ≤ 3 then

$\qquad\quad$ Increment round by 1

$\qquad\quad$ Repeat "PIV_Request"

$\qquad$ else

$\qquad\quad$ "Node Captured. Process Revocation"

Fig. 4. Node authentication and program integrity verification protocol

Figure 4 presents the details of the protocol for node authentication and program integrity verification by TVS.

Once node A is successfully authenticated and its program integrity is verified by TVS i, both A and i delete the nonce values shared. The new key K_A $(= K_I)$ computed will now serve as the new secret between TVS i and node A. In case, node A moves out of the cluster headed by TVS i, it informs i about the move and the new cluster it joins that is headed by some TVS j. TVS i, then informs all nodes in its cluster about this move and also informs the new cluster head j. TVS i also shares the new secret K_A $(= K_I)$ of node A secretly with the new cluster head j using the pair wise shared key between these two TVSs.

4 Analysis

4.1 Security Analysis

The protocol security analysis is carried out against the adversary model as given below:

Adversary Model. The proposed protocol considers the existence of an adaptive adversary who is capable of tapping all the links in the wireless network with sufficient resources at his disposal for computation, communication and storage. The adversary can record the messages being transmitted on the communication channel and has adequate energy needed to steal the secret information from a captured node. Once the adversary gets hold of the node physically and obtains the secret information of the node, the adversary can take part in the network operations by assuming the identity of a valid node. Adversary is also capable of reprogramming and redeploying the captured nodes in order to launch various insider attacks such as Sybil attack and selective forwarding. Although, an adversary having adequate hardware resources and time at his disposal can carry out medium attacks, in this protocol, we assume that the adversary does not have enough hardware support and time to add memory to a captured node.

The security analysis is carried out using the formal analysis tool ProVerif [22] to prove the security of the proposed protocol against man-in-the-middle attack, impersonation attack and threats due to redeployment of the node after capture and reprogramming. The results are presented in the form of theorems. The notations used in the proof of a theorem are as given below:

$Attacker(S)$ - Attacker has access to S (S may be some term/name/variable/channel)	
c - Public channel	
NV_A - Node A has passed the Authentication and PIV by TVS i	
$W \wedge V$ - Logical AND operation on W and V	

The protocol claims that if the TVS itself is captured, then any modification in its platform configuration makes it invalid and the TVS authentication by node would fail. Similarly, if the node is captured, then any alteration in its program would result in the failure of node authentication and its program integrity verification by TVS.

Theorem 1. *A reprogrammed captured node does not pass the node authentication and program integrity verification by a valid TVS.*

Proof. The proof of the theorem is shown using *proof by contradiction* technique. The attacker's knowledge at various states, before and during the execution of the protocol, is given to reach the conclusion.

Initial State. In the initial state, the attacker knows unique identities of nodes and TVSs through network topology. So, the attacker knows the identities of node A and the TVS i. Attacker also knows the public functions and has access to a public channel used in the protocol run. Thus:

Attacker(ID_A)	... (1.1)
Attacker(CH_i)	... (1.2)
Attacker($h()$)	... (1.3)
Attacker(c)	... (1.4)

Intermediate State. After capturing a node A, an adversary gets the secret K (i.e. hash code of node's program memory $h(P_A)$). As the attacker reprograms this node, the program memory P_A changes to $Pnew_A$ because memory constraint does not allow an attacker to keep both the original and the modified program. Since the free space in the memory is filled by incompressible random bitstrings, an adversary can not insert code pieces while keeping the original program intact. Therefore:

Attacker(K)	... (1.5)
Attacker($MAC_K()$)	... (1.6)
Not Attacker(P_A)	... (1.7)

It is claimed that since TVS is valid, the attacker successfully authenticates TVS i and obtains nonce N_i from TVS i to further achieve its goal of authentication and program integrity verification for captured node A. To prove this claim, protocol steps are traced back as below:

Attacker(N_i)
$\Rightarrow$ Attacker($N_i \oplus K$)
$\Rightarrow$ Attacker(n_0) $\wedge$ Attacker(K)
$\Rightarrow$ Attacker(c) $\wedge$ Attacker(K) [from Step 5 of protocol provided in Fig. 3]
$\Rightarrow$ True [using assertions 1.4 and 1.5]

As a result, the attacker has N_i.

Attacker(N_i)	... (1.8)

Now, it is assumed that the attacker achieves its goal of authentication and program integrity verification for a captured node A by valid TVS i after reprogramming the captured node. With this assumption and above stated assertions, node authentication and program integrity verification protocol is traced back to resolve the assumption to be true.

Attacker(NV_A)
$\Rightarrow$ Attacker($M_A(=M_I)$)
$\Rightarrow$ Attacker($K_A(=K_I)$) $\wedge$ Attacker($MAC_K()$) $\wedge$ Attacker(ID_A)
  $\wedge$ Attacker(CH_i) $\wedge$ Attacker(N_i)
$\Rightarrow$ Attacker($h(P_A, N_i)$ $\wedge$ True [using assertions 1.6, 1.1, 1.2 and 1.8 respectively]
$\Rightarrow$ Attacker($h()$) $\wedge$ Attacker(P_A) $\wedge$ Attacker(N_i)
$\Rightarrow$ True $\wedge$ False $\wedge$ True [using assertions 1.3, 1.7 and 1.8 respectively]
$\Rightarrow$ False

This is a contradiction. Thus, the assumption that the attacker successfully gets the authentication and program integrity verification for captured node A by a valid TVS i even after reprogramming the captured node is false.

Therefore, the theorem is proved   □

Lemma 1. *Node program integrity verification fails, if an adversary inserts a new piece of code into program memory.*

Proof. As assumed in the adversarial model, the adversary is not capable of adding memory to the node. The free space in the program memory is filled with incompressible bit strings, so the adversary can not use the free space to insert the code. Therefore, to insert a new piece of code, an adversary needs to either modify the program code or replace the incompressible bit strings. Either of these actions would result in the change in the program memory content i.e. for a node A, the program memory content will change from P_A to $P_{A_{new}}$. The new computed hash would be different than expected by the verification server and the verification protocol fails. Thus, an attempt to insert a new piece of code into program memory would result in the failure of node program integrity verification.

Theorem 2. *A compromised TVS does not pass the authentication by a valid node.*

Proof. The proof is given using *proof by contradiction* technique. The attacker's knowledge at various states is given below:

Initial State. In the initial state, the attacker knows unique identities of nodes and TVSs through network topology. So, the attacker knows the unique identities of node A and the TVS i. Attacker also knows the public functions and public channel. Moreover, TVS i is TPM enabled, so any changes in the TVS program results in the change in the platform configuration of TPM on TVS i and also attacker does not have access to the platform configuration stored in PCRs. Thus:

Attacker(ID_A)	... (2.1)
Attacker(CH_i)	... (2.2)
Attacker($h()$)	... (2.3)
Attacker(c)	... (2.4)
Not Attacker(PC_i^0)	... (2.5)

Intermediate State. The attacker has compromised the TVS, i, so its platform configuration has changed.

It is assumed that the attacker achieves its goal of successfully passing the authentication of an invalid/captured TVS i by a valid node A. This implies that attacker can send the "PIV_challenge" message to node A and receives the "PIV_response" from A. With this assumption and above stated assertions, TVS authentication is traced back to resolve the assumption to be true.

Attacker(PIV_Response)
$\Rightarrow$ Attacker(c) $\wedge$ Attacker(ID_A) $\wedge$ Attacker(CH_i) $\wedge$ Attacker(m_1) $\wedge$
    Attacker(M_A)

$\Rightarrow$ True $\land$ Attacker(m_1) $\land$ Attacker(M_A) [using assertions 2.4, 2.1, 2.2 respectively]

$\Rightarrow$ Attacker(K) (only if attacker had key K, it could compute m_1 and M_A)

$\Rightarrow$ Attacker($h()$) $\land$ Attacker(P_A)

$\Rightarrow$ True $\land$ Attacker($PC_i^t(=PC_i^0)$)) [using assertion 2.3]

$\Rightarrow$ False [using assertion 2.5]

This is a contradiction. Thus, the assumption that the attacker successfully passes the authentication of an invalid/captured TVS i by a valid node A is false.

Therefore, the theorem is proved $\square$

If a node is captured, its aim is to pass its own authentication and program integrity verification. Whether a TVS is authenticated or not, is of no significance to a captured node.

Theorem 3. *Capturing a node will not reveal the secret hash code of any other node.*

Proof. The free space of program memory of a node is filled with some unique random incompressible bit strings. Therefore, even if the application program code is same for any two nodes, the overall program memory content remains unique to each node. Thus, for any node X other than node A in the network the overall program memory content is different. Now, Assume that an attacker captures a node A. Thus:

Attacker(P_A)	... (3.1)
Attacker($h()$)	... (3.2)
Attacker($P_A (\neq P_X)$)	... (3.3)

Let us suppose that capture of node A reveals the hash code of another node B.

$\Rightarrow$ Attacker($h(P_B)$)

$\Rightarrow$ Attacker($h(P_A)=h(P_B)$) $\lor$ (Attacker($h()$) $\land$ Attacker(P_B))

$\Rightarrow$ False $\lor$ (Attacker($h()$) $\land$ Attacker(P_B)) [by definition of $h()$]

$\Rightarrow$ True $\land$ Attacker(P_B)) [using assertion 3.2]

$\Rightarrow$ Attacker($P_B(=P_A)$))

$\Rightarrow$ False [using assertion 3.1 and 3.3]

Thus, even if an adversary captures one node, the secret hash code of any other node is not revealed to adversary.

Therefore, the theorem is proved $\square$

4.2 Performance Analysis

The proposed protocol is analyzed with respect to storage, computation and communication overhead and compared with existing protocols. The Table 4 gives the comparison of the proposed protocol with other related protocols. The terms used in the comparison table are described below.

T_m	- Time to perform a Message Authentication Code(MAC) operation
T_h	- Time to perform an Unkeyed Hash operation
T_x	- Time to perform a XOR operation
T_p	- Time to compute Polynomial based pair-wise key [15]
T_u	- Time to perform Unseal operation in TPM
T_e	- Time to perform Symmetric Encryption
T_d	- Time to perform Symmetric Decryption
T_s	- Time to perform Signature Generation in TPM [19]
T_v	- Time to perform Signature Verification in TPM [19]
T_{rv}	- Time to Read Value from TPM [19]
q	- large prime number
k	- Degree of polynomial used for generating secret share [15]
s	- Total PIVSs in network [15]
N_{auth}	- Number of Authentication tickets needed by a PIVS [15]

In this comparison, the overhead that occurs at the verifier and the prover end, for the purpose of program memory integrity verification and TVS authentication associated with the verification, is considered.

The proposed protocol allows a resource constrained sensor node to carry out TVS authentication and pass the node program integrity verification process with only one XOR, three MAC and two un-keyed hash operations. These operations are computationally efficient [20,21] as compared to encryption, decryption, signature generation and verification required in the existing protocols. The node needs to transmit just one message for the complete protocol. This is a significant reduction in communication cost as compared to the existing software based program integrity verification [15]. Furthermore, the proposed protocol does not require any pair-wise or group key to be stored in the node unlike in [15] where a unique polynomial share is stored at each node and node needs to compute the pair-wise key for $N_{Auth} + 1$ PIVSs to complete the protocol. Since the capture of node would reveal the key to the adversary along with its program code, we saved on the cost of storing and computing the keys using polynomial operations. With the TPM enabled TVS, the overall performance and security as compared to the software based scheme such as [15] is improved and at the same time the cost of equipping all the nodes with the TPM chip as in [19] is saved.

Simulation Results. A simulation has been carried out using *Castalia* Simulator [23] to compare the performance of the existing software based Distributed Authentication and PIV protocol(DAPP) [15] and the proposed protocol. A uniformly distributed clustered network set up is considered, in which some nodes designated as clustered heads are made to behave as verification servers and

Table 4. Performance comparison

Features → Protocol ↓	Prover or verifier	Storage (bits)	Computation	Communication (No. of messages transmitted)
Distributed program integrity verification (DAPP) [15]	Verifier	$(k+s)\log q$	$(N_{auth}+s+5)^*T_m+2t_e + T_h+(s+1)^*T_p$	$N_{auth}+6$
	Prover	$(k+N_{auth}+2) \log q)$	$(N_{auth}+4)^*T_m+2T_d +T_h+(N_{auth}+1)^*T_p$	6
TPM enabled server attestation [18][a]	Verifier	$\log q$	$T_u+T_d+T_e$	1
	Prover	$\log q$	T_d+T_e	1
TPM enabled mutual attestation [19]	Verifier	$3^*\log q$	$T_u+2T_d+T_e+T_{rv}+T_v$	2
	Prover	$\log q$	$T_u+T_d+T_e+T_{rv}+T_s$	1
Proposed protocol	Verifier	$\log q$	$2T_u+2T_h+T_x+2T_m$	1
	Prover	$\log q$	$2T_h+T_x+3T_m$	1

[a] As the scheme given in [18] does not describe the node program integrity verification by the Verifier, the data in the comparison includes only the overhead incurred during verifier authentication process for that scheme.

Table 5. Simulation parameters

Parameter	Value
Simulation time	100 s
Node transmission output power	0 dBm
CCA threshold	−95 dBm
Field size	100 X 100 m^2
Radio range	25 m
Node deployment	Uniform

the remaining nodes act as normal nodes whose program integrity verification is to be done. The node-to-server and server-to-server communication takes place at one-hop distance which is determined by the radio transmission range. The simulation parameters used are given in Table 5.

The simulation is carried out with varied number of nodes with 10 servers in a field of size 100 by 100. Under the similar network conditions, we measured the performance in terms of average energy consumption and the average communication latency for both the protocols (DAPP and proposed). The communication latency is the communication time taken starting from sending the first message and receiving the last message to complete one run of the protocol. The average energy consumption includes the radio energy plus the static node baseline power of 6 mW (as specified in the simulator used). The graphs in Fig. 5 show that with the TPIV protocol, while the average energy consumption

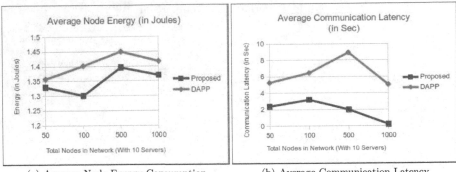

(a) Average Node Energy Consumption   (b) Average Communication Latency

Fig. 5. Performance comparison of proposed protocol and DAPP [15]

reduction is about 4 % (Fig. 5(a)), the communication latency improvement is more than 100 % (Fig. 5(b)). The reason is that in DAPP protocol, a complete run of protocol needs 4 rounds of to and from communication between the node and the server, whereas, in TPIV protocol, only 1 round is needed. As we are using TMAC as MAC protocol in this simulation, the sleep schedule of nodes affects the latency. When the number of nodes is too high (say 1000), almost all the nodes remain awake for most of the time, as they are continuously getting signals from the neighboring nodes. In TPIV, a node can respond back to the server challenge immediately, while in DAPP, the node still has to wait for the server to collect authentication tickets from other servers.

5   Conclusion

We discussed a protocol to verify the integrity of a sensor node program to detect node capture attack in a distributed WSN setup. We analyzed the proposed protocol for security and performance and found that the protocol provides authentication of a node and verification of the program integrity that helps detecting the node capture attack (capture, reprogramming and redeployment of a node) with less overhead as compared to the existing program integrity verification protocols. Prior to node program integrity verification, a node can authenticate the verification server. Since each verification server is equipped with trusted platform module (TPM), the proposed protocol also overcomes the threat of attacker knowing the node program stored at the verifier. The protocol also ensures that capture of a node does not reveal the secret of any other node in the network. Thus, additional security is provided as compared to the pure software based protocols with significant reduction in communication, computation and storage overhead on the nodes as evident from the performance analysis. The simulation results also verify the performance improvement in program integrity verification with proposed protocol. Moreover, the cost of equipping all the nodes with the TPM chip is saved, resulting in the overall reduced cost of network deployment and maintenance.

References

1. Menezes, A., van Oorschot, P., Vanstone, A.: Handbook of Applied Cryptography. CRC Press, Boca Raton (1996)
2. Benenson, Z., Cholewinski, P., Felix, C.: Wireless sensor network security. In: Vulnerabilities and Attacks in Wireless Sensor Networks, pp. 22–43. IOS Press, Amsterdam (2008)
3. Kim, J., Caytiles, R., Kim, K.: A review of the vulnerabilities and attacks for wireless sensor networks. J. Secur. Eng. 9(3), 241–250 (2012)
4. Becher, A., Benenson, Z., Dornseif, M.: Tampering with motes: real-world attacks on wireless sensor networks. In: Proceedings of 3rd International Conference on Security in Pervasive Computing, pp. 104–118 (2006)
5. Groups, T.C.: Trusted Platform Module (TPM) Summary (2009). http://www.trustedcomputinggroup.org/resources/trusted_platform_module_tpm_summary. Accessed 07 May 2015
6. Trusted computing group. https://www.trustedcomputinggroup.org/. Accessed 07 May 2015
7. Tomlinson, A.: Chapter: Introduction to TPM riptsize. http://www.researchgate.net/publication/227039163_Introduction_to_the_TPM/links/00b49523aba9d7bc97000000.pdf. Accessed 07 May 2015
8. Junior, W., Hao, T., Wong, C., Loureiro, A.: Malicious node detection in wireless sensor networks. In: Proceedings of the 18th International Parallel and Distributed Processing Symposium, vol. 4, pp. 24–30 (2004)
9. Mathews, M., Song, M., Shetty, S., McKenzie, R.: Detecting compromised nodes in wireless sensor networks. In: Proceedings of 8th ACIS International Conference on Software Engineering, Artificial Intelligence, Networking, and Parallel/Distributed Computing, vol. 1, pp. 273–278 (2007)
10. Conti, M., Pietro, R., Mancini, L., Mei, A.: Emergent properties: detection of the node-capture attack in mobile wireless sensor networks. In: Proceedings of 1st ACM Conference on Wireless Network Security, pp. 214–219 (2008)
11. Conti, M., Pietro, R., Mancini, L., Mei, A.: Mobility and cooperation to thwart node capture attacks in MANETs. EURASIP J. Wirel. Commun. Netw., 2009(8) (2009)
12. Ding, W., Laha, B., Yenduri, S.: First stage detection of compromised nodes in sensor networks. In: Proceedings of Sensors Applications Symposium, pp. 20–24 (2009)
13. Lin, X.: CAT: building couples to early detect node compromise attack in wireless sensor networks. In: Proceedings of 28th IEEE Conference on Global Telecommunications, pp. 1–6 (2009)
14. Park, T., Shin, K.: Soft-tamper-proofing via program integrity verification in wireless sensor networks. IEEE Trans. Mob. Comput. 4(3), 297–309 (2005)
15. Chang, K., Shin, K.: Distributed authentication of program integrity verification in wireless sensor networks. In: ACM Transactions on Information and Systems Security, vol. 11, No. 3, Article 14 (2008)
16. Seshadri, A., Perrig, A., Doorn, L., Khosla, P.: SWATT: SoftWare-based ATTestation for embedded devices. In: Proceedings of the 2004 IEEE Symposium on Security and Privacy, pp. 272–282 (2004)
17. Seshadri, A., Luk, M., Perrig, A., Doorn, L., Khosla, P.: SCUBA: secure code update by attestation in sensor networks. In: Proceedings of ACM Workshop on Wireless Security (WiSe), pp. 85–94 (2006)

18. Krauß, C., Stumpf, F., Eckert, C.: Detecting node compromise in hybrid wireless sensor networks using attestation techniques. In: Stajano, F., Meadows, C., Capkun, S., Moore, T. (eds.) ESAS 2007. LNCS, vol. 4572, pp. 203–217. Springer, Heidelberg (2007)

19. Tan, H., Hu, W., Jha, S.: A TPM-enabled remote attestation protocol(TRAP) in wireless sensor networks. In: Proceedings of the 6th ACM Workshop on Performance Monitoring and Measurement of Heterogeneous Wireless and Wired Networks, pp. 9–16 (2011)

20. http://www.cryptopp.com/benchmarks.html. Accessed 7 May 2015

21. Lee, J., Kapitanova, K., Son, S.: The price of security in wireless sensor networks. Comput. Netw. (Elsevier) **54**, 2967–2978 (2010)

22. Blanchet, B., Smyth, B., Cheval, V.: ProVerif 1.87beta6: Automatic Cryptographic Protocol Verifier, User Manual and Tutorial (2013)

23. Boulis, A.: Castalia - A simulator for Wireless Sensor Networks and Body Area Networks - User's Manual, Version 3.2 (2011)

Attack-Resistant Trust-Based Weighted Majority Game Rule for Spectrum Sensing in Cognitive Radio Networks

Suchismita Bhattacharjee$^{(\boxtimes)}$ and Ningrinla Marchang

Department of CSE, NERIST, Nirjuli 791109, Arunachal Pradesh, India
getsuchi87@gmail.com, nm@nerist.ac.in

Abstract. In collaborative sensing, a cognitive radio node cooperates with others in the spectrum sensing process for a more accurate sensing decision. A malicious node may launch Spectrum Sensing Data Falsification (SSDF) in which the local sensing report is falsified before it reaches the fusion center (FC). The task of FC is to aggregate local sensing reports from the collaborating nodes, thereby arriving at a final sensing decision. In this paper, we propose two attack-resistant trust-based decision rules: WMR (Weighted Majority Rule) and WMRR (Weighted Majority Rule with Redemption). These rules are based on the weighted majority game. The key feature in these rules is that the contribution of a sensing report in the final decision depends not merely on the report but also on the trust that the FC has on the node sending out the report. We support the validity of the proposed rules through extensive simulation results.

Keywords: Cognitive radio network · Collaborative spectrum sensing · SSDF attack · Decision rule

1 Introduction

Cognitive Radio Network is a rapidly emerging technology that holds promises for solving the wireless spectrum scarcity problem. The available frequency spectrum is limited and is divided into licensed and license-free bands. With the proliferation of technologies that offer services which operate in the license-free bands, making bands crowded which will eventually lead to a radio traffic jam. On the other hand, we only expect more technologies that operate in the license-free bands to increase in the future. Added to this, population of wireless devices is on the rise. Thus, the spectrum scarcity problem is a significant challenge that researchers face.

A Cognitive Radio Network (CRN) is a network of wireless cognitive radio devices [1,2]. These devices are called cognitive because they can sense the environment and adapt to it. They make opportunistic use of the licensed bands. When a device finds that the frequency band it is using currently is no longer available, it can search for a free band and use it. Thus, it can hop opportunistically from

© Springer International Publishing Switzerland 2015
S. Jajodia and C. Mazumdar (Eds.): ICISS 2015, LNCS 9478, pp. 441–460, 2015.
DOI: 10.1007/978-3-319-26961-0_26

band to band instead of sticking to a particular band. CRN is becoming a reality with the 802.22 standard established by FCC (USA), for opportunistically availing of TV white spaces [3]. The users who have been allocated the licensed bands are known as primary users (PUs) whereas those who make opportunistic use of the licensed bands are known as secondary users (SUs).

One important function of a cognitive radio is spectrum sensing, i.e., sensing spectrum to determine whether a particular channel is free or not. An erroneous sensing decision will result in a channel being used when it is busy causing unwanted interference to the PU, or not using a channel when it is free leading to lower utilization. A cognitive radio senses the spectrum using techniques such as energy detection [4]. Since energy detection method is the simplest, it is used most widely. Instead of depending on its sensing decision alone, a cognitive radio (Secondary User) may cooperate with others to come to a decision. For this reason, in a infrastructure-based CRN, a fusion center (FC) takes care of combining the individual sensing decisions and generating the final decision. Several decision schemes are available in the literature such as OR rule, Majority rule, etc. Most of these are variants of the k-out-of-n decision Rule. In this rule, if the number of results reporting 'channel busy' is at least k out of the n Secondary Users (SUs), then the final decision is 'channel busy', otherwise the final decision is 'channel idle'.

One major disadvantage of the above group of decision rules is that the FC simply uses the sensing reports from the SUs regardless of the trustworthiness of the SUs who send them. This gives ample room for malicious SUs to falsify sensing reports with the aim of disrupting the final sensing decision. However, we contend that the sensing reports sent by the SUs must not carry the same weight, just as the way it is in social relationships. In social relationships, information coming from a trusted friend has more weight than the same information from an acquaintance. In other words, we give more weight to a sensing report from a more trustworthy SU than to a sensing report from a less trustworthy SU. The trustworthiness of an SU can be established by monitoring its past behavior. In our proposed approach, we learn about the trustworthiness of SUs through the reports they send to the FC over time. We measure the trustworthiness of SUs using weights, and dynamically update the weights based on their behaviour.

The contribution of our work can be summarized as follows:

- We propose two attack-resistant trust-based decision rules: WMR (Weighted Majority Rule) and WMRR (Weighted Majority Rule with Redemption) based on the weighted majority game.
- We propose an algorithm for updating of trust values such that the power index of a malicious node in the weighted majority game is minimized.
- We show the validity of the proposed schemes through extensive simulation and also conclude that colluding attacks degrade performance more than independent attacks.

Furthermore, the reports provided by the SUs to the FC can be of two types: (a) continuous (e.g. power estimation from an energy detector) or (b) binary (e.g. PU signal is absent/present). Our work is for binary-type reporting.

2   Recent Works

In recent days, spectrum sensing security in CRN has attracted the attention of many researchers. Some binary-reporting schemes that propose to handle the SSDF attack are reported. Wang et al. [6] proposed a two-type robust detection scheme that combines the suspicious level and the trustworthiness of the users. However, only one adversary is considered. Rawat et al. [7] presented a scheme in which multiple attackers are considered. Moreover, limits in terms on the fraction of the attackers that can make the FC inoperable are presented. However, the reputation metric is not restored. A detection scheme is presented by Chen et al. in [8]. In this scheme, the reputation metric is restored and multiple attackers are considered. Like in our work, a weighted reputation scheme is used so not all users' observations are treated equally. However this scheme uses WSPRT. Noon et al. [9] proposed a technique in which an attacker with an adaptive strategy is used, the number of the attackers vary. However, the disadvantage is that the reputation metric is not restored. Moreover, it is assumed that the attacker successfully eavesdrops on the other users and the FC. Another detection scheme is given by Li et al. [10] in which two attack strategies are considered depending on whether attacker knows the reports sent by other users. Besides, multiple attackers are considered and SUs are regarded as adversaries if their behavior is very close to that of the correctly behaving users, which may increase the false alarm rate.

Several detection schemes for continuous reporting are also found in the literature [13,14]. Many trust and reputation management schemes have been proposed to combat vicious behavior of malicious users in CRNs [15–19]. A trust management model is proposed in [20], in which energy efficiency is achieved by reducing total number of sensing reports. Another trust based scheme is proposed in [21], where malicious users are deterred efficiently from reporting false sensing result under different attack scenarios. In [22], a dynamic trust management scheme is proposed to dependably detect and extenuate SSDF attack. A malicious behaviour resistance mechanism is presented in [23], where the authors have stated that without any prior knowledge on users' reputation, forbidding malicious behavior of an intelligent malicious users can be difficult, since, genuine users may be misjudged as malicious user.

Our proposed work is for binary reporting. We have considered multiple attackers. Restoration of reputation is also considered in our approach. It is based on the weighted majority game [5] and is simple to compute.

The rest of the paper is organized as follows: In Sect. 3, we define the system model, which is followed by the attack model in Sect. 4. Then, the proposed schemes are presented in Sect. 5. Section 6 gives the simulation performance and analysis. Finally, conclusions are drawn in Sect. 7 suffixed by references.

3   System Model

We consider a cognitive radio network consisting of n secondary users. A single-channel system is assumed for simplicity. A SU senses the spectrum to determine the presence of the PU signal. For each SU, each frame slot is divided into three sub-frame slots: (a) sensing sub-slot for spectrum sensing, (b) reporting sub-slot for reporting the result to FC, and (c) transmission sub-slot for transmitting data. We assume that each SU employs an energy detector [4] locally to sense the presence of the PU and sends it sensing report to the FC. The FC aggregates the sensing reports, makes a decision using a decision rule and then feeds it back to the SU. We assume a dedicated and reliable control channel for carrying the reports and decision to and fro the SUs and the FC.

The FC has no information about whether malicious SUs are present. Further, if they are present, it has no idea how many are present. We assume that the SUs and the FC are located together in a small area and hence they have the same spectrum occupancy. We denote by P_{pu} the probability that the PU signal is present. We assume that the local observations at different SUs are mutually independent. Moreover the misdetection (P_m) and false alarm (P_{fa}) probabilities of the local detection at the SUs are the same. During any frame slot, the channel can be in either one of the two states: busy (1), i.e., PU is transmitting, or idle (0), i.e., PU is not transmitting. The sensing result of a SU during the slot can be either one of the two: busy (1) or idle (0).

4   Attack Model

Several types of SSDF attacks are found in the literature [11,15]. The following attacks are considered in our work.

- *"Always Yes"* Attack: The malicious node always sends the sensing report '1' to the FC, whatever may be its local sensing result. This is done with the intention that the FC will be possibly influenced into making the final sensing result as '1'. Thus, even when the channel is free, it may be left free by the other SUs. This free channel then may be used by the malicious node or wasted.
- *"Always No"* Attack: The malicious node always sends the sensing report '0' to the FC, whatever may be its local sensing result. This is done with the intention that the FC will be possibly influenced into making the final sensing result as '0'. Thus, even when the channel is busy, other SUs may try to use it causing interference to the PU.
- *"Always False"* Attack: The malicious node sends a report to the FC which is opposite of its local sensing decision. In this case, both misdetection and false alarm rates are expected to rise. Both user interference and resource wastage are expected to occur.
- *"Randomly False"* Attack: The malicious node sends a report to the FC which is opposite of its local sensing decision with a probability of β. Thus, *"Always False"* attack is a special case of *"Randomly False"* attack in which $\beta = 1$.
- *"Randomly Yes"* Attack: The malicious node sends the sensing report '1' to the FC regardless of its local sensing result with a probability of β. Thus, *"Always Yes"* attack is a special case of *"Randomly Yes"* attack in which $\beta = 1$.

– *"Randomly No"* Attack: The malicious node sends the sensing report '0' to the FC regardless of its local sensing result with a probability of β. Thus, *"Always No"* attack is a special case of *"Randomly No"* attack in which $\beta = 1$.

Attacks may again be classified based on the collaboration between the attackers as follows:

– *Independent attack:* Malicious users are autonomous i.e. they launch attacks based on their own decision. They do not require to have any prior knowledge about the report of other SUs or any reports from other existing malicious users.
– *Colluding attack:* Malicious users work in cooperation to launch an attack [24].

There is no difference in the effects of launching the first three attacks: *"Always Yes"*, *"Always No"* and *"Always False"* either independently or collaboratively. Hence, we focus on the other attacks. In the independent attack scenario, each malicious SU launches the *"Randomly False"*, *"Randomly Yes"* and *"Randomly No"* independently as shown above. However, the malicious nodes could collude to launch the following attacks. We assume that they share a covert channel through which they are able to convey information to each other.

– *Colluding Randomly False attack:* Here, one of the colluding nodes acts as a leader and inverts its sensing result with a probability of α. Then, the rest of the colluding nodes copy the leader's sensing report.
– *Colluding Randomly No attack:* In this attack, the leader among the colluding nodes updates its sensing result as '0' with a probability of α. Then, the rest of the colluding nodes copy the leader's sensing report.
– *Colluding Randomly Yes attack:* In this attack, the leader among the colluding nodes updates its sensing result as '1' with a probability of α. Then, the rest of the colluding nodes copy the leader's sensing report.

5   Weighted Majority Game Rule

We propose a spectrum sensing rule based on the weighted majority game [5]. A weighted majority game, written $[q; w_1, w_2, .., w_n]$ is a game (N, v), where $w_1 \geq 0, w_2 \geq 0, .., w_n \geq 0$ and

$$v(S) = \begin{cases} 1 \text{ if (the sum of the weight of S)} \geq q \\ 0 \qquad\qquad\qquad\qquad \text{otherwise} \end{cases} \tag{1}$$

where N is the set of players in the game and $S \subset N$. Here, N is the set of SUs. Here, S is a winning coalition if $v(S) = 1$.

We apply the weighted majority game to collaborative sensing with some modification. A weighted majority game is associated with each sensing slot.

In each slot k, the FC maintains a trust value (weight) for each of the n SUs, represented by a vector $(w_1^k, w_2^k, .., w_n^k)$. Hence, the weighted majority game associated with slot k is given by $\{q, w_1^k, w_2^k, .., w_n^k\}$. For determining the final decision by the FC, we consider the set S of weights of SUs which report '1' to the FC. If S forms a wining coalition, (i.e., $v(S) = 1$), then the final decision of the FC is '1', otherwise it is '0'.

We consider $q = n/2$ and initially set the value of each weight to 1. Thus, the sum of weights of all SUs is n. At each slot, the weights of the SUs are updated so that a new weighted game is generated for the next slot. A larger weight denotes higher trust, whereas a smaller weight denotes lower trust. The trust value of a SU reduces if its sensing report is different from the final sensing result. When the weight of a SU is reduced by a certain amount, this amount is equally distributed to the rest of the SUs. This is done so that the sum of the weights of the SUs remain the same (i.e., n) throughout the slots. Moreover, this depicts the situation in which when the trust of a player in a group goes down due to bad behaviour, the trust of others go up.

5.1   Updation of Weights

Let the sensing reports received by the FC in a slot k be represented by a vector $(r_1^k, r_2^k, .., r_n^k)$. If a sensing report is not received from SU in slot k, then we consider $r_i^k = 0$. Let X_k denote the final decision at slot k.

The updation of w_i^k of SU i in slot k is performed as follows:

Weight Updation Algorithm:-

Step 1. $count = 0$;
  for each SU i
      if $r_i^k \neq X_k$ then begin
          $count = count + 1$;
          $w_i^k = w_i^k - \epsilon$;
      end
Step 2.
  for each SU i
      if $r_i^k = X_k$ then begin
          $w_i^k = w_i^k + (count \times \epsilon)/(n - count)$;
      end

In the above algorithm, the variable $count$ gives a count of the number of SUs whose sensing reports do not match the final decision. In step 1, $count$ is initialized to 0. Then, for each SU whose sensing report does not match the final decision, the value of ϵ is deducted from its weight. Here, ϵ is a predefined value $(0 < \epsilon < 1)$, which denotes the reduction in the amount of trust the FC has on a SU under the said condition. In step 2, the total amount that is deducted in step 1 (i.e., $count \times \epsilon$) is distributed among the SUs whose report match the final decision. The above updation scheme ensures that sum of the weights of the SUs remain the same throughout the lifetime of the network. The weight of each SU is initialized to 1. Hence, the sum of the weights remains n throughout. The idea behind this is to normalize the weights. Hence, in the scenario where no malicious SUs are present and the sensing reports are affected only by local sensing error, the weights of the SUs will remain more or less the same. However, when malicious SUs are present, there will be data skew in the weights.

The running time of the updation algorithm is $O(n)$ since the frequency of execution of the for loop in step 1 as well as in step 2 is n.

5.2 Shapley-Shubik Power Index

The shapley value of a player in a weighted majority game constitutes a good index of the player's power in the game [5]. This index is known as the Shapley-Shubik power index. Numerical analysis of this index for the proposed weighted majority game supports the validity of the algorithm for updation of weights discussed in the last subsection. In a weighted majority game of n players, a player's Shapley value is [5]:

Frequency with which player is pivotal over all possible orders

$$= \frac{number\ of\ times\ player\ is\ pirotal}{number\ of\ possible\ orders(n!)} \tag{2}$$

A player is called a pivotal player in a certain order, if his marginal contribution in that order is 1 [5].

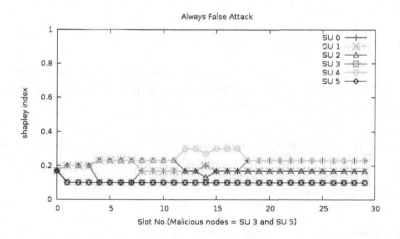

Fig. 1. Shapley index vs. slot numbers

To illustrate, we consider a game of 5 players (SUs) in which SU3 and SU5 are malicious and launch the always yes attack while the rest are legitimate SUs.

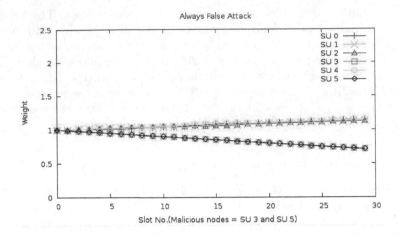

Fig. 2. Weight vs. slot numbers

The weights are updated using the algorithm in the last section. We assume ϵ to be 0.01. As the weights of the SUs get updated at each slot, a new weighted majority game emerges at each slot. Here, $P_{pu} = 0.4$, $P_{fa} = P_m = 0.05$.

Figure 1 shows the shapley value of each SU at different slots. From the graph, we observe that the shapley values of the malicious SUs, SU3 and SU5 become less than those of the other honest SUs. This illustrates the reduction in the power of the malicious SUs, which in turn minimizes the influence of the malicious SUs in the final sensing decision. The corresponding changes in the weights of the SUs is shown in Fig. 2.

5.3   Detection of Malicious Nodes

Once the weight of a SU becomes 0, it is detected as malicious and it automatically stops contributing to the final decision. We proposed the following schemes for handling nodes detected as malicious.

Isolation. Once the weight of any SU becomes 0, it remains 0. In other words, its contribution to the final decision process is nil henceforth. Moreover it is isolated from the weight updation process. This scheme follows the policy: *once convicted, convicted forever.*

Redemption. One disadvantage with the *Isolation* method is that once the FC has lost trust completely on a SU (weight becomes 0), improvement in the behavior of the SU at later instances is disregarded. Hence, in instances such as the hidden terminal problem, the SU may be 'convicted' as malicious forever. A hidden terminal problem is one in which the PU signal is hidden from a SU, whereas the SU is able to send reports to the FC.

To overcome this disadvantage, we introduce the *Redemption* method in which a 'convicted' SU can be later 'redeemed' if its behavior improves. In this method, once the weight of a SU becomes zero, we observe the behavior of the SU for the next S slots and calculate the estimated true positive rate, $(ETPR_S)$ and the estimated true negative rate $(ETNR_S)$ corresponding to the SU. Hence, the following algorithm is implemented S slots after the weight w_i^k of SU i has become 0.

Here, $ETPR_S$ is a ratio. It is the number of slots out of the S slots in which the SU reports 1 when the final decision is 1 divided by S. Similarly, $ETNR_S$ is a ratio. It is the number of slots out of the S slots in which the SU reports 0 when the final decision is 0 divided by S. We also define accepted $ETPR_S$ and $ETNR_S$ values which are denoted by λ_1 and λ_2 respectively. If $ETPR_S \geq \lambda_1$ and $ETNR_S \geq \lambda_2$, then the weight of the SU is set to δ in the current slot. Here, δ ($0 < \delta \leq 1$) is assigned as the weight of the SU to let it start over again as it showed normal behavior in the past S slots. Then, an amount δ/b is deducted from each *benign* SU (i.e., whose weights are greater than 0) where b is the number of benign SUs. Moreover, λ_1, λ_2, δ and S are predefined thresholds. Here, λ_1 and λ_2 represent the acceptable true positive and true negative rates.

The above process is repeated until the convicted SU is redeemed (i.e., weight is set to δ) or the lifetime of the SU is over (i.e., the SU persistently shows malicious behavior and thus is never redeemed).

Redemption Algorithm:-

repeat until $w_i^k \neq 0$ [k denotes the current slot]
begin
    Calculate $ETPR_S$ and $ETNR_S$;
    if $ETPR_S \geq \lambda_1$ and $ETNR_S \geq \lambda_2$
      $w_i^k = \delta$;
end

---

6 Simulation and Performance Evaluation

In this section, we present the numerical simulation results of the proposed schemes for a CRN of 20 SUs. Let P_m, P_f and P_{pu} denote the local misdetection probability, the local false alarm probability and the probability of presence of the PU signal respectively. In our simulations, we let $P_m = 0.05$, $P_f = 0.05$ (as P_m and P_f must be less than 0.1 [12]) and $P_{pu} = 0.50$. Moreover, $\lambda_1 = 0.95$, $\lambda_2 = 0.95$, $\delta = 0.5$ and $s = 20$. The results shown are averaged over 100 iterations.

The SU's report their local decisions to the FC. We present the simulation results for the scenarios when FC employs the proposed schemes viz., *weighted majority rule* (WMR) and *weighted majority rule with redemption* (WMRR) as compared to that of *majority rule* (MR). In majority rule, FC concludes that the PU signal is present if the number of 1's received from the SU's is greater than or equal to $n/2$, where n is the number of SUs. The number of slots used in the simulation is 160. In each slot, SU's report the local sensing decisions to the FC, which subsequently arrives at the final decision depending on the fusion rule being employed. The performance metrics used are the detection rate (true positive rate, TPR) and the false detection rate (false positive rate, FPR). The detection rate is the ratio of the number of slots for which the final decision is '1' when the PU signal is actually present to the number of slots during which the PU signal is actually present. The false detection rate is the ratio of the number of slots for which the final decision is '1' when the PU signal is actually absent to the number of slots during which the PU signal is actually absent.

We assume a simulation scenario in which the percentage (%) of malicious nodes increases w.r.t. time. This is done to check whether the proposed schemes adapt well to the increase in the percentage of malicious nodes. Initially, we start with 10 % of the total number of SUs being malicious. This is based on the assumption that in the initial stages of the lifetime of a CRN, we don't expect a heavy presence of malicious SUs. Since the number of benign nodes (90 %) is more that the number of malicious nodes, the malicious nodes are correctly identified and assigned appropriate weights. If the % of malicious nodes in the initial stage is higher than that of benign nodes, the final sensing decision would be erroneous and consequently, there will be a reduction in the weight (trust) of benign nodes and an increase in the weight (trust) of malicious nodes. The updation of weights in the initial stages is significant since the updation of weights in later stages depends on it.

The simulation results are divided into two parts. First, we illustrate the performance comparison of the three rules under the independent attack scenario for the following attack types: *always yes*, *always no*, *always false* and *randomly false* in Figs. 3, 4, 5, 6, 7, 8, 9 and 10. Next, we show the same under both the independent and the colluding attack scenarios for the following attack types: *randomly yes*, *randomly no* and *randomly false* in Figs. 11, 12, 13 and 14.

First, we consider only independent attacks. Figure 3 illustrates the TPR vs. % of malicious nodes for the *always yes* attack. In the graph, the plot labeled 'MR' denotes the plot when the basic majority rule is used. The plots labeled 'WMR' and 'WMR-R' denote the plots when the proposed weighted majority rule is used without redemption and with redemption respectively.

At slot number 20, the % of malicious SUs is 10 %, which increases to 20 % at slot number 40 and so on. The True Positive Rate (TPR) shown at slot number 20 is based on the sensing reports received by the FC from slot number 1 to 20. Similarly, the detection rate shown at slot number 40 is based on the sensing reports received by the FC from slot numbers 21 to 40, and so on. As the % of malicious nodes increases from 10 % to 80 %, the detection rate remains the same at 1 for all the three rules. In the *always yes* attack, the malicious SUs report always 1 whatever may be their local sensing decision. Hence, the number of 1's increases as the % of malicious SUs increases and consequently, the detection rate is very good under all three rules.

Figure 4 illustrates the FPR vs. % of malicious nodes for the *always yes* attack. Here, we observe that WMRR gives the best false detection rate. Even when the % of malicious nodes is 80 %, the FPR is only 0.05. The weighted

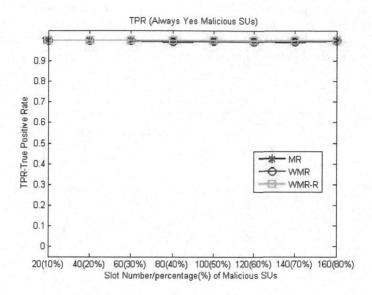

Fig. 3. True Positive Rate (TPR) vs. % presence of malicious SUs

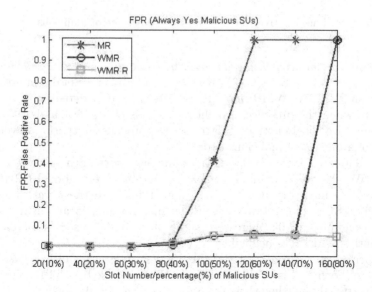

Fig. 4. False Positive Rate (FPR) vs. % presence of malicious SUs

majority rule shows good FPR of 0.05 up to 70 % presence of malicious nodes. In comparison, majority rule performs the worst. It shows acceptable FPR (about 0.05) only up to when the % of malicious SUs is less that 50 %. Hence, we see that WMRR and WMR outperform MR when the % of malicious nodes goes beyond 50 % in the *always yes* attack scenario.

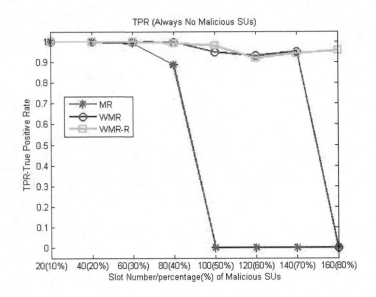

Fig. 5. True Positive Rate (TPR) vs. % presence of malicious SUs

Next, we compare the performance of the three rules in the *always no* attack scenario. Figure 5 illustrates the TPR as the % of malicious nodes increases. We observe that WMRR, WMR and MR maintain a good detection rate (about 0.95) up to when the presence of malicious SUs is 80 %, 70 % and 30 % respectively. Hence, we conclude that our proposed approaches outperform even in the presence of a high % of malicious nodes.

Figure 6 illustrates the FPR vs. % of malicious nodes in the *always no* attack scenario. We observe that all three rules maintain a very good FPR (0) even when the % of malicious nodes is very high (80 %). In the *always no* attack, the malicious SUs report always 0 whatever may be their local sensing decision. Hence, the number of 0's increases as the % of malicious SUs increases and consequently, the FPR is negligible.

The performance results of the three rules under the *always false* attack scenario are shown in Figs. 7 and 8. The WMRR give the best TPR as compared to the other two. Even when there is a 50 % presence of malicious nodes, it gives a TPR of about 1, which decreases minimally to about 0.9 when the % of malicious SUs is 80 %. However, WMR and MR give TPR of 0.93 and 0.90 at 50 % and 40 % presence of malicious nodes respectively.

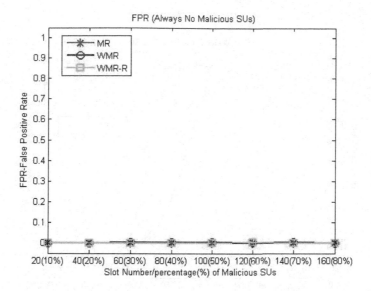

Fig. 6. False Positive Rate (FPR) vs. % presence of malicious SUs

Figure 8 illustrates the FPR vs. % of malicious nodes under the *always false* attack scenario. Here, we observe that WMRR outperforms the other two rules. Even when the % of malicious nodes is 80 %, this rule gives a FPR of about 0.05 while maintaining a FPR of 0 till 50 % presence of malicious nodes. Both WMR and MR maintain a FPR of 0 till 40 % presence of malicious nodes. The *weighted majority rule* maintains good FPR (0) up to 40 % presence of malicious nodes, but shows a FPR of 0.05 when there is 50 % presence of malicious nodes. In comparison, majority rule performs the worst. It maintains a FPR of 0 up to 40 % presence of malicious nodes, but the FPR degrades very severely beyond 40 %.

Figures 9 and 10 shows the effect of changing the value of β under *randomly* attack case. Due to lack of space, we show only the *randomly false* attack scenario. We show the results for $\beta = 0.70$ and $\beta = 0.30$. As explained earlier, β is the probability with which a malicious SU inverts (i.e., from 0(1) to 1(0)) its local sensing report before sending it to the FC. When $\beta = 0.30$, all three rules maintain good TPR (about 1) for varying presence of malicious SUs (Fig. 9). Since the proportion of sensing reports being inverted is less (0.30), it does not affect the TPR. However, when $\beta = 0.70$, both WMRR and WMR maintain a good TPR (about 1) up to when the presence of malicious SUs is 80 % and 70 % respectively. Comparatively, a TPR of about 1 is generated by MR only up to when the % of malicious nodes is 40 %.

Figure 10 shows the FPR vs. % of malicious nodes as the number of malicious nodes increases under the *randomly false* attack scenario. We observe that when $\beta = 0.30$, all the three rules exhibit good FPR (around 0). This is because

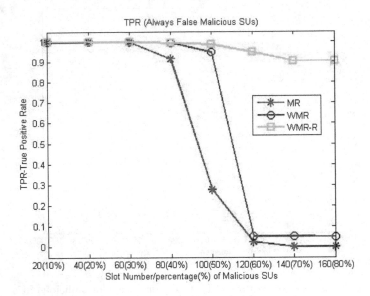

Fig. 7. True Positive Rate (TPR) vs. % presence of malicious SUs

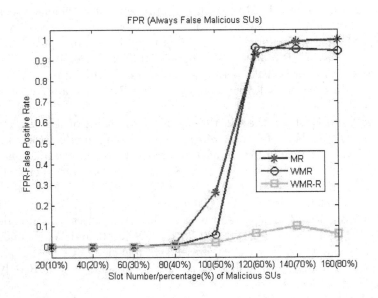

Fig. 8. False Positive Rate (FPR) vs. % presence of malicious SUs

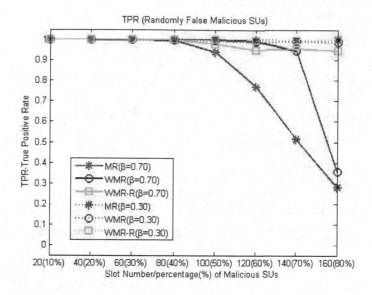

Fig. 9. True Positive Rate (TPR) vs. % presence of malicious SUs

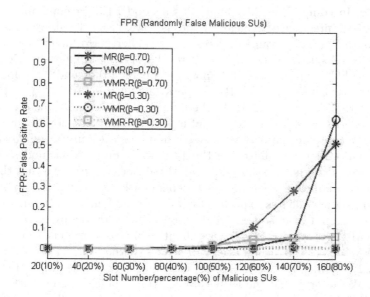

Fig. 10. False Positive Rate (FPR) vs. % presence of malicious SUs

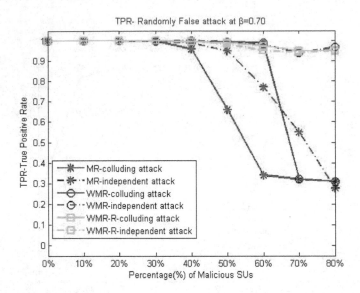

Fig. 11. True Positive Rate (TPR) vs. % presence of malicious SUs

a lower value of β results in generation of less number of false reports, which consequently does not affect the performance. However, when $\beta = 0.70$, both *Weighted Majority rule* and MR maintain a good FPR (a maximum of 0.05) up to 70 %. In comparison, MR maintains a good FPR (a maximum of 0.05) only up to 50 % presence of malicious nodes is 40 %. From the above two graphs, we observe that a higher value of β results in higher performance degradation. This is expected since a higher value of β results in more number of false reports reaching the FC. From the above graphs, we conclude that under the four independent attacks considered, WMRR outperforms both WMR and MR. Besides, WMR performs better than MR. In the following graphs, we show the effect of colluding attacks as compared to that of independent attacks for all three rules.

First, We compare the performance of the three rules in the *randomly false* attack scenario. Figure 11 illustrates the TPR vs. % of malicious nodes for both independent and colluding attacks. For all three rules, we observe that the TPR is higher when malicious nodes attack independently as compared to when they collude and attack. This is expected as collusion is done so as to increase the adverse effect on the final sensing decision. Under randomly false colluding attack, WMRR gives the best TPR (about 1 till 80 % presence of malicious nodes), WMR gives the second best TPR and MR the least TPR.

Figure 12 shows the FPR vs. % of malicious nodes under the same attack scenarios. We observe that the FPR is lower when malicious nodes attack independently as compared to when they collude and attack for all three rules. The reason is as explained earlier. Under randomly false colluding attack, WMRR gives the best FPR (not more that 0.06 till 80 % malicious presence) as compared

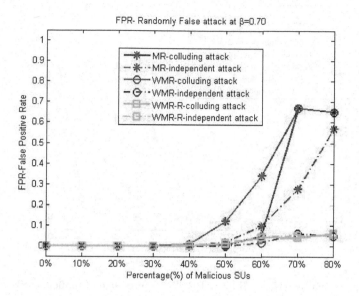

Fig. 12. False Positive Rate (FPR) vs. % presence of malicious SUs

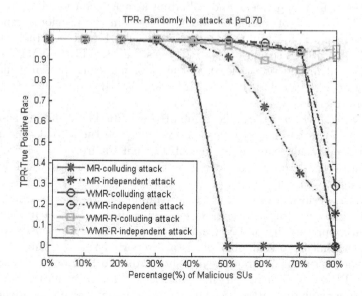

Fig. 13. True Positive Rate (TPR) vs. % presence of malicious SUs

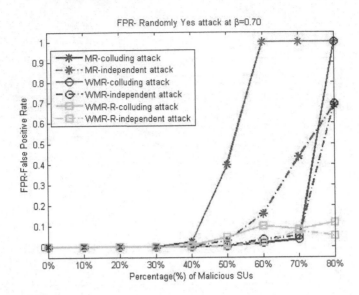

Fig. 14. False Positive Rate (FPR) vs. % presence of malicious SUs

to WMR and MR. However, WMR gives a better FPR than MR as the % of presence of malicious nodes increases.

Next, we compare the performance of the three rules for the *randomly no* attack in both the independent and colluding attack scenarios. Figure 13 illustrates the TPR vs. % of malicious nodes. As seen in the previous results, colluding attack is more harmful than independent attack for this attack type too. Under colluding attack scenario, WMRR gives the best TPR, WMR gives the second best and MR gives the least as the % of malicious presence increases. From the graph, we conclude that WMMR and WMR are resilient to a heavy presence of attackers.

In this *randomly no* attack, the value of β is 0.70. Thus, the malicious SUs report 0 with a probability of 0.70 whatever may be their local sensing decision. Consequently, much more number of 0's than 1's are reported and hence, the FPR for both colluding and independent attack scenarios are both low. The graphs are not shown due to lack of space.

Finally, the performance comparison for the *randomly yes* attack in both the independent and colluding attack scenarios is given in Fig. 14. The malicious SUs report 1 with a probability of 0.70 whatever may be their local sensing decision. Consequently, much more number of 1's are reported than 0's and hence, the TPR is 1 for all rules.The graph is not shown due to lack of space. Figure 14 shows the FPR vs. % of malicious nodes under the above scenario. We observe that FPR under colluding attack scenario is more than under independent attack scenario for all rules. Under randomly yes colluding attack, WMRR gives the best FPR (not more that 0.1 till 80 % malicious presence) as compared to WMR and MR. However, WMR gives a better FPR than MR as the % of presence of malicious nodes increases. From the performance analysis given above, we conclude that WMRR gives the best performance, WMR gives the second best performance and MR gives the lowest performance under all the considered attack scenarios (both independent and colluding). We also find that WMMR and WMR are resilient to a heavy presence of attackers.

7   Conclusion

Based on the weighted majority game, we propose two attack-resistant trust-based fusion rules: WMR (Weighted Majority Rule) and WMRR (Weighted Majority Rule with Redemption). The trust values of the SUs are represented by the weights in the game. These weights are updated by monitoring its past behaviour in such a way that the power index of an attacker is minimized in the game. This is turn minimizes the effect of an attacker in the final sensing decision. Through simulation results, we conclude that our proposed schemes provide a secure way of aggregation of the sensing reports such that even when more than half of the SUs are malicious, the true positive rate and the false positive rate are quite good. Moreover, even when malicious SUs collude, still the proposed schemes show good performance. Additionally, we conclude that colluding attacks degrade the performance of decision rules more than independent attacks.

References

1. Mitola, J.: Cognitive radio for flexible mobile multimedia communications. In: Proceedings of the IEEE International Workshop on Mobile Communications, pp. 3–10 (1999)
2. Mitola, J.: Cognitive Radio: An integrated agent architecture for software defined radio, Ph.D. thesis in Royal Institute of Technology (KTH) (2000)
3. Carlos, C., Challapali, K., Birru, D., Sai Shankar, N.: IEEE 802.22: the first worldwide wireless standard based on cognitive radios. In: Proceedings of the First IEEE International Symposium on New Frontiers in Dynamic Spectrum Access Networks, DySPAN 2005, pp. 328–337 (2005). doi:10.1109/DYSPAN.2005.1542649
4. Shen, J., Liu, S., Zhang, R., Liu, Y.: Soft versus hard cooperative energy detection under low SNR. In: Proceedings of the Third International Conference on Communications and Networking in China, pp. 128–131 (2008)
5. Gura, E.-Y., Maschler, M.B.: Insights into Game Theory. Cambridge University Press, Cambridge (2008)
6. Wang, W., Li, H., Sun, Y., Han, Z.: Attack-proof collaborative spectrum sensing in cognitive radio networks. In: Proceedings of CISS, pp. 130–134 (2009)
7. Rawat, A., Anand, P., Chen, H., Varshney, P.: Countering byzantine attacks in cognitive radio networks. In: Proceedings of ICASSP, pp. 3098–3101 (2010)
8. Chen, R., Park, J., Bian, K.: Robust distributed spectrum sensing in cognitive radio networks. In: Proceedings of Milcom, pp. 1876–1884 (2008)
9. Noon, E., Li, H.: Defending against hit-and-run attackers in collaborative spectrum sensing of cognitive radio networks: a point system. In: VTC, pp. 1–5 (2010)

10. Li, H., Han, Z.: Catching attacker(s) for collaborative spectrum sensing in cognitive radio systems: an abnormality detection approach. In: DySPAN, pp. 1–12 (2010)
11. Li, H., Han, Z.: Catch me if you can: an abnormality detection approach for collaborative spectrum sensing in cognitive radio networks. IEEE Trans. Wirel. Commun. **9**(11), 3554–3565 (2010)
12. Kang, X., Liang, Y.-C., Garg, H.K., Zhang, L.: Sensing-based spectrum sharing in cognitive radio networks. IEEE Trans. Veh. Technol. **58**(8), 4649–4654 (2009)
13. Min, A., Shin, K., Hu, X.: Attack-tolerant distributed sensing for dynamic spectrum access networks. In: Proceedings of ICNP, pp. 294–303 (2009)
14. Zhu, F., Seo, S.: Enhanced robust cooperative spectrum sensing in cognitive radio. J. Commun. Netw. **11**, 122–133 (2009)
15. Wang, W., Li, H., Sun, Y., Han, Z.: CatchIt: detect malicious nodes in collaborative spectrum sensing. In: Proceedings of the 28th IEEE Conference on Global Telecommunications, GLOBECOM 2009, pp. 5071–5076 (2009). ISBN- 978-1-4244-4147-1
16. Yu, H., Shen, Z., Miao, C., Leung, C., Niyato, D.: A survey of trust and reputation management systems in wireless communications. Proc. IEEE **98**(10), 1755–1772 (2010)
17. Chen, R., Park, J.-M., Hou, Y.T., Reed, J.H.: Toward secure distributed spectrum sensing in cognitive radio networks. IEEE Commun. Mag. **46**(4), 50–55 (2008)
18. Yifeng, C., Liu, C., Pelechrinis, K., Krishnamurthy, P., Weiss, M.B.H., Mo, Y.: Decoupling trust and wireless channel induced effects on collaborative sensing attacks. In: 2014 IEEE International Symposium on Dynamic Spectrum Access Nteworks (DYSPAN), pp. 224–235, 1–4 April 2014
19. Abdelhakim, M., Zhang, L., Ren, J., Li, T.: Cooperative sensing in cognitive networks under malicious attack. In: 2011 IEEE International Conference on Acoustics, Speech Processing (ICASSP), pp. 3004–3007, 22–27 May 2011
20. Mousavifar, S.A., Leung, C.: Energy efficient collaborative spectrum sensing based on trust managemnt in cognitive radio networks. IEEE Trans. Wirel. Commun. **14**(4), 1927–1939 (2015)
21. Wang, J., Chen, I.-R.: Trust-based data fusion mechanism design in cognitive radio networks. In: 2014 IEEE Conference on Communications and Network Security (CNS), pp. 53–59, 29–31 Oct 2014
22. Sagduyu, Y.E.: Securing cognitive radio networks with dynamic trust against spectrum sensing data falsification. In: 2014 IEEE Military Communications Conference (MILCOM), pp. 235–241, 6–8 Oct 2014
23. Wang, W., Chen, L., Shin, K.G., Duan, L.: Thwarting intelligent malicious behaviours in cooperative spectrum sensing. IEEE Trans. Mob. Comput. **14**, 2392–2405 (2015)
24. Bhattacharjee, S., Rajkumari, R., Marchang, N.: Effect of colluding attack in collaborative spectrum sensing. In: 2015 IEEE 2nd International Conference on Signal Processing and Integrated Networks (SPIN), pp. 223–227, 19–20 Feb 2015

Watermarking and Steganography

Watermark Removal Attack Extended to Forgery Against Correlation-Based Watermarking Schemes

Toshanlal Meenpal[1][(✉)] and A.K. Bhattacharjee[2]

[1] National Institute of Technology, Raipur 492010, India
tmeenpal.etc@nitrr.ac.in
[2] Reactor Control Division, BARC Mumbai, Mumbai 400094, India
anup@barc.gov.in

Abstract. It is well known that correlation based watermarking schemes are vulnerable to attacks specifically designed for it. One such attack was proposed in Das et al. [11]. Subsequently, they also proposed a robust Modified Differential Energy Watermarking (MDEW) scheme in the same paper. However, we could show that so called robust schemes like MDEW, which is specifically designed to overcome those vulnerabilities is also not secure. In this paper we show that generic watermark removal attack on a correlation-based watermarking scheme may be extended to a general to forgery attack even if the watermark removal strategy is a weak one. We prove our case by mounting such an attack on MDEW.

Keywords: Correlation-based scheme · Digital Watermarking · Forgery attack · Watermark removal · Cryptanalysis

1 Introduction

Digital Watermarking is a method to insert secret user-specific information in a digital object (e.g., image, video, audio, etc.) that may later be used to ensure authenticity of the content. For some of the security aspects like forgery or traitor tracing, an image watermarking scheme produces marked copies $I^{(1)}, I^{(2)}, \ldots, I^{(n)}$ of an original image I, to be sold to authentic buyers $B_1, B_2, \ldots, B_n$, respectively. There are many standard image processing benchmarks to study whether an image watermarking scheme is robust or not [4] and most of the proposed schemes pass those benchmarks. However, from the point of view of cryptology, the scenario is considerably different, as the standard benchmarks mostly work on general image processing ideas, and are not customized to attack a specific watermarking scheme.

In case of a correlation-based watermarking scheme, the marked copies are created from the original image I as follows. For each authentic buyer B_i,

---

T. Meenpal—This research has been carried out at HBNI Mumbai during the course of PhD research work.

© Springer International Publishing Switzerland 2015
S. Jajodia and C. Mazumdar (Eds.): ICISS 2015, LNCS 9478, pp. 463–479, 2015.
DOI: 10.1007/978-3-319-26961-0_27

where $i = 1, 2, \ldots, n$, the owner of the image I first fixes a buyer-specific fingerprint $s^{(i)}$. Using the watermarking algorithm W, the i-th buyer-specific fingerprint $s^{(i)}$ is inserted within the original image I to produce the watermarked copy $I^{(i)} \leftarrow W(I, s^{(i)})$, specifically to be sold to the i-th buyer B_i. For each buyer B_i, fingerprint $s^{(i)}$, and hence the marked copy $I^{(i)}$, is unique.

From the point of view of cryptanalysis, it is assumed that the watermarking algorithm W is public and only the watermark information or the fingerprint $s^{(i)}$ is secret. It is also assumed that an attacker possesses one or more watermarked copy of the original image I. This may be possible if an authentic buyer turns out to be a potential attacker, or if a group of authentic buyers collude to produce pirated copies of the image. The correlation based watermarking techniques are known to be vulnerable to collusion attack [3]. This strategy, however, requires $O(\sqrt{n \ln n})$ number of watermarked copies of the original image, where n is the effective length of the document. Naturally, if n is large, then the required number of copies is also large, and this many copies may not be available to the attacker. Thus it is more practical to consider attacks based on a single watermarked copy.

The general objective of a single-copy attack against the correlation-based schemes is either of the following.

- *Watermark Removal:* Given a single watermarked image $I^{(i)}$, remove the watermark information $s^{(i)}$ from the copy, and retrieve the original image I.
- *Watermark Forgery:* Given a single watermarked image $I^{(i)}$, produce a forged watermarked image $I^{(i,\#)}$ such that the forgery cannot be traced back to its origin, $I^{(i)}$.

The attacker, assumed to be B_i in our case, has complete information about the watermarking algorithm W, and his/her own watermarked copy $I^{(i)}$. However, B_i does not possess any information about the secret fingerprint $s^{(i)}$, or any other secret buyer-specific bits used in the process of watermarking. Of course, B_i does not possess the original image I either, or otherwise the attacks would be trivial.

Our Motivation: For correlation-based watermarking sche-mes, some *single-copy attacks* are already studied in the literature [10–12]. Especially, in [10], the authors have proposed a single-copy forgery attack on correlation-based watermarking schemes. They had illustrated the effectiveness of their strategy by attacking the Cox-Kilian-Leighton-Shamoon (CKLS) algorithm, and later extended the same idea in [11] to cryptanalyse the optimal Differential Energy Watermarking (DEW) scheme, proposed in [5]. However, the attack model proposed in [10,11] is not completely general, as it does not work against the watermarking scheme they have themselves proposed in [11] – the MDEW watermarking algorithm. In fact, the authors of [11] have presented the MDEW scheme as a conscious design to avoid this kind of attacks. It remains an open question whether there exists a general strategy to cryptanalyse correlation-based watermarking schemes, and mount single-copy forgery attacks on them. We tackle this question in our current work.

Our Result: In this paper, we propose a strategy that converts a single-copy watermark removal attack on any correlation-based scheme to a single-copy forgery attack on the same. In particular, we show that if a correlation-based watermarking scheme, like MDEW [11], has the chance of even a very weak single-copy watermark removal attack, the same strategy may be extended to obtain a strong single-copy forgery attack.

We choose MDEW as our target as it has a conscious design principle that tries to avoid straight-forward but customized single-copy forgery attacks, as claimed in [11] by the designers of MDEW. However, the conscious design of MDEW [11] scheme, towards having better security, is shown to be vulnerable against our general watermark removal-to-forgery attack.

Organization of the Paper: In Sect. 2, we present our idea for extending a watermark removal strategy to forgery against a specific example – MDEW watermarking scheme, as proposed in [11]. In Sect. 3, we present detailed experimental results, and extend our strategy to propose similar attack against correlation-based watermarking schemes in general. Finally, Sect. 4 concludes our paper.

2   Forgery Against MDEW Watermarking Scheme

MDEW [11] works alike most of the correlation-based watermarking schemes, as in [5,6]. Let the original image be I, and the owner wants to sell authentic copies of I to buyers $B_1, B_2, \ldots$. Then, the embedding and extraction of the watermark is performed by the owner as follows.

2.1   Watermark Embedding and Extraction in MDEW

Let the size of the original image I be $N \times N$. First the owner applies 8×8 block-wise DCT on I to get the DCT-transformed image I_d. Then, the owner performs a random grouping on the 8×8 DCT blocks of I_d, considering it as a two-dimensional array. One may perform this random grouping using a random permutation P on the blocks of I_d. An example of the random grouping, as a result of applying the random permutation P on I_d, is illustrated in Fig. 1 over a matrix of size 8×8. The groups, each consisting of n blocks, are termed as 'lc-regions', and in Fig. 1, we have four $n = 16$ size lc-regions marked with different colors.

Every lc-region is again subdivided into two lc-subregions A and B, as illustrated in Fig. 1 by the symbols $*$ and $\$$ respectively, and the energies E_A and E_B of the lc-subregions are calculated. The expressions for the energies are given by

$$E_A(q, n) = \sum_{b=0}^{\frac{n}{2}-1} \sum_{j=1}^{q} |\theta_{j,b}|, \quad E_B(q, n) = \sum_{b=\frac{n}{2}}^{n-1} \sum_{j=1}^{q} |\theta_{j,b}| \tag{1}$$

where $|\theta_{j,b}|$ is the absolute value of DCT coefficient of the 8×8 DCT block b in that lc-subregion (A or B), corresponding to frequency j, where $j = 0$ means the DC coefficient of the block that is not considered in the sum. Note that we write

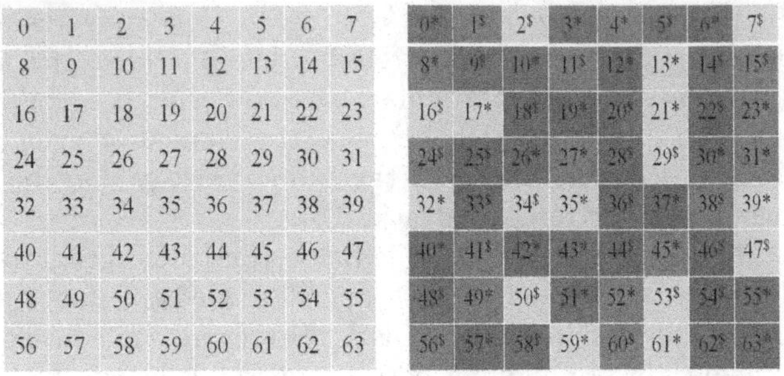

0	1	2	3	4	5	6	7
8	9	10	11	12	13	14	15
16	17	18	19	20	21	22	23
24	25	26	27	28	29	30	31
32	33	34	35	36	37	38	39
40	41	42	43	44	45	46	47
48	49	50	51	52	53	54	55
56	57	58	59	60	61	62	63

(a) DCT Image   (b) Permuted DCT Image

Fig. 1. DCT images where numerals represent blocks of 8×8.

$E_A(q,n), E_B(q,n)$ as E_A, E_B, where the values of n, q are implicitly understood for a specific image I.

The condition in MDEW is that the initial random grouping P and the subdivision into lc-subregions A and B for the DCT image I_d has to be performed in such a fashion that

$$|E_A - E_B| \leq \Delta, \qquad (2)$$

where Δ is a predetermined small threshold. In fact, all that we require is a margin with which the condition $E_A \approx E_B$ is satisfied after grouping. This may not be true for all random permutations, and hence P is chosen over a few iterations such that this condition is satisfied. The information regarding this lc-region and lc-subregion distribution can be stored in a matrix, π, say. This information, π, is determined by the owner for every image I, and is kept secret during the whole process. In fact, π is the same for all the buyers of image I, and serves as the primary key for the MDEW scheme.

For each legitimate buyer B_i, the watermark signal or fingerprint is generated as a pseudo-random bit string $s^{(i)}$ of length l, where $l = G/n$ denotes the number of lc-regions in the DCT image I_d, which has a total G number of 8×8 DCT blocks and each lc-region is of size n. Now, the goal of watermark embedding is to insert each bit of $s^{(i)}$ into one lc-region of I_d. This modified DCT image, $I_d^{(i)}$, may then be subjected to inverse DCT transform to obtain the watermarked image $I^{(i)}$, to be sold to buyer B_i.

Note that we have $E_A \approx E_B$ for each lc-region of I_d, after grouping according to π. To embed a bit of $s^{(i)}$ in an lc-region, the owner introduces the following modifications in the energies of the individual blocks:

$$\text{Embed 0:} \qquad E'_A(q,n) = \sum_{b=0}^{\frac{n}{2}-1} \sum_{j=1}^{q} (1+\alpha_1)|\theta_{j,b}|, \text{ and}$$

$$E'_B(q,n) = \sum_{b=\frac{n}{2}}^{n-1} \sum_{j=1}^{q} (1-\alpha_2)|\theta_{j,b}|; \qquad (3)$$

Embed 1: $$E'_A(q,n) = \sum_{b=0}^{\frac{n}{2}-1} \sum_{j=1}^{q} (1-\alpha_2)|\theta_{j,b}|, \text{ and}$$

$$E'_B(q,n) = \sum_{b=\frac{n}{2}}^{n-1} \sum_{j=1}^{q} (1+\alpha_1)|\theta_{j,b}|, \tag{4}$$

where $\alpha_1, \alpha_2 > 0$ are chosen such that $E'_A - E'_B > \Delta'$ if bit 0 is embedded, and $E'_B - E'_A > \Delta'$ if bit 1 is embedded, where Δ' is once again a predetermined threshold. The parameters α_1, α_2 should be small so that after the modification of the DCT values, the image quality is not degraded.

During watermark extraction for the i-th buyer, note that the owner does not specifically require the original image I. All he/she requires is the grouping information (or the secret key) π, the predetermined threshold Δ', and the watermarked image $I^{(i)}$ corresponding to the i-the buyer B_i. To extract the fingerprint $s^{(i)}$, the owner first takes the DCT-transform of $I^{(i)}$ to obtain $I_d^{(i)}$, say. Then the owner may apply the grouping π on $I_d^{(i)}$, and examine the polarity of $E'_A - E'_B$ with respect to Δ' in each lc-region. This will reveal the exact bitstream $s^{(i)}$ embedded in the image, and the owner may now verify the identity of the buyer by searching for this $s^{(i)}$ in the database of legitimate buyers. If $s^{(i)}$ does not match with any fingerprint produced by the owner, then it may be concluded that the specific watermarked copy $I^{(i)}$ is not created by the owner and that $I^{(i)}$ may be a forged copy.

2.2   Formal Model of Forgery Attack on MDEW

Based on the discussion so far, we may frame the model of forgery attack on MDEW scheme as follows. The watermark embedding algorithm is denoted as W, and the watermark extraction algorithm is denoted by W^{-1}, to imply the inverse of the embedding process. Let F denote the algorithm for forgery, as used by an attacker, and T be the algorithm that the owner uses to trace the attacker in case a forgery has been made. If there are N_B legitimate buyers in total, including the attacker, then the advantage of the owner in tracing the attacker from a forged copy of the image $F(I^{(i)})$ may be defined as

$$\text{Adv}(I^{(i,\#)}) := \left| \Pr\left(T\left(W^{-1}(F(I^{(i)}))\right) = B_i\right) - \frac{1}{N_B} \right|.$$

In general terms, the above expression denotes the probability with which the owner can trace back the attacker, above the probability of a random guess, $\frac{1}{N_B}$. The goal of a forger is to lower the value of owner's advantage, $\text{Adv}(I^{(i,\#)})$, and the attack is completely successful if $\text{Adv}(I^{(i,\#)}) = 0$.

In general, the algorithm T that the owner uses to trace the attacker in such case of forgery is as follows:

1. Step I: Extract the watermark fingerprint from the forged image $I^{(i,\#)} = F(I^{(i)})$ to get $s^{(i,\#)} \leftarrow W^{-1}(I^{(i,\#)})$.

2. Step II: Find the correlations between $s^{(i,\#)}$ and all valid owner-generated $s^{(i)}$ in the buyer database.
3. Step III: Identify B_j as the attacker if $s^{(i,\#)}$ has significantly high (far from 0) correlation with $s^{(j)}$.

Under this consideration, we may simplify the attack model to say that the attacker will be successful in forgery if the correlation between $s^{(i,\#)}$ and $s^{(i)}$ is considerably low, that is, numerically close enough to 0, and the advantage of the owner may be expressed as:

$$\text{Adv}(I^{(i,\#)}) := \left| \text{Cor}\left(s^{(i)}, W^{-1}(F(I^{(i)})) \right) \right|. \tag{5}$$

The attacker, B_i in this case, will be successful in untraceable forgery if there exists a j for which

$$\left| \text{Cor}\left(s^{(j)}, W^{-1}(F(I^{(i)})) \right) \right| > \text{Adv}(I^{(i,\#)}).$$

However, we impose a stricter condition than what is required, and call a forgery F successful only if $\text{Adv}(I^{(i,\#)}) \approx 0$.

2.3 General Forgery Attack on MDEW

The performance of MDEW scheme is quite robust against the standard signal processing attacks, as experimented in [11]. Certain statistical analysis had also been made in [11] to explain the security parameters. We further perform some analysis on MDEW to set the base for a general forgery attack. For a simplified analysis, we assume $\alpha_1 = \alpha_2 = \alpha$.

Note that the DCT values of neighboring blocks in an image may be correlated, but after the random distribution π is made, the values in the DCT blocks, whether or not neighboring, can always be assumed to be independent. We assume that the energies of the 8×8 DCT blocks of I_d are *i.i.d.* random variables X_b, for $0 \leq b \leq G - 1$, satisfying

$$X_b \sim N\left(\mu = \frac{1}{G} \sum_{b=0}^{G-1} X_b, \sigma^2 = \frac{1}{G-1} \sum_{b=0}^{G-1} (X_b - \mu)^2 \right).$$

The energy difference D between the two lc-subregions A and B within a specific lc-region is given by

$$D = \sum_{k=1}^{n/2} X_{A_k} - \sum_{k=1}^{n/2} X_{B_k}, \tag{6}$$

where X_{A_k} is the energy of the k-th block of the subregion A and X_{B_k} is the energy of the k-th block of subregion B. D is a linear combination of *i.i.d.* random variables, and thus itself a random variable satisfying $D \sim N(0, n\sigma^2)$ (see [11] for details). After inserting watermark bits, the energy difference in the lc-region will change to

$$D' = \sum_{k=1}^{n/2} X_{A_k}(1+\alpha) - \sum_{k=1}^{n/2} X_{B_k}(1-\alpha), \tag{7}$$

where the value of α could be positive or negative depending on whether 0 or 1 is inserted in the corresponding region. The expectation of D', the modified energy difference, will be

$$E(D') = E\left(\sum_{k=1}^{n/2} X_{A_k}(1+\alpha) - \sum_{k=1}^{n/2} X_{B_k}(1-\alpha) \right) = n\alpha\mu, \tag{8}$$

and the variance of D' will be

$$V(D') = V\left(\sum_{k=1}^{n/2} X_{A_k}(1+\alpha) - \sum_{k=1}^{n/2} X_{B_k}(1-\alpha) \right)$$

$$= \sum_{k=1}^{n/2} \left((1+\alpha)^2 V(X_{A_k}) + (1-\alpha)^2 V(X_{B_k}) \right)$$

$$= n(1+\alpha^2)\sigma^2. \tag{9}$$

Now that we have all statistical properties of the important parameters, we may device and analyze a naive forgery attack on the MDEW scheme.

First note that the distribution of lc-regions/subregions is coded in a permutation π, unknown to the attacker. After taking the DCT transform of watermarked image $I^{(i)}$, suppose that the attacker finds $G = 2^\omega$ many 8×8 DCT blocks in $I_d^{(i)}$, and let each lc-region consists of $n = 2^{\frac{\omega}{2}}$ such blocks. In this case, the number of all possible groupings comes to

$$\binom{G}{n} \cdot \binom{G-n}{n} \cdot \binom{G-2n}{n} \cdots \binom{n}{n} = \frac{(2^\omega)!}{((2^{\frac{\omega}{2}})!)2^{\frac{\omega}{2}}}.$$

For large values of ω (≥ 4), we have $\frac{(2^\omega)!}{((2^{\frac{\omega}{2}})!)2^{\frac{\omega}{2}}} > 2^{2^\omega}$. One should further consider the possibilities of creating two subregions inside each lc-region. Naturally, this makes a naive guessing of π impossible in all respects, and we may safely assume that π remains an unknown random permutation of the DCT blocks from the point of view of the attacker.

Once the distribution π is unknown, the attacker has only one choice left – that is to look into each of the blocks and try to modify the energies. The idea for forgery is as follows.

General Forgery Attack on MDEW
Input – Authentic watermarked image $I^{(i)}$
Output – Forged watermarked image $I^{(i,\#)}$
Preprocessing – Take DCT transform of $I^{(i)}$ to get $I_d^{(i)}$

Algorithm – For each block of $I_d^{(i)}$, do the following

- Guess whether the energy of the block had been increased or decreased during watermark embedding.
- Depending on the guess, modify the DCT values to reverse the effects of watermark embedding. That is, if the energy of the block was increased (respectively decreased), then decrease (respectively increase) the energy.

The effectiveness of this forgery will directly depend on the correctness of the initial guess for each block. If the attacker knew π, each of these guesses would be correct, and the attacker could completely reverse the effect of watermarking. However, with π an unknown random permutation, the guessing strategy is of prime importance.

2.4 Forgery on MDEW Using Random Guess

An adversary can obviously try a naive approach of random guessing. In random guessing the probability of every correct guess is $\frac{1}{2}$. In this strategy, we randomly decide, with equal probability, whether to increase or decrease the DCT values of each 8×8 DCT block in $I_d^{(i)}$, and construct the forged image $I^{(i,\#)}$, as illustrated in Algorithm 1.

Algorithm 1. Forgery on MDEW using Random Guess

1: Apply 8×8 DCT on $I^{(i)}$ to obtain $I_d^{(i)}$.
2: **for** $y = 1$ to G **do**
3:     Generate a random bit d by tossing an unbiased coin.
4:     **if** $d = 1$ **then**
5:         Decrease DCT values $\theta_{j,y} \leftarrow \theta_{j,y} \cdot (1 - \alpha_1')$ for the known subset of coefficients $j = 1, 2, \ldots, q$.
6:     **else**
7:         Increase DCT values $\theta_{j,y} \leftarrow \theta_{j,y} \cdot (1 + \alpha_2')$ for the known subset of coefficients $j = 1, 2, \ldots, q$.
8:     **end if**
9: **end for**
10: Apply inverse 8×8 DCT to construct forged image $I^{(i,\#)}$.

We model the random guess strategy by a binomial random variable Z, where $Z = 1$ if the guess is correct and $Z = -1$ if the guess is incorrect. Thus the distribution of Z is as follows:

$$Z = \begin{cases} 1 \; ; & \text{prob.} = 1/2 \qquad E(Z) = 0 \\ -1 \; ; & \text{prob.} = 1/2 \qquad V(Z) = 1 \end{cases}$$

If after forgery, the energy difference between the lc-subregions A and B is denoted by D'', then Eq. (10) represents the effect of Z on D'', where we assume $\alpha_1' = \alpha_2' = \alpha'$.

$$D'' = \sum_{k=1}^{n/2} X_{A_k}(1+\alpha)(1-\mathrm{sgn}(\alpha)\alpha' Z_k)$$

$$- \sum_{k=1}^{n/2} X_{B_k}(1-\alpha)(1+\mathrm{sgn}(\alpha)\alpha' Z_k'). \tag{10}$$

Here $0 < \alpha' < 1$, and sgn(.) is the signum function, i.e., $\mathrm{sgn}(\alpha) = 1$ if $\alpha > 0$ and $\mathrm{sgn}(\alpha) = -1$ if $\alpha < 0$. Furthermore, Z_k, Z_k' (where $1 \leq k \leq \frac{n}{2}$) are $i.i.d.$ random variables with the same distribution as Z, i.e., $E(Z_k) = E(Z_k') = 0$, $V(Z_k) = V(Z_k') = 1$. Then,

$$E(D'') = E\left(\sum_{k=1}^{n/2} X_{A_k}(1+\alpha)(1-\mathrm{sgn}(\alpha)\alpha' Z_k) \right.$$

$$\left. - \sum_{k=1}^{n/2} X_{B_k}(1-\alpha)(1+\mathrm{sgn}(\alpha)\alpha' Z_k') \right)$$

$$= n\mu\left(\alpha - \mathrm{sgn}(\alpha)\alpha' E(Z_k)\right) = n\alpha\mu = E(D'), \tag{11}$$

and the variance of D'' is

$$V(D'') = V\left(\sum_{k=1}^{n/2} X_{A_k}(1+\alpha)(1-\mathrm{sgn}(\alpha)\alpha' Z_k) \right.$$

$$\left. - \sum_{k=1}^{n/2} X_{B_k}(1-\alpha)(1+\mathrm{sgn}(\alpha)\alpha' Z_k') \right)$$

$$= \sum_{k=1}^{n/2} \left((1+\alpha)^2 V(X_{A_k}(1-\mathrm{sgn}(\alpha)\alpha' Z_k)) \right.$$

$$+ (1-\alpha)^2 V(X_{B_k}(1+\mathrm{sgn}(\alpha)\alpha' Z_k')). \tag{12}$$

Now, we may compute the variance $V(X_{A_k}(1 - \mathrm{sgn}(\alpha)\alpha' Z_k))$ rigorously as $E(X_{A_k}^2)E((1-\mathrm{sgn}(\alpha)\alpha' Z_k)^2) - (E(X_{A_k})E(1-\mathrm{sgn}(\alpha)\alpha' Z_k))^2 = \sigma^2\alpha'^2 + \mu^2\alpha'^2 + \sigma^2$, and similarly obtain $V(X_{A_k}(1+\mathrm{sgn}(\alpha)\alpha' Z_k)) = \sigma^2\alpha'^2 + \mu^2\alpha'^2 + \sigma^2$. From Eq. (12), we get

$$V(D'') = \frac{n}{2}\left((1+\alpha)^2 + (1-\alpha)^2\right)(\sigma^2\alpha'^2 + \mu^2\alpha'^2 + \sigma^2)$$

$$= n(1+\alpha^2)(\sigma^2\alpha'^2 + \mu^2\alpha'^2 + \sigma^2). \tag{13}$$

In the above analysis, we have considered a random region [SR(A), SR(B)] and analyzed the effect of forgery based on random guess. Since the expectation of the energy difference D'' in case of the forged image $I^{(i,\#)}$ is the same as that in case of the authentic copy $I^{(i)}$, the reversal of energy polarity $(E'_A - E'_B)$ in the lc-region considered above will be insignificant. Thus, the correlation between $s^{(i)} \leftarrow W^{-1}(I^{(i)})$ and $s^{(i,\#)} \leftarrow W^{-1}(I^{(i,\#)})$ will be considerably high, and hence we prove that the random guess strategy is not useful for mounting a forgery attack on MDEW.

The variance of D'' changes from that of D', and the change is proportional to the square of the parameter α' which is used to reverse the effect of α. The change in variance only signifies the increased dispersion of energies in the forged image.

2.5   Forgery on MDEW Using Informed Guess

Suppose that there is some information available to the attacker that helps him/her to guess the increase/decrease in energy per block with probability slightly higher than that in case of random guess. In particular, the attacker can guess correctly, whether the DCT values in a block has been increased or decreased, with probability $\frac{1}{2} + \epsilon$, for some non-negligible $\epsilon > 0$. That is, the distribution of the random variable Z, in this strategy, is:

$$
Z = \begin{cases} 1 \; ; & \text{prob.} = \frac{1}{2} + \epsilon \\ -1 \; ; & \text{prob.} = \frac{1}{2} - \epsilon \end{cases} \qquad \begin{array}{l} E(Z) = 2\epsilon \\ V(Z) = 1 - 4\epsilon^2 \end{array}
$$

In this case of an informed guess, the expectation of D'' is

$$
\begin{aligned}
E(D'') &= E\left(\sum_{k=1}^{n/2} X_{A_k}(1+\alpha)(1 - \text{sgn}(\alpha)\alpha' Z_k) \right. \\
&\qquad\qquad \left. - \sum_{k=1}^{n/2} X_{B_k}(1-\alpha)(1 + \text{sgn}(\alpha)\alpha' Z'_k) \right) \\
&= \sum_{k=1}^{n/2} ((1+\alpha)E(X_{A_k})(1 - \text{sgn}(\alpha)\alpha' E(Z_k)) \\
&\qquad\qquad - (1-\alpha)E(X_{B_k})(1 + \text{sgn}(\alpha)\alpha' E(Z'_k))) \\
&= \frac{n\mu}{2}((1+\alpha)(1 - 2\text{sgn}(\alpha)\alpha'\epsilon) \\
&\qquad\qquad - (1-\alpha)(1 + 2\text{sgn}(\alpha)\alpha'\epsilon)) \\
&= n\mu(\alpha - 2\text{sgn}(\alpha)\alpha'\epsilon) \\
&= E(D') - 2\text{sgn}(\alpha)n\mu\epsilon\alpha', \qquad\qquad\qquad\qquad (14)
\end{aligned}
$$

and the variance of D'' is given by

$$V(D'') = V\left(\sum_{k=1}^{n/2} X_{A_k}(1+\alpha)(1-\text{sgn}(\alpha)\alpha'Z_k)\right.$$

$$\left. -\sum_{k=1}^{n/2} X_{B_k}(1-\alpha)(1+\text{sgn}(\alpha)\alpha'Z_k')\right)$$

$$= \sum_{k=1}^{n/2} \left((1+\alpha)^2 V(X_{A_k}(1-\text{sgn}(\alpha)\alpha'Z_k))\right.$$

$$\left. +(1-\alpha)^2 V(X_{B_k}(1+\text{sgn}(\alpha)\alpha'Z_k'))\right). \tag{15}$$

After simplifying the above expression, we get $V(D'')$ as $n(\mu^2\alpha'^2(1+\alpha^2)(1-4\epsilon^2) + \sigma^2((1+\alpha^2)(1+\alpha'^2) - 8\text{sgn}(\alpha)\alpha\alpha'\epsilon))$.

From Eq. (14), it is obvious that expectation of D'' differs from that of D', and the difference depends on ϵ, α, μ and α'. Among these parameters, the attacker has control only over α', the amount of increase/decrease in the DCT values while forging the image. The other parameters α, μ and ϵ are fixed, either by the owner of the image, or by the information the attacker has got to base his/her guesses on.

If the attacker can obtain any significant information that makes $\epsilon > 0$, he/she may tune the parameter α' to create a large enough difference between D' and D'', possibly to the extent that the energy difference polarity is reversed. This helps the attacker to mount a successful forgery attack on the MDEW scheme, and constitutes the main theme of our work.

2.6   Watermark Removal Attack Extended to Forgery on MDEW

So far we have seen that if the attacker gets a good guessing probability for each block of the DCT domain image $I_d^{(i)}$, by some strategy, then the probability of success for the forgery increases. Suppose that there exists a weak watermark removal attack against MDEW that produces a not-so-good approximation of the original image I from $I^{(i)}$. Let us denote the estimate of I as I^C. If the attacker possesses both $I^{(i)}$ and the approximate original image I^C, then he/she may transform both to the DCT domain, compare $I_d^{(i)}$ with I_d^C block by block, and take a good guess as to whether the DCT values for each block were increased or decreased during watermark embedding. The closer the approximate image I^C is to I, the better will be the guess probability, that is, ϵ, for the attacker. We know from the previous subsection that even if the watermark removal attack is weak, that is, even if it provides only a very small ϵ, the attacker may still magnify its effects in the final forgery attack, by tuning other parameters.

This provides a general platform to extend any watermark removal attack on MDEW to a forgery attack on the same scheme. In fact, even a very weak and practically unusable watermark removal technique for MDEW can be exploited against the scheme, quite effectively, in such a forgery attack. We substantiate our claim through the following example.

2.7   Median Filter Based Forgery on MDEW

Watermark embedding on any image I is generally considered as adding noise in the image where the watermark fingerprint is treated as noise. Thus, any suitable noise removal filter may work as a naive watermark removal strategy that approximates I from a marked copy $I^{(i)}$. Median filter is one of the simplest examples that could be applied on the noisy image $I^{(i)}$ to get back I^C, a very crude approximation of I.

The attacker may now exploit the knowledge of $I^{(i)}$ and I^C together to form his/her guesses. The attacker takes both the images $I^{(i)}$ and I^C to the transformed domain by applying 8×8 DCT. In the DCT domain, he/she compares the energy X of the corresponding blocks in both the images and tries to guess whether the energy of that specific block has been increased or decreased during watermark embedding process. After the guess is finalized, the attacker may try to reverse the embedding effect by modifying the DCT values towards the opposite polarity with respect to the embedding process, so that a forged copy $I^{(i,\#)}$ is created.

Let $|\theta_j^w|$ and $|\theta_j^m|$ represent the absolute values of the DCT coefficients corresponding to frequency j in a specific block of $I^{(i)}$ and I^C, respectively. Similarly, let X_Φ and X_Ψ represent the energy corresponding to a specific block of $I^{(i)}$ and I^C, respectively. Then the median filter based forgery may be summarized as in Algorithm 2.

Algorithm 2. Median Filter based Forgery on MDEW

1: Apply median filter with dimensions $r \times s$ on $I^{(i)}$ and store the resultant image as I^C, an approximation to I.
2: Apply 8×8 DCT on both $I^{(i)}, I^C$ to obtain $I_d^{(i)}$ and I_d^C.
3: **for** $y = 1$ to G **do**
4:     Calculate $X_{\Phi,y} = \sum_{j=1}^q |\theta_{j,y}^{(i)}|$, $X_{\Psi,y} = \sum_{j=1}^q |\theta_{j,y}^C|$.
5:     **if** $X_{\Phi,y} > X_{\Psi,y}$ **then**
6:         Decrease DCT values $\theta_{j,y}^w \leftarrow \theta_{j,y}^w \cdot (1 - \alpha_1')$ for the known subset of coefficients $j = 1, 2, \ldots, q$.
7:     **else**
8:         Increase DCT values $\theta_{j,y}^w \leftarrow \theta_{j,y}^w \cdot (1 + \alpha_2')$ for the known subset of coefficients $j = 1, 2, \ldots, q$.
9:     **end if**
10: **end for**
11: Apply inverse 8×8 DCT to construct forged image $I^{(i,\#)}$.

In case of median filtering, we notice that the extra margin in the probability of guessing, ϵ, is not just a constant, but it depends directly on the energy of a block, that is X. In fact, ϵ behaves proportional to the value of X, and gives a better guessing probability for the high energy blocks. From our experiments, we have found that the relation between ϵ and X can be modeled as $\epsilon = \frac{X}{2M}$, where $M = \max\{X\}$. Thus, the bias in the guessing probability can be modeled as

$$Z = \begin{cases} 1 ; & \text{prob.} = \frac{1}{2} + \frac{X}{2M} \\ -1 ; & \text{prob.} = \frac{1}{2} - \frac{X}{2M}, \end{cases}$$

and the expectation and variance of Z can be computed as

$$E(Z) = E(E(Z|X)) = E(X)/M = \mu/M, \quad \text{and}$$
$$V(Z) = E(Z^2) - (E(Z))^2 = E(E(Z^2|X)) - (E(E(Z|X))^2$$
$$= V(X)/M^2 = \sigma^2/M^2.$$

Now we may calculate the expected value of D'' as follows:

$$E(D'') = E\left(\sum_{k=0}^{n/2} X_{A_k}(1+\alpha)(1 - \text{sgn}(\alpha)\alpha' Z_k) \right.$$
$$\left. - \sum_{k=0}^{n/2} X_{B_k}(1-\alpha)(1 + \text{sgn}(\alpha)\alpha' Z_k') \right)$$
$$= \sum_{k=0}^{n/2} ((1+\alpha)E(X_{A_k}(1 - \text{sgn}(\alpha)\alpha' Z_k))$$
$$- (1-\alpha)E(X_{B_k}(1 + \text{sgn}(\alpha)\alpha' Z_k'))).$$

We have the distribution of Z_i and Z_i' identical to Z, and hence dependent on X. Thus, we may compute $E(D'')$ as

$$E(D'') = \sum_{k=0}^{n/2} ((1+\alpha)E(E(X_{A_k}(1 - \text{sgn}(\alpha)\alpha' Z_k)|X_{A_k}))$$
$$- (1-\alpha)E(E(X_{B_k}(1 + \text{sgn}(\alpha)\alpha' Z_k')|X_{B_k})))$$
$$= \sum_{k=0}^{n/2} ((1+\alpha)E(X_{A_k})(1 - \text{sgn}(\alpha)\alpha' E(X_{A_k}/M))$$
$$- (1-\alpha)E(X_{B_k})(1 + \text{sgn}(\alpha)\alpha' E(X_{B_k}/M))),$$

which, in turn, provides

$$E(D'') = \frac{n\mu}{2} ((1+\alpha)(1 - \text{sgn}(\alpha)\alpha'\mu/M))$$
$$- (1-\alpha)(1 + \text{sgn}(\alpha)\beta\mu/M))$$
$$= n\mu (\alpha - \text{sgn}(\alpha)\alpha'\mu/M)$$
$$= E(D') - \text{sgn}(\alpha)n\alpha'\mu^2/M. \tag{16}$$

Since the mean value of $E(D'')$ is changed from $E(D')$ by the factor proportional to $\alpha'\mu/M$. So if the attacker chooses the parameter $\alpha' > |\frac{\alpha M}{\mu}|$, the polarity of the energy difference in the specific lc-region will get reversed.

Note that we want the probability of polarity reversal in the lc-regions to be close to $\frac{1}{2}$, as in that case, the two watermark fingerprints $s^{(i)} \leftarrow W^{-1}(I^{(i)})$ and $s^{(i,\#)} \leftarrow W^{-1}(I^{(i,\#)})$ will have about half of the bits matching. This condition makes the correlation between $s^{(i)}$ and $s^{(i,\#)}$ close to zero, or negligible, as desired in a forgery attack.

In the next section, we present the experimental results of our forgery attacks on MDEW, in both cases – random guess and median filter based guess – to illustrate the power of extending a weak watermark removal technique to a strong forgery attack on correlation-based watermarking schemes.

3   Experimental Results and Generalized Model

Tables 1 and 2 enlist our experimental observations. We have used some benchmark gray level test images of size 512×512 available in uncompressed TIFF at [7]. We choose the watermark embedding parameters $\alpha_1 = \alpha_2 = 0.1$, and various values for the forgery parameters α'_1 and α'_2 such that the image quality remains acceptable. The quality of the forged image $I^{(i,\#)}$ is tested against the original image I and the watermarked copy $I^{(i)}$, using the perceptual quality parameters $Q^{(\#)}$ and $Q^{(i,\#)}$ respectively, represented in terms of PSNR in dB (see [9], p. 112). $\text{Cor}(s^{(i)}, s^{(i,\#)})$ is calculated as $\frac{\beta-\delta}{l}$ where β and δ represent the number of matches and mismatches between the corresponding bits of $s^{(i,\#)}$ and $s^{(i)}$ respectively, and l represents the total bit-length of the fingerprints. The last two columns illustrate the experimental values of ϵ, the bias in correct guess, on an average, as well as for the high energy blocks, which have more effect on the polarity reversal process of the energy difference.

Table 1. Results of forgery attack on MDEW based on random guess

Image	Forgery values		Quality factors (dB)		$\text{Cor}(s^{(i)}, s^{(i,\#)})$		Guess probability $(1/2 + \epsilon)$	
	α'_1	α'_2	$Q^{(\#)}$	$Q^{(i,\#)}$	(mean)	(SD)	(mean)	(high energy blocks)
Watermark embedding parameters: $\alpha_1 = 0.1$ and $\alpha_2 = 0.1$.								
Lena	0.200	0.200	37.800	38.760	0.980	0.010	0.501	0.500
Lena	0.270	0.270	35.620	36.180	0.970	0.020	0.500	0.500
Cameraman	0.270	0.270	34.400	34.800	0.870	0.040	0.500	0.500
Lake	0.270	0.270	33.000	33.440	0.970	0.020	0.500	0.500
Peppers	0.270	0.270	35.300	35.800	0.920	0.030	0.500	0.500
Jetplane	0.270	0.270	34.100	34.660	0.940	0.030	0.500	0.500
Lena	0.300	0.300	34.820	35.280	0.960	0.020	0.500	0.500
Cameraman	0.300	0.300	33.550	34.000	0.790	0.050	0.500	0.500
Lake	0.300	0.300	32.100	32.540	0.930	0.040	0.500	0.500
Peppers	0.300	0.300	34.500	34.930	0.910	0.040	0.499	0.499
Jetplane	0.300	0.300	33.300	33.800	0.870	0.040	0.500	0.500

Table 2. Results of forgery attacks on MDEW based on median filter guess

Image	Forgery values		Quality factors (dB)		$\text{Cor}(s^{(i)}, s^{(i,\#)})$		Guess probability $(1/2 + \epsilon)$	
	α'_1	α'_2	$Q^{(\#)}$	$Q^{(i,\#)}$	(mean)	(SD)	(mean)	(high energy blocks)
Watermark embesdding parameters: $\alpha_1 = 0.1$ and $\alpha_2 = 0.1$.								
Lena	0.200	0.200	39.660	38.740	0.660	0.080	0.590	0.659
Lena	0.270	0.270	37.100	36.150	-0.050	0.100	0.590	0.660
Cameraman	0.270	0.270	35.120	34.500	0.300	0.090	0.540	0.610
Lake	0.270	0.270	34.050	33.390	0.340	0.100	0.575	0.637
Peppers	0.270	0.270	37.000	35.670	-0.300	0.090	0.600	0.696
Jetplane	0.270	0.270	35.400	34.600	0.140	0.100	0.560	0.642
Lena	0.300	0.300	36.130	35.240	-0.240	0.120	0.590	0.651
Cameraman	0.300	0.300	34.190	33.600	0.200	0.100	0.540	0.609
Lake	0.300	0.300	33.120	32.500	0.200	0.110	0.570	0.639
Peppers	0.300	0.300	36.000	34.770	-0.450	0.090	0.600	0.700
Jetplane	0.300	0.300	34.500	33.690	-0.010	0.100	0.560	0.635

Each row in Tables 1 and 2 represents the mean and SD of the data for over 100 iterations of the forgery algorithms, with different random watermark fingerprint $s^{(i)}$ in each case. The image key π is calculated uniquely for each image, and then maintained over all the iterations with that image. The values $l = 64$, $\Delta = 100$, and $q = 5$ are kept fixed for all cases. In all experiments listed in Table 2, the additional parameters $r = 3$, $s = 3$ are chosen to perform the median filtering.

Discussion on Table 1: One may note that the guessing probability in each case is approximately 0.5, including that for the higher energy blocks. This implies that $\epsilon \approx 0$, which is in line with the relation derived in Eq. (11). $\text{Cor}(s^{(i)}, s^{(i,\#)})$ is quite significant in each case, and hence, the forgery can easily be traced back to the attacker. This proves the robustness of MDEW against naive based on random guess.

Discussion on Table 2: One may note that the probability of correct guess, $(1/2 + \epsilon)$, is significantly greater than 0.5 in all the cases and the mean value of ϵ is approximately 0.07. It is high enough to assist the attacker in guessing whether the significant DCT coefficients of a block have been increased or decreased. The value of ϵ is even greater for the high energy blocks. High energy blocks contribute more significantly to create energy differences D' with a particular polarity. So if the attacker can guess those blocks correctly and apply forgery on the same, then the chances of reversing the polarity of D'' with respect to D' increases significantly. This, in turn, leads to significant decrease in the value of $\text{Cor}(s^{(i)}, s^{(i,\#)})$, as evident from the data. The value of $\text{Cor}(s^{(i)}, s^{(i,\#)})$ ranges close to 0 in most of the cases, thus making attacker-tracing very hard. Values of $Q^{(\#)}$ and $Q^{(i,\#)}$ are significantly greater than 30 dB in all cases, keeping the image quality satisfactory even after the forgery attack.

Generalized Model: Consider the space of all possible watermark fingerprints $s^{(i)}$ to be S. The origin in space S may be defined as $s^{(0)} \equiv \overline{0}$, the zero vector, which represents the original image I. Suppose that there exists a definition of distance between two fingerprints $s^{(i)}$ and $s^{(j)}$ in S, which, in case of MDEW, is the regular Hamming distance between vectors. Then, our generalized forgery model proposes that

If there exists a single-copy watermark removal method that reduces the distance $d(s^{(0)}, s^{(i)})$ from the knowledge of only the watermarked image $I^{(i)} \leftarrow W(I, s^{(i)})$, then the same technique can be amplified to mount a single-copy that reduces the distance $d(s^{(j)}, s^{(i)})$, for any arbitrary j, using only the knowledge of $I^{(i)}$.

This may be exploited against any correlation based scheme, similar to the attack that we have proposed for MDEW. Only the details of forgery implementation have to be customized for each scheme, and every other principle of this attack will remain the same as our general approach. To the best of our knowledge, such a general scheme for extending a single-copy watermark removal method to a single-copy on correlation based watermarking schemes has not been proposed in the literature. It will be interesting to observe the ramifications of this attack on the new dirty-paper-based watermarking schemes [1,2,8,13], if any at all.

4   Conclusion

In this paper, we have proposed a general framework that converts a single-copy watermark removal attack on any correlation-based scheme to a single-copy forgery attack on the same. We like to point out here that such a strategy assumes significance when the watermark removal strategy itself is a weak one and may not succeed in removing the watermark completely. However, in this scenario also, one could use our strategy for mounting a successful . We have substantiated our claims through an attack on MDEW, and complete theoretical analysis and experimental verification of the same. Success of our strategy raises serious doubt about the very existence of correlation based watermarking methods proposed elsewhere and in future, we need a paradigm shift in the design of new watermarking schemes.

References

1. Abrardo, A., Barni, M.: Informed watermarking by means of orthogonal and quasi-orthogonal dirty paper coding. IEEE Trans. Signal Process. **53**(2), 824–833 (2005)
2. Wang, C., Ni, J., Huang, J.: An informed watermarking scheme using hidden Markov model in the wavelet domain. IEEE Trans. Inf. Forensics Secur. **7**(3), 853–867 (2012)
3. Ergun, F., Kilian, J., Kumar, R.: A note on the limits of collusion-resistant watermarks. In: Stern, J. (ed.) EUROCRYPT 1999. LNCS, vol. 1592, pp. 140–149. Springer, Heidelberg (1999)

4. Petitcolas, F.A.P., Anderson, R.J.: Evaluation of copyright marking systems. In: IEEE Multimedia Systems, Florence, Italy (1999)
5. Langelaar, G.C., Lagendijk, R.L.: Optimal differential energy watermarking of DCT encoded images and video. IEEE Trans. Image Process. **10**(1), 148–158 (2001)
6. Cox, I.J., Kilian, J., Leighton, T., Shamoon, T.: Secure spread spectrum watermarking for multimedia. IEEE Trans. Image Process. **6**(12), 1673–1687 (1997)
7. Image Databases. http://www.imageprocessingplace.com/root_files_V3/image_databases.htm
8. Miller, M.L., Doerr, G.J., Cox, I.J.: Applying informed coding and embedding to design a robust high-capacity watermark. IEEE Trans. Image Process. **13**(6), 792–807 (2004)
9. Katzenbeisser, S., Petitcolas, F.A.P. (eds.): Information Hiding Techniques for Steganography and Digital Watermarking. Artech House, Norwell (2000)
10. Das, T.K., Maitra, S.: Cryptanalysis of correlation based watermarking scheme using single watermarked copy. IEEE Signal Process. Lett. **11**(4), 446–449 (2004)
11. Das, T.K., Maitra, S., Mitra, J.: Cryptanalysis of optimal differential energy watermarking (DEW) and a modified robust scheme. IEEE Trans. Signal Process. **53**(2), 768–775 (2005)
12. Das, T.K., Maitra, S., Zhou, J.: Cryptanalysis of Chu's DCT based watermarking scheme. IEEE Trans. Multimedia **8**(3), 629–632 (2006)
13. Xiaotian, X., Guan, Y.L., Teh, K.C.: Performance analysis of binned orthogonal/bi-orthogonal block code as dirty-paper code for digital watermarking application. IEEE Signal Process. Lett. **16**(3), 208–211 (2009)

Reversible Color Image Watermarking in the YCoCg-R Color Space

Aniket Roy[1](✉), Rajat Subhra Chakraborty[1], and Ruchira Naskar[2]

[1] Secured Embedded Architecture Laboratory (SEAL),
Department of Computer Science and Engineering, Indian Institute of Technology,
Kharagpur 721302, West Bengal, India
aniketroy@iitkgp.ac.in, rschakraborty@cse.iitkgp.ernet.in
[2] Department of Computer Science and Engineering,
National Institute of Technology, Rourkela 769008, Odisha, India
naskarr@nitrkl.ac.in

Abstract. *Reversible Image Watermarking* is a technique to losslessly embed and retrieve information (in the form of a watermark) in a cover image. We have proposed and implemented a reversible color image watermarking algorithm in the YCoCg-R color space, based on *histogram bin shifting* of the prediction errors, using *weighted mean based prediction* technique to predict the pixel values. The motivations for choosing the YCoCg-R color space lies in the fact that its transformation from the traditional RGB color space is reversible, with higher transform coding gain and near to optimal compression performance than the RGB and other reversible color spaces, resulting in considerably higher embedding capacity. We demonstrate through information theoretic analysis and experimental results that reversible watermarking in the YCoCg-R color space results in higher embedding capacity at lower distortion than RGB and several other color space representations.

1 Introduction

Digital watermarking [1] is an important technique adopted for copyright protection and authentication. Digital watermarking is the act of hiding secret information (termed a "watermark") into a digital "cover" medium (image, audio or video), such that this information may be extracted later for authentication of the cover. However, the process of watermark embedding in the cover medium usually leads to distortion of the latter, even if it is perceptually negligible. *Reversible watermarking* [2,3,10] is a special class of digital watermarking, whereby after watermark extraction, both the watermark and the cover medium remain unmodified, bit-by-bit. In traditional reversible watermarking schemes, the watermark to be embedded is usually generated as a cryptographic hash of the cover image. Reversible watermarking is most widely used in industries dealing with highly sensitive data, such as the military, medical and legal industries, where data integrity is the major concern for users [10]. In this paper we focus on reversible watermarking algorithms for digital images.

© Springer International Publishing Switzerland 2015
S. Jajodia and C. Mazumdar (Eds.): ICISS 2015, LNCS 9478, pp. 480–498, 2015.
DOI: 10.1007/978-3-319-26961-0_28

A large number of reversible image watermarking algorithms have been previously proposed [2–4]. Most of them have been developed for grayscale images. Although the algorithms developed for grayscale images may trivially be modified to work with for color images, most of the times the performance achieved by such trivial extension is not satisfactory. Relatively few works have been proposed for reversible color image watermarking. Moreover, in the existing literature, almost all reversible color image watermarking algorithms [4–7] utilize the RGB color space. Tian et al. [2] introduced *Difference Expansion* based reversible watermarking for grayscale images. Allatar used that concept for reversibly watermarking color images using difference expansion of triplets [5], quads [6], and later formulated a generalised integer transform [4]. However, these schemes embed watermark into the individual color components of the RGB color space. Li et al. [7] proposed a prediction error expansion based color image watermarking algorithm where prediction accuracy is enhanced by exploiting the correlation between color components of the RGB color space. Published literature on reversible color image watermarking in other (non-RGB) color spaces are very rare. Investigation of color image watermarking in a non-RGB color space is something that we aim to investigate in this paper.

In this paper, we propose a reversible watermarking technique, specifically meant for color images, providing considerably high embedding capacity, by systematically investigating the following questions:

1. What theoretical considerations should determine selection of a color space for reversible watermarking of color images?
2. Which color space is practically the best suited in this context?
3. Is there any additional constraint for selecting color space to ensure *reversibility* of the watermarking scheme?

Our key observation in this paper is that, instead of the traditional RGB color space, if we choose a color space having higher transform coding gain (i.e., better compression performance), then the reversible watermarking capacity will be increased significantly. Moreover, better compression along color components increases intra-correlation of individual color components. Hence, prediction accuracy of such prediction based watermarking scheme improves, which additionally enhances the embedding capacity of the reversible watermarking scheme.

In this paper, we propose a reversible watermarking algorithm for color images, which utilizes the YCoCg-R color space (a modification of the YCoCg color space) having higher transform coding gain and near to optimal compression performance. The transformation from RGB to YCoCg-R, and the reverse transformation from YCoCg-R to RGB, are integer-to-integer transforms which guarantee reversibility [8], and are also implementable very efficiently. The proposed algorithm is based on the principle of *histogram–bin–shifting*, which is computationally one of the simplest reversible watermarking technique. Specifically, we use a newer and more efficient enhancement of histogram-bin-shifting, which performs histogram modification of pixel prediction errors [2,9]. In this technique image pixel values are predicted from their neighbourhood pixel values, and the prediction error histogram bins are shifted to embed the watermark bits. This technique provides much higher embedding capacity compared to the traditional frequency-histogram shifting.

The rest of the paper is organised as follows. We investigate an information theoretic analysis of watermarking embedding capacity maximization in Sect. 2. The proposed reversible watermarking algorithm is presented in Sect. 3. Experimental results and related discussions are presented in Sect. 4. We conclude in Sect. 5 with some future research directions.

2   Principle of Embedding Capacity Maximization

Embedding capacity maximization is one of the major challenges in reversible watermarking, given the reversibility criterion. In this section, we explore successively two approaches to enhance embedding capacity:

1. Selection of the target color space offering higher watermarking performance, and,
2. Selection of the watermark embedding algorithm.

2.1   Color Space Selection

We consider the selection of the color space from three perspectives: information theory, reversibility and compressibility in the transformed color space, and ease of implementation of the color space transformation. We start with the review a relevant information theoretic result.

Information Theoretic Justification. The following theorem is of fundamental importance:

Theorem 1 (Sepain-Wolf Coding Theorem). *Given two correlated finite alphabet random sequences X and Y, the theoretical bound for lossless coding rate for distributed coding of two sources are related by:*

$$\begin{aligned} R_X &\geq H(X|Y), \\ R_Y &\geq H(Y|X), \\ R_X + R_Y &\geq H(X,Y). \end{aligned} \tag{1}$$

Thus, ideally the minimum total rate $(R_{X,Y})$ necessary for lossless encoding of the two correlated random sequences X and Y, is equal to their joint entropy $(H(X,Y))$, i.e. $R_{X,Y} = H(X,Y)$.

The significance of the above result is that for three correlated random sequences X, Y, Z, the total rate $R_{X,Y,Z} = H(X,Y,Z)$ is sufficient for an ideal lossless encoding. This theorem can be extended to a finite number of correlated sources. It can be shown that the same result holds even for the i.i.d and ergodic processes [11].

We make the following proposition related to the selection of color space on the embedding capacity of reversible watermarking:

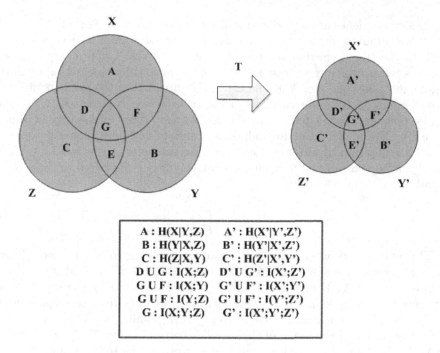

A : H(X|Y,Z)	A' : H(X'|Y',Z')
B : H(Y|X,Z)	B' : H(Y'|X',Z')
C : H(Z|X,Y)	C' : H(Z'|X',Y')
D U G : I(X;Z)	D' U G' : I(X';Z')
G U F : I(X;Y)	G' U F' : I(X';Y')
G U F : I(Y;Z)	G' U F' : I(Y';Z')
G : I(X;Y;Z)	G' : I(X';Y';Z')

Fig. 1. Venn diagram to explain the impact of color space transformation on entropy and mutual information.

Proposition 1. *If the cover color image is (losslessly) converted into a different color space with higher coding gain (i.e. better compression performance) before watermark embedding, then the watermark embedding capacity in the transformed color space is greater than the original color space.*

Consider the color components for color images to be finite discrete random variables. Let X,Y,Z be three random variables as depicted in a Venn diagram in Fig. 1, where the area of each circle (corresponding to each random variable) is proportional to its entropy, and the areas of the intersecting segments are proportional to the corresponding mutual information values of the relevant random variables.

Now consider a bijective transformation **T** applied to the point (X,Y,Z) in the original sample space, to transform it to another point (X',Y',Z') in the transformed sample space, corresponding to the three random variables X',Y',Z':

$$\mathbf{T} : (X,Y,Z) \rightarrow (X',Y',Z') \tag{2}$$

such that the image in the transformed sample space has higher coding gain. Since higher coding gain implies better compression performance, hence, each element of X',Y' and Z' is the compressed version of the corresponding element in X, Y and Y respectively. Moreover, let **T** be an invertible, lossless and it maps integers to integers.

As a consequence of the properties of the transformation $\mathbf{T}$, both the sample spaces are discrete and contain the same number of points. The values of the pixels in the transformed color space (i.e. X', Y' and Z') get "closer" to each other, as these are the compressed version of the pixel color channel values in the original sample space (i.e. X, Y and Z). This implies that the random variables corresponding to the color channels in the transformed color space (X', Y' and Z'), become more correlated among themselves than those in the original sample space (X, Y and Z). Since for individual random variables higher correlation between values implies lesser entropy [11], the entropies of the variables X', Y' and Z' in the transformed domain are relatively lesser compared to those of X, Y and Z. i.e.,

$$H(X') \leq H(X)$$
$$H(Y') \leq H(Y) \quad\quad\quad (3)$$
$$H(Z') \leq H(Z)$$

This is depicted by having the circles corresponding to X', Y' and Z' have lesser areas compared to the circles corresponding to X, Y and Z in Fig. 1. Joint entropy of X, Y and Z, i.e., $H(X, Y, Z)$ is depicted by the union of the three circles corresponding to X, Y and Z. Now, as the circles corresponding to X', Y' and Z' have lesser areas than those corresponding to X, Y and Z, it is evident that area of the union of these circles corresponding X', Y' and Z' (i.e., $H(X', Y', Z')$), must be smaller than that corresponding to X, Y and Z, i.e.,

$$H(X', Y', Z') \leq H(X, Y, Z) \quad\quad\quad (4)$$

We can draw an analogy between lossless (reversible) watermarking and lossless encoding, since in reversible watermarking, we have to losslessly encode the cover image into the watermarked image such that the cover image can be retrieved bit by bit. So, in that sense we can apply the Sepian-Wolf Theorem to estimate the embedding capacity of the reversible watermarking scheme. For lossless encoding of a color image I consisting of color channels X, Y and Z, we need a coding rate greater than equal to $H(X, Y, Z)$. The total size of the cover image is a constant, say N bits. Then, after an ideal lossless encoding of the image I which can encode it in $H(X, Y, Z)$ bits, there remains $(N - H(X, Y, Z))$ bits of space for auxiliary data embedding. Hence, theoretical embedding capacity of the reversible watermarking schemes in the two color spaces are given by:

$$C = N - H(X, Y, Z) \quad\quad\quad (5)$$

and

$$C' = N - H(X', Y', Z') \quad\quad\quad (6)$$

Since $H(X', Y', Z') \leq H(X, Y, Z)$, hence we can conclude that $C' \geq C$. Hence, we conclude that a color space transformation $\mathbf{T}$ with certain characteristics can result in higher embedding capacity.

Compressibility in Transformed Color Space and Reversibility of Transformation. When we transform the representation of a color image from one color space to another, the *Transform Coding Gain* is defined as the ratio of the arithmetic mean to the geometric mean of the variances of the variables in the new transformed domain coordinates, scaled by the norms of the synthesis basis functions for non-unitary transformations [8]. It is usually measured in dB. Transform coding gain is a metric to estimate compression performance [8] – higher transform coding gain implies more compression among the color channels of a color image representation. In general, the *Karhunen-Loeve Transform* (KL Transform), *Principle Component Analysis* (PCA) etc. might also be used to decorrelate color channels. **However, for reversible watermarking we need to choose an integer-to-integer linear transformation.** If $C_1 = (X, Y, Z)^T$ denote the color components in the original color space, and $C_2 = (X', Y', Z')^T$ denote the color components in the transformed color space after a linear transformation, then we can write $C_2 = TC_1$, where T is the transformation matrix. Similarly, the reverse transformation is expressed as $C_1 = T^{-1}C_2$, It is desirable that $\det T = 1$, which is a necessary condition for optimal lossless compression performance [8].

Ease of Color Space Transformation. Color space transformation during watermark embedding/extraction processes is a computational overhead. Another consideration that determines the selection of a candidate color space is the ease of implementation of the computations involved in the color space transformation, i.e. multiplication by the transformation matrix T. If the operations involved are only integer addition/subtractions and shifts, the color space transformation can be implemented extremely efficiently in both software and hardware.

From the discussion so far, our color space selection for performing the reversible watermarking operations is guided by the following criteria:

- Lower correlation among the color channels.
- Reversibility of transformation from the RGB color space.
- Higher transform coding gain, and,
- Ease of implementation of the transformation.

Some of the reversible color space transformations available in the literature [13,14] are described below in brief.

RCT Color Space. *Reversible Color Transform* (RCT) is used for lossless color transformation in JPEG 2000 standard [14]. It is also known as "reversible YUV color space". This color space transformation equations are simple, integer-to-integer and invertible:

$$\begin{cases} Y_r = \left\lfloor \dfrac{R + 2G + B}{4} \right\rfloor \\ U_r = R - G \\ V_r = B - G \end{cases} \iff \begin{cases} G = Y_r - \left\lfloor \dfrac{U_r + V_r}{4} \right\rfloor \\ R = U_r + G \\ B = V_r + G \end{cases} \tag{7}$$

O1O2O3 Color Space. This is another color space with higher compression performance, while maintaining integer-to-integer reversibility [13]. Here, the R, G, and B color channels are transformed into $O1$, $O2$, $O3$ color channels, and conversely:

$$
\begin{cases}
O1 = \left\lfloor \dfrac{R+G+B}{3} + 0.5 \right\rfloor \\[2mm]
O2 = \left\lfloor \dfrac{R-B}{2} + 0.5 \right\rfloor \\[2mm]
O3 = B - 2G + R
\end{cases}
\iff
\begin{cases}
B = O1 - O2 + \left\lfloor \dfrac{O3}{2} + 0.5 \right\rfloor - \left\lfloor \dfrac{O3}{2} + 0.5 \right\rfloor \\[2mm]
G = O1 - \left\lfloor \dfrac{O3}{3} + 0.5 \right\rfloor \\[2mm]
R = O1 + O2 + O3 - \left\lfloor \dfrac{O3}{2} + 0.5 \right\rfloor - \left\lfloor \dfrac{O3}{2} + 0.5 \right\rfloor
\end{cases}
\tag{8}
$$

Our Selection: The YCoCg-R Color Space. In our case, X, Y and Z correspond to the R, G and B color channels of the RGB color space, and X', Y' and Z' correspond to the Y, Co and Cg color channels in the YCoCg-R color space. The well-known YCoCg color space decomposes a color image into three components – *Luminance* (Y), *Chrominance orange* (Co) and *Chrominance green* (Cg) respectively. YCoCg-R is the integer to integer reversible version of YCoCg. The transformation T (for RGB to YCoCg-R), and the inverse transformation are given by [8]:

$$
\begin{aligned}
Co &= R - B, \\
t &= B + \left\lfloor \tfrac{Co}{2} \right\rfloor, \\
Cg &= G - t, \\
Y &= t + \left\lfloor \tfrac{Cg}{2} \right\rfloor
\end{aligned}
\tag{9}
$$

and similarly,

$$
\begin{aligned}
t &= Y - \left\lfloor \tfrac{Cg}{2} \right\rfloor, \\
G &= Cg + t, \\
B &= t - \left\lfloor \tfrac{Co}{2} \right\rfloor, \\
R &= B + Co
\end{aligned}
\tag{10}
$$

Notice that rolling out the above transformation equations allows us to write the direct transformation equations:

$$
\begin{bmatrix} Co \\ Cg \\ Y \end{bmatrix} = \mathbf{T} \begin{bmatrix} R \\ G \\ B \end{bmatrix} = \begin{bmatrix} 1 & 0 & -1 \\ -\tfrac{1}{2} & 1 & -\tfrac{1}{2} \\ \tfrac{1}{4} & \tfrac{1}{2} & \tfrac{1}{4} \end{bmatrix} \begin{bmatrix} R \\ G \\ B \end{bmatrix}
\tag{11}
$$

and hence $\det \mathbf{T} = 1$, which is desirable for achieving optimal compression ratio, as mentioned in Sect. 2.1. A close look would reveal that the transformations are nothing but repeated difference expansion of the color channels.

To summarize, selection of the YCoCg-R color space has the following consequences:

– Repeated difference expansion of the color channels makes the resultant color channels less correlated in the YCoCg-R color space. It is known that the YCoCg-R representation has higher coding gain [8].

- The RGB to YCoCg-R transformation is an integer-to-integer reversible transform.
- YCoCg-R achieves close to optimal compression performance [8].
- The arithmetic operations of the transformation are simple integer additions/subtractions and shifts, and hence extremely efficiently implementable in hardware and software.

We establish the superiority of our choice of the YCoCg-R color space over other color space representations through detailed experimental results in Sect. 4. We next discuss the impact of the embedding scheme on the embedding capacity. We justify the selection of a scheme used by us, which is a combination of the well-known *histogram-bin-shifting* scheme with pixel prediction techniques.

2.2 Embedding Scheme Selection for Capacity Enhancement

Ni et al. [3] introduced the histogram-bin-shifting based reversible watermarking scheme for grayscale images. In this scheme, first the statistical *mode* of the distribution, i.e., the most frequently occurring grayscale value, is determined from the frequency histogram of the pixel values, let us call the pixel value to be the "peak point". Now, the pixels with grayscale value greater than the peak value are searched, and their corresponding grayscale values are incremented by one. This is equivalent to right shifting the frequency histogram for the pixels having grayscale value greater than the peak point by one unit. Generally, all images from natural sources have one of more pixel values which are absent in the images, let us call these "zero points". The existence of zero points ensure that the partial shift of the frequency histogram do not cause any irreversible change in the pixel values. The shift results in an empty frequency bin just next to the peak point in the image frequency histogram. Next, the whole image is scanned sequentially and the watermark is embedded into the pixels having grayscale value equal to the peak point. When the watermark bit to be embedded is '1', the watermarked pixel occupies the empty bin just next to the peak value in the histogram, and when it is '0', the watermarked pixel value is left unmodified at the peak point. The embedding capacity of the scheme is limited by the number of pixels having the peak grayscale value. Figure 2 shows an example of the classical histogram-bin-shifting based watermarking scheme for an 8-bit grayscale image, where the peak point is 2 and the zero point is 7.

To improve the embedding capacity histogram-bin-shifting is blended with pixel prediction method [9]. In the pixel prediction technique, some of the cover image pixel values are predicted based on their neighbourhood pixel values. Such prediction gives prediction errors with respect to the original cover image. Generally, the frequency distribution of such prediction error resembles an Laplacian distribution [9], with peak value at zero as shown in Fig. 3. Watermarking bits are embedded into the prediction errors by histogram shifting of bins "close to zero", where the closeness is pre-defined with respect to some threshold. The bins that are "close to zero" in the prediction error histogram can be both right or left shifted to embed watermark bits. This two-way histogram shifting enhances

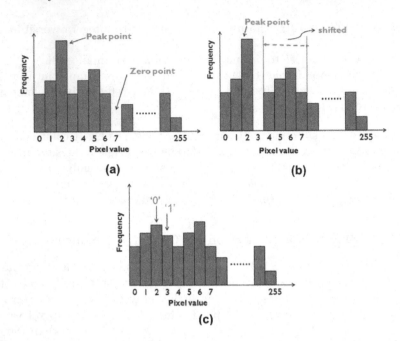

Fig. 2. Operations in the *Histogram-bin-shifting* reversible scheme proposed by Ni. et. al [3]: (a) histogram before shifting with peak point=2 and zero point=7; (b) histogram after shifting the pixels; (c) histogram after watermark embedding.

the capacity of the scheme significantly, compared to the classical histogram-bin-shifting case. The embedding in error histogram is shown in Fig. 3. During extraction, prediction errors are computed from the watermarked image, and the watermark bits are extracted from the errors. After watermark extraction, the error histogram bins are shifted back to their original position. The retrieved errors are combined with the predicted pixel values to get back the original cover image losslessly.

3   Proposed Algorithm

Our proposed algorithm consists of the following main steps:

1. Transformation of the cover color image from RGB color space to the YCoCg-R color space, using transformation-(9).
2. Pixel prediction based watermark embedding in the YCoCg-R color space.
3. Watermark extraction and lossless retrieval of original cover image.
4. Reconversion from YCoCg-R color space to RGB color space, using transformation-(10).

The first and the last steps have already been discussed. We now describe the remaining steps.

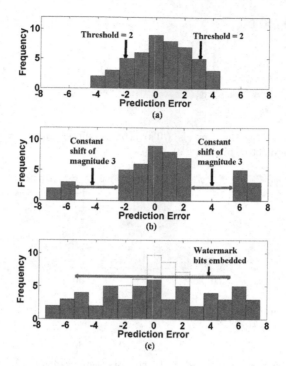

Fig. 3. Steps of watermark embedding using histogram shifting of prediction error: (a) prediction error histogram; (b) histogram shifting; (c) watermark embedding.

3.1 Pixel Prediction Based Watermark Embedding

We use *Weighted Mean based Prediction* [2] in the proposed scheme. In this scheme two levels of predicted pixel values are calculated exploiting the correlation between the neighboring pixels. One out of every four pixels in the original cover image is chosen as a "base pixel", as shown in Fig. 4, and the values of these pixels are used to predict the values of their neighboring pixels. Positions of next levels of predicted pixels are also shown in Fig. 4. Neighborhood of the pixels are partitioned into two directional subsets which are orthogonal to each other. We calculate the "first level predicted pixels" and the "second level predicted pixels" by interpolating the "base pixels" along two orthogonal directions: the 45° diagonal and the 135° diagonal as shown in Fig. 5. The first level predicted pixels, occupying coordinates $(2i, 2j)$ are computed as follows:

1. First, interpolated values along directions 45° and 135° are calculated. Let these values be denoted by p'_{45} and p'_{135}, and calculated as shown in Fig. 5:

$$p'_{45} = (p(i, j + 1) + p(i + 1, j))/2$$
$$p'_{135} = (p(i, j) + p(i + 1, j + 1))/2 \tag{12}$$

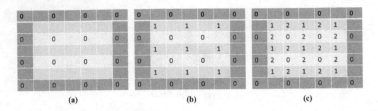

Fig. 4. Locations of (a) base pixels ('0's), (b) predicted first set of pixels ('1's), (c) predicted second set of pixels ('2's).

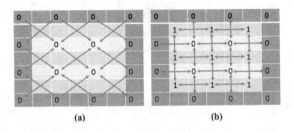

Fig. 5. (a) Prediction along 45° and 135° diagonal direction; (b) Prediction along 0° and 90° diagonal direction.

2. Interpolation error corresponding to the pixel at position $(2i, 2j)$ along directions 45° and 135° are calculated as:

$$
\begin{aligned}
e_{45}(2i, 2j) &= p'_{45} - p(2i, 2j) \\
e_{135}(2i, 2j) &= p'_{135} - p(2i, 2j)
\end{aligned}
\tag{13}
$$

3. Sets S_{45} and S_{135} contain the neighbouring pixels of the first level predicted pixel along the 45° and 135° directions respectively, i.e.,

$$
\begin{aligned}
S_{45} &= \{p(i, j+1), p'_{45}, p(i+1, j)\} \\
S_{135} &= \{p(i, j), p'_{135}, p(i+1, j+1)\}
\end{aligned}
\tag{14}
$$

4. The mean value of the base pixels around the pixel to be predicted, is denoted by u, and calculated as:

$$
u = \tfrac{p(i,j)+p(i+1,j)+p(i,j+1)+p(i+1,j+1)}{4}
\tag{15}
$$

5. In the weighted mean based prediction, weights of the means are calculated using variance along both diagonal direction. Variance along 45° and 135° are denoted as $\sigma(e_{45})$ and $\sigma(e_{135})$, and calculated as:

$$
\sigma(e_{45}) = \frac{1}{3} \sum_{k=1}^{3} (S_{45}(k) - u)^2
\tag{16}
$$

and

$$
\sigma(e_{135}) = \frac{1}{3} \sum_{k=1}^{3} (S_{135}(k) - u)^2
\tag{17}
$$

6. Weights of the means along $45°$ and $135°$ directions are denoted by w_{45} and w_{135}, and calculated as

$$w_{45} = \frac{\sigma(e_{135})}{\sigma(e_{45} + \sigma(e_{135}))}$$
$$w_{135} = 1 - w_{45}$$

(18)

7. We estimate the first level predicted pixel value p', as a weighted mean of the diagonal interpolation terms p'_{45} and p'_{135}:

$$p' = \text{round}\left(w_{45} \cdot p'_{45} + w_{135} \cdot p'_{135}\right)$$

(19)

Once the first level pixel values are predicted, the values of the second level pixels can be computed from the base pixels and the first level predicted pixels. A similar procedure as described above is used, but now pixel values along the horizontal and vertical directions are used for prediction, i.e. the values along the $0°$ and $90°$ directions are used, as shown in Fig. 5. In this way, we can predict the entire image (other than the base pixels) using interpolation and weighted mean of interpolated pixels along two mutually orthogonal directions.

Embedding Algorithm. After the given color cover image is transformed into the YCoCg-R color space, the given watermark bits are embedded into the color channels Co, Cg and Y in order. We preferentially embed watermarks into the *Chroma* components (Co and Cg), and then to the *Luma* component (Y),

---

Algorithm 1. *EMBED_WATERMARK*

/* Embed watermark bits into the prediction errors */
Input: Color cover image of size $M \times N$ pixels in YCoCg-R color space (I), Watermark bits (W),
   Embedding Threshold (T)
Output: Watermarked image I_{wm} in the YCoCg-R color space
1: **for** Color channels $P \in \{Co, Cg, Y\}$ in order **do**
2:   **if** W is not empty **then**
3:     **for** $i = 1\ to\ M$ **do**
4:       **for** $j = 1\ to\ N$ **do**
5:         **if** $P(i, j)$ is not a base pixel **then**
6:           $P'(i, j) \leftarrow Predict_{weightedmean} P(i, j)$
7:           Compute prediction error $e_P(i, j) = P(i, j) - P'(i, j)$
8:           **if** $e_P(i, j) \geq 0$ **then**
9:             $\text{sign}(e_P(i, j)) \leftarrow 1$
10:          **else**
11:            $\text{sign}(e_P(i, j)) \leftarrow -1$
12:          **end if**
13:          **if** $|e_P(i, j)| \leq T$ **then**
14:            $e'_P(i, j) \leftarrow \text{sign}(e_P(i, j)) \times [2 \times |e_P(i, j)| + \text{next bit of } W]$
15:          **else**
16:            $e'_P(i, j) \leftarrow \text{sign}(e_P(i, j)) \times [|e_P(i, j)| + T + 1]$
17:          **end if**
18:          $P_{wm}(i, j) \leftarrow P'(i, j) + e'_P(i, j)$
19:        **else**
20:          $P_{wm}(i, j) \leftarrow P(i, j)$
21:        **end if**
22:      **end for**
23:    **end for**
24: **end if**
25: **end for**
26: Obtain watermarked image I_{wm} by combining the watermarked color channels Y_{wm}, Co_{wm} and Cg_{wm}.

---

to minimize the visual distortion. Moreover, as human vision is least sensitive to changes in the blue color [12], so among the chroma components, the Co component (mainly combination of orange and blue) is embedded first, and then we embed in the Cg component (mainly combination of green and violet).

In each of the color channels, we apply the weighted mean based pixel prediction technique separately. Let $P(i,j)$ denote the value of the color channel at coordinate (i,j) with $P \in \{Co, Cg, Y\}$, and let $P'(i,j)$ be the corresponding predicted value of $P(i,j)$:

$$P'(i,j) \leftarrow Predict_{weightedmean}(P(i,j)) \qquad (20)$$

Then, the prediction error at the (i,j) pixel position for the P color channel is given by:

$$e_P(i,j) = P(i,j) - P'(i,j), \text{ where } P, P' \in \{C_o, C_g, Y\} \qquad (21)$$

Next the frequency histograms of the prediction errors are constructed. For watermark embedding, prediction errors which are close to zero are selected considering a threshold $T \geq 0$. Hence, the frequency histogram of the prediction errors in the range $[-T, T]$ are histogram-bin-shifted to embed the watermark bits. Rest of the histogram-bins are shifted away from zero by a constant amount of $(T+1)$ to avoid any overlap of absolute error values.

For embedding watermark bits, prediction errors $e_P(i,j)$ are modified due to histogram shifting to $e'_P(i,j)$ according to the following equation:

$$e'_P(i,j) = \begin{cases} \text{sign}(e_P(i,j)) \times [2 \times |e_P(i,j)| + b] & \text{if } |e_P(i,j)| \leq T \\ \text{sign}(e_P(i,j)) \times [|e_P(i,j)| + T + 1] & \text{otherwise} \end{cases} \qquad (22)$$

where $b \in [0,1]$ is the next watermarking bit to be embedded, and $\text{sign}(e_P(i,j))$ is defined as:

$$\text{sign}(e_P(i,j)) = \begin{cases} +1 & \text{if } e_P(i,j) \geq 0 \\ -1 & \text{otherwise} \end{cases} \qquad (23)$$

Finally, the modified prediction errors $e'_P(i,j)$ are combined with the predicted pixels $P'(i,j)$ in the corresponding color space to obtain the watermarked pixels $P_{wm}(i,j)$:

$$P_{wm}(i,j) = P'(i,j) + e'_P(i,j) \qquad (24)$$

The same procedure is applied in the three color channels (C_o, C_g, Y) of YCoCg-R color space. Hence, YCoCg-R color channels are watermarked. Now we transform P_{wm} from $YCoCg-R$ to RGB losslessly by Eq. 10 to finally obtain the watermarked image I_{wm}.

The proposed watermark embedding algorithm is presented as Algorithm 1.

3.2   Extraction Algorithm

The extraction algorithm just reverses the steps of the embedding algorithm. Watermark extraction is done in order from the Co, Cg and Y color channels respectively as used for embedding. In the extraction phase, we also predict the pixels except the base pixels for each color channel $P \in \{Co, Cg, Y\}$. At each pixel position (i, j) of color channel P of the watermarked image, $P'_{wm}(i, j)$ is calculated to be the predicted value of $P_{wm}(i, j)$:

$$P'_{wm}(i, j) \leftarrow Predict_{weightedmean}(P_{wm}(i, j))) \tag{25}$$

Then prediction error at (i, j)-th position of the P color channel is denoted by $e_{P_{wm}}(i, j)$. Then,

$$e_{P_{wm}}(i, j) = P'_{wm}(i, j) - P_{wm}(i, j) \tag{26}$$

Then the prediction error frequency histogram is generated and the watermark bits are extracted from the frequency histogram bins close to zero, as defined by the embedding threshold T:

$$|e_{P_{wm}}(i, j)| \leq (2T + 1) \tag{27}$$

Hence, the watermark bit b is extracted as:

$$b = |e_{P_{wm}}(i, j)| - 2 \times \lfloor \tfrac{|e_{P_{wm}}(i,j)|}{2} \rfloor \quad \text{if } |e_{P_{wm}}(i, j)| \leq (2T + 1) \tag{28}$$

After extraction, all bins are shifted back to their original positions, so the prediction errors in their original form are restored as given in following equation:

$$e'_{P_{wm}}(i, j) = \begin{cases} \text{sign}(e_{P_{wm}}(i, j)) \times \lfloor \tfrac{|e_{P_{wm}}(i,j)|}{2} \rfloor & \text{if } |e_{P_{wm}}(i, j)| \leq (2T + 1) \\ \text{sign}(e_{P_{wm}}(i, j)) \times (|e_{P_{wm}}(i, j)| - T - 1) & \text{otherwise} \end{cases} \tag{29}$$

where the restored error $e'_{P_{wm}}(i, j)$ is exactly same as the prediction error $e_P(i, j)$.

Next, the predicted pixels $(P'_{wm}(i, j))$ are combined with the restored errors $(e'_{P_{wm}}(i, j))$ to obtain each of the retrieved color channels $(P_{ret}(i, j))$ losslessly,

$$P_{ret}(i, j) = P'_{wm}(i, j) + e'_{P_{wm}}(i, j) = P'_{wm}(i, j) + e_P(i, j) = P(i, j) \tag{30}$$

where $P \in \{Co, Cg, Y\}$. After we retrieve the color channels Y, Co and Cg losslessly, we transform the cover image to the RGB color space by the lossless YCoCg-R to RGB transformation. The extraction algorithm is presented as Algorithm 2.

3.3   Handling of Overflow and Underflow

An overflow or underflow is said to have occurred if the watermark pixel $P_{wm}(i, j)$ as obtained in Eq. 24 is such that $P_{wm}(i, j) \notin \{0, 255\}$. The underflow condition is: $P_{wm}(i, j) < 0$ and the overflow condition is : $P_{wm}(i, j) > 255$. In embedding phase, we do not embed watermark into such above stated pixels to avoid overflow and underflow.

In extraction phase, we first find out which of the pixels cause overflow and underflow. These pixels indicate two types of possibilities:

Algorithm 2. *EXTRACT_WATERMARK*

/* Embed watermark bits into the prediction errors */

Input: Color watermarked image of size $M \times N$ pixels in YCoCg-R color space (I_{wm}), Embedding Threshold (T)

Output: Retrieved cover image (I_{ret}), Watermark (W)

1: **for** Color channels $P \in \{Co, Cg, Y\}$ in order **do**
2:    **for** $i = 1$ *to* M **do**
3:       **for** $j = 1$ *to* N **do**
4:          **if** $P_{wm}(i,j)$ is not a base pixel **then**
5:             $P'_{wm}(i,j) \leftarrow Predict_{weightedmean} P_{wm}(i,j)$
6:             Compute prediction error $e_{P_{wm}}(i,j) \leftarrow P_{wm}(i,j) - P'_{wm}(i,j)$
7:             **if** $e_{P_{wm}}(i,j) \geq 0$ **then**
8:                $sign(e_{P_{wm}}(i,j)) \leftarrow 1$
9:             **else**
10:                $sign(e_{P_{wm}}(i,j)) \leftarrow -1$
11:             **end if**
12:             **if** $|e_{P_{wm}}(i,j)| \leq (2T+1)$ **then**
13:                (Next bit of W) $\leftarrow |e_{P_{wm}}(i,j)| - 2 \times \lfloor \frac{|e_{P_{wm}}(i,j)|}{2} \rfloor$
14:                $e'_{P_{wm}}(i,j) \leftarrow sign(e_{P_{wm}}(i,j)) \times \lfloor \frac{|e_{P_{wm}}(i,j)|}{2} \rfloor$
15:             **else**
16:                $e'_{P_{wm}}(i,j) = sign(e_{P_{wm}}(i,j)) \times [|e_{P_{wm}}(i,j)| - T - 1]$
17:             **end if**
18:             $P_{ret}(i,j) = P'_{wm}(i,j) + e'_{P_{wm}}(i,j)$
19:          **else**
20:             $P_{ret}(i,j) = P_{wm}(i,j)$
21:          **end if**
22:       **end for**
23:    **end for**
24: **end for**
25: Obtain original cover image I_{ret} in YCoCg-R color space by combining the Y_{ret}, Co_{ret} and Cg_{ret} color components

Fig. 6. Test images used in our experiments: (a) Bird; (b) Cap; (c) Cycle; (d) House; (e) Sea; and (f) Nature.

1. During embedding, it caused overflow or underflow, and hence was not used for embedding.
2. Previously the pixel did not causes overflow or underflow, hence watermark bit was embedded. However, after watermark embedding the pixel causes overflow or underflow.

To correctly distinguish between which one of the cases have occurred, a binary bit stream, called a *location map* is generally used [9,10]. We assign '0' for the first case and '1' for the second case respectively, in the location map. If none of the cases occur the location map remains empty. Now during extraction, if a pixel with overflow or underflow occurs we check the next location map. If the location map bit is '0', we do not use the corresponding pixel for extraction and it remains unchanged. On the other hand, if the location map bit is '1', we use the corresponding pixel for extraction using Algorithm 2. Size of the location map is generally small and we can further reduce the size of the location map using lossless compression. The compressed location map is then inserted into the LSBs of the base pixels starting from the last base pixel. The original base pixel LSBs are concatenated at the beginning of the watermark and embedded into the cover image, before replacement with the location map bits.

4   Results and Discussion

The proposed algorithm was implemented in MATLAB and tested on several images from the *Kodak Image Database* [15]: *Bird, Cap, Cycle, House, Sea* and *Nature*, as shown in Fig. 6. The performance measurement for our proposed scheme is done with respect to the following:

1. Maximum embedding capacity, and,
2. distortion of the watermarked image with respect to the original cover image.

Maximum embedding capacity can be estimated as the number of pure watermark bits that can be embedded into the original cover image. To make the comparison independent of the size of the cover image, we normalized the embedding capacity with respect to the size of the cover image, and report it as the average number of bits that can be embedded per pixel, measured in units of

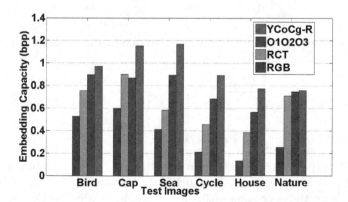

Fig. 7. Comparison of embedding capacity in different color space for several test images.

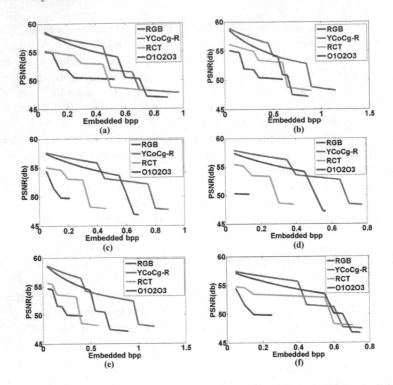

Fig. 8. Distortion characteristics of test images: (a) Bird; (b) Cap; (c) Cycle; (d) House; (e) Sea; and (f) Nature.

bits-per-pixel (bpp). Distortion of the watermarked image is estimated by the "Peak-Signal-to-Noise-Ratio" (PSNR), which is defined as:

$$PSNR = 10 \log_{10} \left(\frac{MAX^2}{MSE} \right) \text{dB} \tag{31}$$

where MAX represent the maximum possible pixel value. "Mean Square Error" (MSE) for color images is defined as:

$$MSE = \frac{1}{3 \cdot M \cdot N} \sum_{i=1}^{M} \sum_{j=1}^{N} [(R(i,j) - R'(i,j))^2 + (G(i,j) - G'(i,j))^2$$
$$+ (B(i,j) - B'(i,j))^2] \tag{32}$$

where $R(i,j)$, $G(i,j)$ and $B(i,j)$ represent the red, green and blue color component values at location (i,j) of the original cover image; $R'(i,j)$, $G'(i,j)$ and $B'(i,j)$ represent the corresponding color component values of the watermarked image, and the color image is of size $M \times N$.

The result of watermarking in the YCoCg-R color space using the proposed algorithm, and those obtained by watermarking using the same prediction-based histogram-bin-shifting scheme in the RGB, RCT [14] and O1O2O3 [13] color space representations are compared for the test images, as given in Fig. 7. The comparison clearly demonstrates that the embedding capacity is higher in the YCoCg-R color space representation than the RGB, RCT and O1O2O3 color spaces.

Distortion characteristics (i.e., variation of PSNR vs. Embedded bpp) for several test images are shown in Fig. 8. Note that the maximum bpp value attempted for each color space corresponds to their embedding capacity. The plots also suggest that the distortion of the images with increasing amount of embedded watermark bits is the least for the YCoCg-R color space representation in most cases. Since no color space representation can reach the embedding capacity of the YCoCg-R representation, overall we can conclude that the YCoCg-R color space is the best choice for reversible watermarking of color images. This observation was found to hold for most of the images in the Kodak image database [15].

5   Conclusions

In this paper we have proposed a novel reversible watermarking scheme for color images using histogram-bin-shifting of prediction errors in the YCoCg-R color space. We used a weighted mean based prediction scheme to predict the pixel values, and watermark bits were embedded by histogram-bin-shifting of the prediction errors in each color channel of the YCoCg-R color space. The motivations for the choice of the YCoCg-R color space over other color space representations were justified through detailed theoretical arguments and experimental results for several standard test images. Our future work would be directed towards exploiting other color space representations, and comparison of watermarking performance among them through theoretical and empirical techniques.

References

1. Cox, I.J., Miller, M.L., Bloom, J.A., Fridrich, J., Kalker, T.: Digital Watermarking and Steganography. Morgan Kaufmann Publishers, San Francisc (2008)
2. Tian, J.: Reversible data embedding using a difference expansion. IEEE Trans. Circuits Syst. Video Technol. **13**(8), 890–896 (2003)
3. Ni, Z., Shi, Y.-Q., Ansari, N., Su, W.: Reversible data hiding. IEEE Trans. Circuits Syst. Video Technol. **16**(3), 354–362 (2006)
4. Alattar, A.M.: Reversible watermark using the difference expansion of a generalized integer transform. IEEE Trans. Image Process. **13**(8), 1147–1156 (2004)
5. Alattar, A.M.: Reversible watermark using difference expansion of triplets. In: Proceedings of International Conference on Image Processing, vol. 1 (2003)
6. Alattar, A.M.: Reversible watermark using difference expansion of quads. In: Proceedings of International Conference on Acoustics, Speech, and Signal Processing, vol. 3 (2004)
7. Li, J., Li, Xi., Yang, B.: A new PEE-based reversible watermarking algorithm for color image. In: Proceedings of International Conference on Image Processing (2012)

8. Malvar, H.S., Sullivan, G.J., Srinivasan, S.: Lifting-based reversible color transformations for image compression. In: Proceedings of Optical Engineering and Applications (2008)

9. Naskar, R., Chakraborty, R.S.: Histogram-bin-shifting-based reversible watermarking for colour images. IET Image Process. **7**(2), 99–110 (2013)

10. Naskar, R., Chakraborty, R.S.: Fuzzy inference rule based reversible watermarking for digital images. In: Venkatakrishnan, V., Goswami, D. (eds.) ICISS 2012. LNCS, vol. 7671, pp. 149–163. Springer, Heidelberg (2012)

11. Cover, T.M., Thomas, J.A.: Elements of Information Theory. Wiley, Hoboken (2012)

12. Kandel, E.R., Schwartz, J.H., Jessell, T.M.: Principles of Neural Science. McGraw-Hill, New York (2000)

13. Nakachi, T., Fujii, T., Suzuki, J.: Lossless and near-lossless compression of still color images. In: Proceedings of International Conference on Image Processing, vol. 1. IEEE (1999)

14. Acharya, T., Tsai, P.-S.: JPEG2000 Standard for Image Compression: Concepts, Algorithms and VLSI Architectures. Wiley-Interscience, New York (2004)

15. Kodak lossless true color image suite. http://r0k.us/graphics/kodak/

Short Papers

A Study of Web Application Firewall Solutions

Stefan Prandl, Mihai Lazarescu, and Duc-Son Pham[✉]

Department of Computing, Curtin University, Perth, WA, Australia
stefan.prandl@student.curtin.edu.au, mihai.lazarescu@curtin.edu.au,
dspham@ieee.org

Abstract. Web application firewalls (WAFs) are the primary front-end protection mechanism for Internet-based infrastructure which is constantly under attack. This paper therefore aims to provide more insights into the performance of the most popular open-source WAFs, including ModSecurity, WebKnight, and Guardian, which we hope will complement existing knowledge. The key contribution of this work is an in-depth approach for conducting such a study. Specifically, we combine three testing frameworks: the Imperva's proprietary benchmark, a generic benchmark using both FuzzDB and Burp test-beds, and testing for common vulnerabilities and exposures (CVE) known exploits. Our experiments show that open source WAFs are not yet totally reliable for protecting web applications despite many advances in the field. ModSecurity appears to be the most balanced open-source solution.

Keywords: Web application firewalls · Information security · ModSecurity · WebKnight · Guardian · Imperva WAF testing framework

1 Introduction

The last decade has seen an increasing popularity of web applications as primary delivery of services over the Internet [6]. This popularity has been built on an evolution of web technologies such as Javascript, Java, Flash, Silversight, XML (client side) and PHP, Ajax (server side). These technologies allow sophisticated and content-rich applications to be built upon and delivered ubiquitously and simply through a web browser, which provides seamless experience to users [14]. The rising popularity of web applications also comes with serious security concerns. Web applications are now the primary targets of cyber attacks, causing financial losses, disruption of services [7]. Popular types of attacks such as cross-site scripting (XSS), SQL injection, and remote command execution are now the most challenging problem for web application developers and Internet security personnels [15]. In the early days, the security responsibility primarily belonged to the web application developers and/or owners. In the academic literature, the focus was largely on developing tools and methods for detecting vulnerabilities with web applications [5,9–12].

More recently, the focus has transitioned from developing those tools for checking vulnerabilities in web applications to firewalls, which take a more

© Springer International Publishing Switzerland 2015
S. Jajodia and C. Mazumdar (Eds.): ICISS 2015, LNCS 9478, pp. 501–510, 2015.
DOI: 10.1007/978-3-319-26961-0_29

pro-active defence role [4,6]. However, existing knowledge on how actually the existing WAFs perform is presently dispersed in somewhat fragmented and limited academic studies and industry-based technical whitepapers. Furthermore, as sophisticated attacks also evolve rapidly, more frequent and up-to-date studies on existing WAFs are of urgent need.

Motivated by such a need, this work presents such an in-depth study of several popular open-source WAFs, including ModSecurity [2], WebKnight [3], and Guardian [1]. They are selected for their popularity, strong community support, and sufficient documentation. The approach we use in this particular study is to measure the performance of these WAFs using a wide range of latest testing frameworks. This means that the types of attacks to be simulated are more comprehensive and thorough than studies that were based on a single testing benchmark. In addition, we also construct specialized scripts to generate friendly and non-trivial traffic that is challenging for over-conservative WAFs. By examining WAFs from these different perspectives, we argue that more detailed pictures can be revealed. In addition, we also focus on the qualitative analysis of the results with in-depth discussions to be given subsequently. Our intensive tests reveal that none of the WAFs produced ideal performance that is absolutely reliable. Each of the solutions still have their own strengths and weaknesses, though ModSecurity appears to be the most balanced overall.

The paper is organized as follows. Section 2 discusses in more detail the proposed study and network setup. Experimental results are provided in Sect. 3. Further discussion is given in Sect. 4 before concluding remarks are detailed in Sect. 5.

2 Proposed Study

We propose to investigate the functionality of three popular web application firewalls. These firewalls are ModSecurity [2], WebKnight [3], and Guardian [1]. The firewalls would be tested with a combination of both generic attacks, including XSS, SQL injection, RFI/LFI, and LDAP attacks; and also known exploits as tested in previous studies [8,13]. Generic attacks would be sourced from Imperva's Web Application Firewall Testing Framework, and from the FuzzDB web application exploit database. Known exploits would be sourced from previous studies and exploit database websites.

2.1 Motivation

There are two questions we would like to address in this work are:

- *How effective are the freeware WAF solutions currently available and can they be considered as a real alternative to commercial WAFs?*
- *Are there any classes of attacks that the freeware WAFs are effective at blocking and are there any types of malicious patterns that consistently manage to bypass the WAFs?*

In order to determine the effectiveness of these free WAFs, we have built a set of test patterns that thoroughly covers the types of attacks which have been deployed against web applications. The evaluation was done based on four criteria: (1) the number of attacks that were blocked by the WAFs, (2) the number of errors made by the respective defences in term of missed attacks, (3) the number of errors in terms of blocked friendly traffic, and (4) the delay introduced by the traffic analysis.

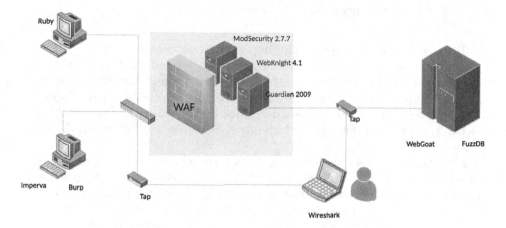

Fig. 1. Network setup for the study.

2.2 Detailed Setup

Tests were performed in a miniature network of virtualised machines as shown in Fig. 1. The setup consisted of a network consisting of four virtual machines connected to a central virtual router: an attack machine, a WAF gateway machine, a webserver machine, and a network analysis machine. The network analysis machine was configured with Wireshark and promiscuous mode networking such that all packets on the network would be routed to the network analysis machine as well as their intended destinations.

The WAFs were configured with their *default* security settings. For Guardian and WebKnight, this meant no alterations of the starting configuration or rules. For ModSecurity, this meant loading the "`Base`" OWASP rules configuration folder `Tests` consisted of five parts; Imperva Web Application Firewall testing attacks, Fuzz-DB project based attacks, Burp project based XSS and SQLi attacks, friendly traffic, and finally known exploits.

2.3 Combined Approach

The testing process involved the use of Imperva Testing Framework and the Burp Suite Community version software tools.

Imperva WAF Testing Framework. The Imperva Web Application Firewall testing suite was used as a starting point in our analysis. The framework provides a good range of malicious patterns but attacks classes such as LDAP are not covered. The Imperva framework also generates friendly traffic, but it should be noted that the friendly traffic is designed to fully test the WAF's capacity to distinguish malicious activities from normal traffic. The key to providing a detailed evaluation is the thoroughness of the testing patterns. For this reason, we have generated an additional separate test set that covered attacks that were not included in the Imperva testing suite.

Additional WAF Test Sets. The Imperva test set was augmented by using a combination of two other test sets: the Burp test set and the FuzzDB test set. There was an overlap between the three sets in the sense that all covered the XSS, SQL Injection and RFI types of attacks. The reason for the overlap was to try and determine if there was a difference between the way that the WAFs react to the attacks in Fuzz-DB, which are more readily available than the ones in Imperva's framework.

The LDAP, directory disclosure, integer overflow types of attacks used in our testing were only found in the Burp and FuzzDB sets. The attacks sets generated by using Imperva, Burp and FuzzDB required only single-stage interactions with the target system (such as a basic SQLi POST query). In addition to evaluating how the single-stage attacks were handled, we were also interested in determining whether the free WAFs had the capacity to handle multi-stage malicious traffic as well as to detect some well-known web-based exploits that were not found in the patterns provided by either Imperva, Burp or FuzzDB. For this reason, we added a set of patterns that included login & service access traffic to the target system, and we have also used a set of four exploits that are well established in the web application testing community.

The known exploit attacks consisted of four known exploits selected from previous papers [8,13]. The chosen attacks were the Practico CMS 13.7 Auth bypass SQL attack, the CLansphere 2011.3 Local File Inclusion attack, the Seo Panel 2.2.0 cookie-rendered persistant XSS attack, and the WebsiteBaker 2.6.5 SQL injection attack. All exploits were executed in the manner stated on their exploit report.

In addition to the Imperva friendly traffic, we also generated normal traffic that used POST or GET queries based on four templates. The aim was to emulate real user usage, rather than traffic that specifically attempts to break the WAF, something that we believe that Imperva's test suite lacked. The vulnerable application running on the target machine took the form of a simple guestbook, and thus the GET requests were to the index, to a page with a select element (that was vulnerable to cookie tampering and query string XSS injection), or to a page that allowed the viewing of the guestbook entries. The POST request followed a users posting to the guestbook, first making a textttGET request to the guestbook form page, then posting to the guestbook post page, and then making a GET request to the view guestbook page. Each step was broken up by a delay of up to 10 s, trying to emulate an actual user.

Friendly traffic was simulated using a custom built friendly traffic simulator that performed POST and GET requests using random selections from a full dictionary of English words against the same vulnerable web application as the previous two tests. Friendly traffic also included tests for known web applications, in this case PHPMyAdmin and Wordpress.

The results obtained from the three test sets are covered in detail in the next section followed by a discussion on the overall effectiveness of each of the three WAFs.

3 Experimental Results

3.1 Imperva Testing Framework Suite Results

The results from the first set of test done using the Imperva Test Framework are shown in Tables 1 and 2. From Table 1, we can see that both WebKnight ModSecurity were able to block all attacks generated by the test suite whereas Guardian failed to detect any of the attacks. The friendly traffic testing produced a contrasting set of results. All WAFs blocked friendly traffic with WebKnight being the worst performing solution. ModSecurity blocked 52 % of the crafted friendly packets with Guardian allowing blocking only around 5 % of the packets.

Overall, ModSecurity has the best performance as it blocked the attacks generated by the Imperva Framework but it also blocked a large number of friendly packets. This is **significant** as an effective WAF needs to allows friendly traffic through otherwise the user experience will be severely affected. WebKnight was effective at blocking the attacks but also blocked all but one of the specially crafted friendly traffic packets which indicates that its usefulness with real applications would be severely limited. Guardian was the worst performing WAF overall for this test set. Though it did not generate so many false positives, Guardian was the only solution that generated false negatives instead, missing all of the attacks generated.

Table 1. Performance of open-source Web Application Firewalls against Imperva test framework attacks

Imperva Attack Tests	Mod Security	WebKnight	Guardian@Jumperz
Total XSS tests	22	22	22
XSS Bypased	0	0	22
XSS Blocked	22	22	0
Total SQLi tests	19	19	19
SQLi Bypased	0	0	19
SQLi Blocked	19	19	0
Total RFI/LFI tests	19	19	19
RFI/LFI Bypased	0	0	19
RFI/LFI Blocked	19	19	0

Table 2. Performance of open-source Web Application Firewalls against Imperva test framework friendly packets

Imperva Friendly Tests	Mod Security	WebKnight	Guardian@Jumperz
Total Friendly tests	148	148	148
Friendly Blocked	76.5	147	6.1
Friendly Passed	71.5	1	141.9

3.2   Additional Test Results

The second set of patterns used for testing consisted of the patterns from the Fuzz-DB site while the third set was the Burp Suite in built one. Unlike the previous set of results, we present the friendly traffic results in a combined format as in both cases the same type of traffic was used.

FuzzDB and Burp Combined Attack Patterns Results. The combined results obtained from the Burp and Fuzz-DB sets are shown in Table 3. The results show that WebKnight has overall the best performance blocking 85.6 % of the attacks. ModSecurity has as lightly lower performance with 79.7 % of the attacks blocked. Guardian, however, performed poorly with most attacks with an overall blocking rate of 56 %.

Given the significant differences between the combined results from Fuzz-DB & Burp and the Imperva Testing Framework, it was important to determine the cause of the differences observed.

When considering the three types of attacks - XSS, SQLi and RFI/LFI, the results show that the WebKnight and ModSecurity's effectiveness is very similar to the one observed in the Imperva tests. WebKnight has overall the best performance blocking 99.93 % of the attacks. ModSecurity has similar performance with 99.89 % of the attacks blocked.

Friendly Traffic Results. The results from the friendly traffic are shown in Tables 4 and 5 and cover both single-stage interactions as well as multi-stage application specific usage traffic.

Table 4 shows that again WebKnight had major difficulties in distinguishing between normal and malicious traffic. Specifically, even with less difficult to categorise friendly traffic, WebKnight blocked slightly more than half of all randomly generated normal traffic. ModSecurity, on the other hand, did not generate any false positives and thus is clearly the best performing WAFs from the point of view of friendly traffic.

In terms of web application usage shown in Table 5, WebKnight and ModSecurity both blocked login and post attempts on Wordpress. In PHPMyAdmin however, ModSecurity allow the log in, while WebKnight blocked everything owing to it's proclivity to block POST requests. Guardian did not block any friendly traffic.

Table 3. Overall performance of open-source Web Application Firewalls

WAF Tests	Mod Security	WebKnight	Guardian@Jumperz
Total XXS tests	223	223	223
XSS Bypased	3	1	89
XSS Blocked	220	222	134
Total SQLi tests	43	43	43
SQLi Bypased	0	1	24
SQLi Blocked	43	42	19
Total RFI/LFI tests	26	26	26
RFI/LFI Bypased	0	0	26
RFI/LFI Blocked	26	26	0
Total Debug/Admin Flag Attacks	40	40	40
Debug/Admin Flag Bypased	40	40	40
Debug/Admin Flag Blocked	0	0	0
Total Directory Disclosure Attacks	10	10	10
Directory Disclosure Bypased	9	5	9
Directory Disclosure Blocked	1	5	1
Total HTTP Manipulation Attacks	115	115	115
HTTP Manipulation Bypased	25	0	0
HTTP Manipulation Blocked	98	115	115
Total Integer Overflow Attacks	36	36	36
Integer Overflow Bypased	13	28	36
Integer Overflow Blocked	23	8	0
Total LDAP Attacks	27	27	27
LDAP Bypased	16	0	15
LDAP Blocked	11	27	12

Table 4. WAF performance with randomly generated friendly traffic.

Friendly Traffic Types	Mod Security	WebKnight	Guardian@Jumperz
Total Random GET/POST Traffic	2369	3681	3467
Random GET/POST Traffic Blocked	0	1865	89
False Positive Rate	0%	50.60%	0%

Table 5. WAF performance with basic application authentication traffic.

Friendly Traffic Types	Mod Security	WebKnight	Guardian@Jumperz
Wordpress Login	Blocked	Blocked	Passed
Wordpress Post Submission	Blocked	Blocked	Passed
PHPMyAdmin Login	Passed	Blocked	Passed
PHPMyAdmin Query	Blocked	Blocked	Passed

3.3   Known Exploits

The final set of tests involved four well known web application exploits and the results are show in Table 6. Both ModSecurity and WebKnight were successful in blocking all the known exploit attacks. However, it should be noted that in all cases WebKnight blocked the attack by blocking application functionality. ModSecurity blocked the attack, but still allowed the application to function. Guardian did not succeed in blocking any of the four known exploit attacks.

Table 6. WAF performance with well known web application exploits.

Application & Vulnerability	Mod Security	WebKnight	Guardian
Practico CMS 13.7 AuthBypass SQL Injection	Blocked	Blocked	Passed
Clansphere 2011.3 Local File Inclusion	Blocked	Blocked	Passed
Seo Panel 2.2.0 Cookie-Rendered Persistent XSS	Blocked	Blocked	Passed
WebsiteBaker Version¡2.6.5 SQL Injection	Blocked	Blocked	Passed

4   Discussion

When considering the results from all tests, the best overall free WAF is ModSecurity. It offers the best balance between blocking malicious traffic and allowing normal traffic through. If one compares ModSecurity with WebKnight from the point of view of attack blocking, ModSecurity is less effective with a substantially larger number of attacks bypassing it. However, WebKnight has a tendency to block a large proportion of the traffic observed by default.

Our tests also show that Guardian is not an effective solution but this was not unexpected given that is rule set does not cover the more recent malicious patterns. Guardian allowed through a large number of malicious packets, and was not successful in blocking any known exploits. In addition, it was also very slow in our tests, adding about a second of time in routing the packets to the application server. This slowdown is enough to be noticeable, and could have negative user experience implications, as well as not actually defending against known attacks. This contrasts markedly with the performance of the ModSecurity and WebKnight, which showed no significant slowdown in the traffic.

WebKnight is also not an effective solution. It was the most effective in blocking malicious attacks, however, WebKnight was discovered to be blocking all POST requests, regardless of their content. While this allows it to be more effective at defending against malicious attacks, it also results in an unacceptably large number of false positives. In summary, WebKnight may block nearly all incoming attacks, but does so at the cost of application functionality.

The question of whether ModSecurity is a possible alternative to a commercial solution is dependant largely on the type of application to be protected and the overall setup. If the application is likely to face SQL, XSS or RFI/LFI attacks, then ModSecurity will provide a very effective option. From this point of view, the block success rate is very similar to the commercial solutions outlined in the NSS labs report which showed that most solutions had a detection rate of over 98 %. On the other hand, if the application is likely to face LDAP or Integer Overflow attacks, then ModSecurity falls well short of the level of performance seen in commercial solutions. However, it should be stressed that if a malicious packet was able to pass through the WAF does not necessarily result in the application being compromised and in many cases knowing the type of patterns cause the WAF failure can be handled with other mitigation measures on the target server.

5   Conclusion

We have investigated the performance of three free Web Applications Firewalls (WebKnight, ModSecurity and Guardian) with a number of test sets covering both malicious and friendly traffic. Our aim was determine how effective free WAFs are overall and whether they could be considered as viable alternatives to commercial solutions. The results have shown that ModSecurity is the best free WAF solution available as it can handle a significant number of attacks while generating a small number of false alarms. When compared with the commercial solutions, ModSecurity is less effective with the commercial WAFs reportedly blocking on average over 99 % of the attacks whereas ModSecurity could only block around 80 % of the attacks generated for this investigation. ModSecurity is very effective at blocking commonly occurring attacks such as XSS, SQLi and RFI/LFI but does not fare well when faced with attacks involving HTTP Manipulation, Integer Overflow or Debug/Admin flags.

However, despite the problems that ModSecurity has with some less common types of attacks, it can still provide a substantial amount of protection against popular attacks such as XSS. The other two free WAFs on the other hand, WebKnight and Guardian could not be considered as being effective or applicable enough in real world scenarios. WebKnight's drawback is that does not have the capacity to handle friendly traffic whereas Guardian offers very little protection from a wide range of attacks.

References

1. Guardian. http://guardian.jumperz.net/index.html
2. ModSecurity. https://www.modsecurity.org/
3. Web Knight. https://www.aqtronix.com/?PageID=99
4. Balock, R., Jaffery, T.: Modern Web Application Firewalls Fingerprinting and Bypassing XSS Filters. Technical report, Rhainfosec (2013), White Paper
5. Bau, J., Bursztein, E., Gupta, D., Mitchell, J.: State of the art: automated black-box web application vulnerability testing. In: 2010 IEEE Symposium on Security and Privacy (SP), pp. 332–345. IEEE (2010)
6. Becher, M.: Web Application Firewalls. VDM Verlag, Saarbrücken (2007)

7. Bojinov, H., Bursztein, E., Boneh, D.: Xcs: cross channel scripting and its impact on web applications. In: Proceedings of the 16th ACM Conference on Computer and Communications Security, pp. 420–431. ACM (2009)

8. Cabrera, H., Krstic, G., Petrushevski, S.: CloudFlare vs Incapsula: Round 2. Technical report, Zero Science Lab (2013). http://zeroscience.mk/files/wafreport2013v2.pdf. Accessed 16 July 2015

9. Doupé, A., Cova, M., Vigna, G.: Why Johnny can't pentest: an analysis of black-box web vulnerability scanners. In: Kreibich, C., Jahnke, M. (eds.) DIMVA 2010. LNCS, vol. 6201, pp. 111–131. Springer, Heidelberg (2010)

10. Huang, Y.W., Yu, F., Hang, C., Tsai, C.H., Lee, D.T., Kuo, S.Y.: Securing web application code by static analysis and runtime protection. In: Proceedings of the 13th International Conference on World Wide Web, pp. 40–52. ACM (2004)

11. Jovanovic, N., Kruegel, C., Kirda, E.: Pixy: a static analysis tool for detecting web application vulnerabilities. In: Proceedings of the IEEE Symposium on Security and Privacy. IEEE (2006)

12. Nguyen-Tuong, A., Guarnieri, S., Greene, D., Shirley, J., Evans, D.: Automatically hardening web applications using precise tainting. In: Sasaki, R., Qing, S., Okamoto, E., Yoshiura, H. (eds.) Proceedings of the 20th IFIP International Information Security Conference, vol. 181, pp. 295–307. Springer, US (2005)

13. Tibom, P.: Incapsula vs. CloudFlare: Security Review & Comparison. Technical report, Personal Review (2012). https://www.computerscience.se/downloads/Full-Review.pdf. Accessed 16 July 2015

14. Torrano-Gimenez, C., Perez-Villegas, A., Alvarez, G.: A self-learning anomaly-based web application firewall. In: Herrero, Á., Gastaldo, P., Zunino, R., Corchado, E. (eds.) Proceedings of the Conference on Computational Intelligence in Security for Information Systems, vol. 63, pp. 85–92. Springer, Heidelberg (2009)

15. Vernotte, A., Dadeau, F., Lebeau, F., Legeard, B., Peureux, F., Piat, F.: Efficient detection of multi-step cross-site scripting vulnerabilities. In: Prakash, A., Shyamasundar, R. (eds.) ICISS 2014. LNCS, vol. 8880, pp. 358–377. Springer, Heidelberg (2014)

Attacks on Branch Predictors: An Empirical Exploration

Moumita Das[1]([✉]), Bhaskar Sardar[2], and Ansuman Banerjee[3]

[1] Meghnad Saha Institute of Technology, Kolkata, India
moumita.it@gmail.com
[2] Jadavpur University, Kolkata, India
[3] Indian Statistical Institute, Kolkata, India

Abstract. Branch predictors play a critical role in achieving high performance in many modern pipeline processors. A branch predictor at runtime predicts the direction which a branch instruction will take and begins fetching, decoding and executing instructions using this prediction even before the result of the branch condition is known. This greatly reduces delay and increases CPI (cycles per instruction) of a program. The branch predictor is therefore, a crucial piece inside any modern pipelined processor. This paper presents an empirical exploration of different state-of-the-art branch predictors with respect to their vulnerabilities and the resulting effect on processor performance.

1 Introduction

Branch predictors play a critical role in achieving high performance in many modern pipeline processors. Modern processors do not wait till the direction of a branch condition gets resolved as taken or not-taken. In contrast, they use a speculative strategy to guess the branch direction even before the branch condition is actually evaluated. However, if a processor incorrectly predicts a branch target direction, it may cause a serious problem. As a penalty of incorrect prediction, the pipeline has to be flushed for all the incorrectly speculated instructions and results and instructions from the correct branch target addresses have to be fetched and executed. Flushing of instructions and results from a pipeline is expensive and causes a delay of several cycles. This delay significantly degrades system performance, if these incorrect predictions occur frequently. For example, in the Pentium 4 family of processors, branch mis-predictions are much more expensive than on previous generations of microprocessors and it takes a substantial number of processor cycles to recover from a mis-prediction [2]. Designing efficient branch predictors with low mis-prediction rate is therefore, a fundamental research challenge in computer architecture.

Dynamic branch predictors which reside inside the processor and operate at run-time, keep different pieces of information about branches and their correlations to be able to accurately predict the direction of future branches. These information may vary from the direction of a branch to the history of preceding branches, with the motivation of being able to predict correctly the direction of

S. Jajodia and C. Mazumdar (Eds.): ICISS 2015, LNCS 9478, pp. 511–520, 2015.
DOI: 10.1007/978-3-319-26961-0_30

a future branch using this information, since studies have shown a substantial degree of correlation among branch directions [7]. The information is stored in processor registers. The objective of this study is to analyze the effect of an attack on these internal registers with respect to their effect on processor performance and accuracy of prediction. A simple piece of malware which is active when a given program runs, may tamper the contents of the processor registers and easily achieve this objective. An illegal change in the contents of a register which a predictor uses for keeping information can alter the number of correct predictions, and thereby, increase the mis-prediction rate, and affect the overall performance of execution of a given user program. In this paper, we perform a detailed empirical study on the effect of an attack on the branch predictor on a processor's performance. We consider a number of contemporary branch predictors and identify the amount of information needed at runtime (which the processor needs to store) for these predictors to work correctly. We change these registers in a controlled fashion, and show the resulting change in prediction and performance. To the best of our knowledge, this is the first such work which attempts to study the effect of an attack on the branch prediction piece inside the processor hardware. We observe the performance variations for different branch predictors using an architectural simulator. Specifically, we alter the register contents inside the simulator and observe the outcomes. The simulation outputs for every predictor are measured in terms of performance in respect of prediction accuracy, number of processor cycles needed and power consumption for that processor.

The rest of the paper is organized as follows: Sect. 2 describes the backgrounds and related works done on this theme. In Sect. 3, we have identified different types of attacks on different branch predictors. Section 4 describes the experimental set-up used as well as the results of our experiment. Section 5 concludes the paper and introduces new ideas for future research.

2 Background and Related Work

In a pipelined architecture, instructions typically go through an assembly line while a program executes, as shown in Fig. 1. Figure 1 shows a simplified view of a pipelined processor, wherein each instruction goes through different stages (omitted the memory stage for simplicity) to reach the end of execution. Thus every clock cycle, a new instruction can be fetched, while other instructions transit through the different stages inside the pipeline. This leads to improved execution by overlapping instruction latencies and different instructions can be in flight, resulting in improved performance. Branch instructions in this pipeline typically get resolved in the second/third stage, thus it is a tricky task to decide which instruction to fetch next, when a branch instruction is encountered as the current instruction. The processor may still go ahead and load instructions from the immediate next instruction, but if the branch gets resolved in the else-path, the entire instruction stream loaded has to be flushed off. To improve the performance of program execution, efficient predictors are employed inside a

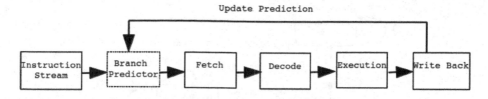

Fig. 1. Architecture of a pipelined processor

modern processor which guide the processor to predict the direction of a branch and start fetching, decoding and executing instructions before the result of the branch condition is evaluated as shown in Fig. 1.

It is observed that incorrect predictions can cause significant performance degradation due to high mis-prediction penalty. For example, P4 and P4E processors take minimum 24 clock cycles and around 45 micro-operations as a mis-prediction penalty [2]. Apparently, the processor cannot cancel an unnecessary micro-operation before it has reached the retirement stage. This means that if we have a lot of micro-operations with long latency or poor throughput, then the penalty for a mis-prediction may be as high as 100 clock cycles or more. In the discussion below, we present a brief summary of the underlying principles of some of the state-of-the-art branch predictors.

2.1   Branch Prediction

In this paper, two popular state-of-the-art dynamic branch predictors, namely, the Two-Level Adaptive Branch Predictor and the TAGE predictor are chosen to perform this study. In this section, we describe the internal configurations of these predictors which are needed at the time of prediction and can be considered as the targets of different attacks.

Two-Level Adaptive Branch Predictor: The Two-Level Adaptive Branch Predictor was proposed by Yah and Patt in 1991 [10,11] to make the prediction using two levels of branch history information. The first level stores the history of the last n branches encountered. The second level is the branch behavior for the last k occurrences of the same pattern of these n branches. Prediction is done on the basis of branch behavior for the last k occurrences of the pattern. This predictor uses two main data structures, the Branch History Register (BHR) and the Pattern History Table (PHT). BHR is a n bit shift register which shifts in bits to represent the branch outcomes of the most recent n branches (or the last n occurrences of the same branch). Since, the BHR has n bits, at most 2^n different patterns can appear in this history register. For each of these 2^n patterns, there is a corresponding entry in the PHT which is achieved by using an indexing function. Each PHT entry contains the branch result for the last k times the same output of the indexing function appears. A two bit saturating up-down counter [4] is used to perform this operation. When a conditional branch

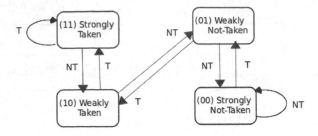

Fig. 2. Two-bit saturating counter

is predicted, the content of the BHR is used as one of the inputs of the indexing function to address the pattern history table. The pattern history bits at that particular address in the PHT are then used for predicting the branch. After a conditional branch is resolved (at a later stage in the pipeline when the actual branch direction gets known exactly), the BHR is left shifted by one bit and the branch outcome is recorded at the least significant bit position in the BHR. This new updated BHR is also used to update the corresponding pattern history table entry by changing the current state of the saturating counter.

The two-bit saturating counter is considered as a finite state machine for most of the branch predictor designs since it was introduced for dynamic branch prediction [10,11]. It has four different states (00, 01, 10 and 11) defined by the 2 bits of it as shown in Fig. 2. The counter transitions from one state to another in response to a taken (T) or not-taken (NT) outcome resulting from the execution of one or more branch instructions that are assigned to the index value of the predictor. Each bit of the two-bit counter plays a different role. The most significant bit, called the direction bit is used to track the direction of branches. If the counter is in states 01 or 00, the branch is predicted as NT. When it is in states 10 and 11, the prediction is T. The least significant bit provides a hysteresis which prevents the direction bit from immediately changing when a mis-prediction occurs.

In our work, we consider Two-Level Adaptive Branch Prediction, and in particular, the GShare and PAp predictors.

TAgged GEometric (TAGE) History Length Branch Predictor: TAGE is considered as the state-of-the-art branch predictor which uses several different history lengths to capture the correlation from very remote branch outcomes as well as very recent branch history [9]. The TAGE predictor uses a base predictor T0 and a set of (partially) tagged components Ti. The base predictor is a simple PC-indexed 2-bit counter which is used to provide the default prediction. The tagged predictor components Ti, $1 \leq i \leq M$ are indexed using different history lengths that form a geometric series [8]. Each entry of a tagged component contains a partial tag, an unsigned counter u and a signed counter ctr with the sign providing the prediction. At prediction time, the base predictor and the tagged components are accessed simultaneously. If no matching in the tagged component is found, the base predictor is used to provide the default prediction. In the next section, we discuss the vulnerabilities of these predictors in more detail.

2.2 Related Work

In past years, several articles have addressed the problem of finding different hardware resources which are sensitive to an attack and different types of attacks which can be performed on them. For example, in 2000, John Kelsey, Bruce Schneier, David Wagner, and Chris Hall introduced *cache attacks*, which proved that a cache memory is vulnerable to side-channel attacks [3]. Debdeep et al. [1] showed that Linear Feedback Shift Registers (LFSRs), which are used as a building block of many stream ciphers are also vulnerable to power attacks. To the best of our knowledge, this is the first study that addresses this theme.

3 Detailed Methodology

For branch prediction, almost every branch predictor uses the two-bit saturating counter, the BHR, the PC and the PHT, as discussed in Sect. 2. This gave us the motivation to explore how a branch prediction policy gets affected by attacking and changing these data structures in the following way-

- **Target of an attack: two-bit saturating counter.** The two bit counter is very crucial for branch prediction since it provides the final prediction for branch direction. Some of the possible ways in which this counter can be affected are as described below-
  - Most Significant Bit (MSB) of all states are flipped: As explained already, the MSB provides the direction for a branch prediction. If we flip this bit, the branch direction is inverted. So taken branches now become not-taken branches and vice versa and this is expected to have an impact on branch prediction accuracy.
  - Least Significant Bit (LSB) of all states are flipped: The LSB, when paired with the direction bit, provides hysteresis which prevents the direction bit from immediately changing when a mis-prediction occurs. If we flip this bit, it changes the current state of this two-bit counter and a strongly taken:00 (strongly not-taken:01) state becomes a weakly taken:01 (weakly not-taken:10) state and vice versa. As a result, states which used to take two consecutive mis-predictions to alter the branch direction, now take only one mis-prediction. This again has an impact on prediction accuracy and performance.
  - Counter length changed: The two-bit saturating counter can also be replaced by any n-bit counter (n ≠ 2). We already discussed the effect it has if the two-bit counter is changed to a 1-bit one, However, if the counter length is increased, there is a chance to improve the prediction accuracy as well as overall system performance. We did this in our experiments and found interesting consequences.

– **Target of an attack: BHR.** BHR is a n-bit shift register which stores the history of the last n branches (global history) or the last n outcomes of the same branch instruction (local history). For example, to do the prediction, the GShare and the TAGE predictors use the global history whereas the PAp predictor uses the local history. The BHR is used to address an entry in a PHT which keeps a two-bit counter to give the final prediction. If this BHR is changed, the branch predictor will index a wrong PHT entry to get the final prediction. This BHR can be affected by its content or its length as discussed below-

  • MSB or LSB of BHR is flipped: This flipping changes the original value of the BHR and a different PHT entry is accessed by the predictor to get the final prediction for branch direction. For example, a 4-bit BHR with a value 1001 becomes 0001, if MSB is flipped. Now in a PAp predictor, instead of an entry in 1001, 0001 entry will be accessed to get the prediction for a branch, which can vary prediction accuracy. So, this change can be taken as an attack to fluctuate the overall performance.

  • Length of BHR is changed: If BHR length is changed, the indexing used to address an entry in PHT can differ and as a result a wrong PHT entry will be picked up for the final prediction. For example, consider a 8-bit BHR with a value 11101001. In a PAp predictor, this 8-bit is used to index an entry in a 2^8 entry PHT. If we select only the lower 4 bits of this BHR i.e. 1001 to index a PHT entry, then instead of 11101001, the 00001001 entry will be accessed for prediction. So this can alter the prediction accuracy as well.

– **Target of an attack: PC.** The program counter contains the branch address and is used by different prediction mechanisms. In PAp, each PC has its own BHR as well as own PHT. If the number of bits of a PC which are taken to select this Branch History Table (BHT) and PHT is changed, a different BHT entry (or BHR) and as well as PHT will be accessed to get the final prediction. However, in case of the GShare predictor, this PC value is used as one input of an indexing function to find an entry in the PHT. So this length change of PC will result in a different output for the same indexing function and as a result, a wrong PHT entry will be chosen to give the prediction. Similarly, for the case of the TAGE predictor, a wrong predictor component or incorrect entry of the base predictor will be accessed for the branch prediction. So this change also can be taken as an attack to alter the performance.

Along with these, the TAGE predictor also has tagged components whose signed counter (sign bit) is used to make the prediction. Any change on this counter (e.g. flipping of sign bit) will make an impact on the prediction accuracy.

4   Experiments and Results

In this section, we present the details of our simulation framework, along with a discussion on the benchmark datasets used for experimentation.

Table 1. Performance statistics for GShare Predictor (MSB Flipped): Performance degradations seen for all benchmarks

Benchmark	Prediction accuracy(%)		Clock cycles		Energy	
	Original MSB	Flipped MSB	Original MSB	Flipped MSB	Original MSB	Flipped MSB
403.gcc	66.27	33.6931	86754099	96932134	2454452.3728	2635708.1682
400.perlbench	63.75	36.2364	11766325	12867838	339602.8584	359208.8278
458.sjeng	99.92	0.0706	283822066	497448050	5526430.3942	9328972.9094

Table 2. Performance statistics for PAp, TAGE Predictor (MSB of Counter Flipped): Performances are varied for all benchmarks

Predictor	Benchmark	Prediction accuracy(%)		Clock cycles		Energy	
		Original MSB	Flipped MSB	Original MSB	Flipped MSB	Original MSB	Flipped MSB
PAp	403.gcc	75.346	24.6208	83385248	99911660	2394376.5798	2688633.8706
	400.perlbench	69.8519	30.1486	11389779	13426984	332899.9548	369160.4722
	458.sjeng	99.947	0.053	283502111	497505905	5520735.1952	9330002.7284
TAGE	403.gcc	85.93	88.0023	80209030	79442840	2337946.489	2324347.3642
	400.perlbench	83.23	86.4732	10589517	10720538	318653.5596	320985.7334
	458.sjeng	99.93	99.9307	283196974	283122778	5515303.7566	5513983.0678

Table 3. Performance statistics for GShare Predictor (LSB Flipped): Performance degradations seen for all benchmarks except 429.mcf

Benchmark	Prediction accuracy(%)		Clock cycles		Energy	
	Original MSB	Flipped MSB	Original MSB	Flipped MSB	Original MSB	Flipped MSB
403.gcc	66.27	64.0966	86754099	87023273	2454452.3728	2459165.9404
400.perlbench	63.75	63.0858	11766325	11796034	339602.8584	340131.2938
458.sjeng	99.92	0.2276	283822066	497415305	5526430.3942	9328390.0484

4.1 Experimental Setup

For performing the attack simulations, we used the Tejas architectural simulator. Tejas [5] is an open source, Java based multicore architectural simulator. At the end of each execution, it reports various statistics related to cache utilization, branch prediction accuracy, energy expenditure, etc.

We used Tejas to generate the branch profile for the SPEC CPU 2000 benchmark. The simulator was modified to record the behavior of each branch for different prediction strategies with different configurations. In this work, we considered three different branch prediction strategies, namely, Gshare [6], PAp [11] and TAGE [9]. However, to limit simulation time, only the first 30 million instructions from each benchmark were simulated.

Table 4. Performance statistics for PAp and TAGE Predictors (LSB of Counter Flipped): Performance variations seen for all benchmarks

Predictor	Benchmark	Prediction accuracy(%)		Clock cycles		Energy	
		Original MSB	Flipped MSB	Original MSB	Flipped MSB	Original MSB	Flipped MSB
PAp	403.gcc	75.346	64.0929	83385248	87046670	2394376.5798	2459550.2762
	400.perlbench	69.8519	63.1424	11389779	11781463	332899.9548	339871.3528
	458.sjeng	99.947	0.2631	283502111	497379990	5520735.1952	9327761.4414
TAGE	403.gcc	85.93	86.3175	80209030	79715714	2337946.489	2329132.7562
	400.perlbench	83.23	84.1727	10589517	10636708	318653.5596	319495.6758
	458.sjeng	99.93	99.9299	283196974	283338969	5515303.7566	5517831.2676

Table 5. Performance statistics for GShare, PAp, TAGE Predictor (Counter Length Changed): Performances are varied with counter lengths

Predictor	Benchmark	Prediction accuracy(%)				Clock cycles			
		1-bit	2-bit	3-bit	4-bit	1-bit	2-bit	3-bit	4-bit
GShare	403.gcc	61.96	66.27	67.92	68.62	87517041	86754099	86322007	85356433
	400.perlbench	58.8	63.75	66.27	66.4	11660939	11766325	11357031	11593328
	458.sjeng	99.89	99.92	99.92	99.92	283320350	283822066	283552210	283606701
PAp	403.gcc	69.8066	75.346	76.9188	76.85	85849140	83385248	82786622	83092197
	400.perlbench	65.244	69.8519	72.3361	72.6049	11326321	11389779	11121986	11252867
	458.sjeng	99.9348	99.947	99.9416	99.9338	283460925	283502111	283202229	283268135
TAGE	403.gcc	79.83	85.93	87.44	87.6	82189182	80209030	79472066	79754141
	400.perlbench	74.9	83.23	85.97	86.56	11175555	10589517	10754710	10422707
	458.sjeng	99.91	99.93	99.93	99.93	283681764	283196974	283581362	283144095

Table 6. Performance statistics for GShare, PAP, TAGE Predictors (Counter Length Changed)

Branch predictor	Benchmark	Energy			
		1-bit	2-bit	3-bit	4-bit
GShare	403.gcc	2467992.3364	2454452.3728	2446727.0804	2429563.9132
	400.perlbench	337726.9876	339602.8584	332318.0024	336524.089
	458.sjeng	5517499.8494	5526430.3942	5521626.9574	5522596.8972
PAp	403.gcc	2438333.713	2394376.5798	2383780.681	2389245.1204
	400.perlbench	331770.4024	332899.9548	328132.6622	330462.344
	458.sjeng	5520002.0844	5520735.1952	5515397.2956	5516570.4224
TAGE	403.gcc	2373177.2254	2337946.489	2324840.8434	2329799.6332
	400.perlbench	329085.036	318653.5596	321593.995	315684.3416
	458.sjeng	5523933.0186	5515303.7566	5522145.863	5514362.5104

Table 7. Performance statistics for GShare and PAp Predictors (LSB of BHR is Flipped) little improvements seen for all benchmarks (except 429.mcf for PAp)

Predictor	Benchmark	Prediction accuracy(%)		Clock cycles		Energy	
		Original MSB	Flipped MSB	Original MSB	Flipped MSB	Original MSB	Flipped MSB
GShare	403.gcc	66.27	66.2889	86754099	86186566	2454452.3728	2444335.47
	400.perlbench	63.75	63.7644	11766325	11508252	339602.8584	335007.04
PAp	403.gcc	75.346	75.3677	83385248	83209708	2394376.5798	2391358.1726
	400.perlbench	69.8519	69.853	11389779	11589839	332899.9548	336459.2912

Table 8. Performance statistics for GShare, PAp, TAGE Predictors (Length PC and BHR Changed): Performances are varied with lengths of PC and BHR

Predictor	Benchmark	Prediction accuracy(%)				Clock cycles			
		N = 1	N = 4	N = 6	N = 8	N = 1	N = 4	N = 6	N = 8
GShare	403.gcc	61.4186	66.2913	71.474	77.2345	87836252	85920228	84338856	82805824
	400.perlbench	59.9311	63.7636	68.0441	74.5646	11628160	11707093	11614214	10895872
PAp	403.gcc	64.7491	75.346	84.8665	89.1641	86674276	83385248	80058058	79309951
	400.perlbench	61.8533	69.8519	78.422	81.6467	11425903	11389779	11202170	11097707
TAGE	403.gcc	85.5172	85.9951	87.2236	89.0868	80540126	80209030	79766975	79398784
	400.perlbench	83.3496	83.4818	85.5783	87.907	10651077	10589517	10557308	10612129

Table 9. Performance statistics for GShare, PAp, TAGE Predictor (Length PC and BHR Changed)

Predictor	Benchmark	Energy			
		N = 1	N = 4	N = 6	N = 8
GShare	403.gcc	2473697.9574	2439608.3146	2411368.8878	2384063.4098
	400.perlbench	337143.1366	338547.5668	336894.8978	324107.833
PAp	403.gcc	2452949.1762	2394376.5798	2335240.717	2321893.436
	400.perlbench	333542.962	332899.9548	329560.5146	327701.0732
TAGE	403.gcc	2343866.1642	2337946.489	2330080.9884	2323536.6162
	400.perlbench	319750.482	318653.5596	318081.971	319057.7848

Table 10. Performance statistics for TAGE Predictor (Sign Bit for Prediction component is Flipped): Significant performance degradations seen for all benchmarks

Benchmark	Prediction accuracy(%)		Clock cycles		Energy	
	Original sign-bit	Flipped sign-bit	Original sign-bit	Flipped sign-bit	Original sign-bit	Flipped sign-bit
403.gcc	85.93	43.4541	80209030	94350717	2337946.489	2589703.342
400.perlbench	83.23	48.7298	10589517	12224435	318653.5596	347757.7936
458.sjeng	99.93	98.5902	283196974	283495606	5515303.7566	5520619.4062

4.2 Experimental Results

We now report our experience of using our methods on the GShare, PAp and TAGE predictors on the benchmarks. Performances are shown in terms of prediction accuracy, number of processor cycles needed and energy consumption. In all the tables, the column labeled as energy shows the dynamic energy expenditure in nanojoules measured by Tejas. We present below the results of our experiments performed for the different predictors using the different attack methodologies on different registers (Tables 1, 2, 3, 4, 5, 6, 7, 8, 9, and 10).

As can be seen from the experimental records, a significant amount of performance and prediction accuracy changes are observed when these attacks are performed.

5 Conclusion and Future Work

In this paper, our experiment shows, how vulnerable a branch predictor can be in response to an attack. We also present a methodology to identify which internal registers can be selected as the target of an attack. Going forward, we plan to do this experiments on more branch predictors and investigate these attacks in real hardware. We will also explore the correlation of our attacks with side channel analysis.

References

1. Burman, S., Mukhopadhyay, D., Veezhinathan, K.: LFSR based stream ciphers are vulnerable to power attacks. In: Srinathan, K., Rangan, C.P., Yung, M. (eds.) INDOCRYPT 2007. LNCS, vol. 4859, pp. 384–392. Springer, Heidelberg (2007)
2. Fog, A.: The microarchitecture of Intel, AMD and VIA CPUs (2011)
3. Kelsey, J., Schneier, B., Wagner, D., Hall, C.: Side channel cryptanalysis of product ciphers. J. Comput. Secur. **8**(2/3), 141–158 (2000)
4. Loh, G.H., Henry, D.S., Krishnamurthy, A.: Exploiting bias in the hysteresis bit of 2-bit saturating counters in branch predictors. J. Instr.-Level Parallelism **5**, 1–32 (2003)
5. Malhotra, G., Aggarwal, P., Sagar, A., Sarangi, S.R.: ParTejas: a parallel simulator for multicore processors. In: ISPASS (2014)
6. McFarling, S.: Combining branch predictors (1993)
7. Pan, S.-T., So, K., Rahmeh, J.T.: Improving the accuracy of dynamic branch prediction using branch correlation. ACM Sigplan Not. **27**(9), 76–84 (1992)
8. Seznec, A.: Analysis of the O-GEometric history length branch predictor. In: ISCA, pp. 394–405 (2005)
9. Seznec, A., Michaud, P.: A case for (partially) tagged geometric history length branch prediction. J. Instr. Level Parallelism **8**, 1–23 (2006)
10. Yeh, T.-Y., Patt, Y.N.: Two-level adaptive training branch prediction. In: MICRO, pp. 51–61 (1991)
11. Yeh, T.-Y., Patt, Y.N.: Alternative implementations of two-level adaptive branch prediction. In: SIGARCH, vol. 20(2), pp. 124–134 (1992)

Privacy-Preserving Decentralized Key-Policy Attribute-Based Encryption Schemes with Fast Decryption

Y. Sreenivasa Rao[✉]

Department of Mathematics, Indian Institute of Technology Kharagpur,
Kharagpur 721302, India
y.sreenivasarao2008@gmail.com

Abstract. We present an efficient decentralized Attribute-Based Encryption (ABE) that supports any Monotone Access Structure (MAS) with faster decryption capability in the key-policy setting. We further extend our MAS construction to Non-Monotone Access Structure (nonMAS) in order to support negative attributes. A notable advantage of our non-MAS construction is that the computation cost during encryption and decryption, and the size of ciphertext are linear to the number of authorities involved in the system, not to the number of attributes used in the respective process unlike existing schemes. In addition, our schemes provide user privacy, enabling any user to obtain secret keys without disclosing its unique identity to the authorities. The security reduction of both the schemes rely on the decisional Bilinear Diffie-Hellman Exponent problem.

Keywords: Key-policy · Decentralized · Attribute-Based · User privacy

1 Introduction

Chase [4] devised the first *collusion-resistant* multi-authority Attribute-Based Encryption (ABE) to address the key escrow problem in single Central Authority (CA) based schemes where the CA is able to decrypt every ciphertext since it holds the system's master secret. However, Chase assumed multiple (attribute) authorities and one fully trusted CA. Consequently, the scheme is subject to the key escrow problem. The first *CA-free* or *decentralized* multi-authority ABE was suggested by Lin et al. [3]. Thereafter, Chase and Chow [1] removed the functionality of the CA from [4]. Interestingly, they addressed the notion of *user privacy*, where the authority cannot get any information regarding user's identity during key generation phase. Han et al. [2] proposed a novel decentralized multi-authority ABE with user privacy, where all authorities work independently. However, Ge et al. [6] showed that this scheme is vulnerable to collusion attacks. All the above multi-authority ABE are in key-policy setting (termed as KP-ABE) that support only threshold policies and selectively secure under decisional Bilinear Diffie-Hellman (dBDH) problem. Li et al. [5] introduced a decentralized KP-ABE for expressive Non-Monotone Access Structure (nonMAS), the

S. Jajodia and C. Mazumdar (Eds.): ICISS 2015, LNCS 9478, pp. 521–531, 2015.
DOI: 10.1007/978-3-319-26961-0_31

Table 1. Comparison of computation cost and ciphertext-size

		Key generation	Encryption	Decryption		Ciphertext-Size
		Exp.	Exp.	Exp.	Pair	
MAS	[3]	$\mathcal{O}(N\cdot\phi_k)$	$\mathcal{O}(N\cdot\phi_c)$	$\mathcal{O}(N\cdot\phi_d)$	$\mathcal{O}(N\cdot\phi_d)$	$B_{\mathbb{G}_T}+\mathcal{O}(N\cdot\phi_c)\cdot B_{\mathbb{G}}$
	[2]	$\mathcal{O}(N\cdot\phi_k)$	$\mathcal{O}(N\cdot\phi_c)$	$\mathcal{O}(N\cdot\phi_d)$	$\mathcal{O}(N\cdot\phi_d)$	$B_{\mathbb{G}_T}+\mathcal{O}(N\cdot\phi_c)\cdot B_{\mathbb{G}}$
	[1]	$\mathcal{O}(N^2+N\cdot\phi_k)$	$\mathcal{O}(N\cdot\phi_c)$	$\mathcal{O}(N\cdot\phi_d)$	$\mathcal{O}(N\cdot\phi_d)$	$B_{\mathbb{G}_T}+\mathcal{O}(N\cdot\phi_c)\cdot B_{\mathbb{G}_2}$
	Our	$\mathcal{O}(N^2+N\cdot\phi_k^2)$	$\mathcal{O}(N\cdot\phi_c)$	-	$\mathcal{O}(N)$	$B_{\mathbb{G}_T}+B_{\mathbb{G}_2}+\mathcal{O}(N\cdot\phi_c)\cdot B_{\mathbb{G}_1}$
nonMAS	[5]	$\mathcal{O}(N^2+N\cdot\overline{n}^2)$	$\mathcal{O}(N\cdot\phi_c)$	$\mathcal{O}(N\cdot\phi_c)$	$\mathcal{O}(N)$	$B_{\mathbb{G}_T}+B_{\mathbb{G}_2}+\mathcal{O}(1)\cdot B_{\mathbb{G}_1}$
	Our	$\mathcal{O}(N^2+N\cdot u_{max}^2)$	$\mathcal{O}(N)$	-	$\mathcal{O}(N)$	$B_{\mathbb{G}_T}+B_{\mathbb{G}_2}+\mathcal{O}(N)\cdot B_{\mathbb{G}_1}$

N = number of authorities, ϕ_k = maximum number of attributes that user holds from each authority, ϕ_c = maximum number of ciphertext attributes from each authority, ϕ_d = minimum number of attributes required for decryption from each authority, $\overline{n}$ = maximum bound for the number of ciphertext attributes $(N\cdot\phi_c\leq\overline{n})$ and u_{max} = maximum number of attributes managed by every authority and $B_{\mathbb{D}}$ = bit size of an element in a group $\mathbb{D}$, where $\mathbb{D}\in\{\mathbb{G}_1,\mathbb{G}_2,\mathbb{G}_T\}$.

selective security of which relies on decisional Bilinear Diffie-Hellman Exponent (dBDHE) assumption.

Our Contribution: In this article, we focus on constructing a decentralized KP-ABE inspired by [1] with lower computation cost during encryption and decryption, still realizing expressive access policies. We first propose a decentralized KP-ABE that works for monotone access structure (MAS). In our construction, the key generation algorithm generates user personalized secret key (other than attribute related keys) jointly by conducting *anonymous key issuing protocol* (AKIP) following [1] between user and authorities, whereas the attribute secret keys are computed solely according to Linear Secret-Sharing Scheme (LSSS) realizable MAS over user attributes. Our scheme leads to better decryption efficiency than previous schemes [1–3] as illustrated in Table 1. More precisely, the proposed scheme executes only $2N+1$ pairings to decrypt any ciphertext, thus computation cost is independent of the number of underlying attributes, where N is the number of authorities. This is significantly better than the decryption requirements for existing schemes which consist of $\mathcal{O}(N\cdot\phi_d)$ exponentiations and $\mathcal{O}(N\cdot\phi_d)$ pairings. Here ϕ_d is the minimum number of attributes required for decryption from each authority. The complexity of encryption is similar to that of [1–3]. However, the size of secret key increases by a factor of ϕ_k, the maximum number of attributes that user holds from each authority. The security holds under dBDHE assumption in the selective model.

We further extend the decentralized KP-ABE for MAS employing the technique that represents nonMASs in terms of MASs with negative attributes. The selective security of this scheme is proved under dBDHE assumption. The construction in [5] for nonMAS achieves constant-size ciphertext. However, the encryption and decryption are very costly in terms of exponentiations due to the fact that the scheme additionally requires $\mathcal{O}(N\cdot\phi_c)$ exponentiations to encrypt a message or decrypt a ciphertext, where ϕ_c is maximum number of attributes from each authority listed in ciphertext. As illustrated in Tables 1 and 2, the proposed new schemes are of independent interest as they exhibit

Table 2. Comparison of different properties

		AAs communication during setup	User privacy	Access structure	Security model	Assumption
MAS	[3]	Yes	No	Threshold	Selective	dBDH
	[2]	No	Yes	Threshold	Selective	dBDH
	[1]	Yes	Yes	Threshold	Selective	dBDH
	Our	Yes	Yes	LSSS realizable	Selective	dBDHE
nonMAS	[5], Our	Yes	Yes	LSSS realizable	Selective	dBDHE

AA = attribute authority and dBDH(E) = decisional Bilinear Diffie-Hellman (Exponent).

significant performance in terms of both computation and communication overhead than the best known solutions [1–3,5] so far with similar security levels.

2 Preliminaries

Notation: $x \in_R X$ denote x is randomly selected from the set X, $[N] = \{1, 2, \ldots, N\}$, $[N \setminus j] = [N] \setminus \{j\}$ and $[N \setminus j_1, j_2] = [N] \setminus \{j_1, j_2\}$.

Access Structure. Let U be the universe of attributes. Let $\mathcal{P}(U)$ be the collection of all subsets of U. Every non-empty subset of $\mathcal{P}(U) \setminus \{\emptyset\}$ is called an *access structure*. An access structure $\mathbb{A}$ is said to be *monotone access structure* (MAS) if $\{C \in \mathcal{P}(U) : C \supseteq B, \text{ for some } B \in \mathbb{A}\} \subseteq \mathbb{A}$.

Linear Secret-Sharing Scheme (LSSS). A secret-sharing scheme $\Pi_{\mathbb{A}}$ for the access structure $\mathbb{A}$ over U is called *linear* (in $\mathbb{Z}_p$) if $\Pi_{\mathbb{A}}$ consists of the following two polynomial-time algorithms, where $\mathbb{M}$ is a matrix of size $\ell \times \tau$, called the *share-generating matrix* for $\Pi_{\mathbb{A}}$ and $\rho : [\ell] \to I_U$ is a row labeling function that maps each row of $\mathbb{M}$ to an attribute in $\mathbb{A}$, I_U being the index set of U.

- Distribute($\mathbb{M}, \rho, \alpha$): This algorithm takes as input the share-generating matrix $\mathbb{M}$, row labeling function ρ and a secret $\alpha \in \mathbb{Z}_p$ which is to be shared. It randomly selects $z_2, z_3, \ldots, z_\tau \in_R \mathbb{Z}_p$ and sets $v = (\alpha, z_2, z_3, \ldots, z_\tau) \in \mathbb{Z}_p^\tau$. It outputs a set $\{\boldsymbol{M}_i \cdot v : i \in [\ell]\}$ of ℓ shares, where $\boldsymbol{M}_i \in \mathbb{Z}_p^\tau$ is the i-th row of matrix $\mathbb{M}$. The share $\lambda_{\rho(i)} = \boldsymbol{M}_i \cdot v$ belongs to an attribute $\rho(i)$.
- Reconstruct($\mathbb{M}, \rho, W$): This algorithm will accept as input $\mathbb{M}, \rho$ and a set of attributes $W \in \mathbb{A}$. Let $I = \{i \in [\ell] : \rho(i) \in I_W\}$, where I_W is index set of the attribute set W. It returns a set $\{\omega_i : i \in I\}$ of secret reconstruction constants such that $\sum_{i \in I} \omega_i \lambda_{\rho(i)} = \alpha$, if $\{\lambda_{\rho(i)} : i \in I\}$ is a valid set of shares of the secret α according to $\Pi_{\mathbb{A}}$.

Bilinear Maps. Let $\mathbb{G}_1, \mathbb{G}_2, \mathbb{G}_T$ be multiplicative cyclic groups of same prime order p and g_1, g_2 be generators of $\mathbb{G}_1, \mathbb{G}_2$, respectively. A mapping $e : \mathbb{G}_1 \times \mathbb{G}_2 \to \mathbb{G}_T$ is said to be *bilinear* if $e(u^a, v^b) = e(u, v)^{ab}$, for all $u \in \mathbb{G}_1, v \in \mathbb{G}_2$ and $a, b \in \mathbb{Z}_p$ and non-degenerate if $e(g_1, g_2) \neq 1_T$, where 1_T is the unit element in $\mathbb{G}_T$. Let $F_{2,1} : \mathbb{G}_2 \to \mathbb{G}_1$ be efficiently computable isomorphisms with $F_{2,1}(g_2) = g_1$.

User u (with ID)		Authority A (with α, β, γ)
1. $\vartheta_1 \in_R \mathbb{Z}_p$	$\xrightarrow{\quad 2PC \quad}$	$\sigma = (\beta + \text{ID})\vartheta_1$
2.	$\xleftarrow{B_1, B_2, \text{PoK}(\alpha, \tau, \sigma)}$	$\tau \in_R \mathbb{Z}_p, B_1 = g^{\tau/\sigma}, B_2 = h^{\alpha\tau}$
3. $\vartheta_2 \in_R \mathbb{Z}_p, \widetilde{B} = (B_1^{\vartheta_1} B_2)^{\vartheta_2}$	$\xrightarrow{\widetilde{B}, \text{PoK}(\vartheta_2)}$	
4.	$\xleftarrow{\widetilde{B}', \text{PoK}(\gamma, \tau)}$	$\widetilde{B}' = \widetilde{B}^{\gamma/\tau}$
5. $D = (\widetilde{B}')^{1/\vartheta_2} = (h^\alpha g^{1/(\beta+\text{ID})})^\gamma$		

Fig. 1. Anonymous key issuing protocol (AKIP) [1]

We employ the following anonymous key issuing protocol from [1] to achieve user privacy.

Anonymous Key Issuing Protocol (AKIP). In this protocol, a user u with identity $\text{ID} \in \mathbb{Z}_p$ (which is treated as its secret value) and an authority A with secret parameters $\alpha, \beta, \gamma \in \mathbb{Z}_p$ are jointly compute the term $D = (h^\alpha g^{1/(\beta+\text{ID})})^\gamma$ for commonly known $g, h \in \mathbb{G}_1$. Only the user receives the final output D. The protocol is presented in Fig. 1, where PoK denotes a proof of knowledge of the secret values used in the computation and the statements being proved are omitted for simplicity. The overview of the protocol is as follows.

1. The user u and the authority A engage in a secure (arithmetic) 2PC protocol that takes (ID, ϑ_1) from u and β from A, and sends the secret output $\sigma = (\beta + \text{ID})\vartheta_1$ to A.
2. A samples $\tau \in_R \mathbb{Z}_p$ and computes $B_1 = g^{\tau/\sigma}, B_2 = h^{\alpha\tau}$. A sends (B_1, B_2) to the user and proves that it knows (α, τ, σ) in zero-knowledge.
3. If the proof is correct, u selects $\vartheta_2 \in_R \mathbb{Z}_p$ and sends $\widetilde{B} = (B_1^{\vartheta_1} B_2)^{\vartheta_2}$ to the authority. The user proves that it knows ϑ_2 to A in zero-knowledge.
4. Again, if the proof is correct, A sends $\widetilde{B}' = \widetilde{B}^{\gamma/\tau}$ and proves that it knows (γ, τ) to u in zero-knowledge.
5. If the proof is correct, the user can compute its secret key $D = (\widetilde{B}')^{1/\vartheta_2} = (h^\alpha g^{1/(\beta+\text{ID})})^\gamma$.

3 Our Decentralized KP-ABE Scheme for MAS

In this section, we present a decentralized KP-ABE construction that uses LSSS realizable access structures to generate attribute related user secret keys adapting the multi-authority framework of [1].

A decentralized KP-ABE system is composed mainly of a set $\mathcal{A}$ of authorities, a trusted initializer (TI) and users. The *only* responsibility of TI is generation of system global public parameters GP once during system initialization, which are system wide public parameters available to every entity in the system. We fix the set of authorities involved in the system ahead of time.

All authorities pairwise communicate once in the initial system setup to decide on system public parameters PubK. Each authority $A_j \in \mathcal{A}$ controls a different set U^j of attributes and issues corresponding secret attribute keys to users. Each user in the system is identified with a unique global identity ID and is allowed to request secret attribute keys from the different authorities. To achieve *user privacy* while obtaining secret key from authorities, each user performs the *anonymous key issuing protocol* (AKIP) [1] with the authority and gets personalized secret key (other than attribute keys) without exposing its identity ID to the authority. Consequently, *key escrow* is eliminated as multiple authorities together cannot recognize the complete key structure of any user in the system and hence unable to decrypt any ciphertext. This makes our scheme user privacy-preserving. On the other hand, the attribute secret keys are computed solely by authority according to suitable access structure.

Let $\mathcal{A} = \{A_1, A_2, \ldots, A_N\}$ be the set of authorities participated in the system and $U^j = \{a_{j,t}\}$ be the set of attributes managed by the authority A_j. In the attribute $a_{j,t} \in U^j$, the subscript j indicates an identifier of the controlling authority A_j and t denotes the index of the attribute within the set U^j. Let the user identity space be $\mathbb{Z}_p$. Secure communication channels are assumed between every pair of authorities $(A_j, A_k), j, k \in [N]$. Our N-authority decentralized KP-ABE scheme is a set of the following five algorithms that works as described below.

System Initialization$(\kappa, \mathcal{A})$: The TI generates global public parameters GP $= (p, \mathbb{G}_1, g_1, \mathbb{G}_2, g_2, \mathbb{G}_T, e, F_{2,1})$ according to the implicit security parameter κ and are made available to every entity in the system.

- Each authority A_j samples $\alpha_j \in_R \mathbb{Z}_p$ and transmits $Y_j = e(g_1, g_2)^{\alpha_j}$ to all other authorities. Consequently, every authority individually can compute $Y = \prod_{j \in [N]} Y_j = e(g_1, g_2)^{\sum_{j \in [N]} \alpha_j}$ which, with some randomness, is used to bind every message in the system.
- In addition, each A_j picks $x_j \in_R \mathbb{Z}_p$ and sets $y_j = g_1^{x_j}$. The parameter y_j is made public and x_j is kept secret by A_j.
- Every pair (A_j, A_k) of authorities agrees on a pseudorandom function (PRF) seed s_{jk}, defined as $s_{jk} = s_{kj}$, via a 2-party key exchange protocol that is only known to them but not to any other $A_i \notin \{A_j, A_k\}$. Define a PRF, $\mathsf{PRF}_{jk}(\xi) = g_1^{x_j x_k/(s_{jk} + \xi)}$. The authority A_j can compute the PRF as $\mathsf{PRF}_{jk}(\xi) = y_k^{x_j/(s_{jk} + \xi)}$, while the same for A_k is $\mathsf{PRF}_{kj}(\xi) = y_j^{x_k/(s_{kj} + \xi)}$. Note that $\mathsf{PRF}_{jk}(\xi) = \mathsf{PRF}_{kj}(\xi)$ provided $s_{jk} = s_{kj}$. Consequently, $\mathsf{PRF}_{jk}(\xi)$ is computable only by A_j and A_k which have the common PRF seed s_{jk}.
- The system public parameters are published as PubK $= \langle$GP$, Y, y_1, y_2, \ldots, y_N \rangle$ and each authority A_j keeps MkA$_j = \langle \alpha_j, x_j, \{s_{jk} : k \in [N \setminus j]\} \rangle$ as its master secret key. (Note that the parameters $\{y_j : j \in [N]\}$ are only used by the authorities in order to compute PRFs.)

Authority Setup(GP$, U^j$): Every authority runs autonomously this algorithm during system setup. Each $A_j \in \mathcal{A}$ controls a set of attributes U^j. For each attribute $a_{j,t} \in U^j$, A_j selects $h_{j,t} \in_R \mathbb{G}_1$ and outputs its public key as $\mathsf{PubA}_j = \{h_{j,t} : a_{j,t} \in U^j\}$.

Authority KeyGen($\mathsf{PubK}, \mathsf{ID}, (\mathbb{M}_j, \rho_j), \mathsf{MkA}_j$)**:** It is performed in two phases.

Personalized Secret Key Generation. Similar to [1], when a user u wishes to obtain the decryption key from A_j without revealing its identity $\mathsf{ID} \in \mathbb{Z}_p$ to the authority, it performs AKIP executions with A_j for each authority $k \in [N \setminus j]$, and obtains the personalized secret key component D_{jk} which is an output of the AKIP for $g = y_k^{x_j}, h = g_1, \alpha = \delta_{jk} R_{jk}, \beta = s_{jk}, \gamma = \delta_{jk}$, where $R_{jk} \in_R \mathbb{Z}_p$ is sampled by A_j and $\delta_{jk} = 1$ if $j > k$ and -1 otherwise. Hence,

$$D_{jk} = \begin{cases} g_1^{R_{jk}} \cdot y_k^{x_j/(s_{jk}+\mathsf{ID})} = g_1^{R_{jk}} \cdot \mathsf{PRF}_{jk}(\mathsf{ID}), & \text{if } j > k, \\ g_1^{R_{jk}} / y_k^{x_j/(s_{jk}+\mathsf{ID})} = g_1^{R_{jk}} / \mathsf{PRF}_{jk}(\mathsf{ID}), & \text{if } j < k. \end{cases}$$

Finally, the user with identity ID gets its personalized secret key as $\widetilde{D}_j = \{D_{jk} : k \in [N \setminus j]\}$ from the authority A_j.

Attribute Secret Key Generation. Authority A_j creates a LSSS realizable access structure $(\mathbb{M}_j, \rho_j)$ over the attribute set U^j according to the role of user in the system and computes the attribute secret keys as follows. Here $\mathbb{M}_j$ is a share-generating matrix of size, say, $\ell_j \times \tau_j$ and ρ_j is a mapping from each row i of $\mathbb{M}_j$ (denoted as $\boldsymbol{M}_{j,i}$) to an attribute $a_{j,\rho_j(i)}$.

- Set $\alpha_{j,\mathsf{ID}} = \alpha_j - \sum_{k \in [N \setminus j]} R_{jk}$ as its master secret share for the user with identity ID.
- Run Distribute($\mathbb{M}_j, \rho_j, \alpha_{j,\mathsf{ID}}$) and obtain a set $\{\lambda_{\rho_j(i)} = \boldsymbol{M}_{j,i} \cdot \boldsymbol{v}_j : i \in [\ell_j]\}$ of ℓ_j shares one for each row of $\mathbb{M}_j$, where $\boldsymbol{v}_j \in_R \mathbb{Z}_p^{\tau_j}$ such that $\boldsymbol{v}_j \cdot \boldsymbol{1} = \alpha_{j,\mathsf{ID}}$, $\boldsymbol{1} = (1, 0, \ldots, 0)$ being a vector of length τ_j.
- For each row $i \in [\ell_j]$, select $r_{j,i} \in_R \mathbb{Z}_p$ and compute $B_{j,i} = g_1^{\lambda_{\rho_j(i)}} h_{j,\rho_j(i)}^{r_{j,i}}$,

$$B'_{j,i} = g_2^{r_{j,i}}, B''_{j,i} = \{B''_{j,i,t} : B''_{j,i,t} = h_{j,t}^{r_{j,i}}, \forall a_{j,t} \in L_j \setminus \{a_{j,\rho_j(i)}\}\},$$

where L_j is the set of attributes used in the access structure $(\mathbb{M}_j, \rho_j)$.
- Set $\mathsf{SK}_{(\mathbb{M}_j,\rho_j)} = \langle (\mathbb{M}_j, \rho_j), \{B_{j,i}, B'_{j,i}, B''_{j,i} : i \in [\ell_j]\} \rangle$ and send the secret key $\mathsf{SK}_{(\mathbb{M}_j,\rho_j)}$ to the user u with identity ID.

Let $\mathsf{SK}_{j,\mathsf{ID}} = \langle \widetilde{D}_j, \mathsf{SK}_{(\mathbb{M}_j,\rho_j)} \rangle$ be the secret key of a user u with identity ID received from the authority A_j. After receiving all $\{\mathsf{SK}_{j,\mathsf{ID}} : j \in [N]\}$, the user u computes

$$D_{\mathsf{ID}} = \prod_{j \in [N]} \prod_{D_{jk} \in \widetilde{D}_j} D_{jk} = \prod_{(j,k) \in [N] \times [N \setminus j]} D_{jk} = g_1^{\sum_{(j,k) \in [N] \times [N \setminus j]} R_{jk}}.$$

All the PRF terms are cancelled due to the choice of δ_{jk} and finally the user obtains its whole secret key as $\mathsf{SK}_{\mathsf{ID}} = \langle D_{\mathsf{ID}}, \{\mathsf{SK}_{(\mathbb{M}_j,\rho_j)} : j \in [N]\} \rangle$.

Encrypt($\mathsf{PubK}, M, W, \{\mathsf{PubA}_j\}_{j \in [N]}$)**:** To encrypt a message $M \in \mathbb{G}_T$ under a set of attributes $W = \{W_1, W_2, \ldots, W_N\}$, where $W_j \subset U^j$, the encryptor samples $s \in_R \mathbb{Z}_p$ and constructs a ciphertext $\mathsf{CT} = \langle W, C, C_1, \{C_{2,j} : j \in [N]\}\rangle$ using system public parameters and public key of each authority by setting $C = MY^s, C_1 = g_2^s, C_{2,j} = \{C_{2,j,t} : C_{2,j,t} = h_{j,t}^s, \forall a_{j,t} \in W_j\}$.

Decrypt$(\mathsf{GP}, \mathsf{CT}, \mathsf{SK}_{\mathsf{ID}})$: When a decryptor with identity ID receives a ciphertext CT, the decryptor first checks whether each access structure $(\mathbb{M}_j, \rho_j)$ associated with its secret key $\mathsf{SK}_{\mathsf{ID}}$ accepts the corresponding attribute set W_j embedded in CT. If some $(\mathbb{M}_j, \rho_j)$ is not satisfied by respective W_j, decryption will fail. Otherwise, the decryptor performs the following steps for each $A_j, j \in [N]$.

- run $\mathsf{Reconstruct}(\mathbb{M}_j, \rho_j, W_j)$ and obtain a set $\{\omega_{j,i} : i \in I_j\}$ of secret reconstruction constants, where $I_j = \{i \in [\ell_j] : a_{j,\rho_j(i)} \in W_j\}$. Note that since W_j satisfies the access structure $(\mathbb{M}_j, \rho_j)$, $\sum_{i \in I_j} \omega_{j,i} \lambda_{\rho_j(i)} = \alpha_{j,\mathsf{ID}} = \alpha_j - \sum_{k \in [N \setminus j]} R_{jk}$. The secret shares $\{\lambda_{\rho_j(i)}\}_{i \in I_j}$ are not known to the decryptor.
- compute $E_{1,j} = \prod_{i \in I_j} \left(B_{j,i} \cdot \prod_{a_{j,t} \in W_j', t \neq \rho_j(i)} B_{j,i,t}''\right)^{\omega_{j,i}}$, $E_{2,j} = \prod_{i \in I_j} (B_{j,i}')^{\omega_{j,i}}$, $C_{2,j}' = \prod_{a_{j,t} \in W_j'} C_{2,j,t}$, where $W_j' = \{a_{j,t} \in W_j : \exists i \in I_j \ni \rho_j(i) = t\}$.
- extract $Z_j = e(g_1, g_2)^{s(\alpha_j - \sum_{k \in [N \setminus j]} R_{jk})}$ by computing $e(E_{1,j}, C_1)/e(C_{2,j}', E_{2,j})$.

Finally, the message M is recovered by computing $\dfrac{C}{e(D_{\mathsf{ID}}, C_1) \cdot \prod_{j \in [N]} Z_j} = M$.

Note that for boolean formulas, $\omega_{j,i}$ are either 0 or 1 and hence the decryption is free from exponentiations.

Correctness. For each $j \in [N]$, W_j satisfies $(\mathbb{M}_j, \rho_j)$, we have $\sum_{i \in I_j} \omega_{j,i} \lambda_{\rho_j(i)} = \alpha_j - \sum_{k \in [N \setminus j]} R_{jk}$.

$$E_{1,j} = \prod_{i \in I_j} \left(g_1^{\lambda_{\rho_j(i)}} h_{j, \rho_j(i)}^{r_{j,i}} \cdot \prod_{a_{j,l} \in W_j', t \neq \rho_j(i)} h_{j,t}^{r_{j,i}}\right)^{\omega_{j,i}}$$

$$= g_1^{\sum_{i \in I_j} \omega_{j,i} \lambda_{\rho_j(i)}} \prod_{i \in I_j} \left(\prod_{a_{j,t} \in W_j'} h_{j,t}^{r_{j,i}}\right)^{\omega_{j,i}} = g_1^{\alpha_j - \sum_{k \in [N \setminus j]} R_{jk}} \left(\prod_{a_{j,t} \in W_j'} h_{j,t}\right)^{\sum_{i \in I_j} r_{j,i} \omega_{j,i}}$$

$$E_{2,j} = \prod_{i \in I_j} (B_{j,i}')^{\omega_{j,i}} = \prod_{i \in I_j} g_2^{r_{j,i} \omega_{j,i}} = g_2^{\sum_{i \in I_j} r_{j,i} \omega_{j,i}}$$

$$C_{2,j}' = \prod_{a_{j,t} \in W_j'} C_{2,j,t} = \prod_{a_{j,t} \in W_j'} h_{j,t}^s = \left(\prod_{a_{j,t} \in W_j'} h_{j,t}\right)^s$$

$$Z_j = \frac{e(E_{1,j}, C_1)}{e(C_{2,j}', E_{2,j})} = e(g_1, g_2)^{s(\alpha_j - \sum_{k \in [N \setminus j]} R_{jk})}$$

$$\frac{C}{e(D_{\mathsf{ID}}, C_1) \cdot \prod_{j \in [N]} Z_j} = \frac{MY^s}{e(g_1^{\sum_{(j,k) \in [N] \times [N \setminus j]} R_{jk}}, g_2^s) \cdot \prod_{j \in [N]} e(g_1, g_2)^{s(\alpha_j - \sum_{k \in [N \setminus j]} R_{jk})}}$$

$$= \frac{M \cdot e(g_1, g_2)^{s \sum_{j \in [N]} \alpha_j}}{\prod_{j \in [N]} e(g_1, g_2)^{s \alpha_j}} = M.$$

3.1   Proof of Security

The following selective ciphertext indistinguishability under chosen plaintext attack (IND-CPA) security game is similar to the one described in [1,2]. The challenger plays the role of all authorities and answers the adversary's queries by executing relevant algorithms of N-authority KP-ABE system as follows.

Init. The adversary ADV announces an attribute set $W^* = \{W_1^*, W_2^*, \ldots, W_N^*\}$, where $W_j^* \subset U^j$, and a set of corrupt authorities $\mathcal{A}_{corr} \subset \mathcal{A}$. Let I_{corr} be the index set of $\mathcal{A}_{corr}$, i.e., $I_{corr} \subset [N]$.

Setup. The challenger $\mathcal{C}$ performs System Initialization and Authority Setup algorithms of KP-ABE, and sends the information including PubK, $\{\mathsf{PubA}_j\}_{j\in[N]}$, $\{\mathsf{MkA}_j\}_{j\in I_{corr}}$ to ADV.

Key Query Phase 1. The adversary ADV can request secret keys for the sets of access structures coupled with user global identities such as $(\mathsf{ID}_1, \{\mathbb{A}_{1,j}\}_{j\in[N]})$, $(\mathsf{ID}_2, \{\mathbb{A}_{2,j}\}_{j\in[N]}), \ldots, (\mathsf{ID}_{q_1}, \{\mathbb{A}_{q_1,j}\}_{j\in[N]})$ with the restriction that for each secret key query $(\mathsf{ID}_r, \{\mathbb{A}_{r,j}\}_{j\in[N]})$, there must be at least one *honest* authority $A_k \in \mathcal{A} \setminus \mathcal{A}_{corr}$ such that W_k^* does not satisfy $\mathbb{A}_{r,k}$.

Challenge. ADV sends two equal length messages M_0 and M_1 to $\mathcal{C}$. The challenger flips a random coin $\mu \in \{0,1\}$ and encrypts M_μ under W^*. The resulting challenge ciphertext CT^* is given to ADV.

Key Query Phase 2. The adversary can obtain more secret keys for user identity, set of access structures pairs $(\mathsf{ID}_{q_1+1}, \{\mathbb{A}_{q_1+1,j}\}_{j\in[N]})$, $(\mathsf{ID}_{q_1+2}, \{\mathbb{A}_{q_1+2,j}\}_{j\in[N]})$, $\ldots, (\mathsf{ID}_q, \{\mathbb{A}_{q,j}\}_{j\in[N]})$ subject to same constraint stated in Key Query Phase 1.

Guess. ADV outputs a guess bit $\mu' \in \{0,1\}$ for μ and wins if $\mu' = \mu$.

The advantage of an adversary in the above selective IND-CPA game is defined to be $|\Pr[\mu' = \mu] - \frac{1}{2}|$, where the probability is taken over all random coin tosses of both adversary and challenger.

Definition 1. An N-authority KP-ABE system is said to be $(\mathcal{T}, n, q_{\mathsf{SK}}, \epsilon)$-IND-sCPA secure if all $\mathcal{T}$-time adversaries corrupting at most n $(n < N)$ authorities that make at most q_{SK} secret key queries have advantage at most ϵ in the above selective IND-CPA game.

The proofs of the following theorems will be given in full version of this paper.

Theorem 1. *If each honest authority controls at most m attributes, then our N-authority decentralized KP-ABE system is $(\mathcal{T}, N-2, q_{\mathsf{SK}}, \epsilon)$-IND-sCPA secure, assuming that the decisional m-BDHE problem in $(\mathbb{G}_1, \mathbb{G}_2, \mathbb{G}_T)$ is $(\mathcal{T}', \epsilon/2)$-hard. Where $\mathcal{T}' = \mathcal{T} + \mathcal{O}\left(N \cdot \Gamma + q_{\mathsf{SK}} \cdot (N^2 + N \cdot \ell_{max}^2)\right) \cdot \mathcal{T}_{exp} + 5 \cdot \mathcal{T}_{pair}$, here $\Gamma = max\{m, |U^j| : A_j$ is a corrupt authority\}, ℓ_{max} is the maximum number of attributes queried by the adversary for all authorities among all secret key queries, $\mathcal{T}_{exp}$ denotes the maximum of running time for an exponentiation in $\mathbb{G}_1$ and that in $\mathbb{G}_2$, and $\mathcal{T}_{pair}$ denotes the running time of one pairing in $\mathbb{G}_T$.*

Theorem 2. [1] *The AKIP is a secure 2PC protocol for computing the component* $D = (h^{\alpha}g^{1/(\beta+\text{ID})})^{\gamma}$, *assuming the underlying (arithmetic) 2PC and zero-knowledge proofs are secure. It is also secure against corrupt user under the eXternal Diffie-Hellman (XDH) assumption.*

From Theorems 1 and 2, we have the following theorem.

Theorem 3. *Our N-authority privacy-preserving decentralized KP-ABE construction for MAS is secure in the selective security model when at most $N - 2$ authorities are corrupted, under m-BDHE and XDH assumptions, and the assumption that the underlying (arithmetic) 2PC and zero-knowledge proofs are secure.*

4   Our Decentralized KP-ABE Scheme for nonMAS

In order to handle *negative* attributes in user's secret key policy, called as Non-Monotone Access Structure (nonMAS), we exploit the technique that represents nonMASs in terms of MASs with negative attributes. We denote the negative attribute of a (positive) attribute iciss as ¬iciss. Let U be a set of positive attributes.

Given a family $\mathfrak{F} = \{\Pi_{\mathbb{A}} : \mathbb{A} \in \text{MA}\}$ of LSSSs for a set MA of possible MASs and $\widetilde{U} = U \bigcup \{\neg a : a \in U\}$ is the underlying attribute universe for each MAS $\mathbb{A} \in \text{MA}$, a family NM of nonMASs can be defined as follows. For each access structure $\mathbb{A} \in \text{MA}$ over $\widetilde{U}$, one defines a possibly nonMAS $\text{N}_{\mathbb{A}}$ over U in the following way–(i) For every set $W \subset U$, set $\text{N}(W) = W \bigcup \{\neg a : a \in U \setminus W\} \subset \widetilde{U}$. (ii) Define $\text{N}_{\mathbb{A}}$ by saying that W satisfies $\text{N}_{\mathbb{A}}$ iff $\text{N}(W)$ satisfies $\mathbb{A}$, i.e., $W \models \text{N}_{\mathbb{A}}$ iff $\text{N}(W) \models \mathbb{A}$. The family of nonMASs is $\text{NM} = \{\text{N}_{\mathbb{A}} : \Pi_{\mathbb{A}} \in \mathfrak{F}\}$. The nonMAS $\text{N}_{\mathbb{A}}$ will have only positive attributes in its access sets.

System Initialization($\kappa, \mathcal{A}$)**:** We refer to System Initialization in Sect. 3.

Authority Setup(GP, U^j)**:** For each attribute $a_{j,t} \in U^j$, A_j selects $h_{j,t}, h'_{j,t}, \in_R \mathbb{G}_1$ and outputs its public key as $\text{PubA}_j = \{h_{j,t}, h'_{j,t}, : a_{j,t} \in U^j\}$.

Authority KeyGen($\text{PubK}, \text{ID}, \widetilde{\mathbb{A}}_j, \text{MkA}_j$)**:** This is similar to Authority KeyGen of MAS construction given in Sect. 3, but the attribute secret key generation is performed *differently* as described subsequently. The authority A_j

- creates a nonMAS $\widetilde{\mathbb{A}}_j$ such that $\widetilde{\mathbb{A}}_j = \text{N}_{\mathbb{A}_j}$ for some MAS $\mathbb{A}_j$ over the attribute set $\widetilde{U}^j = \{a_{j,t}, \neg a_{j,t} : a_{j,t} \in U^j\}$ and associated with a LSSS $\Pi_{\mathbb{A}_j} = (\mathbb{M}_j, \rho_j)$, where $\mathbb{M}_j$ is a matrix of size $\ell_j \times \tau_j$ and the mapping ρ_j assigns each row i of $\mathbb{M}_j$, $\boldsymbol{M}_{j,i}$ to an attribute $\widetilde{a}_{j,\rho_j(i)} \in \{a_{j,\rho_j(i)}, \neg a_{j,\rho_j(i)}\}$.
- calls Distribute($\mathbb{M}_j, \rho_j, \alpha_{j,\text{ID}}$), where $\alpha_{j,\text{ID}} = \alpha_j - \sum_{k \in [N \setminus j]} R_{jk}$, and obtains $\{\lambda_{\rho_j(i)} = \boldsymbol{M}_{j,i} \cdot \boldsymbol{v}_j : i \in [\ell_j]\}$, where $\boldsymbol{v}_j \in_R \mathbb{Z}_p^{\tau_j}$ such that $\boldsymbol{v}_j \cdot \boldsymbol{1} = \alpha_{j,\text{ID}}$.
- samples $r_{j,i} \in_R \mathbb{Z}_p$ for each row $i \in [\ell_j]$ and compute $B_{j,i} = g_1^{\lambda_{\rho_j(i)}} \widetilde{h}_{j,\rho_j(i)}^{r_{j,i}}$, $B'_{j,i} = g_2^{r_{j,i}}, B''_{j,i} = \{B''_{j,i,t} : B''_{j,i,t} = \widetilde{h}_{j,t}^{r_{j,i}}, \forall a_{j,t} \in U^j \setminus \{a_{j,\rho_j(i)}\}\}$,

  where, for each $a_{j,t} \in U^j$, $\widetilde{h}_{j,t} = \begin{cases} h_{j,t}, \text{ if } \widetilde{a}_{j,\rho_j(i)} = a_{j,\rho_j(i)}, \\ h'_{j,t}, \text{ if } \widetilde{a}_{j,\rho_j(i)} = \neg a_{j,\rho_j(i)}. \end{cases}$

- sets $\mathsf{SK}_{\widetilde{\mathbb{A}}_j} = \langle \widetilde{\mathbb{A}}_j, \{B_{j,i}, B'_{j,i}, B''_{j,i} : i \in [\ell_j]\}\rangle$ and send the secret key $\mathsf{SK}_{\widetilde{\mathbb{A}}_j}$ to the user u with identity ID.

Encrypt($\mathsf{PubK}, M, W, \{\mathsf{PubA}_j\}_{j\in[N]}$): To encrypt a message $M \in \mathbb{G}_T$ for $W = \{W_1, W_2, \ldots, W_N\}$, where $W_j \subset U^j$, the encryptor chooses $s \in_R \mathbb{Z}_p$ and computes $C = MY^s, C_1 = g_2^s, C_{2,j} = \left(\prod_{a_{j,t}\in W_j} h_{j,t}\right)^s, C_{3,j} = \left(\prod_{a_{j,t}\in W_j} h'_{j,t}\right)^s, \forall j \in [N]$. The ciphertext is $\mathsf{CT} = \langle W, C, C_1, \{C_{2,j}, C_{3,j} : j \in [N]\}\rangle$.

Note that the size of ciphertext is $B_{\mathbb{G}_T} + B_{\mathbb{G}_2} + 2N \cdot B_{\mathbb{G}_1}$ which is independent of the number of attributes used in the encryption.

Decrypt($\mathsf{GP}, \mathsf{CT}, \mathsf{SK}_{\mathsf{ID}}$): The secret key is parsed as $\mathsf{SK}_{\mathsf{ID}} = \langle D_{\mathsf{ID}}, \{\mathsf{SK}_{\widetilde{\mathbb{A}}_j} : j \in [N]\}\rangle$ and the ciphertext CT is parsed as above. If some $W_j \not\models \widetilde{\mathbb{A}}_j$, the decryption fails. Otherwise, since $\widetilde{\mathbb{A}}_j = \mathsf{N}_{\mathbb{A}_j}$ for some MAS $\mathbb{A}_j$ over $\widetilde{U}^j$ associated with a LSSS $\Pi_{\mathbb{A}_j} = (\mathbb{M}_j, \rho_j)$, we have $\mathsf{N}(W_j) \models \mathbb{A}_j$, for each $j \in [N]$. The decryptor carries out the following steps for each authority $A_j, j \in [N]$.

Execute $\mathsf{Reconstruct}(\mathbb{M}_j, \rho_j, \mathsf{N}(W_j))$ and receive a set $\{\omega_{j,i} : i \in I_j\}$ of reconstruction constants such that $\sum_{i\in I_j} \omega_{j,i}\lambda_{\rho_j(i)} = \alpha_{j,\mathsf{ID}} = \alpha_j - \sum_{k\in[N\backslash j]} R_{jk}$, where $I_j = \{i \in [\ell_j] : \widetilde{a}_{j,\rho_j(i)} \in \mathsf{N}(W_j)\}$.

Let $I_j^+ = \{i \in [\ell_j] : \widetilde{a}_{j,\rho_j(i)} = a_{j,\rho_j(i)} \in \mathsf{N}(W_j)\}$ and $I_j^- = \{i \in [\ell_j] : \widetilde{a}_{j,\rho_j(i)} = \neg a_{j,\rho_j(i)} \in \mathsf{N}(W_j)\}$. Then $I_j = I_j^+ \bigcup I_j^-$. Compute $E_{3,j} = \prod_{i\in I_j^-}(B'_{j,i})^{\omega_{j,i}}, E_{1,j} = \prod_{i\in I_j}\left(B_{j,i} \cdot \prod_{a_{j,t}\in W_j, t\neq\rho_j(i)} B''_{j,i,t}\right)^{\omega_{j,i}}, E_{2,j} = \prod_{i\in I_j^+}(B'_{j,i})^{\omega_{j,i}}$.

Obtain $Z_j = e(g_1, g_2)^{s(\alpha_j - \sum_{k\in[N\backslash j]} R_{jk})} = e(E_{1,j}, C_1)/(e(C_{2,j}, E_{2,j})e(C_{3,j}, E_{3,j}))$.

The message M is obtained by computing $\dfrac{C}{e(D_{\mathsf{ID}}, C_1) \cdot \prod_{j\in[N]} Z_j} = M$.

Theorem 4. If each honest authority controls at most m attributes, then our N-authority decentralized KP-ABE system for nonMAS is $(\mathcal{T}, N-2, q_{\mathsf{SK}}, \epsilon)$-IND-sCPA secure, assuming that the decisional m-BDHE problem in $(\mathbb{G}_1, \mathbb{G}_2, \mathbb{G}_T)$ is $(\mathcal{T}', \epsilon/2)$-hard. Where $\mathcal{T}' = \mathcal{T} + \mathcal{O}\left(N \cdot \Gamma + q_{\mathsf{SK}} \cdot (N^2 + N \cdot \ell_{max}^2)\right)\cdot\mathcal{T}_{exp} + 5\cdot\mathcal{T}_{pair}$.

Theorem 5. Our N-authority privacy-preserving decentralized KP-ABE for nonMAS is secure in the selective security model when at most $N-2$ authorities are corrupted, under m-BDHE and XDH assumptions, and the assumption that the underlying (arithmetic) 2PC and zero-knowledge proofs are secure.

5   Conclusion

In this paper, we propose efficient privacy-preserving decentralized KP-ABE schemes for both MAS and nonMAS wherein the number of pairings is independent of the number of underlying attributes. CPA security against selective adversary is reduced to the dBDHE problem in standard model. Proposed schemes outperform the existing schemes in terms of computation cost during encryption and decryption.

Acknowledgement. The authors would like to thank the anonymous reviewers of this paper for their valuable comments and suggestions.

References

1. Chase, M., Chow, S.S.M.: Improving privacy and security in multi-authority attribute-based encryption. In: ACM Conference on Computer and Communications Security, pp. 121–130. ACM, New York (2009)
2. Han, J., Susilo, W., Mu, Y., Yan, J.: Privacy-preserving decentralized key-policy attribute-based encryption. IEEE Trans. Parallel Distrib. Syst. **23**(11), 2150–2162 (2012)
3. Lin, H., Cao, Z.-F., Liang, X., Shao, J.: Secure threshold multi authority attribute based encryption without a central authority. In: Chowdhury, D.R., Rijmen, V., Das, A. (eds.) INDOCRYPT 2008. LNCS, vol. 5365, pp. 426–436. Springer, Heidelberg (2008)
4. Chase, M.: Multi-authority attribute based encryption. In: Vadhan, S.P. (ed.) TCC 2007. LNCS, vol. 4392, pp. 515–534. Springer, Heidelberg (2007)
5. Li, Q.Y., Xiong, H., Zhang, F.L., Zeng, S.K.: An expressive decentralizing KP-ABE scheme with constant-size ciphertext. Int. J. Netw. Secur. **15**(3), 131–140 (2013)
6. Ge, A., Zhang, J., Zhang, R., Ma, C., Zhang, Z.: Security analysis of a privacy-preserving decentralized key-policy attribute-based encryption scheme. IEEE Trans. Parallel Distrib. Syst. **24**(11), 2319–2321 (2013)

A (k, n) Multi Secret Sharing Scheme Using Two Variable One Way Function with Less Public Values

Shyamalendu Kandar[1](✉) and Bibhas Chandra Dhara[2]

[1] Department of Information Technology, Indian Institute of Engineering Science and Technology, Shibpur 711103, West Bengal, India
shyamalenduk@it.iiests.ac.in
[2] Department of Information Technology, Jadavpur Univesity, Salt Lake Campus, Kolkata 700098, West Bengal, India
bibhas@it.jusl.ac.in

Abstract. In this paper we have proposed a perfect (k, n) multi secret sharing scheme based on YCH scheme. The YCH method shares m secrets at a time and it publishes $(n + 1)$ data (or $(n + m - k + 1)$ data) as public values when $m \leq k$ (or $m > k$). Our method requires to publish no public values for $m \leq k$ and $(m - k)$ public values for $m > k$. In the proposed method a special binary matrix is used to generate the secret shadows for the participants. The secret shadows are generated in such a way that the GCD of k or more such shadows generate r while less than k such generate $r.d$, where $d > 1$. We have also proved that the scheme is a secure one.

Keywords: Multi secret sharing · One way function · Secret shadow · GCD_n

1 Introduction

Secret sharing is a technique to protect sensitive information from getting lost or misuse by wrong hands. Secret sharing started its journey as a research wing in the field of information security after the individual proposals by Shamir [1] and Blakley [2] in 1979. The former proposal [1] is based on polynomial interpolation and the later [2] is based on hyperplane geometry. Both the proposals are (k, n) threshold secret sharing scheme, where n is the number of participant and k is the minimum number of participant to reconstruct the secret. In threshold secret sharing scheme secret holder is known as dealer and s/he has the authority of generating shares and distribute them among the authenticated participants.

S. Kandar—Please note that the LNCS Editorial assumes that all authors have used the western naming convention, with given names preceding surnames. This determines the structure of the names in the running heads and the author index.

© Springer International Publishing Switzerland 2015
S. Jajodia and C. Mazumdar (Eds.): ICISS 2015, LNCS 9478, pp. 532–541, 2015.
DOI: 10.1007/978-3-319-26961-0_32

Person having the right to reconstruct the secret is known as combiner. In information theoretic sense Shamir scheme is a perfect secret sharing as $(k - 1)$ or fewer participants cannot get any information about the secret from their shares.

Multi-secret sharing scheme shares multiple secrets in one sharing process [3]. This has several advantages like (i) sharing more than one secret among the same group of participants (ii) the amount of data needed to share more than one secret is same as sharing a single secret. Multi secret sharing scheme can be classified into two types- one time use scheme and multi use scheme [4]. In one time use scheme fresh shares are issued by the dealer to every participant after reconstruction of some or all secrets. But in multi use scheme every participant only need to keep one share.

A multistage secret sharing (MSS) using one way function and public shift technique is presented in [5] where $m.n$ data are published as public values (m is the number of secrets to be shared). Public shift technique is used to obtain the true shadows and the secret is reconstructed stage by stage in a special order by successive use of one way function. A proposal on dynamic multi secret sharing using two variable one way function is available in [6]. Authors proved that the method prevents disclosing the secret shadows among the participants. A proposal of multi secret sharing by Chien et al. [3] came up with systematic block codes. It is a matrix based method with the application of two variable one way function and has several advantages like parallel reconstruction of secrets, multi use scheme, dynamic determination of the distributed shares etc. The method has few public values but computation cost is high due to the reconstruction of several simultaneous equations constructed from the matrix. In 2004 another multi secret sharing scheme was proposed by Yang, Chang and Hwang [7] (known as YCH scheme). Two variable one way function is used as backbone in YCH scheme. The scheme has two parts (i) $m \leq k$ and (ii) $m > k$, where m is the number of secrets to be shared. Number of public values required for case (i) is $(n + 1)$ and for case (ii) is $(n + m - l + 1)$. Pang et al. [8] proposed another multi secret sharing scheme based on Shamir method [1]. A Hermite interpolation based multi secret sharing scheme is presented in [9]. This scheme also uses two variable one way function but fails to put light for the case when number of secrets is more than the threshold value. A dynamic multi secret sharing scheme is presented in [10]. In the scheme each participant need to keep only one master secret share, using which different group secrets are reconstructed based on the number of threshold values. The scheme provides security by applying successive one way hash function and the exclusive OR operation. In [11] a multi use multi secret sharing scheme is presented. The scheme is based on the one way collision resistant hash function which provides securities against conspiracy attacks even by somehow pseudo-secret shares are compromised. Bai [12] proposed a multi secret sharing in form of image secret sharing based on matrix projection. In the method, a random matrix is taken and its projection is calculated. The projection is subtracted from another matrix containing the image pixel. The resultant is known as remainder matrix. The main disadvantage of the scheme is that the secret matrix and the projection matrix are square matrices and thus the remainder is also square. A modified version of multi secret sharing based on matrix projection is available in [13]. In [14] a new multi secret sharing scheme is proposed where each secret has constant length. The scheme has been used to derive two new cryptographic functionalities, multi policy signature and multi policy decryption. A perfect multi secret sharing based on monotone span programs (MSP) is proposed in [15]. Few recent proposals [16–18] on multi secret sharing schemes came up with Chinese Remainder Theorem. Few multi image secret sharing schemes are available in [19, 20].

Verifiability in secret sharing is an important issue. It covers the identification of cheater or any type of cheating done in secret sharing process. Few proposals have included verifiability with multi secret sharing to make it sure that right secrets are retrieved in reconstruction process. Tentu et al. [21] proposed a verifiable multi secret sharing based on YCH scheme. LFSR based public key cryptosystem is used in [22] to detect a variety of forgery or cheating actions in multi secret sharing performed by Lagrange interpolation. An updated version of this scheme is presented in [23] which uses non-homogeneous linear recursions with LFSR based public key cryptosystem. One dimensional cellular automata can be used in verifiable multi secret sharing [24]. The authors have proved that the sharing can be done in linear time complexity using this method.

In the paper we have proposed a multi secret sharing scheme which uses YCH scheme. The proposed scheme publishes no public value for $m \leq k$ and $(m - k)$ public values for $m > k$. We have used a binary participation matrix to generate the secret shadows sw_i. For any subset of k or more secret shadows GCD is r but any subset of less than k such give GCD as $r.d$ where $d > 1$. r is one variable of the two variable one way function and it need not to be made public. We have also proved that the proposed scheme is secure and a perfect secret sharing scheme.

The rest of the paper is organized as follows. YCH method is described in Sect. 2. The proposed scheme is presented in Sect. 3. Security analysis of the proposed method is made in Sect. 4. Finally the conclusion is drawn in Sect. 5.

2   YCH Method

Yang, Chang and Hwang proposed a multi secret sharing scheme which is well known as YCH scheme [7]. The share generation of this scheme is based on the application of two variable one way function in polynomial.

A two variable one way function is an important primitive, mainly used in cryptography. This type of functions is easy to compute but hard to find inverse. The following properties make it suitable for application in cryptographic techniques. For a two variable one way function $f(r, s)$

(a) It is easy to compute $f(r, s)$ for a given r and s.
(b) It is hard to find r if $f(r, s)$ and s are known.
(c) r is known. Till computation of $f(r, s)$ is hard without any knowledge of s.
(d) For a given s it is hard to find two distinct r such that $f(r_i, s) = f(r_j, s)$.
(e) It is hard to find s for a given r and $f(r, s)$.
(f) For a given pair r_i and $f(r_i, s)$, it is difficult to compute $f(r', s)$ for $r' \neq r_i$.

In YCH multi secret sharing scheme a two variable one way function $f(r, s)$ maps a public value r and a secret shadow s to a fixed length bit string. According to the scheme $(S_1, S_2, \ldots, S_m)$ are m secrets (belong to prime field q) to be shared among n participants. In the secret sharing process the dealer chooses n secret shadows $(sw_1, sw_2, \ldots, sw_n)$ randomly and sent sw_i to $participant_i$ using a secret channel.

(I) If $m \leq k$
  (a) Dealer construct a $(k - 1)$th degree polynomial $h(x) mod\ q$ as follows

$$h(x) = S_1 + S_2 x^1 + \cdots + S_m x^{m-1} + c_1 x^m + c_2 x^{m+1} + \cdots + c_{k-m} x^{k-1} mod\ q \tag{1}$$

  (b) $y_i = h(f(r, sw_i)) mod\ q$ is computed for $i = 1, 2, \ldots, n$
  (c) $(r, y_1, y_2, \ldots, y_n)$ are published using some authenticated manner such that those are in [25, 26].
  Total number of public values is $(n + 1)$.
(II) if $m > k$
  (a) Dealer constructs a $(m - 1)$ degree polynomial $h(x) mod\ q$ as follows

$$h(x) = S_1 + S_2 x^1 + \cdots + S_m x^{m-1} mod\ q \tag{2}$$

  (b) $y_i = h(f(r, sw_i)) mod\ q$ is computed for $i = 1, 2, \ldots, n$.
  (c) $h(i) mod\ q$ for $i = 1, 2, \ldots, (m - k)$ is computed.
  (d) Using some authenticated manner $(r, h(1), h(2), \ldots, h(m - k), y_1, y_2, \ldots, y_n)$ are published such that those are in [25, 26].
  Total number of public values is $(n + m - k + 1)$.

3   Proposed Scheme

In this paper we have proposed a multi secret sharing scheme which publishes less data as public values than YCH scheme. In the proposed scheme the secret shadows sw_i, $i = 1, 2, \ldots, n$ are computed by the dealer, except choosing them randomly. To generate sw_i we have taken a binary random matrix and secret shadows are generated in such a way that any subset of k or more sw_i give r as GCD while any subset of less than such shadows produce $r.d$, *where* $d > 1$ as GCD. In reconstruction phase r is calculated by cyclic GCD computation from sw_i, belonging to the chosen subset of participants. There is no need to make the integer r as public.

Following subsections present the proposed method in detail.

3.1   Share Generation

The share generation process of the proposed secret sharing scheme is divided into two steps

(A) Secret shadow generation.
(B) Final Share generation.

(A) **Secret shadow generation.** The secret shadow generation process starts with construction of n distinct keys. Each key is production of some prime numbers $\in pr$ and obeys the following two properties. Let key_i is the key for generating secret shadow for $partitipant_i$. Then

(a) $GCD(key_{i_1}, key_{i_2}, \ldots, key_{i_{k-u}}) > 1$ for $u \geq 1$ and

(b) $GCD(key_{i_1}, key_{i_2}, \ldots, key_{i_{k+u}}) = 1$ for $u \geq 0$

The participance of the prime numbers $\in pr$ in the key generation process is represented by a binary matrix $M_{n \times c}$. The ith row of M define key_i for sw_i and key_i is computed as

$$key_i = \prod_{1 \leq j \leq r, m_{i,j}=1} p_j \tag{3}$$

It must be noted that if the jth column of M is 1 then pr_j contributes as a factor of key_i. If each column of M contains $(k-1)$ 1's and $n-(k-1)$ 0's then the condition that the GCD of any k keys is 1, is ensured. With this condition satisfied there will be $\binom{n}{k-1}$ different combinations, hence $c = \binom{n}{k-1}$. If pr_i is a factor of key_i then the occurrence of pr_i^t, $t \geq 1$ as a factor in key_i does not violate the above two conditions. Therefore the binary matrix M is modified to M' by replacing the non-zero entries of M by arbitrary integers. The key construction process for $n=5$ and $k=3$ and the matrices $M_{5 \times 10}$ and $M'_{5 \times 10}$ are presented in Tables 1 and 2.

Table 1. The matrix M for $(n = 5, k = 3)$

Rows	Prime numbers									
	pr_1	pr_2	pr_3	pr_4	pr_5	pr_6	pr_7	pr_8	pr_9	pr_{10}
1	1	1	1	1	0	0	0	0	0	0
2	1	0	0	0	1	1	1	0	0	0
3	0	1	0	0	1	0	0	1	1	0
4	0	0	1	0	0	1	0	1	0	1
5	0	0	0	1	0	0	1	0	1	1

The keys constructed from Table 2 are as follows:

$key_1 = pr_1^2.pr_2^3.pr_3^2.pr_4^4$
$key_2 = pr_1^2.pr_5^3.pr_6^2.pr_7^5$
$key_3 = pr_2^2.pr_5.pr_8^3.pr_9$
$key_4 = pr_3^4.pr_6.pr_8^5.pr_{10}$
$key_5 = pr_4^4.pr_7^3.pr_9.pr_{10}^2$

From the matrix given in Tables 1 and 2 it is clear that no prime number is a common factor of any 3 or more keys but a single prime number is a

Table 2. The matrix M' for $(n = 5, k = 3)$

Participant	Prime numbers									
	pr_1	pr_2	pr_3	pr_4	pr_5	pr_6	pr_7	pr_8	pr_9	pr_{10}
1	2	3	2	4	0	0	0	0	0	0
2	2	0	0	0	3	2	5	0	0	0
3	0	2	0	0	1	0	0	3	1	0
4	0	0	4	0	0	1	0	5	0	1
5	0	0	0	4	0	0	3	0	1	2

common factor of any two keys. A randomly selected number r is multiplied with each key to get the secret shadow.

$$sw_i = key_i * r \tag{4}$$

This ensures that r will be found as GCD for any k or more secret shadows but less than k secret shadows generate some number $> r$ as GCD. The prime field q is chosen in such a way that all sw_i are member of it. Finally sw_i is sent to $participant_i$ through a secret channel.

(B) **Final Share Generation.** Let $(S_1, S_2, \ldots S_m)$ are m secrets to be shared among n participants with threshold value k. $f(x, y)$ is a two variable one way function. In the share generation process two cases may appear (I) $m \leq k$ and (II) $m > k$.

Case I: $m \leq k$:
(a) Dealer constructs a $(k-1)$th degree polynomial $h(x) mod\ q$ as follows

$$h(x) = S_1 + S_2 x^1 + \cdots + S_m x^{m-1} + c_1 x^m + c_2 x^{m+1} + \cdots + c_{k-m} x^{k-1} mod\ q \tag{5}$$

where c_i are random co-efficients.
(b) $Sh_i = h(f(r, sw_i)) mod\ q$ is computed for $i = 1, 2, \ldots, n$
(c) Sh_i is sent to $participant_i$.

Case II: $m > k$:
(a) Dealer constructs a $(m-1)$ degree polynomial $h(x)$ mod q as follows

$$h(x) = S_1 + S_2 x^1 + \cdots + S_m x^{m-1} mod\ q \tag{6}$$

(b) $Sh_i = h(f(r, sw_i)) mod\ q$ is computed for $i = 1, 2, \ldots, n$
(c) $h(i) mod\ q$ is computed for $i = 1, 2, \ldots, (m-k)$
(d) Sh_i is sent to $participant_i$ and $h(1), h(2), \ldots, h(m-k)$ are made public.

It is noted that each participant are assigned a distinct participant number from $1, 2, \ldots, n$ and the number is known to the participant. This number is required in secret reconstruction phase while computing the GCD of the sw_is belonging to their possession.

3.2   Secret Retrieval

In retrieval phase the trusted combiner selects k or more participants. The selected participants retrieve r from the sw_is belonging to their possession. From the available two variable one way function each participant computes $f(r, sw_i)$ for $i = 1, 2, \ldots, k$. Finally Sh_i and $f(r, sw_i)$ for $i = 1, 2, \ldots, k$ are sent to the combiner. The GCD computation and the secret retrieval are discussed in the following subsections.

3.2.1   GCD Computation

Selected participants communicate themselves and arrange themselves in ascending order according to their participant number. The participant with first rank in the list sends its sw to the second rank holder. This person computes the GCD of the two secret shadows, let as r'. r' is sent to the third rank holder and it computes the GCD of its sw and r'. Let the GCD is r'' and it is send to the fourth rank holder. This process continues upto k^{th} participant and the final GCD r is found. The process can be represented mathematically as follow.

$$r = GCD(\ldots (GCD(GCD(sw_1, sw_2), sw_3)\ldots), sw_k) \tag{7}$$

r is send to each selected participant by $participant_k$. Now $participant_i$ computes $f(r, sw_i)$ and it is sent to the combiner along with Sh_i.

Like share generation, two cases are possible for secret retrieval.

Case I: $m \le k$

(a) Combiner collects the pair $(f(r, sw_i), Sh_i)$ for $i = 1, \ldots, k$ from k participants.
(b) The secrets are collected from the co-efficients of the polynomial generated using Lagrange Interpolation from $(f(r, sw_i), y_i)$. It is denoted as follows.

$$h(x) = \sum_{i=1}^{k} Sh_i \prod_{j=1, j \ne i}^{k} \frac{x - f(r, sw_j)}{f(r, sw_i) - f(r, sw_j)} mod\ q$$

$$= S_1 + S_2 x^1 + \cdots + S_m x^{m-1} + c_1 x^m + c_2 x^{m+1} + \cdots + c_{k-m} x^{k-1} mod\ q$$

Case II: $m > k$

(a) Combiner collects the pair $(f(r, sw_i), Sh_i)$ for $i = 1, \ldots, k$ from k participants.
(b) $(m - k)$ public values $h(i)$ are pooled by the combiner.
(c) The $(t - 1)$ degree polynomial $h(x)$ is uniquely determined using k pairs of $(f(r, sw_i), Sh_i)$ and $(m - k)$ pairs of $(i, h(i))$ as follows.

$$h(x) = \sum_{i=1}^{k} Sh_i \prod_{j=1, j \ne i}^{k} \frac{x - f(r, sw_j)}{f(r, sw_i) - f(r, sw_j)} + \sum_{i=1}^{m-k} h(i) \prod_{j=1, j \ne i}^{m-k} \frac{x - j}{i - j} mod\ q$$

$$= S_1 + S_2 x^1 + \cdots + S_m x^{m-1} mod\ q$$

4   Security Analysis

The share generation and secret reconstruction of our scheme is like YCH scheme but requires less number of values to be made public. In the following section we have analyzed the security of our scheme.

(1) In our scheme if $m \leq k$ then number of public values is 0. In the retrieval process trusted combiner only chooses k or more participants. Participants communicate themselves to find r. Finally pair of $(f(r, sw_i), Sh_i)$ are collected from at least k participants (as done in shamir method) by the combiner. If $m > k$ then number of public values is $(m - k)$ and all those are required in the reconstruction process.

(2) If $(k - 1)$ or fewer participants are chosen by the combiner, the computed GCD will be $r' = r.d$ where $(d > 1)$. This generates $f(r', sw_i)$ which fails to retrieve the secrets as there is no sufficient number of pairs to generate $(k - 1)$ degree polynomial. Thus less than k subset of participants has no information about the secrets. This makes the scheme a perfect secret sharing scheme.

(3) Participants communicate with themselves to find r only. The shares Sh_i hold by them are not disclosed to each other. The combiner is sent the pair $(f(r, sw_i), Sh_i)$, hence the value of r and sw_i are not available outside the participant group. The combiner only knows the set of participants in the secret sharing process. Polynomial is constructed by the trusted combiner and no participant has any role (except sending the pair $(f(r, sw_i), Sh_i)$) in the reconstruction process. Hence there is no chance of disclosure of the secrets by corrupted participant/s.

5   Conclusion

In this paper we have proposed a multi secret sharing scheme based on YCH scheme. A special binary matrix is used to generate the secret shadows except taking them random. Any subset of k or more such secret shadows generate r as GCD but any subset of less than k such produce $r.d$ where $(d > 1)$ as GCD. This r is used in the computation of values from two variable one way function and there is no need to make r as public. When the participants pool their secret shadows and retrieve the secret there is a chance to disclosure of the secrets to some unauthorized persons by some corrupted participant. Assigning a trusted combiner in our scheme removes this threat. Less number of public values makes the scheme simple and easy to handle. In the retrieval process two groups are assigned for two separate jobs. The group of k participants generate r, and $f(r, sw_i)$ is computed by each participant; whereas combiner retrieves the secrets. $participant_i$ have no information about the shares of $participant_j$, $j \neq i$. So no participant can get any information about secrets. Combiner also have no information about r and sw_i. The main disadvantage of the scheme is the computation of sw_i by the dealer and the distribution of fresh sw_i to each participants before a new secret sharing process. Disclosure of sw_i to $participant_j$ (where i

and j are first two participants in the selected subset of participant) at the time of GCD computation is another disadvantage of our scheme.

Cheating by the participants is a great concern in secret sharing scheme. Development of a cheating detection and cheater identification technique over the proposed scheme is left for future work.

References

1. Shamir, A.: How to share a secret. Commun. ACM **22**(11), 612–613 (1979)
2. Blakley, G.R.: Safeguarding cryptographic keys: Proc. Natl. Comput. Conf. **48**, 313–317 (1979)
3. Chien, H.-Y., Jan, J.-K., Tseng, Y.-M.: A practical (t, n) multi-secret sharing scheme. IEICE Trans. Fundam. Electron. Commun. Comput. Sci. **83**(12), 2762–2765 (2000)
4. Jackson, W.-A., Martin, K.M., O'Keefe, C.M.: On sharing many secrets. In: Safavi-Naini, R., Pieprzyk, J.P. (eds.) ASIACRYPT 1994. LNCS, vol. 917. Springer, Heidelberg (1995)
5. He, J., Dawson, E.: Multistage secret sharing based on one-way function. Electron. Lett. **30**(19), 1591–1592 (1994)
6. He, J., Dawson, E.: Multisecret-sharing scheme based on one-way function. Electron. Lett. **31**(2), 93–95 (1995)
7. Yang, C.-C., Chang, T.-Y., Hwang, M.-S.: A (t, n) multi-secret sharing scheme. Appl. Math. Comput. **151**(2), 483–490 (2004)
8. Pang, L.-J., Wang, Y.-M.: A new (t, n) multi-secret sharing scheme based on shamir's secret sharing. Appl. Math. Comput. **167**(2), 840–848 (2005)
9. Tan, X., Wang, Z.: A new (t, n) multi-secret sharing scheme. In: ICCEE 2008 Computer and Electrical Engineering, pp. 861–865. IEEE (2008)
10. Lin, H.-Y., Yeh, Y.-S.: Dynamic multi-secret sharing scheme. Int. J. Contemp. Math. Sci. **3**(1), 37–42 (2008)
11. Das, A., Adhikari, A.: An efficient multi-use multi-secret sharing scheme based on hash function. Appl. Math. Lett. **23**(9), 993–996 (2010)
12. Bai, L.: A reliable (k, n) image secret sharing scheme. In: 2nd IEEE International Symposium on Dependable, Autonomic and Secure Computing, pp. 31–36. IEEE (2006)
13. Radu, V.: Application. In: Radu, V. (ed.) Stochastic Modeling of Thermal Fatigue Crack Growth. ACM, vol. 1, pp. 63–70. Springer, Heidelberg (2015)
14. Herranz, J., Ruiz, A., Sez, G.: New results and applications for multi-secret sharing schemes. Des. Codes Crypt. **73**(3), 841–864 (2014)
15. Hsu, C.-F., Cheng, Q., Tang, X., Zeng, B.: An ideal multi-secret sharing scheme based on MSP. Inf. Sci. **181**(7), 1403–1409 (2011)
16. Subha, R., Bhagvati, C.: CRT based threshold multi secret sharing scheme. Int. J. Netw. Secur. **16**(4), 249–255 (2014)
17. Dong, X.: A multi-secret sharing scheme based on the CRT and RSA. Int. J. Netw. Secur. **2**(2), 69–72 (2015)
18. Endurthi, A., Bidyapati Chanu, O., Naidu Tentu, A., Venkaiah, V.C.: Reusable multi-stage multi-secret sharing schemes based on CRT. J. Commun. Softw. Syst. **11**(1), 15–24 (2015)
19. Dastanian, R., Shahhoseini, H.S.: Multi secret sharing scheme for encrypting two secret images into two shares. In: International Conference on Information and Electronics Engineering IPCSIT, vol. 6. IEEE, Washington (2011)

20. Chen, T.-H., Chang-Sian, W.: Efficient multi-secret image sharing based on boolean operations. Sig. Process. **91**(1), 90–97 (2011)
21. Tentu, A.N., Rao, A.A.: Efficient verifiable multi-secret sharing based on YCH scheme. In: Cryptography and Security Systems, pp. 100–109. Springer, Heidelberg (2014)
22. Hu, C., Liao, X., Cheng, X.: Verifiable multi-secret sharing based on LFSR sequences. Theoret. Comput. Sci. **445**, 52–62 (2012)
23. Mashhadi, S., Dehkordi, M.H.: Two verifiable multi secret sharing schemes based on nonhomogeneous linear recursion and LFSR public-key cryptosystem. Inf. Sci. **294**, 31–40 (2015)
24. Eslami, Z., Ahmadabadi, J.Z.: A verifiable multi-secret sharing scheme based on cellular automata. Inf. Sci. **180**(15), 2889–2894 (2010)
25. ElGamal, T.: A public key cryptosystem and a signature scheme based on discrete logarithms. Adv. Cryptology, pp. 10–18. Springer, Heidelberg (1985)
26. Rivest, R.L., Shamir, A., Adleman, L.: A method for obtaining digital signatures and public-key cryptosystems. Commun. ACM **21**(2), 120–126 (1978)

Robustness of Score Normalization in Multibiometric Systems

Radhey Shyam[✉] and Yogendra Narain Singh

Department of Computer Science and Engineering,
Institute of Engineering and Technology, 226 021 Lucknow, India
{shyam0058,singhyn}@gmail.com

Abstract. This paper presents an evaluation of normalization techniques of matching scores on the recognition performance of a multibiometric system. We present two score normalization techniques, namely modified-linear-tanh-linear (MLTL) and four-segments-double-sigmoid (FSDS) that are found to be robust in achieving the recognition performance to the optimum value. The techniques are tested in fusion of the two face recognition methods Fisherface and A-LBP on the dataset of uncontrolled environments. In particular, AT & T (ORL) face dataset is used in this experiment. The performance of the MLTL and FSDS score normalization techniques are compared with the existing normalization techniques, for instance min-max, tanh and linear-tanh-linear (LTL). The proposed normalization techniques show the significant improvement in the recognition performance of the multibiometric system over the known techniques.

Keywords: Face recognition · Multibiometric · Normalization · Identification

1 Introduction

The unibiometric system that is based on a single source of information suffers from the problems like lack of uniqueness, non-universality, and spoofing attacks. On the contrary, a multibiometric system harnesses relevant information obtained from multiple biometric cues. A strategic combination of these relevant information obtained from multiple biometric cues may overcome some of the problems of unibiometric systems [1–3].

Our concern is to combine several unibiometric systems to achieve a multibiometric system that meets the characteristics of a robust system i.e., optimum recognition accuracy and less falsifications [4–6]. In order to achieve these characteristics the matching scores obtained from different unibiometric systems need transformation and mapping before their fusion. The objective of transformation and mapping operations that refers the normalization process in the biometric terminology, is to supplement the information received at the matching score level of the biometric systems, so that the performance of the combined system improves. Therefore, score normalization is an intrinsic problem. It plays a

© Springer International Publishing Switzerland 2015
S. Jajodia and C. Mazumdar (Eds.): ICISS 2015, LNCS 9478, pp. 542–550, 2015.
DOI: 10.1007/978-3-319-26961-0_33

peculiar role in transforming and mapping the heterogeneous scores of distinct biometric cues into a homogeneous scale.

In literature, the normalization techniques has been found congenial in transforming the heterogeneous score to a homogeneous scale. An evaluation of normalization techniques of matching scores in multibiometric systems has been done by Singh and Gupta [7]. They reported the performance of linear-tanh-linear(LTL) and four-segments-piecewise-linear (FSPL) are better than min-max (MM), z-score and tanh normalization techniques. They also found that MM and z-score normalization techniques are susceptible to outliers. Therefore, it is needed to devise robust and efficient normalization technique that achieves optimum accuracy results.

In [7], let $O_k^T = \{r_{k_1}^T, r_{k_2}^T, ..., r_{k_N}^T\}$ be the set of true scores of N individuals and $O_k^I = \{r_{k_1}^I, r_{k_2}^I, ..., r_{k_n}^I\}$ be the set of impostor scores of those individuals where, $n = N \times (N - 1)$ for biometric cue k. The composite set of matching scores is denoted as O_k (i.e., $O_k = O_k^T \cup O_k^I$ and $|O_k^T \cup O_k^I| = N + n = N^2$).

The distance scores (r_{k_i}') of user i for biometric cue k can be converted into similarity scores in the typical scale, suppose it should be $[0, 1]$ using the formula:

$$r_{k_i} = \frac{max(O_k^T, O_k^I) - r_{k_i}'}{max(O_k^T, O_k^I) - min(O_k^T, O_k^I)} \tag{1}$$

whereas r_{k_i} is the similarity scores of biometric cue k. Otherwise, if the distance scores lies in the range $[min(O_k), max(O_k)]$ then they are simply converted to similarity scores by subtracting them from $max(O_k)$ (e.g., $max(O_k - r_{k_i}')$). The precise summarization of these normalization techniques which transform the raw scores in the typical range of $[0, 1]$, including double-sigmoid (DS), piecewise-linear (PL) are rendered in Table 1.

This paper proposes two new normalization techniques and evaluated their performance by fusing two face recognition methods in uncontrolled environments, namely Fisherface and augmented local binary pattern (A-LBP) [8–13]. The description of techniques are given in Sect. 2. A short discussion of fusion techniques is found in Sect. 3. The effect of normalization techniques on recognition performance achieved by a multibiometric system is reported in Sect. 4. Finally, the conclusions are outlined in Sect. 5.

2   Proposed Score Normalization Techniques

This section proposes two new normalization techniques that transform heterogeneous scores to homogeneous scores. The new formulations of normalizing the matching scores are named as: (i) Modified-linear-tanh-linear (MLTL) which is formulated over tanh and linear-tanh-linear (LTL) normalization techniques along with the conversion of linear function into sigmoid function and (ii) Four-segments-double-sigmoid (FSDS) cleaves the regions of true and impostor scores into four segments and map each segment using piecewise sigmoid functions.

Table 1. Summary of the existing normalization techniques

Normalization Technique	Formula
Min-max(MM)	$n_{k_i} = \dfrac{r_{k_i} - min(O_k)}{max(O_k) - min(O_k)}$
Z-score	$n_{k_i} = \dfrac{r_{k_i} - \mu O_k}{\sigma O_k}$
DS	$n_{k_i} = \begin{cases} \dfrac{1}{1+exp\left(-2\left(\frac{r_{k_i}-t_k}{t_{k_L}}\right)\right)} & \text{if } r_{k_i} < t_k, \\[2em] \dfrac{1}{1+exp\left(-2\left(\frac{r_{k_i}-t_k}{t_{k_R}}\right)\right)} & \text{otherwise.} \end{cases}$
Tanh	$n_{k_i} = \dfrac{1}{2} * \left[tanh\left\{ 0.01 * \left(\dfrac{r_{k_i} - \mu_{O_k^T}}{\sigma_{O_k^T}} \right) \right\} + 1 \right]$
PL	$n_{k_i} = \begin{cases} 0 & \text{if } r_{k_i} \leq min(O_k^T), \\ 1 & \text{if } r_{k_i} \geq max(O_k^I), \\ \dfrac{r_{k_i}-min(O_k^T)}{max(O_k^I)-min(O_k^T)} & \text{otherwise.} \end{cases}$
LTL	$n_{k_i} = \begin{cases} 0 & \text{if } r_{k_i} \leq min(O_k^T), \\ 1 & \text{if } r_{k_i} \geq max(O_k^I), \\ \dfrac{1}{2} * \left[tanh\left\{ 0.01 * \left(\dfrac{r_{k_i} - \mu_{O_k^T}}{\delta_{O_k^T}} \right) \right\} + 1.5 \right] & \text{otherwise.} \end{cases}$
FSPL	$n_{k_i} = \begin{cases} 0 & \text{if } r_{k_i} \leq min(O_k^T), \\ \dfrac{r_{k_i} - min(O_k^T)}{t_k - min(O_k^T)} & \text{if } min(O_k^T) < r_{k_i} \leq t_k, \\ 1 + \dfrac{r_{k_i} - t_k}{max(O_k^I) - t_k} & \text{if } t_k < r_{k_i} \leq max(O_k^I), \\ 2 & \text{if } r_{k_i} > max(O_k^I). \end{cases}$

2.1 Modified-Linear-Tanh-Linear (MLTL)

This normalization technique reinforce the strength of the characteristic resulted from tanh and linear-tanh-linear (LTL) function as illustrated in Fig. 1(a). Normalization function of it corresponds the non overlap region of the impostor scores to a constant value 0 and non overlap region of the true scores to a constant value 1. The overlapped region between O_k^I and O_k^T is mapped to a sigmoid function using tanh and LTL evaluator as,

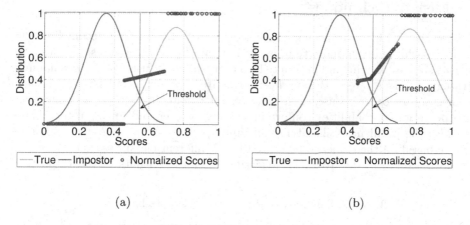

Fig. 1. Proposed score normalization techniques (a) Modified-linear-tanh-linear (MLTL), and (b) Four-segments-piecewise-sigmoid (MSPS).

$$n_{k_i} = \begin{cases} 0 & \text{if } r_{k_i} < min(O_k^T), \\ 1 & \text{if } r_{k_i} > max(O_k^I), \\ \dfrac{1}{(1 + \exp(-2 * (0.1 * z)))} & \text{otherwise.} \end{cases} \qquad (2)$$

where $z = \dfrac{r_{k_i} - \mu O_k^T}{\delta O_k^T}$; and $\mu_{O_k^T}$, $\sigma_{O_k^T}$ are respectively the mean and standard deviation of the true matching scores of biometric cue k. The n_{k_i} is the normalized scores of biometric cue k.

2.2   Four-Segments-Double-Sigmoid (FSDS)

FSDS normalization technique cleaves the regions of true and impostor scores into four segments and map each segment using piecewise sigmoid functions as illustrated in Fig. 1(b). A reference point t_k is chosen between the overlapping regions of O_k^T and O_k^I. The scores between two extremities of the overlap region are mapped using two sigmoid functions separately in the range of $[0, 1]$ towards left and right of t_k accordingly as,

$$n_{k_i} = \begin{cases} 0 & \text{if } r_{k_i} < min(O_k^T), \\ \dfrac{1}{(1 + \exp(-2 * (0.1 * z)))} & min(O_k^T) \leq r_{k_i} \leq t_k, \\ \dfrac{1}{(1 + \exp(-2 * (0.5 * p)))} & t_k < r_{k_i} \leq max(O_k^I), \\ 1 & \text{if } r_{k_i} > max(O_k^I) \end{cases} \qquad (3)$$

where $z = \dfrac{r_{k_i} - \mu O_k^T}{\delta O_k^T}$ and $p = 2 * \left(\dfrac{r_{k_i} - min(O_k^T)}{max(O_k^I) - min(O_k^T)} \right) - 1$, the t_k is the threshold of biometric cue k.

3   Fusion Techniques

Kittler *et al.* [14], have developed a theoretical framework for reconciling the evidence achieved from more than one classifier schemes. These fusion rules are, such as sum, max, min, and product. Two more different fusion strategies namely strategy A and strategy B have been evaluated by Singh and Gupta in their studies [7]. In order to use these schemes, the matching scores are converted into posteriori probabilities conforming to a true user and an impostor. They consider the problem of classifying an input pattern Z into one of m possible classes based on the evidence presented by R different classifiers. Let $\boldsymbol{x_i}$ be the feature vector provided to the ith classifier. Let the outputs of the respective

Table 2. Summary of the existing fusion techniques

Fusion Rule	Formula
Sum	$c = \underset{j}{\operatorname{argmax}} \sum_{i=1}^{R} p(w_j|\boldsymbol{x_i})$
Max	$c = \underset{j}{\operatorname{argmax}} \underset{i}{\max}\, p(w_j|\boldsymbol{x_i})$
Min	$c = \underset{j}{\operatorname{argmax}} \underset{i}{\min}\, p(w_j|\boldsymbol{x_i})$
Product	$c = \underset{j}{\operatorname{argmax}} \prod_{i=1}^{R} p(w_j|\boldsymbol{x_i})$
Fusion Strategy A [7]	$w_k = \left(\sum_{k=1}^{t} \frac{1}{e_k} \right)^{-1} * \frac{1}{e_k}$
Fusion Strategy B [7]	$d_k = \dfrac{\mu_{O_k^T} - \mu_{O_k^I}}{\sqrt{\left(\sigma_{O_k^T}\right)^2 + \left(\sigma_{O_k^I}\right)^2}}$ and $w_k = \left(\sum_{k=1}^{t} d_k \right)^{-1} * d_k$ where the fused score f_i for user i is computed as follows: $f_i = \sum_{k=1}^{t} w_k * n_{k_i}; (\forall i)$ where, $0 \le w_k \le 1, (\forall k); \sum_{k=1}^{t} w_k = 1$

classifiers be $p(w_j|\boldsymbol{x_i})$, *i.e.*, the posteriori probability of the pattern Z belonging to class w_j given the feature vector $\boldsymbol{x_i}$. Let $c \in \{1, 2, ..., m\}$ be the class to which the input pattern Z is finally assigned. Whereas in verification (one to one map) the value of m is 2 and in identification (one to many) the value of m is $n - 1$. The following fusion rules have been simplified by Jain *et al.* [15] for computing the value of class c that are given Table 2.

4 Experimental Results

The efficacy of the proposed normalization techniques are tested on fusion of the two face recognition methods in uncontrolled environments on AT & T (ORL) face dataset [16]. The images of this dataset suffers from the variations, such as pose, facial expression, and eye glasses. A total of 400 images are used to recognize 40 distinct individuals from the dataset. The system is trained for independent dataset composed of 40 true scores and 40×39 (i.e., 1560) impostor scores, whereas the test image is selected randomly from the given images for each individual and the performance is computed. The threshold value t_k is computed as the median of overlapped true and impostor scores. The performance of the proposed normalization technique is analyzed using equal error rate that is an error where the likelihood of acceptance is assumed to be same as to the likelihood of rejection of the people who should be correctly verified. This error is subtracted from 100 to compute the recognition accuracy. The performance of the proposed normalization techniques are also verified by the receiver operating characteristic (ROC) curves. The ROC curve is a two dimensional measure of classification performance that plots the likelihood of the true acceptance rate (TAR) against the likelihood of the false acceptance rate (FAR).

The recognition accuracies achieved by the score normalization techniques are rendered in Table 3. The accuracy values (%) for our proposed score normalization techniques i.e., FSDS (MLTL) are found better than other existing normalization techniques. For example, these values are 99.62(98.11), 97.21(96.89),

Table 3. Performance accuracies (%) of normalization techniques under different fusion criterions on AT & T (ORL) face dataset.

Methods	Normalization techniques	Accuracies(%)					
		Fusion techniques					
		Sum	Max	Min	Product	Strategy A	Strategy B
	Min-max	97.95	97.50	97.50	97.92	97.98	97.98
Fisherface	Tanh	98.01	96.86	97.50	98.01	97.92	97.98
+	LTL	95.64	96.86	96.31	96.31	97.50	97.47
A-LBP	MLTL	**98.11**	**96.89**	**97.56**	**98.11**	**97.98**	**98.11**
	FSDS	**99.62**	**97.21**	**97.79**	**99.62**	**99.55**	**99.65**

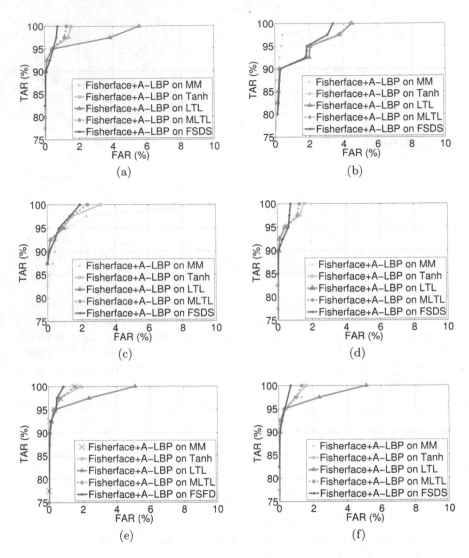

Fig. 2. Receiver operating characteristic curves show the performance of different normalization techniques of matching scores obtained from Fisherfaces and A-LBP methods using different fusion criterions on AT & T (ORL) face dataset.

97.79(97.56), 99.62(98.11), 99.55(97.98), 99.65(98.1), respectively for the fusion techniques, such as sum, max, min, product, strategy A and strategy B.

The receiver operating characteristic curves of the proposed score normalization techniques are plotted in accordance with their fusion techniques i.e., sum, max, min, product, strategy A, and strategy B as shown in Fig. 2. For example using sum rule, the proposed techniques FSDS (MLTL) render the TAR value of 80 % (83 %) at 0 % of FAR. The TAR value reaches to 100 % at 0.5 % (1.2 %)

of FAR for FSDS (MLTL) normalization technique. These values of TAR are far better than the other existing score normalization techniques as shown in Fig. 2(a). Next, under max rule of fusion the proposed technique FSDS (MLTL) shows the TAR value of 80 % (83 %) at 0.2 % of FAR. The TAR value reaches to 100 % at 3.3 % (4.4 %) of FAR for FSDS (MLTL) normalization technique. These values of TAR are better than the other existing normalization techniques as shown in Fig. 2(b).

Similarly, using min rule of fusion the proposed technique FSDS (MLTL) renders the TAR of 83 % (87 %) at 0 % of FAR. The TAR value reaches to 100 % at 1.9 % (2.1 %) of FAR for FSDS (MLTL) normalization technique. These values of TAR are far better than the other existing normalization techniques as shown in Fig. 2(c). The proposed technique FSDS (MLTL) shows the TAR value of 85 % (83 %) at 0 % of FAR using product rule of fusion. The TAR value reaches to 100 % at 0.9 % (1.4 %) of FAR for FSDS (MLTL) normalization technique. The reported values of TAR are better than the other existing normalization techniques using product rule as shown in Fig. 2(d).

For fusion strategy A, the normalization technique FSDS (MLTL) shows the TAR of 77 % (75 %) at 0 % of FAR. The TAR value reaches to 100 % at 0.8 % (1.7 %) of FAR for FSDS (MLTL) normalization technique. These values of TAR are better than the other normalization techniques as shown in Fig. 2(e). Same results are also reported for fusion strategy B e.g., the FSDS (MLTL) normalization technique reported the TAR of 83 % (80 %) at 0 % of FAR. The TAR reaches to 100 % at 0.7 % (1.3 %) of FAR for FSDS (MLTL). The reported values of TAR are found better than the other normalization techniques using the fusion strategy B as shown in Fig. 2(f).

The recognition accuracy results of the suggested techniques i.e., MLTL and FSDS indicate that these score normalization techniques can contribute a peculiar role in the design of a robust multibiometric system.

5   Conclusion

This paper has presented two novel techniques of score normalization namely, modified-linear-tanh-linear (MLTL) and four-segments-double-sigmoid (FSDS). The performance of these proposed score normalization techniques has been evaluated and the fusion of face recognition methods Fisherface and A-LBP. The performance of the proposed score normalization techniques have found better than the existing min-max, tanh and linear-tanh-linear (LTL) normalization techniques. This evaluation of score normalization techniques of matching scores insinuates that the proposed techniques may play an important role in evaluating the performance of a multibiometric system.

Acknowledgements. The authors acknowledge the Institute of Engineering and Technology (IET), Lucknow, Uttar Pradesh Technical University (UPTU), Lucknow for their partial financial support to carry out this research under the Technical Education Quality Improvement Programme (TEQIP-II) grant.

References

1. Jain, A.K., Ross, A.: Multibiometric systems. Commun. ACM **47**(1), 34–40 (2004)
2. Snelick, R., Uludag, U., Mink, A., Indovina, M., Jain, A.: Large scale evaluation of multimodal biometric authentication using state-of-the-art systems. IEEE Trans. Pattern Anal. Mach. Intell. **27**(3), 450–455 (2005)
3. Bolle, R.M., Ratha, N.K., Pankanti, S.: Error analysis of pattern recognition systems the subsets bootstrap. Comput. Vis. Image Underst. **93**(1), 1–33 (2004)
4. Shyam, R., Singh, Y.N.: Identifying individuals using multimodal face recognition techniques. Procedia Comput. Sci. Elsevier **48**, 666–672 (2015)
5. Singh, Y.N., Singh, S.K., Gupta, P.: Fusion of electrocardiogram with unobtrusive biometrics: an efficient individual authentication system. Pattern Recogn. Lett. Elsevier **33**(11), 1932–1941 (2012)
6. Singh, Y.N.: Human recognition using fisher's discriminant analysis of heartbeat interval features and ECG morphology. Neurocomputing Elsevier **167**(2015), 322–335 (2015)
7. Singh, Y.N., Gupta, P.: Quantitative evaluation of normalization techniques of matching scores in multimodal biometric systems. In: Lee, Seong-Whan, Li, Stan Z. (eds.) ICB 2007. LNCS, vol. 4642, pp. 574–583. Springer, Heidelberg (2007)
8. Shyam, R., Singh, Y.N.: A taxonomy of 2D and 3D face recognition methods. In: Proceedings of 1st International Conference on Signal Processing and Integrated Networks (SPIN 2014), pp. 749–754. IEEE, February 2014
9. Shyam, R., Singh, Y.N.: Evaluation of eigenfaces and fisherfaces using bray curtis dissimilarity metric. In: Proceedings of 9th IEEE International Conference on Industrial and Information Systems (ICIIS 2014), pp. 1–6. IEEE, Gwalior, December 2014
10. Shyam, R., Singh, Y.N.: Face recognition using augmented local binary patterns and bray curtis dissimilarity metric. In: Proceedings of 2nd International Conference on Signal Processing and Integrated Networks (SPIN 2015), pp. 779–784. IEEE, Noida, February 2015
11. Shyam, R., Singh, Y.N.: Analysis of local descriptors for human face recognition. In: Smart Innovation, Systems and Technologies, vol. 43, pp. 263–269. Springer, October 2015
12. Shyam, R., Singh, Y.N.: Automatic face recognition in digital world. Adv. Comput. Sci. Inf. Technol. (ACSIT) **2**(1), 64–70 (2015)
13. Shyam, R., Singh, Y.N.: Recognizing individuals from unconstrained facial images. Adv. Intell. Syst. Comput. Ser. Springer **384**, 383–392 (2015)
14. Kittler, J., Hatef, M., Duin, R., Matas, J.: On combining classifiers. IEEE Trans. Pattern Anal. Mach. Intell. **20**(3), 226–239 (1998)
15. Jain, A., Nandakumar, K., Ross, A.: Score normalization in multimodal biometric systems. Pattern Recogn. **38**(12), 2270–2285 (2005)
16. Samaria, F., Harter, A.: Parameterisation of a stochastic model for human face identification. In: Proceedings of 2nd IEEE Workshop on Applications of Computer Vision, Sarasota, FL, December 1994

Enforcing Secure Data Sharing in Web Application Development Frameworks Like Django Through Information Flow Control

S. Susheel[1], N.V. Narendra Kumar[2](✉), and R.K. Shyamasundar[3]

[1] P.E.S Institute of Technology, Bengaluru, India
susheel.suresh@gmail.com
[2] Tata Institute of Fundamental Research, Mumbai, India
naren.nelabhotla@gmail.com
[3] Indian Institute of Technology, Mumbai, India
rkss@cse.iitb.ac.in

Abstract. The primary aim of web application development frameworks like Django is to provide a platform for developers to realize applications from concepts to launch as quickly as possible. While Django framework provides hooks that enable the developer to avoid the common security mistakes, there is no systematic way to assure compliance of a security policy while developing an application from various components. In this paper, we show the security flaws that arise by considering different versions of an application package and then show how, these mistakes that arise due to incorrect flow of information can be overcome using the Readers-Writers Flow Model that has the ability to manage the release and subsequent propagation of information.

1 Introduction

Web applications are increasingly becoming the primary curators of personal and corporate data. Social media applications like Facebook [2], LinkedIn [3] and Twitter [4] have transformed how users communicate with each other, while online document suites like Google Docs [5] or Office Online [6] have made online collaboration the norm. Much of the success of such Web applications is due to the flexibility in allowing third-party vendors to extend user experiences.

Most of today's web applications do not give users end-to-end security on their data. Lampson [7] describes most of the real word problems regarding the gold standard: authentication, authorization and auditing. This means that if a user A decides to share a piece of important/private information with another user B in the system, there is no way of tracking an information leak if, user B decides to make it public or share it with C, who could benefit from it and in turn harm or invade A's privacy.

In the age of a social web and semantic web [8], data belonging to one user might be accessible to an application installed by another user, introducing even more complexity. Due to the complex interactions that are possible in collaborative systems such as social networks, it is important to not only control the

© Springer International Publishing Switzerland 2015
S. Jajodia and C. Mazumdar (Eds.): ICISS 2015, LNCS 9478, pp. 551–561, 2015.
DOI: 10.1007/978-3-319-26961-0_34

release of information (achieved through access controls), but also to control the flow of information among the various stakeholders involved. This is achieved through information flow control (IFC). It is a well established fact that the traditional discretionary access controls are prone to attacks by Trojan horses that can cause indirect usage of data beyond the observation of access controls. IFC which is a form of mandatory access control prevents these types of indirect data misuse.

In this paper, we first experimentally demonstrate that current access controls in web applications are prone to Trojan horses. Then, we demonstrate how addition of simple checks using the RWFM model on the application permits us to enforce information flow control that resist Trojan horses. Fewer than 120 lines of code was needed to achieve this, and more importantly this is all the code needed to protect any application, thus, leading to an extremely scalable solution.

A summary of the contributions of this paper follows:

- Established that Trojan horse type attacks are very much possible in current security architectures.
- Provided an effective way in which practical concepts of authorization are mapped onto the label model.
- Illustrated the simplicity and efficiency of RWFM for securing data sharing in web applications; even the interference between two sessions of the same user are prevented.
- Simplified policy compliance and audit trials.

The rest of the paper is organized as follows: Sect. 2 provides an overview of current approaches to secure data sharing in web applications. Section 3 presents a quick introduction to our RWFM model. Experimental demonstration of the possibility of Trojan horse like attacks in an open source Django based web application, and its mitigation using RWFM are discussed in Sect. 4. Section 5 provides concluding remarks.

2   Overview of Currently Used Access Controls in Web Applications

Historically, access control [9–11] has been the main means of preventing information from being disseminated. One of ways in which web development teams handle security policies is by decoupling their business logic from their authorization logic by externalizing authorization [12]. Externalizing authorization is possible using many access control paradigms like, XACML (eXtensible Access Control Markup Language) [13], ACL (Access Control Lists), and RBAC [10].

However, for simplicity web developers often use ad-hoc security to enforce and implement complex policies, that leads to a lot of problems like:

- the specified policy is intertwined throughout code which is error prone and is not scalable,

– makes the policy of an application difficult to "prove" for audit or quality assurance purpose, and
– causes new code to be pushed each time an access control policy needs to be changed.

The rapid progress of Web 2.0 [14] technologies have brought in a whole new category of web services which are content rich and allow users to interact and share information with each other easily. In addition, web applications publish APIs that enable software developers to easily integrate existing data and functions to create mashups which provide users enriched experience instead of building them by themselves. A lot of research is being conducted for securing web applications from third party extensions and mashups [15–18].

This calls for a model which is able to track and regulate information flow in a web application. An IFC model with a consistent labelling framework unifying both mandatory and discretionary access control is required. In the web setting, it must also enable formal assessment of conformance to security and privacy policies. Further, as advocated by Woo and Lam [30], and Abadi [29], the label must capture the entire essence of the transaction history in a succinct manner to cater to the practical performance.

3   Readers-Writers Flow Model

The first mathematical model for tracking information flow was given by Denning [26]. The lattice model was the first step in the right direction to understand the dynamic nature of information flows. A lot of work has been done in this field and a large body of literature has sprung up [19–22], yet information flow based enforcement/implementation mechanisms have not been used widely in the industry. Steve Zdancewic [23] presents the challenges for practical implementation of IFC.

In this section, we introduce the Readers-Writers Flow Model (RWFM) [27,28] which is a novel model for information flow control. RWFM is obtained by recasting the Denning's label model [26], and has a label structure that: (i) explicitly captures the readers and writers of information, (ii) makes the semantics of labels explicit, and (iii) immediately provides an intuition for its position in the lattice flow policy.

Definition 1 (Readers-Writers Flow Model (RWFM)). *RWFM is defined as a five-tuple* $(S, O, S \times 2^S \times 2^S, (*, \supseteq, \subseteq), (*, \cap, \cup))$, *where* S *and* O *denote the set of subjects and objects in the information system respectively,* $S \times 2^S \times 2^S$ *is the set of security labels,* $(*, \supseteq, \subseteq)$ *denotes the can-flow-to ordering amongst labels, and* $(*, \cap, \cup)$ *denotes the label combining operator.*

The first component of a RWFM label denotes the ownership of information, second component denotes the permissible readers of information, and third component denotes the set of principals that influenced the information. For example, the RWFM label of *Alice*'s private key would be $(S, \{A\}, \{A, S\})$, indicating that S created it, A is the only permissible reader of it, and both A and

S have influenced it, where A denotes *Alice* and S denotes key server/certificate authority.

Theorem 1 (Completeness). RWFM *is a complete model, w.r.to Denning's lattice model, for studying information flows in an information system.*

RWFM follows a floating-label approach for subjects, with $(s, S, \{s\})$ and $(s, \{s\}, S)$ as the "**default label**" and "**clearance**" for a subject s respectively, where S is the set of all the subjects in the system. RWFM follows a static labelling approach for objects, with the exception of downgrading, which is allowed to change the label of an object by adding readers.

RWFM provides a semantics of secure information flow through *Information Flow Diagram* (IFD), which presents significant advantages and preserves useful invariants. IFD is a state transition system defined as follows:

Definition 2 (State of Information System). *State of an information system is defined by the triple* (S, O, λ) *denoting the set of current subjects and objects in the system together with their current labels.*

State transitions of an information system are defined by RWFM considering the need for supporting the following operations: (i) subject reads an object, (ii) subject writes an object, (iii) subject downgrades an object, and (iv) subject creates a new object.

RWFM describes the conditions under which an operation is safe as follows:

READ Rule. *Subject s with label* (s_1, R_1, W_1) *requests read access to an object o with label* (s_2, R_2, W_2).
If $(s \in R_2)$ then
    change the label of s to $(s_1, R_1 \cap R_2, W_1 \cup W_2)$
    ALLOW
Else
    DENY

WRITE Rule. *Subject s with label* (s_1, R_1, W_1) *requests write access to an object o with label* (s_2, R_2, W_2).
If $(s \in W_2 \land R_1 \supseteq R_2 \land W_1 \subseteq W_2)$ then
    ALLOW
Else
    DENY

DOWNGRADE Rule. *Subject s with label* (s_1, R_1, W_1) *requests to downgrade an object o from its current label* (s_2, R_2, W_2) *to* (s_3, R_3, W_3).
If $(s \in R_2 \land s_1 = s_2 = s_3 \land R_1 = R_2 \land W_1 = W_2 = W_3 \land R_2 \subseteq R_3 \land (W_1 = \{s_1\} \lor (R_3 - R_2 \subseteq W_2)))$ then
    ALLOW
Else
    DENY

CREATE Rule. *Subject s labelled* (s_1, R_1, W_1) *requests to create an object o.* Create a new object o, label it as (s_1, R_1, W_1) and add it to the set of objects O.

Given an initial set of objects on a lattice, IFD accurately computes the labels for the newly created information at various stages of the transaction/workflow.

4   Securing Information Flow Among Users in Web Applications with RWFM

In this section, we illustrate simultaneously the simplicity and the power of RWFM for controlling and tracking information flow among users in web applications. Simplicity of RWFM enables an intuitive mapping of actions in the application to the operations of read and write in the abstract model.

For demonstrating the information flow control imposed by RWFM we chose an open source web application called DBpatterns [24][1] written in python using Django, a high-level Python Web Framework. We choose Django because it encourages rapid development, has a clean pragmatic design and is very popular among web developers. DBpatterns is an application that allows users to create, share and explore database schemas on the web. Further, this application supports features like collaboration with remote users, sharing information with fellow users, and ability to make information public or private, and also embodies a RESTful design by giving API endpoints for accessing data and certain functions. This fits well with the problem discussed before. By analysing the flow of information in this system and applying the RWFM, we show that a series of attacks that exists in the current architectures are resolved and propose that this model is easy to use and can be integrated with any web application.

4.1   Overview of DBpatterns

DBpatterns is web application which helps users in creating, sharing and exploring database schemas or models. The main features of the application are:

– User account creation and user authentication.
– User can explore database schemas which are public using public feed.
– User has the ability to fork public viewable schemas created by other members.
– User can create schemas and can set visibility to either public or private.
– User can add collaborators for a schema, and can grant view, edit permission or both.
– Users receive notification if they have been assigned any access in private or public schema documents.

---

[1] DBpatterns is a service that allows you to create, share, and explore database models on the web. Uses Django, Tastypie, Backbone and MongoDB.

Access Control Logic in DBpatterns. The access control policy is written using ad-hoc security policies. The main access control related definitions are stored in the database with the schema document itself. It consists of,

- *is*Public is a boolean value which specifies the visibility of the document.
- Assignees is an array which holds the assigned users for the document with their access permission like *can*View or *can*Edit.

Using these two attributes, access control checks are implemented throughout the application. This kind of implementation common in many web applications.

We have studied the access control logic implementation and experimented on possible attacks that might occur targeting the application's lack of controlling information flow. Section 4.2 gives a detailed account for the possible attack scenarios.

4.2   Attack Scenarios in DBpatterns

Here we give a brief summary of the kind of attacks that were carried out on the DBpatterns web application.

Let the users of the system be Jack, Alice and Bob.

Attack 1 (Read - Attack). Jack shares a document, say D_1, with Alice. Alice forks D_1 and makes a local copy, call it D_2. Alice now owns D_2 and can set access restrictions on it. Alice gives read permission on D_2 to Bob. This way Jack will be unaware of an information leak and Bob who did not have authorization to view D_1 can now read D_2 which essentially has the same information as D_1. These kind of attacks that bypass access control logic are called Trojan horses. The screenshots of attack 1 are depicted in Fig. 1.

Note that the attacks described in this section are possible on any discretionary access control mechanism, and are not specific to this web application.

4.3   Mitigating the Attacks Using RWFM

The flaws discussed in Sect. 4.2 exist in most web applications. Using an IFC based approach, we have successfully implemented RWFM in conjunction with the existing access control logic of DBpatterns and our implementation of RWFM will help web developers mitigate such attacks and also give them a clear picture of both subject and object labels at any given point of time.

RWFM automatically labels subjects and objects as the information flows in the system, given the initial state of DBpatterns application. Using the read, write, and create rules of RWFM, our implementation efficiently tracks information flow for all possible user interactions with the application and successfully resists the attacks presented in Sect. 4.2.

According to OWASP Top 10 Security Vulnerabilities of 2013 [25], Broken Authentication and Session Management was ranked second, our implementation takes into account, user sessions and protects the application from IFC related attacks through session fixation and manages multiple sessions from the same

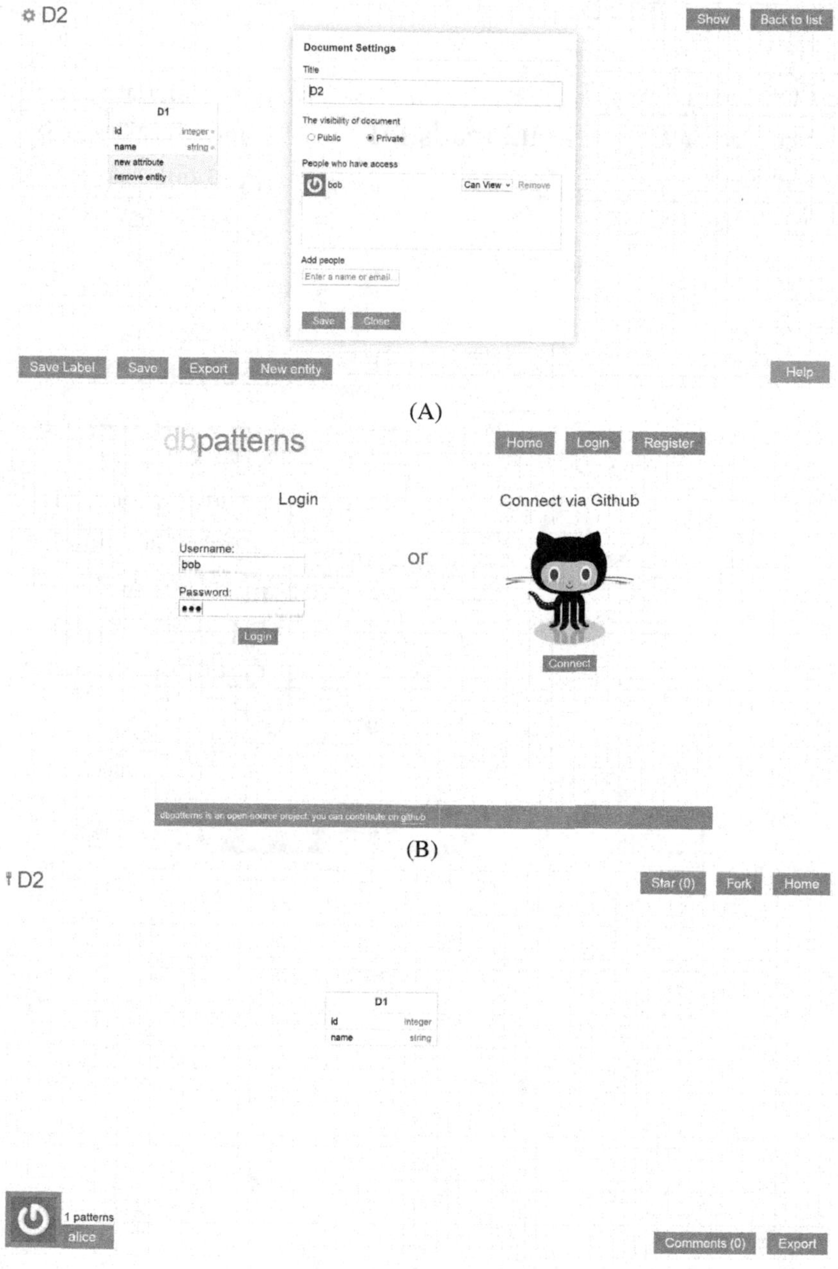

(A)

(B)

(C)

Fig. 1. (A) Alice grants Bob read access to document D_2. (B) Bob logs into the application, and (C) views schema document D_2.

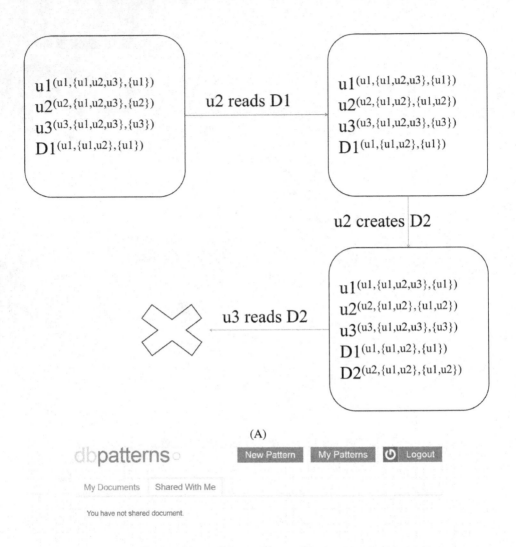

(A)

(B)

Fig. 2. (A) Information flow diagram for attack 1. (B) RWFM mitigates attack 1, by not showing D_2 in Bob's view.

user. In our implementation on DBpatterns, user sessions are treated as subjects, and documents are treated as objects.

Notation: u_1, u_2 and u_3 denote Jack, Alice, and Bob respectively. $S = \{u_1, u_2, u_3\}$ denotes the set of all the users of the system. Entity (subject or object) e with label l is denoted e^l.

Information flow diagram for the scenario of attack 1 and its mitigation by RWFM is depicted in Fig. 2. Note that in the last transition in Fig. 2(A), u_3 is not allowed to read D_2, because u_3 is not a member of readers of D_2 (second component of its label). The screenshot in Fig. 2(B) shows that our implementation denies user u_3 view of D_2. Compare this to the original application screenshot in Fig. 1(C), where u_3 is permitted to view D_2.

4.4 Discussion

In [14], authors show how cross-domain access to sensitive information can be enabled by using IFC on the client side. However, their approach forbids propagation of sensitive information which limits its usability. Their technique facilitates DOM (Document Object Model) operations and function calls within scripts at the add-on level, thus, enabling effective control over existing channels for cross-domain communication. A further limitation of their approach is that users will have to label and identify information important to them, thus resulting in a huge burden.

Client side mashup security is discussed in [16]. A security lattice of syntactic labels is used to label the classified objects, where an object's label corresponds to the origin from which it is loaded, and are used to track information flow within the browser. Their approach supports usage of a range of techniques, such as static and/or dynamic analysis to ensure that information from one origin does not flow to another one unless the information has been declassified. Using syntactic labels and purely discretionary downgrading rules leads to corrosion of flow lattice.

Salient Features of RWFM Implementation are:

1. Our implementation complements the existing access control logic.
2. No major code revisions have to be done for implementing this model.
3. Our implementation does works with any access control mechanism.
4. Subject and Object labels can be accessed at any point of time, this can play a vital role during a security audit.
5. RWFM accurately handles dynamic label changes automatically.
6. This model can scale on par with any web application project with minimal development overhead.

5 Conclusions

In this paper, through a case study, we have clearly demonstrated the possible attacks that might occur in web applications if we don't follow proper information flow control, and demonstrated how these can be overcome easily by using the RWFM model. Based on the experiences of this work, we plan to build a general-purpose re-usable IFC implementation to protect information flow in web applications developed using Django, such that any Django web application developer with the knowledge of information entering and leaving the objects in the system can easily and automatically enforce proper information flow restrictions by invoking this package at appropriate points in the application.

References

1. Django. https://www.djangoproject.com
2. Facebook. http://www.facebook.com
3. LinkedIn. http://linkedin.com
4. Twitter.com. http://twitter.com
5. Google docs. https://www.google.co.in/docs/about/
6. Microsoft office online. https://office.live.com
7. Lampson, B.W.: Computer security in the real world. Computer **37**(6), 37–46 (2004)
8. Gruber, T.: Collective knowledge systems: where the social web meets the semantic web. Web Semant.: Sci. Serv. Agents World Wide Web **6**, 4–13 (2008)
9. Harrison, M.A., Ruzzo, W.L., Ullman, J.D.: Protection in operating systems. CACM **19**(8), 461–471 (1976)
10. Ferraiolo, D., Kuhn, R.: Role-based access control. In: 15th NIST-NCSC, pp. 554–563 (1992)
11. Barkley, J., Cincotta, A., Ferraiolo, D., Gavrila, S., Kuhn, D.R.: Role based access control for the world wide web. In: 20th NCSC, pp. 331–340, April 1997
12. Kreizman, G.: Technology overview for externalized authorization management. https://www.gartner.com/doc/2358815/technology-overview-externalized-authorization-management
13. eXtensible access control markup language (XACML) version 3.0. http://docs.oasis-open.org/xacml/3.0/xacml-3.0-core-spec-os-en.html
14. Murugesan, S.: Understanding web 2.0. IT Prof. **9**(4), 34–41 (2007)
15. Li, Z., Zhang, K., Wang, X.: Mash-IF: practical information-flow control within client-side mashups. In: IEEE/IFIP DSN (2010)
16. Ter Louw, M., Lim, J.S., Venkatakrishnan, V.N.: Enhancing web browser security against malware extensions. J. Comput. Virol. **4**(3), 179–195 (2008)
17. Magazinius, J., Askarov, A., Sabelfeld, A.: A lattice-based approach to mashup security. In: ACM 5th ASIACCS (2010)
18. De Ryck, P., Decat, M., Desmet, L., Piessens, F., Joosen, W.: Security of web mashups: a survey. In: Aura, T., Järvinen, K., Nyberg, K. (eds.) NordSec 2010. LNCS, vol. 7127, pp. 223–238. Springer, Heidelberg (2012)
19. Myers, A.C., Liskov, B.: A decentralized model for information flow control. In: ACM 16th SOSP, pp. 129–142 (1997)
20. Denning, D.E.: Cryptography and Data Security. Addison-Wesley, Reading (1982)
21. Krohn, M., Yip, A., Brodsky, M., Cliffer, N., Frans Kaashoek, M., Kohler, E., Morris, R.: Information flow control for standard OS abstractions. In: ACM SIGOPS Operating Systems Review, vol. 41, no. 6, pp. 321–334. ACM (2007)
22. Sabelfeld, A., Myers, A.C.: Language-based information-flow security. IEEE J. Sel. Areas Commun. **21**(1), 5–19 (2003)

23. Zdancewic, S.: Challenges for information-flow security. In: Proceedings of the 1st International Workshop on the Programming Language Interference and Dependence (PLID04) (2004)
24. DBpatterns. http://www.dbpatterns.com
25. OWASP. https://www.owasp.org
26. Denning, D.E.: A lattice model of secure information flow. Commun. ACM **19**(5), 236–243 (1976)
27. Narendra Kumar, N.V., Shyamasundar, R.K.: Realizing purpose-based privacy policies succinctly via information-flow labels. In: IEEE 4th BdCloud, pp. 753–760 (2014)
28. Narendra Kumar, N.V., Shyamasundar, R.K.: POSTER: dynamic labelling for analyzing security protocols. In: ACM 22nd CCS (2015)
29. Abadi, M.: Security protocols and their properties. In: Foundations of Secure Computation. NATO Science Series, pp. 39–60. IOS Press (2000)
30. Woo, T.Y.C., Lam, S.S.: A lesson on authentication protocol design. SIGOPS Oper. Syst. Rev. **28**(3), 24–37 (1994)

A New Threshold Certification Scheme Based Defense Against Sybil Attack for Sensor Networks

Satyajit Banerjee[1], Debapriyay Mukhopadhyay[2]([✉]), and Suman Roy[3]

[1] Infoworks.io, Bangalore, India
satyajitb@gmail.com
[2] Ixia Technologies Pvt Ltd, Kolkata 700091, India
debapriyaym@gmail.com
[3] Infosys Ltd, 44 Electronics City, Hosur Road, Bangalore 560100, India
suman_roy@infosys.com

Abstract. Security is a major concern for a large fraction of sensor network applications. Douceur first introduced the notion of Sybil attack [5], where a single entity (node) illegitimately presents multiple identities. As the nodes in sensor networks can be physically captured by an adversary, Sybil attack can manifest in a severe form leading to the malfunction of basic operational protocols. It is also pointed out in [5] that Sybil attack could be prevented if each honest identity possesses an unforgeable certificate issued by a trusted authority. The identity is mandated to produce the certificate as a proof of authenticity before it takes part in any network activity. Since ordinary certification schemes are not suitable for sensor networks due to some typical incompatibility features, we propose a symmetric key based threshold certification scheme specially designed to defend Sybil attack in sensor networks.

Keywords: Sybil attack · Symmetric key cryptography · Threshold scheme · Secret share · Certificate

1 Introduction

Sensor networks are now being widely deployed in planned or ad hoc basis to monitor and protect different targeted infrastructures including life-critical applications such as wildlife monitoring, military target tracking, home security monitoring and scientific exploration in hazardous environments. Unlike in general data networks, the nodes of sensor networks may be physically captured by an adversary and thus can induce different modes of harmful attacks in addition to active and passive eavesdropping. This typical feature also makes the design of cryptographic primitives for sensor networks extremely challenging. Douceur

---

Most of this work were done when the authors were with HTSL, Bangalore during 2004 - 2006.

© Springer International Publishing Switzerland 2015
S. Jajodia and C. Mazumdar (Eds.): ICISS 2015, LNCS 9478, pp. 562–572, 2015.
DOI: 10.1007/978-3-319-26961-0_35

first introduced the notion of Sybil attack [5], where a single entity illegitimately claims multiple identities. Physically captured nodes claiming superfluous misbehaving identities could control a substantial fraction of the system leading to malfunction of basic operational protocols including routing, resource allocation and misbehavior detection. An excellent taxonomy of Sybil attacks in sensor networks and their detrimental effects are presented in [9], along with some defense mechanisms.

Sybil attack could be prevented if each honest identity possesses an unforgeable certificate issued by some trusted Certifying Authority (CA) and it is mandated to produce that certificate as a proof of authenticity before the identity takes part in any network activity. This condition implies that for inducing Sybil attack the adversary has to necessarily forge valid certificates. It is also clearly pointed out in [5] that the existence of a logically trusted CA is a must to defend Sybil attack except under extreme and unrealistic assumptions. But certification schemes designed for general purpose networks are not suitable for sensor networks due to some typical incompatibility features. So, our basic motivation is to suitably design a certification scheme for sensor network so that it can defend Sybil attack.

In public key cryptography, forgery of identity by fake nodes is prevented by having a trusted CA that issues a digital certificate to each node. The certificate is a node's identity and its public key information signed by the secret key of the CA. Each node in the network can verify the validity of any other node's certificate with the CA's public key. Typically, the nodes of a sensor network are resource constrained devices in terms of storage, computation and transmission power as they are battery powered. A public key based scheme requires expensive computation and long message transmission that quickly depletes the battery of the sensor nodes. On the other hand, symmetric key based schemes are orders of magnitude cheaper and thus are well suited for sensor network applications.

Another typical property of sensor networks that creates trouble in providing security services is its inherent intrusion model. There can be physical capture of the nodes by an adversary in addition to active or passive eavesdropping. So, a centralized trusted CA is not suitable, since the CA node could be physically captured leading to a single point of failure. Therefore, aim should be to logically distribute CA's functionality uniformly to each sensor node in the network. Thus we choose to adopt a (t, n) threshold technique for our certification scheme. Any t out of n nodes in the sensor network together can perform the functions of a trusted CA and provide individually verifiable certificate for each honest identity in the network. The network continues to function correctly as long as number of captured nodes are less than t.

Again, nodes in sensor networks are generally deployed in large numbers and can join or leave the network on the fly at any time. So while designing the certification scheme we need to make sure that the scheme is scalable and also robust in a dynamic network. Finally, as a node needs to get its certificate validated every time it initiates some network activity, the validation procedure should be reasonably fast so that the network performance is not too compromised. However, the scheme can afford to be a bit expensive while generating such certificates, as this activity is carried out infrequently.

Summarizing all the points, what we are looking for is a symmetric key based threshold certification scheme with some special features for sensor networks. In this paper, we propose realization of such a scheme. The organization of the paper is as follows. Section 2 describes a summary of the existing works and Sect. 3 presents the basic concepts and terminologies. Section 4 illustrates the proposed certification scheme along with an evaluation of its effectiveness with respect to typical attack model. And finally Sect. 5 concludes this work.

2   Related Work

Sybil attack was first introduced by Douceur in [5], wherein a direct valida-tion method of a node's identity, based on resource testing, was proposed. The basic idea of the scheme is to estimate the resource (*e.g.,* computation, storage and communication) associated with each identity and thereby deciding whether each identity possesses an exclusive hardware piece. Though the scheme works fine for general P2P networks, it is not appropriate for sensor networks where an adversary may bring in very powerful devices, in terms of computation, stor-age and communication, to defeat the scheme. Karlof *et al.* analyzed different attacks including Sybil attack in [6] for wireless sensor network and described some countermeasures against them. In their scheme each node is provided with a unique symmetric key which it shares with a trusted base station. Two nodes then verify each other's identity using symmetric Needham-Schroeder [1] proto-col. The solution thus relies on the existence of a trusted third party. However, there are some attacks [3] against Needham-Schroeder protocol in which case the proposed solution fails.

Wang *et al.* [7], introduced the concept of trust graph in mobile ad hoc net-work, which facilitates establishing trust relationship between communicating nodes and considers the possibility of having heterogeneous CAs. Assumption here is that if CA_i trusts CA_j then CA_i also trusts identities certified by CA_j. It is interesting to note here that this assumption and mechanism can safeguard against Sybil attack as long as none of the CAs is compromised. Their scheme also demands each node to have moderately high storage and computational capability and also charges high communication cost and thus remains unsuit-able for sensor networks. Newsome *et al.* in their work [9] established a taxonomy of different kinds of Sybil attack and have provided a series of methods including radio resource testing, key validation for random key pre-distribution, position verification and registration, to verify whether a node's identity is a Sybil iden-tity.

Kong *et al.* proposed a public key cryptography based distributed threshold certification scheme [4] which establishes trust relationship between communicat-ing nodes via unforgeable, renewable and globally verifiable certificates carried by each node in the network. Though not explicitly mentioned in their work, it can stand against Sybil attack, as otherwise attacker has to guess valid certificate of the claimed identity. But, their work is based on public key cryptography and targeted to meet the needs of wireless ad hoc networks. It does not readily suit well in resource constrained sensor networks. [8, 11] also talks about defending sybil attack using public key cryptography and authentication mechanism and in these solutions signatures are combined with digital signatures. But in sensor networks, it is difficult to deploy PKI since there is no gurantee of the presence of appropriate infrastucture and also individual nodes are computationally resource constrained devices.

Zhang *et al.* in [10] have proposed an identity certificate based scheme to defend against Sybil attack in sensor networks. Their method associates each node's identity with an unique identity certificate, where Merkle hash tree has been used as the basic means of computing identity certificates. Main drawback of the scheme is that it it is not scalable as it does not allow nodes to join the network on the fly because of huge computational overhead. Method also can not stand against Sybil attack launched by colluding nodes. We follow a similar line as that of Kong *et al.* to prevent Sybil attack and propose a symmetric key cryptography based threshold certification scheme specially designed for sensor networks.

3 Preliminaries

We first define some of the pivotal concepts that will be used frequently in the subsequent sections. We also point out some terminologies essential to properly qualify them.

3.1 Symmetric Key Based Certificates

The concept of certificates is well established in asymmetric key cryptography. On the other hand, in symmetric key cryptography the concept of signature is hazy. We can view a certificate in symmetric key cryptography domain as some unforgeable object provided by the trusted CA to each entity that validates only the authenticity of its identity. But the problem is, once a node X produces its certificate to some other node Y for validation, unlike in public key domain, Y can pretend as identity X to some other node Z with X's certificate and get successfully validated. So, it is customary to get this validation done with partial information about the certificate, *i.e.*, X only produces the partial information that is of interest to Y and Y validates based on that. This prevents Y to pretend as X, since Y does not know about the partial information of X's certificate that is of interest to Z. Since it turns out to be a partial validation of certificate, the scheme needs to ensure that it is reasonably improbable for some fake nodes to convince others. One more problem is that every time a particular node X is validated by different nodes $A_1, A_2, \ldots, A_k$, some partial information about the certificate is leaked and thus the whole certificate of X would be revealed in course of time. The scheme can stand in spite of such a phenomenon, if refreshment of certificate related information in regular interval be possible.

3.2 Threshold Certification Scheme

Nodes of a sensor network can be physically captured and thus keeping a centralized CA may lead to single point of failure. Thus our basic aim is to distribute the CA's functionality uniformly among each of the n nodes of the sensor network (in terms of some "secret-shares" provided by a trusted Dealer) so that, any s, $s \geq t$, nodes together can issue valid certificates to new nodes. We would like to go one step further to rule out the existence of a central trusted Dealer who provides secret-shares to each node. In fact, the functionality of the trusted Dealer also would be uniformly distributed amongst the nodes with a similar condition, *i.e.,* any s, $s \geq t$, nodes together can issue valid secret-shares to new nodes. These two features qualify the certification scheme to be truly distributed and self-sufficient. Let us define a few terms before we proceed further.

1. **Identity Certificate (IC) and Secret Share (SS):** Each working node contains both of these components. IC is basically an analog of certificate in the symmetric key domain. Each working node in the sensor network holds an IC and other nodes rely on those ICs to validate the authenticity of the nodes. The sole purpose of SS is to validate and generate ICs.
2. **Partial Certificate (PC) and Partial Share (PS):** PC and PS are the partial information about a node's IC and SS. A requesting node receives PC (or PS) from t other nodes, and can uniquely construct its IC (or SS) with those t different PCs (or PSs). The helping nodes construct the PCs (or PSs) for the requesting node using their respective SS (or IC) without revealing the SS (or IC) itself.
3. **Per Node Certificate Information (PNCI):** As each working node contains both IC and SS as its certificate related information, we will refer them together as PNCI. The components IC and SS are complementary to each other as one validates and generates the other.

Basic purpose of a certification scheme is to provide a mechanism for each node to validate others certificate (IC) individually. But, since our certification scheme will use the notion of threshold cryptography in the symmetric key domain, so following additional points are required to be addressed.

1. **Any s, $s \geq t$, out of n honest nodes should be able to provide a unforgeable certificate to a requesting node:** This is to replace a central CA from the network and distribute the functionality of CA uniformly across the nodes so that any t out of n nodes together can perform like CA whereas less than t nodes can not perform the same.
2. **Any s, $s \geq t$, out of n working nodes should be able to provide a SS to a new node:** This feature rules out the existence of a central trusted Dealer who provides secret shares to each node. Rather, the functionality of the Dealer is also uniformly distributed across the nodes. Here also the same restriction is enforced, *i.e.,* any t out of n nodes cumulatively can perform like a Dealer whereas less than t nodes can not.

3. **Any t out of n working nodes should be able to initiate a PNCI refreshment phase:** As any (t, n) threshold scheme can withstand at most $(t-1)$ number of physical capture of the nodes. It is necessary to refresh the PNCI at regular intervals. Given an unbounded time-window, an adversary can gradually break into the network and physically capture t or more nodes. On the other hand, a regular PNCI refreshment policy leaves small quantum of time for the adversary to physically capture t or more nodes within that refreshment interval. This triggers the need to tune the refreshment interval that suits a particular sensor network the best.

4. **The requesting node should be able to verify the received PCs and PSs individually:** This is to ensure that the requesting node should be able to verify the correctness of the PC or PS received from each of the nodes of a chosen t member coalition for constructing its IC or SS. Otherwise, the requesting node could be cheated in the process leading to incorrect construction of IC or SS and will not be reliable and functional.

4   The Certification Scheme

Before describing the scheme, we will list down the set of underlying assumptions which are kept at a very minimal and reasonable set, as mentioned below.

1. Every node has in its possession a unique identification (ID) which we assume to be tamper-resistant. It is reasonable to assume that the IDs are unique even though the nodes are manufactured by different vendors.

2. Depending on the spatial density of nodes and vulnerability of the deployed region, the threshold parameter t can be chosen to make sure each node in the sensor network has at least t number of 1-hop neighboring nodes. Thus a new node can choose a group of t 1-hop away working nodes around it, to construct its SS and IC.

3. There is no man-in-the-middle attack. Since there are standard cryptographic primitives to handle it independently.

Our scheme is based on an extension of Shamir's threshold secret sharing scheme [2]. Unlike using $(t-1)$ degree single-variate polynomial, here we use a bi-variate polynomial of degree $(t-1)$ both in x and y as the pivotal element of the scheme.

$$f(x,y) = \sum_{i=0}^{t-1}\sum_{j=0}^{t-1} a_{ij}x^i y^j (\mathrm{mod}\ p),$$

where p is a large prime and a_{ij}s are randomly chosen from $\mathbb{Z}_p^*$ for all i, j. We do not require the bi-variate polynomial to be symmetric unlike many other cryptographic protocols [12].

Each working node k (*i.e.*, node having ID $= k, 1 \le k < p$) in the network holds two $(t-1)$ degree single-variate secret polynomials, namely $S_k(x)$ and $C_k(y)$, acting respectively as SS and IC, and are defined as $S_k(x) = f(x, k)$ and

$C_k(y) = f(k, y)$. Note that, since f is not symmetric, so $S_k(j) \neq C_k(j)$, but $S_k(j) = C_j(k) = f(j, k)$. $S_k(x)$ and $C_k(y)$ are both single variate polynomials of degree $(t-1)$. Hence each node has to store t coefficients for each of SS and IC, *i.e.*, associated space complexity per node is $O(t)$.

It is worth observing that the family of ICs and SSs form a grid like structure. Any t number of SS can provide t number of points on a particular IC and thus can uniquely construct it by Lagrange's interpolation method, since each IC is a $(t-1)$ degree single variable polynomial. The argument equally holds to justify that any t number of IC can uniquely construct any SS. These two fundamental properties are explored to get rid off trusted CA and Dealer. Note that (t, n) threshold scheme works independently only when there are already at least t working nodes. Thus initializing the first t nodes has to be carried out under human supervision. We will now show how the scheme serves the set of requirements spelt out so far and present the associated security features.

4.1 Certificate Should be Individually Verifiable

Suppose, an honest node A wants to verify node B's certificate. Node A first calculates $S_A(B)$ and then asks node B to furnish $C_B(A)$. Node A accepts node B's certificate if $C_B(A)$ matches with $S_A(B)$, since $S_A(B) = C_B(A) = f(B, A)$. Otherwise A rejects B's certificate. Here node A verifies node B's certificate at $y = A$ only and thus the verification process is very fast.

On verifying the value of B's IC at a single point A accepts the fact that B actually possesses the appropriate IC, namely $C_B(y)$. But it really does not weaken the scheme as $C_k(y)$s, $1 \leq k < p$, are derived from the original random bi-variate polynomial $f(x, y)$ and thus $C_B(A)$ can assume any value in $\mathbb{Z}_p^*$ with uniform probability. Thus B can convince A, without really possessing the IC, namely, $C_B(y)$, with probability $\frac{1}{p-1}$, since $|\mathbb{Z}_p^*| = p - 1$. The probability is reasonably low as it decreases exponentially with the size of p. This remains true even if up to $(t-1)$ misbehaving nodes form a coalition transparently and try to convince node A that they possess B's IC (without really having it). Since the coalition can at most manage to get $(t-1)$ different points on $C_B(y)$ with their respective SSs, they can not uniquely construct $C_B(y)$. In fact the coalition gets no information about the value of $C_B(A)$. So the probability of a valid certificate being forged by a group of $(t-1)$ misbehaving nodes does not improve and the scheme justifies it to be a perfect[1] scheme.

Another important criterion is how long an honest node can get its IC validated before the IC itself is revealed. An honest node would delete the PC information once the validation is over, misbehaving nodes might present different identities to a targeted node and try to accumulate as much partial information (*i.e.*, points on its IC polynomial) as possible about its IC. So as soon as the misbehaving nodes together accumulate t different points on the IC, they

---

[1] A (t, n) threshold scheme is perfect if the probability of guessing some secret with $(t-1)$ or less number of partial information about the secret is identical to the probability of guessing the secret with no information.

can uniquely construct it using Lagrange's interpolation method. So, our scheme exhibits $(t-1)$-tolerance against the IC exposure problem. Let us estimate how many successful validations a node's IC can withstand before it is suspected to be exposed.

We model the scenario with the following assumptions:

1. If node X wants to talk to node Y, it is node X who has to get its certificate validated by Y. This is a realistic scenario and it rules out the possibility for the misbehaving nodes to take initiative to get some honest nodes IC exposed.
2. Number of already captured nodes is $(t-1)$ and they transparently form a coalition so that they are indistinguishable.

Now the probability of an honest node's certificate getting validated by some captured node is $\frac{t-1}{n-1}$. Let us now calculate the probability P_i that an honest node's certificate is getting exposed by the captured nodes at the ith, $i \geq t$, validation of its certificate. P_i can then be viewed as, an honest node's IC being validated by captured nodes $(t-1)$ times (in any order) in the first $(i-1)$ Bernoulli trials followed by the ith validation once again by some captured node. Hence, from binomial probability distribution it follows,

$$P_i = \binom{i-1}{t-1}\left(\frac{t-1}{n-1}\right)^{t-1}\left(\frac{n-t}{n-1}\right)^{i-t}\left(\frac{t-1}{n-1}\right)$$

Hence, the expected Number of Validations (NoV) required to expose an honest node's certificate is given by,

$$E(NoV) = \sum_{i=t}^{\infty} i.P_i = \sum_{i=t}^{\infty} i\binom{i-1}{t-1}\left(\frac{t-1}{n-1}\right)^{t}\left(\frac{n-t}{n-1}\right)^{i-t}$$

The series evaluates to $\left(\frac{t}{t-1}\right)(n-1) = \Theta(n)$, for $t \geq 2$. As nodes of the sensor networks are generally deployed in a large scale, typically the value of n is pretty huge. Thus the worst case analysis illustrates that an honest node can safely get its IC validated, even if misbehaving nodes are around, for a reasonably large number of times in a typical scenario.

4.2   Any t Out of n Nodes Should be Capable to Generate an IC

We assume that SS is the first thing that is given to a new node followed by IC. So, when a node requests for IC, it already holds the SS. Let, B be a new node and A_is, $1 \leq i \leq t-1$, be the one-hop neighbors jointly issuing IC to B, *i.e.*, they work together to help node B construct $C_B(y)$. On verifying the authenticity of the node B, each node $A_i, 1 \leq i \leq (t-1)$, individually calculates the PC for B, namely, $S_{A_i}(B)$ and sends it to the new node B as their respective contribution and B itself calculates $S_B(B)$ with its SS. Node B thus receives t

ordered pairs $(A_i, S_{A_i}(B)), 1 \leq i \leq (t-1)$ and $(B, S_B(B))$. Since $S_X(B) = C_B(X)$, these ordered pairs all correspond to different points on B's IC, namely $C_B(y)$. Knowledge of t points on a $(t-1)$ degree single variable polynomial is sufficient to construct the polynomial uniquely using Lagrange's interpolation method. Thus B can successfully generate its IC with these t ordered pairs. Note that, $(t-1)$ other nodes are needed, since B can generate one PC for itself with its SS. But the scheme remains a (t, n) threshold scheme as the requesting node also participates in the process with other $(t-1)$ helping nodes.

Since t many different points on the polynomial $C_B(y)$ are necessary to uniquely construct it and a fewer number of points simply do not reveal any information about the certificate - it is not possible for any coalition of $(t-1)$ or fewer nodes to issue a certificate to a new node as well as to guess other's certificate. On the other hand, B can not guess $S_{A_i}(x)$s also with the received PCs, due to same reason as presented in Sect. 4.1. This certificate issuing scheme clearly demonstrates that it can cope up with the scenario where nodes of a sensor network join and drop out on the fly. The certificate construction operation is slightly expensive but happens very infrequently.

4.3   Any t Out of n Nodes Should be Capable to Generate a SS

When a node requests for SS, it does not hold any certificate related information at this time and so has to rely on t other nodes to help it construct its SS. Let, B be a new node and A_is, $1 \leq i \leq t$, be the one-hop neighbors jointly issuing a SS to B, i.e., they will work together to help node B calculate $S_B(x)$. The process of constructing SS is similar in nature with creation of IC. Here on verifying node's authenticity, each node $A_i, 1 \leq i \leq t$, individually calculates the PS for B, namely $C_{A_i}(B)$, and sends it to the new node B as their respective contribution. Thus node B receives t ordered pairs $(A_i, C_{A_i}(B))$. These ordered pairs all correspond to t different points on the SS of B, namely $S_B(x)$, since $C_{A_i}(B) = S_B(A_i)$. Now as $S_B(x)$ is a $(t-1)$ degree single variable polynomial, B can uniquely construct it using Lagrange's interpolation method.

Since t many points on the polynomial $S_B(x)$ are necessary to uniquely construct it, it is impossible for any coalition of $(t-1)$ or fewer nodes to issue SS to a new node and to guess other's SS as well. Here also, B can not guess $C_{A_i}(y)$s with the PS received, due to same reason as presented in Sect. 4.1. This mechanism also can cope up with the situation where the nodes join or leave on the fly, as long as the number of working nodes are at least t. This operation also happens very infrequently, when some new node joins the network and at the beginning of each PNCI refreshment interval.

4.4   Any t Out of n Nodes Should be Able to Start PNCI Refreshment

Let, A_is, $1 \leq i \leq t$, be the t nodes who would like to initiate a PNCI refreshment phase. They would securely form a coalition under human supervision and randomly choose another bi-variate polynomial of degree $(t-1)$ in both

x and y, say, $f_{ref}(x, y)$ over $\mathbb{Z}_p^*$ as the pivotal element. Then each node of the coalition calculates its SS and IC with the original restriction $S_{A_i}(x) = f_{ref}(x, A_i)$ and $C_{A_i}(y) = f_{ref}(A_i, y)$ and becomes refreshed. Each of the remaining nodes then behaves as a new node and gets its SS and IC from already refreshed nodes in the same way as described in Sects. 4.2 and 4.3.

4.5 PC and PS Should be Individually Verifiable

As the authenticity of a new node can be verified by some out-of-bound physical proof or biometric measures by the group of t member it chooses, the new node in turn can also adopt the same strategy to verify whether each member of the coalition is also authentic, *i.e.*, they would not cheat while giving their contributions to the new node.

The performance of the certification scheme is dependent on the selection of the threshold parameter. The parameter t has to be judiciously chosen, since its choice influences a number of important components of the scheme like - (i) per node storage requirement; (ii) computation cost while creating IC and SS; (iii) expected number of times an honest node can get its IC validated, before the IC itself is compromised and (iv) PNCI refreshment interval.

5   Conclusion

In this paper we have justified that the certification scheme that best suits for sensor networks to defend Sybil attack should be based on symmetric key and threshold cryptography. In fact we have defined certificate in the symmetric key cryptographic domain and presented a realization of a symmetric key based (t, n) threshold certification scheme specially designed for sensor networks. A few important issues related to the proposed certification scheme have also been addressed. The effectiveness of the proposed scheme is also quantitatively measured under typical attack model. We have plan in future to simulate the proposed certification scheme to evaluate its performance in a parameterized setting.

References

1. Needham, R., Schroeder, M.: Using encryption for authentication in large networks of computers. Commun. ACM **21**(12), 993–999 (1978)
2. Shamir, A.: How to share a secret. Commun. ACM **22**(11), 612–613 (1979)
3. Denning, D., Sacco, G.: Timestamps in key distribution protocols. Commun. ACM **25**, 533–536 (1982)
4. Kong, J., Zerfos, P., Luo, H., Lu, S., Zhang, L.: Providing robust and ubiquitous security support for mobile ad-hoc networks. In: Proceedings of International conference on Network Protocols (2001)
5. Douceur, J.R.: The sybil attack. In: Druschel, P., Kaashoek, M.F., Rowstron, A. (eds.) IPTPS 2002. LNCS, vol. 2429, pp. 251–260. Springer, Heidelberg (2002)

6. Karlof, C., Wagner, D.: Secure routing in wireless sensor networks: attacks and countermeasures. In: First IEEE International Workshop on Sensor Network Protocols and Applications, May 2003

7. Wang, W., Zhu, Y., Li, B.: Self-managed heterogeneous certification in mobile ad hoc networks. In: Proceedings of IEEE Vehicular Technology Conference (2003)

8. Khalili, A., Katz, J., Arbaugh, W.: Toward secure key distribution in truly ad-hoc networks. In: Proceedings of the IEEE Workshop on Security and Assurance in Ad hoc Networks, Orlando, FL, 28 January 2003

9. Newsome, J., Shi, E., Song, D., Perrig, A.: The sybil attack in sensor networks: analysis and defenses. In: Proceedings of Third International Symposium on Information Processing in Sensor Networks, April 2004

10. Zhang, Q., Wang, P., Reeves, D.S., Ning, P.: Defending sybil attacks in sensor networks. In: Proceedings of the International Workshop on Security in Distributed Computing Systems (SDCS-2005), June 2005

11. Raya, M., Hubaux, J.-P.: Securing vehicular ad hoc networks. J. Comput. Secur. **15**(1), 39–68 (2007)

12. Saxena, N., Yi, J.H.: Non-interactive self-certification for long-lived mobile ad hoc networks. IEEE Trans. Inf. Forensics Secur. (TIFS) **4**(4), 946–955 (2009)

DWT Difference Modulation Based Novel Steganographic Algorithm

Imon Mukherjee[1]($\boxtimes$), Biswajita Datta[1], Reeturaj Banerjee[2], and Srijan Das[3]

[1] Department of Computer Science and Engineering, St. Thomas' College of Engineering and Technology, Kolkata 700 023, India
{mukherjee.imon,biswa.jita}@gmail.com
[2] T.A. Pai Management Institute, Manipal 576 104, India
reeturajbanerjee@gmail.com
[3] Department of Computer Science and Engineering, National Institute of Technology, Rourkela 769 008, India
srijandas07@gmail.com

Abstract. Data security means protecting data, such as a database, file, from destructive forces and the unwanted actions of unauthorized users. Since the use of internet is getting popular day by day, data security for efficient and reliable communication has become an important issue. This is the first step towards the introduction of modern day *cryptography*, *steganography* and *watermarking*. Discrete Wavelet Transform Difference Modulation (DWTDM) can be used to embed data by adjusting the pixel values and thus the data can be hidden and the human eye will not be able to notice the hidden text in the cover image. This paper explains the DWTDM with some modified strategies in order to minimize the distortion of the stego image from the cover image. We also show that our work withstand the statistical attacks as well as the benchmark like stirmark.

Keywords: Data hiding · Discrete wavelet transformation · Frequency domain · Seed matrix · Steganography

1 Introduction

Digital data transmission is now posing serious problems as the transmitted data can be retrieved by any third party for exploitation purpose. So, some efficient techniques are required to be developed in order to embed these data to be transmitted through a medium so that no third party is able to retrieve this data. Cryptography plays an important role in this field of security. Along with it, a new technique steganography throws challenges towards data security. Data security techniques like cryptography, steganography, digital watermarking has gained its importance over the time due to the increasing demand of securing the data to be transmitted.

Cryptographic methods try to protect the data to be transmitted simply by modifying it whereas Steganography deals with hiding the data to be transmitted in such a way so that only the sender and the receiver know about the

S. Jajodia and C. Mazumdar (Eds.): ICISS 2015, LNCS 9478, pp. 573–582, 2015.
DOI: 10.1007/978-3-319-26961-0_36

existence of the message [9]. Hiding messages in the pixel intensities of an image has been popular. If these messages are embedded in selective part of the image, particularly in the places where a large change in intensity occurs. This ensure minimal visual disturbance [10]. This basic idea is based on the lattice spin glass model of Ising of physics [4]. But these data security methods can be more useful when applied in the transformation domain. One such method is called Discrete Wavelet Transformation (DWT). The DWT is a linear transformation that operates on a data vector whose length is an integer power of two. It transforms the data vector into a numerically different data vector of the same length [3]. It is a tool that separates data into different frequency components, and then studies each component with resolution matched to its scale.

For a long period of time, Least Significant Bit (LSB) substitution has been in use for hiding the secret message to be transmitted. In LSB substitution, the least significant bit of the pixel is modified as per the bits of the secret message in a certain pattern. Here the LSB of each pixel of the cover image is replaced with the binary bits of the secret message. This ensures that the change in each pixel is minimum since the LSB is substituted and hence restoring the quality of the image [11]. Hossain et al. have proposed a method on pixel value differencing and LSB substitution. This proposed method increases the embedding capacity and decreases the image degradation making it a better method for hiding data [6]. Chan et al. have proposed a data hiding scheme by applying an optimal pixel adjustment process to the stego-image obtained by the simple LSB substitution method which improves the image quality of the stego image with extra computational complexity [2]. Masud Karim et al. have enhanced the existing LSB substitution method by substituting the LSB of RGB true color image. Their method suggests an encryption of a secret key in the LSB of the pixels of the image from which the actual position of the hidden information can be retrieved, thus their method provides an extra layer of protection with good Peak Signal-to-Noise Ratio (PSNR) [8]. DWT is preferred over Discrete Cosine Transforms (DCT) because image in low frequency at various levels can offer corresponding resolution needed. A one dimensional DWT is a repeated filter bank algorithm, and the input is convolved with high pass filter and a low pass filter [5]. In DWT, time domain is passed through low-pass and high pass filters and the high and low frequency wavelet coefficients are generated by taking the difference and average of the two pixel values respectively. The operation of Haar DWT on the cover image results in the formation of 4 sub-bands, namely the approximate band (LL), horizontal band (HL), vertical band (LH) and the diagonal band (HH). The approximate band contains the most significant information of the spatial domain image and other bands contain the high frequency information such as edge details. Thus, the DWT technique describes the decomposition of the image in four non overlapping sub-bands with multi-resolution [7]. Verma et al. have proposed a method for implementing image steganography using 2-Level DWT Technique. DWT is performed on the input image and then again DWT is performed on the approximation matrix obtained from the first level DWT. The embedding of secret message will take place in the matrices obtained from the 2-level DWT. This will ensure more secured transmission of data [13]. Torres et al. proposed an image steganography method in which the data hiding is realized in bit planes of sub band wavelets coefficients using Integer Wavelet Transform (IWT). This proposed method shows a high data embedding capacity while restoring the fidelity of the stego image [12].

2   Proposed Method

The proposed method concentrates on embedding data in frequency domain using DWT. A discrete wavelet transform (DWT) is a transform for which the wavelets are discretely sampled. As with other transforms, a key advantage is that it can captures both frequency and location information (location in time). The existing paper [1] implemented the embedding of data in the frequency domain using DWT but with greater deviations from the original image. In this work, the secret message is embedded by adjusting the range of difference between the adjacent pixels in the seed matrix. The extraction method involves checking of the range of the difference between the adjacent pixels in the transform domain and hence retrieving the data. In our proposed work, we have tried to minimize the deviation of the stego image from the cover image. Here we discuss the embedding procedure followed by the extraction procedure.

2.1   Embedding Method

In this proposed work the secret text is taken in the form of a string and 7 bit ASCII of each character is considered. During embedding 8 bits are inserted within a seed matrix at a time. Thus after concatenating 7 bits of each character if the bit stream is not multiple of 8 then pad one 0 at the end to make it multiples of 8. Three major steps are followed during embedding those are Seed Matrix Generation, position identification for data hiding and the last the data embedding.

(i) **Seed Matrix Generation:** Here during embedding the 2-level DWT transform of cover image is done. This will result in the formation of four bands, i.e., LL, HL, LH and HH shown in Fig. 1. Then we take HL, LH and HH matrices and select a 4×4 seed matrix from these bands such that no two seed matrix overlaps each other as shown in Fig. 2. Here seeds are identified by X.

(ii) **Position Identification for Data Embedding:** Now for each 3×3 seed matrix all the pixel except the seed pixel is selected for hiding the secret data. Each adjacent pixels within the seed matrix are selected. Suppose $D_1 D_2 D_3 D_4 D_5 D_6 D_7 D_8$ are eight bits from target bit stream. Now these are embedded within the seed matrix according to the following Fig. 3.

(iii) **Data Embedding:** Now for each of the message bits, we have to calculate (B-A). If the difference is according to the Table 1 then leave these pixels without any modification otherwise modify them according to the sign and magnitude of Table 1.

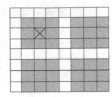

Fig. 1. 2-Level DWT.   **Fig. 2.** Selection of the   **Fig. 3.** Embedding the
                            seeds.   data.

Input: Cover Image (size $M \times N$), Secret Text.
Output: Stego Image.

1 Convert the secret message into bit stream (length should be divisible by 8) by considering 7 bit for each character;
2 Perform the 2-level Discrete Wavelet Transformation (DWT) of the cover image with haar wavelet, to obtain the four components of DWT namely [LL, LH, HL, HH] each of size $M/2 \times N/2$;
3 For each component LL, LH, HL and HH starting with LH and leaving LL, theres going to be $[M \times N/256]$ blocks within each of the DWT components and normalize the DWT coefficients;
4 Do step 5-7, until the entire secret message characters are embedded successfully on LH, HL and HH matrices;
5 Identify 3×3 seed matrix such that no two seed matrices overlap;
6 Now virtually enumerate the coefficients as given in Figure 1;
7 Perform subtraction between two adjacent pixels shown in Figure 3 and adjust the difference according to Table 1;
8 After mapping is complete, restore the fractional components of DWT coefficients and transform back from wavelet domain to spatial domain by inverse DWT to get Stego Image;
9 Output the transformed image component;

Algorithm 1. Embedding Algorithm

Now in this way, we adjust all the 3×3 matrices until the entire secret data is embedded. Then IDWT (Inverse DWT) is performed to get the Stego image and send it to the receiver side.

2.2   Extracting Method

Extraction also follows the three steps Seed Matrix Generation, Position Identification for data hiding and the data extraction. Here also before applying these steps stego image is transform into its Discrete Wavelet form two times.

Table 1. DWT coefficients while Encoding.

Message bit	Decimal equivalent	Modified sign of DWT difference	Modified magnitude of DWT difference
00	0	Negative	2
01	1	Positive	7
10	2	Negative	7
11	3	Positive	2

Input: Stego Image.
Output: Secret Text.

1 Perform the DWT of the cover image with haar wavelet to get LL, LH, HL and HH matrices and normalize the DWT coefficients;
2 Repeat the remaining steps until the entire secret message characters are extracted on LH, HL and HH matrices;
3 Identify 3 × 3 seed matrix such that no two seed matrices overlap;
4 Now assume the coefficients to be named as given in Figure 3;
5 From each [A B] combination extract 2 bits of secret binary message stream as given in Figure 3 and Table 2 and store the extracted bits in an array;
6 Now characters of secret message are formed to get actual secret message at the receiver side;
7 Output the transformed image component;

Algorithm 2. Extraction Algorithm

(i) Seed Matrix Identification. At the receiver side, we have taken the Stego image in which the hidden message is embedded. Now we apply 2-level DWT to the image. After DWT, we get 4 sub matrix of the Image, [LL LH HL HH] respectively. Now we select 3 × 3 seed matrices from LH, HL and IIH matrices (bands) as shown in Fig. 1.

(ii) Position Identification for Data Extraction. Now we select all the adjoining elements of each seeds. So we get the 3 × 3 matrices. Now for each matrix, we select all the elements except the seed elements shown in Fig. 2.

(iii) Retrieving the Data. Now, for each B and A, calculate $(B - A)$ and extract the message bits according to Table 2. Repeat this process until the end of the matrix of the cover image.

Table 2. DWT coefficients while Decoding.

Sign of DWT difference	Magnitude of DWT difference	Extracted message bits
Positive	−4 to 0	00
Negative	5 to 9	01
Negative	−9 to −5	10
Positive	0 to 4	11

3 Experimental Result and Analysis

The efficiency of proposed techniques is tested based on 300 images [14] and more. Out of which some of them are shown in Fig. 4. Also the quality of stego images are analyzed based on MSE, PSNR, NK. At the same time the performance is also tested based on StirMark benchmark 4.0. If embedding is done by considering CA block then the quality of the stego audio will be hampered. Thus this technique is also modified by not considering CA block during embedding as well as extraction but in this time the capacity of stego image is compromised.

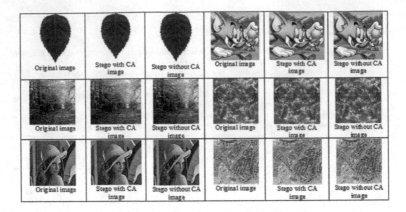

Fig. 4. Cover images (at left), stego images with CA (at center) and stego images without CA (at right).

3.1 Capacity Analysis

The proposed method consists of two types of embedding data-one is embedding data with approximation matrix obtained on applying DWT on the cover image. Since the approximation (CA) matrix contains the most of the information the image so, embedding data by adjusting the difference between two consecutive pixels in the seed matrix brings about a comparable changes in the stego image. On the other hand, restricting the embedding of data in the CA matrix would improve the image quality, but at the same time decreases the embedding capacity. In the normal case, for each 3×3 seed matrix out of 4×4 selected matrix only 8 bits of the binary form of the secret message can be embedded. Thus a character can be embedded for every 4×4 matrix.

3.2 Histogram Analysis

In image processing, histogram of an image refers the histogram of its intensity values. Histogram of an image shows the number of pixels in the image at each different intensity value. Figure 5 shows the histogram of a cover image and its corresponding stego image. Both the histograms are almost same, which shows that the deviation of the stego image from the cover image is less.

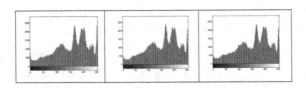

Fig. 5. Histogram of cover image (at left), stego image with CA (at center)and stego image without CA (at right).

3.3 Bit Plane Analysis

Bit plane slicing consists on splitting the original image with 256 gray levels into its equivalent 8 binary images. The method is used for true RGB color images by displaying each color plane as a gray scale image and applying the same algorithm for the former case to convert any intensity level into a byte of 8 bits. Figure 6 depicts the bit planes 0 to 7 of a cover image on the left, its corresponding stego image with CA at the center and stego image without CA on the right respectively.

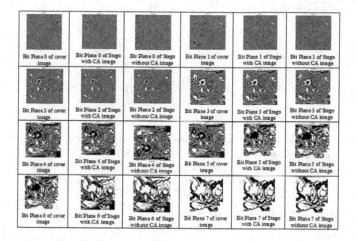

Fig. 6. Bit planes of cover image (left), stego image with CA (center), stego image without CA (right).

3.4 MSE and PSNR

The quality of the stego image is measured by calculation of certain quality measurement metrics.

Mean Square error (MSE) is defined as the average of the square of the difference between the intensities of the stego image and the cover image.

$$MSE = \frac{1}{MN} \sum_{i=1}^{M} \sum_{j=1}^{N} (f(i,j) - f'(i,j))^2 \tag{1}$$

where $f(i,j)$ is the cover image, $f'(i,j)$ is the stego image, M and N are the dimension of the cover image. Table 4 depicts the calculated MSE values of the pair of cover and stego images obtained from the existing algorithm and new algorithm. Table 3 demonstrate these values.

Peak Signal to Noise Ratio (PSNR) is a metric used to distinguish between the cover image and the stego image. More the PSNR value, more preferred is

Table 3. MSE values of different Images

Image	Existing algorithm			Proposed algorithm with LL			ProposedAlgorithm without LL		
	Small	Medium	Large	Small	Medium	Large	Small	Medium	Large
Landscape	97.851	171.570	230.651	48.190	84.395	112.872	21.774	37.267	53.801
Text	1231.4	1231.4	1231.4	240.089	487.450	659.960	66.537	139.268	213.358
Map	310.43	310.43	310.43	56.407	117.222	151.580	16.687	36.985	53.106
Lena	72.822	72.822	72.822	8.566	24.422	32.367	1.639	3.670	4.828
Object	48.504	48.504	48.504	9.601	17.420	22.548	2.891	4.986	6.439
Crowd	168.99	168.99	168.99	7.539	62.464	84.296	7.003	21.447	23.638
Fire	93.622	93.622	93.622	14.403	29.343	42.553	6.382	12.616	22.024
Cartoon	196.95	196.95	196.95	28.369	73.016	96.871	7.340	15.749	24.024
Fast	64.458	64.458	64.458	3.832	25.673	28.335	1.128	6.691	7.336

the stego image.

$$PSNR = 10 \log \frac{255^2}{MSE} \tag{2}$$

Table 4. PSNR values of different Images

Image	Existing algorithm			Proposed algorithm with LL			ProposedAlgorithm without LL		
	Small	Medium	Large	Small	Medium	Large	Small	Medium	Large
Landscape	28.259	25.820	24.535	31.335	28.901	27.638	34.785	32.451	30.856
Text	17.260	17.260	17.260	24.361	21.285	19.969	29.934	26.726	24.873
Map	23.245	23.245	23.245	30.651	27.474	26.358	35.940	32.484	30.913
Lena	29.542	29.542	29.542	38.836	34.286	33.063	46.018	42.517	41.326
Object	31.307	31.307	31.307	38.341	35.754	34.633	43.554	41.186	40.076
Crowd	25.886	25.886	25.886	39.391	30.208	28.906	39.711	34.850	34.428
Fire	28.451	28.451	28.451	36.580	33.489	31.875	40.114	37.155	34.735
Cartoon	25.221	25.221	25.221	33.636	29.530	28.302	39.507	36.192	34.358
Fast	30.071	30.071	30.071	42.329	34.069	33.641	47.638	39.909	39.510

Table 4 depicts the PSNR values of the pair of cover and stego images obtained from the existing [1] and new Algorithm which consists of two types, one in which data is embedded in the approximation matrix obtained on applying DWT and the other in which data is not embedded in approximation matrix for restoring the quality of the stego image obtained. The Existing [1] algorithm uses a wide range of values to be adjusted between the adjacent pixels resulting in more deviation of the stego image.

The proposed algorithm works with only two magnitude values of DWT difference compared to four magnitude values of DWT difference in the existing work as evident from Table 1. This also results in less deviation of the stego image from the cover image which is evident from the values of MSE, PSNR and NK of the cover and stego images obtained from both the algorithms (existing as well as proposed) as shown in Tables 3 and 4. In this proposed work the cover image may be .bmp as well as .jpg and the most highlighting features that the target text is extracted correctly from .jpg stego image also.

Normalised Correlation (NK) measures the similarity between the two images, i.e. the original image and the stego image. Larger values of NK indicate poorer image quality. Its value tends to one as the difference between the two images tends to zero. Normalised Correlation is formulated as:

$$NK = \frac{\sum_{i=1}^{M} \sum_{j=1}^{N} [f(i.j).f'(i,j)]}{\sum_{i=1}^{M} \sum_{j=1}^{N} f(i,j)^2} \tag{3}$$

The Normalised Correlation is calculated for stego images obtained from the existing algorithms and it is concluded that the value of NK for most of the stego images comes to 1. Moreover the difference between the NK of the cover and the stego image comes to zero which is preferred.

Table 5. Benchmark values of sample test images

Analysed Image	Existing				Proposed with LL				Proposed without LL			
	Cropping (20)	Add Noise (20)	Remove lines (40)	Rotation (10)	Cropping (20)	Add Noise (20)	Remove lines (40)	Rotation (10)	Cropping (20)	Add Noise (20)	Remove lines (40)	Rotation (10)
Landscape	76.34	58.1	109.38	81.76	76.26	58.74	108.97	81.44	76.24	58.77	58.19	81.44
Map	155.54	86.81	163.01	121.95	155.14	86.75	162.42	121.5	155.09	86.62	74.7	121.5
Lena	119.57	59.01	112.04	83.81	119.66	59.25	112.08	83.84	119.62	58.97	59.04	83.85
Object	47.72	99.08	176.98	132.38	47.35	99.38	176.86	132.29	47.35	99.33	79.06	111.6
Crowd	93.43	82.23	149.17	111.56	93.47	82.31	149.21	111.6	93.49	82.35	70.76	134.88
Cartoon	179.78	89.77	165.97	124.14	179.84	89.78	166.08	124.17	105.49	89.43	75.71	124.17

3.5 StirMark Benchmark Analysis

In computing, a benchmark is the act of running a computer program, a set of programs, or other operations, in order to assess the relative performance of an object, normally by running a number of standard tests and trials against it. The term "benchmark" is also mostly utilized for the purposes of elaborately designed benchmarking programs themselves. Below table shows the benchmarking values of some test pictures. Table 5 demonstrates the values of Existing Algorithm, Proposed Algorithm with CA and Proposed Algorithm without CA.

4 Conclusion

The proposed algorithm is much more efficient than the state-of-the-art works. Though, the capacity of embedding data is reduced by restricting the embedding data in the CA matrix obtained on applying DWT on the cover image. This is done to ensure the quality of the stego image. Hence the distortion in the stego image is less than that obtained from the existing algorithm. Moreover, the range to be adjusted for embedding the data in frequency domain is less as compared to the existing paper in order to have less distortion.

References

1. Bhattacharyya, S., Sanyal, G.: A robust image steganography using DWT difference modulation (DWTDM). Int. J. Comput. Netw. Inf. Secur. **4**, 27–40 (2012)
2. Chan, C.K., Cheng, L.M.: Hiding data in images by simple LSB substitution. J. Pattern Recogn. Soc. **37**, 469–474 (2004)
3. Chen, P.Y., Lin, H.J.: A DWT based approach for image steganography. Int. J. Appl. Sci. Eng. **4**, 275–290 (2006)
4. Cipra, B.: An introduction to the Ising model. Am. Math. Mon. **94**(10), 937–959 (1987)
5. Elfouly, H.F., Mahmoud, M.I., Dessouky, M.I.M., Deyab, S.: Comparison between Haar and DaubechiesWavelet Transformations on FPGA Technology. Int. J. Electr. Robot. Electron. Commun. Eng **2**, 133–137 (2008)
6. Hossain, S.M., Haque, M.S.: A block based data hiding method in images using pixel value differencing and LSB substitution method. In: Proceedings of the 15th International Conference on Computer and Information Technology (ICCIT), pp. 168–172 (2012)
7. Kocioek, M., Materka, A., Strzelecki, M., Szczypiski, P.: Discrete wavelet transform derived features for digital image texture analysis. Int. J. Eng. Technol., 833–841 (2014)
8. Masud Karim, S.M., Rahman, M.S., Hossain, M.I.: A new approach for LSB based image steganography using secret key. In: Proceedings of the 14th International Conference Computer and Information Technology (ICCIT), pp. 286–291 (2011)
9. Pahati, O.J.: Confounding Carnivore: How to Protect Your Online Privacy (2008)
10. Paul, G., Davidson, I., Mukherjee, I., Ravi, S.S.: Keyless steganography in spatial domain using *Energetic* pixels. In: Venkatakrishnan, V., Goswami, D. (eds.) ICISS 2012. LNCS, vol. 7671, pp. 134–148. Springer, Heidelberg (2012)
11. Reddy, V.L., Subramanyam, A., Reddy, P.C.: Implementation of LSB steganography and its evaluation for various file formats. Int. J. Adv. Netw. Appl. **2**, 868–872 (2011)
12. Torres, S., Nakano-Miyatake, M., Perez-Meana, H.: An image steganography systems based on BPCS and IWT. In: 16th International Conference Electronics, Communications and Computers, CONIELECOMP 2006 (2006)
13. Verma, A., Nolkha, R., Singh, A., Jaiswal, G.: Implementation of image steganography using 2-level DWT technique. Int. J. Comput. Sci. Bus. Inform. **1**, 1–14 (2013)
14. www.imageprocessingplace.com

Author Index

Printed in the United States
By Bookmasters